Final Drafts

suicides

of world-famous

authors

Mark Seinfelt

Foreword by Paul West

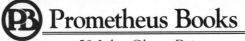

Prometheus Books

59 John Glenn Drive
Amherst, New York 14228-2197

Published 1999 by Prometheus Books

Inquiries should be addressed to
Prometheus Books, 59 John Glenn Drive, Amherst, New York 14228–2197.
VOICE: 716–691–0133, ext. 207.
FAX: 716–564–2711.
WWW.PROMETHEUSBOOKS.COM

03 02 01 00 99   5 4 3 2 1

Library of Congress Cataloging-in-Publication Data

Seinfelt, Mark.
        Final drafts : suicides of world-famous authors / Mark Seinfelt ;
foreword by Paul West.
            p.   cm.
        Includes bibliographical references.
        ISBN 1–57392–741–4 (cloth : alk. paper)
        1. Authors—Suicidal behavior. 2. Suicide victims Biography.
3. Authors Biography. 4. Authors—Death. I. Title.
PN452.S45   1999
809—dc21
[B]   99–31378
                                                                CIP

Printed in the United States of America on acid-free paper

Contents

Acknowledgments

THE AUTHOR IS GRATEFUL TO THE FOLLOWING PUBLISHERS AND RIGHTS holders for granting permission to reprint from the works of the authors listed below:

JOHN BERRYMAN

Reprinted by permission of Farrar, Straus & Giroux, Inc.: #6 from "Eleven Addresses to the Lord," "The Ball Poem," "Henry's Understanding," and "Of Suicide" from COLLECTED POEMS 1937–1971 by John Berryman. Copyright © 1989 by Kate Donahue Berryman.

Excerpts from #42, #162, #384 from THE DREAM SONGS by John Berryman. Copyright © 1969 by John Berryman. Copyright renewed © 1997 by Kate Donahue Berryman.

Excerpts from "At this point in time, million of souls collect" and from "I didn't. And I didn't. Sharp the Spanish blade" from HENRY'S FATE AND OTHER POEMS 1967–1971 by John Berryman. Copyright © 1977 by Kate Berryman.

Excerpts from the unpublished work of John Berryman. Copyright © 1999 by Kate Donahue Berryman. Reprinted by permission of Farrar, Straus and Giroux, LLC, on behalf of the Estate of John Berryman.

PAUL CELAN

Reprinted by permission of John Felstiner:

"From the bridge—," "Water Needles," and an excerpt from "Death Fugue" by Paul Celan, translated by John Felstiner, from PAUL CELAN: POET, SURVIVOR, JEW by John Felstiner. Yale University Press. Copyright © 1995.

The author wishes to thank Eugene O'Connor, R. J. Winchell, and Fred and Laura Seinfelt for their careful and kind assistance in preparing the manuscript for publication, and Daniel B. Bezilla of NCI Technologies for the transfer of data and the preparation of computer diskettes for delivery to the publisher.

$\mathcal{F}$oreword

$\mathcal{P}$aul $\mathcal{W}$est

FOR YEARS NOW, MARK SEINFELT HAS LIVED WITH HIS MATERNAL grandfather atop a mountain in Central Pennsylvania, no doubt initiating himself into hypoxia and strengthening his already intense regard for Thomas Mann.

Up there, as well as composing half a dozen novels, he has prepared a *magnum opus* devoted (in the fullest sense) to literary suicides of the late nineteenth and twentieth centuries. This could have been a mawkish and monotonous undertaking, yet it has not turned out that way. Mr. Seinfelt has no ax to grind, no emptily charismatic academic theory, making tidy what is messy and unknown. Instead, he allows his suicides their full autonomy in a series of candid portraits that, while telling us as much as we need, reveals his subjects in the full dignity of their internal commotion: deciding to think again, then deciding again to think no more, Hamlets of self-infliction, Prufrocks of the profane.

I know of no other such book, done with un-Procrustean passion and knowledgeable balance. Mr. Seinfelt does not stereotype or group his people, and he casts a humane eye on those whose alcoholism, say, seems a suicide of chronic contrivance, or even on such a canker of nature as Hitler, whose destructive habits had a self-destructive core. This is not psychological criticism, though Mr. Seinfelt movingly explores his suicides' minds, the manger of their dismal deaths. Nor is the book prissy moralizing, though its author is clearly on the side of life, the angels even (as Disraeli said), averring in his very first sentence that "If our sweetest songs are those that tell of saddest thoughts, then perhaps our saddest songs are those that tell of sweetest." Human paradoxicality is his theme and, to lift a title from that all but forgotten novelist C. P. Snow, "variety of men" (and women).

His ideal introducer would be one of his own ill-fated dramatis personae: vain hope. He takes full account of the suicidal impulse in most human beings, studying and tracking it in twenty-five exponents of *felo de se* as if it were a gift, in some the inevitable cost of a stance or vision too near the edge, too obsessed with the unknown region. Too hopeful, too desperate. Above all, this is not a case of samples fudged up by a didactic witchdoctor hawking the cowflop and dust of a sometime Ph.D. dissertation. Instead, it is that noble assembly, too little honored in our dumbdown time, the collection of compatible essays, set up to evince the culpable severity of the pensive life, the sometimes mordant sensitivity of the constant observer, the self-elegist apostrophizing self from amid the wreckage of a life too fervent or too fierce, or conducted with a limp wrist, a muddled eye. The human capacity for getting things wrong (expecting too much or too little) is Mr. Seinfelt's Wagnerian *Leitmotif*, and he discusses his entrants and their exits with worldly concession, always aware that life is a given, a gift, ever available for being snuffed out.

A sentient reader, who has not trodden any crack of this fatal path, will no doubt develop favorites and pet peeves by book's end, perhaps even coming to believe there is a decorum of suicide, a finesse of drab finality. Mr. Seinfelt gets into little of this, remaining the well-educated bracelet of bright hair about these bones. His is a young man's book of the dead, and refreshingly so, in which he unpacks his bags in the morgue and sets up his own bright stall, with an uncommonly large and varied array of literary wares at his disposal, almost, as it were, learning his trade from those it killed.

The familiar quietuses of Woolf, Crane, Berryman, Mishima and Hemingway appear here, as they must, in the context of less familiar ones—Trakl, Teasdale, Zweig, Lockridge, Lowry, Kawabata, Gary, and Kosinski—the whole procedure acquiring a frantic normalcy as the record continues, making the reader wonder perhaps why we don't all do it, having had our say and not profited spiritually from it. Among the forgotten there hovers Tom McHale, author of *Farragan's Retreat* and other sprightly novels, reviled in a glossy magazine's perfunctory obituary paragraph for having quit the kitchen, unable to stand the heat. Read this book and be astounded how many authors have done away with themselves: the poisoned, the burned, the beheaded-by-friends; jumpers, danglers, asphyxiants, not to mention lushes and junkies committed to the inevitability of gradualness, with the absurd of old always in the offing. One comes away from Mr. Seinfelt's honorable roll-call mystified by the prodigious thing these people, we authors, keep trying to do: justify the ways of God to man, after Milton, or transcend the human condition altogether. Perhaps we shall see more such exits as profit-mad publishers of no taste lean on their most bellelettristic performers, people of consummate gift for whom an entertainment-hungry society has no further use amid the shenanigans of how-to, celeb non-books, and airline reading that amounts to a tooled vacancy wrapped in simply worded covers. Maybe, one day soon, rejection slips will have a cyanide spot which the unhappy recipients will be invited to lick. The fate of the thoughtful among the thoughtless has always been a nightmare, and Mr. Seinfelt sharply brings us up to speed on our own time's version of it. He sets us wondering all over again: What kills? Indifference or stress?

Someone from another, superior planet might wonder at this trade of letters that kills more than do stockbroking, teaching, or aeronautical design. Mr. Seinfelt brings many drear, cumulative moments to life, proffering the idea, perhaps, that suicides are self-saviors, survivors are the real suicides, the difference between them being mainly a matter of emphasis. One wonders. As Boethius says in *The Consolation of Philosophy*, he who wants his wound healed must first expose it. Here then are miscellaneous wounds exposed as much as possible, culminating in what many now refer to with solecistic fecklessness as the *coup de gras* (a lot of dead ducks). Ultimately, Mr. Seinfelt seems to seek in these baleful memorials a precise account of the grace (*coup de grâce*) administered to oneself, whether it works any better than arranging pain, flux, and joy into words for fifty years or so. Whoever bites the bullet need not eat the gun.

Introduction

I F OUR SWEETEST SONGS ARE THOSE THAT TELL OF SADDEST THOUGHTS, then perhaps our saddest songs are those that tell of sweetest. Suicide has fascinated writers for centuries as a literary topic. From ancient times to the present, authors have related the suicides of both historical figures and of fictitious characters, the former often with so much embellishment and literary license that it would be more accurate to characterize a great many, if not most, of these portrayals not as factual accounts (even when presented as such) but as creations of the imagination. Who would dispute that Shakespeare's Brutus, Cassius, Mark Antony, and Cleopatra are not the Bard's unique constructions, *his* characters above all else? Shakespeare's Roman impersonations tell us as much, if not vastly more, about him than they do about the historical figures on whom they were based. It is Shakespeare himself, of course, who actually deliberates and ponders life's eternal questions in *Hamlet*. Like Romeo attending a Capulet ball, he dons a mask. He uses a mouthpiece and speaks through Hamlet. Might one not go further? Is it so startling to suggest that Hamlet is Shakespeare? Many scholars would, of course, vehemently disagree, arguing that Shakespeare was such a universal genius that he could give tongue to any mood or temperament and that much of his verse is aery and gay, exuberant and triumphant. Could not the happy swains of the comedies reflect his nature as much, or more so, than the brooding Dane, and is there any way of telling which of his creations he himself most resembled? There is merit to this argument, and it is probably safe to assume that Shakespeare, like so many other creative personalities past and present, had both his sunnier and darker natures, that he found life both sweet and sad.[1] What is inconceivable, however, is that he did not himself ever anxiously ponder what awaited us beyond the grave or that, at some point of crisis in his life, did not ask himself:

> Then is it sin
> To rush into the secret house of death,
> Ere death dare come to us ?

From the beginning, writers have romanticized history's suicides or imbued them with a mythic aura. If not a total fiction, the Samson of Judges surely bears little resemblance to his historical counterpart. In addition to the death of the long-haired slayer of the Philistines, the authors of the Old Testament chronicle three more suicides, those of Saul, Abimelech and Achitophel. The accuracy of the scriptures, written centuries after the events chronicled, is once again questionable. In the New Testament, the death of Judas is recounted in Matthew and Acts. In Matthew, Judas throws down the thirty silver coins he had been paid to betray Jesus, scattering them on the floor of the Temple. He then goes off and hangs himself. The priests pick up the coins. As it was unlawful to put blood money in the temple treasury, they use the money to buy Potter's Field as a cemetery for foreigners. In Acts a somewhat different story is told. Judas himself purchases the "field of blood." From a precipice overlooking this land, he leaps headlong to his death. His insides spatter on the ground, giving the field its name.

Like the Hebrew scribes of Israel, Greek and Roman writers also wrote vivid accounts of suicides which had actually or reputedly occurred. Greek myth is full of self-murderers. Leukakas leaps to her death in order to avoid the carnal embraces of Apollo. Jocasta slays herself upon learning Oedipus's identity as her son. Thinking that Theseus has been killed by the Minotaur, Aegeus walks into the sea that henceforth will bear his name and drowns himself. Greek historians recorded (and no doubt embellished) the suicides of actual kings and lawgivers such as Codrus of Athens and Lycurgus of Sparta. These heroes usually sacrificed themselves to save their people from destruction or to impart a moral lesson to their followers. Rhetoricians and philosophers also took their lives with some frequency in ancient Greece, or so the records would indicate. Once again the suicides killed themselves in furtherance of a noble cause or in order to make an ethical point. The famous Greek orator Demosthenes championed a rebellion against the Macedonian general Antipater. After the coup failed, he took poison so as to avoid capture by his adversaries. Socrates chose to drink hemlock rather than be exiled from his native Athens after he had been accused at age seventy of corrupting the youth of the city. Our knowledge of him, however, comes primarily from Plato's account of his trial, imprisonment, and death in the three short dialogues *Apology*, *Crito*, and *Phaedo*. Socrates himself wrote nothing. Some scholars feel that Plato espouses his own philosophy in these works, making his famous teacher a ventriloquist's dummy for his own ideas. Certainly Socrates is somewhat idealized in the dialogues, which are dramatic and stylized works of art and not by any means verbatim transcriptions of Socrates's actual teachings. Other Greek philosophers of note who took their own lives include Zeno, the founder of Stoicism, and his successor, Cleanthes.[2]

The Romans viewed suicide as manly and noble. Seneca belonged to the Stoic school. He called suicide the "end of evils" and wrote that it led to liberty. The road to freedom, he argued, could be found in every vein of one's body. Roman stoic writing is replete with elegant apologias for suicide. The act is also portrayed as a noble recourse in all the notable literature of the period. Dido dies of a self-inflicted wound in the *Aeneid*. Although she is the queen of Carthage, and thus stands opposed to the destiny of the Roman people, Vergil makes her a tragic and noble heroine. Her plight continues to elicit compassion and understanding from readers of the poem today. Three renowned Roman writers, the epic poet Lucan, the satirist Petronius, and the dramatist and essayist Seneca, were either ordered to commit suicide by the emperor Nero or preemptorily stabbed themselves to avoid his vengeance. Due to Nero's jealousy, Lucan, a member of the Imperial court and a public official, was prohibited from publishing. He joined a conspiracy against the tyrant. When it was uncovered, he was given the option of slaying himself or being executed. He chose the former. Petronius ended his life after he had come under suspicion of treason. Seneca, on the other hand, was formally charged with sedition in 65 C.E. Tacitus describes the Stoic's death in his famous *Annals*. Two earlier Roman authors of note, the comic dramatist Terence (ca. 195–159 B.C.E.) and the philosophical poet Lucretius (ca. 94–55 B.C.E.) may have killed themselves. Historical accounts of their deaths differ. Some sources indicate that they committed suicide, others that they died natural deaths. Although he did not slay himself, the lyric poet Catullus (ca. 84-54 B.C.E.) remains an archetype of the poet whose life runs to ruin because of rejection in love. In his poems to Lesbia, he wrote that death could not possibly be more bitter than, indeed would be sweeter and preferable to, Clodia's rebuff.[3]

As A. Alvarez amply demonstrates in his justly celebrated 1971 study, *The Savage God*, "suicide has permeated Western culture like a dye that cannot be washed out."[4] Alvarez documents how, throughout history, in all major literary periods of the last two millennia, writers in the West have continued to be intrigued by the ultimate taboo of human behavior. In his comprehensive investigation, he traces this literary fascination from the Middle Ages and the Renaissance through the Age of Reason and the Romantic era to the first great period of modernism following World War I. Indeed, many of the most memorable characters in nineteenth- and twentieth-century literature either die by their own hand or, like Hamlet, are so guilt- and death-obsessed, that, although they do not actually kill themselves, they hasten and bring on their final end through reckless abandon. Emma Bovary takes poison as do Thérèse and Laurent in *Thérèse Raquin*. Anna Karenina throws herself under a train, as does Mrs. Emily Sinico in "A Painful Case." The half-witted Smerdyakov, the natural son of old Karamazov, hangs himself after murdering his father. Jude and Arabella's young son Little Father Time also dies at the end of a rope. He hangs himself as well as Jude and Sue's two younger children after becoming convinced that he and his half-siblings have become a burden to their parents. Arkady Ivanovitch Svidrigailov shoots himself in front of an unsuspecting bystander. Martin Decoud also uses a bullet to end his life after being left alone on the Great Isabel island by Nostromo. After goading Ludovico Settembrini into a duel, Leo Naphta, in a rage, turns his gun on himself when Settembrini fires his weapon into the air, while Mynheer Peeperkorn injects himself with snake venom upon discovering that he has grown impotent. The war-traumatized Septimus Warren Smith jumps out a window and falls to his death in a London Street. Edna Pontellier swims out into the Gulf of Mexico in order to drown herself and thereby undergo a triumphant transfiguration. Rhoda, one of the six protagonists in *The Waves*, leaps from a precipice into the ocean, likewise to seek release. Because he hates the South, because he is angered and hurt by his sister Candace's promiscuity and because he wants to stop time, Quentin Compson throws himself in the Charles River. A number of Hermann Hesse's heroes also choose death by water. Lord Jim remains on the island of Patusan knowing full well that Dain Waris's father Doramin is bound by honor to slay him. Gustave von Aschenbach stays on in Venice to meet his fate even though he knows that plague has broken out in the city. Hans Castorp leaves the Magic Mountain to fight in the German army, happy in the realization that he will, in all likelihood, face death on the battlefield.

Still other characters, like Wagner's Tristan and Isolde, seek sexual consummation in death and darkness. Some attempt suicide and fail, usually to turn their lives around afterward, while still others make a game of courting death. Only when their lives are in danger do they feel most alive. Isolde expires by sheer willpower. For years, Heathcliff longs to be reunited with Cathy on the Other Side and looks forward to his own death. Gregor Samsa longs for extinction in *The Metamorphosis*. His loathing and self-hatred and his unnatural lust for his blonde-haired, blue-eyed sister, Grete, not only cause his transformation into an insect but also, in the end, lie behind his determination to die and free his family from the awful burden of his presence. Like Isolde, he, too, "wills" his death. A number of Leo Tolstoy's characters attempt or contemplate taking their own lives, including Vronsky and Levin in *Anna Karenina*, Pierre Bezukhov in *War and Peace*, and Katerina Maslova in *Resurrection*. Unlike Anna, they conquer their despair and opt for life. Nonetheless, Leo Tolstoy, even in his devout old age, held the view that suicide was the inalienable right of every individual.[5] Hemingway's heroes stare death in the face and defy it to the bitter end. They feel compelled to keep putting themselves at risk. Only by courting death can they conquer their fear of it.

Despite the fact that suicide has always fascinated writers and that, over the centuries, a number of prominent authors, including John Donne, Michel Eyquem de Montaigne, Giacomo Leopardi, and Leo Tolstoy, defended the act as moral and honorable, relatively few writers took their own lives in past epochs. After the deaths of Lucan, Petronius, and Lucius Seneca, the next significant suicide wave did not occur until the late eighteenth and early nineteenth centuries. The British poet Thomas Chatterton killed himself with arsenic in 1770 when he was not quite eighteen. One of the greatest of literary forgers, Chatterton ascribed his poems to a fictitious fifteenth-century poet-priest, Thomas Rowley. He wrote enough verse to fill three volumes. Chatterton claimed that he had unearthed Rowley's poems in the parish archives of St. Mary Redcliffe's church in Bristol, where members of his family were hereditary sextons. He offered some of the verse to Horace Walpole and represented himself as the discoverer and translator of the poems. Walpole originally accepted the authenticity of the works and agreed to become Chatterton's patron, but withdrew his support when William Mason declared Chatterton a fraud, thus leaving the poet to die in poverty and despair. Facing starvation, he chose to end his life and swallowed arsenic.

In 1811, the Prussian dramatist and novella writer Heinrich von Kleist entered into a suicide pact with Henrietta Vogel on the shore of Wannsee, near Potsdam. In despair over the failure of his last venture, the political newspaper *Die Abendblätter*, Kleist shot Vogel and then himself.[6] Ten years later, in 1821, the poet John William Polidori, Lord Byron's traveling companion and doctor, poisoned himself by ingesting prussic acid after his dismissal by Byron, who had constantly belittled Polidori during his period of service. Polidori is an outstanding example of a writer who was overshadowed by someone else of far greater stature and achievement and thus felt dwarfed to the point where he decided to take his own life.

Three other significant literary suicides occurred later in the nineteenth century. In 1855, Gérard de Nerval, the French translator of Goethe's *Faust* and the darling of a generation of German Romantics, hanged himself in Paris, unable to complete his treatise on madness, *Aurélia*. Nerval had been obsessed with suicide all his life. As a much younger man, during an evening stroll by the Danube, he remarked that the river would make a fine grave for himself. At the end of his life, while working on *Aurélia*, Nerval went insane. He hanged himself with an apron string, which he believed was "the girdle Mme. de Maintenon wore when she acted at Saint Cyr in *Esther*."[7] In 1894, the grandniece of James Fenimore Cooper and confidante of Henry James, American novelist Constance F. Woolson, leaped to her death from a window of her house in Venice. Not only did she feel that she had been eclipsed as a writer by James, she was despondent and frustrated by her inability to make him respond to her romantically. The following year saw the suicide of the Colombian poet José Asunción Silva. Known for his innovative, musical, broodingly pessimistic verse and as one of the chief figures of South America's *modernismo* movement, Silva was driven to suicide at age thirty-one by the deaths of both his father and a beloved sister. Silva inherited all his father's debts and found himself unable to pay them. Shortly before his death, he also lost a manuscript in a shipwreck after having found a publisher for it in France.

In past centuries, however, numerous writers led their lives in such a reckless, self-destructive manner that they could be accurately classified as "psychological suicides," as their habits and vices led to their premature deaths. Others, such as Goethe[8] and Flaubert, felt the urge to kill themselves at some time in their lives, but withstood the temptation "to put down the final period" and wrote perceptively about suicide in their works instead. Still others attempted suicide but did not succeed, including Guy de Maupassant (1850–1893), who tried twice due to fear of insanity, and the English poet Frances Thompson (1859–1907), who, addicted to opium and destitute, in 1885, lay down in the middle of a London street hoping to be run over by a carriage. A woman passerby took pity on him and gave him temporary shelter. Years before commencing his writing career, Joseph Conrad attempted to end his life in March of 1878. Stranded in Marseilles without money, unwilling to ask his uncle for yet another loan, Conrad borrowed eight hundred francs from a friend then proceeded to Villefranche, between Nice and Monaco, where he tried to enlist in the United States Navy but was rejected as a foreigner. Before leaving Villefranche, Conrad lost the money he had borrowed gambling at a casino. He returned to Marseilles, where he shot himself in the chest, missing the heart and other vital organs. Nonetheless a telegram was sent to Conrad's uncle in Poland, who once more came to his nephew's aid. For the sake of family honor, he would later inform Conrad's relatives that the wound had been received in a duel.[9] Sir Thomas More, the English statesman and author of *Utopia*, sacrificed his life for a moral cause. He chose to go to the block because of his conviction that Henry VIII's divorce from his first wife, Catherine of Aragon, was morally wrong and invalid. He also would not swear to the Act of Supremacy oath, which made Henry and not the pope head of the church in England. The king did not desire More's death, but More would not budge or be persuaded from his high-minded but in effect suicidal stance. Evidently, for More, death was sweeter than abandoning principle.

Throughout history, addictions have led to the early deaths of authors with a sad regularity. Some accounts indicate that Shakespeare succumbed after a bout of heavy drinking in Avon. The Elizabethan dramatist Robert Greene (ca. 1558–1592) reputedly died from "a surfeit of pickled herring and Rhenish wine."[10] The English poet laureate and famous butt of Dryden's "MacFlecknoe," Thomas Shadwell (ca. 1642–1692), died as result of an opium overdose. He started taking the drug to relieve his pain from gout and became quickly and progressively addicted to it. Years of opium smoking also shortened the life of the death-haunted American short-story writer, poet, and critic Edgar Allan Poe, who was found unconscious in a Baltimore street and died in a hospital there in 1849 at the age of forty. The French dramatist and lyric poet Alfred de Musset (1810–1857) spent the last ten years of his life seeking forgetfulness in drink and debauchery after being spurned in love by the author George Sand. The affair left him inconsolable and his heavy drinking hastened his death at forty-seven. Saint-Beuve summarized the height de Musset had attained and fallen from with the mot: "What a light! What an eclipse!"[11] Illustrator and poet Dante Gabriel Rossetti (1828–1882) became addicted to chloral and eventually died from ingestion of it. The nineteenth-century French symbolist Paul Verlaine (1844–1896) also died as a result of alcoholism, as did English poet Ernest Dowson (1867–1900). Dowson fell in love with a waitress who did not care for him but who manipulated and exploited his infatuation for her. Finding himself in a "Human Bondage" type of situation, Dowson grieved and despaired and drank his way to an early grave.

Byron supported the Greek fight for independence and died while training troops. Although his physical condition did not fit him for the rigors of military life, he devoted himself unsparingly to the cause, and, in some months' time, he became mortally ill. Several other prominent writers were killed in duels, putting their lives at risk for trivial and inconsequential reasons. Their willingness to do so perhaps shows a suicidal inclination or at least a callous disregard for their own safety. Poet and dramatist Christopher Marlowe (1564–1593) was a frequent bar brawler who eventually died in a tavern fight. Alexander Pushkin was slain defending the honor of his wife, a stunningly flirtatious femme fatale who, by Pushkin's own count, was woman No. 113 in his life. After they married, both continued to engage in romantic affairs with others. Pushkin knew his wife had been unfaithful to him, but felt injured and slighted when this fact was brought to his attention. He died at the age of thirty-eight in 1837. The Russian novelist Mikhail Yurievitch Lermontov (1814–1841) was killed in a duel by a fellow soldier over a small, easily forgotten offense.

"To die" was a coy Elizabethan expression meaning to have an orgasm. The dangers of venereal disease were well known, even to illiterate, uneducated members of the populace. One risked one's life every time one made "the beast with two backs," especially if one trafficked with drabs and trollops. The dramatist George Peele (1556–1596), who had a reputation for being a roistering, thriftless character, died of syphilis at the age of forty. John Keats (1795–1821) contracted the disease after his first sexual encounter with a Scottish prostitute. He would later medicate himself with opium and laudanum. Peele and Keats perhaps were merely unlucky. No doubt many men took the same risks and were never infected. Certainly both men knew the danger they were running—were more aware of it than the common john. Peele was a university wit educated at Christ's Hospital and at Christ Church, Oxford. Keats had been apprenticed to a surgeon-apothecary and studied medicine at a number of London hospitals. Both knew the terror of the pox before catching it themselves. Keats's venereal disease and the drugs contributed to his death from tuberculosis at twenty-five years and four months. Keats recognized the blood in his sputum as arterial and realized that his fate was sealed, that he must die.

Pride, the determination to pursue his art at whatever cost, has also brought down many an author and led him to a precipitous and sad end—a bleak and shabby death. History provides several instances of writers who had such a strong sense of vocation that they would not turn from the craft, even when all their income had dried up and they were plunged into penury. These men resolutely wore blinders and continued to write even though their efforts met with no success. Furthermore, they steadfastly refused to earn a livelihood by other, more practical means. Chatterton angrily declared that his place was not among servants. He wrote: "It is my PRIDE, my damn'd, native, unconquerable Pride, that plunges me into Distraction.

You must know that 19–20th of my Composition is Pride. I must either live a Slave, a Servant; to have no Will of my own, no Sentiments of my own which I may freely declare as such;—or DIE—perplexing alternative."[12] Chatterton preferred to live on air rather than put on livery. Having no bread, he ate arsenic. The Restoration dramatist Thomas Otway (1652–1685), whose heroic tragedies became almost as popular as Shakespeare's plays in the eighteenth and nineteenth centuries, died destitute in a London alehouse. The English poet Christopher Smart (1722–1771) died in debtor's prison. He suffered from madness and religious mania at the close of his life, writing some of his finest poems during his incarceration, when he no longer had to worry about his material well-being. These verses were largely ignored in the eighteenth century but are highly regarded today.

Even if we include these last problematic "psychologicals" in our catalog of pre-twentieth century author-suicides, our list still remains short. While only a small number of writers took their own lives in the past, the twentieth century has seen a profusion of such deaths, a plague comparable in scope to the slew of Hollywood actresses from the 1940s through the 1960s who killed themselves by overdosing on barbiturates or sleeping pills. Surprisingly—especially as the emotional torture that so frequently accompanies literary genius is a subject of perennial interest—no study seriously exploring the collective frustrations, agonies, and suicides of this group of modern writers, or their differing reasons for doing themselves in, has to date been written. I first saw the need for such a work in 1994, after reading, in *Sheer Fiction III*, Paul West's essay "Tan Salaam and the Aga Khan" concerning West's reflexive relationship with publisher and editor George Plimpton. In the essay, West reveals Plimpton's idea for a novel, a book that Plimpton eventually gave up on, having found it impossible to execute:

> At some point in our discussions, George told me about the novel he had never been able to write: about a photographer who (if I recall aright) chased around the world in pursuit of spectacular photographic coups, but was always too late, an absentee in spite of himself. I thought such a personage would eventually develop a keen sense of the unmediated texture of diurnal life, looking for a seasonal or meaningful time but finding only mere chronicity. That's what I would have done, I said; but George was groping for some philosopher's stone, some catalytic knob of chalk, some way of parading a series of timely shots, with always, I thought, the cliché looming of the well-timed photographer, paparazzo as perfectionist who starts with Werther and supplies the visual equivalent of Goethe's "The ball has almost reached the brain." How about a book of famous literary suicides revisited?[13]

Final Drafts examines, in the form of individual chapters, twenty-five authors who elected to end themselves between 1894 and 1991. Each chapter attempts not only to relate the facts of the particular author's life and death but to capture his mindset at the moment when he decided "to rush into the secret house of death, ere death came to him," the mental and emotional equivalent of Goethe's "The ball has almost reached the brain." I hope to have caught this moment, to have clicked "the photo" at precisely the right time. Each case also provides another kind of snapshot, a sort of window on the decade of the author's suicide. The twenty-five chronologically arranged chapters constitute a continuous narrative reflecting the history of our times. The major historical events of the last one hundred years have affected millions of lives; they certainly had an impact on many of these authors' decisions to die. So many writers have chosen to slay themselves since 1894 that I have of necessity had to be selective. Although not an exhaustive overview of all the other literary suicides which took place during the course of this century, the final section of this book offers a glimpse at the sad ends of an additional twenty-four authors, the last being J. Anthony Lukas who died by his own hand in June of 1997. It also examines the perplexing cases of seven writers whose deaths may or may not have been the result of suicide.

Like other literary eras, the twentieth century has had its share of self-destructive authors who, although they did not commit suicide, engaged in dangerous behavior that considerably shortened their lives. The list of those who chronically abused alcohol seems endless and would include such luminaries as F. Scott Fitzgerald, William Faulkner, Dylan Thomas, and Truman Capote. Drugs did many others in, especially in the second half of the century. Finally there is the case of Michel Foucault, the noted French critic and philosopher who continued engaging in unsafe sex after the AIDS epidemic had already begun, and who eventually contracted and died of the disease. The last one hundred years have also seen a number of unsuccessful suicide attempts by authors: Dorothy Parker, Eugene O'Neill, Raymond Chandler, Jean Genet, and A. Alvarez all tried. Ironically, O'Neill was saved by his college roommate, who later successfully committed suicide himself.[14] Finally, a number of important twentieth-century writers had close family members who committed suicide. Thomas Mann had two sisters, a sister-in-law, and two sons who killed themselves. Hugo von Hofmannsthal, Eugene O'Neill, and Robert Frost each experienced the suicide of a son. Hofmannsthal died at his home in Rodaun, a Viennese suburb, shortly after his son's death. As interesting as these related cases undoubtedly are, they are beyond the scope of this study. To examine them all would necessitate a book twice this length.

The stature of the twenty-five author-suicides profiled in depth in *Final Drafts* varies greatly. Several, including Virginia Woolf and Yukio Mishima, come from the highest ranks: their place on Parnassus is secure. Others such as Constance Woolson and Charles Jackson wrote popular works that were financial successes in their time but could hardly be classed as enduring. Still others—Klaus Mann and Ross Lockridge, for example—produced works of considerable achievement that are now neglected and largely forgotten. In part, it is the aim of this book to renew interest in these writers and their works.

Each of the authors who took his or her life did so for unique personal reasons. Certain distinct categories or subgroups, however, emerge upon investigation.

Some of the writers committed suicide because they could no longer produce. They felt that their abilities had atrophied and believed themselves unable to write work that equalled or excelled their previous efforts. Several decided that they were failures because of a lack of recognition or their inability to break into print. Others saw their deaths as political statements; they killed themselves because they felt hopeless. Some chose to die because they had a debilitating illness or because they feared that they were going insane. Still others decided upon death because they were spurned in love or because they tragically had lost their beloved to death. A number of the writers were gay, lesbian, or bisexual. Problems arising from their sexual orientation made suicide seem that much more attractive to them. Hart Crane wanted to return to the magical kingdom to which he had gained entry after undergoing anesthesia in a dental chair. A number of Jewish authors felt survivors' guilt for not perishing with their brethren in the Holocaust.

Although the writers in this study had widely divergent and highly individual reasons for ending their lives, they also shared certain vocational problems common to all members of the guild. In addition, they each faced quandaries and dilemmas peculiar to the modern era and thus were all children of the times. Artists suffer. The agonies and frustrations of composition are well known to anyone who has ever tried to create something out of nothing. While it is true that many writers speak of sudden flights of fancy, when the dam breaks and words come at lightning speed, they also tell of days when each sentence is a struggle. Often an artist is not able to judge his work objectively. He may not always be able to distinguish between his best and his second-best material. Depending on his mood, his opinions of himself and what he produces necessarily fluctuate. As he so closely identifies himself with what he produces, his self-esteem is often dependent on the reception of his work. He is prone to inflated feelings of self-importance. He feels a special calling and narcissistically views himself as an especially blessed being, as one set aside, a Sunday child. His expectations are correspondingly high. He feels that he should be compensated in love and material rewards for the sacrifices he is making, yet all too often he experiences nothing but rejection and rebuff. Manic hours alternate with periods of low self-esteem and depression. A writer's life is usually always one of peaks and valleys.

Authors have always been peculiarly susceptible to the suicidal impulse, the most gifted and successful as well as the least talented and the least prosperous. In other eras, suicide was far less tolerated than it is in modern times. The stigma which was formerly attached to taking one's life was so great that it restrained many from rushing into the secret house of death. Our attitude has shifted. We are much more broad-minded and accepting of suicide today than our ancestors were a century ago. Not only has the modern era seen the disintegration and collapse of traditional values, it has seen the most disastrous and bloody wars in all of recorded human history. After Auschwitz and Hiroshima, the worthiness of mankind to continue to exist has itself been called into question. Many of the writers who took their own lives during this time saw themselves as exemplars of what was best in their society's culture. The bloody events of this century called the value of these very cultures into question.

In Hart Crane's poem of mystic connection, *The Bridge*, a transcontinental train, the 20th-Century Limited, not only carries it passengers across the nation, it transports them back in time. Crane maintains that to fathom modern America, one must also comprehend her past and see the interconnection between yesterday and tomorrow. To understand the phenomenon of modern literary suicide, we also must first move backward. So let us board Hart's train and slip back before the turn of the nineteenth century. Our first suicide occurs in 1894. . . .

Notes

1. For more on Shakespeare's disposition and temperament, see S. Schoenbaum, *William Shakespeare: A Compact Documentary Life* (New York: Oxford University Press, 1977), pp. 255–59.

2. See A. Alvarez, *The Savage God* (New York: W.W. Norton, 1990), pp. 63–93 and Edith Hamilton, *The Greek Way* (New York: W.W. Norton, 1964), *passim*.

3. See Alvarez, *The Savage God*, pp. 63-93 and Edith Hamilton, *The Roman Way* (New York: W.W. Norton, 1967), *passim*.

4. Alvarez, *The Savage God*, p. 235.

5. See Henri Troyat, *Tolstoy* (New York: Doubleday, 1967), pp. 373–414.

6. For more information on the Kleist-Vogel suicide pact, see Joachim Maass, *Kleist: A Biography*, trans. Ralph Manheim (New York: Farrar, Straus and Giroux, 1983), pp. 262–87.

7. Alvarez, *The Savage God*, p 232.

8. For more on Goethe's thoughts of suicide, see Albert Bielschowsky, *The Life of Goethe*, vol. 1 (New York: Haskell House Publishers, 1969), pp. 184–87.

9. Roger Tennant, *Joseph Conrad* (New York: Atheneum, 1981), p. 24.

10. David Daiches, Malcolm Bradbury, and Eric Mottram, eds., *The Avenel Companion to English and American Literature, Britain and the Commonwealth* (New York: Avenel Books, 1981), p. 225.

11. Lillian Herlands Hornstein, G. D. Percy, Sterling A. Brown, eds., *The Reader's Companion to World Literature*, 2nd ed. (New York: New American Library, 1973), p. 359.

12. Alvarez, *The Savage God*, pp. 213–14.

13. Paul West, "Tan Salaam and the Aga Khan," *Sheer Fiction*, vol. 3 (Kingston, N.Y.: McPherson, 1994), pp. 88–89.

14. Travis Bogard, "Notes and Chronology," in Eugene O'Neill, *Complete Plays*, vol. 1 (New York: Library of America, 1988), p. 1066.

Constance J. Woolson

HER MOTHER WAS A NIECE OF JAMES FENIMORE COOPER, HER father a Yankee businessman who throughout his life suffered from chronic depression, a susceptibility which she would inherit from him. In later life, she claimed that her own melancholia was a sort of family curse. She felt particularly vulnerable in winter and preferred the warmth and brightness of southern climes to the dark and chill of the north. "Every year proves to me more and more decidedly . . . that it is entirely a matter of warmth. . . . The minute it is warm, all the wretchedness, no matter what serious and dignified name it may have borne, vanishes into nothing, and never comes back until it is cold again."[1] She also suffered from a distressing physical affliction. For much of her life, Woolson was extremely hard of hearing. Completely deaf in one ear, she would constantly have to turn her head so her good side faced anyone speaking to her. Her condition chagrined and embarrassed her. She felt isolated and cut off from others, especially when caught in a crowd or while attending a social function where many people were speaking simultaneously. For a great many years, Constance F. Woolson led a solitary, lonely life.

Born in New Hampshire in 1840, she was the sixth of nine children, eight of whom were girls. When she was a small child, her family relocated to Cleveland, Ohio. Until 1879, she would dwell not only in the American North and Midwest but also, for fifteen years, in the deep South. She came to know all three regions intimately, describing each with meticulous exactness in her prose. Adept at evoking local color through minute description, Woolson discovered her literary vocation early in life. Prior to attending finishing school in New York City, she already knew she wanted to be a writer, to follow the trail blazed by her granduncle. As a young girl, she accompanied her father on his many business trips. Together, in his buggy, they crisscrossed the Lake Country, often wandering deep into isolated and secluded neighborhoods. As a result of these excursions, not only would she develop a knowledge of both the plant and wildlife of the area—while her father dickered and bargained with the locals, she would traipse down Indian trials leading to Erie's marshy shores—but her imagination would carry her backwards into time. As a result of these transports and revels, Woolson began, in her own fanciful romantic fashion, to fathom the self-sacrificing character and pioneer spirit of the first colonists, the early settlers her granduncle had written about, those hearty explorers and frontiersmen who had foraged in the wild and braved the unknown. She had an inkling of the great solitude in which these men and women abode and suffered. Having found her corner of the country, she began to work it in the manner of her granduncle. Her Northern sketches started appearing in fashionable American periodicals in the 1870s. They were favorably received and brought her to the attention of John Hay and William Dean Howells, who would promote and publish her future work. She achieved recognition and popular success, but that was not enough for her. She aspired to lasting literary achievement.

After her father's death, Woolson devoted her best years to the care of her mother. Thinking that a more temperate climate would be beneficial to that lady's delicate health, she persuaded her to take up residence in Florida and accompanied her there, acting as her nurse and companion. At first hand, Woolson observed the devastation wrought by the Civil War and the struggle of the Southerners to reconstruct their society. She grew to admire the rugged determination of the vanquished enemy who had suffered so bitterly both during and then following the war. She vowed that, despite her Yankee heritage and her resultant prejudices, she would provide a tongue for all the mute, conquered mouths she encountered on her Southern travels. She could "hear" their silent lament, and it saddened her that no artist had taken up the theme, that the Southern song had largely gone untranscribed. She would do her best to remedy this in her subsequent work. At the same time, she remained sympathetic to the negro. Despite her hearing defect, Woolson was among the first American writers to reproduce faithfully black speech patterns in her prose. She made a proper philological study of black dialect, and in her writing tried especially hard to "take their words straight from their lips."[2] While much of what she saw in the South seemed bleak and sad—the ruined plantations, the endless war cemeteries which she went out of her way to visit and described to Thomas Bailey Aldrich as "poor lonely unvisited spots, the very perfection of their order only increasing their solitariness"[3]—she also found great natural beauty in the region and attempted to depict it faithfully in the tales and sketches that she set there. Again, her precise attention to detail and her talent for close observation served her well, just as they had previously done in her Northern sketches. On a regular basis, she took long walks by herself, even on the hottest afternoons, through the rice fields and on to the rim of the huge, brackish swamps, the home of beautiful birds such as the green and the blue heron but also of poisonous snakes and short and broad-snouted crocodilians. She took in everything that she could on these excursions and with time developed an intimate knowledge of Woolson's surroundings. The great friend of her later years would praise Woolson's Southern stories by remarking that she knew "every vague odour and sound, the song and flight of every bird, every tint of the sky and murmur of the forest."[4] Her writing was marked and distinguished by its verisimilitude, by its many minute touches and fine nuances.

After the death of her mother, new possibilities opened for Woolson, but by then she had reached an age where the prospect for marriage and motherhood had greatly diminished if not altogether disappeared. The handicap of her near deafness, she realized, also lessened the likelihood of anyone asking for her hand. Her sisters had married and she had been blessed with numerous nieces and nephews. It appeared, however, that she would never have a child of her own. Still, she had her vocation and could nonetheless be fertile in her own way. Apart from the numerous tales and sketches which had appeared in the magazines, she had, by 1879, published both a long narrative poem entitled *Two Women* and a collection of her Northern stories, *Castle Nowhere*, whose title perhaps reflected a feeling of rootlessness on Woolson's part, of her not having a home to call her own. At this time, she was also putting the finishing touches to a volume of Southern tales, *Rodham the Keeper*, which would bring her more recognition than any of her previous efforts. Moreover, she had that year reached a major crossroad in her life. At age thirty-nine, with the encouragement of Hay and William Dean Howells, she had come to the decision to make an Atlantic crossing, to leave the United States, and take up permanent residence in Europe.

Prior to leaving America, Woolson had made the acquaintance of the work of an American author, three years younger than herself, who had already been living abroad for quite some time, and whose works dealing with the adventures of American expatriates living in Europe had excited her unlike those of any other contemporary she had previously encountered. Woolson was prescient enough to realize that he already possessed a mastery of style that rivaled, perhaps already surpassed, that of any other American, living or dead. She had gushed and effused about his work—albeit anonymously—in the "Contributor's Club" of the *Atlantic*, and she desperately wanted to meet this man, whose prose she had pondered and studied, and whose style she had already tried to emulate in her own writing. Prior to embarking on her ocean voyage, she obtained a letter of introduction to Henry James from his cousin Henrietta Pell-Clark, the sister of Minny Temple, the favorite cousin of James's youth who had died nine years before. In 1879, Mrs. Pell-Clark resided in Cooperstown, New York, the town founded on Otsego Lake by the father of Woolson's famous granduncle, and where the latter, as a young man, gained his insight into frontier life and learned the ways and virtues of the American Indian. When Woolson arrived in London that winter, she took rooms in Clarges Street which abutted Bolton Street, the avenue where James maintained his

London flat. Armed with Pell-Clark's document, she strode up to his front door to present herself, only to be told that Henry James was currently not at home, but in Paris. She would not catch up with him until the following spring. Since he was on the continent and England proved as bleak, damp, and cold as the Lake Country of her girlhood, she headed southward almost immediately, stopping for the next several months at a hotel on the Riviera, where the climate was much more to her satisfaction. Here she had the opportunity to observe closely the various wealthy European types who congregated there and to travel and sightsee, but she also applied herself to her various writing projects, diligently spending her mornings working. She drafted poems and composed stories, but also began a novel, *Anne*, which would prove to be her greatest popular success and yet also the work Henry James considered her weakest. He found the early chapters set in a country boarding house full of promise and thought the novel's heroine, Tita Douglas, exerted great charm on the reader, but felt that Woolson had her marry far too early in the book. He wrote that Woolson resorted to the device of marriage altogether too often in her fiction: "She likes the unmarried, as I have mentioned, but she likes marriages even better, and also sometimes hurries them forward in advance of the reader's exaction."[5]

Constance F. Woolson's and Henry James's paths would finally cross in Florence in April 1880. Just prior to their meeting, she would finish one of her better stories, "Miss Grief," published in the May 1880 issue of *Lippincott's*. Set in Rome, it concerned the first encounter between a world-famous male author and a forty-three-year-old spinster, Aarona Moncrief—or Crief, as the novelist dubs her—who has literary pretensions herself and who, although she greatly admires the work of the novelist—indeed, she has read every word that he has written—nonetheless feels that she can compete with him when it comes to literary endeavors. After she recites a scene from one of the writer's books by heart, the author comes to the conclusion that she understands him perhaps better than he understands himself. She lends him the manuscript of one of her plays, he reads it, and compliments her on her work. Afterward she confesses to him that she would have committed suicide had he not found the play to his liking. Privately, the author feels that one of the lesser characters is poorly drawn and, editing the play, attempts to remove this character but discovers that "to take him out was like taking out one especial figure in the carpet: that it is impossible unless you unravel the whole."[6] At one point in the story, Crief tells her friend that while he had greater success in his career, she had "greater power."[7] After her death he concedes this. However, he notes that he, with less power, succeeded, whereas she, with more, failed. A number of years later, James would give one of his most famous stories the title "The Figure in the Carpet."

They were both in the same European city. Resignedly, James felt that he had to meet Woolson, but he considered it an unpleasant social obligation forced upon him from outside. He wrote to his sister Alice that Florence was "a place where one is liable to tea-parties. I have to call, for instance, on Constance Fenimore Woolson, who has been pursuing me through Europe with a letter of introduction from (of all people in the world!) Henrietta Pell-Clark."[8] Undoubtedly expecting the very worse, he mustered his courage and paid a visit to her pension, where much to his surprise instead of the dilettante dowager he expected to find, he discovered a not unattractive, intelligent kindred spirit, a true admirer of his work. She could be witty and ironic and had a somewhat exalted sense of her own worth as an author. Additionally, her manner was a touch pert: she did not hesitate to tweak him a little, but he rather liked that, and was in fact used to being pilloried both by his relations at home and in the American press for his somewhat stuffy pretensions. Moreover, James had arrived in Florence in April 1880 at an emotional ebb. He had come to Italy to reestablish his friendship with Paul Joukovski, a Russian painter he had been introduced to by Turgenev in Paris some five years before, and who now resided in the Naples suburb of Posillippo. To James's profound disappointment, Joukovski had degenerated into the slavish minion of the composer Richard Wagner. If the painter's hero worship was off-putting, his personal habits and fixations left even more to be desired. Joukovski had become openly homosexual. A number of the hangers-on in the composer's entourage shared the same tendency, if not Wagner himself. Joukovski wanted badly to introduce James to his idol, but Henry declined his offer and abruptly left Posillippo after spending only a few days there. The new acquaintance with Woolson helped to heal his still fresh wound. She moved in and filled the void left by the Russian, and he could rest assured that his relationship with her had a sure footing—was well within proper bounds. Their attachment would appear seemly and tasteful to all eyes, and he would emerge as a model of decorum and propriety. Finding Constance Woolson to his liking, James took on, in short order, the role of her guide and cicerone. Despite his numerous social obligations and his arduous writing schedule, he found time to visit frequently the middle-aged lady novelist and to supervise her sightseeing. They visited the galleries, palaces and churches, and James was amused by the fact that his new friend blushed at the nude statues in the sacristies. While James was always the perfect gentleman, his manner was nonetheless detached, altogether dispassionate. Despite his reserve, with time, he developed, in his own tepid fashion, a great fondness and liking for Woolson, or Fenimore as he came to call her, but it was "a virtuous attachment"[9] on his part, whereas she had been enamored of James even before they met and afterward acquired an even greater passion for him as both writer and man. She knew that her feelings weren't reciprocated in the manner that she wished, but she was patient and hoped to win him over with time.

They would not meet again until the autumn of 1883, when Woolson would take up residence in England. Despite her dislike of the weather, she would stay three years and see James at regular, discreet intervals. They attended the theater together and, in each other's company, once paid a visit to Stonehenge. Woolson also made many excursions on her own to famous sites and spots throughout the English countryside and started working on a new novel, *East Angels*. James found this work her best production to date and said that it was "a substantial contribution to American letters,"[10] a novel that equalled that of any of her male contemporaries. It concerns a group of wealthy New Englanders who winter in Florida and who travel back and forth between Europe and the United States on a frequent basis. The novel shifts effortlessly between its various locales. The heroine is the self-sacrificing Margaret Harold who remains loyal to an unworthy husband instead of falling into the arms of the man who loves her and whom she herself secretly loves. To prevent forever the possibility of a lapse on her part, she contrives to bring about the marriage of her admirer to another woman. Although James felt that among the characters in *East Angels*, the "tender sentiment" usurped "a place even greater perhaps than that which it holds in life,"[11] he considered the "long, comprehensive, copious" work much more "elaborate than her other elaborations."[12] It gave the definite promise of future high accomplishment. Despite her sightseeing and literary success, Woolson's chief compensation in England was her proximity to James. Nonetheless, after three years, she again felt the call of Italy. Perhaps her health dictated the move. When Woolson returned to Florence in the spring of 1886, James wrote his friend Francis Duveneck to keep an eye on her.

During the years that followed, there would be a number of private trysts and rendezvous between the two writers. Either James would travel to the continent or she would come to England. Beginning in 1890, she would for several years once more make her home there, at the end of which she would retreat to Italy a final time. James would be cajoled into promising annual visits prior to this last departure. However, for most of their lives, and even after Woolson had returned to England, the two remained largely apart. They maintained contact though letters. In later years, James insisted that they destroy each other's correspondence, and, as we shall see, after his friend's death, he retrieved those of his letters that she was unwilling to commit to her fireplace but spared instead as treasured mementoes and keepsakes. Despite Henry's scrupulosity when it came to destroying his personal correspondence, four of Woolson's early letters to him were inadvertently preserved among William James's papers in America—the only survivors of what must have been a voluminous correspondence. They date from the period of Henry James's and Constance Woolson's earliest acquaintance, from the years between their first meeting in Florence and their subsequent reassociation in England. At the time, Henry was traveling in America. The letters were forwarded to his brother's address in Cambridge. They are long and diffuse. She harries him unmercifully for his neglect of her and protests that he is never in Italy but always either in England or America and she objects that he only writes her infrequently and not at length. She recognizes the value of his work and praises it lavishly, but nonetheless makes frequent criticisms as well—complains that he doesn't understand how a woman feels or thinks. She asks why he does not give his readers a female character for whom they can feel a real love. She writes "let her love very much, and let us see that she does. . . . If you will only care for her yourself, as you describe her, the thing is done."[13] Despite the harshness of some of Woolson's remarks concerning James's writing, it is also evident that, not only does she stand in perfect awe of his ability, she is, in fact, quite envious of it. She despairs that he writes as well as he does at the first draft, whereas she revises constantly and to no avail; she laments that he is underappreciated. Others do not recognize his worth. "We little fish did!" she writes, "We little fish became worn to skeletons owing to the constant admonitions we received to regard the beauty, the grace, the incomparable perfection . . . of the proud salmon of the pond; we ended by hating the salmon."[14]

In December 1886, ten months after Woolson's abrupt flight from England following her first three-year residency there, James followed her to Florence, where he became her tenant for the remainder of the month, subletting rooms from her at the villa Brichieri-Colombi on the hilltop of the Bellosquardo. She had recently taken the villa on a two-year lease but presently was residing in an adjoining chateau, the villa Castellani, where she had rooms rented until the new year. Once her contract there expired, she would move into the Brichieri and Henry would take lodgings at a Florentine hotel. They were in close proximity to one another both during his tenancy of the villa when they were next-door neighbors and then, living somewhat farther apart, during his residency in town. He stayed in Florence until late February when he departed to Venice for seven weeks, at the end of which time (mid-April), he returned to Florence and moved back into Woolson's villa, where he would stay until the beginning of June. He and Woolson now lived under the same roof, and this, his second stay on the Bellosquardo, would mark the closest James would ever come in his life to entering a traditional domestic arrangement. She resided on the first floor of the spacious three-story mansion, he on the ground. They took their meals together, but spent much of the day apart, each at work writing. It was at this time that James first noticed what a "pack rat" Woolson had become. Apparently she never discarded anything. Her rooms were stuffed with trunks and boxes. She kept clothes she never wore, old magazines and books she never read. James marveled that she had managed to squirrel away so much having lived the migratory life she had. As he had never given her ground to hope, he had assumed that they had long come to a truce in their personal relations. James accepted Woolson as a sister artist, a gentlewoman of great sensibility. But now it became evident to him that she still perhaps cherished the idea of marriage. Both his outward circumstance and his private anxieties at that time are surely reflected in the novella he began writing and all but finished while living with Woolson in Florence: "The Aspern Papers." The narrator of the tale learns that certain papers of the famed American author Jeffrey Aspern are in the possession of his lover, the now very elderly Juliana Bordereau. She resides in a dilapidated

Venetian palace with her grandniece Tita. Determined to come into possession of
the papers, the narrator rents a suite of rooms from the elder Bordereau and courts
the younger. Tita, however, realizes that his interest in her is feigned and, after her
aunt's death, will give the narrator the papers only on the condition that he take her
hand in marriage. Unwilling to take this step, he flees Venice, realizing that he had
"unwittingly but none the less deplorably trifled."[15] Woolson was, of course, the
grandniece of James Fenimore Cooper, like the fictional Aspern, an early giant of
American literature. Moreover, Tita was the first name of the heroine of her novel
Anne. In a late revision of the story, perhaps out of guilt, Henry James changed the
younger Bordereau's name to Tina. While Woolson's tenant in Florence, James
came to the conclusion that he, too, had "deplorably trifled" and left Florence the
beginning of June.

For the next several years, Woolson still continued to hope. She kept writing
and composed a series of international tales in the manner of her idol and beloved.
Her productions never attained to his level of perfection, but were somewhat
crasser and "magazineish" in character; in short they were usually nothing more
than pale imitations or pastiches of James's earlier work. She had long realized that
she would come out the loser in any literary competition between the two, but kept
working anyway. When she took up residence in England a second time in 1890,
Woolson elected to live near Oxford in the town of Cheltenham, where she began
work on her last novel, *Horace Chase*. She and James would continue to exchange
letters and he would pay her the occasional visit. At this time, Henry James's sister
Alice was suffering through the last stages of her prolonged, final illness. Woolson
had made Alice's acquaintance during her earlier stay in England, and the two got
along famously from the first. Alice realized the extent of Woolson's attachment to
her brother and during the last years of her life repeatedly urged Henry to marry
her. Woolson grasped that, like herself, Alice stood in Henry's wide shadow, that
his brilliance and striking success had obscured Alice's own great intellectual
attainment; that she, too, had taken a backseat to him. Woolson summed up her
sentiments to Alice's physician: "If she had had any health at all, what a brilliant
woman she would have been."[16] One day before her death on March 6, 1892, Alice
James had her companion Kate Loring read her one of Woolson's stories. Alice's illness is reflected in the pages of the novel that Woolson was then writing. The
heroine of *Horace Chase* and wife of the title character has an invalid sister who
makes great demands on her time but serves as her advisor and confidante.
Knowing that Mrs. Chase is not in love with her elderly husband but another,
younger man who does not return her sentiment but for whom she nonetheless is
willing to risk all, she sympathizes with her sister's predicament and comforts her
the best that she can.

A year later, Constance Woolson wrote her nephew Samuel Mather that she
would in the near future be leaving England and returning to Italy as she was "giving
up being near [her] kind friend Mr. James."[17] Before her departure, she had obtained

his promise that he would visit her at least once a year. Perhaps, as a compensation for a failed union elsewhere, he had also offered to collaborate on a play with her, the only time in his career that he ever proposed to undertake such a joint venture.

The projected work would never be written. Woolson left England in June of 1893 ill with influenza. She had decided not to go to Florence—the city held too many sad memories for her—but to try to find happiness in Venice instead. When she arrived late in June, she rented a suite of rooms in the Casa Biodetti where she had a beautiful view of the Grand Canal. During the summer months, she arose at 4:30 A.M., wrote until breakfast, and then continued writing until late into the afternoon. The final installments of the serial of *Horace Chase* had appeared and now she was extensively revising the novel for publication in book form. At 4 P.M., she would lay aside her work and hire a gondola to ferry her out to the Lido, where she would swim. She would return to the casa to dine, then spend the evening on the canals listening to music and looking at the marble palaces. Her quarters at the Biodetti were too cramped for her taste, so she eventually moved into the Casa Semitecolo near the Palazzo Dario where she was able to lease two entire floors. For companionship, she purchased a small Pomeranian dog she named Tello. Woolson finished her revision of *Horace Chase* early in January and sent the manuscript to the publishers. As had often been the case when she finished a book, she grew melancholy and depressed, a psychical response shared by Virginia Woolf and others. When "a book is done," she wrote "I am pretty nearly done myself."[18] In a letter to her nephew, Woolson confessed that it was her daily prayer that she would not live to be old. Although Christmas had been unseasonably warm, the weather had taken a turn for the worse in January. The casa was cold and she was subject to her usual winter despondency. "This deadly enemy of mine creeps in, and once in, he is master," she wrote to a friend. "I try to conquer it and sometimes I succeed, sometimes I don't."[19] By the middle of the month, Woolson had again contracted influenza and ran a high fever. A nurse had to be called in. A little after 1:00 A.M. on the morning of January 24, 1894, Woolson sent the nurse out of her room on the pretext of having her bring some article or other from one of the nearby drawing rooms. After she had left, Woolson got out of bed, opened the window of her second-story room and threw herself down to the cobbles below. She was still alive when her body was discovered by two men walking in the *calle*. Their shouts roused the servants, and Woolson was quickly carried back into the house and placed in her bed. A doctor was summoned but could do nothing for her. She died before daybreak.

At the news of Woolson's death, Henry James was greatly grieved and tormented. At first, he thought that she had expired from natural causes and made travel plans to attend her funeral in Rome, but, in short order, the circumstance of her death was made known to him. His grief turned to dread and horror, and he could no longer bring himself to attend her funeral. He wrote John Hay that he had utterly collapsed with the "dreadful image" of Woolson's body before him: "I felt an intense nearness of participation in every circumstance of her tragic end and in every detail of the sequel. But it is just this nearness of emotion that has made—since yesterday—the immediate horrified rush to personally meet these things impossible to me."[20] No doubt James felt that, at least in some measure, he could be held personally accountable for her death, realizing as he did that his inability over the years to respond romantically to her was one of the chief frustrations of Woolson's life, if not the root cause of her late unhappiness. Although he did not attend the ceremony, he had flowers sent to her grave in his name. Woolson was interred in the Protestant Cemetery in Rome, where James had laid his fictional heroine Daisy Miller to rest many years before.

The following March, James traveled to Venice where he offered Woolson's sister his assistance in sorting through her cluttered effects and abundant belongings. He would also examine the literary remains of his late colleague. Going through her papers, he retrieved the letters of his which she had kept as mementoes and promptly destroyed them. He also examined her notebooks and journals to see if there were any references there to her unhappiness at their problematical relations. He read her numerous reflections on art and literature and the sketches and notes she had made for future stories. He must have winced in self-recognition when he read the following jotting:

> Imagine a man endowed with an absolutely unswerving will; extremely intelligent, he *comprehends* passion, affection, unselfishness and self-sacrifice etc. perfectly, though he is himself cold and a pure egotist. He has a charming face, a charming voice, and he can, when he pleases, counterfeit all these feelings so exactly that he gets all the benefits that are to be obtained by them.[21]

It was in another of her notes, however, that James would find the seed for a future story. It is in Woolson's journal that we discover the genesis of *The Beast in the Jungle*:

> To imagine a man spending his life looking for and waiting for his "splendid moment." "Is this my moment?" "Will this state of things bring it to me?" But the moment never comes. When he is old and infirm it comes to a neighbour who never thought of it or cared for it. The comment of the first upon this.[22]

He would take her idea and make it his own.

After finishing with her papers, James had one last sad office to render her grieving relations—to dispose of his friend's seemingly endless black dresses. She had so many of them that, during her later years, she must have seemed to be in perpetual mourning. James had the dresses stacked into a gondola and then took a seat beside them. He had the gondolier row him and his cargo out into the middle of the lagoon, where, one by one, he tossed the dresses into the water. The garments, however, filling with air, immediately bobbed to the surface. With a stick, James tried to beat them under, but they kept coming up like hideous black balloons. Soon the gondola was surrounded by them. He struck at the dresses frantically but they simply refused to sink.[23]

Notes

1. Quoted by Fred Kaplan, *Henry James: The Imagination of Genius* (New York: William Morrow, 1992), pp. 222–23.

2. Henry James, "Miss Woolson," *Literary Criticism*, vol. 2 (New York: Library of America, 1984), p. 641.

3. Quoted by Leon Edel, *Henry James: The Complete Biography*, vol. 2 (New York: Avon Books, 1978), p. 408.

4. James, "Miss Woolson," p. 641.

5. Ibid., p. 642.

6. Quoted by Edel, *James*, vol. 2, p. 416.

7. Ibid.

8. Ibid., p. 410.

9. Ibid., p. 417.

10. Ibid., p. 645.

11. Ibid., p. 646.

12. Ibid., p. 645.

13. Quoted by Edel, *James*, vol. 3, p. 89.

14. Ibid., p. 90.

15. Ibid., p. 225.

16. Quoted by Jean Strouse, *Alice James* (Boston: Houghton Mifflin, 1980), p. 307.

17. Quoted by Edel, *James*, vol. 3, p. 317.

18. Quoted by Kaplan, *Henry James*, p. 382.

19. Ibid, pp. 382–83.

20. Ibid, p. 380.

21. Quoted by Edel, *James*, vol. 3, p. 370.

22. Ibid.

23. Kaplan, *Henry James*, p. 386.

John Davidson

THE SCOTTISH POET, PLAYWRIGHT, AND NOVELIST JOHN DAVIDSON LEFT his rented home at 6 Coulson's Terrace, Penzance, England, on the coast of Cornwall, at about half past six in the evening on Tuesday, March 23, 1909. He had just completed a new collection of verse entitled *Fleet Street and Other Poems* and went out, ostensibly, to post the manuscript as well as another parcel containing reader's reports (he supplemented his meager income by evaluating manuscripts) to his publisher Grant Richards in London. At least, his wife Maggie thought that this was his intention. Subsequently only the parcel containing the reader's reports would arrive at Richards' Carlton Street office. Davidson seemed to be in a festive mood. He had finished his manuscript evaluations earlier in the day and had prepared both packages for delivery. Before leaving the house, he scribbled a menu for a sumptuous dinner on a porcelain writing tablet. He scrawled his bill of fare in French:

Crème aux Pommes de Terre
Boeuf à la Schottishe
Du Pain
Choufleur au Gratin
De l'Eau
Pouding de Riz.[1]

His handwriting was uncharacteristically sloppy, and he joked to his wife that this was due to the fact that he had been writing all day. Passersby observed Davidson in the post office and then inside the Star Hotel where he drank a glass of whiskey and purchased a choice cigar. The telegraphist at the Western Union Cable office saw him exit the hotel. He headed homeward, puffing on the stogie. This was the final authenticated sighting of the fifty-one-year-old poet. It had been Davidson's habit to take long evening strolls, especially after a full day of work, so his absence that evening at first did not cause any particular alarm. As the hours passed, however, his wife grew increasingly concerned. She feared that her husband had perhaps taken a heart attack or had met with some accident. When he walked, he became so engaged in his thoughts that he did not pay attention to his surroundings. Only a month earlier, he had walked off a raised pavement and fallen to the ground. It was only a four feet drop but he had nonetheless badly bruised himself. Could he have perhaps likewise walked over the edge of one of the coastal cliffs and fallen into the English Channel below?

At 10:00 P.M., Maggie Davidson and their son Menzies went to a neighbor's house to ask for help. The Ashtons ushered Mrs. Davidson into their parlor and dispatched their boy to go along with Menzies in search of his father. The two young men scoured the vicinity. They looked for Davidson both in town and on the public walk along the shore in the direction of the village of Mousehole, where Davidson would have been most apt to stroll. Their search was without success. The following morning, Mrs. Davidson cabled both Grant Richards and her other son Alexander in London to see if her husband had gone to the city without informing her. He had not shown up at either's residence. Maggie would telegram Richards a second time in the afternoon. He would wire her back that only a single package had been delivered to his office. He also recommended that Mrs. Davidson contact the local police. When the constables arrived at 6 Coulson's Terrace, they asked Mrs. Davidson if she had searched the house for a suicide note. It was well known that, for a number of years, Davidson had showed signs of psychological disturbance. He had suffered health problems for quite some time and recently he had experienced marked difficulty in breathing as a result of asthma and chronic bronchitis. At various times during 1908, he had also appeared to be suffering from acute depression, and in August of that year he had drawn up his will.

Also in 1908, he had published the last of his five *Testaments*, a series of lengthy philosophical poems that reflect (as do a number of his popular ballads of the nineties such as "Thirty Bob a Week") the ideas of Arthur Schopenhauer, Ernst Haeckel, and Friedrich Nietzsche. Davidson came to believe that life was nothing more than a grand cosmic jest. Existence was replete with false dualities such as body and soul, man and woman, time and space, and day and night. Such antitheses could be abolished only in death. The riddle of the universe was solved through the nebular hypothesis. The cosmos is governed by strict scientific laws: a material truth that cannot be gainsaid. Davidson came to believe that all human beings secretly long for extinction, to return to the state or the primal condition which still persists in the infinitude of interstellar space. All bothersome antitheses are resolved in the unconscious energies of creation. In man, a potent, natural force expedites the abandonment of the will to live and the return to nonexistence. We all ache to revert to the primary ether, the elementary nebular substance out of which inorganic matter, the stars, and the planets arose. Eons later, animate organisms began to emerge and develop from inorganic compounds. Evolution at last culminated in man, and consciousness was lifted to its highest level. This end, however, had been the unconscious goal from the very beginning of the process as the following stanzas from "Thirty Bob a Week" clearly indicate:

> And it's this way that I make it out to be:
> No fathers, mothers, countries, climates—none;
> Not Adam was responsible for me,
> Nor society, nor systems, nary one:
> A little sleeping seed, I woke—I did, indeed—
> A million years before the blooming sun.
>
> I woke because I thought the time had come;
> Beyond my will there was no other cause;
> And everywhere I found myself at home,
> Because I chose to be the thing I was:
> And in whatever shape of mollusc or of ape
> I always went according to the laws.
>
> I was the love that chose my mother out;
> I joined two lives and from the union burst;
> My weakness and my strength without a doubt
> Are mine alone for ever from the first.
> It's just the very same with a difference in the name
> As "Thy will be done." You say it if you durst![2]

Consciousness attains its pinnacle in man, and despite all the false divisions that he perceives and daily must contend with, man, for a time, suffers from the delusion that he is God. Once he frees himself from this illusion, he achieves self-knowledge. When he comes to terms with his mortality, man not only learns his true nature but the universe comes to understand itself, for man is star stuff, inseparable from the rest of creation. With this revelation, however, the individual begins to experience the powerful allure of death and negation, for perception and awareness are a burden which he longs to be rid of. Consciousness disappears with life, and the star stuff that constitutes the human individual is once again free to merge back into the primary ether.

Davidson's dark philosophical preoccupations permeate the two plays that he authored during the years 1907 and 1908: *The Triumph of Mammon* and *Mammon and His Message*, the first and second installments of a projected trilogy to be entitled *God and Mammon* which Davidson had hoped would be his masterpiece. Davidson intended the two works to serve as vehicles to express his social and political concerns (indeed, Davidson's readers have generally found the plays bothersomely preachy and pedantic on that account) as well as to explore larger ontological issues. Behind all the political and economic baggage lie Davidson's materialist doctrine and his new philosophical discoveries. Mammon speaks for the author when, pointing out the false dualities that plague existence, he declares: "Time's a liar/ And space a trick."[3] Davidson had systematically developed and set forth his social and materialistic ideas in the first four of his *Testaments*, those, respectively, of "a Vivisector," "a Man Forbid," "an Empire-Builder," and "a Prime Minister." As always, he espouses the cause of the poor and downtrodden in England, yet at the same time he champions British imperialism, savagely attacks conventional morality and the Christian religion, and prophesies the rise of a Nietzschean superman.

The fifth poem in the series was much more personal, as its title, "The Testament of John Davidson," will immediately suggest. While the earlier *Testaments* had explored the wider social applications of his materialistic philosophy, the final poem which runs over two thousand lines, was Davidson's "personal utterance on the Universe become conscious. . . ."[4] He examines how an individual can be empowered by the revelation that the facts of existence are sufficiently explained by the actuality of matter and by the certainty that no "other world" or spiritual realm exists anywhere but inside our minds. In the opening lines of the poem, Davidson justifies and excuses suicide. He argues that faced with the physical and mental deterioration that comes with old age, an individual should be able to end his life without fear or the recrimination of society. Under such circumstances, a person exhibits bravery and shrewdness by taking the reins of fate into his own hands. Again in control, once more the master of his destiny, he actually cheats death by killing himself, for he saves himself from unnecessary suffering and spares his friends and family the spectacle of a protracted demise. Davidson intimates that his own end is near but that he, for one, will not allow death to defeat and degrade him:

> "None should outlive his power," I said. "Who kills
> Himself subdues the conqueror of kings:
> Exempt from death is he who takes his life:
> My time has come."[5]

He holds back, however, because he realizes that, through him and through him alone, the universe has finally gained consciousness of its existence, and that, with his demise, the universe would cease to know itself.

The bulk of the poem concerns the seduction of Diana, the goddess of chastity, by the *Testament*'s protagonist, an epic hero who, as it happens, shares the name of the poem's author. He conquers the virgin and thus metaphorically emancipates mankind from the false concepts of body and soul. By bringing back together what never should have been separated in the first place, he reestablishes the primal unity of the universe, and, in his hubris, he believes that he is God. For this sin, this "Pernicious slander of material truth,"[6] he must undergo crucifixion in hell. As the *Testament* closes, he returns to earth convinced of his error and now in a state of complete enlightenment. He realizes that the insights that he has attained will perish with him, but he accepts this resignedly as one of Nature's unconditional laws.

The *Testament* has both a prologue and epilogue. Davidson characterized these as "the two most personal poems I have written as a brother man"[7] and stated that he intended the first to depict the "dawn" and the latter to portray the "close" of his life. The former, "Honeymoon," is a reworking of his early poem "For Lovers," and venerates and exalts the delights of sexual intimacy. The latter, "The Last Journey," portrays a man at peace with his approaching death. During his time on this planet, he has walked great distances to see and experience all that life has to offer. Now, however, he will undertake the last journey. "The way is steep," he says, but "alone I climb/ The rugged path that leads me out of time—/Out of time and out of all. . . ."[8] We see a man who has accepted his fate and who is determined not to outlast his welcome or "outlive his power." His hour has come. He will melt back into the Infinite, return to the elemental resting place from which all life had originally sprung. Death will thus be a sort of homecoming. His voice will be stilled, but others will come after him and sing their songs in turn. Although the universe is in a state of constant flux, mutability is in itself a sort of constant. For all its manifold changes, the universe abides. The cycles of birth and death repeat themselves eternally, and, if individual men aren't immortal, matter and consciousness nonetheless are:

> I felt the world a-spinning on its nave,
> I felt it sheering blindly round the sun;
> I felt the time had come to find a grave:
> I knew it in my heart my days were done.
> I took my staff in hand; I took the road,
> And wandered out to seek my last abode.
> Hearts of gold and hearts of lead
> Sing it yet in sun and rain,
> 'Heel and toe from dawn to dusk,
> Round the world and home again.'[9]

> . . . .

> Farewell the hope that mocked, farewell despair
> That went before me still and made the pace.
> The earth is full of graves, and mine was there
> Before my life began, my resting-place;
> And I shall find it out and with the dead
> Lie down forever, all my sayings said—
> Deeds all done and songs all sung,
> While others chant in sun and rain,
> "Heel to toe from dawn to dusk,
> Round the world and home again."[10]

As a poet, John Davidson reached the height of his popularity in the early to mid-nineties. His depictions of city life in his first two collections, *In a Music Hall and Other Poems* (1891) and *Fleet Street Eclogues*, won him wide acclaim. After reading the first volume, William Butler Yeats called Davidson one of the leading poetic innovators in England at the close of the nineteenth century. The paradoxically titled second collection juxtaposes a London street with a term (eclogue) which, since its application to Vergil's *Bucolics*, has come to mean a pastoral idyll featuring shepherds as speakers. The volume was Davidson's first real popular success, going into a second edition in three months' time. Despite the book's notoriety and his new-won fame, like the Grub Street types he celebrates and lionizes in these so-called eclogues, Davidson did not make a sufficient income from his poems to devote himself solely to his art and therefore had to earn his livelihood by working as an editor, critic and a literary reviewer—a life of drudgery and endless hack work. He contributed articles to more than eighteen newspapers and literary journals, writing a weekly column for one and serving as the assistant editor of another. Nonetheless, he gained membership to both the Rhymers' Club (to which Yeats also belonged) and the Bodley Head. At the height of his fame, Davidson appeared to be living a charmed life. He associated with all the literary lights of the period—Edmund Gosse, Arthur Symons, Grant Allen, and Yeats, among others. He frequented the theaters and music halls and drank absinthe late into the night. Yet, always short of money, even after the publication of his best and most highly regarded work, *Ballads and Songs*, in 1894, Davidson found himself under pressure to write more and more. He had to keep producing in order to make ends meet. Turning to the theater to supplement his income, he translated a number of European plays into English, notably François Coppée's *Pour la couronne* and Victor Hugo's *Ruy Blas*. He also wrote a stage adaption of Alphonse Daudet novel's *Sappho* as well as a number of original plays, including *Godfrida: A Play in Four Acts*, *Self's The Man: A Tragi-Comedy*, and *The Knight of the Maypole: A Comedy in Four Acts*. His version of *Pour la couronne*, *For the Crown*, which opened at the Lyceum on February 27, 1896, was a critical triumph. His other plays—adaptions and originals both—were not nearly so successful. Many were published but never produced. Others had only short runs. In his will, Davidson stipulated that, along with all his letters, the manuscripts of seven unpublished plays and adaptations, including a Lancelot drama he had undertaken in 1902, be committed to the fireplace. Apparently his instructions were carried out.

From the beginning, Davidson's poems dealt with the sordid realities of modern life. He had a low opinion of most Victorian poetry because it failed to take into account the rampant human suffering occurring in England at the time. Nor would it deal with the country's economic inequities and caste system then prevailing. He demanded a new aesthetic. "Poetry is not always an army on parade," he wrote. "Sometimes it is an army coming back from wars, epaulettes and pipeclay all gone, shoeless, ragged, wounded, starved but with victory on its brows. All the woe of the world is to be uttered at last. Poetry has been democratized. Nothing could prevent that. The songs are of the highways and byways. The city slums and the deserted villages are haunted by sorrowful figures, men of power and endurance, feeding their melancholy not with heroic fable, the beauty of the moon, and the studious cloisters, but with the actual sight of the misery in which so many millions live. To this mood the vaunted sweetness and light of the ineffective apostle of culture are like a faded rose in a charnel house, a flash of moonlight on the Dead Sea."[11]

For the most part, Davidson's own life was one of struggle and disappointment. Plagued with monetary difficulties that forced him to adopt a Spartan manner of living and beset by personal tragedies throughout his life, he could empathize with the lower classes who, because of high unemployment and low wages, frequently lost all hope and ambition. Giving into despair, such individuals often drowned their sorrows in alcohol or, with a chip on their shoulders, drifted into crime, perhaps dreaming of someday violently striking back at society. Davidson understood such a mindset. He did not demand, however, that the poet confine himself to the topic of human misery, but required that the poet give the subject a place in his work proportional to its place in life. He had a painter's eye and in the same poem could convey both the rugged grandeur of the environs of Greenock on the Firth of Clyde and the dearth and grime of the industrial shipping port itself. The city has a weird sort of beauty despite its squalor and wretchedness. A beauty due, in part, ironically to its soot and smoke:

> I need
> No world more spacious than the region here:
> The foam-embroidered firth, a purple path
> For argosies that still on pinions speed.
> Or fiery-hearted cleave with iron limbs
> And bows precipitous the pliant sea;
> The sloping shores that fringe the velvet tides
> With heavy buillion and with golden lace
> Of restless pebble woven and fine spun sand;
> The villages that sleep the winter through,
> And, wakening with the spring keep festival
> All Summer and all autumn: this grey town
> That pipes the morning up before the lark
> With shrieking steam, and from a hundred stalks
> Lacquers the sooty sky; where hammers clang
> On iron hulls, and cranes in harbours creak
> Rattle and swing, whole cargoes on their necks;
> Where men sweat gold that others hoard or spend,
> And lurk like vermin in their narrow streets:
> This old grey town, this firth, the further strand
> Spangled with hamlets, and the wooded steeps,
> Whose rocky tops behind each other press,
> Fantastically carved like antique helms
> High-hung in heaven's cloudy armoury,
> Is world enough for me.[12]

Born April 11, 1857, in Barrhead, Renfrewshire, in southwestern Scotland, John Davidson was the fourth child and first son born to Alexander and Helen Crockett Davidson. His father was an ordained minister in the Evangelical Union Church, whereas his maternal grandfather had earned his livelihood as a school-teacher. In 1859, the family moved to Glasgow, some six miles north of Barrhead, after Reverend Davidson was named pastor of the Evangelical Church in Montrose Street. A few years later, Alexander Davidson was again transferred, this time to the port city of Greenock. In conversation, the younger Davidson always remained respectful and deferential toward his father. He maintained that the older man had a reputation for delivering memorable sermons and, recalling the latter's deep, resonant voice, said that people from other parishes would leave their own churches early in order to hear Alexander Davidson offer up the benediction at the close of his own service. Davidson also considered his father to be something of a courageous rebel, due to the fact that, as a young man, he had forsaken his parent church in order to join the Evangelical Union. No doubt the anti-Christian stance the poet later developed had much to do with the severity and sternness of his father's chosen denomination. Young John saw the Reverend Davidson as a demanding and forbidding authority figure, and, from an early age he rebelled against the strictures of his father's sect. While Alexander Davidson had given a heated temperance speech at the age of fifteen, his son, at an equally young age, would develop a penchant for whiskey and cigars as well as the poetry of Algernon Charles Swinburne, and, in his spare hours, would inevitably be found frequenting Greenock's saloons and music halls. Davidson's true attitude toward his father is perhaps best expressed in "A Ballad in Blank Verse," written in 1894 after the Reverend Davidson's death. The poem concerns a narrow-minded and self-righteous Calvinist, who is so set in his ways that he has become blind and indifferent to the anguish and distress of the world about him. The elder Davidson also had a puritanical attitude toward sex. Davidson probably modeled the character of the castrating king in *The Triumph of Mammon*, at least in part, on his father.

John Davidson had been something of an infant prodigy or *Wunderkind*. He attended the Highlander's Academy in Greenock, where he proved to be an excellent student. At the age of nine, he was able to participate in an involved debate concerning predestination. A few years later, he had memorized all of Shakespeare's sonnets as well as Milton's "Comus" and large sections of the *Morte Darthur*. He wrote his first poem in 1869, "a sturdy ballad on the defeat of the Moors by Pamiro king of Spain." Even though he left school in 1870 to work in the chemical laboratory of Walker's Sugar factory, he continued writing both poems and playlets in his spare time. The following year, when the Food Adulteration Act passed in Parliament, Davidson became an assistant to the public analyst in Greenock. In 1872, he was appointed a student teacher at Highlander's Academy. He remained in this post for four years and read voraciously. During this time, he acquainted himself not only with all the major writers of the English canon but read a great deal of European literature in translation as well. In 1876 he studied briefly at Edinburgh University. The following year he wrote his first full-length play, *An Unhistorical Pastoral*, and took a position at Alexander's Charity School in Glasgow. He attended university classes in the city and eventually became the protégé of John Nichol, a professor of English at the university there. Nichol would introduce Davidson to Algernon Swinburne in 1878. Supposedly, Swinburne declaimed some of Davidson's early verse, and, impressed by what he read, extended his hand, touched the younger man's shoulder and pronounced him poet. Encouraged by the great man's regard for him, Davidson joined the Glasgow Ballad Club, where he made the acquaintances of a number of individuals, including John Cramb, William Canton, and W. S. McCormick, whose friendships would later prove beneficial to him in London.

From 1878 to 1881, Davidson served as English master at Perth Academy. While in Perth, Davidson probably met his future wife, Margaret Cameron MacArthur, the daughter of a bobbin factory owner who at one time had been mayor of the city. Aside from teaching, Davidson performed at a series of local entertainments, reciting traditional ballads such as "Tam o'Shanter." This conduct was found unbecoming by the school authorities, who dismissed Davidson on account of it. He next taught at Kelvinside Academy, Glasgow, and in 1883 took a position at Hutchinson Charity School in Paisley. On October 23, 1884, he married Margaret and during the first year of their married life worked as a clerk in a Glasgow thread company. He published both a journeyman novel, *The North Wall*, and a verse drama, *Diabolus Amans*, in 1885. Also that year, he resumed his career as a teacher, accepting a position at Morrison's academy at Crieff. He would remain at the school until 1888. His first son, Alexander, would be born in Crieff in 1887.

Davidson would later claim that he hated teaching, deriding the profession as "mental boot-blacking"[13] and "hellish drudgery."[14] Yet one of Davidson's colleagues at Morrison's Academy, Rudolf von Liebich, claimed that Davidson "was far and away the most popular of all the teachers" at the school. Von Liebich wrote that the students "listened with delight to his illuminating lectures on poetry and seemed to devour his every word, entranced."[15] While in Crieff, Davidson managed to produce two more plays, the historical drama *Bruce* (1886) and *Smith, A Tragic Farce* (1888), which most critics consider his first important piece of writing. The latter work foreshadows his later philosophical thought, especially its Nietzschean aspects. In the play, Davidson argues that individuals should obey their own natures and defy authority. While there is no evidence that Davidson had yet read the German philosopher, he himself took arms against authority, namely, the rector at Morrison's Academy, during his last year in Crieff. Davidson observed the head of the school horribly mistreating schoolchildren on numerous occasions. He would later write about such a despotic and cruel individual in his short story "The Schoolboy's Tragedy." The story depicts a sadistic teacher who abuses and mistreats a bright young pupil until he completely destroys him. Perhaps Davidson saw elements of his own father in the rector. At any rate, he sided with the pupils and

enjoined his fellow teachers to take action against the headmaster. As a result of
his defiance, he and von Liebich were both fired, and Davidson, for a time, became
a traveling actor, giving dramatic and musical recitals in various Scottish towns and
cities. Eventually, Davidson found employment at a private school in Greenock.
His second son, Menzies, was born in 1889. The following year, Davidson and his
family moved to London so that he could take up his literary pursuits full time. His
second novel, *Perfervid*, appeared that year, and as we have already seen, his first
two collections of verse appeared respectively in 1891 and 1893.

In 1894, Davidson broke new ground with his third volume of verse, *Ballads
and Songs*. A number of these poems, including "Ballad of a Nun," had earlier
appeared in the periodical *Yellow Book* and had caused a sensation. The book itself
had an immediate following. In the *Bookman*, Jane Stoddart referred to *Ballads
and Songs* as "the poems of the hour."[16] Many years later, T. S. Eliot spoke about
Davidson's "Thirty Bob a Week." He said that the poem had been crucial in his
own development because it proved that "one could write poetry in English such
as one would speak oneself."[17] He contended that the poem marked a seminal
breakthrough in English verse. What is true of "Thirty Bob a Week," however, is
equally valid for the other poems in *Ballads and Songs*: they are all written as "one
would speak." The difference between Davidson's new kind of verse and the poetry
of, say, Alfred Tennyson is immediately evident, however, in the opening stanzas of
"Thirty Bob a Week." Eliot claimed that the voice of Davidson's clerk haunted him
the first time he read the poem and that it would continue to haunt him for the
remainder of his life:

> I couldn't touch a stop and turn a screw,
>   And set the blooming world a-work for me,
> Like such as cut the teeth—I hope, like you—
>   On the handle of a skeleton gold key;
> I cut mine on a leek, which I eat it every week:
>   I'm a clerk at thirty bob as you can see.
>
> But I don't allow it's luck and all a toss;
>   There's no such thing as being starred and crossed;
> It's just the power of some to be a boss,
>   And the bally power of others to be bossed:
> I face the music, sir; you bet I ain't a cur;
>   Strike me lucky if I don't believe I'm lost!
>
> For like a mole I journey in the dark,
>   A-travelling along the underground
> From my Pillar'd Halls and broad Surburbean Park,
>   To come the daily dull official round:
> And home again at night with my pipe all alight,
>   A-scheming how to count ten bob a pound.

> And it's often very cold and very wet;
>   And my missis stitches towels for a hunks;
> And the Pillar'd Halls is half to let—
>   Three rooms about the size of travelling trunks.
> And we cough, my wife and I, to dislocate a sigh,
>   When the noisy little kids are in their bunks.[18]

Davidson's ballads gained such a popular following that for a time he was considered Tennyson's likely successor as Poet Laureate. He would write two additional collections of such poems, *New Ballads* (1897) and *The Last Ballad and Other Poems* (1899). These volumes contained some of his finest work and increased his fame, but they also came to be something of an albatross around Davidson's neck. His readers wanted him to continue writing ballads, and he alienated and disappointed them when he produced his *Testaments* instead. Most of Davidson's contemporary readers found the later works rambling and incoherent. A few admitted admiring selected passages from the *Testaments* due to the high caliber of the writing. Others attacked the works as impious and obscene. Some even went so far as to allege that Davidson was advocating a kind of Satanism.

During the height of his popularity, Davidson not only provided for his wife and children in London, he also subsidized his mother and sister in Edinburgh. About a year before his mother's death in September 1896, Davidson's younger brother, an alcoholic with an explosive temper who throughout his life had shown signs of mental disturbance, had attempted, in a fit of rage, to murder Helen Davidson and, as a result, had to be confined at Garthneven Asylum. As a result of his brother's committal, Davidson had to completely maintain his mother and sister until the former's death. Thereupon, he saw to his brother's release from the asylum and arranged his emigration to Australia and welcomed his sister into his own household. Shortly thereafter Davidson suffered an emotional collapse and left London for the Sussex Coast. He stayed in the village of Shoreham for a year and a half and devoted himself to the study of Schopenhauer and Nietzsche. As a child, he had memorized Sir Thomas Malory, Milton, and Shakespeare. Now he learned verbatim long passages from *Thus Spake Zarathustra* and *Beyond Good and Evil*. Like Nietzsche had done before him, Davidson, in his own apocalyptic writings, would adopt a biblical form— "the solemn covenant" or testament—to deliver a decidedly anti-Christian message. In a newspaper article, he explained his newfound philosophical preoccupation as follows: "When a Scotsman finds himself at cross purposes with life . . . he either sits down and drinks deeply, thoughtfully, systematically, of the amber spirit of his country, or he reads philosophy."[19] During his convalescence in Shoreham, Davidson began to develop his own materialist ideology. His explicitly materialistic writings would not appear, however, until after the turn of the century. He continued to experience financial difficulties in the early 1900s. He would eventually be granted a 100 pound annual Civil List Pension in 1906 (Edmund Gosse and William Symington

McCormick had attempted to secure Davidson a pension as early as 1900 but without success); but the amount was inadequate for Davidson's needs, and he had to supplement his income by reading manuscripts for Grant Richards. He had to write Richards begging for the position, and, although the publisher had reservations about hiring Davidson, who had by then taken up residence in Penzance, due to the fact that he lived so far from London, Richards nonetheless agreed in 1908 to make Davidson his "literary advisor" and pay him 100 pounds a year. He did so in part out of fear, for Davidson had hinted at suicide in his correspondence to him. In a February 1908 letter to Richards pleading for the position of manuscript evaluator, Davidson wrote: "I should like to leave my affairs in some shape behind me: I have had very distinct notice that I have barely a year or two to live in now."[20]

Although many of Davidson's readers turned against him when he began expounding his materialist ideas, George Bernard Shaw was intrigued with Davidson's thought and, in 1901, offered him 250 pounds to write an original play expressing his philosophical convictions. Davidson took up the challenge with great enthusiasm. The resulting play, *The Game of Life*, did not, however, impress Shaw. Davidson wanted to write a popular success, so he attempted to convey his dark philosophical ideas in a Shavian farce, a strange hybrid which Shaw characterized as "not popular enough for a popular theatre; and . . . not advanced enough for a coterie theatre."[21] The play was never produced and was among the works that Davidson ordered burned in his will. In 1905, he did publish a serious drama concerning atheistic materialism, *The Theatrocrat: A Tragic Play of Church and Stage*. Set in London, the work relates the plight of an actor-manager trying to save his theater. He produces only serious works, not frivolous American-style comedies, and therefore has little commercial success. During the course of the play, he befriends the Bishop of St. James, who has abandoned the Christian faith and written a powerful drama expressing his new materialist doctrine. Steadfast in his convictions, the manager immediately agrees to mount it. When the work is staged, the audience becomes so inflamed that, during the prologue, they leap from their seats and rush the stage. They murder the bishop, trample the set, and tear down the backdrop. Davidson's own play was attacked and vilified by the press. It and his other materialist works, the Testaments and the *Mammon* plays, were little to the liking of either the critics or the general readership. Davidson's depression in 1908 was due in part to the negative reception of what he considered to be his most significant work. One magazine in particular, *Academy*, attacked him on a regular basis. He was labeled as a "despairing sort of posturer" and denigrated as a socialist. The magazine went so far as to suggest that Davidson be stripped of his state pension:

> Considering *The Testament of John Davidson* in all its ghastly bumptious enormity, we for our part fail to comprehend how it comes to pass that in a Christian country it should be possible for a person who considers himself a poet to be writing at his leisure such dangerous and stupid twaddle on a pension which is paid to him quarterly out of the Treasury of a Nonconformist Government. . . . The

> King is the Defender of the Faith, and we consider that it is against public policy
> and decency that Mr. Davidson be allowed to huckster offensive atheism from a
> booth subsidized out of the State purse.[22]

The continued attacks unhinged Davidson and plunged him into despondency.
Health problems and financial woes—his income was less than four pounds a
week; the only luxury he could afford was an occasional cigar—contributed to
Davidson's despair. In August of 1908, he made out his will. In November, he again
wrote Richards of his approaching death, but his mood improved with the new year
and the coming of spring.

When the police arrived at Coulson's Terrace in March 1909 and requested
that Maggie Davidson go through her husband's papers, she found his handwritten
will, but because of the August 1908 date, she did not read through the document.
The will, in her opinion, did not reflect Davidson's current state of mind, and she
did not mention the document's existence to the constables. She reported only that
she had not found a suicide note. A missing person's notice was issued to all the
constabularies in Cornwall, Devonshire, and Dorset as well as to a number of
important towns in England and Scotland. A description of the poet's physical
appearance would subsequently also be given out. On the evening of March 25,
Alexander Davidson reported his father's disappearance to the *Daily Mail*. The
story appeared in the London papers the following day. By then, the police had
determined the identities of the five passengers who had boarded the only train
departing Penzance the night of Davidson's disappearance. The poet had not been
one of them. The coast guard had been notified that Davidson was missing and had
orders to watch the waters around Mount's Bay for signs of a corpse. It was proposed that the lock be dredged, but as the wind had been coming in from the sea
since the night Davidson vanished, it was thought that, had he fallen into the
channel and drowned, his body would have been washed ashore. The police eventually arranged a manhunt of the district, but no signs of the poet were found. The
superintendent suggested that Davidson might have fallen down an abandoned
mine shaft. If such were the case, there was little likelihood of the body ever being
recovered. In any case, the family would have to bear the costs of any additional
search. Alexander Davidson went to his father's bank to withdraw whatever funds
his father had managed to lay aside. From the bank manager he learned that the
account was overdrawn in the amount of twelve pounds and that seven pounds in
rent money was past due for the Coulson Terrace house. Davidson's quarterly pension had been scheduled to be paid on April 1, but due to the poet's disappearance
the remittance would likely be held up. Alexander had no other recourse but to
turn to the *Daily Mail*. In exchange for exclusive interviews with the family, the
newspaper agreed to shoulder the costs of a private search. While the *Daily Mail*
spared no expense in trying to locate Davidson, in its articles covering the poet's
disappearance, the newspaper suggested that Davidson had either killed himself

(lines from "The Last Journey" were quoted in one feature story) or that he had purposely deserted his family. The *Daily Mail* also broke the news that the Davidson family had discovered that the poet's revolver was missing from the house. As time went on, Maggie Davidson became more and more persuaded that her husband had accidentally fallen off one of the coastal cliffs and drowned. Nonetheless, in the coming months, a number of people reported sighting Davidson in various locations. Four individuals claimed to have seen him walking the streets of the neighboring town of Hayle. A man answering his description was spotted farther down the coast at Cabis Bay. A Saint Ives railroad agent reported selling a man who might have been Davidson a train ticket for London and recalled the gentleman asking if, instead of traveling straight on to his destination, he might leave the train at Truro then board a later train for London. A ship steward named Willis, who had previously been acquainted with Davidson, reported seeing the poet in Truro. He claimed that Davidson recognized and tried to elude him. Nonetheless Willis managed to follow the poet to the train station and heard him book passage to Falmouth. Willis claimed that Davidson wore new clothes and clean boots. A barber reported shaving the poet in the village of St. Austell. Alexander Davidson became convinced that his father was alive and was perhaps suffering from some sort of mental disturbance. Grant Richards offered a reward of twenty pounds for information on Davidson's whereabouts, but requested that no one lay "violent hands"[23] on him. The publisher came to believe that the author had, in fact, abandoned his family. Further sightings were reported, but Maggie Davidson remained skeptical. Her husband had only two pounds in his pocket on the evening of March 23.

Alexander Davidson contacted an old friend of his father, Sir Arthur Conan Doyle, to see if he could shed any light on Davidson's disappearance. It was the opinion of the creator of Sherlock Holmes that the alleged sightings of Davidson were both irresponsible and unreliable. From the evidence of the missing revolver and the Davidsons' later revelation that two bullets had also been removed from the cartridge case, Doyle surmised that Davidson had probably killed himself. The fact that Davidson had not finished his *Mammon* trilogy, however, kept the case open in Doyle's mind. Shortly after Alexander solicited Doyle for his opinion, Menzies Davidson, going through his father's effects and papers, discovered the second package the poet had made up on March 23—the one he hadn't posted to Grant Richards. It contained the manuscript of *Fleet Street and Other Poems* and the following note:

> The time has come to make an end. There are several motives. I find my pension is not enough. I have therefore still to turn aside and attempt things for which people will pay. My health also counts. Asthma and other annoyances I have tolerated for years; but I cannot put up with cancer.[24]

The parcel also contained a letter to Davidson's agent A. P. Watt which read: "This will be my last book. Please forward it to Grant Richards and arrange with him upon the usual terms. I have appointed Grant Richards my literary executor to account to you and my heirs."[25]

Maggie Davidson hoped to cover up the suicide of her husband. She knew she would not receive Davidson's insurance if his death was ruled a suicide. Nor did she feel that the verse in *Fleet Street and Other Poems* would appreciably add to her husband's fame. She did not wish to see the volume published if the truth about her husband's death would thereby be revealed. Despite her efforts to conceal her son's discovery, the truth would shortly out. The same week that Menzies happened on his father's manuscript, *Lloyd's Weekly* would report that Davidson had committed suicide. Davidson's will would subsequently be published in the *Times* together with an obituary. In the will, Davidson requested that no biography ever be written about him. He enjoined all men, however, to "study and discuss in private and public my poems and plays, especially my Testaments and Tragedies."[26]

Problems continued to haunt the family because Davidson's body still had not been recovered. Nor did any doctor step forward to admit that he had diagnosed Davidson with cancer. The Davidsons' family physician had recently treated the poet for hemorrhoids but for nothing more serious. Grant Richards published an advertisement in the *Lancet* calling for any doctor whom Davidson might have called upon to break his silence and reveal the results of his examination. He received no responses to the notice. Menzies Davidson would later reveal that shortly before his death his father had used nitric acid to burn a sebaceous cyst from his scalp. In retrospect, Menzies came to believe that his father had suffered from hypochondria, that he suspected that he had cancer when in actual fact he did not have the disease.

Fleet Street and Other Poems would appear in August 1909 with Davidson's suicide note as a preface. William Butler Yeats was correct in seeing Davidson as an important poetic innovator. As Howard Mumford Jones maintained, he "strove all his life against the limits of form."[27] Throughout his career, Davidson would employ traditional forms only to undermine and sabotage them. He struggled continually to break new ground and develop a style altogether his own. T. S. Eliot maintained that English poetry made a giant advance when Davidson adopted the traditional ballad to his own purposes. He made another leap forward with *Fleet Street and Other Poems*. To contemporary readers, the verse seemed fragmentary, disjointed, and bursting with strange idioms. According to the *Times Literary Supplement*, Davidson's last poem exhibited the "suicidal futility"[28] of their author and precious little else. A more kindly disposed reviewer in the *Star* wrote that many separate voices were "swallowed up in [Davidson's] singing voice," that the poet had in effect created a new language, "Davidsonese,"[29] which was part street slang and part arcane scientific argot. Today, however, most critics agree that *Fleet Street and Other Poems* is Davidson's most inventive book and that its juxtaposition of styles, its looser verse forms, and the conversational quality of many of the individual poems anticipate the modernist innovations of Pound and Eliot.

The sea at last would tell. On Saturday September 18, 1909, two fishermen saw a number of gulls congregating over something floating in the water a mile off of Mousehole. The tide brought the object in closer to their boat, and they could see that it was a badly decomposed body dressed in a dark overcoat. They towed the corpse into port and summoned the local policeman. The remains were carried via stretcher to Penzance. Someone fetched Menzies Davidson. From the coat and various articles found in its pockets—a briar pipe, a bone paper knife, a packet of tobacco, and a silver matchbox—Menzies identified the remains as his father. An inquest was subsequently held at Mousehole. Menzies repeated the familiar story about his father's disappearance and related how the family had later found that his revolver and two of his cartridges were also missing. The examining physician stated that the remains had been in the water for approximately six months. He said that, in all likelihood, the body had been snared underwater near where it had been spotted and that, a short time before its discovery, it had worked itself free from where it had been trapped. He also noted a small hole in the right temple and a much larger opening, directly opposite it. These looked suspiciously like entrance and exit wounds made by a bullet, but, because of the body's state of decomposition, he could not say for certain whether or not Davidson had shot himself. The skull had also sustained a severe fracture, perhaps from striking a rock or being hit by a ship's keel. In the interest of the family, despite overwhelming evidence to the contrary, the local coroner would subsequently rule the death accidental.

On September 21, John Davidson's body would be committed to the waves off Cornwall. His body was placed in a coffin of plain pitch pine with brass mountings. The breastplate bore the inscription: "John Davidson, died March 23, 1909, aged 52."[30] Davidson had always wanted to be buried at sea. His family at first planned to bury him off the coast between Mousehole and Newlyn, but the local fishermen objected. After some delay, the body was taken by hearse to Penzance Harbour. In the presence of a crowd of onlookers, the coffin was taken to the water's edge, placed in a ship's boat, and towed to the steam launch *Nora*. The poet's two sons and several of his personal friends followed close behind in a punt. The vicar of Newlyn, the Reverend Patrick Fagan, had been retained to read the burial service and accompanied the mourners. They boarded the launch in the middle of the harbor. The boat carrying the coffin was attached to a launch which flew its little flag at half mast. It was towed well out into the bay. A weight was then attached to the coffin, and it was committed to the sea.

Notes

1. John Sloan, *John Davidson: First of the Moderns* (Oxford, New York: Clarendon Press, 1995), pp. 272–73.

2. John Davidson, "Thirty Bob a Week," *Selected Poems and Prose of John Davidson,* ed. John Sloan (Oxford, New York: Clarendon Press, 1995), p. 43. This poem appeared in *Ballads and Songs* in 1894.

3. John Davidson, *God and Mammon: Mammon and His Message* (London: G. Richards, 1908), p. 55.

4. Quoted by Sloan, *John Davidson,* p. 267.

5. Ibid., p 266. Here Sloan quotes from Davidson's long poem *The Testament of John Davidson* published in London in 1908.

6. Ibid.

7. Ibid., p. 267.

8. Davidson, "The Last Journey," *Selected Poems,* p. 152. This poem was first published in *The Testament of John Davidson* as an epilogue.

9. Ibid.

10. Ibid., pp. 152–53.

11. John Davidson, *The Man Forbid and Other Essays,* ed. E.J. O'Brien (Boston: Ball Publishing, 1910), pp. 33–34.

12. Davidson, "A Ballad in Blank Verse of the Making of a Poet," *Selected Poems,* pp. 51–52. This poem appeared in *Ballads and Songs.*

13. Quoted by Mary O'Connor, *John Davidson* (Edinburgh: Scottish Academic Press, 1987), p. 3.

14. Ibid.

15. Ibid, p. 4.

16. Jane Stoddart, "An Interview with John Davidson," *Bookman,* February 1895, p. 85.

17. Quoted by Richard Ellmann and Richard O'Clair, eds., *The Norton Anthology of Modern Poetry* (New York: W. W. Norton, 1973), p. 91. Eliot's remark appeared in his preface to *John Davidson: A Selection of His Poems,* ed. Maurice Lindsay (London, 1961), p. 9.

18. "Thirty Bob," p. 41.

19. Quoted by O'Connor, *John Davidson,* p. 7.

20. Quoted by Sloan, *John Davidson,* p. 265.

21. Quoted by Caroll V. Peterson, *John Davidson* (New York: Twayne Publishers, 1972), p. 11.

22. "An Epistle of Davidson," *Academy* 75 (14 November 1908): 462–63.

23. Quoted by Sloan, *John Davidson,* p. 276.

24. Ibid., p. 279.

25. Ibid.

26. Ibid., p. 280.

27. Howard Mumford Jones, "A Minor Prometheus," *Freeman* (25 October 1922): 153.

28. Quoted by Sloan, *John Davidson,* p. 282.

29. Ibid.

30. Ibid., p. 285.

Georg Trakl

HIS HUNDRED-ODD POEMS HAVE BEEN VARIOUSLY CHARACTERIZED AS macabre and decadent, elusive and hermetic, life-affirming and sensual, as well as dreamlike and otherworldly. His hallucinatory, enigmatic verse with its recurring color imagery and its unadorned, simple language is singularly open to interpretation and can readily accommodate the many different, often conflicting, constructions that have been conferred and bestowed on it over the years. Yet, as Rilke realized early on, no interpretation of the poems can be called definitive, that "even a close spectator sees the poet's vision and insights as through a window-pane and as if shut outside."[1] Rilke realized that Trakl's accomplishment lay in the "liberation of the poetic image;"[2] that the startling, gruesome, yet nonetheless weirdly beautiful, images that comprise his poetry were in and of themselves of prime importance and not any symbolic significance, metaphysical truth, or subjective emotion that was incidentally attached to them by reader or author. While others concentrated on the darkness of Trakl's vision and the morbidity of the poems, Rilke recognized a strange inversion in Trakl's work. In it, he wrote, "falling is the pretext for the most continuous ascension." Rilke believed that Trakl's poetry was, in the final analysis, basically affirmative. He wrote that Trakl's books "mapped out a new dimension of the spirit and . . . disproved that prejudice that judges poetry only in terms of feeling and content." For Rilke, Trakl's poetry was above all, "an object of sublime existence."[3] Trakl's anonymous patron, the philosopher Ludwig Wittgenstein, likewise maintained that the poems could not be comprehended in any regular sense, conceding that exegesis of the verse was beyond him, that, although he loved Trakl's work, he did not understand it. Despite his inability to make conventional sense of the verse, to find any precise meaning in it, he nonetheless delighted in the poetry's "tone"; it was, he wrote, "the tone of a man of real genius."[4]

Tellingly, both Rilke and Wittgenstein speak of the poems collectively. Indeed, to truly appreciate Trakl, one must read his entire oeuvre, for all the poems in his small body of work are interconnected by his repetitive, haunting imagery. A single poem, cut off from its fellows, yields little and may even appear vapid, but when read along with the rest (though not necessarily in any special order or sequence— the poems must merely be read together) it takes its place among the others in an almost fugal fashion, as yet another variation on the poet's single, obsessive musical theme, a melancholy and ghostly melody written in a minor key that lulls and invites the reader, that keeps him reading even though meaning eludes him. Trakl's song is as suggestive, mysterious, and enticing as that of the sirens and perhaps just as dangerous. As the reader proceeds from poem to poem, he keeps hearing its continuous echo and reverberation. The same words, the same autonomous, self-reliant images, recur again and again but they are transformed and modified according to the various contexts in which they are used. Trakl's technique, so reminiscent of Wagnerian leitmotiv, is one of ongoing mutation and alteration. Martin Heidegger asserted that each poem is part of a whole, a single unwritable ode to Being, to a transitory mutable "Isness"[5] that is simultaneously an occasion for both rejoicing and lament. Those who have been captivated by his song do not risk sailing into rocky shoals. They do, however, run the danger of forgetting themselves and following Trakl too far. Into the very mouth of madness itself.

The poets of the German Expressionist movement championed Trakl's work and saw him as one of their own, indeed even as a sort of paragon or type of the visionary or Orphic poet. In 1913, after coming across his poems in the literary journal *Der Brenner*, the poet and playwright Franz Werfel, a reader for the Kurt Wolff press and one of the early exponents of Expressionism, arranged for the publication of Trakl's first volume, handpicking the verse that went in it. Up until that time, Trakl had little or no contact with the Expressionist poets, most of whom lived in Berlin, and there is no indication that he had read either their poems or their numerous tracts and manifestoes. While his lyrics are equally cryptic as Benn's, Stadler's, or Hoddis's, they are not nearly as exclamatory but are, for all their eerie unearthliness, elegiac and wistful—incantatory and hushed. Trakl referred to his poetry as an "imperfect penance" for "unabsolved guilt."[6] His verse sometimes has the quality of mumbled prayer. Tellingly, he classified three of his short poems as "Rosenkranz-lieder" or "Rosary Songs." Indeed, while the Berlin poets strove to express their inner turmoil and turbulence in dynamic, aggressive fashion, Trakl endeavored to cover and hide all trace of himself, to disappear completely behind his images. Like the Expressionists, however, he revered Nietzsche, and he shared their profound distrust of modern civilization. In his poems, the city is an infernal place, whereas the rustic wild offers release and redemption. Returning to the forest represents a return to innocence. Pastoral or country life is preferable to that of the city in that it is less developed, less evolved. Throughout Trakl's poetry, that which dies (and thus is permanently arrested) in its youth—that which, to use his term, is only "half

born"⁷—is blessed. For to be fully born, to reach maturity, is to become self-aware
and to gain knowledge of one's sinfulness, to experience guilt. The agrarian way of
life is in its simplicity and purity analogous to childhood and innocence.

In addition to Nietzsche, Trakl's thought was informed by Dostoevski and
Kierkegaard. His lifelong search for personal redemption, his attempt to do
penance for the "unabsolved guilt" that burdened him, had its inspiration and
source in the works of the Danish religious writer and the Russian novelist. Near
the end of his life, when he decided that he must renounce reading and books,
Trakl found Dostoevski's work the most difficult to forgo. His poetical influences
are also clear. He owes a great debt to the French Symbolist poets Baudelaire, Verlaine, and Rimbaud whose work he discovered as a youth after he was taught
French by an Alsatian governess. Like the Symbolists, he employed words in
painterly fashion, striving to distill beauty from what had hitherto been considered
morbid and ugly and to create a dreamlike world of mirage and unreality through
the careful juxtaposition of images. At times, again in the manner of Baudelaire
and Verlaine, he tried to invest certain of these images with symbolical significance
(though more often than not he lets an image stand on it own, self-sufficient and
independent). A symbolical meaning whenever he does apply it to an image, however, is never applied with any sort of rigor or consistency. The next time the image
appears, it might very well be invested with an entirely different metaphorical significance or none at all. Through the agency of words, Trakl tries to evoke and
convey sense perceptions. The smell of apples in a cupboard. The hiss of grass and
the rustle of leaves. The dark flutter of jackdaws. Rose-red clouds on a hill. Any
meaning such phenomena has is intrinsic and not symbolical. The pealing of a
churchbell is usually just the pealing of a churchbell. It is the arrangement and
grouping—the flight—of such images, however, that gives Trakl's verse its peculiar effect. His visions can be serene and bucolic. A radiant pit of sunlight. Deer
herding under trees. Water racing over a rock bed. A blackbird singing in the
forest. A luminous moon rising in a starfilled sky. Or they can be nightmarish and
horrific. Furniture molders and rots before the reader's eye. A child's skeleton
smashes against a bare wall. Plump rats gnaw cupboards and doors. Vultures tear
the flesh of metal hearts. Blood spills over doorsteps in the moonlight and brown
pearls trickle through dead fingers (a doomed Trakl at his poetry penance, telling
his rosary beads, stringing discrete images together as if he were threading
pearls?). Trakl's verse has the streamlike character of automatic or free associa-
tional writing. In Symbolist fashion, one image follows another. The serene and
pretty transforms itself itself into the grisly and frightful—and vice versa—as the
verse purls limpidly on. Ghosts and malign spirits of all sorts haunt Trakl's atmos-
pheric landscapes. His poetry often has the spooky feel of a drug-induced vision.
Dead eyelids lift and blue poppy-eyes—no doubt bleary and bloodshot—open to
behold a wide array of apparitions. Angels strangle red wolves. Fiery wheels roll
through a woman's hair. Shadows of the long-departed hover and float over the

countryside as a boy's hyacinth voice descants over a bone footbridge. Trakl's poetry has an immediate visual and sonic appeal. It is stunning and surreal.

In addition to the French Symbolists, Trakl's work bears the stamp of a number of German poets. His early verse shows the great influence of the Romantic Austrian lyricist Nikolaus Lenau, whose melancholic, anguished nature poems Trakl greatly admired as a youth. During his apprenticeship years, Trakl acknowledged his debt to Lenau, calling his predecessor and countryman his first master. Throughout his life, Trakl developed a penchant and affinity for poets, such as Lenau, who had in the course of their lives suffered in love and had, as a result, become incurably insane, no doubt seeing their predicaments as analogous to his own. While Lenau fell in love with the wife of a close friend, a woman he could not hope to marry and as result became mad, Trakl suffered from a hopeless incestuous attraction to his younger sister Margarete, who resembled him in appearance, temperament, and artistic aspiration (as an adult, she became an accomplished concert pianist). The unnamed sister figure who appears again and again in his poetry was, no doubt, at least in part, modeled on her. This sister's presence is continually felt in the poems, for it is to her that the poet directs his *sanfe Gesang* or "gentle song." The source of Trakl's unabsolved guilt lay in his unnatural attachment to Margarete. He showed signs of mental illness throughout his short life and, shortly before his suicide, was diagnosed as schizophrenic. Trakl no doubt saw Lenau as a type of himself, but he also found much to admire in his predecessor's verse. He realized that Lenau's depictions of gloomy landscapes, primeval forests, and towering alpine panoramas functioned as reflections—metaphors and images—of the Austrian nobleman's own dark moods. From Lenau, Trakl learned the art of projection. However, he was not content merely to make a mirror of nature. He felt such a deep identification with the mountains and pastures of his native Salzburg, he longed and wished for a complete mystical merging with them. The cost for such a union, he realized, was high, but he was prepared to pay it even if it entailed the disintegration of his personality or, ultimately, the loss of his life. Indeed, at the time of his suicide, Trakl felt absolutely compelled to make the necessary outlay as he witnessed firsthand the horrors of the World War I. He had to return home. He had to escape.

Besides Lenau, other German-language poets Trakl owed a debt to include Mörike, Hofmannsthal and Stefan George, but it is to the elegies and hymns of Hölderlin (another poet who suffered from mental illness brought on by a love that could never be realized) that Trakl's last poems, written in free verse, revert and harken most. Trakl not only mimics the rhythmic flow of Hölderlin's lines, he borrows his syntax and imagery as well, but he transmutes and changes what he expropriates and commandeers for his own highly original purposes. He does not merely quote, he continues and builds upon. He re-creates and replaces Hölderlin, much as he re-creates and replaces himself, falling back as he inevitably does on the same cluster of images, the same phrases, meters and cadences, that he had previously employed in his earlier poems. However, like an alchemist converting base metals into silver and gold, he transmutes what he appropriates from his earlier work and gives it new life. Similarly, whatever he borrows from other poets, he makes totally new, totally his own. His art is one of continual regeneration, and his poems—read one by one—recall the fluctuating images viewed in a kaleidoscope. They are indeed hymns to transience.

From the testimony of his friends and acquaintances, it is known that Trakl deeply identified with the legendary figure of Kaspar Hauser, the sixteen-year-old boy who suddenly materialized in the city of Nuremberg in 1828 after being liberated from a cellar where he had been kept imprisoned all his life. According to witnesses, Hauser could hardly walk upon emerging from his artificial womb and could only utter one enigmatic sentence: "I want to be a horseman."[8] Adopted and educated by Anselm von Feuerbach, the foundling would later state that, until the time of his escape, he saw the chains that bound him and the dungeon in which he was held as extensions of himself, as parts of his own body. Hauser's end proved as mysterious as his beginning. He was murdered in 1883—stabbed by an unknown assassin. Trakl celebrated the foundling's strange life in his "Kaspar Hauser Lied." The following is David Luke's English translation:

Caspar Hauser Song

He truly adored the sun, as crimson, it sank from the hilltop,
The paths of the forest, the blackbird singing
And the joy of the green.

Serious was his habitation in the tree shade
And pure his face.
God spoke a gentle flame into his heart:
O man!

His silent footstep found the city at evening;
The dark lament of his mouth:
I want to be a horseman.

But bush and beast pursued him,
House and pallid garden of pallid men,
And his murderer sought him.

Beautifully the spring and summer and the autumn
Of the righteous man, his soft footfall
Beside the dark rooms of dreamers.
By night he stayed alone with his star,

Saw snow falling through bare branches,
And in the dusking hall his murderer's shadow.

Silver it fell, the head of the not-yet-born.[9]

"Kaspar Hauser Lied" is one of Trakl's least opaque poems; it reveals much about the poet's own peculiar pathology, indeed provides a key to understanding his mental kinks and defects. In Trakl's version of the tale, time is telescoped and the course of events quickened. Hauser is already pursued by his stalker and murderer as he enters the city. This figure is actually a deliverer, for he saves Hauser from becoming completely self-aware. As Frank Graziano notes, at the time of his death, Trakl's Hauser still has a "perceptual rather than conceptual approach to reality."[10] Therefore, he remains "not-yet-born" and thus is still oblivious of his human sin and guilt. Moreover, he has only just begun to experience separation from the natural world. This process of estrangement commences as he enters the city and it is the cause of his lament. Nonetheless, he remains a righteous man, even in the heart of the city. As he moves through enemy territory, he is "still at one with his star" and thus able to perceive beauty. He is enthralled by snowflakes descending through the limbs of a leafless tree. Therefore, in the hostile, infernal region he has somehow drifted into, he immediately becomes a target for destruction, a marked man, as it were. Bush and beast pursue him and his murderer lies in wait.

In a letter to his friend Erhard Buschbeck, Trakl wrote that he would always remain "a poor Kaspar Hauser."[11] However, he did point out a significant difference between this poetical persona and himself. Hauser remained "not yet born," where he was further along on the road to self-awareness—"half born"—and thus he was detached and sequestered from the natural world to a far greater degree. As deeply as Trakl identifies with Hauser, on one level another part of his personality clearly associates itself with the knife-wielding deliverer, the savior who blots out self-awareness and thus prevents the loss of Paradise. As a writer, Trakl tried to recover the oneness with the world that he had previously experienced but had now lost. His poems reflect, perhaps even attempt to duplicate, a state of intensified sensation—of unalloyed being, where all perception of self vanishes and total integration with the world is possible. We experience such oneness in infancy, but, as our personality develops, we grow increasingly aware of our own distinct and detached condition, begin to become aware of boundaries and limits, and to develop the concept of individuality. Someone with Trakl's mindset, however, would view this process quite negatively, as a sort of fall from grace through which we are trapped within our own bodies. As Graziano points out, schizophrenia is often thought to have its beginnings in early childhood, specifically in "a child's failure to resolve his symbiotic relationship with his mother."[12] In many of his poems, Trakl identifies the child's first condition—to his mind, a state of grace which we literally grow out of—with the color blue. In his poem "Kindheit," he states that childhood is "lived in a blue cave."[13] It is to this same cave to which he aspires to return. He is able to do so in a variety of ways, albeit only briefly. There are many examples of "blue moments"—flashes of short-lived rapture—in his poetry; in "Kindheit" he defines the essence of such an instance. It is, he writes, "purely and simply soul." One illustration of such bliss and elation is found in the following lines from the poem "Wayfaring," here translated by Christopher Middleton:

Your eyelids are heavy with poppy and dream softly against my forehead.
Gentle bells tremble through the heart. A blue cloud,
Your face has sunk over me in the twilight.

A song for the guitar, sounding in a strange tavern.
Wild elderbushes there, a long bygone day in November,
Familiar steps on the dusky stair, the sight of beams tanned brown,

An open window, at which a sweet hope stayed behind—
Unspeakable it all is, O God, one is overwhelmed and falls on one's knees.[14]

Such moments of grace might naturally occur—they could be occasioned, perhaps by listening to music, to one's sister "playing a Schubert sonata,"[15] or by immersing oneself in nature, by rambling through the woods and mountains—but they were rare and short-lived. Trakl additionally realized that one might lose all awareness of self in the throes of physical intimacy, for he writes in "Elis" that the "languor of lovers"[16] is blue, but here, too, the blue moment is ephemeral. More sinisterly, Trakl knew other ways—decidedly unnatural and unhealthy methods—to induce ecstatic bliss. He learned that, by drinking wine or by ingesting narcotics in sufficient quantities, one could likewise for a time obliterate all sense of self. Many such artificially realized "blue moments" are celebrated in his poetry, such as the following one from "To The Boy Elis." The translation is by Kate Flores:

> You go with gentle tread still within the night,
> Hung full with purple grapes,
> And move your arms more beautifully in blue.
> . . . .
> Your body is a hyacinth,
> In which at times a monk a waxen finger dips.
> Our silence is a cave of black,
>
> From which at times a gentle doe steps out
> And closes slowly heavy lids.
> Upon your temples drips black dew,
>
> Last gold of shattered stars.[17]

Trakl, however, understood just how evanescent and fleeting, not to mention how self-destructive, such moments of bliss were, that the soul's music quickly "fades and dies" when the "wine-drunk head sinks down to the gutter."[18] One could steal a taste of the paradisal fruit but could not perpetually feast on it. Only in death might one acquire lasting blueness. The color is associated with early death in a number of Trakl's poems. The following lines are from "An Einen Frühverstorbenen" or "To One Who Died Young." The English translation is again by Middleton:

> But the other descended the stone steps of the Mönchsberg,
> A blue smile on his face, and strangely ensheathed
> In his quieter childhood, and died;
> And the silver face of his friend stayed behind in the garden,
> Listening in the leaves or the ancient stones.[19]

Trakl grew increasingly aware that after each blue moment, each instance of pure being that one experienced in life, there was a corresponding coming down or fall. A return to normalcy or sobriety, a plummet or plunge out of the momentary condition of grace, after which the individual once again feels trapped within his own skin, cruelly cut off and detached from the rest of the world.

It is in the title poem of his posthumously published second volume of verse, *Sebastian in Dream*, that Trakl explores the theme of the fall in most detail. The poem begins with the child's birth. The memory of the boy (at least in dreams or reverie) can stretch backward to this primal, turbulent scene. Later in the poem, we will see that he is also clairvoyant and can glimpse the sad but glorious end that awaits him in the future. He has uncanny abilities akin to those of Günter Grass's Oskar Matzerath, who remembered everything, including the peace and serenity he experienced as a fetus inside his mother's womb. Oskar never wished to be born. Nor apparently did Sebastian. The first two verses of the poem (here translated into English by Kate Flores) are reminiscent of the opening paragraphs of James Joyce's *A Portrait of the Artist As a Young Man* in that both beginnings have embedded in them a son's memory of a father looking down at him, Stephen of his father peering at him either through a pair of spectacles or from behind a window—at any rate through a barrier of glass—Sebastian of his father looking at his wife in labor, at his son's violent entrance into the world, if not from the heights of heaven (Sebastian's mother gives birth to her child under the moon in the family garden). then from inside the adjoining house and, like Simon Dedalus also "through a glass." The father in Trakl's poem, just like Joyce's, has a hairy face:

> Mother bore this child in the white moon,
> In the shade of the nut tree, of the primitive elder,
> Drunk with the poppy's juice, the lament of the thrush;
> And quiet
> In compassion bent above her a bearded face
>
> Soft in the window's dimness; and old household things
> Handed down the years
> Lay in neglect; love and autumnal reverie.[20]

Next, Sebastian recalls a suicide attempt he made in early childhood. A person receives a special dispensation when he is willing to sacrifice himself. He perceives his destiny and realizes that he is one of the elect:

When stonily he threw himself before onrushing horses,
In the gray night his star came over him.[21]

After this, Sebastian recollects his growing awareness of death as a child. He remembers walking with his mother through St. Peter's autumnal graveyard at dusk and, on another occasion, seeing a corpse laid out in a dark room. Although death's presence was close at hand on both these occasions, Sebastian's unity and oneness with his environment was not affected. If anything it was increased:

A fragile corpse lay tranquil in the darkness of the room
And to it he lifted cold eyelids.

But he was a little bird upon a barren twig.
The bell tolling all through the November evening long,
The stillness of the father as he went down the winding stairway in the dark.[22]

The following stanza elaborates upon the inner peace the boy feels. He relates the serenity he experiences at viewing a corpse to the tranquility of another special child a long time before. That child, too, was at one with his surroundings and Trakl paints a suitably beatific tableau:

Peace of soul. Lonely winter evening,
The darkling figures of shepherds beside the ancient pool;
The babe in the hut of straw; O how softly
Sank his face into black fever.
Holy night.[23]

In the next verse, Sebastian is walking with his father. Clutching his father's hand, he perceives that he will die young. Once again he identifies with Jesus, and, in the subsequent stanzas, he again experiences great ecstasy and elation. He associates this joy with the little garden where his mother gave birth to him. In that magical realm, in the shadow of the two trees, he caught a glimpse of an angel:

Or when holding to the father's hardened hand
In silence he ascended the gloom of Calvary Hill,
And in shadowy niches of rock
Humanity's blue figure came into his legend;
From the wound beneath the heart purple ran the blood.
O in the darkness of his soul how tender rose the Cross.

Love. Then the snow in black corners melted,
Joyously a blue breeze caught in the ancient elder,
In the nut tree's arch of shadow;
And soft his rosy angel appeared before the boy;

> Joy. An evening sonata sounding in cool rooms,
> In the dark brown of the rafters
> Came from its silver chrysalis an azure butterfly.[24]

Once more Sebastian detects "the nearness of death"[25] and he is electrified. He intuits that when one goes through what Henry James called "the Great Change," one undergoes a mysterious metamorphosis, a subtle refining and alchemical transformation, and as a result exchanges an inferior state of being for a more transcendent one. The lowly wormlike caterpillar emerges as a blue butterfly. Something similar awaits us, Sebastian realizes, when we cut through death's cocoon. However, the small boy does not die then and there and achieve his destiny, however much he would like to. He continues walking with his father. It quickly becomes clear that he is being led out of the earthly paradise. Father and son walk to the "city's crumbling walls at twilight"[26] before turning homeward. When they return to the garden, however, everything has changed—the bower of bliss has been ravaged and despoiled—for only now is Sebastian's birth complete. Although he walks by his father's side (the father is now depicted as old and wizened), he is also at the same time the "pink baby" held by the self-same sire, swaddled in his overcoat:

> He held to the bony hand of the old man
> Who carried a pink baby in his black overcoat;
> In the shadow of the nut tree the spirit of evil appeared.
>
> Groping across the green steps of summer. O how quietly
> The garden in the brown stillness of autumn fell to ruin,
> Fragrance and sadness of the immemorial elder,
> When in Sebastian's shadow the silver voice of the angel faded away.[27]

Like Kaspar Hauser, Sebastian has ventured out of Eden and gone to the city. Upon his return home, he has a conceptual rather than a perceptual approach to reality. He is thus a fallen creature and the garden shaded by the two trees no longer holds its former magic. Satan has made his appearance in paradise. Green has turned to brown, and Sebastian can no longer detect the presence of his angel. He has eaten the fruit of the tree of knowledge of good and evil instead of the fruit hanging from the boughs of the tree of life.

Life and death, however, are subject to an idiosyncratic inversion in Trakl's garden. Death is a reversion to pure Being, whereas continued existence in the fallen world, life and breath, are nothing short of animate death. Trakl's central idea may be succinctly put—we may taste of the tree of life only in death.

Georg Trakl was born February 3, 1887, in the city of Salzburg. He was the fourth of six children born to Tobias and Maria Halik Trakl. Both his parents were of Slav descent; his father's ancestors had emigrated from Hungary while his mother's people had moved to Austria (at a far later date) from Bohemia. Maria was Tobias's second wife. She was fifteen years younger than the widowed Tobias and had carried on an affair with him while married to another man. She divorced her first husband—a Catholic—after being impregnated by Trakl's father, a Protestant, and changed her religion shortly before her second marriage. Trakl's father owned a successful hardware store and dealt primarily in iron goods. His mother had a mania for antiques and filled the family house with period furniture and *objets d'art*. In addition to his beautiful yet nonetheless affected and high-flown residence, Tobias owned a small garden in another part of the city. Both home and garden feature prominently in Trakl's poetry, especially in "Sebastian in Dream," where, however, they are depicted as being adjacent. While Trakl's father was a confirmed bourgeois, Maria Trakl appears to have had a more refined nature. Nevertheless, she suffered from acute depression and it has been suggested by some Trakl scholars (though denied by others) that at the time of Trakl's birth she was addicted to opium, as seems to be indicated in "Sebastian in Dream." Both father and mother had a relaxed, nonchalant attitude toward their six offspring, taking only a perfunctory or token interest in their happiness and well-being. They were far too absorbed in their own pursuits and pastimes—the father running his business, the mother collecting her antiques—to pay much notice to any of their children.

Georg was a docile, gentle child for the most part, and he seemed fond of his parents despite their neglect; yet, before the age of ten, he tried to do grave bodily harm to himself on several occasions. At six or seven, he walked into a pond and submerged himself completely in the ice-cold water. His hat, however, slipped from his head and bobbed to the surface, alerting his caretaker, who by then had missed him, to his perilous situation. A few years later, he threw himself before onrushing horses, a suicide attempt that he would later memorialize in "Sebastian in Dream," and on a third occasion, he attempted to jump in front of an oncoming train. A doctor who treated him at around this time would later relate that, "He did not believe his father was his own but rather imagined that he descends from a cardinal and that in the future he will become a great man."[28] The doctor also noted that the boy often heard the ringing of nonexistent bells, and that he was affected with visions and imaginary perceptions, frequently seeing objects with no reality and experiencing sensations with no external cause. Trakl would later claim to his friends that until the age of twenty he could not discern any of the physical features in his surroundings except water and that every face he beheld was blurred and clouded; that he could not distinguish one visage from another.

Despite these instances of aberrant and eccentric behavior and signs of obvious mental illness, Trakl enrolled in school at the age of ten and embarked on an ambitious course of study in the humanities with an emphasis on Greek and Latin. His fellow students did not detect anything out of the ordinary about him until he reached late adolescence. At that time, however, he became increasingly withdrawn and anti-social and was subject to violent mood swings. Gentle and childlike at one moment, he could turn wild and berserk the next. From the first, he proved to be a mediocre and indifferent student, the rigor and discipline of the Gymnasium being little to his liking, but now he began to drug himself with chloroform and to smoke cigarettes dipped in opium as well as to drink immoderately and to threaten suicide. It was also during this period that his unnatural attraction to Margarete began to develop. It seemed that only his younger sister could understand and empathize with him. He shared her love of music (not surprising for a boy who claimed descent from a bright-colored songbird) and himself was a talented pianist. He also began attending sessions of a Salzburg literary club called "Apollo" and began producing the first of his prose poems. His talents were all extracurricular. Failing his examinations in the seventh form, and disinclined to take them for a second time, Trakl was forced, at last, to withdraw from school. For a time, he studied under private tutors, but then began a three-year apprenticeship at the White Angel, a Salzburg apothecary's shop, which would be followed by a two-year program in pharmacology at the University of Vienna. No doubt Trakl selected his future profession because of the easy access to drugs it would provide him, a dangerous career choice for a person with his appetites and impulsive and reckless temperament.

During his apprenticeship years, Trakl began publishing book reviews and prose pieces in a Salzburg newspaper, and, encouraged and spurred on by Gustav Streicher, a local playwright and Nietzsche disciple, he wrote two one-act plays, both of which were produced in 1906 at the Salzburg Municipal Theatre. While the first play, the Ibsenesque *Totentag* (*All Souls' Day*) was something of a *succès de scandale*, the second, *Fata Morgana*, had a poor public reception and was lambasted by the critics. Trakl subsequently destroyed the manuscripts of both plays.[29]

In 1908, he commenced his studies in Vienna. He hated the milieu of the city and led a life of dissipation, moving from apartment to apartment and frequenting bar after bar. Sullen and unapproachable, he had few friends and, according to those who knew him at the time, could never be engaged in conversation. If he did condescend to speak with anyone, he would tend to ramble or to launch into monologues of Wagnerian length, never looking directly into the face of the person with whom he was speaking and never giving him a chance to break in and interrupt. He even went so far as to hire an old and run-down prostitute to hear him out when he felt like speaking, handing over her usual fee merely to have her listen to him. He labored on two plays, a puppet piece concerning a Bluebeard murderer and a tragedy about Don Juan. While the marionette play has been preserved, only a fragment of the drama has survived.

Trakl's depression and loneliness in Vienna were assuaged somewhat with the 1909 arrivals of his sister Margarete and his friend Erhard Buschbeck, the former coming to the city to study music, the latter to prepare for a career in the law. In 1910, however, Trakl was plagued with financial difficulties due to the death of his father.

He nonetheless managed to finish his studies, whereupon he was drafted for a one-year term into the Austrian medical corps. He was first stationed at Innsbruck but then posted back to Vienna. His year of service seemed to do him some good, in that it provided his life with structure and regimentation. Nonetheless he transferred to the reserves as soon as he was able. After his discharge, Trakl drifted back and forth from Vienna to Salzburg, working at various pharmacies, including a stint at the White Angel, but never staying long at any one place. Sometimes he would work for as little as two or three days at an apothecary shop before giving notice and moving on. Rootless and restless, he lived a hand-to-mouth existence, relying on handouts from friends to see him through. At one point, he considered emigrating to Borneo. Finally, his finances sank to such a low point that he was forced to reenlist. In April 1912, Trakl was again at Innsbruck, working in the pharmacy of a military hospital.

While in Innsbruck, he encountered a number of young artists and intellectuals, associates of Ludwig von Ficker, the influential editor of *Der Brenner*. Buschbeck arranged for these meetings and introductions, and for the first time in his life, Trakl found himself surrounded by people who recognized his worth and talent. At last, Trakl made the acquaintance of von Ficker himself. The editor quickly became his friend and benefactor and soon Trakl's poems were regularly appearing in Ficker's magazine. Again Trakl left active military service. In January 1913, he accepted a clerical post in Vienna but resigned after only three days and returned once again to Innsbruck, where, thanks to Ficker's patronage, he had no material worries and was able to devote himself exclusively to his poetry. Franz Werfel read *Der Brenner* and was captivated by Trakl's work. Arrangements were soon made to issue a collection of his poems in book form. At last finding acceptance for his art, Trakl entered into his most productive period. At this time, he also began reading Hölderlin. Despite his newfound success, however, he continued to live dangerously. In December 1913, he almost died from an overdose of veronal. On another occasion he collapsed in the snow after a long night of drinking and lay outside all night, an event celebrated in the poem "Winternacht." For all his alcoholic excesses, he had a strong constitution. He suffered no ill effect from his long exposure to the wet and the cold. He woke up the next morning and continued his journey homeward.

Gedichte appeared in July 1913 and a contract for a follow-up volume was quickly issued (*Sebastian im Traum* would appear posthumously in 1915). Aside from writing, Trakl traveled with the Ficker coterie. In the company of his patron, Karl Kraus, Adolf Loos, and Peter Altenberg, he made a memorable journey to Venice, but he also took jaunts to Lake Garda and to diverse resorts and vacation spots throughout Austria. In March 1914, Trakl suffered a grave scare. His life was thrown into disarray and the stability he had just begun to attain shattered when his sister Margarete suffered a miscarriage and as a result became dangerously ill. Living in Berlin, despondent, and, like her brother, addicted to drugs, she was unhappily married to a man nearly twice her age. Trakl hastened to her bedside. To Trakl's great relief, Margrete recovered. While he was in Berlin, she would introduce him to the poet Else Lasker-Schüler, one of the few women other than his sister with whom he was able to relate. He would dedicate one of his best poems, "Occident," to her. In July 1914, Ficker received 100,000 Austrian crowns from the philosopher Ludwig Wittgenstein to distribute to needy German and Austrian authors. The two main beneficiaries of Wittgenstein's endowment were Rilke and Trakl. Ficker allocated 20,000 crowns to each poet. Trakl, however, was so nervous and overwrought when he accompanied Ficker to the bank to draw on the grant, that he fled the scene, drenched in his own sweat, unable or unwilling to complete the transaction. Shortly thereafter Austria declared war on Serbia and World War I began. At first Trakl welcomed the commencement of hostilities. He felt the war resulted from the breakdown and disintegration of the old social order and intuited that the corrupt values of the *ancien régime* could not survive the conflict, that the current political system would fall. Called to service as a medical corps lieutenant, he left Innsbruck for Galicia in Austria-occupied Poland. After the ghastly and horrific battle of Grodek, he was put in charge of ninety wounded men lying in a barn. He did not have the medical expertise to properly treat them, nor did he have sufficient quantities of narcotics to mitigate their suffering. The casualties moaned and screamed and one of the wounded shot himself in the head. Trakl ran to this soldier's side only to see his brains spattered all over the barn's wall. Trakl fled from the building only to behold another horror. Outside the barn the limp bodies of a number of deserters swung from the limbs of several trees. During the disorganized Austrian retreat a few days later, Trakl rose to his feet at dinner and declared that he could no longer endure life. After making this pronouncement, he either threatened or attempted to commit suicide. Restrained by his fellow soldiers, he was sent to a military hospital at Cracow to undergo psychiatric observation. Here he was diagnosed as suffering from schizophrenia. Locked in a cell with another officer suffering from delirium tremens, frightened that he might be shot or hanged as a deserter, Trakl wrote his two last poems, "Lament" and "Grodek." Once again, the translations are by Kate Flores:

Lament

Sleep and death, the darkling eagles
Around the head whirl all the night:
The icy wave of eternity
The golden image of man
Will swallow. His purple blood
On terrible shoals is going to splatter.
And dark the voice
On the sea laments.
Sister of the stormy sorrows,
See a frightened boat go down
Under the stars
The silent face of night.[30]

Grodek

At eventide the autumnal woods
With weapons of death resound, across golden fields
And lakes of blue, solemn the sun
Rolls on; the night embraces
Soldiers dying, the wild lament
Of their shattered mouths.
Still soundlessly from the meadowland
The scarlet clouds of an angry god
Gather the spilled blood up, moonly cool;
Every road leads to black decay.
Under golden boughs of night and the stars
Through the quiet glade moves the sister's shadow,
Greeting the spirits of the heroes, the bleeding heads;
And soft the dark fires of autumn sound in the reeds.
O prouder grief! O altars of brass,
The searing flame of the spirit is fed by a mighty sorrow today,
The grandchildren not to be born.[31]

Both poems express Trakl's gloom. He wants to flee from the front, from his cell in the military hospital, to the peace and serenity of the forest glade. The dead have already escaped there. Like one of Wotan's daughters, the Sister waits upon them, ready to conduct the worthy on to paradise.

Trakl was visited by Ficker during the course of his enforced confinement. Shortly after their meeting, he overdosed on cocaine. He died on November 3, 1914, at the age of twenty-seven. After leaving the garrison hospital, Ficker wrote to Wittgenstein, who was also then serving in Poland, requesting that he, too, visit the anguished and emotionally disturbed Trakl. The philosopher attempted to do so, but he arrived too late, three days after the poet's death. Trakl was buried in Cracow. Two years later, Margarete Trakl Langen shot herself to death while attending a party.

In 1925, her brother's remains were disinterred from their resting place in Poland. Trakl was reburied in his beloved Innsbruck in a cemetery adjacent to the home of his friend and patron Ludwig von Ficker.

Notes

1. John Wakeman, ed. *World Authors, 1950–1970* (New York: H.W. Wilson, 1975), p. 1439.

2. Quoted by Michael Hamburger, "Introduction," *Georg Trakl: A Profile*, ed. Frank Graziano (Durango, Colo.: Logbridge-Rhodes, 1983), p. 14.

3. Ibid.

4. Ibid., p. 12.

5. *World Authors*, p. 1439.

6. Ibid.

7. Quoted by Frank Graziano, "Introduction," *Georg Trakl: A Profile*, ed. Graziano (Manchester: Carcanet, 1984), p. 16.

8. Ibid.

9. Georg Trakl, "Caspar Hauser Song," trans. David Luke, in *An Anthology of German Poetry from Hölderlin to Rilke in English Translation*, ed. Angel Flores (Gloucester, Mass: Peter Smith, 1965), p. 354. All translations were done especially for this volume in 1960.

10. Graziano, *Georg Trakl*, p. 16.

11. Ibid.

12. Ibid., p. 17.

13. Trakl, "Childhood," trans. Christopher Middleton, *Anthology*, p. 349.

14. Trakl, " Wayfaring," trans. Middleton, *Anthology*, p. 347.

15. Ibid.

16. Trakl, "Elis," trans. Kate Flores, *Anthology*, p. 345.

17. Trakl, "To the Boy Elis," trans. Kate Flores, *Anthology*, p. 344.

18. "Wayfaring," p. 348.

19. Trakl, "To One Who Died Young," trans. Middleton, *Anthology*, p. 355.

20. Trakl, "Sebastian in Dream," trans. Kate Flores, *Anthology*, p. 350.

21. Ibid.

22. Ibid.

23. Ibid.

24. Ibid., p. 351.

25. Ibid.

26. Ibid.

27. Ibid.

28. Graziano, "Introduction," *Georg Trakl*, p. 12.

29. Hamburger, "Introduction," *Georg Trakl*, p. 11.

30. Trakl, "Lament," trans. Kate Flores, *Anthology*, p. 367.

31. Trakl, "Grodek," trans. Kate Flores, *Anthology*, p. 368.

Vladimir Mayakovski

ONE OF THE MOST PARADOXICAL AND CONTROVERSIAL FIGURES OF
twentieth-century world literature, Vladimir Mayakovski, became obsessed with the ideas of martyrdom and suicide early in his
career. Although the poet fought hard against his destructive impulses
and repudiated his early nihilism and self-obsession to embrace the
Bolshevik revolution of 1917, his fixation with death abided throughout
his life, as did his exhibitionism and his general anarchistic spirit.
Little else about the man remained constant over the years. Mayakovski's thinking did not run a steady course but underwent a continual
metamorphosis. Following the Russian revolution, his aesthetics would
undergo a drastic shift, a complete flip-flop or hundred-and-eighty
degree turn. One of Russian poetry's greatest formal innovators, known
for his idiosyncratic style and for the subjective focus of his verse (his
early poetry dealt almost exclusively with his personal suffering, especially the tortures inflicted by love), Vladimir Mayakovski would
become a communist polemicist and sloganeer and, blind to the red
terror and Leninist excesses of the early years of the revolution, would,
heart and soul, play Dryden to the devil. While the seventeenth-century
English poet wrote occasional verse glorifying both Cromwell and
Charles II, Mayakovski would extol Vladimir Iliyich Lenin and other
communist leaders. Each man was also something of a turnwheel. After
attacking the doctrine of papal infallibility in the poem *Religio Laici*,
Dryden would convert to Catholicism upon the ascension of James II to
the throne of England and write a moving defense of his new faith, *The
Hind and the Panther*. Mayakovski would also have a change of heart
about communism. In the two years preceding his death in 1930,
Mayakovski would write two satirical plays, *The Bedbug* and *The Bathhouse*, that would expose the failures of the Soviet system, reveal the sad

plight of the individual living in a totalitarian state, and uncover the corruption and labyrinthine inefficiency of "sovbureaucrats" during the Stalin era, as well as attack the reigning dictator himself.

Boris Pasternak described Mayakovski's early lyrics as "poetry molded by a master; proud and daemonic and at the same time infinitely doomed, at the point of death, almost an appeal for help."[1] Mayakovski's central subject was Mayakovski. In the 1915 poem "The Backbone Flute," he saw his life as a sort of high-wire exhibition. He needed a crowd to witness his dance of death. Naturally he would perform without nets, and, when the time came, he would enjoy taking the inevitable nosedive: "I shall plunge head first from the scaffolding of days./Over the abyss I've stretched my soul in a tightrope/ and, juggling with words, totter above it."[2] Although he needed an audience, Mayakovski was dismissive and contemptuous of it. As a youth and young man, he felt deeply alienated from society. Alone, misunderstood, and unhappy, he longs for comprehension and love but is constantly rebuffed. Different from the ordinary run of men, he quickly learns that he can expect no sympathy from the "faceless crowd" and the "bull-featured mass."[3] He depicts his contempt and antagonism to the mob in the "The Way I Became a Dog." Rather than associating with human beings, Mayakovski would prefer to turn into a dog and to consort and fraternize with other hounds. While dogs may be fierce, savage, and bestial, they are never duplicitous. Unlike humans, their motivations and incentives remain abundantly clear. In another early poem, "A Warm Word to Certain Vices," Mayakovski celebrates corruption and depravity and glorifies those who profiteer from the toil of others. The capitalist who amasses rubles understands both the venality and herd-like nature of the public. He leads the myriad-headed louse by the nose and has a fully developed, if ruthless, personality. He is an individual and therefore has the right to utilize and manipulate nonentities as he sees fit. Bilkers and cardsharps likewise deserve to be applauded, for they also take advantage of the stupidity and avarice of the average man.

Estranged from society, feeling powerless in the face of a hostile and loveless world, Mayakovski claimed that he felt dead and unfeeling inside. In order to spur himself out of his lethargy, he would strive to drum up his passions to a fever pitch in order to rouse himself into a frenzy. While his early confessional poetry is highly emotive, Mayakovski admitted that boredom and malaise were his usual state. As he suffered from perpetual ennui, he would do anything to break the monotony. He claimed that he felt truly alive only when his feelings and emotions were pushed to the breaking point, when his pain, anguish, and hatred were at their most intense. He had strongly masochistic inclinations and would invent imaginary torments for himself in his poetry as well as envision himself in the most extreme and harrowing of situations.

Always in search of thrills and stimulation, the world-weary Mayakovski regularly sought diversion in mutually destructive love affairs. The greatest of his loves was probably Lily Brik, the daughter of a prominent Moscow lawyer and wife of the editor and critic Osip Brik. The two met in July 1915 at the Briks' salon. The couple's house was frequented by poets and artists, and Lily found many admirers from the ranks of the avant-garde, including the young Mayakovski. The two would not become lovers, however, until after the revolution. The obliging Brik permitted Mayakovski to move into his and his wife's apartment. Mayakovski continued living with the Briks even after his affair with Lily ended when she abandoned Mayakovski in favor of another lover in 1923. After their relationship had terminated, whenever he traveled away from home, Mayakovski would write letters to Lily pleading for tenderness and renewed attention on her part, even though he had long since begun seeing other women. He addressed her as Kitten and signed the letters Puppy. Brik would finally permit the publication of Mayakovski's letters in 1958. A fickle and hardhearted individual, she remained deaf to his entreaties. He sent several beseeching telegrams to her only a month before his death. To the last of these, she wired back: "I have received your little telegram . . . but I do not understand to whom you are writing—certainly not to me. . . . Please invent a new text for telegrams."[4]

Long before the couple became lovers, indeed immediately after the two met in 1915, Mayakovski began dedicating his poetry to Lily. While he made her his muse, it was not in the ordinary sense. His poems about Lily were almost invariably disparaging and derogatory indictments against her. In the premonitory "The Backbone Flute," written several months after he and Lily met, Mayakovski already portrays himself as Lily Brik's lover—a lover forsaken by her for another man. He feels as if he has been sent into Siberian exile. Nonetheless, his love survives despite her abandonment of him. He boasts that he will scratch Lily's name on his fetters, and, "in the darkness of hard labor,"[5] he promises to kiss his shackles again and again. In "The Backbone Flute," and other similarly misogynistic poems addressed to Lily which, during the early years of his career, he read all over Russia with Brik's consent, Mayakovski again and again poses the question whether suicide would be preferable to his current torment. In "The Backbone Flute," he contemplates using a pistol. In "Man," he writes: "The heart yearns for a bullet/while the throat raves of a razor. . . ."[6] Although he is sorely tempted to do away with himself, he resists the urge to end his life. Instead he celebrates his pain. His love, he avers, is superhuman and will outlast God and the universe both:

> When all will perish,
> swept away,
> He
> to whom love conforms
> from the last suns
> The last weak ray
> will burn
> o'er planet swarms,
> then,
> only sharper still my pain,
> beside,
> below,

above—
I'll stand,
wrapped in undying flame—
unfanciable love.[7]

A handsome man and successful poet and playwright, Mayakovski had no dearth of female admirers. He took many lovers during his life, but he seemed most attracted to women who, like Lily Brik, in some way or the other, could do him the most harm. He forsook women who were nurturing and truly loving in favor of *belle dames sans merci*; on the other hand, he had little compassion or conscience himself in dealing with women who made the mistake of falling in love with him. In his relations with women, he resembled the fictional character Arkady Ivanovitch Svidrigailov, the amoral and debauched sensualist of Dostoevski's *Crime and Punishment* whose every action is driven by his libido, and whose devil-may-care-attitude and his delight in shocking the innocent and uninitiated culminates, after he realizes that the woman he loves will have nothing more to do with him, in his publicly shooting himself before an unsuspecting stranger.

In his most significant poem prior to 1917, "The Cloud in Trousers," which deals with the poet's tortured relations with two women named Maria, Mayakovski depicts himself being impaled on spires, trampled by a mob, set on fire and blown and buffeted by storms. His tribulations serve as metaphors for the torments and anguish of unrequited love. Rebuffed by the first Maria in Part One of this apocalyptical poem, Mayakovski lays hands on himself and tears his body to shreds in order to expose his soul and offer it to the icy, disdainful woman as a bloody trophy; then, as she still won't relent, he proceeds to annihilate and shatter the universe itself. He beheads the stars and bloodies the sky. The Maria of Part Three is likewise depicted as willful, stubborn, and unyielding to Mayakovski. In truth, she was a seventeen-year-old girl whom Mayakovski had abandoned after a short-lived affair. While in the poem, Mayakovski undergoes agonies tantamount to those of Christ on the cross, in actual fact it was the girl who suffered most. Still desperately in love with Mayakovski after he had broken off relations with her, she would kill herself several years later. In a film scenario *How Do You Do?* written in 1926, Mayakovski depicts his reaction to the woman's death. The hero of the film is named Mayakovski. The part was to be enacted by the author. The script opens with the poet reading an account of his lover's suicide in a newspaper. Seated in an armchair, he sips tea as he reads. The girl herself suddenly materializes from off the printed page. She points a revolver at her temple. Mayakovski jumps to his feet and pleads with her not to pull the trigger, but she fires anyway. The newspaper is pierced by the shot. The bullet passes through the pages in the manner of a dog breaking through a paper hoop at the circus. Mayakovski crumples the paper with disgust. He falls back into the chair and within a few seconds his face becomes calm. He shrugs off the girl's suicide, dismissing her death as both a theatrical gesture and a vain, egotistical act.

Mayakovski would develop a very negative attitude toward suicide (especially suicide occasioned by rejection in love) after he accepted his mantle as bard of the proletarian revolution. Some months before writing *How Do You Do?* he bitterly attacked the poet Sergey Yesenin for committing suicide in December 1925. From the first, Mayakovski had viewed Yesenin's poetry with hostility. Yesenin had embraced the communist revolution but had quickly grown disenchanted with the totalitarian Soviet system. He stopped writing poetry with revolutionary themes and again began to produce imagist and neo-romantic verse. After the failure of his marriage to Isadora Duncan in 1923, Yesenin grew increasingly morose. A dipsomaniac for all of his short life, Yesenin had become addicted to both alcohol and drugs. Shortly before his death, he sought happiness in a second marriage to Leo Tolstoy's granddaughter, but, debilitated by years of heavy drinking and growing progressively more and more disillusioned with the historical developments taking place in Russia, Yesenin slit his wrists, wrote a poem or suicide note in his own blood, then hanged himself at the age of thirty in the city of Leningrad. While the poem or note was largely illegible, the two concluding lines were clear: "in this life to die is nothing new/ and, in truth, to live is not much newer."[8] Mayakovski would rebut these lines in his own poem "To Sergey Yesenin." He would later state that his aim in writing the poem was "to deliberately paralyze the action of Yesenin's last lines; to make Yesenin's end uninteresting; to set forth in place of the easy beauty of death, another kind of beauty. For the working class needs strength to continue the revolution which demands . . . that we glorify life and the joy that is to be found along the most difficult of roads—the road towards communism."[9] In his own poem, Mayakovski would rework Yesenin's lines as follows: in this life it is not hard to die,/to mold life is more difficult."[10]

Five years later, however, Mayakovski would also be dead by his own hand. As had earlier been the case with Yesenin, Mayakovski would likewise grow disenchanted with the Soviet system, and shortly before his death he would become enmeshed in another of his impossible love affairs. For all his criticism of Yesenin, Mayakovski recognized the slightly younger man as an essentially kindred spirit. Mayakovski, too, had always been attracted to the "easy beauty of death." No matter how dogmatic his later remarks would become, there was a struggle inside his breast between his two selves: the shameless self-promoter and morbid narcissist obsessed with sex and death—the literary innovator who, absorbed in his own inner world, exults in self-expression—and the selfless communist ideologue, the Utopian idealist who envisioned a better and more equitable world, who struggled to triumph over his personal despair and alienation and aspired to a universal brotherhood, a higher and collective good. During the Bolshevik revolution, Mayakovski underwent an experience akin to that of the Christian being "born again." Throughout his life, the poet displayed an uncanny ability to foretell coming events. He predicted the Russian Revolution in "The Cloud in Trousers," his apocalyptic poem concerning the anguish of love. Because he cannot find love, he wants the entire world to be swept away and destroyed. Love, art, religion all must perish. He looks forward to a time when the foundations of society shall crack and its ramparts topple, and he sees the approaching upheaval in biblical terms—linking the imminent cataclysm to the second coming of Christ, a figure whom Mayakovski throughout his career had identified with himself and whom, in the 1918 play *Mystery-Bouffe*, he depicted as a proto-communist who summons to his side "all you who have calmly stabbed the enemy and walked away with a song on your lips."[11] Mayakovski predicted that the insurrection would occur in 1916. He miscalculated the event by a single year:

> I perceive whom no one sees,
> crossing the mountains of time.
> Where men's eyes stop short,
> there, at the head of hungry hordes,
> the year 1916 cometh
> in the thorny crown of revolutions.[12]

Mayakovski saw the Bolshevik revolution as a new beginning for both himself and the entire world. In the poem "Man," he writes: "Today topples your thousand-year-old Before./ Today the foundations of worlds are revised./ Today,/ to the very last coat-button, you're/ to start remodelling everyone's lives. . . ."[13] Mayakovski realized that a price would have to be paid in order that the slate could be wiped clean, and if that price was the shedding of vast amounts of blood, he was all for the paying of it. Far from being distressed and disturbed by the barbarism and the terror of the Bolsheviks, Mayakovski welcomed the slaughter and chaos of the first years of the communist takeover. Furthermore, he felt that corrupt and degenerate personality traits had to be purged from the individual person just as decadent institutions as well as certain individuals, those enemies of the state who attempted to forestall the revolution, had to be eliminated from society as a whole. Following the fall of the czar and the installation of Lenin as dictator, Mayakovski struggled very hard to suppress what he had now come to perceive as his own personal character flaws, but the old self would not prove as easy to keep down as Mayakovski at first supposed. In "Jubilee Poem," after vowing never again to foist "his melancholic mood on others"[14] but to use his talents exclusively to promote class struggle, he acknowledges that it will be difficult for him to keep his vow:

> But poetry's
> 　　　　　　a damn stubborn thing:
> it's there
> 　　　　　and you can't be destroyed—that's a fact.[15]

Mayakovski's internal struggle would continue to the very end of his life. Although in the 1920s, he produced a large quantity of propagandistic verse and made frequent attacks against love poetry in his various essays, he still wrote lyrical poems in his spare time. He could not help himself, but he was conscience-stricken and contrite afterward. In the early twenties, he continued to write remarkable love poems to Lily, including "I Love" (1922) and "About This" (1923). In 1928, he produced "Letter from Paris to Comrade Kostrov on the Nature of Love." In this late work, Mayakovski declares that love is an equally valid, if not more valid, theme than communism or class struggle. At the time he wrote the poem, he was visiting Paris, where he had just become enamored of Tatiana Yakovlea, the last great love of his life. Asked by his editor to submit a political article excoriating French culture, he sent this poem instead. He chastises Kostrov for thinking that his passion could be checked: "Hurricane,/fire,/water surge forward, rumbling. /Who/can/ control this?/ Can you?/ Try it. . . ."[16] Yet even after writing this admonitory poem and producing his last plays, *The Bedbug* and *The Bathhouse*, which were extremely critical if not of the high ideals of communism then of the stark and brutal realities of the Soviet system of the late 1920s, he would speak out a final time against the writing of "decadent" poetry three weeks before his suicide. At an exhibition of his work, he declared: "Why should I write on Mary's love for Peter instead of considering myself part of the state organ which builds life. The basic goal of the exhibition is . . . to show that the poet is not one who, like a wooly lamb, bleats of lyric-erotic themes, but one who, in our acute class struggle, surrenders his pen to the arsenal of proletarian arms."[17]

The post-revolutionary Mayakovski characterized himself as "a rabble-rouser and a brazen-mouthed ringleader."[18] He professed that art was worthless if it did not have utilitarian or political value. Believing that he had successfully purged the *poète maudit* aspect of his character, Mayakovski took pride in the fact that he had stopped writing what he now derided as self-indulgent verse and "lovesick twaddle"[19] in favor of patriotic jingles and agit-art. In "At the Top of My Voice," he claimed that he had saved himself by subduing himself, by "setting [his] heel on the throat of [his] own song."[20] Mayakovski not only lauded his own act of self-censorship (in itself a kind of suicide), but, in the 1925 poem *Back Home*, he championed the state's right to supervise and control the direction of art and thought. He declared that he needed and welcomed such guidance from above: "I want/ a commissar/with a decree/to lean over the thought of the age./ . . . I want/ the factory committee/to lock/my lips/when the work is done."[21] In keeping with his pronouncement that "the work of a poet of the Revolution was not confined to the writing of books,"[22] Mayakovski would increasingly spend his time writing militant essays and drawing posters and political cartoons to educate the proletariat. He would purposely "write down" for the masses, employing bold, simple imagery that could readily be understood. He had always been attracted to the theater, but, in the 1920s, he became enormously interested in the cinema as well. The prospect of mass audiences excited him, and he wrote over a dozen film scripts and scenarios. Working for ROSTA (the Russian Telegraph Agency), he produced both artwork and captions for cartoons. These agit-posters were mass produced and placed in the streets of all the major Russian cities for all to read. The signs urged the Russian people to shop at government stores such as

Mosselprom, to have faith in Soviet banks, that it was safe to deposit their money there, and to always boil water before drinking it. Mayakovski claimed not only that he considered such work equally important as the writing of poetry, but that he felt that his slogans constituted his finest "art."

Mayakovski would become one of the driving forces behind the new orthodoxy of socialist realism—perhaps the most tendentious, not to say monotonous, movement in the history of all of art, a campaign that demanded complete ideological conformity in its purposive and unconditional disposition to promote the communist point of view. Until the fall of communism in the former Soviet Union, many of Mayakovski's implicitly doctrinaire poems, including the sentimental yet lock-step-allegiant "My Soviet Passport," and his panegyric to the architect of the Bolshevik revolution *Vladimir Ilyich Lenin*, were required reading for schoolchildren from Moscow to Vladivostok. Mayakovski's long elegy to Lenin also served as a combative defense of socialist art:

> Sure,
> "Capitalism" rings
>
> not so very elegant,
> "Nightingale"
> has a far more delicate sound.
> Yet I'll go back to it
> whenever relevant.
> Let stanzas
> like fighting slogans resound!
> I've never
> been lacking in topics—
> you know it,
> but now's
> not time
> for lovesick tattle.
> All
> my thundering power of a poet
> is yours,
> my class
> waging rightful battle![23]

Not all of Mayakovski's later poems are as militant and dogmatic as *Vladimir Ilyich Lenin*. In addition to such fulsome and chauvinistic verses, to his silly slogans, to his doggerel rhymes and to his doctrinaire essays published in *Komsomolskaya Pravda*, Mayakovski also wrote undeniably stirring and emotional poems about the Russian revolution that were inventive both in presentation and content. Although Pasternak would dismiss Mayakovski's political verse, he nonetheless called him the preeminent poet of his time. Paradoxically, the Russian writers who would later resist social realism would also uniformly hold Mayakovski in high esteem. Like Pasternak, they naturally preferred the iconoclasm of his prerevolutionary poetry to his later verse. They also applauded his final plays and such defiant late lyrics as "Letter from Paris to Comrade Kostrov on the Nature of Love"; but they were also forced to admit that, even in his most obviously doctrinaire poems, Mayakovski was able to preserve a measure of his originality. He glorifies the masses, for example, in the poem "150,000,000," which was written after American troops intervened in the Russian civil war in support of the White Russians. Mayakovski spouts the party line that the well-being of the individual is far less important than the prosperity of the populace as a whole. He rattles off a long, dull litany in praise of the Russian proletariat in which the word "millions" appears *ad nauseam*: he writes "endearing verse" for the millions in battle. He sings his song for the millions. All he can see are the millions surging together in joint action. Collectively they can "dynamite" the Old World to bits. His "lyre strings rattle"[24] for the millions, and so on, and so on. He makes no effort to differentiate the individual faces in the crowd. The millions are ant-like; they are indistinguishable and interchangeable. Even the communist critic Alexander Ushakov found the poem crude. "Such unqualified glorification of 'the millions' alone," Ushakov writes, "appears somewhat too biased in favour of the masses, as opposed to the individual. The spirit of anonymity, permeating the poem, was detrimental to the image of the people which it depicted. The poet, as it were, shackled his lyric feeling, not letting it reveal itself to the full."[23] Ushakov is certainly dead to rights when it comes to the litany portion of the poem, but "150,000,000" comes alive when the millions fuse into a single figure, a 150,000,000-headed colossus named Ivan whose arms stretch the entire length of the Neva river and whose heels are as broad and wide as the Caspian steppes. Ivan is so tall he can walk across the ocean bed of the Atlantic without ever becoming submerged. He does so in order to do battle with Woodrow Wilson, who also takes on gigantic proportions in the poem and doffs a top hat as tall as the Eiffel tower.

In his best revolutionary verse, Mayakovski captures the excitement and expectancy of the times like no other poet. There is a sense of destiny, an elemental and emergent force, in his work that reflects the gigantic energies unleashed in Russia by the revolution. The slumbering colossus had at last awakened and there would be consequences for the world. Mayakovski knew that he was a witness to history in the making, but the turbulence and storm that Mayakovski saw in the outside world also mirrored the tempest that swirled within Mayakovski. In his early poetry, he compared his inner agitation to the grand forces of nature. The sun's energy he made his own. Lightning flashed and thunder roared inside him, and he likened his personal turmoil to the surf and spray of a seething ocean. From the first, he also thought of himself as a sort of giant. He stood over six feet tall and had the build of a strapping Russian peasant. Not only did he have the appearance of a primitive throwback, he had an ecstatic, passionate nature befitting his size— or at least he desperately wanted to cultivate such an image, for, as we have seen, he was all too frequently bored and impassive. At the age of twenty-two, in the poem "To His Beloved Self, the Author Dedicates These Lines," Mayakovski attempted to advance such a depiction of himself: "But where can a man/like me/bury my head?/ Where is there shelter for me?/ . . . The gold of all the Californias/will never satisfy the rapacious horde of my lusts./ . . . I shall go by, dragging my burden of love./In what delirious/ and ailing night,/ was I sired by Goliaths—/ I, so large,/so unwanted?"[76] Robert Payne writes, in his introduction to the *Complete Plays of Vladimir Mayakovski*, that the "whirlwind of Mayakovski met the whirlwind of the Revolution head on" and that the two often "seemed to be the same whirlwind. . . ."[27] In the poem "Fine," Mayakovski admits as much:

> This is time
>
> > humming taut
> > > as a telegraph wire
>
> My
>
> > heart
> > > alone with the truth,
> > > > whole and sole.
>
> This happened—
>
> > > with fighters,
> > > > with the country entire,
>
> > in the depth
> > > of my own soul.[28]

A cyclone raged inside the man from the very beginning. Vladimir Mayakovski was born in the Georgian village of Bagdadi in 1893, the son of an indigent Russian nobleman who worked as a forester in order to support both himself and his family. Although he accompanied his father on his rambles through the woods, the young Mayakovski did not share the older man's love of nature. When in the course of one of their patrols, the boy caught sight of an illuminated rivet factory at night, he was astonished and electrified. After seeing such a massive production of power, the result of man's ingenuity and resourcefulness, he later wrote, his interest in the natural world faded completely. "It wasn't up to date enough."[29] Mayakovski hated school as a youth and almost did not pass his entrance exam to the upper forms due to the fact that he mistook a word in Slavonic frequently used in Eastern Orthodox Church ritual for a similar sounding word in Georgian. In the essay "I Myself," Mayakovski noted the effect his embarrassment at making the mistake had on him: "I conceived a hatred for everything ancient, everything churchy, everything Slavonic. Possibly from this spring my futurism, my atheism, and my internationalism."[30] At the age of twelve, the boy became enamored of the idea of revolution and found relief from boredom in stealing his father's shotguns and providing them to Social Democratic radicals and becoming a courier between local party leaders and their functionaries. After his father's death, which left his family totally destitute, Mayakovski, at the age of fifteen, moved from the country to Moscow, where he joined the Bolsheviks and handed out subversive pamphlets to workers. For this offense, he was arrested in 1908 and sentenced to eleven months in jail. The experience sobered him. While in prison, he read Shakespeare, Byron, and Tolstoy. Overwhelmed by the greatness of these three writers, he vowed to forswear politics and pursue the arts. From the first, however, he felt that he would accomplish tremendous things, that he would surpass even those three mighty titans from the past, or so he claims. In his autobiography, with characteristic braggadocio, he writes: "The authors I had read were the so-called great ones, but how easy to write better than they! I had already acquired a correct attitude toward the world. I needed only experience in art."[31] Mayakovski's first artistic efforts were in poetry, but he also tried his hand at abstract painting. On a Moscow street, he met the futurist painter David Burlyuk and asked Burlyuk to read one of his poems, though at the time he disclaimed authorship of the piece. Burlyuk guessed the truth and on the tenuous strength of just a few lines, the painter proclaimed Mayakovski a genius. Mayakovski wrote: "This grandiose and undeserved appellation overjoyed me. That evening quite suddenly I had become a poet."[32] Burlyuk had access to Moscow's various artistic circles and introduced Mayakovski to the leading lights of the day. He presented him as "My friend, the genius, the famous poet, Mayakovski."[33]

At the outset of his career, Vladimir Mayakovski aligned himself with the Russian futurist movement which called for the abrogation of all prevailing artistic genres and conventions in favor of new forms suitable to the machine age. Like other modernists, the Russian futurists desired a "revolutionary" upheaval in the arts. In 1912, Mayakovski signed the group's belligerent manifesto. The document insisted upon the poet's right to an "uncompromising hatred for the [Russian] language as used hitherto. . . ."[34] All writing, every model of style, that had previously been held up for public acclamation should now go into immediate disfavor. The poet's task was to reinvent the language and "enlarge the vocabulary with arbitrary and derivative words."[35] The titans of Russian literature would all have to be knocked from their pedestals. The laurels must be stripped from the brows of the so-called great in order that art might progress: "We alone are the *Face of Our Time*. Time's trumpet blares in our art of words. The Academy and Pushkin are more unintelligible than hieroglyphs. Throw Pushkin, Dostoevski, Tolstoy, etc., overboard from the steamer of modernity. . . . From the height of skyscrapers we look down at their insignificance."[36] Mayakovski retained his anarchic zeal and impatience with the past all his life. Since the futurists' pronouncements were largely hyperbolic, Mayakovski's opinion of the Russian classics would go up and down. He could be reverential or dismissive depending on his mood. His work bears the influence of many past masters, notably Pushkin, Lermontov, Gogol, Dostoevski, and Blok. Knocking the titans of art from their pedestals, however, was a persistent theme of his poetry from the start of his career to its finish. The bullets must whiz through the museums from time to time. The old must give way to the new, and it was best that the slate be washed clean. Periodic fresh beginnings are essential for the development and progress of art. Stagnation and complacency must be avoided at all costs.

The futurists loved to shock and offend. In the 1912 manifesto one of their stated goals was to elicit "cat-calls and indignation."[37] As a young man, in typical futurist fashion, Mayakovski enjoyed making a spectacle of himself. Alone or in the company of others, he liked to don outlandish costumes, daub his face with paint, and disrupt poetry readings, concerts, and painting and art exhibits. The solemnity of such occasions incited the futurists, who preferred to declaim their own verses on street corners or in the middle of public parks, to engage in what others would consider highly scandalous behavior. They, however, knew precisely what they were about. They loved disconcerting the philistines and drawing attention to themselves. To them such disruptive antics were nothing more than playful pranks —a giant lark or one great joke. Naturally their behavior was deeply resented. Ivan Bunin dismissed Mayakovski as a versifying hooligan. In his memoir *Memories and Portraits*, Bunin describes meeting Mayakovski at the opening of a Petrograd exhibition of Finnish artwork. Bunin, Gorky, and the Finnish painter Axel Gallen had just sat down to dinner. Mayakovski pulled a chair up to their table, sat down beside them, and began eating off their plates with his fingers and sipping wine from their glasses. Gallen was so nonplussed he couldn't say a word. The Russian Foreign Minister rose to give the official toast. Mayakovski got up, dashed to the minister's table, leaped onto an empty chair and proceeded to shout the minister down. He swore and blustered until the French ambassador rose to his feet. Mayakovski continued shouting. A number of his supporters and colleagues who had accompanied him to the exhibition all started to carry on. They shouted, clapped their hands and pounded their feet until one of the Finnish painters started to cry and wail from his seat. He kept repeating one of the few Russian words he knew. "Mnogo! Mno-go! Mno-go!" (Too much! Too much! Too much!). Despite all his infantile antics, Mayakovski deeply impressed other artists whenever he publicly recited his own poetry. Not only did he have obvious charisma, he showed real genius as well. On first encountering Mayakovski, Pasternak was stunned by the man's brilliance. Pasternak also had the impression that Mayakovski was himself startled by his own genius. In his memoir *Safe Conduct*, Pasternak writes, "his encounter with it [i.e., his genius] had so astonished him at some time that it had since become his prescribed theme for all time, and he had devoted his whole being to incarnate it without any pity or reserve."[38] Mayakovski never lost his love of performing before a crowd. Shortly before the Bolshevik revolution, he began carrying a megaphone. In the streets of Moscow and in the city's various public halls, he would descant his verse. He carried a gold-topped cane and wore a topcoat and a silk top hat. Instead of a flower, a large wooden spoon protruded from his buttonhole.

Because he was so exhibitionistic, Mayakovski was attracted to the theater right from the start of his career. His first dramatic work was, not surprisingly, entitled *Vladimir Mayakovski, A Tragedy*. The play, which premiered in the Lunar Park Theater in St. Petersburg in 1913, with Mayakovski in the title role, brought the twenty-year-old poet the notoriety and fame he so abundantly craved. The play showcases Mayakovski's love of excess. The author's intention in writing the drama is clear from the moment the curtain rises. Mayakovski's purpose is to sing his own praises, to pronounce himself the poet of the age. Like Napoleon he crowns himself, but also receives tribute from a host of colorful, clownish characters: The Man with Two Kisses, the Man with a Long Drawn-out Face, the Old Man with a Scrawny-Black Cat, the Enormous Woman, the Woman with a Tiny Tear, The Woman with a Tear, The Woman with a Great Big Tear, The Man Without a Head, the Man with One Ear, and the Man with One Eye and One Leg. All these secondary figures, however, are projections of various aspects of Mayakovski's personality. The crying ladies with their different-sized tears, represent the maudlin and bathetic aspects of the poet as well as the pity and tenderness he feels for himself. The comical Old Man with a Scrawny-Black Cat shares Mayakovski's love for technology. He envisions an urban landscape where street cars "will start off in a rush" and lights will burn "in the night like triumphant banners."[39] Instead of squabbling about ontological issues, he is concerned with practical questions, such as supplying enough energy to ensure efficient operation of the trams (he thinks he can furnish a sufficient amount by stroking the backs of his cats). More sinisterly, this character also embodies Mayakovski's revolutionary enthusiasm. He foresees and looks forward to a day of universal destruction. Men will be cut down in great numbers, but as people are no more than "bells on the duncecap of God,"[40] what of it? The Man with a Long Drawn-Out Face represents the love-sick Romanticist, who having loved and lost wishes both to murder love and to taste transcendent bliss, to embrace "the shaggy, sweat-dripping sky and the milky-innocent stars."[41] The Enormous Woman who stands between fifteen and twenty feet tall illustrates the poet's grandiosity, his love of hyperbole and exaggeration. At the play's conclusion, the Mayakovski character states that he dreams of having huge breasts, breasts big enough to suckle all of mankind. The variously mutilated characters embody Mayakovski's personal fears and apprehensions. The passage of time, in particular, distresses Mayakovski. He has to acknowledge that one day he will eventually be snuffed out, swallowed up by time. Despite his genius and for all his superior soul, he, too, is mortal. He will tread the stage for his appointed hour, but then, like everyone else, he will cease to exist. Although some audiences booed the play, it became the talk of Petrograd. Mayakovski eventually took the drama on the road and staged it in theaters all across Russia. Suddenly he was a literary figure of the first magnitude.

Mayakovski's second important drama, *Mystery-Bouffe*, was written during the heady days of the revolution and staged in October 1918. Mayakovski called the work, "a heroic, epic, and satiric representation of our era."[42] As Robert Payne points out, it resembles a medieval morality play, but one set in the twentieth century. As the curtain rises on the first of the play's six acts, the world has been destroyed by flood. Only the North Pole remains above the waters. There are twenty-eight human survivors, seven pairs of Clean and a like number of Unclean. The former are prominent members of the bourgeoisie. Their number include an American tycoon, the Negus of Abyssinia, a Russian speculator who made a fortune trafficking in stocks and bonds, the French statesman Clemenceau, and the British Prime Minister Lloyd George whose moustaches give him the appearance of a walrus and for which animal he is constantly mistaken. The Unclean are all proletarians of different professions. They consist of a carpenter, a laundress, a lamplighter, and a miner, among others. These workers unite to build an ark but are duped into taking on board the capitalists, who immediately assume command of the vessel. The Negus greedily consumes all the food that the Unclean have put aside for the voyage, and the two politicians vie with each other in issuing contradictory commands and orders. The workers revolt and heave most of the Clean overboard. They then set sail for Mount Ararat. As they espy the peak in the distance, Jesus appears and walks across the water toward them. He tells the Unclean that his paradise is for everyone except the poor in spirit and that Heaven is within their reach, then he vanishes into thin air. Not surprisingly, Mayakovski played the role of Christ in the first production of the play. Instead of reaching the heavenly port, the Unclean, through poor navigation, land in Hell. Horned devils quickly sniff out the few Clean still hidden in the hold of the boat and inflict appropriate torments on them. The Unclean thereby, manage to escape Hell quickly, passing through Purgatory to reach the gates of Paradise, where they are greeted by Methuselah, Saint John Chrysostom, Jean-Jacques Rousseau, and Leo Tolstoy. When asked by these worthies how they have managed to ascend to these sacred precincts and august heights, the workers answer: "We ourselves are Christ and Savior."[43] The Unclean do not find Heaven much to their liking. There is no wine to drink and no chairs to sit on. Besides, when compared to elevators, wings don't seem so very special. Once again the crew mounts an escape. Leaving Heaven, they enter Chaos, a region populated with Marxist dialecticians. At last, however, they are delivered from this final unhappy realm. A shiny steam engine materializes. They board it and are taken to the true paradise, a great modern city with skyscrapers, trains, streetcars, and automobiles.

Prior to the revolution, Mayakovski had already garnered a considerable reputation as a poet and playwright. Therefore, when he offered his services to the communists, they welcomed him with open arms. At first, he had only one detractor in the party (which he never officially joined), but nonetheless a very powerful one—its leader, Vladimir Ilyich Lenin. Lenin had a great love for traditional Russian literature and had no time for futurists such as Mayakovski. He found the poet's work bewildering and impenetrable and questioned why the government printing office would issue his work. He asked that publication of Mayakovski's writings be suspended and put the measure to a vote. In a rare instance, the ballots did not go Lenin's way.

Trotsky, on the other hand, greatly esteemed the poet's work. While he found some of Mayakovski's verse affected and grandiose, he wrote admiringly that "Mayakovski describes love as though it were a migration of nations."[44] Due to his stature, Mayakovski was given pretty much of a free reign by the communists until 1928. As early as 1922, he began attacking soviet bureaucrats. In "About Conferences," he laments that each morning the workers are called into conferences of the "A-B-C-D-E-F-G committees re the purchase of a bottle of ink by the provin-

cial co-op."[45] He longs for an end to such asininity: "Oh, for just one more conference re the eradication of all conferences."[46]

From time to time, Mayakovski would occasionally play the peacock in his dealings with Soviet officials. Trotsky asked to interview Mayakovski on the topic of revolutionary poetry for his book *Literature and Revolution*. Mayakovski dutifully came to
the office of the People's Commissar and delineated his ideas on the direction poetry
ought to take. Trotsky rephrased Mayakovski's comments after his own fashion,
desiring to recast the poet's remarks in words that could be taken for his own. He
asked Mayakovski what he thought of his paraphrase, and the poet, playing on the
popular maxim "the first pancake falls like a lump," replied "the first pancake falls
like a People's Commissar" (*pervy blin lyog komom/ pervy blin lyog narkomom*).[47] Such
insolence would not have been tolerated from a person of less eminence. Because of
who he was, Mayakovski had far greater leeway than the average party functionary.

Mayakovski's soul searching began in the mid-nineteen twenties. By that time,
other Soviet writers had begun faulting him for what they perceived as his literary
experimentation. He and other Russian futurists had founded an organization
known as Left Front of Literature or LEF. The group promoted innovative art forms
fit for the new revolutionary and technological epoch and published a progressive,
highly original magazine.[48] So much criticism was leveled against the organization,
however, that it had to stop publication of its periodical and close its offices. Not
even Mayakovski could stop the shutdown.

Disheartened by the collapse of LEF, Mayakovski began traveling widely in the
West. As a correspondent for *Komsomolskaya Pravda* and other Soviet newspapers,
he visited Poland, Czechoslovakia, Germany, Mexico, and the United States. Wherever he traveled, he took note of technological achievement and scientific progress,
but he also wrote of capitalistic exploitation and social injustice. Mayakovski spoke
only Russian, so his reporting was completely dependent on the Russian-speaking
interpreters who accompanied him. In particular, the prospect of traveling in the
United States thrilled him. In the abstract, American cities enthralled and excited
Mayakovski. As a futurist, he was all for industrialization and urbanization, and, in
American cities, he expected to see "the futurism of naked technology" which had
"the enormous task of revolutionizing the paralyzed, obese, and ancient psyche"[49]
definitely confirmed. The workers' Paradise in *Mystery-Bouffe* with its trains, streetcars and automobiles, and its "lattice-like forms of transparent factories and apartment buildings"[50] had been modeled on Manhattan. When Mayakovski arrived in
New York City, however, what he saw frightened and unsettled him. While delighting
in such marvels of construction as the Brooklyn Bridge, Mayakovski found the city
as a whole unpalatable. The filth, he wrote, was worse than Minsk. The pace of life
was too hectic, and the immensity of the place bewildered him. As a result of his
impressions of New York and other American cities such as Chicago, Pittsburgh, and
Detroit, Mayakovski, late in his life, altered his view of technology. It was not an
unmitigated good but had negative as well as positive aspects. His trip to the United

States was highly revelatory in this regard, for while in the past he wholeheartedly
promoted mechanization, after returning home from America, he wrote in his travel-
ogue *My Discovery of America* that the task of futurism was no longer "the hymning
of technology but its control in the interests of humanity."[51]

Unexpectedly, Mayakovski found France far more congenial than the United
States. In the past, the French nation had been a frequent butt of his satire. In the
1923 poem "Paris," for example, he addressed the Eiffel tower. He charged the
structure to incite revolution in the French capital and afterward to run away with
him to Moscow. The workers there, he promises, will take much better care of her
than the debauched and degenerate French. In various other writings, he characterized the French people as the most decadent, self-absorbed, and tradition-bound
populace on the face of the earth, yet he concludes *My Discovery of America* as follows: "In comparison with America's wretched hovels, each inch of land [in France]
has been captured by age-long struggle, exhausted by centuries, and used with
pharmaceutical minuteness to grow violets or lettuce. But even this despised sort
of little house, this little bit of land, this property, even this deliberate clinging for
centuries seemed to me now an unbelievable cultural milieu in comparison with
the bivouac-type set-up and the self-seeking character of American life."[52]

Upon returning home from America, Mayakovski experienced a sudden surge of
patriotism and wrote the insipid poem "Back Home!" where he swears allegiance to
Stalin and upholds the right of the state to control art. His acquiescence to the dictator did not last long. In 1927, Mayakovski attempted once again to establish LEF,
but due to the opposition of RAPP, the conservative Association of Proletarian
writers, his efforts came to naught. Russian intellectuals, futurists in particular, were
being upbraided for "Trotskyist left deviations."[53] Rather than promoting general
anarchism and technological innovation, writers should instead drum up enthusiasm
among the people for Stalin's first five-year plan, or so RAPP impatiently contended.
Having brought about the collectivization of agriculture, the new dictator was now
bent on subduing the intellectuals. Mayakovski saw what was in the works, and in
1928 he wrote his first satire of communist society, the trenchant yet subtly veiled
indictment of sovbureaucracy, *The Bedbug*. During the course of the play's composition, he traveled to Paris. While there, he met the eighteen-year-old White Russian
émigrée Tatiana Yakovleva "a beauty/all inset in furs and beads"[54] and immediately
fell in love. The object of his affection scandalized and shocked his Soviet colleagues.
He, of course, knew that she would and part of his attraction to her no doubt lay in
this foreknowledge, but she had other charms as well.

The niece of the fashionable painter Alexander Yakovlev possessed outstanding beauty. Tall and statuesque, she modeled clothing and posed for *Vogue*. In
addition, she had a strong sense for poetry and a forthright candid manner that dazzled Mayakovski. She stood up to him when she thought she must. Mayakovski
found her bold and winsome. She had a nature very much like his own but unde-
veloped. He took pains in her presence to soften his rough edges. He didn't swear

and grouse in his usual manner but recited lyric poems in fervid fashion. Tatiana had many admirers. She moved freely in French society, making frequent calls at the salons of the famous and the chic. She hobnobbed with both the aristocrats and the *nouveaux riches* and knew artists and painters of stature and repute. Mayakovski's first thought was to spirit her away from such decadent society. He wanted to carry her off to Moscow just as he had formerly desired to take home the Eiffel tower. In a single night, he wrote her a poem "Letter to Tatiana Yakovleva," in which he begged to marry her and bring her back home with him to the Soviet Union. Her presence is craved there: "We need people like you in Moscow,/there's a shortage of long-legged people./It's not for you who walked/in snow drifts and typhus/with those legs of yours/to surrender them/to the caresses/of oil magnates/at banquets/ . . . Come here!/Come to the crossroads/of my large/and clumsy arms./You don't want to?/ Well, stay behind and winter here/ . . . But—all the same/one day/I'll take you—/you alone/or together with Paris."[55]

Mayakovski returned to Moscow without Tatiana. He was, however, miserable and out of sorts. After finishing *The Bedbug* and attending its premiere, he rushed back to Paris. He had grown to love the city. The doors of high society opened to him, and he and Tatiana traveled to seaside resorts, where Mayakovski spent hours at the racecourses and the gaming tables. He purchased expensive suits for himself as well as costly dresses for Lily Brik. He stayed in France until the expiration of his visa in March 1929. Once again he failed to persuade Tatiana to return home with him. He wrote imploring letters to her throughout the spring and summer. He applied for another travel visa but was denied it by Soviet authorities, and in December 1929, he learned Tatiana had married a Frenchman. In grief and anger, Mayakovski began his final play, *The Bathhouse*, his second invective against the Soviet system—a far more direct assault than the earlier *Bedbug*.

Mayakovski's final two plays are informed by the ideas of the nineteenth-century Russian philosopher and librarian Nikolay Fyodorov, a friend of Tolstoy and Soloviev, whose single book, *The Common Cause*, influenced a generation of Russian writers. Dostoevski became acquainted with his ideas while writing *The Brothers Karamazov* and as a result rethought much of the novel. Fyodorov contended that mankind would eventually come to understand all the secrets of the universe. He believed history had one end, man's mastery of the cosmos. Human beings would not only travel to the most distant stars, they would eventually vanquish death and learn to resurrect the dead and return life to even their remotest ancestors. Mayakovski was introduced to Fyodorov's work by his friend the artist Vassily Chekrygin, who painted a resurrection series based on Fyodorov's ideas. The librarian's faith in science and technology appealed to Mayakovski's futurist side. His ideas infected both *The Bedbug* and *The Bathhouse*.

The central figure in the first play is Ivan Prisypkin, an uncouth, sycophantic, hopelessly corrupt Soviet bureaucrat. At the same time he is a caricature of the author Vladimir Mayakovski, who instructed the actor who originally played the part to mimic many of his mannerisms, his most noticeable quirks and tics. Prisypkin comes off as hero and villain both. In the first half of the play, he displays every vice of the bureaucrat as well as all of Mayakovski's personal weaknesses. He grovels and kowtows to the party higher-ups and bullies those beneath him in station. He vows his allegiance to the party too vocally and forever flashes his trade union card. He picks his pimples, belches when he eats, and drinks large quantities of vodka. He entertains himself by singing and playing the guitar. Despite his all-too-evident crudity and his professions of loyalty to the party, he has bourgeois pretensions and changes his name to the more elegant Pierre Skripkin. He drops his proletarian lover, Zoyka Berezkina, for the manicurist and beauty parlor cashier Elzevira Renaissance and is unaffected by Zoyka's subsequent suicide. He proposes to Elzevira who accepts his suit. Her mother rejoices at the prospect of having a Soviet official in the family and plans a sumptuous wedding feast. Elzevira's veil catches fire during the dinner. A horrible conflagration ensues and everyone at the dinner dies in the flames. A half century later, when world communism has been firmly established, an excavation at the site of the fire uncovers Prisypkin's body frozen in ice. The remains are sent to the Institute of Human Resurrection, where the directors debate whether or not to revive Prisypkin. Such a throwback might endanger the world. Who knows what diseases he might carry or what dangerous ideas he might spread? The newspapers of the world call for the reanimation of Prisypkin, so the Institute unthaws him, and, in the process, the bedbug embedded in his flesh is also brought back to life. The worst fears of the Institute are realized. Prisypkin can't possibly be reintegrated into society. All he wants to do is indulge in his old vices. He desires nothing more than to sing and strum his guitar and to chase after women after eating and drinking his full. All such activities have been banned in the new society. As Prisypkin refuses to forsake his crudeness and individuality, there is nothing for the authorities to do but place him in a cage in the local zoo marked *Philistinius vulgaris*.

The Bathhouse also deals with the conflict of past and future. The central figure is the all powerful dictator Pobedonosikov, or "Nose for power," a caricature of Joseph Stalin. Pobedonosikov's state is horribly inefficient. The sign in front of his office reads, "If you haven't been announced don't come in."[56] No real work gets done. The bureaucrats under the Supreme Leader constantly pass the buck onto their colleagues. Letters, reports, studies, minutes of preceding committee meetings are in constant circulation. Pobedonosikov delivers pompous speeches and stamps resolutions. Everyone licks his boots, but, from the top down, everyone in the system does his best to avoid work and responsibility. One of the dictator's favorite activities, for instance, is posing for portraits. He is hostile to all criticism. He becomes enraged when he sees a play that burlesques the stupidities of his government and vents his spleen afterward: "Your theater pretends to be revolutionary but you irritate . . . how do you say . . . you shake up responsible officials. This is not for the masses; workers and peasants won't understand it, and it's just as well they won't understand it, and it shouldn't be explained to them."[57] One of Pobedonosikov's underlings, Chudakov (Wonder-worker), claims to have built a time machine. The invention will enable men to travel into the future at the rate of one year per second. Chudakov desires to escape into the hereafter when man has conquered nature, science has solved the riddle of life, and society has at last been perfected. No funding can be found for Chudakov's project. The bureaucrats refuse to pursue the matter because there aren't any state directives regarding time travel. They refuse to admit Chudakov to the dictator's office, so he is forced to bring his machine to Pobedonosikov's private residence. The device is activated, and a messenger from the year 2030, the Phosphorescent Woman, suddenly appears. She confirms to Pobedonosikov that Chudakov was right about the future and promises to accompany the dictator there. Pobedonosikov and the other bureaucrats quickly board the machine. The dictator is intent on storming the future and reinstituting all the red tape of his present regime. The time machine, however, explodes after it is turned on. Pobedonosikov steps to the front of the stage and utters the final lines of the drama: "What are you trying to say here? That people like me aren't of any use to communism?"[58]

While *The Bedbug* had been critically well received, *The Bathhouse* raised the hackles of party leaders, and the play was bitterly attacked in the press. Mayakovski's loudest detractor was the RAPP spokesman and hack writer Vladimir Ermilov, who in the pages of *Pravda* labeled Mayakovski a Trotskyist. Mayakovski responded by hanging the following banner in the Meinhold, the Moscow theater where the play was being staged:

> It is hard to get rid of
>   The swarms of bureaucrats:
> Not enough bathhouses,
>   Not enough soap,
> Bureaucrats like Ermilov
>   Are comforted by the critics.[59]

Ermilov complained, and RAPP ordered the banner removed. Mayakovski felt that he was being subject to wrongful persecution. He attempted to defend himself in the press, but his health failed him. He was taken to the Kremlin hospital where he was treated for nervous exhaustion. Released after several days, he returned to his apartment where he began playing games of Russian roulette. The writer had always been prescient. He no doubt sensed the purges that were coming. On April 10, 1930, a friend saw him in the lobby of the Meinhold theater and told him of a more sympathetic review of *The Bathhouse* that had recently appeared in *Pravda*, but Mayakovski replied that it was too late now. Four days later, on the morning of April 14, 1930, he would load a single bullet in his revolver, spin the cylinder, and point the weapon at his heart and pull the trigger. On this his third try he lost the game. Earlier in the morning, the poet Semyon Kirsanov telephoned Mayakovski to ask the name of a tailor. Mayakovski promised to join his colleague at the man's shop the following day. He would not keep the appointment. Had he won the game of Russian roulette that he played later in the day he no doubt would have shown up. Twice before he pulled the trigger and lived. After each reprieve, he continued on with his daily routine. Prior to placing the cartridge in the gun Mayakovski changed his shirt. An old Russian superstition dictated that a man face death in fresh linen. He also placed a letter and a poem that he had written several days earlier on his desk. He had laid them out on the two previous occasions that he had played the game, but winning both times he put them away again. The poem read:

> "The incident is closed."
> The love boat has been
> Smashed against conventions.
> I don't owe life anything,
> And nothing will be gained
> By counting over
> Mutual hurts and slights.[60]

The note was more apologetic. It was addressed "to all":

> Do not blame anyone for my death and please do not gossip. The deceased terribly disliked this sort of thing. Mamma, sister, and comrades, forgive me. . . . Comrades of RAPP—do not think me weak-spirited. Seriously—there was nothing else I could do. Greetings.[61]

Had Mayakovski not killed himself at the age of thirty-six, he would no doubt have been one of Stalin's victims in the Soviet purges of the nineteen-thirties, when many of his friends and colleagues were jailed and executed. Ironically, at the height of those depredations, Stalin demanded reverence for the dead poet's work. He proclaimed, "Mayakovski was and remains the best and most talented poet of our Soviet epoch. Indifference to his memory and work is a crime."[62] A subway station was named in the poet's honor and his ashes were removed from their former resting place and buried under a giant red-and-black marble memorial in Moscow's Novo-Devechy Cemetery. As a result of his posthumous elevation at the hands of Stalin, Mayakovski became an official icon of the Soviet state. Boris Pasternak would later write that the works of the foremost Russian poet of the first half of the twentieth century, who saw in the chaos and turmoil of a revolutionary Russia a reflection of his own soul, were forcibly introduced to the Russian reading public "like potatoes under Catharine the Great."[63] According to Pasternak, this was the poet's second death.

Notes

1. Quoted by Patricia Blake, "The Two Deaths of Vladimir Mayakovski," in *The Bedbug and Selected Poetry* by Vladimir Mayakovski (Bloomington: Indiana University

Press, 1975), p. 22. Paternak's remarks are from *An Essay in Autobiography* (London: Collins and Harvill Press, 1959).

2. Vladimir Mayakovski, "The Backbone Flute," trans. George Reavey in *The Bedbug and Selected Poetry*, p. 125. The Bloomington edition is a reprint of the 1960 New York Meridian Books original.

3. Quoted by Alexander Ushakov, "Mayakovski, Poet of a New World," trans. Dorian Rottenberg, foreword to *Selected Works in Three Volumes* by Vladimir Mayakovski (Moscow: Raduga, 1985, 1987), vol. 1, p. 12.

4. Quoted by Blake, trans. Blake, "Two Deaths," *The Bedbug and Selected Poetry*, p. 27.

5. "Backbone Flute," *The Bedbug and Selected Poetry*, p. 123.

6. Quoted by Blake, "The Two Deaths of Vladimir Mayakovski," *The Bedbug and Selected Poetry*, p. 26.

7. Quoted by Ushakov, "Mayakovski, Poet of a New World," *Selected Works*, p. 11.

8. Quoted by Blake, "The Two Deaths of Vladimir Mayakovski," trans. Blake, *The Bedbug and Selected Poetry* p. 28.

9. Ibid., p. 29.

10. Ibid., p. 28.

11. Mayakovski, *Mystery-Bouffe in The Complete Plays of Vladimir Mayakovski*, trans. Guy Daniels with an introduction by Robert Payne (New York: Washington Square Press, 1968), p. 89.

12. Mayakovski, *The Cloud in Trousers*, trans. Reavey, *The Bedbug and Selected Poetry*, p. 83.

13. Quoted by Ushakov, "Mayakovski, Poet of a New World," *Selected Works*, vol. 1, p. 15.

14. Mayakovski, "Jubilee Poem," trans. Peter Tempest, *Selected Works*, vol. 1., p. 105.

15. Ibid.

16. Mayakovski, "Letter From Paris to Comrade Kostrov on the Nature of Love," trans. Reavey, *The Bedbug and Selected Poetry*, p. 219.

17. Quoted by Blake, "The Two Deaths of Vladimir Mayakovski," *The Bedbug and Selected Poetry*, p. 33.

18. Quoted by Ushakov, "Mayakovski, Poet of a New World," *Selected Works*, vol. 1, p. 7.

19. Mayakovski, *Vladimir Ilyich Lenin*, trans. Rottenberg, *Selected Works*, vol. 2, p. 155.

20. Mayakovski, "At the Top of My Voice," trans. Reavey, *The Bedbug and Selected Poetry*, p. 225.

21. Mayakovski, "Back Home," trans. Reavey, *The Bedbug and Selected Poetry*, p. 187.

22. Quoted by Ushakov, "Mayakovski, Poet of a New World," *Selected Works*, vol. 1, p. 18.

23. *Vladimir Ilyich*, pp. 154–55.

24. Quoted by Ushakov, "Mayakovski, Poet of a New World," *Selected Works*, vol. 1, p. 17.

25. Ibid.

26. Mayakovski, "To His Beloved Self, the Author Dedicates These Lines," trans. Reavey, *The Bedbug and Selected Poems*, pp. 133–35.

27. Robert Payne, "Introduction," *The Complete Plays*, p. 2.

28. Mayakovski, *Fine*, trans. Rottenberg, *Selected Works*, vol. 2, p. 208.

29. Quoted by Blake, "The Two Deaths of Vladimir Mayakovski," *The Bedbug and Selected Poetry*, p. 14.

30. Ibid., pp. 14–15. This passage appears in "I Myself," *Mayakovski and His Poetry* (London: Pilot Press, 1942).

31. Quoted by Blake, "The Two Deaths of Vladimir Mayakovski," *The Bedbug and Selected Poetry*, p. 15.

32. Ibid., p. 16.

33. Ibid.

34. Ibid., pp. 17–18. This passage from the Futurist Manifesto of 1912 appears in *The Creative Experiment*, trans. C. M. Bowra (New York: Grove Press, 1948).

35. Ibid, p. 18.

36. Ibid., pp. 17–18.

37. Blake, "The Two Deaths of Vladimir Mayakovski," *The Bedbug and Selected Poetry*, p. 18.

38. Ibid., trans. Reavey, pp. 19–20.

39. Mayakovski, *Vladimir Mayakovski, A Tragedy, Complete Plays*, p. 24.

40. Payne, "Introduction," *The Complete Plays*, p. 4.

41. *Vladimir Mayakovski, A Tragedy*, p. 29.

42. Quoted by Payne, "Introduction," *The Complete Plays*, p. 7.

43. *Mystery-Bouffe*, p. 108.

44. Quoted by Payne, "Introduction," *The Complete Plays, The Bedbug and Selected Poetry*, p. 7.

45. Quoted by Blake, "The Two Deaths of Vladimir Mayakovski," p. 31.

46. Ibid., p. 32.

47. Ibid.

48. Ibid., p.34.

49. Ibid., p. 35. This passage is from *My Discovery of America*, trans. Charles A. Moser.

50. *Mystery-Bouffe*, p. 130.

51. Quoted by Blake, "The Two Deaths of Vladimir Mayakovski," *The Bedbug and Selected Poetry*, p. 35.

52. Ibid., pp. 35–36.

53. Ibid., p. 36.

54. "Letter from Paris to Comrade Kostrov," p. 209.

55. Quoted by Blake, "The Two Deaths of Vladimir Mayakovski," *The Bedbug and Selected Poetry*, p. 42.

56. Mayakovski, *The Bathhouse, Complete Plays*, p. 212.

57. Quoted by Blake, "The Two Deaths of Vladimir Mayakovski," *The Bedbug and Selected Poetry*, p. 44.

58. *The Bathhouse*, p. 264.

59. Quoted by Payne, "Introduction," *The Complete Plays*, p. 16.

60. Ibid.

61. Quoted by Blake, "The Two Deaths of Vladimir Mayakovski," *The Bedbug and Selected Poetry*, p. 47.

62. Ibid., pp. 49–50.

63. Ibid, p. 50. This passage is from Boris Pasternak's *An Essay in Autobiography* (London: Collins and Harvill Press, 1959).

Vachel Lindsay

ONCE HE ACHIEVED FAME AND RECOGNITION AS A POET, VACHEL
Lindsay started giving annual readings at the First Christian
Church in his hometown of Springfield, Illinois. He made no exception
in the year 1931. The evening of November 30, he delivered a short lecture and declaimed selected verse before a large and appreciative audience. Within a week of his last Springfield performance, he died by his
own hand. On December 5, 1931, he drank a bottle of Lysol and expired
in an upstairs bedroom of his Springfield residence. This was the same
house in which he had been born fifty-two years earlier, a dwelling
which stood next door to the gubernatorial mansion of the State of Illinois and which at one time had been owned by a sister-in-law of
Abraham Lincoln (Lincoln's own home was but several blocks distant).

The previous Monday, Lindsay "recited with vigor, enjoyed the
enthusiasm of the large audience, and later was the centre of a demonstration of congratulations."[1] So did the *New York Times* report after his
death (the family had given it out that Lindsay had died of a heart attack;
the newspaper accepted the story and likewise attributed Lindsay's death
to heart failure). The poet, however, was an old and expert hand at reciting
his work and had become more than adept at hiding his inner torment;
indeed, he was a veritable master at public deception. The cracks might
show on occasion during his public lectures and recitations but very
infrequently. He had a dramatic voice and a compelling stage presence.
His best poems were written to be read aloud. Lindsay wrote that he did
not compose by "listening to the inner voice and following the gleam—
but by pounding the table with a ruler and looking out the window at electric lights."[2] Many of his poems were designed according to a musical
scheme. Often he adopted the rhythm and beat of jazz and ragtime in his
verse. Sound was always of equal, if not greater, importance than sense:

Oh, the longhorns from Texas,
The Jay hawks from Kansas,
The plop-eyed bungaroo and giant giassicus,
The varmint, chipmunk, bugaboo,
The horned-toad, prairie-dog and ballyhoo,
From all the newborn states arow,
Bidding the eagles of the west fly on.
Bidding the eagles of the west fly on.
The fawn, prodactyl and thing-a-ma-jig,
The rakaboor, the hellangone,
The whangdoodle, batfowl and pig,
The coyote, wild-cat, and grizzly in a glow,
In a miracle of health and speed, the whole breed abreast,
They leaped the Mississippi, blue-border of the West,
From the Gulf to Canada, two thousand miles long:—
Against the towns of Tubal Cane,
Ah,—sharp was their song.
Against the ways of Tubal Cane, too cunning for the young,
The longhorn calf, the buffalo and wampus gave tongue.[3]

Lindsay consciously wrote performance pieces. He even printed stage directions with certain of his poems. When he read, he half-chanted and half-sang his poetry. He swayed on his feet and gestured with his hands. He knew how to put on a show and please a crowd. As far as outward appearances were concerned, he seemed in fine fettle during his Springfield recital. He read his verse movingly, but for the first time in his career as a public performer he stammered over a few lines. He would later attribute this to the church's poor lighting. From the moment he first spoke, Lindsay perceived a friendly feeling emanating from the audience and he certainly appeared to be basking in his glory as he mingled with his listeners afterward. As an encore that evening, he had read "The Lame Boy and the Fairy." His eyes sought out those of his wife, Elizabeth, who was sitting in the first row. Both struggled to keep from crying as Lindsay read:

We shall see silver ships.
We shall see singing ships,
Valleys of Spray today,
Mountains of foam.
We have been long away.
Far from our wonderland.
Here come the ships of love
Taking us home.[4]

He did not read the poem to the end. Stepping down from the pulpit, he confided to Dr. Cummings, the minister, "I feel that at last I have won Springfield!"[5]

The poet, however, had had a very bad year. He was sick, in debt, and deeply depressed. His critical reputation had gone into a tailspin and the reading public evinced little interest in his more recent volumes. Critics derided some of the verses in *Going-to-the-Sun* (1923) *Going-to-the-Stars* (1926) and *The Candle in the Cabin* (1927) as feminine and ladylike. They found others exuberant and lively in presentation but lacking in substance. The language of such a poem might be flamboyant and high-spirited or even driven and frenzied, but the idea behind it seemed, in the end, inconsequential. The poem was all sound and fury—it signified nothing. The critics carped that Lindsay inflated the importance of his subjects and tried to give cosmic gravity and consequence to everything he wrote. They also perceived increasing didacticism and demagoguery in his work.

Admittedly, from the first, there had been an evangelical fervor to his writing. At the outset of his career, Lindsay became a voluntary hobo, a minstrel or troubadour of the road, who tramped through Florida, Georgia, and the Carolinas "trading rhymes for bread." Convinced that the "people liked poetry as well as the scholars or better,"[6] he saw himself as a sort of trailblazer, a Johnny Appleseed of culture and beauty, who spread the good news about the future America.

In his early verse, he celebrated a veritable pantheon of American heroes. He venerated Lincoln, Springfield's most famous son, above all others, seeing the assassinated president as a Christ-like figure who had envisioned a millennial American utopia. This most optimistic of American poets believed that he himself could help nudge Lincoln's vision into being by taking on the role of strolling player and mendicant minstrel. As a wandering poet, he would assist in creating a national mythos. Building on what he perceived to be a shared heritage, he hoped to establish a communal or national art. Springfield would become the New Jerusalem of a revitalized America, a shining city sacred because of its associations with the slain president. Lindsay revered Lincoln as the great Emancipator, the man who freed the slaves. The future America would need "many Lincoln-hearted men,"[7] he wrote in "On the Building of Springfield." Although his masterpiece, "The Congo," would be deemed (at least in some quarters) politically incorrect in the America of the 1990s, Lindsay was strongly sympathetic toward the American negro, as evidenced by poems such as "John Brown" and "Simon Legree." He always stood for the little man, the factory worker, the homesteader, the itinerant fruit picker, the lost and forlorn individual that General Booth of the Salvation Army would seek to save from perdition. He became the poet of the most notoriously degraded—the "vermin-eaten saints" and the "unwashed legions."[8] These folks—the longhorns, the Jay hawks, the rakaboors and hellangones—would inherit the kingdom, not the plutocrats, "With dollar signs upon their coats,/ Diamond watchchains upon their vests/And spats upon their feet."[9]

Although Lincoln had been a Republican, most of Lindsay's political heroes were Democrats. He revered Thomas Jefferson and celebrated Andrew Jackson as a "friend of the common man."[10] As a youth, he became caught up with the populist cause, which in commentator Mark Harris's words "permitted the simpler idealistic instinct to join itself to political forces composed not only of disgruntled farmers but also of various degrees of sophisticated socialism."[11] At the age of sixteen, Lindsay saw William Jennings Bryan as the hope of the new states of the American West and would later write "Bryan, Bryan, Bryan, Bryan" in his honor. He also lionized Illinois Governor John P. Altgeld, who welcomed the free silver advocate to Springfield in 1896 when the latter had become a candidate for president. Although his surname literally meant "old money" in German, Altgeld was a man of the people and hearkened to Bryan's admonition to the eastern plutocrats: "You shall not crucify mankind/ Upon a cross of gold."[12] He pardoned the anarchist agitators for their part in Chicago's Haymarket riot and criticized President Cleveland for sending federal troops to Chicago during the Pullman strike. Lindsay would memorialize the governor, whose contributions were largely ignored after he left office, in one of his finest poems, "The Eagle That Is Forgotten." In later life, Lindsay would also come to hold Woodrow Wilson in particularly high esteem. He saw the twenty-eighth President of the United States as a modern-day Socrates who tried to plant the seeds of American-style democracy in Europe, only to see his policies repudiated by his fellow countrymen and America denied admission to the League of Nations.

Lindsay did not, however, restrict his heroes to politicians. He wrote about quintessential American types, popular figures of regional folklore such as Johnny Appleseed; Daniel Boone, John Brown, and other historical personages; fictional characters who seemed so real they became a living part of the American consciousness: Mark Twain's Tom Sawyer, for example, or Harriet Beecher Stowe's evil slaveholder Legree; and sports figures and showmen such as heavyweight champion John L. Sullivan and circus barker and ringmaster P. T. Barnum. Indeed, Lindsay felt that America resembled nothing so much as a county fair or circus. He intended his opus to be a sort of big top in which the reader could encounter all the motley figures of our collective culture. With missionary zeal, he determined to spread his twin gospels of beauty and Jeffersonian democracy throughout the United States. He envisioned an entire nation of "artistic democrats" and felt confident that if he could but lay the seed, other greater poets would come after him:

> I certainly am willing to blast the breach in the wall, if you will send the 100 poets in my wake. . . . Say I am the least, the humblest, and you have 99 stronger coming in behind me, and number 99, now hid in the womb of time is the foremost. And please tell the other poets . . . that I expect them to follow me up and do a heap better than I do, that I do not claim a single thing for myself in the way of place or privilege. When I quit I want the 99 to be *well started, singing*.[13]

At the height of his fame, Lindsay felt himself on "the tantalizing verge of converting the *General Public*."[14] Believing that he had won the day in America, he spoke about taking his show to Australia, New Zealand and South Africa. He vowed that he would spread his message to "the edges of the English-speaking world."[15]

"We are planning an Art Revolution," Lindsay wrote. "Once the Poets and Artists are in power, good-bye to the business men, and tariff senators and such forever-more. We must make this a *Republic of Letters*."[16]

Vachel Lindsay searched for a distinctively American rhythm to his poetry, a cadence and beat suitable to his subject and message. This rhythm would not only reflect America's carnival aspects, it would mimic a wide array of different American sounds from the pulse and throb of jazz music to the hoofbeats of buffaloes thundering across the plain, from revival singing in a Campbellite meeting house to the cacophony of automobiles caught in crosstown traffic, horns and cutouts blaring during rush hour. This new American rhythm, pulsing with energy and vigor, was Lindsay's lasting contribution to poetry. His efforts would pave the way for a whole new generation of American poets, including Langston Hughes among others. Lindsay's optimistic message, his gospel of beauty, however, had become threadbare and motheaten by 1931. Ears had grown deaf to it. The poet had been promising pie in the sky for years. Banks failed. Fortunes were lost. Every day, it seemed, a former millionaire, unable to face bankruptcy and financial ruin, was jumping to his death from some office window ledge. The middle classes had it much worse. Thousands lost their jobs. People became hobos out of necessity, not by choice. America didn't seem to have much of a future at all. Lindsay, however, went on preaching the faith. Revising his famous chant "The Ghost of the Buffaloes," he added the clumsy and out-of-place appeal: "Would I might rouse the Lincoln in you all!"[17] By 1931, idealism, confidence and cheerfulness had gone the way of the American bison.

In addition to rejecting Lindsay's message of optimism as outworn and out of date and faulting him for increasing dogmatism, the critics charged that the poet had lost his ability to be self-critical and insisted that he could not tell the difference between his most accomplished poetry and his second-rate productions. Lindsay's increasing financial difficulties indeed drove him to turn out work too quickly. Nonetheless he felt overlooked and slighted. As the years went by, he displayed signs of increasing paranoia. One moment he would appear to be rational and in good spirits, but the next he'd be in a towering rage, full of distrust and suspicion. He charged that everyone was conspiring against him: his family, his publishers, his supposed friends. He groundlessly accused his wife of infidelities and complained that she had sapped his strength and broken his pride. He felt that his father-in-law and others were plotting to murder him, and, toward the end of his life, he grew increasingly discourteous and impudent with his handlers and business associates. His audiences did not see him offstage and thus were not exposed to his increasing nastiness and rudeness. They did not see him threatening violence against himself and others. Nor did they observe the weeping fits which followed his bellicosity.

Due to his failing health and nerves, Lindsay started to doubt his ability as a writer. He became convinced that his muse had grown hoarse and that he would never write the great poems he envisioned in his youth. He had long dreamed of writing larger works and had often projected such future poems with friends. He had been saving himself for them for years; but now, when at last he should be settling down to write "the great poems" which, since the very beginning of his career, he had had sincerely believed he would one day write, he found that he could not commence work on them. His own optimism began to waver. The times themselves were not conducive to such optimism, and Lindsay experienced something akin to a loss of faith. People still flocked to hear him read his old poems, however. He made good money reciting his work, but, unbeknownst to his audiences, the hours he spent in the limelight pained him more than anything else. His self-doubt only grew after such occasions.

Lindsay's auditors seemed most rapt when he recited the poems that had brought him his initial public acclaim, verse that he had written at the very beginning of his career. By 1931 the poet had been giving such recitals for close to two decades, yet in city after city and performance after performance, his audiences still continued to demand that he recite the same signature poems. Everywhere Vachel Lindsay traveled, the public behaved in exactly the same fashion. They preferred the "old chestnuts," as it were, to his newer verse and compelled him to fall back on a tried and tested repertoire of crowd pleasers.

It has been said that there are no second acts in the United States. The adage holds true for our politicians and sports figures and even for our rock-and-roll musicians, but sadly it has no greater bearing or validity than in the case of the American writer. So many of our authors stagnate in mid-career and seem unable to replicate or build upon their first successes. The very work that makes an artist's reputation often becomes the cross on which he is crucified, the albatross dangling from his neck. Forced to mouth the same old words night after night, Lindsay began to doubt the merits of his best labor. The words turned to ash as he endlessly intoned them. He did not, however, let on to his audience who did not discern his self-doubt. He delivered what they wanted and they applauded. But he began thinking of himself as a prostitute. The "broncho that would not be broken"[18] was domesticated at long last. Lindsay's recitations were so popular that recordings were made of him reading "The Congo," "General William Booth Enters Heaven," and "The Chinese Nightingale," among other of his more famous poems, so that the poet's resonant baritone would be "kept for posterity after his death."[19] Because his early verses had gained such notoriety and their popularity overshadowed all his subsequent efforts, Lindsay came to feel that his career was caught in a groove— that he was doomed to endlessly repeat himself. He could not lift the needle by the pick-up clip and move ahead, and in his despair, he came to feel that he was less of a poet and more of a stage entertainer or vaudevillian.

In order to win his audience, Lindsay had consciously incorporated lowbrow and comic elements into his verse, hoping, he said, to create a "Higher Vaudeville imagination." He believed that "America needed the flamboyant to have her soul"[20] and felt the poetry had become far too staid for its own good. He had come to this conclusion, he wrote in his introduction to *The Congo and Other Poems*, after a conversation with William Butler Yeats. In the course of their talk, Yeats, an early admirer of Lindsay, had expressed the opinion that modern poetry was in danger of becoming far too refined and rarefied and posed the following question to his American colleague, the answer to which, Lindsay immediately realized, could he but find it, would provide a new and important direction for his art. "What are we going to do to restore the primitive singing voice of poetry?"[21] Yeats had asked. Lindsay's answer was to compose verse which could be "two-thirds spoken and one-third sung."[22] With *The Congo*, he achieved his breakthrough. It proved difficult for Lindsay, however, to extend or enlarge his art.

Now Lindsay detested life on the road. He had enjoyed his troubadour days when he did not have a penny in his pocket, but once he started earning large sums by giving recitals he decided, and in short order, that he wanted to get out of the business of "entertaining" and to devote himself solely to his writing. To the young Lindsay, money was dung. It soiled and dirtied the person who held on to it. He often told a favorite anecdote concerning one of his tramps through the South, relating how the possession of twenty-five or fifty cents so disconcerted him that he was not happy until he had given it away.

His first three volumes, *General William Booth Enters into Heaven* (1913), *The Congo and Other Poems* (1914), and *The Chinese Nightingale* (1917), were so popular that Lindsay became an instant sensation. He was in demand everywhere. The novelty of his poems' syncopated meters became even more apparent when he declaimed his verse at the podium. Overnight he had bookings from coast to coast. In 1920, at the height of his popularity, Lindsay traveled to England. He was the first American poet to give a reading at Oxford University and he performed in many fashionable clubs in London where he again caused something of a stir. With his Middle Western accent, he seemed as exotic and strange as any of the American critters he listed in "Bryan, Bryan, Bryan, Bryan." London audiences did not know what to make of the "whangdoodle, prodactyl, and wampus."[23] They nonetheless came out in huge numbers to view this rare American bird. They were enthralled and baffled at the same time. "Probably," one exasperated critic wrote, "the Kansas farmer who gave Lindsay a square meal for his poems understood better what they were about than literary London."[24]

As early as 1922, however, Lindsay began expressing his resentment against touring: "how utterly impossible it has become for me to live a private life. . . . I am like a newspaper or the front-door rug for everybody to use."[25] He vowed repeatedly to quit the circuit. In 1922, he pledged to "say good-by to all such schemes by July 1, 1923."[26] In Spokane, in November 1924, he declared, "I am here for all time so far as I know, and haven't the least notion of lecturing or travelling."[27] The following year, he married Elizabeth Conner, a high-school teacher he had met in Spokane. His wife would give birth to two children, Susan Doniphan and Nicholas Case, during the first years of their marriage. Economic necessity spurred Lindsay back on the road just as it drove him to write too much too quickly.

For a time, he considered the possibility of terminating his recitations and supporting himself and his family as a professional illustrator. He said that he just wanted to go home to Springfield and draw. "I am sure I have pictures in me with as long fluid lines as the Congo, once I take a year or two to get the swing of it."[28] Despite making many such statements, he never left the circuit. He continued touring to the very end, crisscrossing the United States by rail, thrilling his audiences by chanting (to his mind) old and worn-out poems, especially that "infectious blend of rhyme, religion and rag-time"[29] which begins:

> Fat black bucks in a wine-barrel room,
> Barrel-house kings, with feet unstable,
> Sagged and reeled and pounded on the table,
> Pounded on the table,
> Beat an empty barrel with the handle of a broom,
> Hard as they were able,
> Boom, boom, Boom,
> With a silk umbrella and the handle of a broom,
> Boomlay, boomlay, boomlay, Boom.
> Then I had religion, Then I had a vision.
> I could not turn from their revel in derision.
> THEN I SAW THE CONGO CREEPING THROUGH THE BLACK,
> CUTTING THROUGH THE FOREST WITH A GOLDEN TRACK.[30]

Although Lindsay offered both "The Congo" and "General Booth" on his circular, he considered performing them a shameful stunt. On March 14, 1931, he finally had enough and refused to read "The Congo" at a preparatory school for boys in Ashville, North Carolina. Afterward his agent reminded him that as he advertised the poem in his handbill, the school might refuse to remit him his fee. In order to receive his check, Lindsay was forced to apologize to the angry headmaster. Afterward he begged his agent to alter his contracts: "I simply can't bear it. . . . Put it in all my contracts that I refuse hereafter to recite 'Booth,' 'The Congo' and any other poems I do not choose to recite."[31] He wrote to Elizabeth: "I will *not* be a *slave* to my yesterdays. I will *not*. I was born a *creator* not a parrot. . . ."[32]

Years before Lindsay realized that he would pay a heavy price for his touring success. It took up too much of his time and kept him from writing. He knew what he had to do if he wanted to develop as a writer, but fate and family prevented him from adopting the only measure that would save him:

> I see that for the most part my contact with the world *must be by deputy*. . . . I *must* learn to live on a penny a day. *It is only on a penny a day that I can write*. I have hardly written a line for six years. I must learn to live on nothing and hide. It is the only way out for me. . . .[33]

Nicholas Vachel Lindsay was born in Springfield on November 10, 1879, the son of Vachel Thomas and Catharine Frazee Lindsay. He was the second of six children and the couple's only son. Three of his sisters would die in infancy. Vachel Thomas Lindsay was a prominent physician who hailed from Kentucky. A Southern Democrat, he despised and detested Abraham Lincoln and attempted to indoctrinate his son with the Southern point of view: "My father had filled me with the notion that, way down in Kentucky, once upon a time a certain Abraham Lincoln came with many soldiers. According to this tale, they stole all the horses from my Grandfather Lindsay's estate, drove off the negroes forever (my grandfather's personal property and mine), burned the crops, and then in a way not mentioned, stole the farm, and left us all to begin again by studying medicine. . . ."[34] While Lindsay's mother held "many Southern ideas," she was "all for Lincoln" and countered Dr. Lindsay's "general view of history."[35] Both parents belonged to the Campbellite sect, and they raised their children in the evangelical tradition. The theatricalism of the church services and revivals he attended as a youth profoundly affected Lindsay. Although he never formally forsook the faith, he became dubious of many of its tenets while still retaining his relish for the sect's flagrant exhibitionism. Religion would increasingly become a rag-and-bones show for Lindsay, and in his recitations, he would show (at least at first) the same proneness to self-complacent display as many a Pentecostal Christian on Sunday. His sister Olive, however, absorbed the message like a sponge. In later life, she would spend many years as a missionary in China.

As a boy, Vachel stood in awe of his father but, as the poem "Doctor Mohawk" indicates, was also frightened and intimidated by him. The boy's birth announcement predicted that one day he would inherit his father's practice and that evidently was Dr. Lindsay's intention. When Vachel was old enough, he was repeatedly warned by his father about the dangers of alcohol, tobacco and venereal diseases. The last of these admonitions was so thoroughly drilled into the young Lindsay's head that he developed phobias concerning women that took him a long time to overcome. Perhaps he never overcame them fully. Toward the end of his life, he began to adopt an increasingly misogynistic attitude toward his wife. His power, he alleged, was taken from him with his virginity and he accused his wife of tyrannizing his life. Lindsay's fear of his father increased immeasurably when he and another boy, playing with matches, accidentally set fire to several outbuildings and storehouses belonging to a local farmer. Lindsay was flogged unmercifully for his misdeed.

Lindsay's father was dark-skinned, his mother fair. As a child, Lindsay became convinced though he had no real evidence to lend credence to his supposition, that Indian blood flowed in his father's veins and thus in him. At the age of forty-three, he attempted to convey "the exact atmosphere" if not the facts of his childhood in the poem "Doctor Mohawk":

> I cried, and held hard to my mother's warm hand.
> And the Mohawk said:—"Red man, your first trial begins."
> And the Mohawk roared:—"Shame to you, coward and
>   mourner!" . . .
>
> I wept with my mother. I kissed and caressed her.
> Then she taught me to sing. Then she taught me to play:—
> The sibyl, the strange one, the white witch of May.[36]

Lindsay wrote elsewhere that his mother "destined me, from the beginning, to be an artist. . . . I am practically the person she made of me when I was eight."[37] Mark Harris details her tremendous influence on her son in his introduction to *Selected Poems of Vachel Lindsay*: "She transmitted to him both religious zeal and civic sense, eventually to become so well assimilated within him that the creation of his poetry would become his votive act, its sheer physical distribution a crusade not less arduous than the sacrifices of his missionary sister, and his final commitment to its necessity the agent of his mortal exhaustion."[38] In his junior year in college, Lindsay complained in a letter to his mother that in her dealings with him she always spoke and acted as if he were "a premature brilliant inspired baby." She responded: "I never want the time to come when I cannot associate you in my mind with the baby I carried on a pillow and watched as his life flickered for months."[39] As an infant, Lindsay became gravely ill due to milk poisoning. Within six months of his birth, Mrs. Lindsay had once again become pregnant. Before recognizing her condition, she continued to breast feed her son. He was sick for over a year.

Lindsay graduated from Springfield High School in 1897. That year, he entered Hiram College, Ohio, to study medicine. He would drop out after three years to enroll in the Art Institute of Chicago. His mother supported his change of vocation and hoped that her son would eventually become a Christian cartoonist. His father also acquiesced to the career switch, albeit more grudgingly. As a student, Lindsay was dependent on his father's financial support. He earned additional money by working as a menial at a variety of low-paying jobs. In 1904, he continued his studies at the New York School of Art, where he studied under William Merritt Chase and Robert Henri. The following year he began handing out copies of his poems on New York street corners. From 1905 to 1908, Lindsay spent his winters lecturing for the West Side YMCA in New York City and his summers lecturing for the YMCA in Springfield. In 1909 and 1910, he toured central Illinois on behalf of the Anti-Saloon League. He set out on his walking tour of the South in 1912, giving away his poems and passing out a pamphlet entitled "Rhymes To Be Traded for Bread." In 1914, he courted the poet Sara Teasdale. In temperament the two were very unsuited to each other. After falling in love with the poet John Hall Wheelock but failing to persuade him to commit himself, Teasdale decided that marriage was still imperative to her. She was willing to forego romantic love in order to find a husband who could support her, since she could not face the prospect of spending the rest of her life with her aging parents in Saint Louis. She loved the cultural milieu of New York City and desperately wanted to leave the Midwest which she found provincial and gauche in comparison with the East Coast. In 1914, Lindsay could hardly support himself much less a wife. As we have seen, he had a strong affinity for the Middle West and hoped to plant the seeds of his communal or national art in the heart of the heart of the country. Moreover, in looking for a wife, he wanted a spiritual helpmeet, someone to share his vision. He confessed that conventional domesticity did not interest him. No woman would pull him from his path or detour him from his purpose. Nonetheless he was attracted to Teasdale for her discipline, wit, and intelligence. Although Teasdale would ultimately reject Lindsay for another suitor, the two would remain lifelong friends.

Lindsay would describe his early troubadour years in two prose volumes, *Adventures While Preaching the Gospel of Beauty* (1914) and *A Handy Guide For Beggars* (1916). In 1915, he wrote one of the first (and best) appreciations of the silent cinema, *The Art of the Moving Picture*. About the same time he developed an interest in Egyptian hieroglyphics, seeing such picture writing as an ancient analog to the modern movie. He spent a great deal of his spare time devising "personal hieroglyphics"[40] for himself and his family. In 1920, he published the visionary novel *The Golden Book of Springfield*, in which he sets forth in his most concrete and tangible terms his millennial vision for America. His final prose work, *The Litany of Washington Street*, which he described as "a kind of Washington's birthday, Lincoln's birthday, Whitman's birthday, Jefferson's birthday book,"[41] appeared in 1929. It takes the form of a series of Fourth of July orations delivered on a mythical Main Street which extends all the way from Connecticut to Calcutta. In the decades following his death, Lindsay's prose work has attracted increasing critical attention. Many commentators now feel that it is superior to the later verse.

Vachel Lindsay spent most of the two days following his reading at the First Christian Church in bed. He left the house early on the morning of December 3 and encountered his father-in-law, the Reverend Franklin Conner, on the corner of Fifth and Jackson Streets. Lindsay raved and cursed and swung his cane in the air. He screamed that Conner was planning to kill him. Believing his son-in-law insane and potentially dangerous, Reverend Conner hastened to the office of Lindsay's physician, Dr. McMeen, to report Lindsay's bizarre behavior. The poet returned home and hysterically embraced his wife, kissing her repeatedly. Crying, he told her to always remember that he loved her no matter what might happen. Later in the day, Lindsay began arranging photographs of his wife and children—pictures he always carried with him when he left home on tours—on the library desk and table. The following morning, he seemed deeply depressed. His wife put him to bed for an afternoon nap. Later she woke him, so he could accompany her to the Abraham Lincoln Hotel, where a small tea was being given in behalf of two female friends. He seemed in a good humor after his nap and joked good-naturedly with his wife on the way to the hotel. Elizabeth left the tea early, excusing her premature departure on the grounds that she had a business appointment. In truth, she went to the office of Dr. McMeen, where her father secretly awaited her. McMeen acknowledged the situation was serious but believed that Lindsay posed no threat to himself or others as long as he could release his anger by raving and shouting. When she arrived home, Elizabeth discovered that her husband had returned before her. Once more he had retired to bed. He wore his pajamas and dressing gown to supper. He wept throughout the meal and entreated his wife not to steal his childhood memories now that he was an old man. He left the table and reclined on a sofa in the hall, continuing to cry all the while. Eventually she coaxed him upstairs. He asked to be left alone and complained that she treated him like a child. Dismissed from his presence, she went back downstairs and rested on a couch in the library. After a short interval, an angry and an emotionally overwrought Lindsay entered the room. He sat down beside the fireplace and once again rattled off his litany of charges and accusations. He claimed that he had been persecuted ever since his childhood when his schoolfellows refused to play with him. He told her that she and the children had destroyed him as a poet and that he would certainly foil her father's plot to kill him. He railed at her one moment, but the next was crying out that she was the best and kindest human being he had ever known. He had tried so hard to please her but had failed miserably. Still he loved her more than she would ever know. At last, he said that he must leave her and the children forever. He needed complete freedom and no familial responsibilities, for only then could he redeem himself as a poet. He would embark on another begging tour across the country. His wife attempted to reason with him. She vowed that she would never stand in his way and would always be ready to come to him should he need her. Who, however, would take care of him on the road? Lindsay replied, "the One who watches over the sparrows."[42] Once more he told her that, when he left town, she would never see him again. "Never, Vachel?" she asked. He looked at her and answered very solemnly: "I'll see you again in *The Golden Book of Springfield*, not before."[43] In all, Lindsay raved three hours. At last, his rage and strength spent, he walked out of the library and mounted the stairs to the bedroom. His wife remained in the library for a time. She suffered from a stabbing headache and feared that her husband had lost all touch with reality. Finally, she, too, went up to the bedroom. Lindsay was reading. From his expression, she knew that she dare not kiss or touch him. She climbed into bed and said goodnight. He got up and proceeded downstairs. After a time, she followed him. She found Lindsay in the dining room. Once more he was setting up his photographs of her and the children, this time on the dining room table. He seemed, she later recalled, "calm, happy, peaceful, and firm."[44] She asked if he was all right. He applied in the affirmative and said that he would be up in a little while. Elizabeth again went upstairs and lay down. Within minutes she was asleep.

After she retired from the dining room, Lindsay continued to arrange the photographs of her and the children on the table. He ordered them in a circle around the table centerpiece. He set two lighted candles before them. On the floor was a pillow and a blanket from the library as well as a photograph of Elizabeth at seventeen propped against a little blue coat belonging to the Lindsays' infant daughter Susan. After setting up this display, Lindsay walked to the bathroom and drained a bottle of Lysol. He poured the poison into a tea-glass and drank from it. Both bottle and glass were later recovered in the bathroom. Apparently, it was Lindsay's intention to lie down on the dining room floor and die amid the artifacts of his life which he had lovingly laid out in that room. The pain from the burn proved too much. Elizabeth Lindsay was awakened by a crash downstairs. She heard heavy footsteps along the lower hall and then the great din of Lindsay scrambling up the stairs on his hand and knees. She rushed from her bedroom, thinking that Lindsay was headed for the nursery. She feared that her husband was so completely out of his mind that he might murder the children in their sleep. She screamed for Irene, the negro maid. When she saw Lindsay running through the upstairs hall, his hands high in the air, his face pale and scared, she knew that it was not the children but he who was in danger. The poet collapsed to the floor. Somehow she got him up and into bed. He asked for water and told his wife that he had attempted to poison himself by drinking Lysol. She brought him the water. He drained the glass, threw it to the floor and, shaking his fist in the air, shouted, "I got them before they could get me—they can just try to explain this, if they can."[45] Elizabeth rushed from the room to telephone Dr. McMeen. By the time she returned to the bedroom, Lindsay was only half conscious. She and the maid administered several emetics but to no avail. By the time, McMeen arrived, Lindsay had ceased breathing and his face had turned blue. The doctor detected a faint pulse, but Lindsay died a few minutes later at 1:00 A.M., December 5, 1931.

Notes

1. *New York Times* Obituary, 6 December 1931.

2. Quoted by Richard Ellmann and Robert O'Clair, eds., *The Norton Anthology of Modern Poetry* (New York: W.W. Norton, 1973), p. 260.

3. Vachel Lindsay, "Bryan, Bryan, Bryan, Bryan," *Collected Poems* (New York: Macmillan, 1941), pp. 97–98. The poem excerpted here previously appeared in *The Golden Whales of California* (New York: Macmillan, 1920).

4. Lindsay, "The Lame Boy and the Fairy," *Collected Poems*, p. 138. The poem excerpted here previously appeared in *The Golden Whales of California*.

5. Eleanor Ruggles, *The West-going Heart: A Life of Vachel Lindsay* (New York: W. W. Norton, 1959), p. 427.

6. Ibid., p. 97.

7. Quoted by Ellmann and O'Clair, *The Norton Anthology*, p. 256.

8. Lindsay, "General William Booth Enters into Heaven," *Collected Poems*, p. 123. The poem excerpted here was copyrighted in 1913.

9. Lindsay, "Bryan," p. 103.

10. Quoted in *The Avenel Companion to English and American Literature, United States of America*, ed. David Daiches, Malcolm Bradbury, and Eric Mottram (New York: Avenel Books, 1981), p. 151.

11. Mark Harris, "Introduction," *Selected Poems of Vachel Lindsay* (New York: Collier Books, 1963), p. xii.

12. Lindsay, "Bryan," p. 102.

13. Quoted by Harris, "Introduction," *Selected Poems of Vachel Lindsay*, p. xix.

14. Ibid.

15. Ibid.

16. Ibid.

17. Quoted by Louis Untermeyer, ed., *Modern American Poetry* (New York: Harcourt Brace, 1950), p. 236.

18. Lindsay, "The Broncho That Would Not be Broken," *Collected Poems*, p. 77. This poem previously appeared in *The Chinese Nightingale and Other Poems* (New York: Macmillan, 1917).

19. *New York Times* obituary.

20. Quoted by Ellmann and O'Clair, *The Norton Anthology*, p. 256.

21. Ibid.

22. Ibid. Endnotes, 20, 21, and 22 refer to Vachel Lindsay's "Introduction" to *The Congo* (New York: Macmillan, 1916).

23. Lindsay, "Bryan," p. 98.

24. *New York Times* obituary.

25. Harris, "Introduction," *Selected Poems of Vachel Lindsay*, p. xx.

26. Ibid.

27. Ibid.

28. Ibid.

29. Untermeyer, *Modern American Poetry*, p. 235.

30. Lindsay, "The Congo," *Collected Poems*, pp. 178–79. This poem was first copyrighted in 1914.

31. Quoted by Ruggles, *The West-going Heart*, p. 411.

32. Ibid., p. 412.

33. Quoted by Harris, "Introduction," *Selected Poems of Vachel Lindsay*, p. xx.

34. Ibid., p. xi.

35. Ibid.

36. Lindsay, "Doctor Mohawk" *Collected Poems*, p. 439. The poem excerpted here previously appeared in the first edition of *Collected Poems* (New York: Macmillan, 1925).

37. Quoted by Harris, "Introduction," *Selected Poems of Vachel Lindsay*, p. x.

38. Quoted by Ruggles, *The West-going Heart*, p. 26.

39. Ibid.

40. Untermeyer, *Modern American Poetry*, p. 237.

41. Ibid., p. 236.

42. Quoted by Ruggles, *The West-going Heart*, p. 430.

43. Ibid.

44. Ibid, p. 431.

45. Ibid, p. 432.

Hart Crane

BOTH HART CRANE AND VIRGINIA WOOLF HAD PIVOTAL EXPERIENCES in dental chairs. Each had an anesthetic vision of a transcendental nature. Woolf, as we shall see, thought she had been vouchsafed an intimation of the moment of death. Crane believed that, for a brief shining instant, he had attained a heightened state of being. Simultaneously he existed in and out of time. He understood the nature of genius and saw that he possessed it, if only for the duration of his dream—-the short interval he was under.

Crane's experience would influence all his subsequent poetry, which would become increasingly visionary and ecstatic. Mere representation of external reality would no longer be enough, for he would now have to approximate the mind expansion and mystic revelation he experienced in certain moments of pure rapture—most sensationally and thrillingly when gas was administered to him in the dentist's office. In his essay "General Aims and Theories," Crane defines his new poetic which he calls Absolutism and differentiates between the impressionistic and the absolutist poet. The former "is interesting as far as he goes—but his goal has been reached when he has succeeded in projecting certain factual details into the reader's consciousness. He is really not interested in the *causes* (metaphysical) of his materials, their emotional derivations or their utmost spiritual consequences. A kind of retinal registration is enough. . . ."[1]

According to Crane, William Blake understood this trap when he faulted art, in which "We are led to believe in a lie/ When we see *with* not *through* the eye."[2] In addition to the unworldly and antirational English poet, painter, and engraver, Crane lists Donne, Baudelaire, and Rimbaud as his absolutist predecessors. Perhaps Rimbaud provides the closest parallel. *The Drunken Boat* (*Bateau ivre*) seems like a prototype for Crane's later interior journeys. Each man's verse can be characterized as a flight or exodus from the real. Both poets were verbal virtuosos, audacious in their use of metaphor and in their employment of multifaceted and elliptical symbols. Each utilized words for their suggestive tone color and musical value, and each purposely distorted syntax to create a dreamy mood—a drunken and delirious ambience—in which a higher reality is suddenly, piercingly, if only intuitively and briefly, apprehended.

At the outset of one of Crane's poems, the reader usually finds himself on firm enough ground. (The first section of "Voyages," for example, is a rather straightforward account of children playing at the seashore.) Sense impressions and visual details are recorded. Indeed they "plunge by"[3] with dizzying speed. At some point, however, delineation and representation end. The poet-voyager is catapulted into a higher realm, and the reader is carried along with him. From the real flashes forth the ideal, but the voyager is most often permitted only a tantalizing glimpse of heaven. For an instant, he steps out of time and experiences a momentary feeling of unity and connection with all things. The vision abruptly fades and the voyager once more finds himself back where he was, isolated and cut off, trapped in his own skin.

Crane wrote that an absolute poet attempts to "go *through* the combined materials of the poem, using our 'real' world somewhat as a spring-board, and to give the poem *as a whole* an orbit or predetermined direction of its own."[4] He takes a stab at a higher truth (true seeing as opposed to mere retinal registration). According to Crane, the aim of absolute poetry is the replication of this higher truth: "Its evocation will not be toward decoration or amusement, but rather toward a state of consciousness, an 'innocence' (Blake) or absolute beauty. In this condition there may be discoverable under new forms certain spiritual illuminations, shining with a morality essentialized from experience directly, and not from previous precepts or preconceptions."[5]

Crane demanded that poetry communicate more than it had hitherto, and "In General Aims and Theories," he detailed the technique whereby the poet could push communication to its absolute limit. The "entire consciousness" of the absolutist poem, Crane wrote, would be "raised on the organic principle of 'a logic of metaphor,' which antedates our so-called pure logic, and which is the genetic basis of all speech, hence consciousness and thought extension."[6] Such a poem would be boldly suggestive and yet somewhat nebulous at the same time, for, paradoxically, the moment of vision, of supreme illumination, is never really absolute, utter, or conclusive. Revelation is always only partial. That which is glimpsed is somewhat fuzzy, always slightly out of focus. While consciousness expands on such occasions, it is only ever in hints and intimations that the eternal reveals itself. At any rate, such was Crane's experience, and he wanted to replicate his perceptions—the rapturous winkings and twinklings of eternity—in his verse. As his first biographer, Philip Horton, succinctly put it, Crane intended his poems "not as descriptions of experience that could be *read about*, but as immediate experiences that the reader could *have*. . . ."[7]

How successful the poet was in realizing his absolutist goals was a matter of intense debate both in his lifetime and in the years following his death. He would have both forceful partisans and vigorous detractors. Eugene O'Neill, Dylan Thomas, and Louis Simpson all found themselves rapt and entranced by Crane's work. O'Neill, who spent two years in the Merchant Marines, thought Crane's sea poems particularly spellbinding. All three would express their genuine if qualified esteem and appreciation of his poetry. Of all Crane's numerous partisans, however, Robert Lowell would prove the most staunch and the most lavish. In the early encomium, "Words for Hart Crane," he called Crane "*Catullus redivivus*" and "the Shelley of my age."[8] His opinion did not alter with the passage of time. In a *Paris Review* interview years later, he unhesitatingly pronounced Crane the finest poet of his generation and spoke of the "tremendous power" and "fulness of experience"[9] of his poems.

Crane's detractors would include R. P. Blackmur and Yvor Winters, as well as Crane's close friend and frequent correspondent, Allen Tate. All three would acknowledge Crane's ability and talent, yet, in the end, Blackmur would dismiss him as a self-indulgent obscurantist and verbal showoff who practiced virtuosity for virtuosity's sake, a dazzling wordsmith but an incoherent thinker; Winters (and to a lesser extent Tate), as a possessed and hysterical irrationalist, a mystic crackpot who foreswore sanity and sense in his pursuit of illusory states of being, a Faustian pleasure-seeker drunk on wine and words and bent on crossing all borders and barriers in search of new and sweeter sensations. There is a certain moral smugness, a puritanical self-righteousness, to Winter's essay on Crane. Nonetheless he shows great psychological penetration in his dissection of the poet's character. Winters alleges that, in the tradition of Emerson and Whitman, Crane saw reason as "the source of all evil" and "the adversary of impulse."[10] For him "the automatic man, the unreflective creature of impulse,"[11] was the ideal, not the rationalist who believed intellect and logic superior to and independent of sense perception. Winters condemns such a stance as morally lax and argues that it leads to the negation of all values or ethical anarchy, yet he acknowledges Crane's ardency and commitment in his pursuit of mystic sensation and calls him "a saint of the wrong religion."[12] Indeed, Crane was willing to risk everything, to "spend" himself out again and again, to "cleave and burn" and "bleed" until "drop by caustic drop" "the bright logic"[13] was won, the higher reality captured, the visionary experience put into words—proclaimed and promulgated in verse. Tate is not nearly so sanctimonious as Winters, yet he also wags an admonitory and cautionary finger, and, while he is more kindly disposed to Crane's mature work, he nonetheless feels that Crane's early verse is superior to the later poems. Of all Crane's verse, he considers the early lyric "Praise for an Urn" his best. As we shall shortly see, it is one of Crane's most pessimistic poems which seems to refute the very ideas of resurrection and mystic transformation that would inform much of his subsequent verse. Referring to "Praise for an Urn," Tate wrote in his memoir, "Although his later development gave us a poetry that his period would be much the less rich for not having, he never again had such perfect mastery of his subject. And I think this was because he never afterwards knew precisely what his subject was. . . . Crane was the archetype of the modern American poet whose fundamental mistake lay in thinking that an irrational surrender of the intellect to the will would be a basis of a new mentality."[14]

In a letter to his friend Gorham Munson, Hart Crane attempted to describe what happened to him in the dentist's office: ". . . under the influence of aether and *amnesia* my mind spiraled to a kind of seventh heaven of consciousness and egotistic dance among the seven spheres—and something like an objective voice kept saying to me—'You have the higher consciousness—you have the higher consciousness. This is something very few have. This is what is called genius.' . . . A happiness, ecstatic such as I have known only twice in 'inspirations' came over me. I felt the two worlds. And at once . . . O Gorham, I have known moments in eternity."[15] The poems Crane wrote after his seminal trip to the dentist concern the divulgence and disclosure of this higher consciousness. As Herbert A. Leibowitz writes, they "record, after the fact, an ascent from dejection to a moment of acute vision or pleasure and its aftermath, a descent into the dark sight or shortsightedness of daily life."[16] The 1925 poem "Passage," of which Crane wrote to Waldo Frank several months after he completed it, "To me it is still the most interesting and conjectural thing I have done,"[17] is perhaps the most striking of Crane's early efforts to transcribe a transcendent moment, the sudden feeling of mystic unity and connection and its equally hasty disappearance. Such an ascent and fall are logged in the poem's first four stanzas:

> Where the cedar leaf divides the sky
> I heard the sea.
> In sapphire arenas of the hills
> I was promised an improved infancy.
>
> Sulking, sanctioning the sun,
> My memory I left in a ravine,—
> Casual louse that tissues the buckwheat,
> Aprons rocks, congregates pears
> In moonlit bushels
> And wakens alleys with a hidden cough.
>
> Dangerous the summer burned
> (I had joined the entrainments of the wind).
> The shadows of boulders lengthened my back:
> In the bronze gongs of my cheeks
> The rain dried without odour.

"It is not long:
See where the red and black
Vine-stanchioned valleys—": but the wind
Died speaking through the ages that you know
And hug, chimney-sooted heart of man!
So was I turned about and back, much as your smoke
Compiles a too well-known biography.[18]

As he hears the rush of the sea and looks out at the "sapphire arena of the hills,"[19] the poet experiences a sense of renewal. He feels the assurance of rebirth as well as a oneness with the world about him. His awareness grows and his sense of being alive increases dramatically. In his surrender to sensation, he leaves Memory (presumably also intellect and reason) behind him, deriding it as a "casual louse"—a parasite that sucks the blood out of a visionary experience—as he "joins the entrainments of the wind"[20] and is carried into the Beyond, the realm of the Ideal, but just as eternity (the red and black vine-stanchioned valley) comes into view, the wind—a recurring symbol of creative strength and power in Crane's poetry—dies down. The vision fades as has happened so many times before. Time (the ages that you know and hug) reasserts itself. Experience again becomes linear and fractionary. Perhaps the poet himself (or a part of him, Hart Crane's own heart of darkness) does not have the courage to let go, but clings to the world of duration. Possibly he is not clean or pure enough to cross over into the promised land and, like Moses, is only able to glimpse it from afar, or, perhaps, because his heart is chimney-sooted, he is a creature of smoke, who must fall from Heaven into the fiery pit. At any rate, the vision fails and the poet finds himself in the same ravine where he previously deposited Memory. Beneath an opening laurel bough—Crane was at long last beginning to receive recognition for his poetry—the poet comes across a thief (i.e., Memory) who has stolen his experiences (in the form of his poems, his volume of verse). The two contend for the laurel and Memory shuts the book. L. S. Dembo interprets this as a reconciliatory gesture and argues that Crane accepts memory as a necessary part of the visionary experience. Upon this acceptance, new and more powerful visions ensue. The poet apprehends both past and future (the sand of the Ptolemies, the unpaced beaches on which the serpent's tongue drums) and hears fountains and icy speeches betokening a new world. The promise of "an improved infancy"[21] has been realized. Memory is so taxed and strained that it breaks after the impossible has been achieved and the poet's vision has been committed to the page. Other critics, however, argue that the poet does not embrace Memory but renounces her a second time and much more forcefully. As the two combatants contend for the laurel wreath, Memory momentarily has the upper hand. Like the Sphinx, the poet is covered over and immobilized by the sands of the past. Once more he is caught in time. As the poem concludes, however, he breaks his bonds and banishes his foe. Freed from mind, intellect, and time, and reveling in pure sensation, he once again regains paradise:

The evening was a spear in the ravine
That throve through very oak. And had I walked
The dozen particular decimals of time?
Touching an open laurel, I found
A thief beneath, my stolen book in hand.

"Why are you back here—smiling an iron coffin?"
"To argue with the laurel," I replied:
"Am justified in transience, fleeing
Under the constant wonder of your eyes—."

He closed the book. And from the Ptolemies
Sand troughed us in a glittering abyss.
A serpent swam a vertex to the sun
—On unpaced beaches leaned its tongue and drummed.
What fountains did I hear? what icy speeches?
Memory, committed to the page, had broke.[22]

After their experiences in dental chairs, both Virginia Woolf and Hart Crane wanted to return to the magical kingdom to which they had gained entry. Woolf made periodic suicide attempts. At first, Crane did not seek death but admission or passage to a terrestrial paradise. He knew of certain "bridges" by means of which he could cross over into his earthly Elysian Fields. He found his way back to Shangri-la, but his visits there were always of brief duration. Once regained, Paradise would inevitably be lost again. The sense of isolation and exclusion would return: "And fold your exile on your back again; Petrushka's valentine pivots on its pin."[23] With time, these links and spans—never very trustworthy to begin with—which on occasion nonetheless gave Crane access to seventh heaven and enabled him to dance among the seven spheres, became less and less reliable; the kingdom, the special state of consciousness, would prove increasingly elusive. Nonetheless, Crane continued his attempts to regain his realm and dominion. After his experience in the dental chair, the idea of resurrection did not seem as far-fetched as it had after the 1921 death of his friend Ernest Nelson, whose passing he commemorated in the early poem Tate so prized, "Praise for an Urn." After his experience, Crane's faith in the power of the poetic word, something Nelson had bequeathed him but which he had come to doubt, was renewed. Once more he believed that language had the ability to transfigure life and give form and spiritual meaning to the world. Once more he hailed the incarnate word in which consciousness, and thus the world itself, reside: the true habitation of each. Ernest had been right after all. Poetry's trumpet could call the vanished one from the ground!

A Norwegian who emigrated to America in his youth, Ernest Nelson attended art school in Washington. He was a promising student, and as a young man had done some fine paintings. He also wrote several striking and highly original poems which were published in *Scribner's* and *Century* magazines. Nonetheless, the aunt who paid his tuition withdrew her patronage after he finished school and forced Nelson "into the prostitution of all his ideals and a cheap lithographic work that he was never able to pull out of afterward. . . . He was one of many broken against the stupidity of American life. . . ."[24] Crane met him in Cleveland a number of years later.

Crane felt America's heartland was an arid wasteland. Nelson was one of the few cultured persons he encountered there as a young man. He was extraordinarily well read and a fierce devotee of Friedrich Nietzsche. Crane rapidly formed a friendship with him, and the two engaged in long conversations about modernist art and philosophy. Crane would later write that Nelson had a lasting influence on him. Crane served as a pallbearer at Nelson's funeral in December 1921. He helped carry the casket to its destination, the crematorium, and wrote that the funeral was one of "the few beautiful things"[25] that happened to him in Cleveland. The poem that he would later write, however, ends in a cheerless and ironic way. In this particular verse, Crane seems to say that death is final and inexorable. He admits the failure of his own elegy: he cannot capture the essence of his friend in verse and thus restore him to life.

In the first stanza of "Praise for an Urn," Crane describes Nelson's physiognomy: "It was a kind and northern face/ That mingled in such exile guise/ The everlasting eyes of Pierrot /And, of Gargantua, the laughter."[26] The key word in the stanza is "exile." The Gallic eyes of Pierrot seem oddly out of place on a Nordic face. It also seems paradoxical that a northerner, ascetic and austere by type, would share Gargantua's ravenous appetites and huge vitality, his love of art, liberty and libidinous gratification. These are warm and sunny Southern qualities. Hyperborean individuals seldom exhibit such largesse and license. Nelson himself, of course, was a double exile. An expatriate who had come to the United States from Norway, he also was a fugitive and outcast from the realm of art, banished to his Cleveland lithography establishment. Instead of painting great works, he produced printed impressions of cheap and tawdry designs. Nonetheless, during his life, Nelson had intimations of immortality. Certain works of art seemed eternal and deathless. Personal immortality could perhaps be achieved if one were able to create such an undying masterpiece. Nelson impressed his thoughts and ideas on the receptive Crane, who was deeply affected by them. Crane came to share his mentor's presentiments concerning an afterlife. Nelson bequeathed his ideas on art to Crane. In the second stanza of his elegy, Crane comes to the conclusion that such "inheritances" are extremely precarious. The clock in the crematory lobby seems to rebut Nelson's ideas on immortality. Nelson's ashes will be scattered and lost and so will the lines ("these well-meant idioms") of Crane's poem. Crane's words do not have the ability to bestow immortality for he is not Christ. Neither author nor subject shall survive death. Poem and corpse will both be reduced to ash:

His thoughts, delivered to me
From the white coverlet and pillow,
I see now, were inheritances—
Delicate riders of the storm.

The slant moon on the slanting hill
Once moved us toward presentiments
Of what the dead keep, living still,
And such assessments of the soul

As, perched in the crematory lobby,
The insistent clock commented on,
Touching as well upon our praise
Of glories proper to the time.

Still, having in mind gold hair,
I cannot see that broken brow
And miss the dry sound of bees
Stretching across a lucid space.

Scatter these well-meant idioms
Into the smoky spring that fills
The suburbs, where they will be lost.
They are no trophies of the sun.[27]

In another early poem, "My Grandmother's Love Letters," Crane recalls his grandmother Elizabeth. She lives in his memory still, but her image has become blurred with the passage of time. In the poem he attempts to find his way back to her, tries to undertake a voyage across the span of years. He must traverse a great distance to reach her and searches for a bridge or conduit (in this instance music) that will carry him over the gulf of lost time. In "My Grandmother's Love Letters," he sounds the great theme of *The Bridge*—the quest for a mystic link or nexus between past and present—in a poignant, personal yet at the same time subdued and quiet, fashion. He knows that the memories he is searching for are evasive. They are on the verge of vanishing forever. Like snow they are liable to melt and disappear: "Over the greatness of such space/ Steps must be gentle/ It is all hung by an invisible white hair./ It trembles as birch limbs webbing the air."[28] He questions whether he can retrieve her from the dark and asks himself: "Are your fingers long enough to play/ Old keys that are but echoes:/Is the silence strong enough/ To carry back the music to its source/ And back to you again? as though to her?"[29] Like "Praise for an Urn," "My Grandmother's Love Letters" ends on a note of futility. Crane continues his attempt to recapture the past. He "stumbles" on, as rain falls on the roof with "a sound of gently pitying laughter."[30]

After momentarily escaping the fetters of time in the dentist's office, renewed and exhilarated and once more sure of himself, Crane again embarked on his poetic quest to transcend space and duration and capture "moments in eternity" in verse.

In "Chaplinesque," an empty ash can in a moonlit alley becomes the holy grail. The garbage container recalls the burial urn of Ernest Nelson. Mystical transformation once more seems possible. To quote Richard Ellmann and Robert O'Clair, "hope and light radiate out of squalor."[31] Most of Crane's subsequent poems express the author's conviction that "spiritual events and possibilities" still existed in the modern world, that they were "as real and powerful now as, say in the time of Blake. . . ."[32] While these works are dominated by his hopefulness, Crane's earlier apprehension and skepticism periodically resurface.

This vacillation is especially apparent in *Key West: An Island Sheaf*, a collection of twenty-two poems Crane was preparing for publication at the time of his death. The volume would never be issued on its own but would appear as part of the *Complete Poems*. Crane had written most of the verse which would ultimately comprise *Key West* during a sojourn to his maternal grandmother's plantation on the Isle of Pines, Cuba, in 1926, one of many times in his career when he felt that his poetic powers had deserted him. Prior to his departure from the island, the poet would witness the near-destruction of the plantation during a hurricane. The storm would revivify and resuscitate him but only for a short while. Several verses in the collection do not date from 1926 but from Crane's last years, a fallow and barren stretch following the 1930 publication of *The Bridge* when the poet felt the most defeated and the most demoralized. He reached his nadir in Mexico, a country which proved equally malevolent and inhospitable to another dipso-scribbler, Malcolm Lowry, but five years later.

Crane wrote a number of other poems after leaving the Isle of Pines, but he was even more dissatisfied with them than those he picked out and settled on for inclusion in *Key West*. As we will see, he was not altogether satisfied or happy with the twenty-two poems comprising his "island sheaf"; nevertheless, he saw these verses as the best work, aside from *The Bridge*, that he had managed to produce during the last six years of his life. Other poems written during this time period appear under the heading of "Uncollected Poems" in *The Complete Poems of Hart Crane*.

The personal and anguished verses Crane wrote during his island retreat in 1926 are, for the most part, firmly grounded in reality. The tropical fecundity of the Isle of Pines, its vast waste and intense beauty, is depicted with all Crane's characteristic verbal vividness, but the poems do not for the most part catalog mystic or ecstatic experiences. In Crane's own terms, they are impressionistic rather than absolutist. All we get is retinal registration, but what retinal registration! The images are nacreous and spellbinding, the poems themselves far more reader friendly than the more visionary verse in *White Buildings*, the Crane collection issued by Boni & Liveright that same year. Precisely for that reason, Crane felt his new verses did not equal his earlier work, poems which had previously seen print in literary magazines but were only just then appearing in book form.

As Monroe K. Spears points out, the lyrics in *Key West: An Island Sheaf* "show a resemblance to the recent trend sometimes called 'poetry of experience' " (Spears was writing in the early 1960s) "—the direct and open-textured poetry similarly related to personal crisis, of Robert Lowell's *Life Studies* and W. D. Snodgrass' *Heart's Needle. . . .*"[33] Crane left his cosmic concerns behind him in New York City and became Crusoe on his island in Cuba. He wrote about his personal anguish, his loss of inspiration, and the perceived atrophy of his ability. In "O Carib Isle!" he expresses his fears and doubts concerning death. It is multiform, colorful and omnipresent in the tropics, but the crawling tarantulas and the "zigzag fiddle crabs/ Side-stilting from the path"[34] are oblivious of it. Unlike man, they do not mourn, nor do they realize that they, too, will one day die. The only way the poet can gainsay death is to celebrate the feast of life on the island. This profusion he strives to put into words, but, as he does so, "The wind that knots itself in one great death—/ Coils and withdraws."[35] Inspiration dissipates when it seems most strong. It slackens like the wind and thus "syllables want breath."[36] The words simply won't come. Crane decides that the God of this creation must be a bloodthirsty pirate such as Captain Kidd, then proceeds to contemplate his own approaching death. He wants to die in a final blaze under the "fiery blossoms"[37] of the poincianas and hopes that his ghost will ascend upward into the blue. However, he realizes that only mock gods reside in the sky and that death will probably take him in some slow and agonizing way. Like the upturned and spiked terrapin on the beach, he shall lie, a victim of the hurricane. Unable to roll over, the turtles will suffer slow evisceration in the hot sun.

Crane's life had always been one of peaks and valleys. Spurts of amazing productivity were followed by long barren stretches in which he could not write. During these intervals, Crane's behavior became extremely self-destructive. Doubt and faith would alternate in Crane's last lyric, the final poem of *Key West*, "The Broken Tower." It was written after Crane became romantically involved with Peggy Baird, the estranged wife of poet and critic Malcolm Cowley and has to do with an autobiographical experience of the author.

Troubled by insomnia, Crane had risen before dawn the morning of January 27, 1932, and walked through the village square in Taxco, Mexico, where he met the Indian bell-ringer of the town, an old friend of his, who invited him to accompany him to the church and ring the angelus, the morning bell commemorating the incarnation of Christ. Crane did so, and as the sun rose over the mountain and the church bells swung and surged and the air reverberated with their sound, Crane experienced a moment of great joy and ecstacy. He felt reborn and vitalized and set to work on the poem after returning to his lodgings, where he refused breakfast and fetched his friend Lesley Simpson. Together they went back to the plaza. Simpson would later reveal that they "sat in the shadow of the church, Hart the while pouring out a magnificent cascade of words."[38] Crane worked rapidly, for he knew the magical moment would not last. His urgency is caught in the poem. There, even as the words come rushing forth, the poet (Crane) is unsure of them. His confidence begins to waver almost immediately. Crane equates the ringing of the church bells with the poet's task and compares the poet (himself) to Christ. Like the Savior, the poet enters "the broken world/ to trace the visionary company of love. . . ."[39] He, too, will suffer crucifixion and in his darkest moment will doubt himself and his mission. It will seem as if his Muse has forsaken him:

> My word I poured. But was it cognate, scored
> Of that tribunal monarch of the air
> Whose thigh embronzes earth, strikes crystal Word
> In wounds pledged once to hope—cleft to despair?[40]

At first it appears that Crane's implied question (Why have you forsaken me?) will not be answered, but at the penultimate moment his potency will suddenly be restored by "she/ Whose sweet mortality stirs latent power."[41] Once again he enters the timeless world within time and is able to erect his tower, not of stone but of words. Reading them, others will be able to share his revelations and intimations, and, like him, they shall stand briefly in both worlds at once. Heaven is not revealed by anything so brazen or showy as a stone edifice. It can be glimpsed only in a "slip of pebbles,"[42] something tiny and easily disregarded. One must glance down instead of looking up. Only then will one detect the eternal in the transient:

> The steep encroachments of my blood left me
> No answer (could blood hold such a lofty tower
> As flings the question true?)—or is it she
> whose sweet mortality stirs latent power?—
>
> And through whose pulse I hear, counting the strokes
> My veins recall and add, revived and sure
> The Angelus of wars my chest evokes:
> What I hold healed, original now, and pure . . .
>
> And builds, within, a tower that is not stone
> (Not stone can jacket heaven)—but slip
> Of pebbles,—visible wings of silence sown
> In azure circles, widening as they dip
>
> The matrix of the heart, lift down the eye
> That shrines the quiet lake and swells a tower . . .
> The commodious, tall decorum of that sky
> Unseals her earth, and lifts love in its shower.[43]

Until he wrote, "The Broken Tower" Crane had been unable to finish a poem for close to two years. Most critics agree that his final lyric is among his best. During the weeks he spent revising the poem, however, Crane came to the conclusion that "The Broken Tower" was a botch and that his creative powers were spent. He drank heavily and frequently threatened suicide. Like Woolf, he came to see death as the ultimate apotheosis. Instead of a terrestrial paradise, he sought a more lasting one. A month after he abandoned the poem, he climbed the railing of the steamer *Orizaba*, the ship bringing him and Peggy Baird home to New York from Vera Cruz, and leapt overboard. He was lost at sea 275 miles north of Havana. He had written frequently about death by water. As Philip Horton, his first biographer noted, "Possibly no other writer but Melville has ever been able to express the mysteries and terrors of the seas with such eloquence and imagination. . . ."[44] Yet Crane had no fear of drowning. It would be a gentle death, and transfiguration would certainly follow. He would undergo a sea change and enter Paradise a final time, never to be expelled again. In "the vortex" of his grave, "The seal's wide spindrift gaze toward paradise"[45] would at last be answered. Fulfillment would be finally found and every secret at last revealed. He would experience "instant apocalypse."

Rilke's famous comment about the Austrian Trakl's poetry, "Falling is the pretext for the most continuous ascension,"[46] is equally, if not more, valid for the visionary verse of the American Crane. When one thinks of Crane's suicide one can't help recalling China's most famous lyric poet Li Po (to whom Rilke also compared Trakl). According to legend, on the night of his death, Li Po, drunk with wine, began reciting poems to the moon. He reached out for its reflection in the Yellow River, fell into the water, and drowned. A dolphin bore him on its back to the world of the immortals. A similar inversion is found in Crane's "At Melville's Tomb," which the author placed before the long poem "Voyages" in his 1926 collection *White Buildings*. In the poem the vortex of a sinking ship is referred to as the "calyx of death's bounty."[47] The clamor and swirl of the whirlpool as it closes over the ship and sucks it down are foretold by the "portent wound in corridors of shells,"[48] the roar one hears when one holds a conch to one's ears, the sound of blood coursing through one's own veins. This sound inspires reverence. One is tempted to lift one's eyes up to the stars in search of the deity, but instead one should turn one's gaze downward toward the sea, for only there is the mystery solved:

> Then in the circuit calm of one vast coil,
> Its lashings charmed and malice reconciled,
> Frosted eyes there were that lifted altars;
> And silent answers crept across the stars.
>
> Compass, quadrant and sextant contrive
> No farther tides. . . . High in the azure steeps
> Monody shall not wake the mariner.
> This fabulous shadow only the sea keeps.[49]

Once one has beheld supreme beauty, there is no escape or turning back. The ideal kills. One cannot look God square in the face. Those who stare too long at the sun are blinded. Crane knew that "few evade full measure of their fate,"[50] yet, in Dembo's words, he continued his "quest for a logos in which the Absolute that he had known in his imagination [would] be made intelligible to the world. . . ."[51] This quest became the theme of his longest and most ambitious poem, *The Bridge*, wherein Crane selected the Brooklyn Bridge as his ultimate symbol of the timeless and Absolute.

Crane began *The Bridge* in 1923 after finishing "For the Marriage of Faustus and Helen" and would continue to tinker and add to it for the next seven years. The two works are closely related. In the earlier poem, while riding a street car (a sort of magical chariot that bridges time as well as shortens space and distance), the poet-voyager has yet another of his visionary experiences. The poem, in Crane's words, records "the transition of the imagination from quotidian details to the universal consideration of beauty."[52] As the poet progresses to his destination, he watches the hubbub and traffic, the blinking pink and green neon signs of the city, through the jerky window frame of the streetcar. As the images fly past, his mind begins to wander and although his body is still "centered in traffic,"[53] his imagination is set free. It eludes life's "daily nets"[54] and travels at speeds far greater than that of the streetcar. The poet experiences a mystic connection (i.e., marriage) between past and present, "a kind of fusion of our own time with the past."[55] In a letter to Waldo Frank concerning the poem, Crane wrote, "Almost every symbol of current significance is matched by a correlative, suggested or actually stated 'of ancient days.' Helen, the symbol of this abstract 'sense of beauty,' Faustus the symbol of myself, the poetic or imaginative man of all times."[56] Many have died and sacrificed themselves in the pursuit of beauty. Crane knows that the "capped arbiter"[57] who sits beside him in the streetcar has led many men—whole cities—to their destruction and that her realm is elusive and as seemingly insubstantial as a castle in the air. Helen saturates with both blessing and dismay. Her disciples are mown down as if by machine gun fire, but others continue to be captivated. Despite all the carnage, the soldiers keep advancing, determined to eventually storm their goal and achieve the impossible. In more sober moments, they know full well that they are Don Quixotes tilting at windmills, that it is impossible to lay siege to Heaven, that the sky will shake down "vertical repeated play of fire"[58] at all who strive to fly upward. Nonetheless, they keep coming. Crane is one of their number. Enrapt with Helen, he will continue to sing her praises, for his eye is "riveted" to Beauty's higher plane where death, warfare, and dismay are all transcended. He may never attain paradise. The vision may always fade and "fall too soon/ And in other ways than as the wind settles/ On the sixteen bridges of the city,"[59] but he will continue to stretch his bleeding hands out toward the unattainable heights, for "The imagination spans beyond despair,/ Outpacing bargain, vocable and prayer."[60]

The Bridge, like "For the Marriage of Faustus and Helen," is a poem of mystic connection. In a letter to his patron Otto H. Kahn, Crane described *The Bridge* as "an organic panorama, showing the continuous and living evidence of the past in the inmost vital substance of the presence."[61] Elsewhere he wrote of the poem: "Very roughly, it concerns a mythical synthesis of 'America.' History and fact, location, etc., all have to be transfigured into abstract form that almost would function independently of its subject matter. The initial impulses of 'our people' will have to be gathered up toward the climax of the bridge, symbol of our constructive future, our unique identity, in which is also included our scientific hopes and achievements of the future. The mystic portent of all this is already flocking through my mind."[62] His letters also make clear that Crane saw *The Bridge* as a sort of counterpoise to T. S. Eliot's *The Wasteland*, a work that Crane admired tremendously from a technical point of view but found unduly pessimistic in its analysis and evaluation of the modern world. In a letter to Allen Tate a year before he commenced work on *The Bridge*, Crane details both his preoccupation with Eliot and his concerted effort to move beyond him and embark on a new poetic course all his own:

> I have been facing him for four years,—and while I haven't discovered a weak spot yet in his armour, I flatter myself a little lately that I have discovered a safe tangent to strike which, if I can possibly explain the position—goes *through* him toward a *different goal*. You see it is such a fearful temptation to imitate him that at times I have been almost distracted. . . . In his own realm Eliot presents us with an absolute *impasse*, yet oddly enough, he can be utilized to lead us to, intelligently point to, other positions and "pastures new." Having absorbed him enough we can trust ourselves as never before, in the air or on the sea. I, for instance would like to leave a few of his "negations" behind me, risk the realm of the obvious more, in quest of new sensations, *humeurs*.[63]

Six months later Crane again stresses his own "more positive, or (if [I] must put it so in a skeptical age) ecstatic goal. . . ." He calls *The Wasteland* a "perfection of death" and writes that now "nothing is possible in motion but a resurrection of some kind."[64]

Eliot's seminal poem consists largely of "broken fragments." Louis Untermeyer rightfully characterized it as "an anthology of assimilations and jumble of quotations."[65] *The Wasteland* is constructed out of bits and pieces and ends and remnants. It contains allusions both well known and obscure, foreign text in a dozen languages, snippets of popular songs and nursery rhymes, as well as allusions to Shakespeare, Vergil, Milton, the operas of Richard Wagner and to religious texts such as the Bible and the Upanishads. These are seemingly haphazardly strung together but are actually strategically and artfully interwoven to suggest the disintegration and sterility of modern times. The world has become a giant junk heap, entropy and disintegration having long ago set in. Unity and wholeness are lost, the Fisher King lies maimed, and the twentieth century has become an arid desert. In Eliot's poem, no Parsifal appears to heal the King and restore the land. The renewal that comes each year with the spring is false and deceptive. April is thus the cruelest month. The fisher can only shore fragments against his ruins. New creation is not possible. Eliot sees the modern poet as nothing more than a magpie. He steals from his illustrious predecessors and tries to refashion what he has purloined into something new. A nest of his own. He fails. Everything comes apart.

London Bridge falls down. In answer to *The Wasteland*, Hart Crane hoped to offer a vision of cohesion and oneness occasioned by another bridge, a proud edifice and architectural marvel in no danger of collapse, a stationary structure spanning river and sea, facilitating passage and movement by connecting far points and thereby defying space and time. When he commenced writing *The Bridge*, Crane thought he had embarked on an epic poem in the classical tradition. As Herbert A. Leibowitz writes, he dreamed "of being the American Vergil, the poet-colonist who would establish the links between his nation's past, present, and future, who would carry its household gods in his utterance to a new civilization where they would flourish. . . ."[66] Crane was impulsive and imprudent in his early comments about his poem-in-progress. He lost faith in *The Bridge* during the course of its composition. For one thing, the poem he was actually writing was not an epic. He later saw that his first claims were far too grandiose; he had completely mischaracterized the piece. Nonetheless, he never retracted his earlier statements. When the poem finally appeared in 1930, Tate and Winters, among others, were quick to point how little the work Crane delivered resembled the one he had promised. *The Bridge* was not an epic, but a patchwork of interconnected lyric poems. Dembo would later call it "a romantic lyric given epic implications."[67] Crane realized the fix Crane was in—that what he was writing was coming out utterly different from what he had initially planned. As early as June 1926, he wrote to Waldo Frank that "intellectually judged the whole theme and project seems more and more absurd."[68] In addition, after beginning work on *The Bridge*, Crane began to read the German philosopher Oswald Spengler. Quietly, he came to the conclusion that Eliot might have been right after all. Despite his reservations and his loss of confidence, Crane nonetheless proceeded to finish the poem. Despite his doubts, he tried to keep true to the positive and ecstatic goals which he had originally set for himself. The poem he produced is indeed kaleidoscopic, but most critics agree that the fine, often great, writing in it unfortunately does not add up to the sum of its parts. It is also the critics' consensus that *The Bridge* is uneven. While it contains some of Crane's choicest poetry, it also features some of his weakest material.

The poem begins with a "proem," a panegyric to the Brooklyn Bridge, whose structure is hailed as divine. Its "guerdon" is as obscure as the "heaven of the Jews." The accolade it bestows is "anonymity," but it also shows "reprieve and pardon."[69] It is "harp and altar of the fury fused" as well as "the prophet's pledge," "the lover's cry" and the "prayer of the pariah."[70] Against "the traffic lights that skim" its "swift unfractioned idiom,"[71] the bridge condenses eternity. The poet views it during the winter under the shadow of the piers. Instead of offering a prayer to the deity, he lifts his supplication to the bridge's parapets and cables: "Unto us lowliest sometimes sweep, descend /And of the curveship lend a myth to God."[72] The poem's first section, "Ave Maria," concerns Columbus' ocean voyage and his discovery of America. He is a type of the quester poet and his destination, Cathay, is the poet's visionary realm. The second part, "Powhatan's Daughter," is itself divided into five sections. Pocahontas serves as Crane's symbol of the primitive American continent awaiting exploration. In "Harbor Dawn," Crane's protagonist dreams of her as he sleeps in modern New York City. Awaking in the metropolis, he becomes Rip Van Winkle and boards the subway, which in the next section of "Powhatan's Daughter," the justly famous "The River," becomes a transcontinental train named "20th-Century Limited." The reader is transported to the Middle West. A journey down the Mississippi ensues. As both hobos and Pullman breakfasters view the mighty waterway which stretches like a lifeline or artery from northern Minnesota to the Gulf of Mexico, they are carried back in time like the streetcar rider in "For the Marriage of Faustus and Helen." There are many metaphoric bridges in Crane's *magnum opus*. The train and river serve as two of them. In "Dance," the final section of "Powhatan's Daughter," the hero undergoes yet another of his metamorphoses and becomes the Indian Maquokeeta. He takes Pocahontas as his bride. Later he is chosen as a sacrificial victim in a ritual dance and is burned at the stake. However, Maquokeeta is the "snake that lives before,/ That casts his pelt, and lives beyond."[73] He will arise again to embrace America—i.e., Pocahontas. The poem's third segment is entitled "Cutty Sark" after an American brand of whiskey whose label depicts a Yankee clipper. In this section of *The Bridge*, Crane evokes the era of the great whaling and merchant ships. Struggling to survive in a world seemingly devoid of spiritual experience, the protagonist, now a drunken sailor, hears the siren call of eternity—a tune emanating from a pianola—as he enters a waterfront saloon. As he staggers home, he spies a convoy of ghost ships from Brooklyn Bridge. The next segment of the poem, "Cape Hatteras," is an ode to the airplane. In Louis Untermeyer's estimation, Crane comes close, here, to realizing his "dream of accustoming poetry to images from contemporary life, of 'acclimatizing' the machine with its 'nasal whine' of power."[74] The poet again sounds his theme of death and resurrection. Technology's great promise can and will be perverted: "The soul, by naphtha fledged into new reaches/ Already knows the closer clasp of Mars,—/ New latitudes, unknotting, soon give place/ To what fierce schedules, rife of doom apace!"[75] Planes will become agents of destruction in war and act as the "dragon's covey."[76] Nonetheless, the aviators have "splintered space" and stormed heaven: "There, meaningful, fledged as the Pleiades,/ With razor sheen they zoom each rapid helix!/ Up-chartered choristers of their own speeding/ They, cavalcade on escapade, shear Cumulus—/ Lay siege and hurdle Cirrus down the skies!"[77] The "Three Songs" of the next segment illustrate the misuse and trivialization of American land and heritage in the twentieth century. In "Quaker Hill," for example, a Friends' Meeting House in Connecticut is turned into a commercial resort hotel. "The Tunnel" depicts the epic hero's obligatory trip to the underworld. In this instance he must descend to the subway and cross under the harbor and East River. If Crane is attempting to raise a bridge that will fuse and link all the pivotal points and transcendent thresholds in American history, he knows that the structure he is erecting will also span deep defiles. In order to ascend, one first must hit bottom. Underground, the protagonist harrows hell: "The phonographs of hades in the brain/ Are tunnels that re-wind themselves, and love, a burnt match skating in a urinal."[78] Like Lazarus, however, the hero will arise. He will emerge from the bowels of the earth to view the bridge. The sight of the transcendent can inspire a man, but it also can drive him mad. Visionary experience often leans to suicide. At the conclusion of "The Tunnel," Crane means the reader to recall the following lines from the proem, "To Brooklyn Bridge," in which another Lazarus comes out of his grave in order to behold the "silver-paced" structure. The sight of the bridge inspires him to mount it, then jump from its parapets to his death:

> Out of some subway scuttle, cell or loft
> A bedlamite speeds to thy parapets,
> Tilting there momentarily, shrill shirt ballooning,
> A jest falls from the speechless caravan.[79]

The poem has now come full circle. The last segment of *The Bridge* is entitled "Atlantis." The poet identifies the fabled lost continent with the long-searched-for paradise. The singer is last seen floating in the sea. Paradise has of course long ago sunken beneath the waves.

In his letter to Gorham Munson, Crane does not elaborate on his two earlier ecstatic episodes, but implies that they were every bit as intense as his experience in the dental chair. What caused or triggered these earlier "inspirations" can't be identified with absolute certainty. Nonetheless, it is clear from Crane's poems what two methods he most frequently employed in his attempts to open the gates between this world and the next in order that he might become, however briefly, a bestriding colossus, a human bridge, with one foot in each. While these two "techniques" would often prove futile and unavailing, drinking and homosexual lovemaking could act, on rare occasions, as catalysts for Crane, expediting excursions beyond "the dozen particular decimals of time"[80] into bliss and seeming eternity. Crane realized that whatever bliss he did attain through drink and sex would inevitably be short-lived. In his poems he portrays both the efficacy and unreliability of these two techniques, the exhilaration they would sometimes occasion, but also the fraudulence and deceitfulness of the altered states of consciousness they would produce as well as, of course, their heartbreaking transience.

In "The Wine Menagerie," Crane writes that wine can "redeem the sight."[81] Drinking grants release. It breaks down barriers and inhibitions and frees the poet from the dullness of everyday experience. Alcohol narrows "the mustard scansions of the eyes"[82] and awakens the latent animal inside the drinker, the part of him most open to sensation. The "leopard" always ranges in the brow but becomes dominant and controlling only under the stimulus of drink. Then he asserts "a vision in the slumbering gaze."[83] As he drinks, the poet is filled with a sense of well-being. He can forget the terrible pain of his youth, the ever present tension and sexual hostility existing between his parents. Sitting at the bar he watches two other patrons, a man and a women, and observes the sexual antagonism developing between them, the predatory lust that awakens in the man and the woman's violent, hysterical rebuff. Her hard-eyed refusal: "Regard the forceps of the smile that takes her./ Percussive sweat is spreading to his hair. Mallets,/ Her eyes, unmake an instant of the world."[84] For a brief moment, as he "nudges a cannister across the bar," he is once again an "urchin"[85] watching his parents, but as he imbibes more wine, he experiences a new serenity. Quotidian concerns and the banal reality of the bar are transcended, and, in a state of visionary drunkenness, the poet experiences:

> New thresholds, new anatomies! Wine talons
> Build freedom up about me and distill
> This competence—to travel in a tear
> Sparkling alone, within another's will.[86]

Seemingly, the poet is propelled beyond himself. He can sense the pain and suffering of those about him. His commiseration and pity increase and he feels as if his spirit can filter through, and permeate into, those of others. No longer cut off and isolated from his fellow man, he can travel as a tear through someone else's will. The experience, however, is nothing more than an illusion. The vision proves false. The poet has not transcended reality: "Ruddy, the tooth implicit of the world/ Has followed you."[87] Alcohol is playing tricks on him and drink has gone to his head. The poet spurs himself to leave the bar: "Rise from the dates and crumbs and walk away. . . ."[88] His spirit has not left his body. The sense of mystic connection he has experienced is false. He is still cut off and isolated from the world. The heads of Holofernes and John the Baptist remain severed from their trunks. "Petrushka's valentine pivots on its pin"[89] and he is sober once again.

Alcohol can also produce hellish visions. "Paraphrase" relates a nightmarish experience of the poet. Awakening from a drunken sleep and blinded by the bright light of dawn, Crane feels death enter his bed and body. Paralysis strikes his toes and limbs. The poem begins with a false note of reassurance. As the poet is in the process of awakening, somewhere between sleep and consciousness, he realizes he is alive. He detects a "record wedged in his soul," the "steady winking between Systole, diastole. . . ."[90] Suddenly, however, his heart is beating much too fast. The palpitations are likened to the spinning "spokes of wheel"[91] which blur into one another and appear to multiply in the rush of their revolution. Death invades the sleeper's limbs and he is immobilized. Light will fill the room and turn the drunk's pillow into an "antarctic blaze" but it "shall not rouse"[92] him. His head will constitute "a white paraphrase" among the "bruised roses"[93] of the wallpaper. The dead face is only a shell, a bad paraphrase of the once living countenance.

According to A. L. Rouse, Crane had his first homosexual encounter in Akron, Ohio. The experience astounded and overwhelmed him: "I have never had devotion returned before like this, nor ever found a soul, mind, and body so worthy of devotion. Probably I never shall again."[94] Until this time, sex had always seemed offputting to Crane. He equated it with the anger and aggression of his father and the misery of his mother.

Crane wrote about his awakening homosexuality in the early poem "Episode of Hands" but also camouflaged and veiled his subject. In the poem, an injured factory worker's hand wound receives unexpected attention from a fellow employee:

> The unexpected interest made him flush.
> Suddenly he seemed to forget the pain,—
> Consented—and held out
> One finger from the others.
> . . . .
> And factory sounds and factory thoughts
> Were banished from him by that larger, quieter hand
> That lay in his with the sun upon it
> And as the bandage knot was tightened
> The two men smiled in each other's eyes.[95]

The affair, however, was short-lived. Within weeks, Crane wrote: "I have gone through a great deal lately—seen love go down through lust to indifference, etc., and also, not very well."[96] The poet drowned his sorrow.

Lovemaking can produce an ecstacy, a possession, comparable to, or greater than, that furnished by alcohol. Sex is yet another gateway to visionary experience. Therefore, despite all his heartache and his always unfulfilled expectation, the poet, propelled by his aching lust, will continue to seek out new assignations. He knows that new affairs and encounters will fail like all the others, but his search for ultimate fulfillment must go on. In "Possessions," Crane vents his frustration at his absurd condition but also reveals the apocalyptic consummation he seeks. His "fixed stone of lust" is "undirected."[97] Keys fit in proper locks and rain falls to earth. But he has yet to find the perfect correlation; the right key, the right lock. In Greenwich Village, he continues his tortured search. He feels as if he is being burned alive, turned "on smoked forking spires."[98] Lust gores him like the horns of a bull. He is certain that he shall die bleeding. "Piteous admissions"[99] will be all that he ever will achieve. Such admissions comprise a "record of rage and partial appetites."[100] Nonetheless, he continues his search for "The pure possession, the inclusive cloud/ Whose heart is fire shall come,—the white wind raze/ All but bright stones wherein our smiling plays."[101] Death.

Crane's longest lasting relationship was with Emil Opffer, a merchant seaman and steward away on eight-week cruises. Crane dedicated to him perhaps his greatest and most successful work, a series of six love-and-sea poems entitled "Voyages." Tellingly the mystic experience the poet details occurs when he and his lover are parted, the sea lying between them. Crane originally entitled the first poem "The Bottom of the Sea Is Cruel" but would later cross it out. He would instead use the phrase as the first section's closing line. As stated earlier, the opening of "Voyages" concerns children: "striped urchins"[102] playing on the beach, digging and giggling and hurling sand at each other. They are oblivious of the sun beating on the waves and the waves folding thunder on the sand. They frisk with their dog and fondle their shells and sticks without realizing ". . . There is a line/ You must never cross nor trust beyond it/ Spry cordage of your bodies to caresses/ Too lichen-faithful from too wide a breast."[103]

The poet will cross that line, for while immersed in the sea he is connected to his lover. He has found his bridge. The sea—it is revealed in the second section— makes exceptions for lovers. They need not fear her like others. Together with poem III, this passage constitutes "the heart" of the entire six poems:

> —And yet this great wink of eternity,
> Of rimless floods, unfettered leewardings,
> Samite sheeted and processioned where
> Her vast belly moonward bends,
> Laughing the wrapt inflections of our love;
>
> Take this Sea, whose diapason knells
> On scrolls of silver snowy sentences,
> The sceptred terror of whose sessions rends
> As her demeanors motion well or ill,
> All but the pieties of lovers' hands.
>
> And onward, as bells off San Salvador
> Salute the crocus lustres of the stars,
> In those poinsettia meadows of her tides,—
> Adagios of islands, O my Prodigal,
> Complete the dark confessions her veins spell.
>
> Mark how her turning shoulders wind the hours,
> And hasten while her penniless rich palms
> Pass superscription of bent foam and waves,—
> Hasten, while they are true,—sleep, death, desire.
> Close round one instant in one floating flower.[104]

The sea is both love and death. According to Monroe K. Spears, in all the world of art, the closest parallel to the second stanza of the third section of "Voyages" is Wagner's *Liebestod*.[105] If the waters don't carry the floating poet to his lover, they will afford him another passage. He will be taken where he most wants to go:

And so, admitted through black swollen gates
That must arrest all distance otherwise,—
Past whirling pillars and lithe pediments,
Light wrestling there incessantly with light,
Star kissing star through wave on wave unto
Your body rocking!
                         and where death, if shed,
Presumes no carnage, but this single change,—
Upon the steep floor flung from dawn to dawn
The silken skilled transmemberment of song;

Permit me voyage, love, into your hands . . .[106]

In Poem IV, the poet is transported in his imagination into the embracing arms of
his lover. The harbor disconnects from the shore. The waves of the sea draw and
pull it to the islands of love, the "Blue latitude and levels"[107] of his lover's eyes.
There he will receive the "secret oars and petals of all love."[108] In stark contrast to
this invented and fictitious encounter, Poem V depicts the actual meeting of poet
and steward after one of the latter's cruises of eight weeks. It is a bitter disappointment for Crane. A "wedge" separates Opffer and him now that they stand side
by side on a moonlit beach. While the seaman is struck by the moon, the poet sees
only "a godless cleft of sky. . . ."[109] To him, the lunar orb resembles nothing so much
as "dead sands flashing":

—As if too brittle or too clear to touch!
The cables of our sleep so swiftly filed,
Already hang, shred ends from remembered stars.
One frozen trackless smile . . . What words
Can strangle this deaf moonlight? For we

Are overtaken. Now no cry, no sword
Can fasten or deflect this tidal wedge,
Slow tyranny of moonlight, moonlight loved
And changed . . . "There's

Nothing like this in the world," you say,
Knowing I cannot touch your hand and look
Too, into that godless cleft of sky
Where nothing turns but dead sands flashing.

"And never to quite understand!" No,
In all the argosy of your bright hair I dreamed
Nothing so flagless as this piracy.[110]

The poet finds himself again in the sea in Part VI. It is the "harbor of the phoenix's
breast."[111] He will drown. He will burn. But he will emerge from his ashes. "Beyond

siroccos harvesting/ The solstice thunders"[112] will have crept away. He will emerge on the shores of the Belle Isle and hear "Creation's blithe and petalled word."[113] "It is the unbetrayable reply/ Whose accent no farewell can know."[114]

Crane was jealous when his friend was away at sea, but often even more hurt when he was at home. A. L. Rouse writes: "one affair does not preclude another. During the ten-day period between voyages Hart and his friend would go to the Metropolitan Opera House and stand in the wings to hear Melchior, who was also a friend of Crane's sea-going friend."[115] Opffer, whose name so resembles the German word for opera, had found himself a better Isolde.

Harold Hart Crane was born in Garretsville, Ohio, a small town close to the Pennsylvania border, on July 21, 1899. He was the only child of Clarence and Grace Hart Crane. During Crane's childhood the family moved twice, first to Warren, Ohio, where Clarence Crane established a maple-syrup plant, and then to Cleveland, where he began his career as a candy manufacturer and founded the Crane company, a successful chain of retail candy stores. Crane's parents separated in 1909, when Crane was ten. Grace Crane promptly suffered a mental and emotional collapse. In several months, however, husband and wife reunited. During their period of estrangement, the boy was packed off to his maternal grandmother.

After reconciling, the Cranes lived together for nine more years, but their union was always shaky and unstable, and their marriage at last ended in divorce in 1917. The two were a poor match, and, as Crane would later write in "Quaker Hill," he was constrained to "shoulder the curse of sundered parentage."[116] Affectionate but quick of temper, Clarence Crane put business and sensual gratification above all else. His wife was high-strung and demanding. She constantly complained and picked quarrels, and, although she was sexually frigid, she knew how to tease and torment Clarence and could work him like a puppet. While battling, she would be aggressive and mocking in turn. Grace was also the last flower of a long line of New England Puritans (the early Harts had belonged to the congregation of Reverend Thomas Hooker, Puritan founder of Connecticut). Quick to perceive affront, she would assume the moral high ground during a row and could feign boiling indignation at the drop of a pin. Clarence Crane felt that his wife did not love him sufficiently or properly appreciate his struggles and exertions as the family breadwinner. Nor did she satisfy his sexual appetites. The couple fought and bickered constantly. The young boy sided with his mother. He was susceptible to her theatrical appeals and teary eyes, and she made him her ally and confidant in her game of marital brinkmanship. The father-foe was a monstrous, demanding beast, an animal not a man. The boy joined with the mother to repel the stalker-and-predator's assaults.

As he grew older, Harold's hatred for his father deepened due to the latter's hostile attitude toward poetry. Clarence Crane felt the writing of verse was an effeminate pursuit. He wanted his son to follow in his footsteps and take over the family business. Grace, on the other hand, encouraged Harold's artistic bent. In terms of temperament and demeanor, Crane felt he had more of his mother—i.e., Hart—in him than Crane. Both his mother and grandmother were staunch advocates of Christian Science, and, as a child, Crane was brought up in the faith. When he bolted to New York City in 1916, one of the few books he took with him was Mary Baker Eddy's *Science and Health with Key to the Scriptures*. Although he would later reject the religion, certain of its tenets would continue to affect him profoundly. Although he could not swallow the sect's "total denial of the animal and organic world,"[117] he felt Christian Science was correct in what it said with regard to mental and nervous ailments. And even though he rejected the faith's doctrine that all matter was an illusion and that the phenomenal world was completely unreal, Christian Science's emphasis on shifting states of consciousness continued to intrigue him. According to the church, all causation is mental. Therefore, states of mind constitute the only reality. Crane's mystic side and his quest for a higher consciousness had much to do with the early religious training he received from Grace. In later life, Crane confessed to his friend Solomon Greenberg that he had once had a dream in which he ripped his mother's belly open and rooted through her entrails as if he were a Greek diviner opening up an animal sacrifice.[118] He cut into her flesh in order to find out the secret of his life. When he began to publish, Crane would drop the first name his father had bestowed on him, adopting his middle name—the maternal surname—in its stead. He took his mother's part in the parental lists until age nineteen, when his good will toward her would also sour, as he began to realize just how much she had dominated and controlled him as a child. One day, he accosted her and angrily charged that for the past eight years, his youth "had been a rather bloody battleground" for her and her husband's "sex life and troubles."[119] A long rupture between mother and son would ensue. After her son's suicide, however, Grace Hart directed all her energy to seeking recognition for Crane's work and securing his reputation as poet. At the same time, she stinted her own needs, scraping out a living as a lowly janitress. After her death in 1947, in a final tribute to her son, she stipulated in her will that her ashes be scattered from the Brooklyn Bridge.

The tension and sexual hostility between his parents frightened Crane and possibly caused him to recoil from heterosexuality. He was, however, randy and wanton in his pursuit of sexual fulfillment with other men. His lust was insatiable, yet Allen Tate could also, with justification, call him "an extreme example of the *unwilling* homosexual."[120] As A. L. Rowse points out, he "did not care for the professionalism of accredited homosexual circles," but found "the willingness of sailors on the sea-front and bars somehow more authentic and more rewarding: they had a physical need, so had he."[121] Crane did not, then, wear his gayness on his sleeve. Usually he had to be well in his cups in order to overcome his inhibitions. His trysts were most often of short duration, casual pick-ups. A soldier or sailor might afford him, at the most, a night or two of bliss. Several of his lovers kept in periodic if infrequent touch. Such "unexpected loyalties"[122] surprised and moved Crane. Once a sailor traveled from Norfolk, Virginia, all the way to the Isle of Pines to see Hart, only to find him not on the island. The sailor had undertaken this odyssey because of two evenings spent with the poet in Brooklyn the previous January. Crane found such incidents "immortally choice and funny and pathetic. I treasure them against many disillusionments made bitter by the fact that faith was given and expected—whereas, with the sailor no faith or such is properly *expected*, and how jolly and cordial and warm the touseling *is* sometimes, after all. Let my lusts be my ruin, then, since all else is a fake and a mockery."[123] On the other hand, cruising for sailors would often prove hazardous and dangerous for Crane. He often came home bleeding and beaten.

In 1916, a year before his parents divorced, at age seventeen, Crane quit high school and left home and Middle West for New York City. He had begun writing poetry three years earlier. The year 1916 also saw Crane's first publication, the poem "C 33," in *Bruno's Weekly*, a small Greenwich Village magazine. Crane used Oscar Wilde's prison number at Reading Gaol for the poem's title. During his early days in Manhattan, Crane studied the writings of Plato and Nietzsche. According to Horton, when reading the works of the Greek philosopher, he underscored in bright red ink the passages concerning the inherent madness of the poet and the concept of the upward progression of beauty from imperfect and mutable earthly imitations of the Forms to the pure and changeless Ideas themselves, existing in a region outside space and time and completely unaffected by fluctuation and decay in the material world. These concepts would influence his later development as poet, as would Nietzsche's assault on conventional morality and championship of the irrational and Dionysian elements of the human character, his reverence for the artist, and his doctrines of "the will to power" and "eternal recurrence."

Crane found an early patron in Mrs. William Vaughn Moody. While Crane was acquainted with the poetry of Whitman, Melville, and Dickinson as well as that of Swinburne, Wilde, Dowson, and Yeats, Mrs. Moody introduced him to the work of Pound and Eliot and other emerging poets of the modernist school as well to the small but courageous literary magazines, such as *Poetry*, *The Dial*, *The Little Review*, *The Egoist*, and *Blast*, that were publishing them. While in New York, Crane also befriended the young painter Carl Schmitt. As we have seen, Crane's poetry was extremely visual. Throughout his career he always found cross-pollination with painters and photographers beneficial and valuable to his art. As an adolescent, he loved painting almost as much as he did poetry. Prints and photographs adorned all the walls of his boyhood room. Schmitt became one of Crane's earliest mentors. According to Horton, he gave Crane weekly poetic assignments and periodically reviewed his work. The two agreed that Crane "should compose a certain number of poems a week simply as technical exercises with the purpose of breaking down formal patterns. These he would bring to his critic as he wrote them, and the two would read them over together, Schmitt illustrating with pencil the rising and falling of cadences, the dramatic effect of caesural breaks, and the general movement of the poem as a whole. . . . Surprisingly enough, this conscious experimentation with verse forms did not lead him, as it might have done during those flourishing days of *vers libre*, to abandon meter and rhyme."[124] The two also composed nonsensical verse to maximize the sound and musical qualities of words.

Crane, who never attended a university, supported himself by odd jobs. He also had difficulty finding a permanent home for himself. He left Manhattan a number of times and lived variously in Cleveland, Akron, and Washington, D.C., but was always drawn back to New York City. Over the years, he was employed variously as an ad agency copywriter, a riveter and defense plant worker, a reporter on the *Cleveland Plain Dealer*, a tea room manager, a bookstore clerk and a door-to-door salesman, and finally as a private secretary to a traveling stockbroker in California. He was jobless, however, much of the time. When money ran short, he returned to Ohio to work in various capacities for his father. In 1919, he moved to Akron to clerk in one of the elder Crane's candy shops there. From 1920 to 1923, he lived in Cleveland, working both for his father (always in some humble and humiliating position) and in advertising. There he befriended Ernest Nelson and the painter William Sommers. Crane's life became increasingly disordered and chaotic. He drank much of the time and continued to have frequent homosexual assignations. In 1925, the banker Otto Kahn offered him financial support to complete *The Bridge*, and, in late 1928, Crane traveled to Europe on an inheritance from his grandmother. He spent the first half of 1929 primarily in Paris where the American poet Harry Crosby and his wife, Caresse, took him under their wing. Harry Crosby was as decadent and debauched and obsessed with death as Crane. The two drank heavily and otherwise indulged their habits. The Crosbys did, however, give Crane the incentive he needed to finish *The Bridge* by agreeing to print the poem at their Black Sun Press in Paris. It would be published both there and in New York the following year. In 1931, Crane lived three months with his father in Chagrin Falls, Ohio. In March he was awarded a Guggenheim Fellowship and, with the funds provided him, went to Mexico to work on a poem about Montezuma and the Spanish Conquest. He lived among a community of artists in Taxco. One of his neighbors was the emerging short story writer, Katherine Anne Porter, whose first collection, *Flowering Judas*, had just appeared.

Crane had great difficulty writing and made little headway with his projected epic. Additionally, he found himself in frequent trouble with the authorities not only for public drunkenness but for sexual encounters with local Indian boys. Nonetheless, Crane found sexuality freer and more spontaneous in Mexico than anywhere else he had traveled. The Indian adolescents he encountered seemed to equally enjoy heterosexual and homosexual experiences. About their sexual practices and physical attractiveness, Crane would write: "Ambidexterity is all in the fullest masculine tradition. I assure you from many trials and observations. The pure Indian type is decidedly the most beautiful animal, including the Polynesian—to which he bears a close resemblance. Even Lawrence couldn't resist some lavish description of their fine proportions."[125]

When Peggy Cowley arrived in Taxco, she and Crane felt a mutual attraction. Perhaps inspired by the indifferent bisexuality of the Indian youths he had encountered, Crane entered into the first heterosexual affair of his life. He tasted love with a woman and felt transformed: "healed, original now, and pure."[126] He attempted living with Cowley, but their relationship proved stormy. Both drank far too much, and they quarrelled on a frequent basis. Crane would often become violent and break and smash anything he could lay his hands on. The poet Witter Bynner, then living in Taxco, observed the couple and the disastrous turn of affairs once the two began keeping house together. "Their household," he wrote, "would have driven anyone mad. When they weren't quarrelling violently with each other they were rowing with the servants. . . . Their continual squabbling invariably ended with Hart moving downtown to a hotel. It would have been impossible for him to do any work in such a hurly-burly. . . ."[127] Crane felt as if he and Cowley were reenacting old scenes originally played out by his parents. Nonetheless, he proposed to Peggy, and the two planned to marry once they returned to New York City. During his last months in Mexico, Crane suffered from frequent mood swings. Exhilaration alternated with despair. The poet could not control his behavior and his grip on sanity slowly began to loosen. This in no way frightened him: poets were of necessity mad. He did fear returning to the United States because he would have nothing to show for his Guggenheim—he had failed to write his epic about Montezuma. After his fights with Cowley, he would seek comfort with various Indian boys and youths of his acquaintance, but now felt great guilt whenever he engaged in homosexual activity. His guilt led him to further drink and further sexual abandon. He threatened suicide on numerous occasions. Once, when two old friends of Mrs. Cowley paid her a visit, he threatened to drink iodine. The women prevented him from carrying out his threat on that occasion. Another time, however, he did succeed in gulping down the contents of a small bottle of Mercurochrome and had to have his stomach pumped.

In April, Crane and Cowley at last left Mexico aboard the ocean liner *Orizaba*. They continued to quarrel during the voyage. Early in the trip, several shiphands beat Crane up after he tried to seduce one of their number. On the morning of April 27, Crane was greatly upset by some casual remark made by Cowley. As several passengers watched, he tried to climb over the railing to leap into the sea but was restrained by a steward and locked in his cabin. For the next few hours he drank heavily. At noon, having somehow escaped his confinement, he made his way to Cowley's cabin dressed only in pajamas and an overcoat. Peggy urged him to go back to his room and put on suitable clothes and then to join her for lunch. Crane replied, "I'm not going to make it, dear. I'm utterly disgraced."[128] She again told him to return to his room and repeated her request that he put on proper dinner clothes. "All right, dear," he said, "Goodbye."[129] After kissing Mrs. Cowley, Crane exited her cabin. Shortly before noon, he made his way to the ship's stern. He took off his coat, climbed over the railing, and slipped into the sea. Life preservers were tossed after him. Accounts differ as to whether he tried to catch hold of them. Within seconds, his head disappeared under the water. Four lifeboats were lowered. The search for the missing man lasted two hours, then was called off.

Hart Crane died a few months shy of his thirty-third birthday.

Notes

1. Quoted by Monroe K. Spears, *Hart Crane* (Minneapolis: University of Minnesota Press, 1965), p. 20.

2. Ibid.

3. Hart Crane, "Legend," *The Complete Poems and Selected Letters and Prose of Hart Crane*, ed. and introduction and notes by Brom Weber (New York: Liveright, 1966), p. 3. The poem quoted here previously appeared in *White Buildings* (New York: Liveright, 1926).

4. Quoted by Spears, *Hart Crane*, p. 20.

5. Ibid., p. 21.

6. Ibid.

7. Ibid., p. 16.

8. Ibid., p. 5.

9. Ibid.

10. Quoted by Herbert A. Leibowitz, *Hart Crane: An Introduction to the Poetry*, foreword by John Unterecker (New York: Columbia University Press, 1968), p. 12.

11. Ibid.

12. Ibid.

13. "Legend," *Complete Poems*, p. 3.

14. Quoted by Louis Untermeyer, ed., *Modern American Poetry* (New York: Harcourt Brace, 1950), pp. 561–62.

15. Quoted by Spears, *Hart Crane*, p. 19.

16. Leibowitz, *Hart Crane: An Introduction to the Poetry*, p. 23.

17. Quoted by Richard Ellmann and Robert O'Clair, eds., *The Norton Anthology of Modern Poetry* (New York: W.W. Norton, 1973), p. 583.

18. Crane, "Passages," *Complete Poems*, p. 21. The poem excerpted here previously appeared in *White Buildings*.

19. Ibid.

20. Ibid.

21. Ibid.

22. Ibid., pp. 21–22.

23. Crane, "The Wine Menagerie," *Complete Poems*, p. 24. The poem quoted here previously appeared in *White Buildings*.

24. Quoted by Ellmann and O'Clair, *The Norton Anthology*, p. 581.

25. Quoted by Spears, *Hart Crane*, p. 18.

26. Crane, "Praise for an Urn," *Complete Poems*, p. 8. This poem previously appeared in *White Buildings*.

27. Ibid.

28. Crane, "My Grandmother's Love Letters," *Complete Poems*, p. 6. The poem excerpted here previously appeared in *White Buildings*.

29. Ibid.

30. Ibid.

31. Ellmann and O'Clair, *The Norton Anthology*, p. 578.

32. Ibid. This letter appears in *The Letters of Hart Crane*, ed. Brom Weber (Los Angeles, 1965), p. 115.

33. Spears, *Hart Crane*, p. 41.

34. Crane. "O Carib Isle," *Complete Poems*, p. 156. The poem excerpted here previously appeared in *The Collected Poems of Hart Crane* (New York: Liveright, 1933).

35. Ibid.

36. Ibid.

37. Ibid.

38. Quoted by John Unterecker, *Voyager, A Life of Hart Crane* (New York: Farrar, Straus, and Giroux, 1969), p. 722.

39. Crane, "The Broken Tower," *Complete Poems*, p. 193. The poem excerpted here previously appeared in *Collected Poems*.

40. Ibid.

41. Ibid, p. 194.

42. Ibid.

43. Ibid.

44. Quoted by Spears, *Hart Crane*, p. 28.

45. Crane, "Voyages," *Complete Poems*, p. 36. "Voyages" previously appeared in *White Buildings*.

46. Quoted by Michael Hamburger, "Introduction," *George Trakl: A Profile*, ed. Frank Graziano (Durango, Colo.: Logbridge-Rhodes, 1983), p. 14.

47. Crane, "At Melville's Tomb," *Complete Poems*, p. 34. This poem previously appeared in *White Buildings*.

48. Ibid.

49. Ibid.

50. Quoted by Leibowitz, *Hart Crane: An Introduction to the Poetry*, p. 7.

51. Quoted by Spears, *Hart Crane*, p. 34.

52. Quoted by Ellmann and O'Clair, *The Norton Anthology*, p. 586.

53. Ibid.

54. Ibid.

55. Ibid.

56. Ibid.

57. Crane, "For the Marriage of Faustus and Helen," *Complete Poems*, p. 32. The poem excepted here previously appeared in *White Buildings*.

58. Ibid.

59. Ibid.

60. Ibid., p. 33.

61. Quoted by Untermeyer, *Modern American Poetry*, p. 560.

62. Quoted by Ellmann and O'Clair, *The Norton Anthology*, p. 594. This letter appears in *The Letters of Hart Crane*, pp. 124–25.

63. Quoted by Ellmann and O'Clair, *The Norton Anthology*, p. 578. This letter appears in *The Letters*, p. 90.

64. Quoted by Ellmann and O'Clair, *The Norton Anthology*, p. 578. This letter appears in *The Letters*, p. 115.

65. Untermeyer, *Modern American Poetry*, p. 394.

66. Leibowitz, *Hart Crane: An Introduction to the Poetry*, p. 20.

67. Quoted by Spears, *Hart Crane*, p. 33.

68. Leibowitz, *Hart Crane: An Introduction to the Poetry*, p. 20.

69. Crane, *The Bridge, Complete Poems*, p. 46. *The Bridge* was previously published under separate cover in 1930 in Paris and New York.

70. Ibid.

71. Ibid.

72. Ibid.

73. Ibid., p. 73.

74. Untermeyer, *Modern American Poetry*, p. 561.

75. *The Bridge, Complete Poems*, p. 90.

76. Ibid., p. 91.

77. Ibid.

78. Ibid., p. 110.

79. Ibid., p. 45.

80. "Passage," *Complete Poems*, p. 21.

81. "The Wine Menagerie," *Complete Poems*, p. 23.

82. Ibid.

83. Ibid.

84. Ibid.

85. Ibid.

86. Ibid, p. 24.

87. Ibid.

88. Ibid.

89. Ibid.

90. Crane, "Paraphrase," *Complete Poems*, p. 17. The poem quoted here previously appeared in *White Buildings*.

91. Ibid.

92. Ibid.

93. Ibid.

94. Quoted by A. L. Rowse, *Homosexuals in History* (New York: Dorset Press, 1983), p. 313.

95. Crane, "Episode of Hands," *Complete Poems*, p. 141.

96. Rowse, *Homosexuals in History*, p. 313.

97. Crane, "Possessions," *Complete Poems*, p. 18. The poem quoted here previously appeared in *White Buildings*.

98. Ibid.

99. Ibid.

100. Ibid.

101. Ibid.

102. "Voyages," *Complete Poems*, p. 35.

103. Ibid.

104. Ibid., p. 36.

105. Spears, *Hart Crane*, p. 30.

106. "Voyages," *Complete Poems*, p. 37.

107. Ibid., p. 38.

108. Ibid.

109. Ibid., p. 39.

110. Ibid.

111. Ibid., p. 40.

112. Ibid.

113. Ibid.

114. Ibid., p. 41.

115. Rowse, *Homosexuals in History*, pp. 314–15.

116. *The Bridge, Complete Poems*, p. 105.

117. Spears, *Hart Crane*, p. 6.

118. Leibowitz, *Hart Crane: An Introduction to the Poetry*, p. 2.

119. Quoted by Spears, *Hart Crane*, p. 7.

120. Ibid., p. 6.

121. Rowse, *Homosexuals in History*, p. 314.

122. Ibid.

123. Ibid.

124. Spears, *Hart Crane*, p. 15.

125. Quoted by Rowse, *Homosexuals in History*, p. 315.

126. "The Broken Tower," *Complete Poems*, p. 194.

127. Quoted by Rowse, *Homosexuals in History*, p. 316.

128. Quoted by Unterecker, *Voyager*, p. 757.

129. Ibid.

Sara Teasdale

A T NINE O'CLOCK IN THE MORNING OF JANUARY 29, 1933, SARA Teasdale's private-duty nurse, Miss Rita Brown, discovered the body of her charge submerged in warm water in the bathtub of her Fifth Avenue apartment in New York City. Brown had been attending the forty-eight-year-old poet since the previous September, when Teasdale returned to the United States from England, where she was researching the life of Christina Rossetti for a proposed biography, the opening forty pages of which she would write before her death. She had contracted pneumonia in London and was grievously ill when she arrived in the States. She expected to die and, as she had longed for death for some time, looked forward to the cessation of her life—to the seeming assurance of her decease. However, despite her desire to die, she recovered, and in December visited Winter Park, Florida, for two weeks, with her friend, the poet and reviewer Jessie Rittenhouse Scollard. Although she regained her health, Teasdale's case was complicated by her severe and recurring depression. Brown had been retained to watch over and guard her—to monitor her emotional and mental condition and do all she could to stabilize it, as well as to minister to her physical needs.

The poet's father had died in 1921, her mother in 1924. Following each parent's death, Teasdale became deeply despondent. Her period of mourning was morbidly protracted: when her father died, she dreamed about him for months afterward. Her grief was so intense that she suffered something akin to a nervous breakdown or mental collapse. Her poetry grew increasingly melancholic, yet at the same time it was also acquiescent and assenting in dealing with death. In Louis Untermeyer's words, Teasdale's songs became "preoccupied with the coming of age, the gathering of night, the mutability of things."[1]

Upon learning of the suicide of her former suitor, Vachel Lindsay, in

December 1931, she suffered another breakdown, one from which she never fully recovered. Lindsay had had the courage to put an end to his suffering. Teasdale had long cherished the notion that peace and comfort came at last with the grave—although at the same time she remained suspicious and skeptical of such a romantic view.

Her 1915 collection, *Rivers to the Sea*, contains a poem titled "I Shall Not Care," which pictures the tomb as the ultimate place of repose for a woman thwarted in love, a site consecrating her preserved chastity, her victory over sin and carnality and the man who had jilted her. This was a common enough conceit among female poets, including Emily Brontë, Elizabeth Barrett, Emily Dickinson, and Christina Rossetti. It had not lost any of its currency in the post-Victorian world of Teasdale's youth and girlhood. A woman spurned in love could turn the tables on her lover by dying. Heathcliff would inevitably be drawn to Cathy's tomb, but now the roles would be reversed and Cathy would have the upper hand. The man would weep and moan and, on his knees, make heartfelt avowals of his love, but the woman, proud, superior, masculine, would remain deaf and disdainful. While such a role reversal greatly appealed to Teasdale, as did the notion that the grave was a bed or bower, a place of rest and repose, she recognized the fallacy of the conceit. The woman would not be conscious of her lover's supplications. She could not enjoy her victory, for death, as the Arabs say, is the Destroyer of Delights: it wipes us out completely. We are struck from the books. Sentience is lost. All that remains is oblivion and nothingness. (Only the living, however, can comprehend such abstract concepts; the dead can't differentiate between self or absence of self, awareness or utter ignorance.) Only someone who is alive can understand what death is. Teasdale understood all too well.

The deceased woman in her poem is "silent and cold-hearted"[2] because she can't hear. She has ceased to be. Death is not slumber, for we are alive when we sleep. Our minds still function; indeed, they are exceedingly active. We dream. All the fetters are magically unloosed. The unconscious mind, primal and barbaric, can romp and play without restraint. Hamlet's fear, on the other hand, of falling into a dream from which he cannot awake after dying, is, of course, baseless. The brain returns to dust. Only the skull in which it is encased survives. Tongue and ears both rot. Ants can crawl all over a dead face. It will not feel because the departed are beyond all care. After life come only oblivion and nothingness:

> When I am dead and over me bright April
> Shakes out her rain-drenched hair,
> Though you should lean above me broken-hearted,
> I shall not care.
>
> I shall have peace, as leafy trees are peaceful
> When rain bends down the bough;
> And I shall be more silent and cold-hearted
> Than you are now.[3]

As the years went by, death gradually shed all its romantic trappings for the coldly realistic Teasdale. She recognized its inevitability early on. As a girl, she put her faith in heaven and God, but the Christian creed of renunciation was not to her taste and the horrors of World War I shattered whatever remaining belief she had in the Almighty. "We cannot live through one of the crucial acts in the drama of civilization," she wrote, "without paying for the privilege."[4] While she had diffi-culty reconciling herself to the grim reality of death, Teasdale sought salvation in writing, for a time harboring the belief that, by leaving a trace of herself behind in words, she would assure herself of a kind of afterlife. In the 1917 poem "The Wine," she posed a question expressing her faint hope that by creating exceptional verse she might somehow be exempt from Nature's general law:

> The rest may die—but is there not
> Some shining strange escape for me
> Who sought in Beauty the bright wine
> Of immortality?[5]

The consolation of language did not, however, last long—her awareness of death's imminence never left her. She realized that the writing of even great poetry, peer-less and incomparable verse far superior to her own, would prove hollow and unsat-isfactory, for while words might be left behind for others to enjoy, the one who penned them would be utterly effaced. One simply had to accept the way of things, the inflexible and rigid rule of the game, that everything that lives also passes out of existence. Life was a snare in which we were all caught. In the end one had no choice but to submit at last to death. Finally, Teasdale made her peace. In life, as a girl and woman, she had previously yielded to parents, husband, and societal conventions. To be fulfilled as a female, she felt that she had to surrender her will to a greater force. Compliance and resignation were the rule of the Universe. Fixed for eons in space, the stars of heaven were "august in their submission" or so she wrote in the unpublished 1921 poem "In the Web":

> Let be, my soul, fold your rebellious pinions,
> There is no way out of the web of things,
> It is a snare that never will be broken,
> And if you struggle you will break your wings.
>
> Be still a while, content to brood on beauty;
> Caught in the trap of space that has no end,
> See how the stars, august in their submission,
> Take Their Great Captor for their changeless friend.[6]

Death would become the final "Great Captor" for Teasdale. The enemy would even-tually turn into a friend. As an adult, she recognized how death overshadows all of life, a revelation which periodically would make all our interim activities, whatever

they might be, seem inconsequential and insignificant. In a letter to her husband
in 1920, she observed: "The more one comes to think about life, the more one realizes it's necessary to get a certain amount of 'kick' out of it. But whether the 'kick'
is obtained from sorrow, or joy, love, war, religion or art makes very little difference
in the end."[7] In the poem "The Crystal Gazer," Teasdale gathers all her scattered
selves together and makes a polished crystal ball of them. She stares into the
future. Realizing that death will come, she is content to watch the passing of time,
a silly and vain show full of people puffed up with pride, forgetting at least for the
moment, the time being, that they, too, are mortal:

> I shall sit like a sibyl, hour after hour intent,
>   Watching the future and the present go—
> And the little shifting pictures of people rushing
>   In tiny self-importance to and fro.[8]

Yet the poems Teasdale wrote after the deaths of her parents, such as the double
quatrain "Epitaph" from the 1926 collection *Dark of the Moon*, begin to show a
placid acceptance of our last end. Death was natural—a part and parcel of creation. The life cycle was as inescapable and inexorable as the agricultural round
and the yearly change of season:

> Serene descent as a red leaf is descending
>   When there is neither wind nor noise of rain.
> But only autumn air and the unending
>   Drawing of all things to the earth again:
>
> So be it: let the snow sift deep and cover
>   All that was drunken once with light and air.
> The earth will not regret her tireless lover.
>   Nor he awake to know that she does not care.[9]

The finality and absolute certainty of death were easier for Teasdale to accept in
the abstract. It was far more difficult for her to acquiesce to the loss and departure
of loved ones. Teasdale understood all too well what death was. Individual instances of it caused her great grief. The irrevocability of the loss overwhelmed her.
She could not come to terms with the deaths of individuals she deeply cared for and
repeatedly felt the urge to follow the loved one who had died. Knowledge and
acceptance were replaced by a desire for oblivion. After his suicide in 1931,
Lindsay seemed to call to her from the Other Side as her parents had earlier done.
"The Flight" appeared in *Dark of the Moon* after the passing of her parents, but the
reader who knows the story of Lindsay's and Teasdale's deaths—how one followed
the other within the space of only thirteen months—naturally will think of the two
poets when he reads the lines:

We are two eagles
Flying together,
Under the heavens,
Over the mountains,
Stretched on the wind.
Sunlight heartens us,
Blind snow baffles us,
Clouds wheel after us,
Raveled and thinned.

We are like eagles;
But when Death harries us,
Human and humbled
When one of us goes,
Let the other follow—
Let the flight be ended,
Let the fire blacken,
Let the book close.[10]

Death had been on Teasdale's mind long before Vachel Lindsay's suicide. She made her will in May 1930. Naming the great friend of her last years, Margaret Conklin, as her literary executor, she stipulated that "no poems or verses of mine shall be published after my death unless my written sanction for such publication appears thereon."[11] But its allure grew all the greater afterward. Teasdale became distraught immediately upon hearing of Lindsay's "heart attack." With him gone, she came to feel that she also was not long for this world and although she was alternatively depressed and filled with anxiety, this certainty ultimately lent her a sort of peace and serenity. Submission gave her peace. Her cognizance of approaching death, of being cornered at last, stimulated her muse, and, during the last two years of her life, she produced some of her finest poems. Sylvia Plath would experience a similar explosion of creativity in the months prior to her death three decades later.

Upon discovering Teasdale's body, Brown summoned Dr. Frederick R. Bailey, one of the two physicians treating the poet since her return from England, to the apartment. He, in turn, telephoned the Medical Examiner's office, reporting Teasdale's death a suicide. Assistant coroner Henry Weinberg was assigned to investigate the case. He interviewed both Bailey and Brown, but even though the nurse had informed him that for several days Teasdale had been in a state of extreme depression and had repeatedly inquired into the most efficacious and painless methods of committing suicide (a subject which Brown tried to turn the conversation from but which Teasdale, not to be put off, returned to with equal persistence again and again), Weinberg refused to issue a death certificate and ordered the body autopsied at the local morgue. Teasdale's sister, Mrs. Joseph Wheless, also of New York City, conceded that the poet had been "in exceptionally poor spirits,"[12] but maintained that this was due to Teasdale's believing that she was about to have a stroke. The day before her death, Teasdale had summoned Wheless to her apartment and had given her power of attorney over her affairs. Wheless claimed that Teasdale had complained of dangerously high blood pressure and that she feared that she would shortly become incapacitated and thus be unable to attend to her affairs herself. In a statement issued to the press, Weinberg said that, although the evidence presented to him by Brown and Bailey pointed to suicide, he was not convinced that the poet had taken her life. Even if tests proved that Teasdale had died by drowning, he cautioned that it would not necessarily mean that she had committed suicide. He said that Teasdale could have suffered either a stroke or a heart attack. In either case, she would have been rendered unconscious and thus would have drowned accidentally. All doubts vanished, however, with the autopsy. Tests indicated that Teasdale had swallowed a lethal quantity of sleeping tablets before stepping into the tub. She had suffered from chronic insomnia since her childhood and had taken Veronal from the early 1920s until the time of her death.

Sara Teasdale was born August 8, 1884, in St. Louis, Missouri, the daughter of John Warren and Mary Elizabeth Willard Teasdale. The unplanned pregnancy had come late in the couple's marriage. The father was a prosperous wholesaler of nuts and dried fruit whose forbears had distinguished themselves as ministers and jurists. The maternal line was even more illustrious. Elizabeth Teasdale traced her lineage back to Simon Willard, one of the founders of Concord, Massachusetts. Her family tree included a signer of the Declaration of Independence and a president of Harvard University. The Willards, like the Teasdales, had also produced several clergyman of regional, if not wider, repute. The Teasdale home was traditionally Victorian and Sara was brought up to respect religion and morality and to know her place. At an early age, she was taught that marriage and motherhood were in her future. Like Christina Rossetti, Teasdale suffered ill health in her early childhood and youth. Her parents coddled and protected the child of their old age; they always treated her as if she were a piece of rare china or some other costly and fragile bauble, and positively encouraged her in her invalidism. She did not begin attending school until age nine. All the parental attention made Teasdale feel as if she belonged on center stage, that others should wait on her and that she should always receive the utmost consideration. She became self-absorbed and narcissistic at an early age, but she also was painfully shy and retiring, comfortable in her cocoon and insistent upon her privacy. A life-long hypochondriac, Teasdale would make periodic retreats to country inns to refresh herself and would frequently check into private sanitoria such as Cromwell Hall. Prone to colds and sore throats, she would spend an inordinate time bundling herself against the weather before going out of doors. In later life, she would go so far as to claim that she had been born with her outermost layer of skin missing. When queried who told her this, she would disingenuously and quite simply reply, one of her physicians.

Teasdale wrote many poems in the last two years of her life that weren't included in the posthumous collection *Strange Victory* (1933). She also left behind a number of poems from earlier in her career which she never saw fit to print. These verses, in the minds of contemporary critics, constitute some of her very best work. As Teasdale's literary executor, Margaret Conklin scrupulously followed her friend's instruction to publish only the verse which Teasdale had authorized. Forty years later, however, Conklin permitted the publication of the withheld poems—over fifty in all—in *Mirror of the Heart: Poems of Sara Teasdale*, a retrospective compilation of Teasdale's verse issued on the centennial of her birth, August 8, 1984. In her lifetime, Teasdale had either thought the unpublished poems too personal, too raw, and too fraught with emotion to see print or feared that they contained private confidences which might embarrass or humiliate friends. In addition, she thought best to keep certain of her views hidden for decorum's sake. In his introduction to *Mirror of the Heart*, William Drake writes that the unauthorized verse reveals "a more somber and troubled psyche than the tenor of her *Collected Poems* suggests," what he calls "the shadow side"[13] of Teasdale. There are repeated references in the poems dating from the poet's last two years to imaginary physical ailments—she frequently writes of a continually bleeding internal wound, for instance—as well as other indications of mental disturbance.

In the unpublished verse, Teasdale details her desperation and despair and her physical exhaustion. She seems always on edge. One senses that she feels hedged in and pinned down from all sides. Life once again appears inconsequential and without meaning to her and she records violent impulses and thoughts which she no longer tries to check or diminish. In the past she expended her destructive energy in the creation of restrained, sad, yet ravishingly beautiful poems. But now sleep constantly eludes her. She feels worthless and weak and registers her rage and heartache without attempting to dilute or transmute it.

Not only did Teasdale find the poems too revelatory, she probably also thought them half finished, not properly turned or spun. While she believed that all poems resulted from "emotional irritation" and that a poem was "written to free the poet from an emotional burden,"[14] she also felt that the finished poem should be sufficiently detached, that it was the poet's task to transform his or her irritation and vexation into something altogether different, a serene and delicate work of art. "As soon as a thing is nicely arranged in rhyme and meter," she once wrote a friend, "it ceases to bother one."[15] From the first, writing verse had been a sort of therapy for Teasdale.

Many years later, in a letter to a friend, she recalled the genesis of the artistic impulse within her. She wrote that as a young girl, lying in bed but unable to sleep, restless and frightened as she watched sheet lightning illuminate the night sky outside her window and listened to a neighbor boy strumming a mandolin from across the street, she would keep her anxiety and uneasiness in check by telling herself stories. The boy became a "minstrel knight"[16] serenading her. Story and song became her safeguards against the night and she was able to soothe her trepidation. Later she wrote poetry to ward off other demons and to placate intense grief. She celebrated what she saw as the transformative power of art in the early poem "Alchemy":

> I lift my heart as spring lifts up
> A yellow daisy to the rain;
> My heart will be a lovely cup
> Altho' it holds but pain.
>
> For I shall learn flower and leaf
> That color every drop they hold,
> To change the lifeless wine of grief
> To living gold.[17]

As much as she loved her father and mother and as safe and sheltered as they made her feel living in their genteel upper-middle-class household, its pedestrian and excessively moralistic atmosphere eventually became stifling and intolerable for her. Inhibited and deeply dependent on her parents' care and ministrations, she nonetheless continued playing the role of ailing daughter, a pale invalid in the family circle, into her late twenties despite gathering feelings of stagnation and suffocation. She saw her parents grow old and fade, and she was desperately in need of a new caretaker when she finally married at age thirty.

As a young woman, aside from writing poetry which the elder Teasdales considered an innocent enough pastime for their daughter as long as she remembered her true vocation in life was to wed and bear children, Sara did not seek to fashion any sort of independent identity for herself. She had no interest in personal autonomy and suppressed any urge or inclination that would meet with her father's or mother's disapproval. Certain behavior was out of bounds; good girls simply did not do certain things. Sara conformed to class norms and expectations and heeded all society's strictures concerning polite behavior. She bent herself completely to the parental will and played the part expected of her on every occasion. In 1903, she graduated from Hosmer Hall, a private school for girls. Only tasteful books, the milder English classics, were on the reading lists. Teasdale made up for the lapses in her formal education by reading on her own. She was largely self-taught.

Although she would later find St. Louis confining and leave it to reside in the East, the city—a cultural and intellectual Mecca in the Midwest with its museums and theaters, its universities, art schools, and opera houses—offered many portals of discovery for young persons bent on learning and knowledge. Then as today, the city had many different faces. Situated on the National river, St. Louis was one of the country's great hubs and points of junction: it had long been known as the gateway to the West. One could travel in and out by riverboat or rail.

A smoky and grimy industrial giant with immense factories and thousands of belching smokestacks, the city had produced its share of millionaires, and in Teasdale's day it had its established aristocracy as well as its working class and its negroes. Children of the highest rank sought their education in the East but returned home to take over family enterprises. They brought the rest of the world back with them and made sure St. Louis kept culturally up to date. The racially diverse city also had a large German ethnic element. This group's love for music and poetry added greatly to the city's cultural milieu. Teasdale's future husband, Ernst Filsinger, an international trade expert and one time vice-president of the Royal Baking Powder Company, was the descendant of German emigrés. He loved the arts and delighted in his wife's fame as poet.

Of course, St. Louis also had (and still retains) a Midwestern squareness. In Teasdale's day, it was full of Puritans and Sunday-go-to-meeting types eager to swallow the fire and brimstone hurled each Sunday from the local pulpits—flatlanders and philistines and self-righteous know-it-alls who wanted the whole world to be as flat and monotonous as the Missouri horizon. Everyday Midwesterners were too provincial, too smug and set in their ways for Teasdale's taste. She detected such a sameness to them all, yet as a girl growing up in St. Louis she had no difficulty encountering other young women who sought and struggled after cultural refinement, with interests similar to hers in the arts and in faraway, fanciful-seeming places such as New York, Paris, and London.

From 1904 to 1907, Teasdale belonged to the Potters, an informal art society of St. Louis women. Its members wrote, painted, took photographs, and put on plays. Each month they put together a handwritten amateur journal known as *The Potter's Wheel*. Teasdale's family was also sufficiently affluent that Teasdale and her mother could travel abroad. From February to May in 1905, they toured the Holy Land, Egypt, Greece, and Italy as well as Spain, England, and France. At last, Teasdale saw something of the world beyond Missouri. Her first volume, *Sonnets to Duse*, appeared in 1907. Her father footed the printing costs. Although she never saw the actress Eleonora Duse on stage, Teasdale idolized the performer as did all the other young women belonging to the Potters. A self-reliant, independent woman who defied convention and rejected a traditionally domestic life to pursue her art, Duse had also carried on a fiery and well-publicized love affair with the Italian author and soldier Gabriele D'Annunzio. Her purported exploits and adventures made the virginal young Potters sigh and swoon. Tears came to their eyes when they thought of her wounded heart. She had suffered (grandly, oh so grandly) for love, the chiseled features of her lovely face seemed "Carved in the silence by the hand of Pain"[18] just as the Venus de Milo's had been. She was the Sappho of her age.

Teasdale secretly longed for a great romantic experience of her own, but, a recluse and wallflower by nature, for years she remained a spectator at the dance. Duse was all that Teasdale was not. In her own life Teasdale could not breach the rules and edicts of polite society. She curbed herself and appeared to all eyes content to remain the sheltered invalid, an observer of life but not a participant, a model of propriety and stern Victorian maidenhood.

Her poetry shows that she was a deeply conflicted and divided person. It became the one vehicle for self-assertion for an otherwise timorous and self-effacing woman. Not one of poetry's innovators in terms of form, she celebrated great women of literature and history who endured pain and humiliation for love's sake in her second volume, *Helen of Troy and Other Poems* (1911), composing dramatic monologues in blank verse for her tragic heroines. The volume also contains a number of picturesque (though thoroughly predictable) quatrains concerning courtly romance. Louis Untermeyer writes that these early verses suffer from too conscious a cleverness and that they seem written in an altogether too predetermined mood, "the mood of languishing roses, silken balconies, moonlight on guitars, and abstract kisses for unreal Colins."[19] In subsequent books, she settled on the short lyric as her principal form. Her poetry, however, became more subjective and probing.

From 1911 on, Teasdale's verse increasingly reflects her inner longings. She eagerly awaits the great experience of love. She will welcome the incumbent pain that love will invariably bring, for pain is part of love and she therefore must experience it. Someday the beast will spring for her and she will at last be cornered by it. She pines for that hour and in the interim vents her frustration that she is a woman. It is impermissible for her to take matters into her own her hand; a man must initiate courtship. But she is bold and to the point in her verse. In the 1911 poem, "A Maiden," she writes: "Oh if I were the velvet rose/ upon the red rose vine,/I'd climb to touch his window/ And make his casements fine./ . . . But since I am a maiden/ I go with downcast eyes,/ And he will never hear the songs/ That he has turned to sighs."[20]

Teasdale's public demeanor did not change, however. She still abided by all the polite rules. Nonetheless, 1911 proved a pivotal year. Very slowly, she began to emerge from the parental cocoon. She traveled for the first time to New York City to attend a meeting of the Poetry Society of America. She had been proposed for membership the previous year and now attended one of the society's inaugural gatherings. She stayed in the city two months and made important contacts with the publishing world. She also wrote her most forthright poem to date, "Union Square," in which she expressed envy for the freedom and the total lack of inhibition of prostitutes who can "ask for love"[21] while she desperately awaits a suitable suitor. The poem, which appeared in *Helen of Troy*, stood out from the other verse. A reviewer in the *New York Times* wrote, "Has the woman who speaks in the very unusual poem, 'Union Square' been always with us but inarticulate?"[22] Teasdale found a new voice. In her future verse, she spoke more honestly and discarded the romantic clichés and trappings of her earlier poems.

Teasdale returned to her parents' home in St. Louis and set up a shrine to Aphrodite in her study, confiding to a friend, "She is more real to me than the Virgin."[23] No husband, however, appeared in the offing and Teasdale longed to take up permanent residence in New York City. In 1912 she traveled to Europe with Jessie Rittenhouse. Aboard ship, she met a young Englishman, Stafford Hatfield, with whom she was immediately taken. She thought that he resembled Percy Bysshe Shelley in appearance. An astute and clever conversationalist but a reckless and brash individual, Hatfield noticed Teasdale's interest and paid court to her. He tried to get her into bed, but at the last moment, she could not follow her heart's desire. In an unpublished poem, she would write, "Like a coward I turned aside."[24] A few years later, in an essay on H. G. Wells published in *The Little Review*, Teasdale would define what she came to see as the modern woman's dilemma. The problem was certainly her own. "Mary Martha," Teasdale wrote, had the conscience of "a little old Victorian lady." She imagined that she was "perfectly free," but the moment she resolved to take action, her conscience checked her by saying "Stop that right now, I'm ashamed of you."[25] Conscience always had the last word.

In 1913, she fell in love again, this time with the poet John Hall Wheelock. He reciprocated her affection but was not marriage minded. Many of the poems in *Rivers to the Sea* (1915) reflect Teasdale's deep feelings for the life-affirming and sensual Wheelock, who remained a lifelong confidant and understanding friend of Teasdale, but who balked at the prospect of a marital alliance. Ironically, within two years, he became as desperately smitten as Sara. Not with Teasdale, of course, but with another woman. A year after her 1914 marriage, she wrote "The India Wharf" concerning a walk the two had taken. Wheelock always would remain the great what-if of her life, the man with whom she just possibly could have found fulfillment in love: "I always felt we could have taken ship/ And crossed the bright green seas/ To dreaming cities set on sacred streams."[26]

After this second romantic disaster, two of Teasdale's friends, Harriet Monroe and Eunice Tietjens, stepped in as matchmakers and each introduced Teasdale to a possible marriage candidate. Enter Lindsay and Filsinger. Each man had a backer and both proposed. The two could not, however, have been more unlike. Lindsay had great flamboyance and exuberance. He courted in grand style, but was as erratic and unpredictable as Hatfield and could frighten Teasdale as well as make her forget about Wheelock. The most disciplined and straightlaced poetess of the era was serenaded by its most reckless, toe-tapping improvisator. The delicate wallflower, the porcelain vase, came face to face with the swirling tornado and giant giassicus. They both claimed to be apostles of beauty, but their aesthetics were continents, if not worlds, apart. Cross pollination, however, might have benefitted each. Lindsay needed discipline and control, Teasdale to be brought to life and swung off her feet. For all his razzmatazz, Lindsay needed a caretaker every bit as much as Teasdale did. As a marriage prospect he made little sense.

Filsinger, the successful businessman and man of means, seemed like a younger version of her father. He had fallen in love with Teasdale long before they ever met through reading her poems and considered himself a patron of the arts. Wheelock had a love of German culture. After graduating from Harvard, he had continued his studies at the University of Göttingen and Berlin and had told Teasdale how deeply appreciative and understanding, how loving and respectful, the German people could be of their artists. Now a Saint Louis German with similar devotions and sensitivities courted her. Lindsay gave her a year to make up her mind; Filsinger pressed for an immediate engagement. Seeing Filsinger as her last hope, Teasdale made the prudent choice. She told Harriet Monroe that she might be all wrong but she couldn't help it. She did not want to become an old maid.

To others their marriage seemed strong and durable. In public they were always deferential to each other. They held similar views and thought alike. Both were avowed if quiet pacifists during the war. In 1916 Filsinger was able to attach himself to a firm in New York City and Teasdale at last was able to take up residence in the metropolis of her heart.

Teasdale's notion of love was so idealized that she was bound to be disappointed. She would later confess to Wheelock that her honeymoon was a fiasco. Early in their marriage, in a letter to his parents, Filsinger, however, ecstatically sang his bride's praises. She was a "glorious, *womanly* woman—no 'female rights' sort of person. . . . Ever since I knew her she put the duties of true womanhood (motherhood and wifehood) above any art and would I believe rather be the fond mother of a child than the author of the most glorious poem in the language."[27] The couple had no children. In 1975, John Hall Wheelock revealed that Teasdale had become pregnant during the early years of her marriage but decided to abort the child because to raise it, she felt she would have to relinquish poetry. No corroborative medical records have been found, however. William Drake, in his introduction to *Mirror of the Heart*, takes Wheelock at his word. He surmises that Teasdale would have destroyed any intimate letters that would have made reference to the termination and he fixes a probable date for the then illegal procedure on the basis of the following unpublished quatrain scribbled by Teasdale in a notebook in August 1917:

> Fool, do not beat the air
>   With miserable hands—
> The wrong is done, the seed is sown,
>   The evil stands.[28]

A short time later, Teasdale admitted herself to Cromwell Hall in Connecticut. She had spent five months there in 1908 and she stayed almost as long now. According to Drake, she was in "a state of physical weakness and severe emotional depression" for almost a year.

She eventually put the experience behind her. In 1917 she compiled *The Answering Voice: One Hundred Love Lyrics by Women*. She also published *Love Songs*, a collection of old and new poems for which she would win the Columbia

Poetry Prize in 1918. A possibly revelatory poem, "Let It Be Forgotten," appears in her 1920 collection, *Flame and Shadow*:

> Let it be forgotten, as a flower is forgotten,
>   Forgotten as a fire that once was singing gold,
> Let it be forgotten for ever and ever,
>   Time is a kind friend, he will make us old.
>
> If anyone asks, say it was forgotten
>   Long and long ago,
> As a flower, as a fire, as a hushed footfall
>   In a long-forgotten snow.[29]

In the early 1920s, Teasdale's verse begins to show a growing sense of independence and self-reliance. "The Solitary" appeared in *Dark of the Moon*:

> My heart has grown rich with the passing of years,
>   I have less need now than when I was young
> To share myself with every comer,
>   Or shape my thoughts into words with my tongue.
>
> It is one to me that they come or go
>   If I have myself and the drive of my will,
> And strength to climb on a summer night
>   And watch the stars swarm over the hill.
>
> Let them think I love them more than I do,
>   Let them think I care, though I go alone,
> If it lifts their pride what is it to me,
>   Who am self-complete as a flower or a stone.[30]

In the subsequent years of their marriage, Filsinger was frequently abroad. In 1920, Sara sublet their New York apartment and retreated to a hotel in Santa Barbara, California, to write. In later years she would check into country inns throughout the Northeast, sometimes for weeks at a time. With her parents's deaths, her poetry became increasingly autumnal. In 1926, she drew close to Margaret Conklin, a college student who had written to her about her poems. Conklin, Teasdale would later say, became the child she never had. The two began living together in 1927. Teasdale would dedicate the last volume she published in her lifetime—a small collection of verse for children, *Stars To-Night*—to Conklin in 1930. A year before she had flown to Reno, after Filsinger set sail to South Africa on another of his protracted business trips, to sue for divorce on grounds of neglect. The shocked and saddened husband gave her her freedom; she would not see him for two years. The unpublished poems she wrote at this time were particularly violent. She writes of black vultures and hawks sweeping down on prey or circling carrion. Houses catch fire and burn. Sinister figures haunt the night. Her own blood flows as does that of others. Writing, she said, seemed "useless as ashes."[31] In 1930, Teasdale decides to rouse herself from her melancholy by writing a biography of Christina Rossetti and takes two trips to England to do research. Between them, she learns of the death of Vachel Lindsay. She contracts pneumonia on her second trip and returns home grievously ill. Her resultant debility contributes to her increasing disinterest in life. After her suicide, in accordance with a frequently expressed wish, her body is cremated and her ashes are scattered at sea.

Notes

1. Louis Untermeyer, ed., *Modern American Poetry* (New York: Harcourt Brace, 1950), p. 285.

2. Sara Teasdale, "I Shall Not Care," *The Collected Poems of Sara Teasdale* (New York: Macmillan, 1966), p. 54. The poem excerpted here previously appeared in *Rivers to the Sea* (New York: Macmillan, 1915).

3. Ibid.

4. Quoted by William Drake, "Introduction," *Mirror of the Heart: Poems of Sara Teasdale*, ed. with an introduction by William Drake (New York: Macmillan, 1984), p. xxi.

5. Teasdale, "The Wine," *Mirror of the Heart*, p. 39. The poem excerpted here was written in 1917 but did not appear in a Teasdale collection until *Mirror of the Heart*.

6. Teasdale, "In the Web," *Mirror of the Heart*, p. 81. The poem excerpted here was written in 1921 but did not appear in a Teasdale collection until *Mirror of the Heart*.

7. Quoted by William Drake, "Introduction," *Mirror of the Heart*, pp. xxxv–vi.

8. Teasdale, "The Crystal Gazer," *Collected Poems*, p. 179. The poem excerpted here previously appeared in *Flame and Shadow* (New York: Macmillan, 1920).

9. Teasdale, "Epitaph," *Collected Poems*, p. 173. This poem previously appeared in *Dark of the Moon* (New York: Macmillan, 1926).

10. Teasdale, "The Flight," *Collected Poems*, p. 193. This poem previously appeared in *Dark of the Moon*.

11. Quoted by Drake, "Introduction," *Mirror of the Heart*, p. xvii.

12. *New York Times* Obituary, 30 January 1933.

13. Drake, "Introduction," *Mirror of the Heart*, p. xviii.

14. Ibid., p. xix.

15. Ibid.

16. Ibid.

17. Teasdale, "Alchemy," *Collected Poems*, p. 57. This poem previously appeared in *Rivers to the Sea*.

18. Quoted by Drake, "Introduction," *Mirror of the Heart*, p. xxiii.

19. Untermeyer, *Modern American Poetry*, p. 284.

20. Teasdale, "A Maiden," *Collected Poems*, pp. 23–24. The poem excerpted here previously appeared in *Helen of Troy and Other Poems* (New York, Putnam, 1911).

21. Teasdale, "Union Square," *Collected Poems*, p. 31. The poem quoted here previously appeared in *Helen of Troy*.

22. Quoted by Drake, "Introduction," *Mirror of the Heart*, p. xxviii.

23. Ibid.

24. Ibid., p. xxix.

25. Ibid., p. xxxiii.

26. Teasdale, "The India Wharf," *Collected Poems*, p. 54. The poem excerpted here previously appeared in *Rivers to the Sea*.

27. Quoted by Drake, "Introduction," *Mirror of the Heart*, p. xxx.

28. Ibid, p. xxxiii.

29. Teasdale, "Let It Be Forgotten," *Collected Poems*, p. 135. This poem previously appeared in *Flame and Shadow*.

30. Teasdale, "The Solitary," *Collected Poems*, p. 179. This poem previously appeared in *Dark of the Moon*.

31. Quoted by Drake, "Introduction," *Mirror of the Heart*, p. xliii.

Virginia Woolf

ALWAYS INTENT ON PORTRAYING THE FLUX, TRYING TO ILLUSTRATE this existence as "a shower of atoms"[1] by capturing the rhythmic ebb and flow of being, life's unremitting pulse, its often fibrillating beat, Virginia Woolf regretted that the one event she would never secure for posterity by pinning it down in her shimmering, iridescent prose would be the subjective experience of her own death. She did, however, in her diaries, letters, and such occasional pieces as her short essays, "Flying Over London" and "Gas," beautifully describe premonitions of it.

That these passages are awesome and full of magic goes without saying. The radiance and splendor of Woolf's imagery often makes one gasp. It seems that nothing is beyond the power of her pen. Yet, paradoxically, in everything she writes she also always seems to be pushing the envelope further in an attempt to catch something that still constantly eludes her, something that more than likely can never be grasped, at least in this life. Perhaps she wanted death to be beautiful because her existence seemed so hard and sordid, fraught with guilt and self-doubt. She suffered from feelings of inadequacy, feared failure, and was always frightened of critics' response to her work. Death would be not only release and escape but (she hoped) something divinely transcendent.

Like the seasons of the agricultural round, the monthly lunar sequence, or the daily shifting of the tides, Woolf's bouts of madness and subsequent reversions to relative sanity were cyclical. Though she often denied her mental state and refused to believe anything was wrong with her, especially at the commencement of one of her periodic descents into hell, she nonetheless could see that there was repetition and pattern to her attacks. Insanity had previously claimed her elder half-sibling Laura Stephen (unlike Virginia, a granddaughter of W. M. Thackeray), who had to be institutionalized for nearly all of her adult life.

In 1925 Virginia Woolf characterized her life as "amphibious." She was speaking here not of the essential androgyny of the artist, a subject she would elsewhere address, but of her productive, healthy hours spent at her writing desk and of her periods of nervous collapse and exhaustion, when she kept to her bed for days on end. At her lowest points, she found living so ugly, so abhorrent, that she longed for annihilation and—she hoped—apotheosis, since, naturally enough, she romanticized her insane visions. Perhaps she would find the answers—the beauty—in death that she had been unable to find in life. Artistic creation, writing, might be nothing more than a wild goose chase. She had said as much at the conclusion of her novel *Orlando*. Ultimately order could not be brought to chaos, the poem her hero/heroine had been working on for centuries remained unfinished, even though it had finally been published, had won prizes, and had gone into seven editions. Writing did not yield the ultimate secret Woolf was in search of. The thing she could not grasp, that eternally gave her the slip just as she thought it would pop into reach, might possibly be apprehended and collared in death. Expiring she perhaps could embrace it: a notion with which the terminally ill Aldous Huxley, in his quest for spiritual revelation, might well have sympathized.

On March 28, 1941, she was again ready to die. Determined to do away with herself, she left her house in Rodmell after having written two letters—one to her husband, Leonard, the other to the lesbian partner of her middle years and fellow writer, Vita Sackville-West—and strode outside. It was a brisk, chilly morning despite a profusion of sun; she made her way down to the river Ouse with her walking stick. At its bank, she placed several small stones in her coat pocket. They might not be heavy enough to hold a thin, frail, angular old woman down against her will, but Woolf planned to breathe water in through her mouth and nose, as if inhaling some anesthetizing gas. Her death would be gentle. Her lungs would begin to fill with cool water and she would stand on the borderline. This time she would cross it. *As always*, she had ample reason to end her life.

She couldn't read. She couldn't write. She felt she was plunging ever closer toward complete insanity. She heard interior voices as she had during several of her earlier breakdowns, including her second serious collapse following the death of her father, the eminent essayist Sir Leslie Stephen, in 1904. At that time, she made her first attempt on her life by jumping to the ground from an upper window of a friend's house (fortunately not a very high one). Confined to her bed, she heard "birds chirping and singing in Greek" as well as "King Edward VII lurking in the azaleas using the foulest possible language."[2] By 1941 she realized that the voices were only parts of her divided mind. Still she couldn't help but listen as they hotly and even coarsely expounded to one another and ultimately to her. They ranted and agonized—not at all like demure, upper-crust ladies attending a splendid dinner party or some other equally genteel event. Woolf found her interior voices as terrifying as the stalwartly patriotic, often belligerent, male ones she heard every day on the radio in 1941, and had been hearing now for years.

Moreover, all her old doubts and uncertainties had resurfaced full force. As in previous unstable periods, the pendulum would slowly swing out to the furthest possible point and then, when her burden became too great, she would make yet another attempt on her life. Guilt oppressed her. With renewed shame, she felt that she hadn't been a good wife, that she held her husband back, a man whose physical advances she had never been able to fully respond to but with whom she remained on affectionate terms nonetheless.

Certainly she was anything but frigid with Vita, whose body she found ample and perfect. She also esteemed Vita's self-assurance and her genteel, proud bearing. In fact, the usually unresponsive, ice-cold Virginia initiated their famous liaison, playing the part of seductress at Vita's home, Long Barn.[3] She attacked her literary friend on a couch. Writing Woolf about it later, Sackville-West reminisced about an "explosion on the sofa in my room when you behaved so disgracefully and acquired me for ever."[4]

Despite his wife's unfaithfulness and the couple's obvious sexual incompatibility, Leonard stood faithfully by Virginia's side and ministered to all her needs whenever she was ill. He founded the Hogarth Press principally for her. That is not to say he did not have his own numerous warts and character deficiencies. Above and beyond these, he was a man and Virginia Woolf had problems with the whole sex, dating back to early childhood traumas in the nursery. Her nineteen-year-old half-brother George Duckworth began molesting her when she was only six. Virginia would later say that he displayed an inordinate interest in exploring her private parts.[5] Her resentment of men was also exacerbated by the fact that she was denied a formal education, unlike her (to her mind) much less deserving brothers. They had other irritating privileges as well. For example, they were permitted to smoke in Sir Leslie Stephen's home whereas Virginia and her sister were not, as her father's house was not a cheap bar.[6] In later life, Virginia would develop a passion for cheroots.

Her distrust of males went further yet. All violent affinities and inclinations discernible in humanity she found inherently masculine, also everything vulgar and scatological. Leonard's lacks were the same as the rest of his sex. Furthermore, true to a Western stereotype of the Jew, he was always penny-pinching, and Virginia dutifully handed over her pitiful earnings from books and reviewing. Whenever she wanted to make a purchase of any kind, she had to beg and was often refused. The decision in the end lay entirely with him.

Leonard's politics were decidedly left of center. Naturally he felt winning the war against Hitler was better than losing it. Despite her strong pacifist bias, Virginia had to agree. She perceived what was in the works in Germany when she traveled there in 1936, and on her return to England attended meetings of Vigilance, an anti-fascist organization. After hostilities broke out, she foresaw a Nazi victory and was afraid for Leonard's and her own safety. She did not want to see him wearing a yellow star on the lapel of his coat. Her trepidation was justified. Both her and her husband's name were on Josef Goebbels's list of undesirables to be arrested after the successful completion of Operation Sea Lion. Still, a part of her couldn't help despising the men on the radio who actually had the effrontery to champion killing, bombing, and maiming. War was a masculine preoccupation; a German loss would not put an end to the practice. She saw the same hubristic qualities in her countrymen, even in her beloved husband, and she often harangued him bitterly.

Nonetheless, what happened outside in the world perfectly mirrored Woolf's inner turbulence. Everything had gone into disarray or was in the process of unraveling. Entropy had set in. In previous breakdowns she alone had gone to pieces. Now it seemed the whole world was headed for a smash: she and it were fragmenting simultaneously. In the past, when the world situation wasn't nearly so grave, her private anxieties and disturbances had been enough to propel her to try to kill herself several times. According to Quentin Bell, mental illness had struck a full decade before her father's death in 1904. The first attack was occasioned by the death of her mother. While there is no evidence that Woolf thought about killing herself then, her fascination with suicide predated her father's death and her first attempt at suicide. On the day of Queen Victoria's funeral in 1901, for example, she asked Jack Hills, the husband of her half-sister Stella Duckworth, if he thought that she would ever attempt killing herself.[7]

Woolf came very close to succeeding in 1913 during one of her very worst periods of mental deterioration. Married only a year before, Virginia swallowed one hundred grains of Veronal while her husband was out consulting with her doctors. She had been suffering from severe headaches and insomnia. She found where Leonard had hidden the medicine, took a lethal dose, and lay down. Prompt medical intervention saved her life. Her stomach was pumped. Still, she almost died during the night and remained unconscious all the next day. There were probably other unsuccessful suicide attempts as well. Leonard Woolf felt she had made at least one abortive bid to drown herself before March 1941 and had learned what and what not to do from that incident.

Virginia Woolf's attacks of madness had a peculiar pathology all their own. The symptoms were always the same. She would grow very nervous and frightened of people. Her pulse would accelerate and her heart would leap and thump. Restless and agitated, she would sit down but be unable to work. She knew something was wrong; she could detect the transition from one state to the other as one can tell when one is dreaming and when one is awake, but she was unable to help herself.[8] Particularly vulnerable whenever she finished a book, she would worry constantly about its reception. A negative review was not just a judgment about her work, it was a judgment about her. As well as being subject to excruciating headaches and bouts of insomnia, she became obsessed with bodily functions, which she found repulsive in the extreme. Eating was a loathsome and unlady-like act— the process of digestion disgusted her—so she starved herself. Then the voices would come. Her attacks could be very sudden, accompanied by enormous mood shifts. She could be fairly happy then abruptly become very depressed or, even worse, catatonic. Often she would turn sarcastic and malicious, attacking the very people who tried to help her most.

For Virginia Woolf, the Second World War was a continuing nightmare. She believed in nonviolence, and criticized her husband for joining the Local Defense Volunteers and wearing an armband just like the uniformed Nazi Germans. Yet she was under no illusion about the enemy. The fascist mentality horrified her. When hostilities broke out, she decided to devote more of her time to journalism and literary criticism as a sort of patriotic gesture but also to supplement the Woolf family income. She and Leonard traveled back and forth from their new London home in Mecklenburgh Square to Monk House, their residence in the country, where Virginia continued to work on her autobiography of Roger Fry and her novel-in-progress, *Pointz Hall*. The war was going badly. Germany attacked Belgium, Holland, and France. Paris fell, and the British Expeditionary forces were humiliated at Dunkirk. A Nazi invasion of Great Britain looked imminent. Knowing what defeat would entail, Leonard and Virginia made plans. If England was occupied, the Woolfs would commit joint suicide, inhaling carbon monoxide fumes inside their car or overdosing on morphine, a sufficient amount of which was obtained from Virginia's younger brother, the Bloomsbury aesthete Adrian. Despite bleak news from the Continent, Virginia was able to finish her book on Fry, which Leonard criticized severely but which Roger's contemporaries enjoyed, saying that Virginia had brought him back to life for them. For her that was enough. But her "little moment of peace" came "in a yawning hollow."[9] The Battle of Britain began in earnest. Both Virginia's and her sister Vanessa Bell's London homes were demolished in air raids on London. Even Rodmell was subject to Axis bombing. Virginia records the following air attack in her diary:

> They came very close. We lay down under the tree. The sound was like someone sawing in the air just above us. We lay flat on our faces, hands behind head. Don't close your teeth, said L. They seemed to be sawing at something stationary. Bombs shook the windows of my lodge. Will it drop I asked? If so, we shall be broken together. I thought, I think, of nothingness—flatness, my mood being flat. Some fear I suppose. Should we take Mabel to garage. Too risky to cross the garden L. said. Then another came from Newhaven. Hum and saw and buzz all round us. A horse neighed in the marsh. Very sultry. Is it thunder? I said. No guns, said L., from Ringmer, from Charleston way. Then slowly the sound lessened. Mabel in kitchen said the windows shook. Air raid still on: distant planes. . . .[10]

As the battle in the air continued, the prospect for a German invasion diminished. From August 1940 into January of the next year, Virginia remained oddly tranquil.

Bombs still fell regularly and there were food shortages, but Mrs. Woolf found the strength to work. She had no splitting headaches or other distresses. Her appetite was hearty. She wrote a glowing letter of thanks to Vita, who was then living on a farm, for the present of a pound of butter. The lazy routine of country life proved therapeutic. One day would follow another. Order was brought to Virginia's existence. After breakfasting in bed and reading for a while, she would bathe and dress. First speaking to her man-servant Louie about his tasks for the day, she would then go out to her garden lodge, perhaps smoke a cigarette or two, and commence work on *Pointz Hall*. She also began a history of English literature which she provisionally titled *Anon*. She would work to mid-day. After lunch she would take a walk, glance at the papers, pick apples or possibly bake bread. She had tea in the afternoon and went to work on her correspondence. Then she would cook dinner and eat. Afterward she would listen to music on the gramophone or embroider or read until she felt tired enough to retire for the evening.

While writing, she would often stop and contemplate the landscape from her lodge. After an air raid in November, the waters of the Ouse poured over their bank and reached right up into her garden. The swamped meadow attracted birds. The river, it seemed, was stretching out a hand to her.

She remained calm and serene until the middle of January, but slowly deteriorated over the next two months. By March, the situation was critical. Although Virginia denied that anything was wrong with her, Leonard persuaded her to see a doctor on March 27. Octavia Wilberforce was a friend of the Woolfs and tried to help. During the consultation, Virginia admitted that she was frightened her illness would reoccur and that she would not be able to continue writing. Dr. Wilberforce told her to take courage from the fact that she had gotten better in the past. Virginia said she didn't want a rest cure, the doctor advised Leonard against hiring a nurse or otherwise putting his wife under surveillance. It seemed to both Wilberforce and Leonard that the session had done Virginia some good. The very next day, however, she drowned herself, "the one experience," as she said to Sackville-West, "I will never describe."[11]

At one time, Woolf daydreamed about returning with all the answers, realizing, of course, that it was impossible. In the end she wanted enlightenment, illumination, if only for herself. To achieve it, she was once more willing to forego living any longer. Her death would be hers and hers alone. In her writings, however, she left behind a number of intriguing guesses of what the moment of death must be like. One has only to think of the poignant suicides of two of her more famous fictional characters, the shell-shocked war cripple Septimus Warren Smith in *Mrs. Dalloway* or Rhoda, one of the six friends in *The Waves*, who on a trip to Spain, while standing on a precipice overlooking the ocean and mesmerized by the lapping water, leaps to her death.

Woolf's essays are even more revealing. In "Flying Over London," an imaginary plane ride metaphorically becomes the last voyage out, the death journey. At takeoff there is transition from one element to another; earth is exchanged for air. The pilot's head "cased in leather"[12] resembles Charon's. The clouds become "a wet sponge which extinguishes"[13] all. Death appears at the summit of life. Extinction turns into, is, consummation. Perhaps the most amazing attempt to describe what dying might be like in her entire oeuvre, however, is Woolf's description of the apparent and seeming death one experiences after undergoing anesthesia and losing consciousness sitting in a dentist's chair. She writes that going under gas at the hands of a dentist is a common experience that almost everyone in modern times has had. It is impossible to board a train and not see adult faces that have not been to some extent transformed by it. Many have been under several times at least in their lives. The same expression is in all the older people's eyes. The process has aged them. The dentist and his anesthetist "manage the embarkations and disembarkations."[14] They forward the patient from the realm of life into the realm of death, then bring him back. At the outset of the journey, the patient is told to breathe deeply and not to resist:

> With each breath one draws in confusion; one draws in darkness, falling scattering, like a cloud of falling soot flakes. And also one puts out to sea; with every breath one leaves the shore, one cleaves the hot waves of some new sulphurous dark existence in which one flounders without support attended only by strange relics of old memories, elongated, stretched out. . . . And as we plunge deeper and deeper away from shore, we seem to be drawn on in the wake of some fast flying always disappearing black object drawn rapidly ahead of us. We become aware of something we could never see in the other world. . . . All the old certainties become smudged and dispersed, because in comparison with this they are unimportant . . . because one needs to be naked, for this chase, this pursuit; all our most cherished beliefs and certainties and loves become like that. Scudding under a low dark sky we fly on the trail of this truth which, if we could grasp it, we should be for ever illuminated. And we rush faster and faster and the whole world becomes spiral and like wheels and circles about us, pressing closer and closer until it seems by its pressure to force us through a central hole, very narrow through which it hurts us, squeezing us with its pressure on the head, to pass.[15]

Woolf must have expected to undergo something similar to this when she walked into the River Ouse that March morning in 1941. She would take a similar excursion out of herself, hoping at long last to catch the rare moth that had always shunned and evaded her (even if it was she herself who was put under the poison jar and not the insect specimen), hoping to finally kiss the ineffable, to reach the far shore. It would be a voyage of discovery and adventure, and she would be just as bold a pioneer as that first English sailor to cross the Atlantic and put boot heel down on the new continent, the hoped-for paradise of virgin forest. A test pilot, she would board her silver biplane and take flight.

Notes

1. Quoted in *The Reader's Companion to World Literature*, 2nd ed., Lillian Herlands Hornstein, G.D. Percy, Sterling A. Brown, eds. (New York: New American Library, 1973), p. 556.

2. Quoted by Quentin Bell, *Virginia Woolf: A Biography* (New York: Harcourt, Brace and Jovanovich, 1972), p. 94.

3. For more on the Sackville-West affair, see Louise De Salvo, " 'Tinder-and-Flint': Virginia Woolf and Vita Sackville-West," *Significant Others: Creativity and Intimate Partnership*, ed. Whitney Chadwick and Isabelle De Courtivron (New York: Thames and Hudson, 1993), pp. 83–95.

4. Ibid., p. 87.

5. Bell, *Virginia Woolf: A Biography*, p. 46.

6. Ibid., p. 79.

7. Ibid., p. 94.

8. Ibid., p. 243.

9. Quoted by Bell, *Virginia Woolf: A Biography*, pp. 452–53.

10. Ibid., pp. 454–55.

11. Ibid., p. 464.

12. Virginia Woolf, "Flying Over London," *The Captain's Death Bed and Other Essays* (New York: Harcourt, Brace and Jovanovich, 1978), p. 206.

13. Ibid.

14. Woolf, "Gas," *Captain's Death Bed*, p. 219.

15. Ibid., p. 220.

Stefan Zweig

I N HIS CELEBRATED BIOGRAPHY OF MARIE-ANTOINETTE, STEFAN ZWEIG depicted a woman who wore blinders for most of her life, a queen who lived a fairy-tale existence in the palace of the Petit Trianon, quite oblivious to the great tide of history, the monumental and weighty events occurring in the spacious but unstable world outside the immediate purview of her miniature realm, her rococo doll's house in Versailles park (so suitable to her amblyopic mode of being) with its silver-and-red garbed servants; its fawning courtiers and pleasure-seeking and fortune-hunting ladies-in waiting; its artificial grottos and waterfalls; its tiny windmills and graceful pavilions; its amateur theatricals; its horse races and high-stake games of chance; its late night revels; its frequent opportunities to play at courtship, to coquet and trifle amorously with her favorites; and its daily round of appointments, lessons with the dancing and music masters, weekly visits from Monsieur Boehmer the jeweler who held his tray of glittering gewgaws and Madame Bertin the dressmaker and Monsieur Léonard the hairdresser who each concocted new stylish designs, flowing gowns and towering tresses, to titillate and tantalize her and cause her to dip deeper and deeper into the king's exchequer—in short, a charmed and untroubled existence, a life of a thousand-and-one fripperies and superficialities.

At last, however, the tiny domain came under siege; the outer world, France and Europe, could no longer be shut out. The diversions, distractions, and amusements abruptly came to an end, and, as the beautiful façade of her life came crashing down before her, this ordinary woman, this silly goose, had to rouse and bestir herself, to shake off sleep and indolence and open her eyes at long last. In Zweig's estimation, Marie-Antoinette met the challenge, and in the wake of revolution and European war, truly became a queen. At the end of her life, at the time of her trial and execution, circumstances thrust greatness upon her. At her hearing before the Revolutionary Tribunal, she stood up to her accusers and offered a spirited yet dignified defense, often outwitting and embarrassing the brutal and coarse prosecutor who put forth the case against her. She knew that the trial was a mere formality, that she would receive the death sentence and be driven to the Place de la Révolution to mount the scaffold no matter what, but, her eye on posterity, she maintained her composure throughout her ordeal, determined to show a nobility and a reserve of manner befitting her station. Having lifted the cudgels against her enemies, she did not let them drop but engaged the foe to the very end.

No one would accuse Zweig of sharing the faults of frivolity and indolence that he ascribes to Marie-Antoinette—his literary output was not only immense but of such a caliber as to make him the most widely read and translated German writer of his day; moreover, between the wars, he worked tirelessly for the causes of pan-Europeanism and international peace as well as on the behalf of needy and destitute artists everywhere. Nevertheless, it can be argued that, like the French queen, for many years he led—at least materially—a care- and worry-free life and that it took historical cataclysm and world holocaust to stir him not only from his dreams and delusions but also from the personal problems of his own making, and to awaken him to the harsh realities of his time. During the period of his English exile in the late 1930s, blinded by his idealism, by the chimera of a united Europe or "manifold homeland," Zweig covered his eyes to the coming catastrophe. Every bit as myopic as the hummingbird-brained queen, he did not perceive the historical forces at work about him and, much to the chagrin of the European émigré community, refused to denounce National Socialism, but maintained a policy of *Abseitsstehen*, or disengagement, from politics until war at last erupted. Although he expressed misgivings about the rise of Fascism in Italy, he initially thought that the Nazi movement could conceivably be an invigorating and rejuvenating force in post–World War I Germany. Before joining the community of nations, the new Europe, she would have to again feel good about herself. A short period of intense nationalism was necessary and inevitable for Germany after her defeat. Such flag-waving would prove cathartic. Guilt and resentment would thereby be dispelled, and afterward a Germany, once again secure in her national identity, could take her rightful place in the manifold homeland, an equal among equals. Anti-Semitism was a by-product of this surge of patriotism. No doubt, such Jew-baiting would be short-lived.

Jewish himself, Zweig even went so far as to maintain that his people were not entirely innocent and guiltless but had done much to bring about their own victimization. He declared that Jewish involvement and interference in politics was the basis for German anti-Semitism and that Jews should refrain from meddling in European affairs. He vowed not to meddle himself and refused to disparage and censure the leaders of the Reich or their policies in the press. When the Nazis rose to power, Zweig had just entered into a collaboration with the composer Richard Strauss. Strauss turned to Zweig after the death of his librettist of many years, Hugo von Hofmannsthal. He had read Zweig's translation of Ben Jonson's *The Silent Woman* and was so enthralled by it that he contacted Zweig and asked him to prepare a libretto from the play which Zweig agreed to do. The resulting book pleased Strauss to no end. He had once again found a fitting and worthy partner. The score was completed in late 1934. By that time Zweig had established a second residence in London but traveled back and forth between Austria and England until the *Anschluss*. Certain functionaries in the Nazi hierarchy did not wish Zweig to be given credit for the libretto at the work's premiere in 1935, but Strauss insisted that his partner "of undesirable race"[1] receive his due, and Goebbels saw the propaganda value of yielding to Strauss on this occasion. The Nazis were not so intolerant after all. The Germans were patrons of the arts and not dyed-in-the-wool racists. Hitler himself authorized production, and the work was performed twice before being banned. Members of the émigré community were shocked and angered that Zweig had allowed himself to be so used. Even after 1938 and the incorporation of Austria into the greater Reich, when Zweig had taken up permanent residence in England, he refused to condemn Germany, perhaps with a view to the Jews still living in his former homeland. Privately, however, he worked tirelessly on behalf of the displaced and donated considerable sums of money to those less fortunate than himself. Nineteen-thirty-eight was a particularly difficult year for Zweig. With the *Anschluss*, he lost his last remaining German-language publisher. Also that year, his mother died in Vienna and his first wife divorced him. Zweig's marital difficulties were entirely of his own making. During the course of his wedded life, he had always been something of a domestic tyrant, transferring all household duties and responsibilities to his long-suffering wife. When he left for England, he charged her to remain behind in Salzburg to see to the sale of his property there and then to tend his ailing mother in the Austrian capital. Moreover, since 1934, he had been engaged in a love affair with his German refugee secretary, Charlotte Altmann, who was only half his age. This had not been, by any means, his first affair. He had written about his propensity to drift into short-lived liaisons in his most celebrated novella, the thinly disguised "Letter from an Unknown Woman." He did not spare himself in this work. The novelist R. is hopelessly self-centered. An incurable philanderer, he shows little regard for the feelings of the women he seduces and blithely proceeds from affair to affair. He receives a posthumous letter from one of his past conquests (they had slept together on three occasions) and learns not only that he had fathered a son who died shortly before its mother, R.'s former mistress, but just how deeply this forgotten or "unknown" woman had loved him. From her letter, he learns that, for years and years, she had held his image in her heart and had selflessly denied herself in the hopes that he would return to her. He had merely trifled whereas she had loved. Zweig explores the psyche of the abandoned woman with finesse and delicacy. Sympathetic and understanding of women in his fiction, he nonetheless was ruthless and domineering with them in life.

When the Nazis seized Austria, they impounded Zweig's beloved collection of bibliophilic rarities and autographs. The items were subsequently sold. Throughout the Reich, Zweig's books were burned on the bonfires. Nonetheless, he remained silent. Not until the invasion of Poland did he at last publicly denounce the Nazis. A few days later, he and Charlotte Altmann wed. In 1940, the couple became naturalized British citizens, but by then life in England had become unbearable for Zweig. He thought British patriotism as invidious as its German counterpart. The distrust and suspicion directed at the German émigrés by the English infuriated him, and he found British officialism and red tape both labyrinthine and mind-numbing. Papers and travel permits caused him no end of grief. He took strong offense when bureaucratic niceties almost caused him to miss Freud's funeral in London on September 26, 1939. (He was then living in Bath.) At a later date, he became enraged when a train delay occasioned by British mobilization efforts made him late for a London appointment. Such incidents show just how near-sighted and self-absorbed Zweig could be—we see him here at his absolute worst. Zweig's depression deepened with the fall of France. He became convinced that there was now no stopping Hitler, that the whole continent was his to plunder. Feeling that England would fall, Zweig and his young wife crossed the Atlantic and took up residence in the Americas. Having escaped from danger himself, he entered the ranks of the exiles opposing Hitler from across the water, yet in his newfound safety he suffered from a depression as black as that of Henry James at the outbreak of the war to end all wars. No doubt, Zweig felt a measure of personal guilt at the turn of events in Europe and at his previous shortsightedness. He was being feted in America while his brethren were being gassed and burned in the camps. Having witnessed the collapse of everything he so fervently believed in and stood for, the peace movement, the internationalist ideal, the vision of a new Europe without armies and frontiers, Stefan Zweig had undergone both shattering disappointment and total disillusionment. He realized that for years he had put his stock in utopias. The future he had foreseen had proven to be one giant mirage. Clearly civilization was not to have a new dawn, humankind did not have a better or higher nature after all. The European spirit that Zweig had championed for so long, the will to progress and enlightenment, had been supplanted by a new barbarism. Everything had been lost. As John Fowles observes in his introduction to *The Royal Game and Other Stories*, Jill Sutcliffe's 1981 translation of Zweig novellas, history had "jackbooted [Zweig's] dreams into oblivion."[2] Although he took up the cudgels, Zweig did not find the strength to carry on the fight for very long. He came to the conclusion that all further effort was futile. Writers and artists could not serve as mediators between nations. Whereas Marie-Antoinette opposed and resisted her enemies to the end, Zweig did not have the strength to do so. The world had become a place in which he could no longer live. Other members of the émigré community—Thomas Mann for one, who, like Zweig, had been initially slow to declare himself against the Nazis—felt deeply betrayed and hurt by his suicide. They vented their opprobrium, if not in public, then privately among themselves. To take one's life at such an hour, they whispered, displayed inner weakness and utter selfishness. It was the obligation of the refugees to stand their ground and fight the good fight—not only to oppose but to *outlast* Naziism. Shining examples of European—and more particularly German—artistic achievement, the exiles lent the importance and weight of their names to the fight against fascism in order to set an example and high road for others to follow and to play, in light of their undeniable aesthetic accomplishments, the very public roles of special envoys and cultural ambassadors from war-torn Europe to the New World, to the Goliath across the water, the United States, in particular. Zweig's suicide seemed sadly mistimed, for in February 1942, when he and his second wife, Charlotte Altmann, chose death rather than perseverance and endurance in the cause of human liberty—when they, so to speak, gave up the struggle— the tide had already begun to turn against the enemies of democracy and civilization. At long last, the United States had entered the war against the Axis. The decisive battle at Alamein was not far off. More losses would have to be suffered; many lives would still have to be sacrificed, but the Allies would soon have the offensive and, with America's entry into the war, they would eventually win the final victory. Zweig's death completely shocked the émigré community because the role of cultural ambassador seemed tailor-made for him. A life-long internationalist and world traveler, he had always styled himself as the "good European," a type that the chauvinistic, saber-waving Thomas Mann of the First World War had contemptuously referred to as civilization's literary man or belletrist, enemy of *Kultur*, music, metaphysical speculation, and native German inwardness. Furthermore, in his single novel, the allegorical *Beware of Pity* (1939), in which he himself is a character, Zweig warned against the dangers of weakness and appeasement. The novel opens in Vienna in 1937. In a café and then subsequently at a social event at a private residence, Zweig encounters Captain Anton Hofmiller who had served in the First World War, first with the cavalry in the "——th Regiment of Imperial Uhlans,"[3] then in the air corps where, on an observation flight over the Piave, he single-handedly shot down three enemy planes, and finally with a machine gun company. Leading his fellow machine-gunners on the battlefield, he had occupied and held for a period of three days a sector of the front. For his services to his country, Hofmiller had been awarded the Order of Maria Theresa by the Emperor Charles—"the most rare of all decorations in the Austrian army."[4] At the party, the guests are talking about the possibility of another world war. The host, a distinguished lawyer, argues that the people could not be tricked by the politicians a second time; not only is war not imminent, it will never come. Zweig protests. While the guests assembled at the lawyer's that evening had been "befuddling (themselves) with Utopias," the ministries and military authorities "had taken full advantage of the interval of peace in order to organize the masses in advance and have them ready to hand, at halfcock. . . ."[5] Factories were turning out munitions at a furious rate and propagandists were employing their craft to instill servility in the masses so that "when the news of mobilization came hurtling through the loud-speakers no opposition could be looked for from any quarter."[6] No one at the party agrees with Zweig, with the sole exception of Captain Hofmiller. Soldiers become automatons, the latter states. They obey their orders without thinking, and the only courage in war, he says, is mass or herd courage. As he and Zweig leave the party, Hofmiller disparages himself. By no means is he a heroic character; his actions on the battlefield were those of a machine. He considers himself unworthy of the Order of Maria Theresa and proceeds to relate an instance of great cowardice on his part. In the months prior to World War I, he had both a military and a social life and as an individual felt strangely bifurcated. On one hand he belonged to the Austrian military caste and had pledged to abide by its special code of honor. There was a special fraternity between him and his fellow officers. They always addressed each other, even if not personally acquainted, in the familiar second person singular *Du* instead of the formal second person plural *Sie*. The men lived by a special code. To breach its unwritten rules of behavior would be unpardonable. At the same time as a private person, Hofmiller had gained entrance into the highest ranks of Austrian society and was befriended by the wealthy Herr von Kekesfalva. When he learned that the old man's crippled daughter Edith had fallen in love with him, out of pity for her impairment and fear for both her physical health and mental well-being, he unthinkingly agreed to an engagement with her, and suddenly his two spheres came into conflict. Immediately he feared his comrades' reactions to his proposal. They would conclude that he was marrying for money and thus not acting like a meritorious officer but doing dishonor to his regiment. Another officer, Balinkay, had done precisely that, and his comrades had never forgiven him. They sneered that he had sold himself to an old Dutch cow. Furthermore, Hofmiller discovered than von Kekesfalva was not really an aristocrat but a masquerading Jew, the former Leopold Kanitz, and thus his intended was not only a cripple on crutches, but a half-Jewess as well. When word of his engagement at last reached his regiment, Hofmiller vigorously denied the news. His disavowal ultimately led to the girl's suicide and the breaking of her father's heart. Zweig writes that there are two kinds of pity: "the weak and sentimental kind, which is really no more than the heart's impatience to be rid as quickly as possible of the painful emotion aroused by the sight of another's unhappiness" and the "kind that counts . . . which knows what it is about and is determined to hold out, in patience and forbearance, to the very limit of its strength and even beyond."[7] Zweig urged his readers in 1939 not to give into weakness but to persevere and to overcome. By 1942, he, too, was unable to persist any longer. He saw himself not as a diplomat but a wandering Jew and a man without a country.

Born in Vienna on November 28, 1882, Stefan Zweig came from a long line of industrialists and bankers. His forbears had found their way to Austria from Bohemia, Moravia, and Italy. There, the family had become large and prosperous. Its branches extended all across Europe by the mid-nineteenth century. Members of the clan transacted business and accrued wealth from various bases in several nations. At the time of his birth, Zweig's father had already made millions in textiles. His mother was a well-known socialite. The Austrian line of the Zweigs had become assimilated generations before. They practiced their religion quietly and, Zweig would later say, with no real zeal. He would eventually come to criticize his parents for this racial and religious indifference, but for most of his life would himself exhibit the same apathy and disinterest, inculcated, as he was from early youth, not to assert his Jewishness but to integrate and adapt as best he could into mainstream Austrian society. If the Zweigs put on airs, these had a decisively European flavor. Certain members of the family pranked in the manner of aristocrats. These individuals saw themselves as high-born bluebloods and, although Jewish, acted in a fashion that would make one think that their lineage could be found in the *Almanac de Gotha* instead. Not of noble birth, they nonetheless had money, estates, and property. Moreover, with all its branches, their family was now as far-flung as any European royal house. The Austrians had relatives and associates in a number of other nations. Three languages—German, French, and English—were spoken in Stefan's parental home. Such a cosmopolitan atmosphere no doubt contributed to Zweig's future internationalist outlook. He benefited from his parent's largesse and spent his first thirty years in the lap of luxury. Due to the fact that he was not his father's first-born son and therefore under no obligation to succeed him as the head of the family business, Stefan could pursue literature not as an avocation but as a calling and career. His father even encouraged him in this direction. If successful, Stefan would bring credit to the family by demonstrating that the Zweigs could be just as successful in the world of art and culture as they had previously been in the spheres of business and commerce. Doors opened and obstacles were cleared for Zweig due to his family's connections and great wealth. He received an excellent and expensive education. Before he finished his university studies in Berlin and Vienna, he had already published two collections of verse. During the first decade of his literary career, he traveled across Europe, seeking and obtaining introductions to the leading writers of the day. To further develop his *Weltperspektive*, he also embarked on long *Auslandsreisen* to India, Africa, and America. An unabashed Francophile, during his apprenticeship years as a writer, he fell under the influence of the internationalist poet Emile Verhaeren and the French novelist Romain Rolland, though he did not subscribe to the former's Marxist views. He set himself up as an authority and exponent of French literature to the German-reading public, completing his first biography, a life of Verlaine, in 1902. From the very outset of his career, Zweig was professing the idea of a Europe without borders and preaching the internationalist ideal.

When war came in August 1914, Zweig's beliefs and convictions were put to the test. Initially, he experienced a surge of patriotism and, despite his Francophile literary tastes, put on an Austrian uniform and worked briefly as a propaganda clerk. His ardor, however, was short-lived. Before the year ended he completed his anti-war play *Jeremiah*, based on the life of the Old Testament prophet. The work would be his first public acknowledgment of his Jewish roots. In the play, Zweig argues that a seer and oracle is always misunderstood and persecuted by his own people. Zweig's Jeremiah makes the case for peace, but his message is ignored by those who hear it. Zweig took the manuscript of the play with him when he crossed the border into Switzerland in 1917 and went into his first exile. Authors and pacifists from numerous nations had gathered there, and Zweig saw a working model in the tiny country—multilingual, peace-loving, and tolerant—for the future Europe. Returning to Austria after the war and settling in Salzburg in 1919, Zweig determined to redouble his efforts in behalf of the internationalist cause. To his great regret, he learned that his old master Verhaeren had lost faith in humankind because of the war (much as Zweig himself would during World War II); but he himself was convinced Europe would have a new dawn, that she was about to experience a great Renaissance. That year he also wed Friderika von Winternitz, with whom he had been carrying on an affair since before the war. Unhappily married but mother to two daughters, Winternitz had had difficulties in obtaining a divorce and keeping custody of her children. Obstacles and complications kept arising to prevent her and Zweig from tying the knot. When he returned from his self-imposed exile, these were at last overcome. The following decade and a half would prove to be Zweig's most fertile period when his readership would mushroom and his popularity soar. His works would be translated into many languages, and he would reach a worldwide audience. Convinced that a new and better world would arise phoenix-like from the ashes of the great disaster that was World War I, Zweig strove to help the process along. Much of his writing had a pedagogic thrust: he would diagnose the societal ills of his age as well as air his personal fears and private anxieties in essays and treatises as well as in certain of his novellas, among them "Angst," "The Flight to God," and "Confusion of Feelings." Although these works hint at the despair that would eventually come to kill him, at the time of their composition, Zweig remained basically hopeful and optimistic in his outlook, maintaining that once a societal danger had been defined—that there is a confusion and loss of values, a deterioration of the soul, in modern times, for example— or a personal weakness confronted—I am prone to unreasonable dread—a solution could be found, the societal ill corrected, and individual debility conquered and overcome. Other of the novellas weren't nearly so didactic. Zweig's early stories, "The Burning Secret" among them (which reflects his difficult relationship with his mother), treat the problems of childhood. Later works, most notably the novellas comprising *Amok: Tales of Violent Feelings*, Zweig's hugely successful 1922 collection, deal with the intense passions of adults and feature sensational or torrid themes, many of a provocative, sexual nature. His most famous story, "Letter from an Unknown Woman," appeared in this volume. In such works, Zweig attempted to unmask bourgeois hypocrisy and investigate the churning whirlpools of libidinous desire. His psychological insight was praised by the critics; his novellas were regarded as both bold and highly illuminating. Zweig himself, however, thought his non-fiction much more important than his tales. Here, he could truly indulge his pedagogical proclivities. Through a series of biographies, he sought to introduce important figures of European history, of diverse nationalities, to his reading public. Each of his subjects was chosen to illustrate a special aspect or national side of the European character. They include the French writers Emile Verhaeren, Romain Rolland, and Marceline Desbordes-Valmore; two queens, Marie-Antoinette and Mary Stuart; the time-serving politician Joseph Fouche, and the enigmatic Dutch scholar Erasmus. The last biography, a work of full maturity, is considered by many critics to be Zweig's best. In Erasmus, Zweig discovered a kindred soul. He uses the biographical form to set down what amounts to his philosophy of life. In addition to the lengthy biographies, Zweig wrote shorter studies— meditative essays and miniature portraits —of other consequential persons. *Three Masters* contains accounts of the lives of Balzac, Dickens, and Dostoevski; *Struggles with the Demon*, essays concerning Hölderlin, Nietzsche, and Kleist; and *Adepts in Self-Portraiture*, depictions of Casanova, Stendhal, and Tolstoy. *Mental Healers* (1931) deals with the scientific advances of Franz Mesmer, Sigmund Freud, and Mary Baker Eddy. In addition to his biographical writings, Zweig recreated twelve important moments in history in *Sternstunden der Menschheit* (*Tide of Fortune*, 1927). He also found time to write plays and poetry and to translate the works of others as well as write countless commemorative essays and treatises on Pan-Europeanism. He attracted many noteworthy and consequential readers throughout the 1920s. Toscanini, Schweizer, Freud, Einstein, Carl Zuckmayer, Richard Friedenthal, Bruno Walter, and Thomas Mann all extolled his work. Even Hermann Göring was a devoted reader.

Zweig would experience another period of notoriety—again becoming a hot property, so to speak—upon his arrival in the United States in 1940. *Beware of Pity* had created a stir the previous year and two of his plays, *Volpone* and *Jeremiah*, had been produced on the New York stage by the Theatre Guild. *Jeremiah*'s plea for peace did not fall on deaf ears in February 1939, but the news from Europe was so bleak that Zweig showed no signs of his youthful idealism. The prophet had begun to doubt his own message of passivity and compassion. Still, disillusioned as he was, he made no effort to repudiate it. The words of the play might ring hollow, but Stefan Zweig would never preach the gospel of violence—even when he came to believe that he was witnessing the end of civilization. He did not stay in the States very long but departed on a lecture tour to South America. He would return to New York in 1941 for a reunion with his first wife, Friderika, and his two stepdaughters, who had managed to escape from France. Zweig did not find the New York émigré world congenial, and in August he and Lotte headed south once more. They rented a home in Petropolis, Brazil, near Rio de Janeiro, where Zweig spent his last months writing. Although he claimed his skills had atrophied, he produced some of his finest work during this time. The people of Brazil afforded him a gracious, even ecstatic, reception. He had access to private libraries and received invitations to countless social and diplomatic functions, yet he also found the solitude which was necessary for his work. When he did appear in public, however, he was greeted as a celebrity. On February 16, 1942, the Zweigs attended Rio's world-famous carnival, but the following day, they learned of the fall of Singapore and immediately returned to Petropolis. Having decided to enter a suicide pact with one another, for five days they prepared. After seeing that their affairs were in order and having written a number of letters to various of their friends, they each ingested a gigantic dose of Veronal the night of February 22 or early in the morning of February 23. Sometime after 4:00 P.M. the following afternoon, the police were called. A servant had knocked on the couple's bedroom door several times during the day but had received no response. At last, he informed the Zweigs' neighbors. They summoned the authorities who proceeded to break into the room. The two bodies lay on the bed. The couple had died in each other's arms. Two empty glasses sat on the bedside table. The room was in perfect order. Among the many letters was the following note addressed to Senator Claudio de Souza, president of the P.E.N. Club of Brazil:

> Before I depart from this life, of my own free will and with a clear mind, I want urgently to fulfil one last duty: I want to give heartfelt thanks to this wonderful country of Brazil which has been for me and my work so good and hospitable a resting place.
>
> Every day I have learned to love this country better, and nowhere would I more gladly have rebuilt my life all over again, now that the world of my native tongue has perished for me and Europe, my spiritual home, is destroying itself. But one would need special powers to begin completely afresh when one has passed one's sixtieth year. And mine have been exhausted by long years of homeless wandering. It seems to me therefore better to put an end, in good time and without humiliation, to a life in which intellectual work has always been an unmixed joy and personal freedom earth's most precious possession.
>
> I greet all my friends! May they live to see the dawn after the long night is over! I, all too impatient, am going on alone.
>
> Stefan Zweig.
Petropolis.
22.2.1942[8]

Brazil's President Getulio Vargas ordered the Zweigs' burial expenses be paid by the government, and he was one of hundreds of Brazilian dignitaries who visited the home to view the bodies as they lay in state.

A few weeks prior to his death, Zweig completed his autobiography, *The World of Yesterday*. The day before his suicide, his American publisher, Viking Press, published *Amerigo: A Comedy of Errors in History*, an inquiry into Vespucci's supposed discovery of America. At the time of his death, Zweig was working simultaneously on several projects, including an expanded biography of Balzac. It appeared posthumously in 1946.

The last decade of his life Stefan Zweig continued to produce work at a phenomenal pace. In *The Right of Heresy: Castellio Against Calvin*, he attacked Protestantism, depicting the anti-Semitism of Luther, Knox, and Calvin. He returned to Old Testament themes in a series of novellas, including "The Buried Candelabrum," a tale of Benjamin, and the powerful "Rachel Arraigns God," a heartfelt indictment of the deity for permitting such unbearable human suffering in the world. Although first published separately, the novellas would be issued together as *Biblical Legends* following Zweig's death. Two other late works of note are *Conqueror of the Sea* (1938), a biography of Magellan, and *Brazil: Land of the Future* (1941).

During the last four months of his life, Zweig wrote one final novelette, *Schachnovelle* or "The Royal Game," which would reach print in 1944. Many critics regard the story as his finest fiction. The novella concerns a chess match pitting Dr. B., an Austrian expatriate who only a short time before had been interrogated and tortured by the Gestapo, against Mirko Czentovic, the conceited world chess champion—a symbol of fascist inhumanity and ruthlessness. Dr. B. had learned how to play chess while he was incarcerated by the Germans. By playing imaginary games against himself in his head, he managed to survive his imprisonment. In his tournament with Czentovic, he takes the first game but has to discontinue play in the second due to mental exhaustion. Zweig concludes that refined sensitivity and benevolent humanitarianism cannot prevail against obstinate persistence and savage intention. The story reflects his own defeat.

Notes

1. Quoted by John Fowles, "Introduction," *The Royal Game and Other Stories*, trans. Jill Sutcliffe (New York: Harmony Books, 1981), p. xi.

2. Ibid., p. viii.

3. Stefan Zweig, *Beware of Pity*, trans. Phyllis and Trevor Blewitt (Evanston, Ill.: Northwestern University Press, 1996), p. 1.

4. Ibid., p. ix.

5. Ibid., p. x.

6. Ibid., p. xi.

7. Ibid., p. vi.

8. Quoted by Elizabeth Allday, *Stefan Zweig: A Critical Biography* (Chicago: J. Philip O'Hara, 1972), p. 238.

Adolf Hitler

ADOLF HITLER'S *MEIN KAMPF* SOLD THOUSANDS AND THOUSANDS OF copies in Germany but was scarcely read. His appeal to the masses had little to do with his turgid prose. Rather, his genius was for oratory and stagecraft. He hypnotized an entire nation with his political addresses. Those who managed to wade through Hitler's book were more than adequately warned. Chillingly he laid out all his plans for genocide and world conquest in this combination autobiography and political testament. Hitler had begun the work in 1922 but had put it aside almost immediately and did not take it up again until his imprisonment in 1924. Sentenced to five years' incarceration for his part in the failed November 1923 *putsch* in Munich, the revolt he and his minions had organized in collaboration with World War I General Erich von Ludendorff, Hitler recommenced dictating the story of his life after entering the prison at Landsberg am Lech.

The botched *coup d'état* had been put down by Bavarian authorities after only a single day. In the great hall of the Burgerbraukeller on the evening of November 8, 1923, the future Führer of Germany announced the start of his revolution and proclaimed his ascension to power after his steel-helmeted storm troopers seized the building. The three thousand people gathered there swigged from their beer steins as Hitler and his clique decided upon government appointments in a back room. The following day, at 11:00 A.M., some fifteen hours after he declared the formation of the provisional government, Hitler issued orders for his National Socialist troops to march into the heart of Munich. He and Ludendorff led the motley procession of private armies, veterans' groups, and rank-and-file party members. The marchers headed for the War Ministry which had already been occupied by Ernst Roehm's Reich War Flag Group, a paramilitary organization of

right-wing extremists which had allied itself to the Hitler-Ludendorff coalition. The
Bavarian authorities had resolved to prevent this linkup at all costs. Without any
great difficulty, however, the procession passed through several police cordons.
The police could not bring themselves to fire on General Ludendorff or else they
were simply swept aside by the Nazis, overwhelmed by their greater numbers.
However, when the National Socialists turned into the narrow Residenzstrasse, a
security force of Green Police led by Freiherr von Godin awaited them. Godin
ordered his men to fire into the ground. The bullets ricocheted from the granite
cobbles and the walls of houses. Splinters and shavings from the paving stones also
went flying into the air. Many of the oncoming Nazis collapsed to the ground, their
bodies pierced by lead or stone. The people in the front rows were mostly spared.
The ricocheting bullets rained down behind them, on the fourth and fifth columns.
Hitler's troops began to break ranks and pandemonium quickly ensued. Some of
the men turned tail and fought their way down the street through the rows of men
marching behind them. Others kicked in the doors of the houses and shops lining
the street to take refuge inside. Still others gained entrance to these buildings by
way of their windows. Ludendorff walked through the police barrier and was taken
into custody. Hitler, who had fallen and dislocated his shoulder in the opening seconds of the melee, fled to the home of his friend Ernst Hanfstaengl in the village of
Uffing. A bodyguard had thrown himself over Hitler's body. Several shots meant for
his master were taken by him—or so National Socialist historians would later
claim. Managing to crawl on his hands and knees through the crowd, Hitler made
his way to Max-Josephplatz where an automobile and driver awaited him. Nazi propagandists maintained that Hitler rescued a wounded boy he saw lying in the
streets just prior to escaping in the car. Despite his injured arm, he supposedly
hoisted the boy off the ground and into the automobile. A policeman tried to club
the youth—or so the story goes—but Hitler protected the boy, using his own body
as a human shield. The driver of the automobile tramped on the gas pedal, but a
green-and-yellow armored car full of machine-gun toting soldiers gave pursuit. The
driver would give the soldiers the slip by turning down a side street.

By the time the car reached the Hanfstaengls', Hitler had become delusional and
incoherent. Ernst Hanfstaengl was not at home, but his pregnant wife welcomed
Hitler into the house in his stead. He stayed in an attic bedroom that night but was
in great pain due to his shoulder. He slept hardly at all, and, the following morning,
in Frau Hanfstaengl's presence, he drew his revolver from his holster and threatened
suicide. He had failed. His career as a politician was at an end, but he would not give
his enemies the satisfaction of capturing him. Death would be preferable to that.
Before Hitler could fire, Frau Hanfstaengl took hold of the barrel of the gun and
wrenched the weapon from his hand. She would later hide it in a tub of flour. Hitler
remained morose throughout the day. He felt that he would certainly be taken, perhaps even summarily executed, so he penned his will and chose his successor as
leader of the party. Hitler spent a second night in the attic, but on the following

evening, two trucks full of Green Police rolled to a stop in front of the Hanfstaengl residence. Hitler ran down the stairway, in one of his towering rages, shortly after a lieutenant and two policemen had been admitted to the house. Ranting and spewing obscenities, he declared himself to be the destined savior of Germany and berated the men for standing in his way. Their actions, he said, would cause the ruination of the country. The officers apprehended him and drove the screaming Hitler away into the night.

How different history might have been had Frau Hanfstaengl not been on hand to intervene when Hitler drew his gun to shoot himself in 1923. That, however, was not the first time he contemplated suicide. According to the friend of his adolescence, August Kubizek, Hitler had become infatuated with a young woman named Stefanie whom he had seen walking along the Landstrasse in Linz in 1906. Hitler told Kubizek that Stefanie was a superior individual like himself. He boasted that whenever she came in close proximity to him, she would recognize his presence— his worth—immediately and that he would not have to utter a single word. Not only would she be irresistibly drawn to him, she'd be able to understand and share his innermost thoughts and dreams, for such exceptional individuals, as they both obviously were, could communicate with each other telepathically. Hitler felt sure his own unspoken messages, or rather his suggestions and commands, could shoot across great distances and through all sorts of impediments and barriers; that he could infiltrate the minds of others and bend them to his will. Yet exert himself as he might, he could not commune with Stefanie. She would not even look into his eyes and exchange glances with him. Hitler became insanely jealous when he learned that she was being courted by an army lieutenant and that she regularly frequented balls, escorted there not only by her favorite but by other beaus as well. Kubizek advised his friend to take matters into his own hands and step forward and introduce himself, but Hitler refused to adopt this simple expedient. He felt that either she or her mother would question him about his profession. He could not yet claim to be a successful painter. Perhaps he could approach her after completing a four-year course of study at the Academy of Art in Vienna. He had not, however, even taken—much less passed—the entrance exam. Therefore, for Hitler, Stefanie remained unreachable, a picture of perfection to be admired only from afar. Perhaps he might kidnap her. Surely she would come to love him once she got to know Hitler. He sounded out Kubizek, who reminded him that he had nothing to live on, that he could not support Stefanie. Plunging into despair, Hitler told Kubizek that he would certainly drown himself as a result of Stefanie's rejection. Stefanie was not Jewish. Her surname, however, was suspicious, one common among both Jews and Aryans, yet Hitler at that time had not yet adopted his gospel of hate, as evidenced by his respect and high regard for his mother's Jewish physician, Dr. Eduard Block. After Klara Hitler's death a year later in December 1907, Hitler would call on Block and tell him that he would be grateful forever for all that he had done for his mother.

In June 1905, two years after the death of her husband, Frau Hitler had moved her little family to Linz after selling their house in the village of Leonding. Adolf loved the city. The two and a half years he spent there prior to his mother's death were among the happiest of his life despite the fact that his passion for Stefanie and the fact that she took no notice of him, preferring the company of her young lieutenant, almost sent him leaping into the Danube. He read deep into the night and rose sometime toward midday. His small room was cluttered with sketchbooks and the trappings and equipment of a painter, for young Adolf had already determined his life vocation. He was going to become a great artist. His talent, however, would not just be limited to drawing and painting. He had grandiose illusions about conquering all the arts. He saw himself as a master architect, a great painter, a magnificent poet, an important philosopher, and an extraordinary and glorious composer all rolled into one. Hitler attended the Linz Opera House on a regular basis and his infatuation with the musical dramas of Richard Wagner began when he heard a performance of *Rienzi*. According to Kubizek, the music so entranced him that after the performance, despite its being very cold, Hitler insisted on a long walk. He strode out of the city with Kubizek in tow, and together they climbed the Freinberg, a small mountain on the outskirts of Linz. Once they reached the top, Hitler told his friend that, like the hero of the opera, he would one day liberate his people from the chains of their servitude. Hitler's confession startled Kubizek, who thought that his friend had no greater goal than becoming an artist: "Now he aspired to something higher, something I could not yet fully understand. All this surprised me, because the vocation of artist was the highest of all goals, the one most worth striving for. But now he was speaking of a mandate he would one day receive from the people...."[1] If Kubizek's story is to be believed, and Hitler's political calling came at such an early date, the young man quickly forsook such dreams and fancies in favor of his older goal of becoming some sort of comprehensive or universal artist, a genius unrestricted in range and versatility, who could cross the boundaries of the separate arts and work in each with equal facility.

Apparently Hitler harbored such fantastic and unrealistic expectations about himself even before he heard the music of Richard Wagner. Indeed, from time to time, such multifaceted geniuses have appeared on the face of the earth. One thinks of Leonardo da Vinci, Michelangelo, and Johann Wolfgang von Goethe. While Michelangelo's knowledge of anatomy undoubtedly had a positive effect upon his art, and while his paintings betray his true identity as a sculptor (he always thought of himself primarily as a worker in marble), he never confused his pursuits but wore his various caps—sculptor, painter, architect, and poet—one at a time. He turned his many-sided genius in a variety of directions but, for the most part, did not try to integrate or unite his efforts, or in other words create the *Gesamtkunstwerk* or "work of total art," a new form or genre in which all the individual arts would combine and crystallize, a crossbreed which would make each of the separate arts uninteresting by comparison. Nor did the two other versatile geniuses mentioned above attempt any such grand-scale fusion of their diverse undertakings. The digging of the Martesana canal had little to do with the painting of *The Last Supper*. Nor did Leonardo's scientific experimentation affect his endeavors as a musician. They were discrete activities, separately pursued. In later life, Goethe even came to the conclusion that polymaths such as himself were rather rare phenomena. While he might strive in a variety of directions and succeed in each, others had best apply themselves to but a single course.

Goethe's change of thinking is reflected in his last novel, *Wilhelm Meister's Journeyman Years*, where he seems to repudiate the very pedagogic principles he espoused with such conviction in his earlier *Wilhelm Meister's Apprenticeship*, to which the *Journeyman Years* serves as a sequel. In the first book, Wilhelm wavers and hesitates about his destiny and the role he is to play in the world. Like Hamlet, he cannot come to a quick conclusion, thus he grows and develops in a variety of directions. He tries his hand at a number of professions, switching roles with actor-like ease; he cannot make up his mind which part suits him best. As a result of all his experimentation, he receives what amounts to a "liberal education" and gradually becomes a well-rounded, multi-faceted individual. In the *Journeyman Years*, however, Goethe argues against such a prolonged and unfocused apprenticeship. He concludes that it is better for a person to master a single skill and not to unnecessarily divide himself. As the novel opens, Wilhelm essays to educate his son Felix in a manner consistent with his broad-minded views, but by midpoint in the book he turns the boy's schooling and training over to the master educators of the Pedagogic Province, who provide rigid structure and organization and direct the child's education toward a specific goal. As the novel concludes, Wilhelm himself even settles on a trade. Instead of actor, merchant, stage manager, poet, or world educator, he will become a surgeon. He will have a practical skill from which society can at last reap benefit. Perhaps from observing the pathetic efforts of his own son August to establish an identity for himself, Goethe belatedly recognized the danger an average man faced when he spread himself too thin. Jack of all trades, after all, is master of none. Goethe certainly did not want to breed dilettanti, and what was the young Hitler if not a dilettante?

In Linz and, later, Vienna, Hitler tried his hand at each of the arts, but he never made steady progress in any direction. In his mind he'd undertake one massive creative project—such as redesigning the entire city of Linz—only to abandon it after several days for something else equally improbable. According to Kubizek, after taking up permanent residence in Vienna in February 1908, Hitler drew up plans for the construction of a new metropolis there as well. Large portions of the old city would perforce have to be torn down. Hitler laid out broad squares and exalted avenues. He envisioned huge apartment complexes, where the workers of the future could be housed cheaply. According to Kubizek, he was always demolishing some building or section of an existing city in his mind and then redesigning a replacement. One chimerical scheme would follow another in rapid succession. Once Hitler

thought about arranging a traveling orchestra that would visit all the small towns and
hamlets in Austria, as he felt that it was unjust that only the big cities could afford
orchestras. He even went so far as to plan programs and draw up rehearsal schedules. When such an improbable idea came to Hitler, for a time, he would act as if
electrified. He'd throw himself completely into a project for a brief interval, but
would overtax himself, then quickly lose interest in the activity. He lacked the discipline to bring any major endeavor to a successful conclusion and he was so impulsive that he would frequently drop an undertaking he had only just begun in favor
of another. Through his reading, he gained a broad knowledge of architecture and
he did possess an above-average skill at drawing (though he had difficulty with perspective and proportion). In Linz he was always sketching something. He had a special talent for architectural drawing but was also adept at caricature and cartoon. He
painted watercolors of still life and country landscapes, but was less successful here
than in his architectural designs. The latter were often bold (some might say
overblown) in concept, yet the quality of his sketching was always erratic. It could
be lackluster and substandard or it could be surprisingly well executed. Hitler could
never tell the difference. He lacked the necessary critical faculty to separate the
wheat from the chaff. On his jaunts through Linz, he carried a black notebook in
which he scribbled poems as well as made sketches and designed buildings to be
erected at some future date. He would dedicate a large portion of this juvenile verse
to Stefanie, and he depicted her constantly in the poems. According to Kubizek, she
would appear clad in a blue velvet mantle riding a white horse over some verdant
meadow, her blonde hair cascading down her shoulders, her blue eyes agleam with
devotion and love. Hitler celebrated her as the epitome of charm and grace. After
moving on to Vienna, Hitler persisted with his literary efforts, writing poetry and setting to work on several plays and librettos, all of which he abandoned. According to
Kubizek, Hitler's writing, like his painting, was very uneven. It could be striking or
dismal, and, once again, Hitler could not tell the difference. Because at the time he
was greatly struck by it, Kubizek memorized the stage setting for the first act of a
verse play Hitler proposed to write but never finished. It is the only fragment of
Hitler's early writing to be preserved:

> In the background the Holy Mountain. In the foreground a huge sacrificial stone
> overshadowed by giant oaks. Two formidable warriors grasp the black sacrificial
> bull firmly by the horns, and press the head of the sacrificial beast toward the
> hollow of the stone. Towering behind them stands the priest in a light-colored rai-
> ment. He grips the battle sword with which he will sacrifice the bull. All around
> him solemn bearded men, leaning on their shields, their lances at the ready, watch
> the festive scene with steady gaze.[2]

Hitler's enthusiasm for opera began in Linz. A dozen or more productions were
put on each month, but the more important Wagner operas were seldom staged
there. In 1906, Hitler's mother gave him a sum of money for his birthday present,

and with it, he took a two-week excursion to Vienna, his goal being to attend as many operas as he could. At last, he saw *Der Fliegende Höllander* and *Tristan und Isolde*. Upon his return to Linz, Hitler persuaded his mother to purchase him an extravagantly costly Heitzmann-Flugel piano and took lessons on the instrument from a Polish music teacher named Josef Prevatzki. Hitler struggled hard at the instrument. Prevatzki liked his students to start lessons at a much younger age, but he had to admit his new pupil's playing improved steadily over the next several months. Hitler, however, had to forgo his lessons in January 1907, when his mother became gravely ill with breast cancer. The tumor would be surgically removed but the cancer would spread. Despite his mother's rapidly deteriorating condition, Hitler journeyed to Vienna in October 1907 to take the entrance exam to the Academy of Fine Arts. His drawings were deemed inferior, and Hitler was not accepted for admission. After his mother's death the following January, Hitler again made for Vienna, this time to stay there permanently. Kubizek, who thought Hitler was attending art classes at the academy, would follow him shortly to study music at the Vienna Conservatory. Hitler attended operatic performances once or twice a week. He heard all the major works in the Wagnerian canon as well as operas by Mozart, Beethoven, and Verdi. Gustav Mahler conducted the Wagner performances. Although Hitler's anti-Semitism began to develop during these years—he took delight in testifying against an East European Jew he saw begging in the street— he spoke highly about Jewish musicians and developed a passion for the symphonic works of Gustav Mahler. Kubizek also remembers Hitler speaking enthusiastically about certain compositions of Felix Mendelssohn. Both composers would be banished from the musical lexicon in Germany after Hitler's meteoric rise to power in 1933. After Kubizek joined Hitler in Vienna, Adolf attempted to compose an opera of his own to be called *Wieland the Smith*. Wagner had once considered basing an opera on the exploits of this legendary Norse hero who avenged himself on the king who had crippled him by raping the king's daughter and murdering both his sons. After using the skulls of the two brothers as drinking chalices, Wieland flies away from the scene of the carnage, for, like the Greek Daedalus, he fashioned himself a set of wings. A partial libretto had been found among the composer's effects after his death. Hitler decided to take up what Wagner had abandoned, and like his hero he would strive to fashion a total work of art. Whereas Wagner had been content to supply the drama and the music and leave the stage design to others, Hitler would not only write the libretto and compose the music but paint the backdrops and design the costumes as well. Hitler asked Kubizek to take down the notes as he hammered at the piano. Hitler had no training in music theory. We have only Kubizek's word for it, but, according to him, Hitler's music nonetheless had a "rough elemental quality that was curiously pleasing."[3] Kubizek claims that Hitler composed a prelude, wrote a libretto for the entire first act, and set a portion of it to music before giving the project over as he had done so many others.

Hitler was a dilettante. Yet, as Thomas Mann observed, poetasters and amateurs, those blusterers who desultorily follow the various branches of knowledge yet who, like perfect fools, affect expertise on every subject and who opine on matters about which they should remain silent, can nonetheless accomplish tremendous things. According to Mann, Richard Wagner's art was nothing other than "dilettantism raised to the level of genius."[4]

History has produced few figures as complex and compelling, and as repugnant and repulsive, as Richard Wagner, the composer to whom both Hitler and Mann felt closest. In his lifetime, the Sorcerer from Saxony struck a variety of poses and donned many hats. Certainly much of his thinking—a gallimaufry of Christian doctrine, racist and socialist ideology, and German nationalism—was half-baked and crude. He had something to say about almost everything and his opinion was often uninformed and misguided. Yet he admitted the stupidity of his remarks: "O, this is my salvation, this ability to transform sense into nonsense."[5] Wagner's wife, Cosima, claimed that he merely aired his vexations, and that he often did not mean what he said but used hyperbole for theatrical effect. Often Wagner would make very discrepant statements. He frequently denigrated French culture as decadent, and, at the beginning of the Franco-Prussian War, declared that Paris should be burned to the ground, yet, in 1859, he stated: "At the outbreak of hostilities between Germany and France, I would take refuge in the capital of the enemy. Believe me, I fear I shall lose all my patriotism, and secretly I might rejoice if the Germans took a proper beating."[6] Certainly he was the chauvinist of all chauvinists, but he could say to Franz Liszt, "It is with horror that I contemplate Germany and my plans for the future there. May God forgive me, but all I can see in Germany is small-mindedness, boorish behavior, pretence and arrogance. . . ."[7] Other surprising contradictions are preserved in Cosima's diary. She dutifully took down each and every one of his declarations. He can be seen one day extolling figures such as Frederick the Great, Shakespeare, and Goethe and the next decrying them as blockheads and brutes. In his operas, he explores both pagan and Christian themes, and, like Tannhäuser, he seems caught somewhere between both worlds. Wagner took so many political positions in his lifetime, one can feel equally justified in labeling him a proto-Marxist or a vestigial fascist. He began his career as an adherent of democracy and ended it a devout monarchist. While he called on the rich to give up their wealth to feed the poor, he himself would dress in only the finest silk, and, although he professed vegetarianism, his coats had to be lined with the best ermine. Certainly, above anything else, Wagner was an opportunist. He would go whichever way the wind blew as long as that wind proved beneficial to him in some way. Of all Wagner's brainless statements, his endless anti-Semitic remarks are most frightening, especially in light of future events in Germany. He once said that all Jews ought to burn to death at a performance of Lessing's *Nathan the Wise*, and he made similarly vile proclamations all his life. His autobiography, *Mein Leben*, reads like a precursor to *Mein Kampf*. Nonetheless, Wagner routinely employed Jewish singers and conductors, who positively doted on him. He attempted unsuccessfully to convert one of the latter,

Hermann Levi, the son of a rabbi, to Christianity; yet he would, on one occasion, tell him that although "the Catholics may think themselves more aristocratic than the Protestants, the Jews were, after all, the oldest, the most aristocratic race."[8] Moreover, Cosima was one-fourth Jewish, making his beloved son Siegfried one-eighth. Despite all his numerous contradictory statements, Wagner's character was fairly consistent. He was arrogant in the extreme, and he behaved in despicable fashion toward one and all, even his closest friends and acquaintances. He rejected and repudiated the music of Brahms, Meyerbeer, Mendelssohn, Verdi, and Schubert, claiming that he alone was a worthy heir to Beethoven. He seduced his friends' wives and had no compunction when it came to avoiding paying his debts. His low character reveals perhaps the greatest of all paradoxes concerning Wagner: how could such an odious man compose such sublime and ravishing music? Thomas Mann states the case succinctly: Richard Wagner was "a dubious character, a theoretical charlatan, a political blusterer,"[9] but he also was "a great artist."[10] Mann also admitted that to pin down the real Wagner was almost impossible. "I can write about him today like this and tomorrow like that," he said.[11]

Mann also used adjectives such as "dubious" and "highly suspect" to describe Wagner's operas. He maintained that Wagner appealed to the diseased and erotic sides of our nature, and he likened his love of Wagner to a drug addiction, joking that once one had really drunk deeply of Wagner's music one became intoxicated for life. Yet he also frequently rhapsodized about the effect Wagner's melodies had upon him. He describes attending a Wagnerian performance thusly: "Wonderful hours of deep and solitary happiness admix the theatre throng, hours filled with *frissons* and brief moments of bliss, with delights for the nerves and intellect alike, and sudden glimpses into things of profound and moving significance, such as only this incomparable art can afford."[12] Wagner's music had an enormous effect on Mann. It altered and changed his mood and touched him physically. From Kubizek, we learn that it affected Adolf Hitler in similar fashion:

> When he listened to the music of Wagner, he was transformed. His violence left him, he became quiet, submissive, tractable. His gaze lost its restlessness, and his daily preoccupations were as though they had never been. His own destiny, however heavily it weighed upon him, no longer appeared to have any importance. He no longer felt lonely, an outlaw, a man kicked around by society. He was in a state of intoxicated ecstasy. Willingly he allowed himself to be carried away into a legendary world more real to him than the world he saw around him every day. From the stale musty prison of the room at the back of the courtyard, he was transported into the blessed regions of German antiquity, which was for him the ideal world, the highest goal of all his endeavors.[13]

Richard Wagner was one of the most influential artists who ever lived. Not only did he influence virtually every composer of the succeeding generation, he also had an enormous impact on the literature of both the nineteenth and twentieth centuries. Baudelaire and the other symbolist poets were fascinated by the concept of the *Gesamtkunstwerk* and strove, in turn, to create "absolute" poetry. As Wagner turned music into literature, the symbolists struggled to make poetry into music. Both George Moore and G. B. Shaw were ardent Wagnerphiles, and Moore attempted in his later years to write prose that had the texture and characteristics of the Master's music. Edouard Dujardin, the originator of the stream-of-consciousness technique, said he found his inspiration in Wagner. Both Mann and Proust worshiped the composer and adopted his leitmotiv technique in their fiction. James Joyce, although he claimed that he did not care for Wagnerian opera, was perhaps the most Wagnerian author of all. *Ulysses* and *Finnegans Wake* are filled with references to the composer's works, and the *Wake* itself is perhaps the ultimate realization of the *Gesamtkunstwerk*. But as Erich Heller has noted, there is also a connection between the total work of art and the total or totalitarian state. In his introduction to *Thomas Mann Pro and Contra Wagner*, Heller writes: "The next step follows with fatal logic. Why not transform the 'desolate reality' itself into a work of art, a pseudo-aesthetic phenomenon, and to treat anything 'real' that would not fit the 'artistic' vision as mere blemishes to be discarded as a painter may paint over what strikes him as mistaken in the design of his canvas, or a writer cross out a phrase that displeases him? Thomas Mann arrived late at the insight that in Richard Wagner there was much 'Hitler,' the failed artist who proceeded from painting inferior pictures to creating a colossally and repulsively total reality."[14]

By 1938, however, Thomas Mann had come to the conclusion that Adolf Hitler was a member of the guild. This man he hated and despised, this ruthless dictator who would plunge the world into total war, nonetheless had the temperament and personality of an artist. He published an essay, *Bruder Hitler* (translated "This Man Is My Brother") in *Esquire* magazine in March of that year. He would later consider the piece nothing more than an ironic jest.[15] Mann was certainly bitter; while working on *Bruder Hitler*, he was also tearfully writing in the *Tagebuchblätter* about the loss of his homeland. He came to see his works as his true home. "Engrossed in them I feel all the familiarity of being at home. These works are language, German language and thought form, my personal development of the tradition of my land and people. Where I am is Germany."[16] Although he implied that there was a vast difference between him and Hitler, that he in fact was the representative of the true Germany, he had to admit that he and Hitler practiced the same craft, although they worked in different mediums. Mann sought total control of words and language. His imprint was on every page, every paragraph, every line of his work. Hitler's imprint was on every facet of the German nation. This realization led Mann to write possibly his greatest book, *Doctor Faustus*.

In *Mein Kampf*, Hitler described the years he spent in Vienna as the most miserable of his life. When he attempted to take the entrance exam to the Academy of Fine Arts a second time, he was not even admitted to the test. Therefore, he set up an appointment with the director of the Academy. Hitler was told that he indeed possessed talent, that, on the basis of the drawings in his portfolio, he would make a strong candidate for the School of Architecture. Hitler's poor performance as a student in the Linz *Realschule* would, however, as Hitler well knew, prevent him from ever being admitted there. Only students with high marks were accepted. Years of poverty and hardship would follow Hitler's rejection from art school, and, during that time, Hitler became increasingly obsessed with the notion of racial purity. He may have even experienced a latent fear that his own blood was tainted. In 1930, at Hitler's behest, Hans Frank investigated rumors that Hitler's grandfather had been the nineteen-year-old son of a Jewish family named Frankenberger for whom Hitler's grandmother Maria Anna Schicklgruber had briefly worked as a maid. Hitler's father, Alois, had been illegitimate. Maria Schicklgruber married Johann Georg Hiedler (the Hitler surname had been spelled in various ways over the years) when the boy was five. Alois always claimed that Hiedler had been his father, although he did not officially change his last name from Schicklgruber until January 1877. Frank claimed that he unearthed letters from the Frankenbergers to Maria Schicklgruber that indicated they regularly made support payments for Alois until his fourteenth year. Hitler was greatly distressed by Frank's findings but was not satisfied as to their veracity. No documents have surfaced in the years following the war to corroborate Frank's story.

After five years in Vienna, Hitler moved to Munich. He enlisted in the German army in 1914 and was awarded the Iron Cross, first class, for carrying messages under heavy machine gun fire. He had been put up for the decoration by a first lieutenant named Hugo Gutmann. Gutmann happened to be a Jew, a fact that Hitler took great pains to conceal. After Germany's defeat, Hitler returned to Munich, where he quickly became active in politics. Shortly before the *putsch*, Hitler made a pilgrimage to Bayreuth, where he was invited to the Villa Wahnfried and met Wagner's widow Cosima (from whom he received a kiss); the composer's son Siegfried; his wife, Winifred, whose background was Danish though she had been adopted and raised in England; and Wagner's son-in-law, the notorious racist Houston Stewart Chamberlain. Hitler felt particularly emboldened after the interview. The elderly Chamberlain told Hitler that he was God-sent. For years Chamberlain had proclaimed a pro-Aryan, anti-Jewish ideology. Although the son of a British admiral, Chamberlain believed that the German race alone could save mankind, and he expressed his ideas in the massive *Foundations of the Nineteenth Century*. His thinking had been considerably influenced not only by the writings of Joseph Arthur, Count de Gobineau, but also, of course, by Richard Wagner's condemnatory statements concerning Jews. A letter from Chamberlain awaited Hitler upon his return to Munich, in which Chamberlain declared Hitler to be the Messiah for whom he had, in the manner of John the Baptist, paved the way. Chamberlain wrote: "At one blow you have transformed my soul. That Germany in the hour of her need has produced a Hitler testifies to its vitality. . . . Now at last I am able to sleep peacefully and I shall have no need to wake up again. God protect you!"[17]

Hitler was puffed up with pride. His head full of exulted notions of his own worth, he attempted his *coup*. But the revolt was put down, and Hitler himself would receive a five-year prison sentence. In point of fact, he would serve less than a year, and he would demand and receive extraordinary special privileges. His cell on the first floor was spacious and sunny, and he was provided with additional space to house his collection of books. Other cells were made available for him to receive visitors. While visitors could call on other inmates only at certain set hours, Hitler was free to entertain company whenever he wished. Party meetings with other National Socialists could thus take place. Like all the other inmates, Hitler was allowed to buy a half-liter of beer or wine a day, and usually chose the former. "Lights out" was at ten o'clock, but Hitler could leave his on for two more hours. His chauffeur, Emil Maurice, was permitted to live at the prison fortress and served as Hitler's valet and also entertained the Führer by strumming his guitar. Hitler dictated the opening chapters of *Mein Kampf* to him, but he was soon supplanted in his role of amanuensis by Rudolf Hess, who followed Hitler to Landsberg as a prisoner. Winifred Wagner supplied Hitler with paper. Editorial assistance was provided by Hess's wife, Ilse, printer Adolf Mueller, and Father Bernhard Stempfle, a friend of the Hess family and editor of an anti-Semitic newspaper who would later be marked for death on the night of the long knives. Ilse Hess claimed that she had struggled with Hitler for countless hours to persuade him to make certain stylistic improvements to the book. He seldom gave in and much of the text went to the publishers just as he had originally dictated it.

Hitler planned to call his autobiography *A Reckoning* but then changed the title to *Four and a Half Years of Struggle against Lies, Stupidity, and Cowardice*. The shorter title *My Struggle* or *My Battle* was proposed by Max Amann, the managing editor of the Nazi newspaper the *Volkischer Beobachter*, and Hitler acquiesced to the change. Hitler relates his life story in the first part of the book. He gives an account of his birth, his early efforts to become an artist, his years of abject poverty in Vienna, his wartime service in the Bavarian army, his early political career, and his revolutionary activities. He states his political aims unequivocally and without disguise in the second half of the book and details the policies he will put into effect upon coming to power. He will forge an absolutely unified state. Everyone from the youngest children to the most elderly will come under his domination. He details the steps he will take to unify the country: An end would be put to free speech. Children would be indoctrinated in state-controlled schools. Both young people and adults would undergo intense physical training, and there would be compulsory military service for young men. Status in the new society would not be conferred by wealth and birth but by merit. People were merely subjects of the state until they earned the right of citizenship, men by completing their proscribed military service, women by marrying a healthy man with a blameless record. With everyone falling into rank behind him, Hitler would turn all of Germany into one giant military camp, for his purpose, ultimately, was to wage war—to avenge the indignity of 1918. Germany had been stabbed in the back by the Jews and the Bolsheviks at the close of World War I. She would have prevailed against her enemies had it not been for the traitorous Jews. In the end, however, Germany would still dominate Europe. Hitler would wage a war of conquest in the east, for the master race needed *Lebensraum* (living space) in which to grow and burgeon. It was the manifest destiny of the Germans to subjugate and crush Russia, just as it had been the destiny of the American settlers to push westward and vanquish the Indians. Communism would be wiped from the face of the earth.

Hitler's favorite author, it should be pointed out, was Karl May, the German Zane Grey. Although May never set foot in America, he wrote a series of novels set in the American West in which his hero, the white Old Shatterhand, battles the evil Ogellallah Indians. He slaughters huge numbers of the wicked Redskins and quotes the Bible to justify his actions. May's descriptions of the landscapes of Texas, Arizona, and New Mexico are fanciful and inaccurate and his plots are dubious and implausible, but he won himself a legion of readers in Austria and Germany and made a fortune with his books. In his conversations with his generals, Hitler always referred to the Russian communists as the "Reds," playing on the word's double meaning. He joked that he saw himself as a sort of Old Shatterhand and thus, in his mind, conflated the primitive barbarians of the East with May's American Indian savages.[18]

Not only did Hitler reveal his plans for eastward expansion in *Mein Kampf*, he also indicated what was in store for Jews and dissidents. Anyone who opposed Hitler would be interred in concentration camps. German Jews would first lose their citizenship then face expulsion from the country.

Much of *Mein Kampf* is rambling and repetitious. Hitler devotes page after page to his attack on the Jews. Many of his arguments come directly from the *Protocols of the Fathers of Zion*: There is a secret Jewish conspiracy to take over the world. The Jews already control world finance, and through infiltration they are attempting to take over individual nations one by one. "Democracy has become," Hitler writes, "the instrument of that race which must hide because of its inner aims from the sun, now and in all future times. . . . Only a Jew can praise an institution which is as dirty and untrue as he is himself."[19] Furthermore, the Jews pander to the vices and weaknesses of the world's other people. They are responsible, among other things, for prostitution and white slavery.

Many of the most inflammatory passages were cut from the abridged English translation published in America in 1933. The German edition ran to 781 pages, while the English translation was only 297 pages in length. Even so, Hitler's message still rang crystal clear.

Although Hitler's prose is generally bombastic and bloated, he occasionally writes with finesse, especially when he becomes anecdotal. The narrative sections of the book are written to hold the reader's interest and often succeed in doing so. The *New York Times* book reviewer who evaluated the book in 1933 correctly labeled it "a hymn of hate,"[20] but nonetheless had to admit that Hitler's account of his early years was "vitally interesting."[21] For the most part, Hitler does not make cogent arguments but simply spews forth his hatred. However, he does display great cunning and intelligence about the uses of propaganda. Hitler had seen how the Americans and the British had dehumanized the Germans in World War I. The enemy was not a person, but a monster who would commit any atrocity. This idea was inculcated so effectively into the minds of the American and British troops that they were "prepared for the horrors of war and preserved from disappointment."[22] Hitler argues that leaders must simplify reality for the masses. If one "tries to show the many facets of a problem, the effect is frittered away, for the masses can neither digest nor retain the material offered to them."[23] The masses can be duped and hoodwinked if the big lie is repeated loudly and with enough persistence. "It is part of the genius of a great leader to make it appear as though even the most distant enemies belong to the same category; for weak and fickle characters, if faced by many different enemies, will easily begin to have doubts about the justice of their cause."[24]

Unfortunately for humankind, *Mein Kampf* was little read. Apparently none of Hitler's future targets delved very deeply into its pages. Nor did the leaders of the free world take the book seriously enough.

As the Soviets pressed inexorably toward Berlin in the spring of 1945, Hitler began making preparations to take his own life. Once again everything had turned to ashes. He would not, however, give his enemies the satisfaction of capturing him; death would be preferable to that. He would marry Eva Braun now that the battle was lost. They would die together. First, however, he would pen his will and choose his successor as leader of the nation. The efficacy of the cyanide would be tested on Blondi, his beloved German shepherd. She had just given birth to a litter of pups. After the mother died, they, too, would be killed. All were shot by Otto Guensche, who was also ordered to collect two hundred liters of gasoline for the Führer's funeral pyre. Hitler would take his final meal, then say his goodbyes. He and Eva retreated to their room. At the last moment, Magda Goebbels, the wife of Germany's Minster of Popular Enlightenment and Propaganda, that other would-be artist, the failed novelist and playwright Joseph Goebbels, attempted to dissuade him. She ran to the door, where Guensche stood guard. All was not lost. There was still hope.[25] Guensche opened the door and asked Hitler if he should admit her. Hitler said no. He did not wish to deal with a second Frau Hanfstaengl. Guensche and

Heinz Linge entered the room after hearing the shot. Hitler had also simultaneously bitten down on a cyanide capsule. The bodies of Hitler and Eva were taken to the Chancellery garden, placed in a shell hole, and set afire as the Soviet guns boomed nearby.

In his last act as Nazi propagandist, Goebbels would announce Hitler's death to the world. The Führer's demise was characterized as his personal apotheosis, an event that would be remembered for generations to come. The curtain had fallen on the last act of *Götterdämmerung*. Siegfried had been placed on his funeral pyre. Now the man who presided over the burning of all the books would follow the Führer in death. He would take his wife and six children with him.

Victory for the Allies was finally at hand, but at what cost! Millions upon millions had died. Hitler adversely affected the lives of countless people—including a large number of important twentieth-century authors. He is the black spider at the middle of everything. No serious discussion of the last hundred years can proceed without his mention, and his dark presence can be felt throughout much of this book.

Notes

1. Quoted by Robert Payne, *The Life and Death of Adolf Hitler* (New York: Dorset Press, 1989), p. 53.

2. Ibid., p. 69.

3. Ibid., p. 67.

4. Thomas Mann, "The Sorrows and Grandeur of Richard Wagner," *Pro and Contra Wagner*, trans. Allan Blunden with introduction by Erich Heller (London: University of Chicago Press, 1985), p. 103.

5. Quoted by Rudolph Sabor, *The Real Wagner* (London: Cardinal, 1989), p. 223.

6. Ibid., p. 208.

7. Ibid.

8. Ibid., p. 214.

9. Quoted by Heller, "Introduction," *Pro and Contra Wagner*, p. 21.

10. Ibid.

11. Ibid.

12. Mann, *Pro and Contra Wagner*, pp. 46–47.

13. Quoted by Payne, *The Life and Death of Adolf Hitler*, pp. 66–67.

14. Heller, "Introduction," *Pro and Contra Wagner*, p. 19.

15. Ronald Hayman *Thomas Mann: A Biography* (New York: Scribner, 1995), pp. 441–42; Anthony Heilbut, *Thomas Mann: Eros and Literature* (New York: Knopf, 1996), p. 569; Donald Prater, *Thomas Mann: A Life* (Oxford, New York: Oxford University Press, 1995), p. 279.

16. Hans Bürgin and Hans-Otto Mayer, *Thomas Mann: A Chronicle of His Life*, trans. Eugene Dobson (Alabama: University of Alabama Press, 1969), p. 133.

17. Quoted by Payne, *The Life and Death of Adolf Hitler*, p. 171.

18. Ibid., pp. 27–28.

19. James W. Gerard, " 'A Hymn of Hate,' *My Battle* by Adolf Hitler," *New York Times Book Review*, 15 October 1933, reprinted in *The New York Times Book Review 100*, 6 October 1996, p. 42.

20. Ibid.

21. Ibid.

22. Quoted by Payne, *The Life and Death of Adolf Hitler*, p. 199.

23. Ibid., p 198.

24. Ibid., p. 199.

25. Ibid., p. 567.

Ross Lockridge

TWO MONTHS AFTER THE PUBLICATION OF HIS ONLY WORK OF FICTION, the mammoth 1,066-page novel *Raintree County*, Ross Lockridge Jr. committed suicide at the age of thirty-three. On the evening of March 6, 1948, Lockridge left his Bloomington, Indiana, home on the pretext of making a trip to the post office. Whether he took his automobile, a brand-new Kaiser, out of his adjacent garage and actually drove to the post office and back or whether he locked himself inside the outbuilding immediately upon leaving the house remains uncertain. Lockridge had built the home and purchased the car with the $150,000 prize money he had won for *Raintree County* in a Metro-Goldwyn-Mayer-sponsored contest to ferret out books that could serve as lucrative movie properties. He received this award after *Raintree County* had already been accepted by the Houghton Mifflin Company but prior to the novel's publication. Lockridge had started work on the book in 1938, but discontinued writing it the following year. He took the manuscript up again in 1941 and struggled with it for the next seven years. The last year of his life, however, he was forced to compromise his artistic vision and substantially revise the novel (originally an even more massive work divided into five volumes) in order to satisfy the requirements of both his publishers and of other interested parties.

Although they unanimously selected *Raintree County* for an in-house prize for the best first novel submitted to the publisher in 1946, the editors at Houghton Mifflin at the same time demanded the first set of extensive revisions, and Metro-Goldwyn-Mayer insisted upon additional alterations as a condition of its awarding Lockridge its $150,000 prize. Likewise the Book-of-the-Month Club (BOMC) agreed to make *Raintree County* a Main Club Selection, providing that the novel be further edited to meet the club's own standards and criteria. Everyone

acknowledged the excellence of the sprawling, highly poetic work, the life story of
an Indiana school teacher and Civil War veteran named John Wickliff Shawnessy.
Nonetheless, everyone wanted to stick their fingers into the pie in order to alter,
adjust, and amend. For one thing, the novel was too long. Fifty thousand words
would have to go at the very minimum. When Lockridge asked Carol Brandt, the
New York and European head of the story department at MGM, if she would consider a condensed version of *War and Peace* superior to the original, she replied that
she certainly would. Lockridge found it difficult to negotiate with such people. The
editors, movie executives, and BOMC people also called for changes and modifica-
tions that, to their minds, would cause the book to attract a larger readership. The
studio went so far as to trumpet the novel as a northern *Gone with the Wind*. They
not only wanted Lockridge to reduce his literary experimentation and thus make the
book more accessible to the layman; they also required that he tone down, at least
to some degree, the novel's more erotic passages and that he likewise abbreviate his
protagonist Shawnessy's theological speculations as these were indicative of the
character's (and author's) materialistic and strongly humanist philosophy of life.

The editors et al. feared that Shawnessy's ideas might appear irreverent and
iconoclastic to the very people who otherwise would be most attracted to the novel,
those public-spirited and civic-minded readers who would approach the book as a
panoramic slice of United States history, a biography of the country itself. Despite
the comprehensive revisions, Lockridge's vision still shines through. Nonetheless,
it would be interesting to see the book as he originally intended it reach print today.
For one thing, the novel had ended in a lengthy dream sequence, all of which was
dropped at the insistence of his editors. This section could easily be restored or
perhaps printed as an appendix.

Lockridge took great umbrage at the various demands made of him, although
he yielded in each instance in order to achieve publication and reap the financial
benefits of his seven years of uninterrupted labor. During the course of all this
rewriting, Lockridge became increasingly depressed. His physical condition deteriorated as well. His growing emotional instability caused his physicians to pre-
scribe a course of electroshock therapy. Lockridge feared the treatments and broke
them off before undergoing the required number. His family also looked askance at
the procedure. They argued that physical exercise and renewed effort on the novel
would serve Lockridge better than the shock therapy.

When the novel finally appeared, on January 4, 1947, Lockridge still had a bad
taste in his mouth and took little pleasure in the novel's long-awaited publication.
He still harbored the notion that his book had been taken away from him. Many contemporary readers and Faulkner scholars find *Flags in the Dust*, the original, uncut
version of *Sartoris*, preferable to the Sherwood Anderson redaction that ultimately
went to press. The same might hold true for *Raintree County*. The novel is a *Bil-
dungsroman* and allegory both. Shawnessy's development from innocent youth into
a distrustful and somewhat cynical adult reflects the passage of America from its

rustic, pastoral beginnings through the Civil War into the modern, industrial age. Likewise this American Adam's quest for regeneration and spiritual awakening at the end of the novel, his longing for a primitive and carefree way of life, an existence of unreflective pagan joy and exuberance and of mythopoeic apotheosis, is symbolic of contemporary man's need for legend and myth and the nostalgia he feels for times long past, the enchantment that our agrarian roots still holds for us in today's hectic world. Shawnessy's sentiments and yearnings are made clear from the very first pages of the novel. Like James Joyce's *Ulysses* (to which Lockridge's novel owes a large and obvious debt), *Raintree County* narrates the events of a single day: July 4, 1892. However, a series of flashbacks trace events reaching as far back as 1844 and encompassing the Civil War, the first eleven years following the conflict, the American Centennial, the Great Railroad Strike, and the formation of the Populist Party, all of which in some manner or fashion lead up to and culminate in the happenings and incidents that take place during the fourth of July celebration of 1892. These flashbacks are not chronological: the reader must assemble the pieces of the puzzle as he goes along. The novel covers a half century of American history. Yet throughout the book there are intimations of an earlier dawn when

Pre-   A   Historic
STRANGE LIGHT WAS OVER
EVERYTHING, SOFT GRAY AND GREEN AND GOLD.[1]

Like deep sea divers coming up from the depths gasping for air, primal images and buried racial memories of this antediluvian morning rise to the surface of Shawnessy's thoughts, interrupting his ordinary deliberations and more matter-of-fact musings. Lockridge clearly concurs with Jung's theory of the collective unconscious, for he depicts the workings of such a wellspring on the person and mind of his protagonist. Perhaps he was also familiar with Thomas Mann's *Joseph and His Brothers* or at least the opening volume of the series, *The Tales of Jacob*, in which Mann hymns the collective unconscious, the deep well out of which all creativity stems, and analyses its effect both on young Joseph and on himself, the author undertaking such a distant plunge into remote antiquity in writing the Joseph cycle. Mann argues that the fabled and legendary past coalesces with a prophetically intimated yet always nebulous future in order to form time's only true state, the eternal present, and that therefore the seeds of myth perpetually abide in our ordinary lives. These enrich and fortify mankind's otherwise routine existence. Mythic connotations are embedded and embodied in almost every page of *Raintree County*. Like the youthful Joseph, John Shawnessy is forever searching for symbolic correspondences between his life and those of legendary and mythic figures from times past.

Many critics have remarked on the startling humanism of Mann's cosmogony. It is not God but "Adam Qadmon" who creates the universe. In doing so, the soul-light man falls from the heavenly circles and takes on material form. Adam's creation is described as a descent into hell and is likened to Mann's own act of making and shaping, the writing of the Joseph cycle, which, as we have already seen, involved another fall—a plummeting both into the great well of the past and into the depths of the collective unconscious. In the last pages of *Raintree County*, Lockridge similarly argues that all generative power exists in man. Through language, John Shawnessy cast and molded his world. Like Adam, he named all living things. Therefore he, not God, is the Shakespeare of creation.

As *Raintree County* opens, John Shawnessy lies dreaming in bed (though the reader, at first, does not realize this). Shawnessy pictures in his mind the activities of the coming morning, and the reader is tricked into believing that Shawnessy has, in fact, arisen from his sleep and that he is attending to his daily business in the little town of Waycross before going on to meet the train of Senator Garwood B. Jones, Raintree County's leading son and Shawnessy's boyhood friend and rival. Shawnessy stops in at the local post office on the way to the station. The woman at the distribution window says that she has been expecting him, and when he asks if he has any mail, she replies cryptically, "Some letters carved on stone. . . . The fragments of a forgotten language. I take my pen in hand and seat myself—."[2] Post office and woman suddenly undergo a miraculous transformation:

> The woman was lying on a stone slab that extended dimly into the space where the window usually was. She lay on her stomach, chin propped on hands. Her hair was dark gold, unloosened. Her eyes were a great cat's, feminine, fountain-green, enigmatic. A dim smile curved her lips.
>
> She was naked, her body palely flowing back from him in an attitude of languor.
>
> He was disturbed by this unexpected, this triumphant nakedness. He was aroused to memory and desire by the stately back and generously sculptured flanks.
>
> —How do you like my costume, Johnny? she asked, her voice tinged with mockery.
>
> —Very becoming, he said.[3]

Once in his life, on the night of his graduation from high school, John Shawnessy actually found himself in the primitive world of his dreams and imaginings. He and his sweetheart, Nell Gaither, stripped naked and went swimming in Paradise Lake. Just as their bodies were about to come together, they heard several of their fellow students calling their names in the far distance. The couple dress quickly and then answer the calls. They meet up with the other students, who inform them that John's mentor, Professor Jerusalem Webster Stiles, the witty and sardonic founder of Raintree County's Academy of Higher Learning, has seduced the minister's wife and is presently being pursued by a posse of do-gooders intent on doing him grave bodily harm. Although Johnny and Nell love each other, and in her he sees the clearest embodiment of the proto-mother-lover-sister-wife of his dreams, they are not destined for one another. What was on the verge of happening on the lake never comes to pass.

Throughout his life, however, John catches glimpses of his imaginary Ur-woman in other females, first in the person of Susanna Drake, a wealthy but orphaned Southern girl who came to Raintree County from New Orleans after inheriting a house there. The two met the day Johnny had his graduation daguerreotype taken. Johnny took her to Paradise Lake on the fourth of July, and the two had sex even though Shawnessy's heart belonged to Nell. Shortly afterward, Susanna left for New Orleans, but she returned after writing to Johnny in October that she was pregnant. He married her in December even though, on the day of the wedding, she told him that she had lied to him in her letter, and despite the fact that the two were at loggerheads politically: Johnny wanted to see slavery abolished while Susanna supported the secessionist cause. The couple went South for their honeymoon, and Shawnessy learned about his wife's past. Susanna's father, James Seymour Drake, had kept a slave mistress named Henrietta Courtney and brought her to live in his antebellum mansion, where his mentally ill wife also resided. The trio died in a fire set by either Mrs. Drake or Henrietta. The bodies were burned beyond recognition. Mr. Drake and one of the women—ostensibly his wife—had been shot together in bed. He was buried with the woman he was found with, but it was bruited about that Mrs. Drake had murdered her husband and his mistress after catching them together in the bedroom and that Henrietta Courtney actually lay beside James Drake in the double grave.

Upon returning North, Susanna gave birth to a son Jim, whom she named after her father. During the first years of the Civil War, however, she became mentally unhinged and on July 4, 1863, she set the house, which she had inherited and in which the Shawnessys now lived, on fire. The child perished in the blaze. Susanna survived but now was completely insane, prompting Shawnessy to send her back to her Southern relations. Shawnessy came to believe that Susanna was actually Henrietta's daughter. All her life, Susanna feared this possibility, but swore it wasn't so. Her bizarre behavior after giving birth settled the question for Shawnessy. She felt that mixing the races was a sin against God and feared that her own child was somehow contaminated and impure.

After sending his wife home, Shawnessy enlisted in the Union Army, where he became a fighting automaton devoid of all his previous humanity. In the final years of the war, he participated in a number of battles and skirmishes; he fought at Chickamauga and marched through doomed Atlanta. In Raintree County, his name was mistakenly reported among the slain, and, in Washington, he witnessed the assassination of Lincoln at Ford's Theater during a performance of *Our American Cousin*. He attended the performance with Jerusalem Webster Stiles, whom he had reencountered during the war. After being chased out of Raintree County, Stiles had become a journalist and was covering the Southern campaign for his paper. He was still the same old rascal and lecher Johnny remembered from his high school days. In Washington, Stiles promised to introduce John to a young actress named Daphne Fountain, Laura Keene's understudy in *An American Cousin*. She got the

Professor and John tickets for that fateful performance. Due to what happened that night, however, John and Daphne never had a chance to meet. Shawnessy remained oddly untouched by his wartime experiences. They seemed like illusions and phantasmagoria—curiously unreal in comparison to his vivid memories of his boyhood years in Raintree Country.

After the war, he returned home and learned that Nell Gaither had married Garwood Jones after hearing that John had been reported dead and that she died during childbirth in May of 1865. John lived at home with his parents, taught school, wrote articles for a local newspaper and verse for himself. He and Jones were rival candidates for the office of Representative to Congress in 1872. After being defeated following an ugly campaign, Shawnessy went back to teaching school children in Shawmucky township. He attended the Centennial celebration in Philadelphia and spent two years in New York City with Jerusalem Stiles. The Professor introduced him to another of his long succession of Eves, the renowned actress Laura Golden. Before achieving her fame and celebrity, she had performed under the stage name Daphne Fountain and thus was the very same woman Shawnessy had hoped to meet in Washington eleven years earlier. This revelation surprised John and caused him to ponder the strange workings of fate. Once again he beheld the Eternal Female in another of her endless guises. For Johnny, New York City would come to mean Laura Golden and nothing but Laura Golden. She was the inspiration for the heroine in the play he was then struggling to write which was entitled *Sphinx Recumbent* and set in the city. Eventually, however, he came to the realization that he did not, in fact, really love the actress. He could not solve the riddle she presented him. She wore so many masks that he could not determine the true Laura, and this unnerved and perplexed him. Thus he could never complete his play, nor would he ever be able to write the poetic epic of his era that he long envisioned. He had vaunting ambitions and, for a time, thought of himself as a second Shakespeare, but, at last, he had to come to the realization that he did not have the stamina and endurance to fulfill his promise and give literary form to his protean visions.

Upon the death of his mother, Shawnessy returned once again to Raintree County and resumed his career as a teacher. He learned that Susanna had run away from her relatives. A woman fitting her description drowned herself in the Mississippi river; her naked body was seen by excursionists aboard the steamboat *Delta Belle*. The body had been in the water several days, which made identification difficult. The face and shoulders, however, appeared to have been scarred by fire. Though he was not absolutely certain that his first wife was dead, John married Esther Root, one of his former students. While Susanna might have been part Negro, Shawnessy's second wife was rumored to be part Indian. Esther's father disapproved of Shawnessy, so the couple eloped. Root considered his son-in-law an atheist and a bigamist and, after her marriage, he never again welcomed his daughter into his house. In Esther, Johnny saw another version of his archetypical woman. He'd behold her yet again in the person of Mrs. Evelina Brown, a local widow who was the presiding grace of the Waycross Literary society. On the night of July 4, 1892, an informal meeting of the society was held at her mansion. The book *The Golden Bough* was the topic of the discussion. Afterward a delegation of torch-bearing marchers from a local revival meeting entered Mrs. Brown's yard. The leader of the group, the Reverend Lloyd G. Jarvey, accuses Shawnessy and Mrs. Brown of having an adulterous affair, but before the gathered crowd Professor Stiles exposes the minister as a hypocritical fraud by revealing the fact that Jarvey had seduced one of his own parishioners. Stiles thus avenges himself for being run out of town by another minister years before. The final Eve of the book is John and Esther's youngest daughter, Eva Alice Shawnessy, who, at twelve years old, experiences an abnormally strong attraction to her father. She recognizes that she is the latest avatar or incarnation of the mother of mankind, the Eve of the first garden. She hears a voice calling to her deep inside herself. It is that of "the very first of the Evas . . . the one who lived in a summer that had no beginning nor any ending, beyond time and memory, beyond and above all the books—most legendary and lost of Evas!"[4]

No summary of the book's plot, however lengthy, can convey the poetic and imaginative qualities of Lockridge's prose or the novel's innovative devices of style and technique. The latter bear the strong influence of the novels of William Faulkner, especially *The Sound and the Fury*; Marcel Proust's *Remembrance of Things Past*; and James Joyce's *Ulysses*—in particular, its "Aeolus," "Cyclops," and "Circe" episodes. *Raintree County* also shares many of the same themes as Faulkner's Yoknapatawpha saga. Lockridge created a mythical county in Indiana just as Faulkner had earlier done in Mississippi. Faulkner depicts Yoknapatawpha as a pristine paradise in works such as *Go Down Moses* and *The Unvanquished*. Slavery, however, was the sin of the South, the snake that lurked in the garden. Because the South had countenanced this evil, Paradise would be lost. Despite its nobility, the old order is doomed to fall. Lockridge sees American history in a similar light. Both authors have an elemental attachment to their native soils and celebrate the fecund, primal earth out of which all life comes. Each explores the problems of racial identity and miscegenation. Susanna Drake has precursors in Joe Christmas of *Light in August* and Charles Bon, the disowned son of Colonel Thomas Sutpen in *Absalom, Absalom*. Both authors see the Civil War as the pivotal event of American history and view America's industrial expansion after the war in a negative light. A new sort of ruthless individual will rise to prominence in the years following the conflict. The soulless and unscrupulous Snopes, their numbers ever increasing in Yoknapatawpha County in the decades following the defeat of the South, will eventually overthrow and vanquish the older aristocratic families of DeSpain, Compson, and Sartoris. John Shawnessy will likewise lose out to the ruthless Garwood Jones, who harbors presidential ambitions and who has the support of the "new men," the "titans of industry, amassers of corrupt fortunes, exploiters of millions, barons of a new feudalism."[5]

While Lockridge did not attempt to put his readers into the stream of consciousness of his characters, his nonlinear narrative in *Raintree County* recalls the Benjy chapter of *The Sound and the Fury*. In both books, the flashbacks are not arranged in order of time or occurrence. Instead they are "involuntary memories" triggered by chance associations—a golfer shouting the word "caddy" causes Benjy to think about his sister; a band playing "Yankee Doodle" on July 4, 1892, brings to mind a similar band playing the same song in 1854 for John Wickliff Shawnessy. Listening to Professor Stiles recite a poem about the South likewise induces Shawnessy to think about the "lazy, lavish journey"[6] he took down the Mississippi river in a steamboat with Susanna shortly after their marriage in 1859. The flashbacks in both novels reflect the indiscriminate and random play of the mind itself.

Raintree County resembles *Remembrance Of Things Past* in that the central characters of both novels are obsessed with reconstructing their earlier lives. Like Proust, Shawnessy feels that he has the ability to summon and recreate the past out of himself. Both novels register the changing and growing perceptions of their two protagonists as they emerge from childhood and adolescence into adulthood and middle age. Both books also feature the theme of transformation and reappearance. Just as Albertine is prefigured in Odette and Marcel in Swann, all the later "Eves" in John Shawnessy's life in some way or the other mirror his first sweetheart, Nell Gaither. Shawnessy eventually takes Jerusalem Stiles's place as Raintree Country's local philosopher, the intellectual light of the community, but also its most morally suspect citizen. The two men share the same initials: JWS.

The influence of James Joyce on Ross Lockridge is even greater than that of Proust or Faulkner. As previously noted, *Raintree County*, like *Ulysses*, narrates the events of a single day. Lockridge's preoccupation with myth parallels Joyce's immersion in and fixation with fable and legend. Just as Joyce equates Stephen with Telemachus and Hamlet and Bloom with Odysseus and Jesus, Lockridge likens John Wickliff Shawnessy to Adam, Christ, Odysseus, and numerous mythic heroes of the Western tradition. Both authors seek to ennoble their protagonists by comparing them to figures from the world's greatest epic literature. The ordinary man's successes and defeats are thus put on a par with the achievements and disappointments of demigods and supermen. At the same time, the reader perceives the vast distance between the average human being and his legendary analogue. Late in *Raintree County*, Professor Stiles tells Shawnessy that his Edenic dream belongs to an innocent day when myths were still believable. He accuses his protégé of "trying to Hellenize America."[7] Early in *Ulysses*, Buck Mulligan tells Stephen Dedalus that they must "hellenize"[8] Ireland. Stephen demurs. He will not be Mulligan's arm, just as earlier he would not play second fiddle to Cranly. Ireland must find her own myth. Similarly, Shawnessy states that he is striving to "Americanize America."[9] "The early Americans," he says, "were poets of the open road. They rediscovered the earth. They uncoiled the Mississippi, they unrolled the Great Plains, they upheaved the Rocky Mountains. They brought the miracle of names to an earth that was nameless, even as Adam did when God bade him name

the earth and its inhabitants. They were the new Adams."[10] The professor replies
in Buck Mulliganesque fashion:

> —Adam, who always slept in the raw,
> Went to bed with an Indian squaw.[11]

Even Lockridge's punctuation recalls Joyce. He imitates the Irish writer by setting
off his dialogue with a dash instead of using quotation marks. *Raintree County* most
recalls *Ulysses* in that the main text is constantly interrupted by a series of parodic
pastiches in a variety of inflated styles. These intrusions are usually journalistic in
nature and feature screaming headlines similar to those employed in the Aeolus
chapter of *Ulysses*. Most of the interpolations in *Raintree County* are "Epic Frag-
ments from the *Mythic Examiner*," a nonexistent newspaper that reflects the gar-
gantuan aspirations of John Wickliff Shawnessy. At one point late in the novel,
Shawnessy tells Professor Stiles that they have lived through epic times and that
this epic period has been recorded in the newspapers of the day. Stiles suggests
Shawnessy write an epic poem in the form of mock newspaper articles and entitle
it the *Mythic Examiner*. In it, he can record the "deeds of these fabulous people,
the Nineteenth Century Americans . . . in a mythical American style."[12] Throughout
the entire novel, the text is punctuated with such "mythical" columns. On July 4,
1854, for instance, Johnny Shawnessy and Flash Perkins race to determine the
fastest runner in *Raintree County*. The *Examiner* articles that appear in the chapter
concerning the race parody a sports column. The opponents are transformed variously into boxers pummeling one another in a ring, into Athenian and Spartan athletes competing for a flagon of wine in an ancient Olympic contest, into the Midnight Express and the Northern Fury, two trains running side by side full blast
toward a signal light (the headline here reads IRON HORSES IN SPEEDTEST), and into
racing New Orleans river boats:

River Race
(Epic Fragment from the *Mythic Examiner*)

The *Red Streak* and the *Comet*, those two wellknown sidewheelers, leaned into the
current, coming together. Crowds lined the shore as the two fastest boats on the river
jostled each other on the last long run into New Orleans. The *Streak* was crammed
with fast burning pine, and a nigger squat on her boiler. "More pine, Mr. Shawnessy?"
"A little more, thank ye, Mr. Burns." The *Comet*, a more durable-looking craft,
though lacking the *Streak's* speedy design, was gathering head, and as they came into
the bend she had a lead of a half length. The banks were lined with shouting thousands, the wealth and beauty of America's sultriest City, as the Mistress of the Delta,
all braceleted with lights, cheered the stacking steamers to their piers. . . .[13]

These journalistic parodies resemble similar mock-epic insertions and burlesques
in the Cyclops chapter of *Ulysses* which takes place in Barney Kiernan's pub. There

Bloom encounters the Citizen, a bigoted Irish Nationalist and his fearsome dog Garryowen. As the chapter comes to an end, the citizen hurls a biscuit tin at Bloom's departing horse-drawn cab outside the bar, and, in a final interpolation, Bloom turns into Elijah and the cab into Elijah's fiery chariot which ascends to heaven before the assembled throng of onlookers. Joyce, however, intersperses such parodic passages in a wide variety of styles throughout the entire Cyclops chapter. The patrons of Kiernan's pub are transformed into, among other things, debating parliamentarians in the House of Commons and Catholic saints. The mongrel Garryowen turns into a smart exhibition dog, Owen Garry, who recites his own poetry to the gathered tipplers. His verse bears "a striking resemblance to the ranns of ancient Celtic bards."[14] In the mock parliamentary debate, Joe Hynes calls for the resurrection of Gaelic sports. His motion is contested by Leopold Bloom, who speaks out against the violence and brutality of most athletic activities and champions the game of lawn tennis as a civilized alternative to other sports. Thereupon Alf Bergan relates how Myler Keogh, an Irishman, knocked out Percy Bennett, a British artilleryman, in a fight promoted by Blazes Boylan. A sports page parody follows. The fight takes on epic proportions as does the race between Flash Perkins and John Shawnessy in *Raintree County*.

A number of mock-dramatic sections also appear in the Lockridge novel. These resemble the extended "Night-town" or Circe section of *Ulysses*. In the *Odyssey*, Circe turned Odysseus' men into swine. Stephen experiences a similar reduction in his mental capabilities (in his case, due to overindulgence in drink) as he staggers into Night-town. The subconscious minds of Joyce's characters come to the fore in this long, nightmarish chapter of *Ulysses*. Their thoughts are put in dramatic form as are outside events. There is no differentiation between the two in terms of presentation; inner and outer realities stand side by side. The characters undergo numerous transformations. Bloom becomes the Messiah, a vaudeville entertainer and his grandfather Lipoti Virag; Stephen turns into Hamlet and Siegfried. Ghosts such as Stephen's mother and Bloom's son appear. Edward VII and Alfred Lord Tennyson both suddenly materialize as do numerous of the book's fictional characters who aren't actually present in Bella Cohen's brothel (though they are being thought about at the time, presumably, by the individuals who are there). Inanimate objects such as Bella's fan are provided with voices and speak as if they were characters in the play. Lockridge adopts many of the same techniques in his own dramatic interpolations. These also suggest the workings of the subconscious mind. Shakespeare appears in one sequence; the Courthouse clock of *Raintree County* ticks in another. Familiar figures in the book undergo spectacular metamorphoses in these dramatic passages, just as Joyce's characters do in Nighttown. A short excerpt from one such sequence will suffice to show Lockridge's immense debt to Joyce:

Emperor Justinian Webster Stiles

leaning from the imperatorial box, pale temples wreathed in vine-leaves, hands hanging languidly down,

    —I've done all I could, boy. But you know the Populus Americanus as well as I do. They *will* have their little pomps and games. After you've been suitably mangled, I'll see that you get a write-up on the front page of the *Sol Quotidianus*. How about it, Senator, can we get this boy off?

Senator Cigarius Bovocacus Jones

Toga, cigar,

    —No one is more concerned about the lot of the Common Man than I. But I wouldn't fairly represent the thousands that have made me their spokesman if—

Laura Golden

costume of Empress Theodora, in Roman attitude of accubation,

    —You are the most maddening man, dear.[15]

For all his technical virtuosity, Lockridge seems to be delivering a fairly simple message in his vast, complex novel.

He argues that modern man must rid himself of all his impediments and hindrances, the thousand and one neuroses that complicate our lives. Like John Shawnessy, we need to shed our clothes and seek contact with our lost heroic selves. Lockridge argues, as do Mann and Joyce, that life is made up of recurrent cycles, but that time is really unbroken—that the mythic past is still with us. We can come in touch with it if we try hard enough. Not only do we identify with heroic historical personages and with mythic figures of classical times and of biblical antiquity. As we grow older, we make a myth out of our own lives. We recall the days of youth and childhood when everything seemed simpler and less burdensome, and we long for the lost Paradise. Lockridge argues that we can find it embedded deep within ourselves, for we are the creators of the world. If he exists anywhere, God exists in us. God is not Michelangelo's elderly patriarch extending his finger to touch that of insentient man. Nor necessarily is he love. God, according to Lockridge, is the perception and consciousness of humankind itself, as embodied in the word, in Adam Qadmon's power and gift of naming all things:

And who was John Wickliff Shawnessy, whose wavering initials had just been signed in smoke in Waycross Station? How deep and broad was the substance of himself, built into this engendering night? Surely there was a being who didn't bear his name but was nonetheless a composite of all that he had ever been or ever could be. How did one find access to this eternal Self-Affirmer, this restless Shakespeare of Creation, hovering in a world Behind the Scenes? What was he doing there? Polishing the lines of the eternal tragi-comedy of life, setting up props, trying on masks, restlessly taking on and off the costumes, assembling the company for endless rehearsals, reviews, redactions? What was he doing there, down there? Weaving a legend of a younger brother, a residual and mortal brother, this innocent and fortunate brother who walked the streets of time.[16]

Once we discover the God in ourselves, we can conquer both death and nothingness. We turn world into word and thus can build everything over again. Through language, we enact the creation a second time and out of night and nescience the Republic of Mankind arises:

> The wall between himself and the world dissolved. He seemed suddenly lost from himself, plucked out of time and space, being both time and space himself, an inclusive being in which all other beings had their being. A vast unrest was in the earth. The Valley of Humanity was turbulent with changing forms. The immense dream trembled on a point of night and nothingness and threatened explosion.
>
> He held tight to the *Atlas* and walked on. Strong yearning possessed him to build again—and better than before—the valorous dream. If it should all expire, he would be able to rebuild it. He would walk on in his old black schoolmaster's suit, shaking from Family Bibles, McGuffey Readers, Histories of America, Latin and Greek Texts, Free Enquirers, Declarations of Independence and Constitutions, the seeds of words, planting the virgin earth of America with springing forms. So each man had to build his world again![17]

Ross F. Lockridge Jr. was born April 25, 1914, the son of Ross and Elsie Shockley Lockridge. The elder Lockridge was a historian and a professor at Indiana University. Although Ross Jr. inherited his father's love of history and from an early age assisted him with his various writing projects, he dedicated his novel to his mother. The book is based, to a large degree, on family history. John Wickliff Shawnessy is modeled on Lockridge's maternal grandfather, Indiana school teacher and poet John Wesley Shockley. The figure of Eva Alice Shawnessy is a portrait of the author's mother as a young girl. On his father's side, Lockridge was related to the best-selling novelist Mary Jane Ward. The two were second cousins. Nine years older than Ross, Ward also suffered from depression and mental illness. She chronicled her breakdown and recovery in the thinly veiled 1946 novel *The Snake Pit*. Ward tried to be a help to her cousin throughout his career and he himself admitted to trading on her name when he first approached Houghton Mifflin.

From a very young age, Ross Lockridge Jr. was a brilliant student. He attended Indiana University where he earned A.B. and M.A. degrees. Dubbed "A-plus Lockridge"[18] by his fellow students, he graduated with the highest grade-point average ever accumulated at the university. While in college, he joined the varsity track team and distinguished himself as a cross-country runner. The Fourth of July race between John Shawnessy and Flash Perkins is one of the most memorable passages in *Raintree County*. When it came to races and running, Lockridge wrote from experience. He and another athlete on the team, Charles Hornbostel, an Olympic finalist in the 880 in 1932, competed with each other for the affections of Vernice Baker, whom Lockridge had previously known in high school and from Methodist church camp. In 1933, while still an undergraduate, Lockridge went to Europe with the Delaware Foreign Study Group, attended classes at the Sorbonne, and traveled widely in France and Italy. He graduated in the spring of 1935 and began taking graduate courses the following summer. Shortly after enrolling for the summer session, however, he fell ill with scarlet fever and was sick for most of the next year. Lockridge joined Indiana University's English department as an instructor in 1936 and earned his Masters degree from Indiana in 1939. He and Vernice wed on July 11, 1937. Lockridge would begin work on a four-hundred-page epic poem, *The Dream of the Flesh of Iron*, in 1939. Conceived as "a spiritual history of twentieth-century American and European consciousness from 1914 . . . to the beginning of the Second World War,"[19] the unpublished work is, according to Lockridge's son Larry, ambitious but unreadable. Lockridge was admitted to Harvard's Ph.D. program in 1940, but instead of completing his doctorate, he began work on his novel. He would also teach at Simmons College in Boston. In its first incarnation, Lockridge's book, then entitled *American Lives*, bore little resemblance to the later *Raintree County*. Both versions concerned Lockridge's mother's family and each draft was massive. *American Lives* ran two thousand pages when Lockridge abandoned it. Although some two hundred pages have been recovered, most of the manuscript is lost, presumably discarded or destroyed by Lockridge after he had embarked on the rewrite. Although one of the book's major characters was based on John Wesley Shockley, the novel's chief protagonist was modeled on Lockridge's Uncle Ernest Vivian Shockley. Like *Raintree County*, the central events of *American Lives* occur in the early 1890s, but the book traced events that had taken place far earlier in the nineteenth century and extended forward in time to the twentieth century as well. The novel consisted of interior monologues of a number of Shockley family members as well as those of several fictitious characters. Reverend Jarvey and Evelina Brown had clear precursors in Reverend Hezekiah Grubb and Mrs. Desmore Brown. Surviving episodes include a boy's sports event and a Decoration Day parade. When he again took up the novel after joining the faculty of Simmons College, Lockridge had reached the conclusion that his strongest character was that of his grandfather John Shockley. He also decided that he would focus the action on a single day, July 4, 1892. Vernice assisted him with the writing and rewriting of *Raintree County* in its various incarnations during the seven years of the novel's composition. During roughly the same period, the couple had four children: Ernest, Jean, Larry, and Ross III. Ernest would become a noted novelist in his own right. Larry would earn a doctorate at Harvard, write two books of criticism, and a biography of his father, *Shade of the Raintree*.

Upon its publication, *Raintree County* won great acclaim from the critics and sold briskly for being such a mammoth work. It also occasioned a fierce attack from the Catholic church. Lockridge's satirical depictions of hypocritical ministers and their easily gulled parishioners also angered Protestants. Both Stiles and Shawnessy detract Christianity throughout the novel. "The typical Christian," Stiles states,

> is just plain crazy. . . . He believes that the universe was made by a grand old man squatting on a cloud. He believes that this old man somehow begot a son without intercourse a few hundred years ago. He believes that this son came down to earth for the express purpose of being executed like a common criminal to purge humanity of its sins. He believes that the world is better for all this, despite the fact that people go on being as no account as ever. He believes that this young man, after being very dead, got up and walked out of the grave. He believes that the old man up there on the cloud is all-good and all-powerful, but that the world of his creation is a world of corruption and death.[20]

Elsewhere the Professor says that God cannot expect to survive "the era of Darwin and the Dynamo."[21] He argues, however, that resurrection does exist and identifies the blessed, consecrated place where the miraculous event occurs. The sacred site is not a tomb but a womb: "The original love-desire is that of the sperm for the egg. This blind little boat loaded with memories goes and goes till the fuel gives out or it touches port. This terrific tadpole is the real bearer of life. It is Aeneas bearing the Golden Bough and overcoming death. And the only sacred place is the dark-walled valley into which it swims. As for us, we're just seedpods with delusions of grandeur."[22]

Such passages were bound to draw fire. Father Alfred J. Barrett of Fordham University derided *Raintree County* as "1,066 pages of bombast, rank obscenity, materialistic philosophy and blasphemous impudicity."[23] The novel, he added, "patently falls within the general prohibition of the Index."[24] At a critics' forum, Father Barrett announced he was canceling his Book-of-the-Month club subscription in protest against the novel. The Houghton Mifflin Company defended the novel against Barrett's charges, arguing that the book contained irreverent characters but was not itself irreverent. According to the Houghton Mifflin publicity department, Lockridge's purpose in writing the novel was "to give the world a legend of moral and spiritual regeneration in an era when hatred and materialism appear to be enveloping the world—or much of it—in fear and irreligious despair."[25]

Barrett's attacks disturbed the sensitive Lockridge but were not unexpected or unanticipated by him. He knew his novel would undoubtedly arouse wrath in some quarters. No doubt he was angry at the power the church exerted in Hollywood. The Catholic Legion of Decency prided itself on policing the entertainment industry. If it did not exert great authority over America's publishing houses or Broadway theater, it had a much more powerful influence in Hollywood. The do's and don'ts of movie making were laid out in the Johnson and Hays Office Code which was longer than the Washington congressional budget. Literary adaptions were subject to silly and contrived censorship in order for the movie versions to meet Code standards and get the seal of approval from the Legion of Decency. Such studio fudging spoiled many serious films. The plot elements had to come out properly whitewashed: the villain must always get his or her just desserts. Murderers inevitably had to be caught and punished if not killed. Characters had to be softened, their "bad" traits minimized and played down, if they were to survive the movie. Often artificial plot elements were foisted on stories or alternative scenarios devised to explain away problems in character motivation and action. Certain subjects, of course, were completely taboo. The Legion of Decency was not responsible for all the script changes. The studio heads were also capricious and fickle as well as arrogant and power-mad. They had agendas of their own and were often more concerned with the demands and whims of their directors and stars than keeping their writers happy, though they had no compunction about cracking the whip and bringing their power to bear on the others as well. Louis B. Mayer was the most powerful of the studio dictators: as far as he and the other studio heads were concerned, directors, actors, actresses, and writers were all just employees. The writer, however, was low man on the totem pole. Authors were a dime a dozen. When a mogul acquired the rights to a work it was his. Dilution and modification would often ensue. The Nazis might burn books, but Messrs. Mayer, Goldwyn, Cohen, Zanuck, and the Brothers Warner also exercised censorship. They doctored and distorted, cleaned up and homogenized as they saw fit. Whether American-born or displaced European refugees, authors who came to Hollywood generally left with a bad taste in their mouths. Gentile writers felt degraded by Hollywood writing mills and Jewish bosses. Empathetic American-born Jewish authors were ashamed of the immigrant studio heads and commiserated with and apologized to their non-Jewish colleagues. Everyone felt harassed, kept down, and put in place. Yet everyone—or almost everyone—complied with the system and did not make waves. Most authors played the game, took the money, and ran. Only the most important literary figures—Ernest Hemingway, for example — could rebuke the system without suffering any negative consequences. David Selznick acquired the rights to *A Farewell to Arms* from Warner Brothers who had in turn purchased them from Paramount, who had bought the book from Hemingway and made the first motion picture version of the novel starring Gary Cooper and Helen Hayes. The loosely adapted Selznick remake would star Rock Hudson and a badly miscast Jennifer Jones. Although Selznick was under no obligation to pay Hemingway anything (he gave the rights to his *Star Is Born* to Warner's in exchange for the rights to *A Farewell to Arms*), Selznick felt Hemingway deserved some money, so he cabled the author that he planned to remit him $50,000 from the film's eventual profits even though legally he did not owe him a nickel. Hemingway replied that as the film featured the forty-year-old Mrs. Selznick in the role of the twenty-four-year-old Catherine, he doubted that it would make a profit, but, if by chance it did, Selznick should have the $50,000 changed into nickels and then he could "shove them up his ass until they came out his ears."[26] Many writers in Hollywood fantasized about dressing down studio heads in a similar fashion, but dared not protest and speak out. Hemingway did, in fact, attend a screening of the Selznick movie, but he left the theater after only half an hour. He would later comment that when a novelist saw a beloved work desecrated at the hands of a Hollywood movie maker it was like "pissing in your father's beer."[27]

Ross Lockridge was in Hollywood a short time before his death to work on the screenplay of *Raintree County*. He was, however, one of the least-suited writers ever to show up in California. He did not have a thick skin but was frequently nervous, and he broke down under pressure. Furthermore, he deeply resented the revisions that he earlier had to make on his novel in order to satisfy the demands of his publisher and MGM. His vision would undergo further change and corruption in the movie, which would come out in 1957. The project had been shelved in 1949, but interest revived in it in 1954, and the script was assigned to Millard Kauffmann, the creator of the cartoon character Mr. Magoo. The studio still wanted to make a northern *Gone with the Wind*. But the film would not prove as successful as the studio executives had hoped. While it features Elizabeth Taylor in perhaps her finest performance as the crazed Susanna, the film is chiefly remembered today due to the disfigurement of Montgomery Cliff's face that took place in mid-production. Cliff, who plays the part of John Shawnessy, broke his nose in an automobile accident and had to undergo extensive plastic surgery, radically altering his appearance. The picture records the change in his looks since it features scenes shot before and after his accident. The disfigurement that Lockridge's novel underwent was not nearly so well noticed. The novel takes place in a single day in 1892. The events of that significant twenty-four hour period, however, are not portrayed in the movie, which ends shortly after the Civil War. Much of the novel deals with the years following the conflict. This material, therefore, is also dropped from the film. Moreover, the movie is far from faithful to the portions of the book it does dramatize. Although many incidents from the novel remain intact, the plot is significantly altered. Shawnessy is made into a more conventional hero. He does not send Susanna home to her people; she runs away. He enlists in the army and goes South in the hopes of finding her. He succeeds in doing so and brings her back to *Raintree County*. She does not kill her son but dies in childbirth. Shawnessy triumphs over Jones and it is intimated at the movie's conclusion that he will eventually win the hand of his first love, Nell. When he left California shortly before his death, Lockridge must have been greatly disillusioned. He had been very well remunerated for the movie rights to *Raintree County*, but he may have felt a little like a prostitute when he realized what was being done with his book in Hollywood.

After finishing his novel, Lockridge seems to have suffered from something akin to postpartum depression. As *Raintree County* draws to its conclusion, John Shawnessy desires to build the world all over again—this time in language. The theme of regeneration, of "beginning anew," is strongly sounded. It seems that a part of Lockridge was eager to do the same. The final pages of *Raintree County* sound like a call to arms. One perceives Lockridge gathering himself to embark on another literary venture; a second book seems to be in the offing. Lockridge expresses the desire he feels to start writing once more. The prospect, however, must have been daunting for the weakened and burnt-out writer. *Raintree County* had a gestation period of seven lean, hard years for its author. Yet, he had persevered and had erected his monument to a past era. While other young Americans were dying in Europe and in the Pacific, Lockridge was writing about another war long past. This, too, must have weighed on him. By all accounts, he was worn and exhausted when he at last stopped work on his novel, and angry and disconsolate about the revisions that he had been forced to make. Yet when he quit writing, he must have experienced a tremendous vacancy. The prospect of starting a new book, however, was too much.

Wondering why it was taking her husband so long to return from the post office, Vernice Lockridge went to the garage shortly before eleven o'clock on March 6, 1948. The Kaiser was inside. She heard the motor running, entered the unlocked side door, and turned on the lights. She saw her husband sitting upright in the back seat. A vacuum cleaner hose ran from the tail pipe to the automobile's left rear window. The garage was full of dense gas fumes. She turned the key in the ignition, threw open the main garage door, then yanked her husband from the back seat of the car and pulled him out of the garage and onto the driveway. She cried out for help, then ran back to the house to summon assistance. City firemen arrived on the scene and worked for an hour in an attempt to revive Lockridge but to no avail. He was dead from carbon monoxide poisoning.

Notes

1. Ross Lockridge Jr., *Raintree County* (Boston: Houghton Mifflin, 1948), p. 1010.
2. Ibid., p. 4.
3. Ibid.
4. Ibid., p. 1005.
5. Ibid., p. 771.
6. Ibid., p. 430.
7. Ibid., p. 887.
8. James Joyce, *Ulysses: The Corrected Text*, ed. Hans Walter Gabler with Wolfhard Steppe and Claus Melchior (New York: Vintage Books, 1986), p. 6.
9. *Raintree County*, p. 887.
10. Ibid.
11. Ibid.
12. Ibid., pp. 888–89.
13. Ibid., p. 908.
14. *Ulysses*, p. 256.

15. *Raintree County*, p. 860.

16. Ibid., p. 1058.

17. Ibid.

18. See Larry Lockridge, *Shade of the Raintree: The Life and Death of Ross Lockridge, Jr.* (New York: Viking, 1994), photo insert facing p. 149.

19. Ibid., p. 183.

20. *Raintree County*, p. 928.

21. Ibid., p. 912.

22. Ibid.

23. Quoted in *New York Times* obituary, 8 March 1948.

24. Ibid.

25. Ibid.

26. Quoted by Bob Thomas, *Selznick* (New York: Pocket Books, 1972), pp. 291-292.

27. Quoted by Edward Z. Epstein, *Portrait of Jennifer* (New York: Simon and Shuster, 1995), p. 350.

Klaus Mann

O N MAY 21, 1949, KLAUS MANN TOOK HIS OWN LIFE IN CANNES, France, by swallowing an overdose of sleeping pills. His parents, Thomas and Katia Mann, and his sister, Erika Auden, learned of his death on their arrival in Sweden, after flying there from Great Britain. Mann Senior had just been awarded an honorary doctorate by Oxford University and, as an acceptance address, had delivered in German his celebrated essay *Goethe and Democracy*.

The *New York Times* reported that the forty-two-year-old Klaus had expired from a heart attack and that his parents had been apprised of his death. The dateline for the article did not read Cannes but Stockholm. The father's whereabouts (the news of *his* being informed of the matter) took precedence over the fact of the son's death.[1]

This was Klaus's second attempt at suicide. The first, in Santa Monica, California, had occurred only ten months earlier, on July 11, 1948, when he had slit his wrists with a razor, ingested sleeping pills, and then attempted to gas himself.[2] Friends rushed him to a hospital where, after his self-inflicted gashes were taped and his stomach was pumped, his condition was ruled not serious. The primary motive for Klaus's act had been the infidelity of his current lover, a dull-witted but (till then) faithful young sailor.

At a very young age Klaus Mann developed what was to be a life-long fascination with death. Indeed, in his youth he was quite the poseur, his death wish in part pure Romantic affectation. To be obsessed with the grave was part of what it meant to be a poet, but death also meant peace and oblivion to Klaus, a cessation of all pain and suffering. In 1930, in his essay *Selbstmörder*, he wrote feelingly about various suicides he had known and described with "what bitter envy"[3] his gaze followed them into the unknown.

In the course of his life, Klaus suffered much. On several occasions he had experienced great physical pain and torment. He was dangerously ill with appendicitis in 1915 and required four excruciating operations. In the late thirties, he underwent a detoxification cure, where he was weaned off morphine and suffered through an agonizing withdrawal. One can see why a gentle painless death—one provided by ingesting many times the normal sleeping pill dose—would appeal to him. His psychological problems, however, caused him even greater pain. He suffered from drug addiction, from the fact that he was homosexual and a German living in the twentieth century, and because he was his father's son. Klaus came to feel that life was nothing but anguish and death the absence of it. The world situation after the war also disheartened him. The Cold War conflict between Russia and the United States, he wrote in his posthumously published memoir, *The Agony of the European Mind*, left "no room for intellectual independence and hope."[4] He called for a suicide wave of European intellectuals to shake the people of the world out of their lethargy and "bring home the deadly seriousness of the plague that man had brought on himself by his stupidity and selfishness."[5]

The years following the war were particularly difficult for Klaus. He had little success with writing and he again began taking drugs. He had sought consolation for a time with the Catholic church during the war, but his interest in Christianity quickly evaporated. Old friends kept him at arm's length. Naziism had, of course, been defeated, but taking up the cudgels against Hitler had been therapeutic for Klaus. It gave him purpose. There had been an urgency to his life. He founded the refugee magazine *Decision*, then he joined the United States Army. Since he experienced difficulty writing in America after the war, he hoped the sunny climate of the French Riviera would be more conducive for work. In a letter set down the day before his suicide, he wrote that he was reasonably well and trying to write.

Upon hearing that his son had taken his own life, Thomas Mann refused to break his lecture engagements. Neither he nor his wife and not even the beloved sister—it must have hurt her to do so, but Erika steadfastly remained at her parents' side like some dutiful Walkyrie—attended the son's funeral. For many years brother and sister had been inseparable, but from 1947 onward, Erika devoted herself exclusively to their father, becoming his amanuensis and editor.

Only Klaus's younger brother Michael appeared at the ceremony as sole representative of the Mann family. In fact, his arrival came as a complete surprise to those attending the service. On tour with Monteux's San Francisco Symphony, he met the funeral procession at the gravesite, removed his viola d'amore from its tiny case and, as his brother's remains were lowered into the earth, played a moving largo. Shortly after Klaus's suicide, in a letter to Hermann Hesse, Thomas Mann confessed that his relationship to Klaus had been "difficult and not without feelings of guilt, for my very existence cast a shadow over him from the start."[6]

Alas, truer words could not have been written.

For most of his life, Klaus felt himself a watered-down, diluted version of his father. Over the years their relations had become strained almost to the breaking point. Thomas acknowledged Klaus's existence only perfunctorily, and usually in a dispassionate manner—feigned, perhaps, but nonetheless icy. There was ample reason for his coolness. Much about the son made the father shudder. A boy of his own blood and ambition, Klaus appeared nonetheless merely a burlesque, a ridiculous lampoon of the world-renowned author. Thomas Mann was far from a humble man. From early on in his career, he considered himself the foremost writer in German of the twentieth century, the modern counterpart of Johann Wolfgang Goethe (and rightly so, history bears him out). Klaus simply didn't measure up.

The son, on the other hand, identified his father in his 1937 novella *Barred Window* not with Goethe but with that other much more controversial German genius, Richard Wagner. Which portrait came closer to the truth? After all, Wagnerian leitmotiv had taught Thomas how to structure. He would transpose the musical method to his medium: words. As a very young man he fell under the evil wizard's spell just as did the future German Führer (a being he reviled but one whom he recognized as a brother artist and fellow member of the guild).[7] While Wagner the man became suspect to Thomas, he continued to adore Wagner's music. Throughout his life, he was always sitting down at the piano. He would play for perhaps an hour or longer, but, as Klaus writes, "It was always the same rhythm, at once drawing and violent; always the swelling, weeping, jubilating song. It was always Tristan."[8]

Despite all that he suffered in life, Thomas Mann had slowly and painfully produced masterpiece after masterpiece. He also took a tremendously courageous stand against the spread of fascism in Europe though, as will be seen, early in his period of exile he made certain compromises with the Nazi government in exchange for publishing concessions in Germany, where he so badly wanted his Joseph novels to appear. The first two volumes of the series *The Tales of Jacob* and *Young Joseph* were indeed printed in Hitler's Berlin.

In his lifetime, the elder Mann received greater international recognition than any of his contemporaries, including such luminaries as Hauptmann, Kafka, Rilke, Musil, Broch, Döblin, Hesse, and, later, Brecht. This is all the more amazing, as in his personal life he heroically overcame—or at least appeared to have thoroughly conquered—individual weaknesses or private "bohemianisms" comparable in destructiveness to the deficiencies that doomed his sisters Julia and Clara to premature death both by suicide, and his elder brother Heinrich, his early rival, far more clear-sighted in political matters perhaps, but not nearly so fine an author as Thomas, to let himself go, write without discipline. Capable of doing much better work, Heinrich turned out over the years many second or even third-rate works, trashy outpourings of cheap eroticism that made Thomas suffer whenever he tried to read them; he had so clearly come out the winner in their personal contest.

With all the skill of a *Feldmarschall*, Thomas Mann defended himself against his numerous self-destructive inclinations. He was extremely self-centered, but he thought his "inwardness" essential to his work. He guarded himself so well, entirely repressing all his suspect tendencies, that to the world he became a symbol of rectitude, the big businessman of Letters, a Hanseatic merchant in the tradition of his respectable Lübeck forebears. He took Goethe's credo to heart; his work was one vast confession. He might write about suspect persons—dilettantes, bohemians, homosexuals, and confidence men—or about the demonic in life, or the deceitfulness of nature, but his style was always that of a great traditionalist, and the life he led before the world was respectably bourgeois. He married the very wealthy and half-Jewish Katia Pringsheim, daughter of the renowned Munich University mathematics professor, arts patron, and one-time friend of Wagner, Alfred Pringsheim, and granddaughter of the celebrated Berlin literary couple of Ernst and Hedwig Dohm. Katia herself was no intellectual slouch. One of the first Bavarian women to pass the *Abitur*, the notoriously difficult secondary school final examination which Thomas Mann had repeatedly failed, she subsequently studied experimental physics under Roentgen at Munich University. The fact that his wife was half-Jewish surely weighed heavily in Thomas Mann's decision to break with Germany upon Hitler's ascension to power in 1933. Divided loyalties and the psychological perplexities arising therefrom would also plague the son, who was born in November 1906, a year to the month after his elder sister Erika.

Like Richard Wagner, who chose to name his son Siegfried after the hero of his *Ring* cycle, Thomas gave his first-born son the name of the hero of his second novel, *Royal Highness*: Klaus Heinrich, but whereas the *Ring* was Wagner's supreme masterpiece, Thomas Mann's second novel, his gently satiric fictionalization of his own courtship of Katia, the male protagonist recast as a German prince of a fairy-tale state, the wife-to-be as a German-American millionairess, is the only work in the Mann canon decidedly inferior. However, Mann defended the book against all its detractors. Although handicapped by a withered arm he must continually hide, Prince Klaus Heinrich is a "Sunday child"[9] who triumphs as ruler when his brother, the Grand Duke Alberich, abdicates in his favor (as in a sense Heinrich Mann did for Thomas in the world of twentieth-century German literature). Prince Klaus succeeds in saving his financially straitened state by his marriage. Indeed, Thomas Mann's own son was raised like a little princeling, but, unlike the hero of the book for which he was named, he could not overcome his own handicaps and achieve greater glory. Yet this half-genius tried! From a young age, he strove very hard to be a writer.

Being Thomas Mann's child had both its advantages and disadvantages. Mann did not have a very nurturing personality. When they were young, his children were allowed to see him only at specified times during the day. As Klaus's younger brother Golo writes in his *Recollections*: "We almost always had to keep quiet—in the morning because father was working; in the afternoon because he first read, then slept; towards evening, because then he worked seriously again. Terrible were the storms if we disturbed him."[10]

Despite Klaus's great desire to emulate his father, he received scant praise.

Nonetheless, being Mann's son undoubtedly smoothed the way for him as a writer; he was already launched at the age of eighteen. As he wrote in his autobiography, *The Turning Point*: "Whatever I had to offer, they took it; they thought it interesting. The best newspapers and magazines printed my short stories, articles, and reflections."[11] While his father wrote very slowly and painstakingly, Klaus turned out work in a variety of genres with stunning speed. He wrote plays, novels, short stories, essays, travel books, and two autobiographical volumes. His three primary works, however, were written after his family had gone into exile. They are *Symphonie Pathétique* (1935), a novel concerning Peter Ilyitch Tchaikovsky; *Mephisto* (1936), his tale of a talented actor and careerist who makes a Faustian pact with Hermann Göring and becomes the manager of the State Theatre in Berlin and a cultural ambassador for National Socialism; and *The Volcano* (1939), his novel concerning the detoxification cure of a drug addict. Yet, as Klaus wrote in his memoir, *Child of the Times*, he "never had unprejudiced readers. Not only the hostile ones, but the friendly as well instinctively make a connection between whatever I write and my father's work. They judge me as my father's son."[12] Of course, in his innermost being, Klaus knew his books, good as some of them might be, could not possibly rank with those of his very great and long-suffering father, the Magician, or *Der Zauberer*, as he and the other Mann children had dubbed him in their childhood.

Klaus knew his father had created and continued to create masterpieces of the highest order, novels and novellas destined to outlive their time. A talented and perceptive critic of the works not only of his father but of many other prominent twentieth-century authors as well, he was painfully aware of his own shortcomings. Like his Uncle Heinrich he rarely bothered to polish anything he had written, but was satisfied with early drafts, despite their sometimes glaring imperfections, and he often wrote while under the influence of drugs. Klaus's sense of inferiority was also exacerbated by the fact that he could not support himself on his earnings as a writer (especially after the family went into exile) but was dependent on stipends from his parents.

As well as his father's literary ambitions, Klaus seemed to have inherited a number of the same destructive tendencies his father had had, but unlike the elder Mann, had been unable (or unwilling) to master them. The fact that he was openly homosexual must have awakened certain deep misgivings on his father's part, trepidations arising from his own repressed desires. Despite homoerotic yearnings in his youth and through much of his adult life, Thomas Mann remained abstemious. He chose respectability, married, and fathered six children, though any sapient reader of his books would see his intellectual interest in inversion. Klaus consummated his homosexuality, reveled in it, and refused to lead a double life.

In many disturbing ways, Mann and his son were much alike. Both men were egotistical in the extreme and often unemotional in their relations with others. Klaus was as cold and unfeeling with his homosexual partners as Thomas had been with his children. His relationships were fervent but short-lived. In the novel *Symphonie Pathétique* Tchaikovsky, reflecting upon his homosexuality, confesses: "I

never loved where there was any hope or danger of its becoming serious, of my
being tied, of my being loved in return and so committed."[13] Klaus's Tchaikovsky
is every bit as much a self-portrait as his father's Goethe and Adrian Leverkühn.
The "hero" of *The Volcano* is yet another avatar of Klaus, who himself became
addicted to morphine in the early thirties just as Germany itself plunged into
national self-destruction.

The son as well as the father could be justly accused of excessive self-absorption; but if he was often narcissistic, Thomas had also throughout his long life cultivated a sense of irony. Klaus, a perpetual adolescent, must have seemed like a
parody of the father's younger indolent, moody self, for Klaus was an actor—a confidence man—constantly changing masks, adopting yet another affected pose. He
was as much of a cipher as his hated brother-in-law, Erika's first husband, the actor
Gustaf Gründgens, upon whom he modeled Hendrik Höfgen, the soulless careerist
of his novel *Mephisto*. One of the accomplishments of that book is that Klaus manages to make his anti-hero, at least in part, human and likable. There is quite as
much Klaus Mann in Hendrik Höfgen as there is Gründgens.

Generally, Thomas Mann "praised" his son's books in only a vague, imprecise,
even fulsome way, devoting at most only a sentence or two, in one of his numerous
letters to his son otherwise devoted to family matters, to whatever work was then in
question. He acknowledged that a book appeared, then said something bland and
patently insincere about it. Only *The Volcano* really impressed him, especially the
section dealing with the morphine addict's detoxification. "For years,"[14] he wrote to
Klaus, "you have not been appreciated at your full worth." But even in this long
and friendly letter, Mann could not forbear to mention: "You are also an heir; your
bed has been made for you."[15] With *Mephisto* (a novel Thomas had barely recognized let alone said anything complimentary about) Klaus actually anticipated (in
a sense paved the way for) his father's last great masterpiece, *Dr. Faustus: The Life
of the German Composer Adrian Leverkühn As Told by a Friend*. While it is true that
long before Klaus wrote *Mephisto*, Thomas had jotted down a sketch about an artist
selling his soul to the devil in exchange for a number of years of fruitful artistic creation, it was the son who first tied the Faust myth to Naziism. Although on the
boards, Höfgen takes on the role of Mephisto, backstage he plays Faust to Göring's
devil. A decade after his son's book was published, Thomas would contrast his
artist Leverkühn's pact to the one the German people made with destiny in the first
half of the twentieth century, to Hitler's meteoric rise and fall. Both Manns wanted
to demonstrate that the same tree of German Romanticism brought forth fruit both
good and evil; that the best and worst in the German character were closely related,
almost one and the same. The father's book is immeasurably greater than the son's.
Mann developed lung cancer while writing it, and saw his personal illness as a
reflection of the world cancer which had its origin in Hitler's Germany and had
metastasized from there across all of Europe. Mann came to feel that everything
German, including his own art, was diseased and rotting from within, a source of

contagion to those otherwise healthy. One criticism frequently made of *Dr. Faustus* is that Mann thoroughly dehumanized Leverkühn, that the composer remains an unfeeling figure of ice. The reader finds it hard to empathize with him until late in the novel his seraphic little nephew Nepomuk develops meningitis and dies after having been given into his charge. In Höfgen, on the other hand, Klaus gave evil a human face, something his father couldn't quite manage. Nonetheless, Klaus couldn't help but feel that his father's novel had made his own superfluous. As usual, he had been dwarfed. In the obituary he wrote for Klaus, Thomas mentions several of his son's books but not *Mephisto*. Not only in taking up the Faust theme did the son precede the father, however. He was also quicker to embrace certain important moral stances.

As a boy, Klaus learned from his father's mistaken political judgments. After Germany's defeat in World War I, Thomas Mann himself underwent his great conversion from his country's most zealous apologist to one of her most fiery critics. Ironically, in 1875, he had been christened Paul Thomas Mann after a maternal uncle—now in middle age he went down his own road to Damascus: out of his Germanness he grew into a European, a citizen of the world.

Klaus remembered the World War I father, Thomas before he conquered his chauvinism. The elder Mann hated politics. He didn't want to devote his attention to anything but his work, but again and again he was forced to take a stand. James Joyce, when asked to comment about the 1938 Munich Conference between Hitler, Chamberlain, and Daladier quipped, "Why don't they read *Finnegans Wake* and leave Czechoslovakia alone."[16] During the First World War, Thomas Mann took an equally Olympian stand. So self-absorbed with his own work and the "wrong" he felt had been done Germany, he stubbornly persisted in writing his great defense of anti-democratic Germanism, *Reflections of a Non-political Man*, taking very little notice the while of all the wasteful death and carnage wrought by the war. He broke with his brother Heinrich, who from the first spoke out against the slaughter and bitterly accused Thomas of having a passion for himself only, of having the inability ever to grasp the real seriousness of anyone's life but his own. Right up until the cessation of hostilities, Thomas maintained that Germany had been unfairly singled out for reproach. Klaus brilliantly captures his father during this period in the following lines from *The Turning Point*:

> This wartime father seems estranged and distant, essentially different from the father I have known before and after those years of struggle and bitterness. The paternal physiognomy that looms up when I recall this period seems devoid of the kindness and irony which both inseparably belong to his character. The face I visualize looks severe and somber—a proud and nervous brow with sensitive temples and sunken cheeks. Curiously enough it is a bearded face, a long haggard oval framed by a hard prickly beard . . . His features, at once proud and worried, resemble those of a Spanish knight and nobleman —the errant hero and dreamer called Don Quixote.[17]

Even after becoming a democrat, Thomas remained politically naive. Not for one moment, however, was Klaus deceived by Hitler or his minions. After the burning of the Reichstag, he and his sister Erika warned their father, who was out of the country on a lecture tour, not to return to Germany. But in exile, Thomas Mann would not speak out against the new regime, as did his brother Heinrich and his son and daughter. He even contemplated a possible return to Germany. His brother and his children were deprived of their German citizenship before he was, and Klaus's and Heinrich's books were burned on the bonfires whereas his were spared, at least for a time. Klaus edited the refugee journal *Die Sammlung* which bitterly attacked the Nazis. Thomas would not contribute to the magazine and publicly disassociated himself from his son. Because he declined to attack Hitler in the foreign press, Thomas Mann's works weren't banned in Germany.[18] Many members of the refugee community felt betrayed by Mann's initial silence. Klaus tried to advise him to cut ties with his German publisher. In a letter to his father, he wrote: "One does not entrust one's treasure to a country that one has left with loathing. They will harry it to death. . . . It is probably too late, and I really have no business interfering and giving you this advice. But I don't want to leave anything untried. The matter is terribly important—objectively and also to me personally. I think it is a grave mistake to let your book be published in this Germany."[18] Mann finally broke his silence in 1936 when, in an open letter to Eduard Korrodi, the literary editor of the *Neue Zürcher Zeitung* who had penned an article claiming that only the Jewish element in German letters had emigrated from Germany, he wrote: "The German, or the German rulers' hatred of the Jews is in the higher sense not directed against Europe and all loftier Germanism; it is directed, as becomes increasingly apparent, against the Christian and classical foundations of western morality."[19] Before he took this step, he received an imploring telegram from Klaus to declare himself: "Urgently request reply how and where you choose to Korrodi's disastrous article stop this time it is really a question of life and death for us all."[20] After a three-year period of silence, Thomas Mann would write countless articles attacking Hitler and fascism. Klaus would also continue his own fight. After becoming a United States citizen, he would volunteer for military service and was assigned to a desk job writing for *Stars and Stripes*.

Ultimately, it is difficult to determine who suffered more in life, Thomas or Klaus Mann. Both men had an intellectual affinity with the dark and demonic and a longing for death, but suicide was not an option for the father. He overcame his youthful romantic infatuations. What mattered most in Thomas's life was his work. He would painfully persist at it even in old age after all artistic endeavor had grown dubious to him. Everything German had been called into question. He even came to feel that most of his work was nothing more "than a morbid and half parodistic echo of German greatness."[21] Privately Mann often said that it would have been better if he had died after he completed *Dr. Faustus*. He judged his subsequent fictions—*The Holy Sinner*, *The Black Swan*, and *The Confessions of Felix Krull*—frivolous. Yet he found within himself somewhere the strength to fight and write on. His son, unfortunately, did not.

Notes

1. *New York Times* obituary, 23 May 1949.

2. See Ronald Hayman, *Thomas Mann: A Biography* (New York: Scribner, 1995), p. 551.

3. Quoted by Marcel Reich-Ranicki, *Thomas Mann and His Family*, trans. Ralph Manheim (London: Collins, 1989), p. 162.

4. Ibid., p. 159.

5. Ibid.

6. Anni Carlson and Volker Michels, eds., *The Hesse / Mann Letters*, trans. Ralph Manheim (New York: Harper and Row, 1975), p. 136.

7. See Thomas Mann, "A Brother," trans. H. T. Lowe Porter, *Order of the Day* (New York: Knopf, 1942), pp. 153-161.

8. Quoted by Nigel Hamilton, *The Brothers Mann* (New Haven: Yale University Press, 1979), p. 44.

9. Ibid., p. 115.

10. Quoted by Reich-Ranicki, *Thomas Mann and His Family*, p. 179.

11. Ibid., p. 164.

12. Ibid., p. 165.

13. Ibid., p. 172.

14. Ibid., p. 170.

15. Ibid., pp. 170-171.

16. Quoted by Paul West, "The Shapelessness of Things to Come," *Sheer Fiction*, vol. 1 (New Paltz, New York: McPherson, 1987), p. 26.

17. Quoted by Hamilton, *The Brothers Mann*, p. 174.

18. Quoted by Reich-Ranicki, *Thomas Mann and His Family*, p. 168.

19. Quoted by Hamilton, *The Brothers Mann*, p. 293.

20. Quoted by Reich-Ranicki, *Thomas Mann and His Family*, p. 168.

21. Ibid., p. 64.

Cesare Pavese

H E WROTE THAT NO ONE EVER LACKED A GOOD REASON FOR SUICIDE, and on August 26, 1950, at the age of forty-two, Cesare Pavese, arguably the most accomplished Italian novelist of his generation, finally made what he believed was the only legitimate gesture open to suffering man: he took his own life by swallowing an overdose of sleeping pills. Yet the cause he gave for killing himself, his brief, unhappy affair with an American woman whom he, with characteristic Piedmontese gallantry, refused to name but referred to only as C—, seemed hardly suitable as a justification for so momentous and decisive an act. Members of the press immediately proposed other reasons for Pavese's action, ranging from his growing political disenchantment (at the time of his death, he appeared ready to break with his one-time allies, the communists) to his supposed mental instability. Indeed there was so much speculation about Pavese's motivations that his suicide rapidly acquired a mythic aura. Despite all the differing assertions made by the newspapermen, all of whom purported to know the hidden "truth," many Italians were taken in by the fable that Pavese himself originated and saw the novelist in the romantic guise of the unrequited lover. During his funeral procession, which had an eerie carnival aspect, a number of women followed his casket weeping, hoping to be taken for his mistress.

Later, when the public learned C—'s identity—Constance Dowling, a minor Hollywood starlet who in the 1940s appeared in a string of insignificant "B" features, such as the Danny Kaye vehicle *Up in Arms*—Pavese's suicide seemed, despite the actress's undeniable sex appeal, pathetic and piteous. In his complete nakedness, the author looked absolutely spineless. Not only did he appear to be a hapless thrall but one subject to a woman entirely unworthy of him, a fool ensnared in the meshes of human bondage. Yet for all her shallowness and superficiality, Dowling—whom Pavese met in 1950 when she was in Italy searching for movie work—is essentially guiltless in Pavese's suicide. The responsibility rests squarely with him. As we shall see, "blame" (if such is the right word) is entirely attributable to the Italian's own shortcomings and character flaws. No doubt Pavese would like us to overlook all his deficiencies and see his suicide as a grand romantic gesture—hardly an original demonstration of supposed devotion but a stirring and touching one nonetheless. The love lyrics or *amoretti* that he addressed to Dowling bolster this counterfeit view, the Italian's own egotistic, virile projection of himself as a man overcome by an overwhelming, annihilating passion. The poems were collected and published after his death under the title *Death Will Stare at Me out of Your Eyes*. The final verse "Last Blues" is written in English. Although hardly a distinguished piece of poetry, it has nonetheless been found very moving by a number of Pavese's commentators as a final note of desperation and farewell:

> 'T was only a flirt
> you sure did know—
> some one was hurt
> long time ago.
>
> All is the same
> time has gone by—
> some day you came
> some day you'll die.
>
> Some one has died
> long time ago—
> some one who tried
> but didn't know.[1]

Despite Pavese's ardent avowals of love for C— (in addition to the final poems, he also dedicated his last novel, *The Moon and the Bonfires*, to her), the genuineness of his feelings is questionable. One rightly suspects that he set out to manufacture a legend, to cast his action in the best possible light. Although she did not extend him intellectual understanding or emotional support, Dowling did clearly grant Pavese something substantial. He likely experienced the best sex of his life with her. For many years, he suffered from premature ejaculation,[2] but had overcome this difficulty prior to his involvement with the movie star. Under her tutelage, he realized his second youth, and, indeed, instead of a mature caring man, the smitten Italian resembles a moody and infatuated adolescent caught in the throes of first love and, like a petulant boy, seems unfit and incapable of true commitment to another human being. If he was in love with anybody, this forty-two-year-old teenager was in love with himself. In the end, his own gratification was all that really mattered to him. At first glance, Pavese's death seems not so much tragic and poignant as irresponsible and rash.

Self-centered and egocentric, the genuine Pavese emerges in the pages of his posthumously published diary, the American edition of which is entitled *The Burning Brand*, though a more exact translation of the Italian title would be *This Business of Living*. He is, for the most part, a thoroughly dislikable individual, vain and vindictive, full of spite and self-pity. Aside from his mother and sister whom he absolves from any blame and responsibility in his problems and difficulties, Pavese condemns and castigates practically everyone else who played any sort of significant role in his life at all. He feels betrayed on all sides and forced unwillingly into the part of stranger and outcast.

The years encompassed by the diary (1935–50) include Italy's most turbulent during this century, yet in the pages of his private journal, Pavese devotes but a single line to the national turmoil, concentrating instead on his own personal pain.[3] Though one would hardly guess the truth from the diary where Pavese materializes as a shallow and selfish individual, uninterested in the welfare of anyone but himself, to his enormous credit, disinclined as he constitutionally was to take on such a heroic role, Pavese did actively participate in the world around him; indeed, he took many courageous political stands in his public life, and was in fact arrested and jailed for resisting Mussolini and fascism. He wore many masks in his career and none of these faces was altogether false, yet he used his myriad identities to cover the hollowness of the innermost self he reveals in the diary.

Throughout its pages, Pavese frequently indulges in the same "sacrosanct Piedmontese misogyny"[4] that he elsewhere decried as one of the chief faults of his countrymen. These often vile attacks differ markedly from the sympathetic depiction of the plight of Italian females in his novels, especially *Among Women Only*, which is staged almost entirely in the feminine arena (men enter the work only peripherally as props for the ladies). The book deals with the various travails of a cluster of Turinese women of divergent age, class, and social background several years after the Second World War. The girls chum around together and, though they are often hard, callous and unsympathetic with each other, they spend hours discussing their various problems. These usually have to do with the men in their lives, who are always maneuvering to dominate and control them. Yet they also feud among themselves and are frequently subject to petty jealousies. Several of the women opt for intimacy with members of their own sex or are bisexual. One of the younger girls, Rosetta, is so discontent with the routine of her life that she commits suicide at the close of the novel after making an earlier, unsuccessful attempt on her life.

In this book, Pavese holds to the view that suicide is something that happens when an individual becomes glutted and satiated with existence. When the person reaches this saturation point, he will try to kill himself just as the ripe fruit will fall from the tree. If someone attempts suicide once and fails, he will inevitably try again until he, at last, succeeds. It is merely a matter of the will. During the course of the novel, Rosetta is not particularly morose or unhappy. At times, she is gay and convivial.

Apart from its sensational themes of suicide and bisexuality, the book argues the case for the emancipation and enfranchisement of women. The central character, Clelia, is content to manage a store for its Roman owners and thereby lead a life of her own. Though friendly men are always at hand to offer her whatever they can, more often than not they would supply her nothing but problems if she entered a lasting relationship with them. Therefore, she flits back and forth between several lovers.

While he is sympathetic to women in his novels, Pavese complains bitterly about their caprices and their inconsistency in his journal. In its pages, he diligently registers the marriages of all the women he had once ached and yearned for, and writes contemptuously of the men they accepted as husbands and of the children produced by these (to his mind) all but adulterous unions. "The last indignity," according to the Pavese of the diaries —and one feels he doesn't wear one of his funny faces here, that he truly means what he says—is the "woman who smells of sperm that is not your own."[5]

It is evident that Pavese had continuing problems with the opposite sex during the entire period he kept his journal. Early childhood traumas partially explain his life-long obstacles in dealing with women. Pavese's father died when he was only six. One feels that, despite the loyalty and deference he displays to them in his journal, the young Pavese received little encouragement and support from either his stern stoical mother or his elder married sister although he lived with the former until her death in 1931 and afterward, for a time, was taken in as a stray by the latter. Tellingly, every romantic relationship Pavese entered into during the years he chronicles failed miserably. Indeed, prior to his ever meeting Dowling, he had a string of unhappy romances, all of which he had managed to survive, if not to learn from. He lets himself be wounded again and again. He is perpetually vulnerable, his guard always down. The affair with Dowling with all its attendant humiliations was merely the last link in a long chain. The question that naturally arises is why she in particular should have developed such a stranglehold on him.

Pavese was probably more infatuated with the actress as a sex goddess and symbol for America than as an actual person. In both these aspects, she stood as a last emblem for ideals he had embraced since youth, the final embodiment of these beloved chimeras in his short, unhappy life. Pavese had pursued desirable and provocative women since his adolescence. She stood for them all, she was the realization of all his dreams and sexual fantasies. More importantly she also represented the land of opportunity and promise that Pavese had never visited but had loved since boyhood. Of all the Italian novelists of his time, he was the most ardent champion of all things American. As a student and academic, he devoted himself to the literature of the United States. During the years before he started writing fiction, when the fascists were in power and he was perhaps afraid to express himself directly, he translated into Italian works by important writers in the American pantheon—Melville, Lewis, Anderson, Stein, Dos Passos, and Faulkner—and published critical essays on their writing as well as that of other Americans such as Whitman (the subject of his thesis at the University of Turin), Fitzgerald, and Hemingway. He exulted not only in American culture but also in its democratic values, which made him suspect to the Duce and his minions. During the war years, his passion for America seemed increasingly fugitive. American values could not be transported to Italian soil, the hereafter could not be implemented in the here. Pavese joined with the communists not out of doctrinaire belief but expedience. They both had a common enemy: the fascists. In the person of Dowling, America reached a hand out to Pavese one last time. Clearly, their relationship had a deep import for him. His diary, however, reveals that he was pondering suicide long before they ever met. The breakup of their short-lived relationship provided him with a convenient excuse to carry out what he had contemplated doing for years.

Most assuredly, the liaison with Pavese didn't have any deep meaning for Dowling but was really just another flirt or fling. She thought that he viewed it in a similar light. After Pavese's death, she claimed that she had never realized that she had meant so much to him. Perhaps, though obtuse (she also candidly disclosed that she had no idea of his high stature in the world of Italian letters; although she understood he was some sort of writer, she had not read, aside from a few of the poems addressed to her, any of his work), Dowling nevertheless was shrewd enough to realize that "she" in fact hadn't really mattered all that much, that it was the sex that had captivated him or her nationality. In the end, we must conclude that while Dowling indeed served as a potent, personal symbol for Pavese, he was in love with an idealized image of his own creation which he projected onto her. The doubters had ample ground for their skepticism. As a motivation for suicide, Dowling's rejection of Pavese appeared baffling and unsatisfactory for a number of reasons.

First, during the course of his life, Pavese had suffered and overcome so much real hurt and affliction prior to his ever meeting the insignificant American starlet that whatever pain his tawdry affair with her, or for that matter those with any of his other inamoratas, could have possibly caused him seemed shallow and inconsequential in comparison. At the time of his death, he was a renowned figure, a hero in the eyes of many, and, of course, his diary had not yet appeared, his personal weaknesses not yet revealed. As earlier stated, he had been arrested for his political activities and exiled for ten months to Brancaleone, Calabria, in 1935. Moreover, during the Mussolini years, Pavese saw a number of his friends put to death by the fascist oppressors as payment for their opposition. After war broke out, he saw still other of his friends killed while fighting with the resistance and experienced allied bombing raids in Turin before he fled to the hills to live a hand-to-mouth existence among the partisans for two long years. He chronicled his experience in the war-torn countryside in perhaps his best and most gripping novel, *The House on the Hill*. After having survived so much, to kill oneself because of a soured love affair seemed patently absurd to many of his friends and colleagues.

Others found Pavese's suicide perplexing because his fictions manifest a great zest for life. Essentially a minimalist, Pavese claimed that the theme of all his works was "the rhythm of what happens."[6] Many commentators have stated that his incantatory style defies translation. His novels, though filled with action and motion, are essentially plotless. His characters enjoy the simple pleasures of life and engage in repetitive activities and constant movement throughout the course of a book. They drive in endless circles through the countryside in their cars, or regularly come together in groups where they chat incessantly with one another about the hard "business of living,"[7] or spend their nights roistering till dawn, going out for yet another round of drinks at yet another tavern and, if they are men, ending their drunken revels by unwelcomely serenading a woman at her window. Pavese's novels are both lyric and panoramic. In all his works he displays his great love for the Italian peasant, the tillers of the soil and the dressers of the vine. Pavese searches for the eternal—the rivers, the hills, the soil—amid the flux. His characters can find solace in the beauties of the natural world during their moments of greatest travail, even during the carnage and bloodshed of the Second World War. His later works became increasingly abstract. The stories, essays, and poems of *Summer Holiday* all deal with three revolving themes (the Sea, the City, and the Vine) which function in the book like musical motives; whereas in the novel *Dialogues with Leucò* action vanishes altogether, characters devolve into "beautiful names, charged with a destiny but not a psychological character," who meet in pairs in order to examine in "their problematic and anguished ambiguity"[8] the myths of antiquity. Of all his novels, the *Dialogues* was Pavese's favorite. A copy of it was found by his bedside when his body was discovered.

Finally Pavese's suicide confounded people because at the time of his death, he seemed to be at the height of his literary powers. From 1941 to 1950, he produced the great body of his creative work which includes nine short novels, many stories and sketches, his poetry and his diary. As A. Alvarez notes in *The Savage God*, just prior to his suicide, Pavese was writing "better than ever before —more richly, more powerfully, more easily."[9] The year prior to his death, Pavese produced two novels, each in less than two months' time. Moreover, his works were also receiving great public acclaim. Indeed, a month before his death, he received Italy's highest literary award, the prestigious Strega Prize. A few days prior to his suicide, Pavese wrote, "I have never been so much alive as now, never so young."[10] Like his fictional character Rosetta, his mood could change abruptly. High could quickly turn into low.

While not resolving all the ambiguities of Pavese's character, his diary nonetheless sheds great light on his suicide. As Alvarez writes, for Pavese, self-murder was "inevitable as the next sunrise."[11] In addition to documenting his befuddlement and despair with women, the journal shows the author's obsessive, life-long attraction to death and his lengthy flirtation with suicide. Ten days before he took the sleeping pills, he wrote: "Today I see clearly that from 1928 until now I have always lived under this shadow."[12] Indeed, from the diary's very first pages, long before his disappointment with Dowling, Pavese toys with the notion of doing away with himself. Again and again, he weighs the possibility of suicide, then retreats from it. Often he bitterly reproaches himself for considering the idea only to upbraid himself several pages later for not having the courage to carry out his resolve. Over the years, death increasingly represented escape and absolute freedom for Pavese. He also came to view suicide as a debt more or less owed to life. "Every luxury must be paid for," he wrote at age thirty, "and everything is a luxury, starting with being in the world."[13] At one point in the diary, Pavese asks himself if it is conceivable to murder someone in order to count for something in that person's life. If the answer is yes, he reasons, it is also possible to kill oneself "so as to count for something in one's own life."[14] Tellingly, he adds that the problem about suicide is that "it is an act of ambition that can be committed only when one has passed beyond ambition."[15]

For many years, Pavese had not "passed beyond ambition" and was able to suppress his desire to kill himself by aspiring to other goals, both political and literary. At the time of his death, however, the fascists had been defeated for half a decade, and in the meantime he had risen to the forefront of Italian letters. He was indeed ripe, ready to fall. For a long time he doubted if one could purge an "inward tragedy"[16] by converting it into a work of art. He felt that most artists who kill themselves "never, in their lyrical effusions, even hint at the deep cancer which is gnawing them."[17] He writes that "liberating pent-up emotions in a work of art" is not "an alternative to suicide . . . the only way to escape from the abyss is to look at it, measure it, sound its depths and go down into it."[18] These remarks notwithstanding, the act of writing itself seemed to serve as a life buoy for Pavese for many years. Perhaps he did not confront his demons on the page and purge them, but he found the act of creation itself life-sustaining. He was determined to make his mark as an author, and he succeeded. His last diary entry, however, shows that in the end not even the healing power of artistic creation could any longer bolster and support him. Having lost the buoy of the written word, he truly had no other option but to seek release in death:

> The thing most feared in secret always happens. . . . All it needs is a little courage. The more the pain grows clear and definite, the more the instinct for life asserts itself and the thought of suicide recedes. It seemed easy when I thought of it. Weak women have done it. It needs humility not pride. I am sickened by all this. Not words. Action. I shall write no more.[19]

Notes

1. Quoted by Paolo Milano, "Pavese's Experiments in the Novel," *New Republic*, 4 May 1953, p. 23.

2. See R. W. Flint, "Introduction," *The Selected Works of Cesare Pavese* (New York: Farrar, Straus and Giroux, 1968), p. xvi.

3. See Leslie Fiedler, "Introducing Cesare Pavese," *Kenyon Review* 16 (Autumn 1954): 543–44.

4. Quoted by Flint, "Introduction," *The Selected Works of Cesare Pavese,* p. xi.

5. Quoted by Fiedler, "Introducing Cesare Pavese," p. 544.

6. Quoted in *Twentieth Century Authors, First Supplement,* ed. Stanley J. Kunitz and Vineta Colby (New York: H. W. Wilson, 1955), p. 763.

7. Quoted by A. Alvarez, *The Savage God: A Study of Suicide* (New York: W. W. Norton, 1990), p. 13.

8. Quoted by Fiedler, "Introducing Cesare Pavese," p. 548.

9. Alvarez, *The Savage God,* p. 149.

10. Ibid., p. 14.

11. Ibid.

12. Ibid., p. 149.

13. Ibid.

14. Ibid., p. 107.

15. Ibid.

16. Ibid., p. 165.

17. Ibid.

18. Ibid.

19. Ibid., p. 286.

Malcolm Lowry

T HE CONSUL WILLED HIMSELF INTO THE PIT—"DOWN, HEADLONG into hades, selfish and florid-faced, into a tumult of fire-spangled fiends, Medusae, and belching monstrosities"[1]—convinced that his personal disaster might, in the end, even be found to contain a certain element of triumph. Hard-hearted as Ahab, proud as Milton's Satan, the Consul nowise desired, indeed spurned, deliverance the final night of his life—the evening of the Day of the Dead—though miraculously it had been offered him. He had prayed for his chance at salvation, momentarily weakening in his self-destructive resolve, twenty-four hours earlier, only several hours before the dawn of the Mexican holiday (November 2, 1938) and Yvonne's unexpected return to Mexico and him.

Late in their debauch the previous night, he and his drinking companion Dr. Vigil, a specialist in the treatment of venereal diseases, had visited a church in Quauhnahuac, and Geoffery Firmin had knelt before a statue of Mary—she is the "Virgin for those with nobody with,"[2] the doctor told him—and prayed and howled for his wife to come back to him. He had been "falling" for years, dying the protracted death of a hopeless alcoholic, but his descent had been exacerbated and hastened by his wife's leaving him. Throughout the novel, he tries to hide behind a front of respectability. Pathetically and ludicrously, he attempts to maintain a proper consular bearing, to preserve the dignity of his office as he downs tequilas and mescals in the various *cantinas* that he haunts; but his dark glasses, his slurred speech, unsteady gait, his sockless, nephritic, feet, and his trembling hands show him up for what he really is. Everyone in Quauhnahuac knows that Firmin is a man who drinks "very much vine."[3] Firmin himself, of course, realizes that he has been a disgrace to the British diplomatic service, that during the course of his career he has been "kicked downstairs into ever remoter consulships, and finally into the sinecure in Quauhnahuac as a position where he was least likely to prove a nuisance to the Empire. . . ."[4]

Lowry's hands shook, too, whether he was drunk or sober. Eventually he could not even use pen or pencil. He would stand at his desk, his palms facing upward on the blotter, the weight of his entire body pressed down upon them so that they could not twitch and quiver, as he dictated to his second wife, the former Margerie Bonner, material for whatever novel he was then working on, whichever part of the single masterwork he saw himself creating, for the novels were all to interrelate, each be a chapter in one great chronicle that Lowry would call *The Voyage That Never Ends*. Indeed, he would agree with his critics that he was a one-novel author. However, he envisioned himself writing a book far vaster in scope than his acknowledged masterpiece, *Under the Volcano*—but one episode in the projected Great Work. When not busy composing or redrafting one of his novels, Lowry could usually be found well into his cups. A prodigious drinker for most of his life, he drew heavily on his own alcoholic experiences to create his fictions. Two activities—writing and boozing—were central to his life and he went at both with reckless abandon. Lowry's drinking bouts lasted for weeks, even months, at a time. When still able to use a pen, he could go for days without ever picking one up. However, when he did write, he worked as if he were a man possessed. He always stood up when he composed, even in the years before his Parkinson's-like hand trembling necessitated that he dictate. Standing at his desk, he would sometimes scribble for sixteen hours straight. As a result of all the time Lowry spent on his feet, he would develop varicose veins in his legs. Eventually these would balloon so badly that he had to undergo painful surgery to have them stripped. During the later years, when his hands shook so uncontrollably that he could not even sign his name, he exerted so much pressure on their backs as he stood and dictated to Margerie (they must keep still! they simply must!), his knuckles became so callused and scabbed as to be hideous looking. Like Ernest Hemingway, Lowry wrote primarily about himself. It has often been said that the secondary characters in his work, especially the women, are sketchy and two-dimensional, that Lowry could not write convincingly from a point of view radically different from his own. All his central characters are male and alcoholic, from Dana Hilliot, the protagonist of *Ultramarine*, on. Each, to some degree, is a self-portrait of Lowry. Only in *Under the Volcano* did he manage to rise above himself and create ancillary figures of some power, though Hugh, the second protagonist of the book, is clearly also Malcolm Lowry, even if a distanced, ironic, portrait of his younger self, a sort of Stephen to Firmin's Bloom.

All Lowry's fictional avatars are haunted by a past iniquity or sin. The Consul's hands shake not only because he has the DTs, but because they are guilty hands, murderer's hands. During the First World War, Firmin had been an officer aboard the *S.S. Samaritan*, a British warship masquerading as an unarmed merchantman. A German U-boat surfaced and attacked her somewhere in the Pacific, fooled by her disguise. The submarine was left burning in the ocean and its crew was taken aboard the *Samaritan*, whose captain had fallen in the engagement. Firmin, a lieu-tenant commander, took charge of the ship after the senior officer's demise, win-ning him the British Distinguished Service Cross. First, however, he would be court-martialed, for the German officers taken aboard the *Samaritan* were kid-napped by the ship's stokers, then thrown into the *Samaritan's* furnaces and burned alive. Firmin had to shoulder the blame for their deaths. He was acquitted at the court-marshal but the stigma of the incident forever attached itself to him as if he were a latter-day Lord Jim.

Lowry himself felt that he had blood to answer for. A fellow student who had fallen deeply in love with the iconoclastic, ukulele-strumming young Malc com-mitted suicide during the pair's college days. The incident would haunt Lowry for years. He blamed himself for not preventing the death and judged himself guilty of a horrible crime, a crime he made himself answer for at the "bar" of judgment. He dealt with the episode at length in his last novel, the posthumously published *October Ferry to Gabriola*, in which the suicide is precipitated by an automobile accident. The Lowry surrogate Ethan Llewelyn and Peter Cordwainer are both at the beginning of their second term in the college of Ixion at the University of Ely. Previously they had attended Stoke-Newington prep school (Edgar Allan Poe's alma mater) and been in the Boy Scouts together. On the evening of October 7, 1929 (October 7 is a day that over the years again and again proves disastrous for Stoke-Newington graduates), Peter burst into his suite of rooms frantic and wild-eyed. Ethan is there, already a little drunk, listening to a new jazz record on the phonograph. Peter, it turns out, has struck a pedestrian in a hit-and-run accident. The man will die but neither Ethan nor Peter knows this. They do realize, however, that Peter will in all likelihood be sent down as a result of the incident. Although Cordwainer is nervous and distraught, Ethan leaves to purchase a second bottle of gin at a nearby pub. When he returns, he sees his friend tying a noose. Thinking him much too theatrical, Ethan upbraids Cordwainer and then tells him to go on and kill himself. He goes so far as to say that his deceased grandmother will be of help to Peter on the other side. Years later, Ethan remembers, perhaps half imag-ines, his and Peter's conversation:

> ("All right, Mr. Peter Bloody Cordwainer . . . Go ahead and do it. Grandmother won't let you down, I'm sure . . . She's got a lot of friends in high office. And besides, the Tibetans say you can be comfortable even in hell, just so long as you're clever. And you are, if not so damn clever as you used to be. I've promised you. I'll get in touch with you through old Goddo's wife on Sunday afternoons." Had he said this? And Peter: "It's almost worth doing it just to see the expression on all those stick-in-the-mud faces at Ixion tomorrow." "You forget you won't be here to see them, old man." "That's right, nor will I. That's funny. But I thought you said . . ." "Not for three days, I think, as a rule." "Will I know I'm dead?" "Only if you reflect on the subject." "Well, Schopenhauer does say it's the one thing a man surely has

an inviolable right to dispose of as he thinks fit." "All right then, dispose. As a realtor for the next world I recommend this choice lot. I didn't mean that about hell either, Peter. I honestly think things are going to be a damned sight better for you over there. Anyway, you're going to do it sooner or later, so why not now? Have another spot of gin, old chap." "Thanks, old man . . . Ethan you come too!" "No, you do it. We'll keep in touch. I'll come later. The same way." "Then before you go, I . . . wouldn't you—?" "None of that." "And don't fail me!" So let the bugger die . . . The excuse would not do. No excuse would do.)[5]

Ethan leaves Peter on his own a second time. He has to run in order to reach his own digs before the midnight curfew. On his way, he passes the hospital where the inquest into Peter's death will be held the following day. The next morning, badly hung over, he finds a farewell note from Peter in his coat pocket. As he fears, Peter is absent at their first lecture. He goes round to Cordwainer's rooms afterward to find that he is dead, his body already cut down. In penance, Llewelyn becomes a lawyer—a public defender—and devotes himself to rescuing murderers from the gallows, if not from long incarceration. He defends criminals because he feels that he is one. Pleading for them, he is, in truth, petitioning for himself. He gives up his practice and severs connections with his firm, however, after saving from the scaffold a "deceitfully benign"[6] watchmaker, whom he erroneously believed to be innocent of a hideous murder. After his victory in the courtroom, Llewelyn once more finds himself engaging in painful self-recrimination. He feels guilty of another terrible crime and thinks that he deserves to stand on the gallows, "locally in this instance a disused prison shaft painted bright yellow."[7] Guilt is brought home to Lowry's protagonists in numerous ways. It so overwhelms them that they are inhibited from pursuing their true calling. Often a Lowry hero is reminded of his sin by something spurious from the outside world.

In *Under the Volcano*, the movie playing at the local cinema at the time of the Consul's death (and once again a year later as the Consul's acquaintance, the French film director M. Laurelle, discusses the fate of his friend with Sr. Bustamente, the proprietor of both the theater and the adjacent *cantina*) is *The Hands of Orlac* starring Peter Lorre, a Hollywood remake of an earlier German film starring Conrad Veidt, concerning an artist who is given the hands of a killer after losing his own. Posters for the film hang everywhere in Quauhnahuac. Lorre's dilemma (he cannot control what his hands do) reflect the Consul's and Lowry's own. Firmin feels that if he could only sober up, if the damned spot would disappear from his hands, he could fulfill his destiny as artist and write a momentous book concerning the lost continent of Atlantis, as his fate and that of the island seem to mirror each other (each is destined to be swallowed up). Not only does Orlac, the artist with a murderer's hands, serve as a symbol for Firmin, he also stands as "the hieroglyphic"[8] of the troubled times, the late nineteen thirties, as well. Early in the novel, Laurelle stares up at one of the movie posters and realizes that it "was Germany itself that, in the gruesome degradation of a bad cartoon, stood over him."[9]

Not only has Firmin drunk himself into a stupor, the entire world, mankind itself, seems equally smashed and out of control. As Hugh, the Consul's half-brother, succinctly observes, "if our civilization were to sober up for a couple of days, it'd die of remorse on the third."[10] Just like the Consul, just like Hugh's lit cigarette, all of humanity seems bent on consuming, destroying, itself in 1938.

Things aren't much better in the late 1940s, the time of *October Ferry*. The fascists have gone down to defeat, but the world has entered the nuclear era, and the Cold War has begun. A new enemy has replaced the old one; the Red scare is in full swing. *Time* and *Life* magazines are full of anti-communist propaganda. Civilization and industry have begun to encroach on the unspoilt wilderness of Canada's great forests. A Shellco refinery, "a lurid flickering City of Dis"[11] stands on the other side of the inlet from the squatters' hamlet of Eridanus, where Ethan Llewelyn and his wife have finally found peace. They have withdrawn from the world into their own primitive paradise. They live in a cabin built on piles which had been sold to them for one hundred dollars and on which they pay no taxes. The other cottages are inhabited seasonally by fishermen. For much of the year, the two enjoy complete privacy in the dense forest. They live simply and purely off the land. In the spring they watch the buds bursting into bloom, and, in the summer, through their casement windows, they observe deer, raccoon, bear, and other wildlife. Existence can be hard and taxing in Eridanus, especially during the harsh winters, but the primitive life the Llewelyns lead there proves restorative and healing for both husband and wife. Ethan, at last, is able to forgo drinking. The rugged physical labor that survival in the wilderness entails satisfies and fulfills him. In his spare hours, he devotes himself to reading novels and poetry instead of legal briefs. If they so desire, he and Jacqueline can sing at the top of their voices, or Ethan can play jazz riffs wildly upon his clarinet at four in the morning without fear of disturbing anyone. However, in May 1947, a campaign to evict everyone living in Eridanus and to tear down the cabins begins, the editors of the Vancouver newspapers "having discovered after a quarter of a century, and in the absence for a few days of suitable headlines concerning sex crimes, or atomic war, that by [the squatters'] continued existence at Eridanus the public were being deprived of the usage themselves of this forest . . . as a public park."[12] Ethan suspects the real object of the campaign is industrial expansion. Facing the inevitable, the Llewelyns pack up their bags and leave their paradise to return to the city. Vancouver is nothing short of hell. It has changed a great deal since the Llewelyns last lived there, having lost much of its former character in the process of modernization. The beautiful steamboat gothic houses have been torn down so that featureless highrises could be built in their place. The Llewelyns' former apartment building has become a home for juvenile delinquents. They find rooms nearby, but they have no view of the mountains from their windows, the view blocked by other buildings. Later Llewelyn learns his new apartment had previously housed a clandestine abortionist's clinic. The present janitor and landlady are both police informers who

relish reporting drunks as well as turning in those who feed the sea gulls against
city ordinance. Sirens wail all through the night. The police seem to be everywhere.
Ethan again begins drinking heavily. He can see only two advantages to living in
the city: "you can take a hot bath in more comfort, and there was a good gas stove,
and both of these seemed equally—the latter irresistibly so and daily to someone
somewhere in the city, if the paper was to be believed—temptations to suicide. . . ."[13] On October 7, 1949, the Llewelyns embark on a Greyhound bus in
search of a new refuge, a second Eridanus.

Both Firmin and Llewelyn, in the course of their lives, seek to punish themselves for their perceived past crimes, though the latter in the end pardons himself
while the former does not. For each man alcohol serves as both a means of escape,
a way to assuage his guilt for a time, and an instrument of torture and retribution,
a weapon to wield against himself in order to carry out a slow execution. While
Llewelyn ultimately seeks redemption and forgiveness, first at Eridanus, then on
the equally primeval, forested island of Gabriola, Firmin doesn't desire a stay of
sentence. He sees himself as a human scorpion. He does not want to be saved; he
feels that he is justly damned and, in the end, he realizes that, just like the scorpion with its segmented tail that ends in a venomous tip, he will sting himself to
death. He takes pride in the fact that he's drinking himself to death, and realizes
that he will have to answer for the spilling of his own blood just as he will for the
deaths of the Germans aboard *The Samaritan*, which was under his command, even
if he himself did not give the order for their execution. Early in the novel, he tells
himself: "All your love is the *cantinas* now: the feeble survival of a love of life now
turned to poison, which only is not wholly poison, and poison has become your
daily food, when in the tavern."[14] Firmin's pride bids him to carry on, to drink to
the bitter end. His will, he claims, is unshakable; even God cannot conquer it. He
will die at his own hand.

On one level, drinking releases the mystical that is bottled up inside the
Consul. It enhances his discernment. Doors of perception open for him, for booze
is a magical elixir. This is also true for Ethan Llewelyn, who in the extraordinary
"The Wandering Jew" chapter of *October Ferry to Gabriola* steals glimpses into
other realities while drinking in a hotel bar and reading from Charles Fort's *Wild
Talents*, a work on magic and psychic phenomena:

> But now he became conscious of something more frightening yet taking place in
> his mind. It was a feeling that permeated the high ill-lit yellow walls of the hotel
> beer parlour, the long dim corridor between the two beer parlours, on which the
> door now seemed to be opened by an invisible hand . . . a feeling which seemed
> a very part of the ugly, sad, red-and-brown tables and chairs, something that was
> in the very beer-smelling air, as if—the feeling perhaps someway arising, trans-
> lated to the surrounding scene, from the words themselves—there was some
> hidden correspondence between these words and this scene, or between some
> ultimate unreality and meaninglessness he seemed to perceive adumbrated by

them (by these words, under their eyes, in the book on the table—and yet for an instant what meaning, what terrifying message flashed from all this meaningless-ness), and his inner perception of this place: no it was as if this place were sud-denly the exact outward representation of his inner state of mind: so that shutting his eyes for a long moment of stillness (in which he imagined he could hear— God—distantly, pounding, the tumultuous cataract of Niagara Falls twenty miles away), he seemed to feel himself merging into it, while equally there was a fading of it into himself: it was as though, having visualized all this with his eyes shut now he *were* it—these walls, these tables, that corridor. . . .[15]

In a few minutes Llewelyn's fear turns into something else entirely:

Why, to the conclusion that he had somehow magically produced it himself, then that any message in it for *them* was necessarily terrifying? Mightn't he equally well consider that he'd been vouchsafed, was so being vouchsafed, a glimpse into the very workings of creation itself?—indeed with this cognition Ethan seemed to see before his eyes whole universes eternally condensing and recondensing them-selves out of the "immaterial" into the "material," and as the continued visual-ization of their Creator, being radiated back again.[16]

The reverse route—from beatific vision to nightmare—is traversed by the Consul when he drinks. At first, everything becomes more beautiful for Geoffrey Firmin. Step by step, mescal by mescal, he'll approach and then at last reach— click!—a special yet problematic state in which his awareness is so amplified that he is, in fact, "sober." He achieves a special, higher consciousness that he desires to return to again and again: "And even if he were not sober now, by what fabulous stages, comparable indeed only to the paths and spheres of the Holy Cabbala itself, had he reached *this* stage again, touched briefly once before this morning, this stage at which alone he could, as [Yvonne] put it, 'cope,' this precarious precious stage, so arduous to maintain, of being drunk in which alone he was sober!"[17] Drinking, he realizes, also brings him close to death. He sees himself engaged in an epic battle with a worthy adversary. Others might deny the greatness of Firmin's struggle, but he knows that it is akin to the death duel between a matador and a prize bull or a boxing match between titans. There are advertisements for such a contest affixed to the sides of buildings all over Quauhnahuac alongside the ubiquitous posters reading *Las Manos de Orlac. Con Peter Lorre*:

—¡Box! Arena Tomalín. Frente Al Jardín Xicotancatl. Domingo, 8 de Noviembre de 1938. 4 Emocionantes Péleas. El Balón vs. El Redondillo.[18]

Signs, advertisements, billboards, and poster hoardings play an important part in all of Lowry's works. Many commentators have found Lowry's novels and novellas profoundly cinematic. As Stephen Spender notes, signs regularly intrude on the text. They appear, often in block letters, the very moment a character catches sight of them, the character's eye functioning as if it were a camera zooming in for a closeup. Furthermore, in *Under the Volcano*, where the placards are in Spanish, the phrases are, in Spender's words, "interpolated into the action like subtitles in a foreign film."[19] Lowry's characters continually glimpse billboards and advertisements as they travel toward their various destinations—the voyage, in truth, never ends; Lowry's people, it seems, are always on their way somewhere, by foot, bus, train, ship, or airplane, and whenever they are walking or, as often is the case, motoring by bus, their attention is ceaselessly diverted by the signs they pass. These precipitate various emotional reactions on the characters' parts. Usually they create trepidation and uneasiness. The signs speak (sometimes directly, on other occasions subliminally) to the characters' deepest anxieties. It is as if personal messages are being written by the hand of God and distributed along the roadside for their special benefit. Like furies, the hoardings and billboards pursue and torment their intended victim, recalling past guilt. Because these victims are usually drunk, slogans sometimes blur for them; they mistake one word for another. The subconscious mind sees what it wants. "Informal Dancing in the Zebra Room" turns into "Infernal Dancing" or "Notice to Destroy Weeds" becomes "Notice to Newlyweds."[20] A legend below a British Columbia license plate appears to read SAFESIDE-SUICIDE[21] as Ethan Llewelyn catches sight of it from the bus he and his wife, Jacqueline, are traveling in from Victoria to Nanaimo in search for a hoped-for haven and sanctuary on the island of Gabriola. During the trip advertisements for MOTHER GETTLE'S KETTLE-SIMMERED SOUPS[22] continually stare Ethan in the face. Cordwainer's father had been managing advertising director of the company. One sign features a depiction of Peter as a fifteen-year-old boy—a twenty times life-size cartoon—gulping a great bowl of steaming soup and saying, "M'mm, Good!"

Four signs menace the Consul: the movie poster for *The Hands of Orlac*; the *Box!* advertisement; a sign that keeps appearing in private and public gardens throughout Quauhnahuac, including the Consul's own (which he has not tended and has let fall to ruin) that is written in Spanish but translated into English reads "You like this garden? Why is it yours? We evict those who destroy!";[23] and an advertisement for the clinic of Dr. Vigil which specializes in the treatment of venereal diseases and male sexual impediments such as premature ejaculation and impotency.

If Firmin drinks to achieve his special state of awareness, he regularly overshoots his mark and is subject to horrific hallucinations. His room shakes with daemonic orchestras. The barking of dogs turn into human voices. Ghostlike figures materialize. At one point he sees three hundred head of cattle, "dead, frozen stiff in the postures of the living."[24] These appear on the slope in front of Laurelle's house, then abruptly vanish. Firmin's sleep is interrupted "by his own name being continually repeated by imaginary parties arriving, the vicious shouting, the strumming, the slamming, the pounding, the battling with insolent archfiends, the avalanche breaking down the door, the proddings from under the bed, and always,

outside, the cries, the wailing, the terrible music, the dark's spinets. . . ."[25] He calls
the imaginary voices his familiars and gives them the names of devils. They taunt
and mock him and urge him on in his self-destruction. Alcohol opens the gate.
Through drinking, the Consul summons these "specialists in casuistry"[26] to his
side. He invites the impertinent, horned familiars to visit him.

Indeed the demoniac seems to be at work throughout both *Under the Volcano*
and *October Ferry to Gabriola*. In one of the former's very first scenes, a year after
the Consul's death, Sr. Bustamente hands M. Laurelle the Consul's volume of Elizabethan plays which Firmin had several years earlier lent Laurelle and which Laurelle had lost. Imitating the Consul who delighted in opening books at random
hoping to find "some correspondence . . . between the subnormal world and the
abnormally suspicious,"[27] Laurelle spreads the covers and shudders as he reads a
passage from Marlowe's *The Tragical History of Doctor Faustus*:

> Cut is the branch that might have grown full straight,
> And burned is Apollo's laurel bough.
> That sometimes grew within this learned man,
> Faustus is gone: regard his hellish fall—[28]

On the day of his death, while at Laurelle's, the Consul leafs through the telephone
directory for the phone number of his physician, Dr. Guzman. He notices two
names—Zuzogoitea and Sanabria—as he turns the pages. The two names, for some
reason, leap out of the book at him. Firmin will encounter these two sinister characters later that night at the wretched *cantina*-brothel El Farolito, quite literally the
end of the line, Hell itself. They are the self-styled, preposterously titled Chief of
Municipality and Chief of Gardens, pro-fascist pseudo-policemen (the true officers
are on strike) who along with another drunken vigilante, the equally terrifying Chief
of Rostrums, will interrogate the Consul, accusing him variously of being a spy, an
escaped prisoner, a North American gangster, a *pelado* (thief), and a Jew. Everything
conspires against the Consul on the Day of the Dead. Shortly after leaving Laurelle's,
an already drunken Firmin will be hounded by children begging for money. He will
board a carnival ride, a *Máquina Infernal*, a huge looping-the-loop machine. As the
cage he is strapped into whirls him upside down, everything in his pockets will fall
to the ground—his wallet, keys, pipe, loose change, dark glasses, and diplomatic
passport. The children pick up the various items and return them to him with the
exception of the passport, the very article that, had he had it on him later that night,
might have saved his life. When asked his name by his three inquisitors, the Consul
drunkenly blurts out that he is William Blackstone, a historical personage Firmin
admires, a Puritan who left his own people to live among the Indians in Massachusetts. Once again malevolent spirits seem to be at work. The letters that Yvonne had
written to the Consul during their separation which he had never opened but had
carried about with him in his coat pocket until he had lost them—he had searched

vainly for them for months—amazingly resurface in the *cantina*, where they can do
him the most harm. The Elephant, the establishment's proprietor, had returned the
stack of envelopes fastened with elastic to the Consul shortly before his confrontation with the policemen. They indicate that his name is Firmin, not Blackstone, and
thus arouse the suspicions of the three "chiefs." Furthermore, instead of his passport, a carbon of Hugh's dispatch to a London newspaper detailing fascist activities
in Mexico has found its way into the Consul's pocket. The document is highly
incriminating to the three vigilantes, who think it sufficient proof that Firmin is a
spy. As the Chief of Rostrums states ominously, "You are no a de wrider, you are de
espider, and we shoota de espiders in Méjico."[29]

In *October Ferry to Gabriola* a malign force also pursues Ethan Llewelyn. He
begins to see "a certain hideous pattern in his life, a sort of curse"[30] for, over the
years, he and his wife had been extremely unlucky in their houses and, as stated earlier, disaster tends to strike graduates of Ethan's prep school on October 7. The most
famous alumnus of Stoke Newington, Edgar Allan Poe, died on October 7, 1849, and
Peter Cordwainer hanged himself on that date in 1929. As for houses, the ones Ethan
and Jacqueline inhabit all seem to call destruction down upon themselves. Their first
home in Oakville, Ontario, had been swallowed up by the lake which had become
polluted and unfit to swim in just before the war. Thirteen months later, in October
1940, shortly after the death of Ethan's father, the couple moved into Ethan's birth-
place in Niagara-on-the-Lake, the Barkerville Arms, a many-roomed mansion and
Canadian tourist attraction built in 1790 by Ethan's great-great-granduncle and
expanded and added on to by subsequent generations of Llewelyns. The structure
would be completely gutted by fire in May 1946, shortly after Ethan's return from
military service in France. Ethan and Jacqueline are in Ixion at the time of the blaze,
the cause of which is mysterious and undetermined. In the ruins of the cellar Ethan
finds a bottle of gin which connects the fire in his mind to the night of Peter's suicide when he abandoned his friend to purchase a similar bottle in an Ixion pub. After
the destruction of the Barkerville Arms, Ethan predictably takes solace in drink and
shortly thereafter is arrested for driving under the influence in Toronto. He and his
wife temporarily check into the Prince of Wales, a hotel in Niagara-on-the-Lake.
During the fortnight between their fire and Ethan's arrest, numerous fires break out
near the Barkerville Arms. After Llewelyn's return from Toronto, four fires occur
close to the Prince of Wales. The element appears to be following Ethan around; a
supernatural force, it seems, is pursuing him. He and Jacqueline flee to Vancouver
and from there find their way to Eridanus, only to be evicted from the beloved her-
mitage. For Ethan, October 7, 1949, seems a particularly inauspicious day to begin
their search for a new home. He tells Jacqueline; "What's the use! What's the God
damn use! Why, of all days, have you dragged us out today to look for a house? Can't
you see there'll be a curse on anything we find."[31] Once again the devils are in control and the only recourse for Llewelyn is liquor and pills.

While Jacqueline tends to forgive Ethan's heavy drinking, the Consul's alco-

holic excesses over the years drive Yvonne into the arms of other men, including the
Consul's half-brother Hugh and M. Laurelle, and ultimately lead her, at least for a
time, to separate from him. Hugh's guilt arises from his repeated adulteries over the
years with the wives of his friends, mentors, and business associates. As a young
man, he tried to be a songwriter, and he went to sea as a publicity stunt for his song-
writing career. Three of his pieces had just been published. Returning to England,
he expects to be something of a celebrity but discovers that his publisher, a Jew
named Bolowski, has cheated him and not promoted his songs at all. In vengeance,
he seduces Bolowski's wife and becomes strongly anti-Semitic for a period of time.
Recognizing that he is a failed artist—later he will compare himself to a young
Adolf Hitler—he goes on to Cambridge, where he has an affair with the Jewish wife
of one of the visiting professors. Years later, he will betray his half-brother with
Yvonne. The Consul says that he is able to forgive him, that he can still love Hugh
and respect him as a man. He confesses, however, that he is unable to wholly pardon
Yvonne. In his mind, Hugh compares himself with Judas. He understands why the
latter found it necessary to hang himself. In recompense for his past misdeeds, the
younger Firmin becomes a fervent Marxist and anti-fascist. He covers the Spanish
Civil War as a journalist and fights with the Loyalists. He joins his brother in Mexico
after being injured in the conflict and after Yvonne has already departed. Yvonne's
affair with Laurelle occurs shortly before she leaves the Consul and returns to the
United States. Not finding the love she needs from Firmin, she looks for it elsewhere, though she still deeply loves her husband. She feels that he will not allow her
to approach him, that the two of them are hopelessly cut off from one another. During
their separation, the Consul does not write her, though she writes continually to him.
She feels that he is "walking on the edge of an abyss"[32] where she may not follow.

All her life, Yvonne has ministered to the needs of others. As a teenager, she
supported her father, who served his country as a captain in the United States Army
during the Spanish American war, then, after failing as a pineapple farmer in Hawaii,
as the American consul to Iquique, Chile, during the First World War. After his diplomatic service, he attempted to earn his livelihood as an inventor and industrialist, but
failed in all his endeavors and at last returned to Hawaii a broken alcoholic. At thirteen, she became a child actress, appearing in serials and B westerns in Hollywood
for a period of five years. She subsidized her father until his death, then went off to
college, married, had a son who died in infancy, divorced, and returned to Hollywood
briefly for an unsuccessful comeback as an adult actress. Firmin reminds her a great
deal of her own father—the other consul. But if Firmin is a father figure to her, he
also inspires her maternal instinct. In his drunken helplessness, he becomes her
child. Significantly, he and her dead son share the first name of Geoffrey.

After a lengthy separation, Yvonne returns to her husband on the Day of the
Dead—as if in answer to his prayer to the "Virgin for those with nobody with."[33]
She plans to spirit him out of Mexico to Canada—indeed to a squatters' community
called Eridanus, the very place that proves so restorative for Ethan Llewelyn in

October Ferry. There she hopes he will be able to overcome his addiction and at last be able to write his book. Initially, things don't go very well between the two. Yvonne finds Firmin in a *cantina* still drinking early in the morning. He confesses that during the time she was away he has lost their car and thus, in the absence of taxis, they must walk. Outside the bar, they pass a public scribe seated on a park bench typing away at his huge machine. The Consul playfully dictates a suicide note: " I am taking the only way out, semicolon. . . . Goody-bye, full stop. Change of paragraph, change of chapter, change of worlds—"[34] Once they arrive home, he attempts to have sex with her. Because of all he has drunk the previous night, his cock will not rise. The incident proves unpleasant for both parties. Hugh's appearance on the scene also complicates matters, but Firmin, at least initially, is elated by his wife's return. The three decide to enjoy the Mexican holiday and to take the bus to Tomalín to watch the bull riding there. First, however, the Consul insists they stop at Laurelle's, much to Yvonne's discomfort. The French director asks Firmin if he is mad. For months, he had whined and cried for his wife to return to him, but now that she has he treats her indifferently. After departing from Laurelle's, the Consul rides the *Máquina Infernal*, then the three board the bus. On the way to Tomalín, their trip is interrupted when Hugh spies an Indian lying on the roadside dying. A white horse with the number seven branded on its rump stands beside the man, whose hat is pulled over his face to hide the bleeding wound on the side of his head. The Consul, Hugh, and Yvonne had at different times all glimpsed the Indian riding his horse in Quauhnahuac earlier in the day. Hugh wants to come to the Indian's aid, but the Consul prevents him. Mexican law would consider him an accessory after the fact. Another passenger on the bus, however, steals the dying man's money, as the Consul notices once the travelers reboard. Three vigilante policemen arrive on the scene as the bus pulls away. Naturally enough, the murder upsets the other trio of Hugh, Geoffrey, and Yvonne, but their spirits revive in Tomalín, where they become quite gay under the influence of alcohol, and Hugh, acting the part of daredevil, even takes part in the bull riding.

As the day wears on, however, the Consul turns bitter and nasty. At the Sálon Ofélia, he upbraids both his wife and his half-brother. He tells Hugh to stop trying to save the world and to accept the state of the planet's affairs. One can't be useful and noble. All action, including fighting for freedom in Spain, is futile. Besides, the communists are just as totalitarian as the fascists. He is even more vicious with Yvonne, telling her: "Where are all the children I might have wanted? You may suppose I might have wanted them. Drowned. To the accompaniment of the rattling of a thousand douche bags."[35] He says, finally, that he loves his alcoholic hell and would never trade it for a sober Paradise, however beguiling that might sometimes appear, then stands up and runs into the forest. Like the proverbial moth to its flame, he is drawn to the Farolito. He calls the *cantina* his true wife. He cannot be faithful to Yvonne and the Farolito both. When he reaches the *cantina*, Firmin will suffer his ultimate degradation and quite literally plunge and plummet downward—his body toppled into a yawning abyss. But first he will have sexual relations with a prostitute named Maria. She is available for those "who have nobody with,"[36] though she is hardly a virgin. In fact, she is probably diseased. At least, Firmin suspects as much when he sees a sign for Dr. Vigil's clinic on one of the *cantina*'s wall. Firmin had not been with prostitutes the entire time Yvonne had been away for fear of catching something, but now he hopes that he is infected. His relations with Maria, he knows, will prevent any chance of reconciliation with Yvonne. He cannot go to bed with her if he has contracted VD.

Lowry himself was deathly afraid of sexually transmitted diseases ever since visiting an anatomical museum in Liverpool with his brother as a youth and seeing plaster casts of infected organs. Later, he feared that he had contracted syphilis during his days as a sailor (for, like Hugh, he went on a sea voyage to the Far East before entering Cambridge). Dana Hilliot, the hero of Lowry's first novel, *Ultramarine*, drinks in order to stave off the temptation to visit Oriental brothels and enjoy the humid pleasures of the comfort women because he fears catching the clap. Ethan Llewelyn feels "his whole life had been like one long malignant disease since Peter's death, ever since he'd forgotten it, forgotten it deliberately like a man who assures himself, after it begins to disappear, that the first lesion of syphilis is simply impetigo—like Thomas Mann's Dr. Faustus, in fact—forgotten it, or pretended to have forgotten it, and carried on as if nothing had happened."[37] It is not incidental that Lowry alludes to the Mann classic in *October Ferry*. There are many affinities between *Under the Volcano* and Mann's novel, both of which appeared in 1947 (it is also interesting to note that the major works of both writers had remarkably similar geneses, beginning as projected short stories or novellas which in the course of their composition, much to the chagrin of their authors, kept growing and growing until they at last mushroomed into full-fledged novels).

After he has sex with Maria and after the Elephant returns to him Yvonne's letters, the Consul steps outside the *cantina* to see the Indian's white horse tied to a small tree. He pats the animal as it crops grass only to have the horse's bridle snatched out of his hands by the Chief of Rostrums, who accuses the Consul of trying to steal "his" horse. Thus begins the course of events that will lead to Geoffrey Firmin's death. After labeling him a gangster, a Jew, and a spy, the Chief of Rostrums will shoot the Consul "wide open from [his] knees up"[38] with a Colt '17. Mortally wounded, though still conscious, Firmin proclaims, "Christ, this is a dingy way to die."[39] A bell tolls: *Dolente . . . dolore!*

The earth will indeed shortly swallow him up. His body will be borne up by a number of hands, and he will be tossed into the great ravine known locally as the *barranca*, a long precipitous cleft, a "general Tartarus and gigantic jakes"[40] running through the unworldly Mexican landscape, ironically nicknamed the Malebolge, after Dante, by the Consul's half-brother Hugh. Dying and falling at the same time, the Consul, descending to Hell *à la* Dr. Faustus, is vouchsafed a glimpse into the near-future, the war-torn Europe of Hitler and Stalin. He sees the world itself

bursting into flame as he plunges out of Time, through "the inconceivable pandemonium of a million tanks . . . the blazing of ten million bodies."[41] Above him, to
the northeast, loom the two volcanoes Popocatepetl and Ixtaccihuatl, Warrior and
Sleeping Woman, mythic lovers of the sad Indian legend, Popocatepetl guarding
Ixtaccihuatl, whom he had found only to lose again almost immediately, in her
eternal sleep, the fires inside him raging and seething forever. Unbeknownst to the
Consul, the Indian's horse which at the sound of the gunfire reared and freed itself,
then galloped neighing into the forest, will strike and kill Yvonne with its hooves
as she and Hugh wend their way up the forest path in search of him. Mexico will
prove as fatal to Firmin and Yvonne as it did to the other foreign couple, the
Emperor Maximilian and his bride. Someone throws a dead dog into the *barranca*
immediately after the Consul's body is tossed into the ravine.

   Finis Operis. Drop curtain.

   Geoffrey Firmin's creator suffered an equally squalid death, an end every bit as
preordained as the one he gave his alter ego and fictional stand-in, and he was just
as ripe for it. *Es inevitable la muerta del Papa*.[42] The irony of place names, their at
times almost demonic appropriateness, had often struck Lowry in life. Drunk and
angry, he had chased his wife, Margerie, away with a broken gin bottle at the close of
yet another of their drawn-out, violent fights, brandishing it as wildly, as drunkenly,
as the Consul did the machete he snatched up from the bar table in his foolhardy,
histrionic attempt to force the return of Yvonne's letters from the pseudo Mexican
authorities interrogating him. Lowry set one bottle down after his wife fled the house
to seek refuge for the night at the landlady's and picked up another, one containing
Margerie's sleeping pills. Florid-faced and as hell-bent as Firmin, Lowry downed a
substantial number of the tablets in the wake of his and Margerie's quarrel. He no
doubt smirked as he did so, knowing that, if he succeeded, if he brought his suicide
off, it would be in an English village with the appropriate name of *Ripe*. He did bring
it off. Margerie would not return until the next morning. Lowry had overdosed on
liquor and pills. During the night he began to regurgitate and choked to death on
his own vomit. A dingy death indeed. He had written the book and was following it
like a script, though, student of the occult that he was, he might argue the book was
actually "writing" him, that he was trapped in his own pages.

   Numerous Lowry characters face similar dilemmas. The posthumously published novel *Dark as the Grave Wherein My Friend Is Laid* chronicles a trip to
Mexico by the novelist Sigbjorn Wilderness and his wife six years after the writer
has finished a book about his earlier disastrous experiences in that country. On his
return visit, Wilderness's former traumas recur. The past is not recaptured, it is
relived, played over again like a favorite record. Often the fate of a character is
eerily foreshadowed in a book or a movie that he or she happens to read or see. The
protagonist can't escape from his or her destiny. It is reflected back to him or her
from all directions, and he or she feels thoroughly snared and netted in it. In
October Ferry, Ethan wonders if this isn't "an almost universal experience":

... you dropped into some lousy movie to get away for an hour or two from yourself, only to discover that, lo and behold, this movie might as well have been a sort
of symbolic projection, a phantasmagoria, of that life of yours, into which you'd
come halfway through.[43]

In *Under the Volcano*, Yvonne's death is prefigured in one of Laurelle's movies. In
retrospect, Ethan and Jacqueline see uncanny resemblances between their life and
that of the young couple in the D. W. Griffith film *Isn't Life Wonderful*. The two saw
the silent classic early in their courtship, long before the Barkerville Arms burnt
to the ground or they were driven from Eridanus. In the movie which is set in the
Balkans, the two young lovers are driven from their home, a hut at the edge of the
forest, by looting soldiers who proceed to set fire to their cabin. At another point in
the novel, Ethan discovers that his life, the play *The Wandering Jew* and its film
version, and a book *Wild Talents* are all spookily interactive; that the imaginary can
steal into "the phase of existence that is called 'real' " and affect it. Malcolm Lowry
wrote his death before he died it. He could not escape the fate he gave himself in
Under the Volcano.

Born in New Brighton, Cheshire, in the northwest of England on July 28, 1909,
Clarence Malcolm Lowry was the youngest of four brothers, the last and least
wanted child—or so, at least, Malcolm asserted—of Arthur Osborne Lowry and his
wife. One cannot, however, trust what Lowry says. His claims must be taken with a
grain of salt, for like William Faulkner, he lied and mythologized, made up his life
as if creating and narrating a great fiction. Many sources list his place of birth as
Merseyside, Cheshire. Others simply state that he was born near Liverpool. Lowry
would smile at the fact that alternate birthplaces have been assigned him, that
sources are slightly at variance. An inveterate mythmaker, he would no doubt
appreciate Conrad Knickerbocker's pronouncement that he was born "within sight
and sound of the sea."[44] It had the right mythopoeic ring, was the proper way to
begin. A wealthy cotton broker, Lowry's father owned large tracts of land, fields
used for the cultivation of the cash crop he dealt in, in places as far flung and exotic
as Egypt, Texas, and Peru—or so Stephen Spender reports in his introduction to
Under the Volcano. (Spender's information came from Margerie Bonner's "Biographical Note on Malcolm Lowry," from "facts" gleaned from Lowry himself.)
Arthur Lowry was fairly well-to-do (and, yes, he was a cotton broker), but perhaps
not quite so well off as Spender's source would suggest. He would support his son
by means of monthly allowances for much of Malcolm's life—first at Cambridge
and then in London, the United States, Mexico, and Canada—and would suffer a
great deal on account of his rebellious, dipsomaniacal boy, who would, over the

years, become something of a financial strain to him. Throughout his life, Lowry regarded his father as a stern authority figure, whom he both feared and needed. Lowry's maternal grandfather, Boden, became another symbol of authority and reverence for the young boy. Malcolm would later profess that this semi-legendary character half-invented by himself, half-invented by others, had been a Norwegian sailing captain who had survived the sinking of several ships before at last going down with a final vessel somewhere in the Far East, a highly romanticized and inaccurate account according to Malcolm's elder brother, Russell. Nonetheless, throughout his life, Lowry was fascinated with all things Scandinavian. One of his early literary influences was the Norwegian writer Nordahl Grieg, whose 1924 novel, *The Ship Sails On*, colored Lowry's own first novel, *Ultramarine*. Lowry wanted to believe the myth he had created about his grandfather. Nordic characters with names like Sigurd, Kristbjorg, and Sigbjorn appear in numerous of his short stories and novellas.

In later years, perhaps in an attempt to explain his alienation as a youth and young man, Lowry insisted that he had suffered through a lonely and wretched childhood, that his parents paid little attention to him, and that his nannies abused and molested him on a continual basis. His characterization of his youth is perhaps most succinctly expressed in his posthumously published poem "Autopsy":

> An autopsy on this childhood then reveals:
> That he was flayed at seven, crucified at eleven.
> And he was blind as well, and jeered at
> For his blindness. Small wonder that the man
> is embittered and full of hate . . .[45]

He did fall off a bike at the age of six, permanently scarring a knee, though he'd later claim that he received the injury when the *Pyrrhus*, the Blue Funnel freighter he signed on as a deckhand at the age of seventeen, sailed into the midst of a Tong war along the China coast. Made to join the Cub Scouts as a boy by his father, Lowry suffered continual harassment at the hands of his peers, who taunted him about his penis size. A harsh exercise regimen—long walks and plunges in cold water—was also inflicted on him as a child, but he would eventually prove adept at athletics, especially at golf—though characteristically he would exaggerate his prowess and in later years would even go so far as to claim that he had been an international schoolboy golf champion for England. His father encouraged such manly pursuits, for he felt sports and competition built character, as did attending church, and the longer the service the better. According to Lowry, anything that could be labeled luxury and extravagance was banned from his father's household. At Christmas, a glass of port would be bestowed on the boy as a holiday indulgence. At the age of eight, Malcolm was shipped off to Caldicott, a prep school in Hertfordshire, just north of London. The following year, he was struck in the eye while playing ball. Lowry would later claim that the injury was never properly attended to and therefore the eye became infected, causing him to lose sight in it for four years. He further said that his mother could not bear the company of her partially blind son; to look at him aroused such guilt in her that he was never allowed to come home for the holidays. Ethan Llewelyn suffers a similar eye injury as a child in *October Ferry to Gabriola*. Russell Lowry dismisses his brother's charges as so much eyewash and alleges that Malcolm suffered from a persecution complex. He never had the vision difficulties that he claimed; it was purely imaginary. From Caldicott, Lowry went on to The Leys, a public school in Cambridge. There he developed a taste for jazz and an interest in anti-establishment journalism. He collaborated on two published songs—the costs of which were footed by his father.

Before going on to university, Lowry demanded to be allowed to go to sea, so his father arranged for him to sail as a common sailor on the *Pyrrhus* which left Liverpool in May 1927. Lowry's head was filled with romantic notions. He saw himself as a young Jack London or Joseph Conrad when he boarded the Blue Funnel freighter. He soon was disabused. The other sailors took offense at his presence, seeing him as a spoiled rich man's son who took a job away from someone who really needed it. They snubbed him for the entire length of the voyage. While at sea, Lowry began to drink—and to drink heavily. He returned to England in September 1927 and entered St Catharine's College, Cambridge, two years later. He had already decided to become a writer by the time his ship dropped anchor. He arrived home too late in 1927 to enroll in Cambridge that year, so he wrote to the American novelist and poet Conrad Aiken, who was then living in England, to see if he could study privately under him. Aiken consented and subsequently became Lowry's single strongest literary influence. His novel *Blue Voyage* served as model for Lowry's own similarly named *Ultramarine*. Not only did Lowry imitate Aiken's ornamented, poeticised, prose style and his nonlinear narrative technique, he emulated his Bohemian manner of living as well. Unlike the temperate Arthur Lowry, Malcolm's new father figure drank, roistered, and womanized, all of which appealed to the unconventional and nonconformist young man. When Aiken returned to America for several months in early 1929, Lowry traveled to Bonn, Germany, to study German. There he became interested in German expressionist cinema. He would later adopt cinematic techniques—particularly montage—in his own writing, once again following Aiken's lead.

In October 1929, Lowry at last entered Cambridge, where he quickly earned a reputation for being a brilliant if unconventional student. Apart from the Elizabethans, he neglected the time-honored writers of the English canon for the works of the modernist masters Joyce, Mann, Eliot, Faulkner, cummings, and Stevens, as well as the novels of Melville and Henry James and the poetry of Dante Alighieri. He continued to cultivate an interest in jazz music, and he dressed with bohemian flair. With Lowry's wit and acumen, and through the sheer force of his personality, he managed to convince his contemporaries that he was a budding young genius and embryonic novelist. Excerpts from *Ultramarine*, his novel-in-progress, appeared in university magazines. During a Cambridge vacation, he may or may not have boarded a freighter bound to Archangel. He claimed that he left the ship to make a pilgrimage to Norway to visit Nordahl Grieg. He would later turn this purported experience into a novel *In Ballast to the White Sea*. The manuscript would be lost in a fire in the 1940s. This was not the only time that a work of his would be lost or destroyed. He was more unlucky in this regard than even Carlyle.

After graduating from Cambridge in the summer of 1932, Lowry lived with the Aikens in Rye, Sussex, for several months before going on to London in the fall. Before moving, he finished *Ultramarine* and submitted it to the publishers Chatto & Windus, who accepted it in September 1932. The manuscript, however, was lost. It was in a suitcase which was stolen from the unlocked car of an editor. The novel had to be reconstructed from former drafts. Lowry submitted the rewritten book to a different publisher, Jonathan Cape, who brought it out in the summer of 1933. Early that year, disgusted at the libertine life his son was leading in London, Arthur Lowry sent Malcolm to Paris to study at the Sorbonne. Lowry did little studying, and in April he left France to travel to Spain with the Aikens. They stopped in Granada, where Lowry drank to excess until June when he met the former American film starlet Jan Gabrial, who was now pursuing a career as a writer. According to Aiken, he behaved like "a mesmerized owl"[46] and stopped drinking entirely. When Gabrial left Spain, Lowry's life once more took a downward spin and his behavior was such that his friendship with his mentor was adversely affected. The Spanish holiday came to an abrupt end.

In October 1933, Lowry again encountered Gabrial in the Alhambra music hall in London. The place of their chance rendezvous seemed significant because the two had originally met at the Moorish palace of the same name in Granada. They would marry on January 6, 1934. Their relationship was fraught with problems from the very beginning. In July, Gabrial left for America; Lowry followed her there in autumn. They reconciled for a time, and Malcolm began work on *In Ballast to the White Sea*. In 1936, the couple again separated and Lowry once more became self-destructive. In June 1936, friends committed him to—or he checked himself into—the Bellevue Hospital in New York, where he spent at least ten days, perhaps as much as three weeks, in the psychiatric ward. Lowry later claimed that he admitted himself in order to gain background to write a novella. He did in fact write about his experiences during his stay at Bellevue in perhaps his best short novel, *Lunar Caustic*. After his hospitalization, the Lowrys reunited and late in 1936 the pair moved west to Los Angeles, where Lowry hoped to find work as a screenwriter. He never lost interest in script writing, for he would later draft incomplete screenplays for both *Moby Dick* and *Tender Is the Night*. He did not, however, find employment as a scriptwriter in 1936, so he and his wife decided to move to Mexico, where the cost of living was not nearly so great. They arrived in Acapulco on the Day of the Dead, then went on to Mexico City before settling in the town of

Cuernavaca. In May 1937, Conrad Aiken visited the couple. He would later claim that Lowry had already completed a draft of *Under the Volcano* at the time of his visit. Aiken's arrival caused tension between Lowry and his wife, for it triggered a prolonged drinking binge by Malcolm. Lowry had stayed relatively sober in Mexico until Aiken appeared. A subsequent visit by another set of friends, the Calder-Marshalls, likewise gave Lowry all the excuse he needed to once again hit the bottle. Jan determined that Malcolm was a hopeless alcoholic, and she left him for the final time in December 1937, returning to the United States while he remained behind in Mexico. During the Christmas holiday, deeply depressed, he journeyed to the town of Oaxaca, where he was arrested by Mexican authorities probably on a drunk-and-disorderly charge. Lowry later claimed that he was interred on suspicion of being a spy and that an unsuccessful attempt to castrate him was made while he was a prisoner.

Lowry remained in Oaxaca, drinking heavily the entire length of his stay, until April 1938, when he managed to pull himself up by his bootstraps and get away to Acapulco. In July, he left Mexico for Los Angeles. He may have been deported by Mexican authorities, though once again the story could be another of his many fabrications. In the United States, he attempted another reconciliation with Jan but was rebuffed. In Los Angeles he met Margerie Bonner, who gave up her job to follow Lowry to Vancouver, where his father had him shipped off to in mid-1939. A year later, Lowry rented a small cottage in the fishing community of Dollartown, where he would live—actually in three different cottages—until 1954. There, in a squatters' settlement similar to the fictional Eridanus, he would work on various drafts of *Lunar Caustic* and *Under the Volcano*. In June 1944, the Lowry's second shack burned to the ground and the manuscript of *In Ballast to the White Sea* was destroyed in the blaze. Margerie managed to retrieve the current draft of *Under the Volcano*. The couple would erect a third cottage with their own hands. Here, after many rewrites, Lowry would at last complete his masterpiece.

The Lowrys left Dollartown on three occasions between 1940 and 1954. In November 1945, they went to Mexico, the trip chronicled in *Dark as the Grave*. There, on April 6, 1946, Lowry learned that *Under the Volcano* had been accepted in England by Jonathan Cape, and simultaneously in the United States by J. P. Lippincott. Both letters came in the same mail. But Lowry encountered one last hurdle. While the American house took the book as it was, the British publisher demanded extensive revisions. Unable to resolve the ensuing dilemma, Lowry attempted suicide. Not succeeding, he wrote a defense of the novel as he had written it, and Cape eventually dropped its demands. The Lowrys' joy, however, was dampened due to difficulties provoked by Mexican immigration authorities. They were deported from Mexico in May of that year. Back in Canada, the Lowrys took a trip to Gabriola Island. Malcolm jotted notes for a long short story.

In November 1946, the Lowrys vacationed in Haiti, but were present in New York for the American publication of *Under the Volcano* on February 19, 1947.

Nine months later they crossed the Atlantic to visit Europe and to sort out problems involving the various translations of *Under the Volcano* then underway. Lowry could not, however, curb his drinking, and the couple returned to Canada and Dollartown in January 1949. In 1953, Random House signed Lowry to a three-year contract, but he could not complete a single work. As a result, Random House canceled his contract, which greatly embittered the novelist. The Lowrys left Canada for Europe in August 1954. For a time, they lived in Italy but then moved on to England. In his last years, Lowry grew very vindictive toward his wife. He became increasingly irrational and violent and was in and out of hospital and jail. He blamed Margerie for his drinking problems; ironically he also becoming more and more dependent on her. Not only did she take his dictation, she also helped revise and rewrite his work, becoming in effect his collaborator. Margerie was a novelist herself and Lowry felt she was slowly effacing him. Indeed she would loyally edit and publish his posthumous work, bring to completion what Malcolm himself could not. In January 1946, the couple moved into a tiny cottage in the little village of Ripe. There on June 26, 1957, Lowry would take his life.

In *October Ferry to Gabriola*, Lowry writes that heaven and hell are really the same place. Existence might often seem "Schopenhauer-wise . . . a stretch in a penitentiary,"[47] but it was also possible to return to Eden, to regain paradise in this life. Like William Blackstone, one had only to venture into the forest. A simple shack raised by one's own hands could in truth become a veritable palace—a home:

> It stood, on wide-girthed strong legs of pine, between the forest of pine and high, high waving alders and tall slim birches, and the sea. There was the narrow path that wound down through the forest from the store, with salmonberries and thimbleberries and wild blackberry bushes that on bright winter nights of frost reflected a million moons; behind the house was a dogwood tree that bloomed twice in the year with white stars. Daffodils and snowdrops grew in the little garden. There was a wide porch where they sat on spring mornings, and a pier going right out into the water. They would build this pier themselves when the tide was out, sinking the posts one by one down the slanting beach. Post by post they'd build it until one day they could dive from the end into the sea. The sea was blue and cold and they would swim every day, and every day climb back up a ladder onto the pier, and run straight along it into their house. She saw the house plainly now; it was small and made of silvery weathered shingles, it had a red door, and casement windows, open to the sun. She saw the curtains she had made herself, the Consul's desk, his favourite old chair, the bed, covered with brilliant Indian blankets, the yellow light of the lamps against the strange blue of long June evenings, the crabapple tree that half supported the open sunny platform where the Consul would work in summer, the wind in the dark trees above and the surf beating along the shore on stormy autumn nights; and the millwheel reflections of sunlight on the water . . . and at night they stood on their pier and watched the constellations, Scorpio and Triangulum, Bootes and the Great Bear, and then the millwheel reflections would be of moonlight on water ceaselessly sliding down the

wooden walls of silver overlapping shingles, the moonlight that on the water also
embroidered their waving windows—[48]

Lowry found such a northern Paradise—such a home—in the squatters' community of Dollartown. There, despite his life-long addiction, he could forgo drinking
and complete his masterpiece about alcoholic hell. In the end, however, Lowry's
paradise proved a chimera. Like the Consul, he found hell more congenial than
heaven. Hard-hearted as Ahab, proud as Milton's Satan, he spurned deliverance
though miraculously it had been offered him.

Notes

1. Malcolm Lowry, *Under the Volcano*, introduction by Stephen Spender (New York
and Scarborough, Ontario: New American Library, 1971), p. 199. The New American
Library edition cited is a reprint of the 1965 J.B. Lippincott issue. *Under the Volcano* was
first published in 1947.

2. Ibid., p. 289.

3. Ibid., p. 56.

4. Ibid., p. 31.

5. Lowry, *October Ferry to Gabriola*, ed. Margerie Lowry (New York, London, and
Scarborough, Ontario: New American Library, 1971), pp. 68–69. The New American Library
edition cited is a reprint of the 1970 first edition by the World Publishing Co.

6. Ibid., p. 7.

7. Ibid.

8. *Under the Volcano*, p. 25.

9. Ibid.

10. Ibid., p. 117.

11. *October Ferry*, p. 159.

12. Ibid, p. 64.

13. Ibid., p. 182.

14. *Under the Volcano*, p. 65.

15. *October Ferry*, p. 145.

16. Ibid., p. 147.

17. *Under the Volcano*, pp. 84–85.

18. Ibid., p. 60.

19. Stephen Spender, "Introduction," *Under the Volcano*, p. xviii.

20. *Under the Volcano*, p. 264.

21. *October Ferry*, p. 75.

22. Ibid., p. 46.

23. *Under the Volcano*, p. 128.

24. Ibid., pp. 208–209.

25. Ibid., p. 342.

26. Ibid., p. 69.

27. Ibid., p. 34.

28. Ibid.

29. Ibid., p. 371.

30. *October Ferry*, p. 211.

31. Ibid., p. 212.

32. *Under the Volcano*, p. 346.

33. Ibid., p. 289.

34. Ibid., p. 53.

35. Ibid., p. 313.

36. Ibid., p. 289.

37. *October Ferry*, p. 216.

38. *Under the Volcano*, p. 373.

39. Ibid.

40. Ibid., p. 131.

41. Ibid., p. 375.

42. Ibid., p. 213.

43. *October Ferry*, p. 132.

44. Quoted by Spender, "Introduction," *Under the Volcano*, p. xxiii.

45. Lowry, "Autopsy," *Canadian Literature* 8 (Spring 1961): 23.

46. Quoted by Tony Bareham, *Malcolm Lowry* (Houndmills, Basingstoke, Hampshire, and London: Macmillan Education Ltd., 1989), p. 8.

47. *October Ferry*, p. 108.

48. *Under the Volcano*, pp. 269–70.

Ernest Hemingway

DESPITE HIS EVIDENT MENTAL DECAY—ALL HIS PARANOID DELUSIONS of harassment and persecution by the FBI, the IRS, and other government agencies during the final years of his life—Ernest Hemingway's resolve to shoot himself seems from a certain perspective lucid and sane, not at all the arbitrary act of a madman. From this standpoint, his suicide can be looked upon, paradoxically, as his ultimate act of bravery instead of the coward's way out to which, for much of his life, he dreaded he might one day finally have recourse. Hemingway shuddered and trembled at the prospect that he might slay himself, for his father, Clarence, had put an end to his life with a bullet, and Hemingway feared that the same "weakness" might lie latent and dormant within himself. According to an attitude toward suicide much more prevalent today than was the case thirty years ago, a point of view now espoused by the Hemlock Society and Dr. Jack Kevorkian, both men were amply justified in their decisions to end their lives, as they suffered from great physical torment caused by chronic illnesses. At the time of his death, the elder Hemingway suffered from diabetic disorders and angina pectoris and had to endure both constant pain and sleep deprivation. Although financial difficulties may have also played a part in his decision, it was his physical debility that in the end determined his action. Physicians have always been more accepting of the idea of euthanasia than most laymen, and the elder Hemingway was a doctor of medicine by profession. Interestingly enough, Clarence Hemingway used a gun which had belonged to his father to put an end to his suffering.

When viewed and interpreted from this slant, Ernest Hemingway's suicide, just as his father's, seems perfectly rational. He saw that his life was over, that there was precious little quality left to his existence, so he did the right thing. The great lover of Being would turn away from the feast when he could no longer enjoy and participate in it. Undoubtedly, Hemingway the mythmaker and shameless self-promoter would be glad if we ultimately reached such a charitable conclusion concerning his death and, in fact, it may not be too wide of the mark, for his suicide was truly an act of self-release. However, it is equally apparent that during the last days of Hemingway's life, the irrational mean-spiritedness that for years and years the author had directed toward others was now aimed squarely at himself. The method he chose to end his life was, at least in part, determined by his extreme self-loathing. He could, quite simply, no longer stand himself and felt that he was a failure because he could not live up to his own high standard. He came to see his entire life as one big lie. He hated his weakness but saw that he could not conquer it. If he had to kill himself, if he could not stop himself from stooping down to his father's level, in his rage, he would rub himself out in the bloodiest, most violent fashion. He had sunk that low. The bitter, resentful paranoid that Hemingway had become was a far cry from the golden boy he had once been. The carefree, thrill-seeking, but often self-injurious child, on the other hand, was clearly sire and progenitor to the malicious, hateful, and above all doomed Old Man. The seeds of his destruction were sown much earlier and mostly by his own hand.

For much of his life, Ernest Hemingway lived by a rigid, masculine code, a set of principles that defined his identity. His father, more than anyone else, helped shape Hemingway's world view during the younger's formative years. Later in life, Hemingway often stated that he never felt closer to anyone than his father. A fisherman and hunter, the elder Hemingway determined to instill in his boy a love for the wild. Father and son spent numerous hours trudging through the woods looking for game. They took summer vacations to Walloon Lake in Michigan in order to fish. Dr. Hemingway raised his son to be courageous and stoical. As a young boy, Ernest shouted that he was "Fraid o' nothing."[1] Brought up to be competitive, Hemingway participated in all the sports in high school, and for his entire life took pride in physical contests. Upon graduation, he decided to embark on a career in journalism instead of attending college and took a job with the *Kansas City Star*. But then he found himself caught in the midst of World War I. The army rejected him because of an old eye injury, so he joined the Red Cross in Italy, where he served as an ambulance driver. Seriously wounded at Fassalta di Piave, he would later be decorated for bravery by the Italian government. Surrounded by the dead and dying, Hemingway saw how frail life was, how quickly it could be snatched from someone, and he realized that he had come close himself to taking the plunge into nothingness. The prospect of the void frightened him. He would recuperate from his wounds first in Italy and then in Michigan. Afterward he would again find work at a newspaper, this time for the *Toronto Star*, and he would quickly head back to Europe, settling in Paris. Any number of Americans took up residence in that city, including Hemingway's mentors Stein and Pound. His first major book, *In Our Time*, a collection of short stories and other bits of imagist prose, appeared in 1925.

The book would attract immediate attention. Hemingway had already developed all the hallmark trademarks of his deceptively simple prose style, but it took his novel *The Sun Also Rises* to cement his reputation. Other novels, short story collections, and nonfiction volumes would follow, including *A Farewell To Arms*, *Men without Women*, *Death in the Afternoon*, *Green Hills of Africa*, *To Have And Have Not*, and *For Whom the Bell Tolls*.

In the course of his life, Hemingway took four wives: Hadley Richardson, Pauline Pfeiffer, Martha Gellhorn, and Mary Welsh. His relations with women were always turbulent, and his first three marriages ended in unhappy divorces. During the years between the wars, he fished, hunted, and attended bull fights. He took part in the Spanish Civil War on the Loyalist side. As a journalist, he accompanied the First Army in World War II, more often acting as an active participant than as a mere correspondent. His reputation as fighter bordered on the legendary.

If on the one hand Hemingway found the impulse to slay himself craven and despicable, on the other he took great pleasure in constantly putting his life at hazard, in positively courting death, whether on the battlefields of Europe or by running with the bulls at Pamplona, or else swimming out into the ocean dangerously far from the coast—in short by any convenient manner that came to hand. He would face the void again and again and thereby conquer his fear of it. He loved living on the edge. A hell raiser by nature, he would pick fights in bars. He drank far too much. He was accident prone. The planes and automobiles he rode in were wrecked with surprising frequency and he came close to being killed on African safari. It seemed the universe kept trying (and failing) to snuff him out. Even so, all his adult life Hemingway felt a mystical affinity with and attraction toward the ultimate adversary just as he did for the animals and fish he hunted or for the enemy soldiers he faced in combat. By constantly putting himself at risk, by again and again coming face to face with death, he felt that he validated his life, that he lived it to the fullest extent, drinking the wine of existence to the lees. Putting a bullet in one's brain as his father had done, even though the man suffered from persistent, agonizing pain, was the conclusive act of cowardice, or so the younger Hemingway had always maintained. The masculine code that he rigidly imposed on himself demanded that he be tough, fearless, and truthful. He would look the grim reaper straight in the eye and never blink. As a youth, Hemingway witnessed man's inhumanity and the ravages of modern warfare and was himself wounded seriously in the leg. As a young novelist, he considered himself the spokesman of a disillusioned lost generation. However, he agreed with Nietzsche that whatever hurt someone but did not kill him also made that person stronger, and, for that, he gave his many wounds thanks. The motto he picked for himself was: *Il faut (d'abord) durer* (One must first of all endure), and for many years he exhibited grace under pressure.[2]

However, during his last days, his vitality sapped, Hemingway could no longer draw strength from the crucible of his afflictions. The will and power to overcome and surmount his various misfortunes and ailments had vanished. Hardship and distress did not spur him on, as they had in the past, to renewal and regeneration through writing. He caved in under their weight. He was nothing but a frail old man. His body was falling apart. He had been thoroughly beaten and was incapable of wrestling with the dreaded yet beloved antagonist any longer. He had grown puny and was no longer a worthwhile opponent. Instead of the robust and vital bull of his youth, he had become a feeble and wizened gelding. He suffered from hypertension and diabetes mellitus. His liver was enlarged from decades of heavy drinking, and he may have suffered from hemochromatosis.[3] He looked much older than his sixty-one years. His old injuries plagued him, and he always felt fatigued or, as he put it, "dead tired."[4] Undoubtedly, he was also a victim of mental illness. He suffered from both severe clinical depression and a terrible persecution complex. He experienced many irrational fears. Things that he took pleasure in one moment would suddenly horrify him the next, and he would detest thoroughly what he formally relished. The shock treatments he received during the final months at the St. Mary's Hospital in Rochester, Minnesota, brought about temporary improvements in his mood. He became gay and convivial for a time. However, a side effect of the procedure—memory loss—caused him much grief and frustration. Moreover, his delusions were not driven from his mind, as was hoped. Temporarily they might disappear, but they would always return.

In addition to his mental and physical impairments, Hemingway realized that his abilities as a fiction writer had greatly declined. Writing had always been difficult for him. If he produced five hundred words in a day, he was lucky. Toward the end, he wrote of an inherent conflict in the writing process "between the living thing you make and the dead hand of the embalmer."[5] The quality of the various things he penned always varied. His career had gone into decline but he always felt himself capable of a comeback.

Although in 1954 *The Old Man and the Sea* had caught and netted him the Nobel Prize for Literature—he had brought in the fish, his stymied career got the big boost it needed from the brief novelette—its predecessor, the much inferior but far longer *Across the River and into the Trees,* had been savaged and harpooned by the critics. The protagonist of the novel and Hemingway stand-in, Richard Cantwell, an American colonel who dies of a heart condition after visiting Venice, romancing his young girlfriend, and reminiscing about his past glories, was aptly named, for Hemingway's writing ability, as the book evidenced, had greatly atrophied. Apparently he "couldn't" any more, the critics said, or at least not well. Moreover, his novels-in-progress *Islands in the Stream* and *The Garden of Eden* were both unfinished and in need of much editorial pruning, especially the latter, which, as Carlos Baker later reported, was "so repetitious it seemed interminable."[6] The master of the pared-down declarative writing style had turned garrulous. He also realized that the short stories he produced after *The Old Man and the Sea* were not particularly distinguished, but seemed like parodies and imitations of his far superior earlier efforts. Even in the genre his talents seemed most suited for, where in the past he had truly distinguished himself, he did not meet with his wonted success. He fared much better with his nonfiction, especially his posthumously published memoir of the Paris of the 1920s, *A Moveable Feast*. The question, however, that arises about this work is how much of it was new and how much reworking—in some instances only minor retouching—of old material. Not only the idea for the book but portions of individual sketches existed many years before Hemingway started writing. As early as 1933, he spoke to Max Perkins about putting down his Paris recollections and again broached the subject with Charles Scribner in 1949. A first draft of the piece on Ford Maddox Ford had been originally intended for inclusion in *The Sun Also Rises*. However, the return to Hemingway in 1956 of two trunks of manuscripts stored for more than twenty-five years in the basement of the Ritz Hotel in Paris, the existence of which he had apparently forgotten, was what really gave impetus to the project. The rediscovery of these old materials greatly facilitated Hemingway's efforts—indeed, probably made the writing of the book possible.

Hemingway's last sustained work was an article on bullfighting commissioned by *Life* magazine entitled "The Dangerous Summer" which was published in 1960. But even here he was revisiting old grounds, for he had written extensively about bullfighting before in *Death in the Afternoon*. Although he had been contracted to write only 10,000 words, the manuscript spun out of control to 120,000 words. Unable to cut it to the requisite length himself, Hemingway called in Aaron Hotchner to help him prune the piece. Together they were able to strike some fifty thousand words, but the condensed version was still too long for *Life*'s needs. However, the magazine agreed to publish extended excerpts. Although he initially seemed satisfied with his and Hotchner's work, new doubts about the article arose after its publication. He thought he had botched the job and that he had been unfair to one of the two rival toreadors he had written about. He shuddered at his photograph on the front cover of the magazine. He said that it was a horrible face. The picture so disturbed him that he could not bear to look at it.

After completing this piece, Hemingway suffered from acute writer's block right up until his death in June 1961. He continued to ponder the order of the Paris sketches, trying to come up with the best possible sequence, but was unable to add any further pages to the text. He hardly ever put pen to paper aside from writing a few sporadic letters. In February of 1961, he was asked to contribute a few hand-written lines for a presentation volume to President Kennedy. It took him over a week to settle on three or four simple sentences of tribute. He wrote pages and pages of material but was not satisfied with anything he produced. Even so small a chore taxed him greatly. His inability to write drove him to tears. He felt completely washed up.

Life had simply become unendurable for Ernest Hemingway. His suffering had reached a point where it seemed absurd to prolong the agony any longer. One would shoot a dog or a horse if its pain reached a certain level. Why should one be less merciful to oneself? The obvious answer was not to be. He pulled both triggers of his shotgun and blew away "the entire cranial vault"[7] to put a period to all his pain and misery. His mental illness greatly contributed to this suffering, but as the attempts the doctors had made to check its progress had all proven futile, what other solution was available to Hemingway but the shotgun? It did not matter that his paranoia was groundless. The fear he experienced was quite real. In addition to believing that the government was targeting him for political reasons—he said the Castro uprising in Cuba had been "very pure and beautiful"[8]—he worried about his finances (he felt he would be unable to pay his income tax) and his health (he believed that he suffered from diseases he did not actually have). Hemingway's paranoia was so great toward the end of his life that he actually maintained that his close friend Bill Davis had purposely wrecked the automobile in which he had chauffeured Hemingway across Spain to cover the bullfights during the summer of 1959, in a brazen attempt on his life, when in reality a tire had merely burst and no one riding in the car had been seriously injured. Characteristically Hemingway exaggerated and mythologized the incident out of all proportion, but he undoubtedly believed his version of events. Throughout his life he could be shrill and vindictive with both friends and lovers. If he detected weakness, he attacked it. He would always strike where his victim was most vulnerable. He also delighted in disparaging the works of contemporary American writers, saving his sharpest barbs for those of competitors who had attained a notoriety comparable to his own. He did not hesitate to engage in personal attacks. He called James Jones a "Battle-fatigue type" and "a whiner,"[9] said that Thomas Wolf was a "glandular giant with the guts of three mice,"[10] and described F. Scott Fitzgerald as a "rummy and a liar with the inbred talent of a dishonest and easily frightened Angel."[11] He particularly liked to snipe at William Faulkner, a writer whom on several occasions he admitted was better than he, referring to him variously as "ole Corndrinking Mellifluous,"[12] and "a no-good son of a bitch,"[13] and saying of Faulkner's work that it "was not even worthy of a place at Ichang, where they shipped the night soil from Chunking."[14] The finest practitioners of the past were also the targets of his wit. Henry James, for example, was a fake. His men all "talked like fairies."[15] He displayed his mean-spiritedness more and more frequently in his last years, particularly venting his frustrations on his fourth wife, Mary Welsh Hemingway. Once he even told her that she would drive him to shoot himself just as another woman had done his father. If it happened, it would be her fault.

Amazingly, in March of 1961, the man who witnessed in his life so much real horror and carnage found a television adaptation of *Macbeth* unbearable to watch. He told Mary that the play was terrible and cruel and that he could not stand it. She had to shut the television off.[16]

The last few months, Hemingway became quite listless and was unable to take pleasure in anything. He would stand at the windows of his house in Ketchum and stare at the cemetery across the river. The concept of the great void, the abyss Goya termed *Nada*, was no longer so frightful as that of a superfluously prolonged existence. His pain was so great that he had, if not overcome, at least thrust aside his lifelong fears of extinction and nothingness and was ready to accept man's ultimate fate. He could and would die.

During his last months, before he finally succeeded in killing himself, Hemingway made repeated suicide attempts, all of which were circumvented by his various retainers. Each time he threatened extreme violence on himself. In April of 1961, Mary caught him one morning, just home from the local hospital, standing in a corner of their living room with a shotgun in his hand. She and his doctor George Saviers, who had quite by chance arrived on the scene, persuaded him to hand over the gun. They drove him back to the infirmary where they had him sedated and then made arrangements to admit him to the Mayo Clinic in Rochester. Before being flown off, he was brought back home under the supervision of hospital personnel to pack. He was able to give the slip to his retainers and go for his guncase. He loaded a shotgun and placed it at his throat, but it was wrestled away from him. After the first leg of his flight, two days later, upon disembarking from his plane, Hemingway searched for a gun at various places in the airport hangar and even managed to check the glove compartments of several of the cars parked outside it. Led back to his plane, he attempted to walk into the propellers of another aircraft nearby. While he was held back, the pilot switched off his engines. They got him safely to Rochester where, again, he seemed to respond well to treatment. Released once more, he and Mary set off for Idaho on June 26, arriving in Ketchum on the 30th. That night the couple dined out, went home early and got ready for bed. Ernest sang an old Italian song while brushing his teeth. Husband and wife retired to separate rooms. Hemingway rose early, and drew his red "Emperor's robe"[17] over his blue pajamas. His guns had been locked in a basement storage room, but he was able to find the keys. He chose a weapon and loaded it, then walked back up the cellar stairs into the living room. From there he entered the foyer with its linoleum tiles and paneled walls. Placing the butt of the gun on the floor and leaning over, he rested his forehead on top of both barrels, then yanked the two triggers. The epic struggle, the death duel that had begun many years before, had finally ended. Poor Mary would discover the body. Some other poor sucker would have to clean up the mess.

Notes

1. Quoted by Carlos Baker, *Ernest Hemingway: A Life Story* (New York: Charles Scribner's Sons, 1969), p. vii.

2. Ibid., p. vii.

3. Ibid., p. 556.

4. Ibid., p. 558.

5. Ibid., p. 546.

6. Ibid., p. 540.

7. Ibid., p. 668.

8. Ibid., p. 544.

9. Ibid., p. 495.

10. Ibid., p. 495.

11. Ibid.

12. Ibid., p. 532.

13. Ibid., p. 534.

14. Ibid., p. 534.

15. Ibid., p. 189.

16. See Mary W. Hemingway, *How It Was* (New York: Knopf, 1976), p. 496.

17. Baker, *Ernest Hemingway: A Life Story*, p. 560.

 Sylvia Plath*

HER DEATH WAS AN ATTEMPT TO REBUT A WORLD GONE WRONG, YET simultaneously a call for help that tragically failed. She thought of herself as "Lady Lazarus," and, ever the gambler, she decided that she would enter the abyss once more. After all, she had lived through previous suicide attempts, had sounded these dark, watery, depths before only to resurface afterward revitalized, transfigured, at least for a time, into a smiling conqueror, a superior self, an even finer Sylvia than any of her previous incarnations, as choice and outstanding as they certainly had been. For Plath had striven for perfection her entire life; she was both an infant prodigy and a classic overachiever. She simply had to be the best at anything and everything she put her hand to. Second-place was simply not good enough for Sylvia Plath. She had developed a strong and positive self-image early in life—this vision was no doubt encouraged and cultivated to a large extent by her mother—and she had to live up to it. She certainly did live up to it academically, earning straight A's from grade school on, publishing her first poem at the age of eight in the *Boston Herald,* and continuing to perfect her craft through her high school and college years. She collected innumerable rejection slips along the way, but bullheadedly persisted in making submissions and in the end placed her work in all the right places, publishing on a regular basis from the age of eighteen. Moreover, throughout her college career and afterward, Plath won numerous scholarships, including one established by the Wellesley Smith Club and another endowed by the popular novelist and author of *Stella Dallas*, Olive Higgins Prouty. During her college years, Plath served on the editorial board of *The Smith Review*, was elected to var-

---

*I have had to paraphrase rather than quote directly Plath's poetry because the Plath estate denied permission to reprint.

ious class offices, and collected numerous awards and honors. She won two Smith poetry prizes and was elected to both Phi Beta Kappa and to the Smith College honorary arts society. Her short story "Sunday at the Mintons" received first place in *Mademoiselle* magazine's 1952 fiction contest and in the summer of 1953 she was selected as a guest editor in *Mademoiselle*'s College Board contest. In 1955, she would graduate summa cum laude from Smith, and the following year she would receive a Fulbright for a year's study abroad at Newnham College at Cambridge University. In junior high, she tested near 160 on an IQ test, a score indicating genius level. In addition to her literary gifts, she also displayed an exceptional talent for drawing, again starting in childhood, and won kudos for her pen-and-ink sketches as well as her poems. Plath's quest for excellence, however, extended well beyond her scholarly and artistic pursuits to reach and color practically every facet of her life from more or less trivial endeavors such as cooking (here, too, as attested by her college roommate Nancy Hunter, she simply had to outshine all others and not only beat, but trounce, the competition)[1] to highly significant matters such as marriage and motherhood. Her unremitting struggle for perfection and the unrealistically high demands and standards she set for herself were bound to bring her grief and disappointment. As a young woman, Plath was anxious to give the appearance of being the stereotypical "good girl" of the 1950s, who worked and lived within the parameters set by the establishment, who both respected authority and who wanted to be a credit to the teachers and mentors who had backed and promoted her—in short, a young woman whose behavior and actions left nothing to be desired and whose morals were beyond reproach. Later she would strive to be the perfect wife and mother. However, when life did not meet her expectations or she herself could not live up to the standard she had set, she invariably became unhinged and, plagued by self-doubt, plunged into a prolonged period of mental and emotional instability. Suddenly she felt that she had no value at all and saw no reason to go on living. After her first breakdown, with professional assistance, she would rebound. The bell jar rose and miraculously all her insecurities had gone, vanishing as if into thin air.

Plath came to believe that only by diving to the blackest bottom could she subsequently be assured of experiencing a corresponding elevation. A pattern had been established in her life, a recurring leitmotiv. She admitted as much in "Lady Lazarus," where she wrote that at least one year in every ten the urge to end her life would become so overpowering that she could not withstand the impulse and would try to kill herself. Something fundamental had changed, however, between her first suicide attempt the summer following her junior year at Smith College and her stint as a guest editor on the College Board of *Mademoiselle* magazine and her successful suicide, ten years later, the morning of February 11, 1963. When she failed, she was in deadly earnest about wanting to kill herself, cleverly planning her suicide attempt well in advance, taking measures to throw her family off guard and confuse the authorities as to what was happening, and deliberately and systematically carrying out her bid to die. Her plans should have gone off without a hitch, but miraculously not only was she found, but her young body was so strong and healthy that even swallowing fifty sleeping pills did not extinguish her life, though she had lain undisturbed for two days, hidden in a remote corner of her mother's basement. Ironically, ten years later, when Plath did manage to kill herself, she truly wanted, deep down, to live, as is evidenced by numerous details about her death. Whereas in 1953, she had aimed to die and arranged everything to that end, in 1963 she had contrived to be saved, for her suicide to be thwarted at the last moment, and devised this attempt so that it would not succeed; others would intervene before it was too late and stop her, so that her bid for death would result, ultimately, in her rescue. She even left a note with the telephone number of her doctor plainly in sight asking that he be summoned. Both times, events concatenated in an unexpected manner. It was miraculous that she survived in 1953, but it is just as astonishing that she succeeded ten years later.

At the time of her suicide, Plath thought that by confronting her demons and fears, she could exorcise them for good. Indeed, she had invoked and summoned all the imps and devils, the personal fiends and vampires, for their presence fed her poetry and made it powerful. They came when bid, but, if she thought she could control them, she was quite mistaken. When she laid her head in the oven after ingesting a large quantity of sleeping pills, she could only hope that perhaps, as in the past, she would emerge from the tomb purified and made whole, not only restored to health and strength but her identities and personae as lioness, Queen Bee, mother, daughter, lover, wife—in short, all the selves she felt that she could not live up to any longer—confirmed and verified as well. Her willingness to dare self-destruction would, in some strange way, substantiate her authenticity, her courage, and her truthfulness. She would "act out the awful little allegory once more"[2] and thereby finally purge her demons. In the process, all her various selves would be validated by the risk she was taking—all, that is, except poet, for that self had no need of reassurance. At the time of her death, Plath had truly come into her own as artist and no longer harbored any doubts concerning her ability and stature, perhaps another reason why she could so cavalierly gamble with her life. She felt her eventual reputation was already secure. The poems would stand on their own; they were their own validation, and she knew it. Not only was she writing her best work to date in a newer, freer style than her earlier verse, she was producing it at top speed. Toward the end, there were days when she wrote up to as many as three poems in the early morning hours she devoted to work before her small children awoke and her duties as mother called. She had the uncommon ability to convert her inner turmoil into art, almost immediately, even as she was experiencing it. She tapped into her anger at the breakup of her marriage to Ted Hughes to produce the poems that would be collected in *Ariel*, most of which were written in one month. She channeled her suffering into her poetry with amazing success. Suddenly, as never before, she was unstoppered. The work simply gushed out of her. Plath wrote about her increased productivity in the poem "Kindness," in which she compared her newfound creativity to a spurting jet of blood. She claimed there could be no stanching of the wound. Yet what is most amazing about these late poems is the fact that she effectively makes her private, inner suffering a metaphor for the misery of the twentieth-century world. The microcosm becomes the macrocosm as her personal hell expands into the hell of Auschwitz and Hiroshima. Her self-destructiveness mirrors the suicidal tendency of a human race on the verge of H-bombing itself out of existence; her anguish and distress are ours. We live her life-in-death as much as she.

Sylvia Plath was born in Boston, Massachusetts, on October 25, 1932. Her father, Otto Emil Plath, an ethnic German, emigrated to America from the Baltic town of Grabow (or Grabowo), which after World War I was incorporated into the Polish corridor. In *The Bell Jar*, Esther Greenwood states that "Her German-speaking father came from some manic-depressive hamlet in the black heart of Prussia."[3] Plath's mother, Aurelia Schober, was the daughter of Austrian immigrants. Both her parents had academic careers, her father being a professor of biology and German at Boston University and an internationally recognized specialist on bees and author of a well-known reference book on the subject, *Bumblebees and Their Ways*. Twenty-one years older than Aurelia—she took his Middle-High German course at Boston University—he was married when they met, though Otto and his wife had long been separated. At the time she enrolled in his class, Aurelia was a high school German and English teacher studying for her Master's degree. She and Otto began dating in 1930. During Christmas vacation in 1931, they drove to Nevada where Otto obtained a divorce from his first wife, and the two were married. Aurelia resigned from her teaching position, and Sylvia was born ten months later. As Ted Hughes later wrote, she "grew up in an atmosphere of tense intellectual competition and Germanic rigour."[4]

Plath spent her first years residing in the seaside town of Winthrop, Massachusetts. Her maternal grandparents lived but a short distance away at Point Shirley, which faced the bay on one side and the ocean on the other. Their home became a place of refuge and safety for Sylvia. The environment was freer and less stiff than at home and she enjoyed capering in the Atlantic, filling empty jelly jars with water. She was particularly close to her grandfather with whom she played, walked, and swam. He pampered and coddled Sylvia at a period when her father was often too busy with his work and scholarship to devote much time to her. When Sylvia was only two, her brother Warren was born. She was angry and jealous: "I who for two and a half years had been the center of a tender universe felt the axis wrench and a polar chill immobilize my bones."[5] Because her mother paid so much notice to the new baby, she maneuvered to win her father's affection. She greeted him when he came home from work and enjoyed watching him correct papers and exams. He did not engage in sport or recreation with her and seldom even read to Sylvia, yet she nonetheless worshiped him. He generally preferred the children out of his way and even went so far as to take his meals at a different hour than they did. Later, as Sylvia grew a bit older and behaved somewhat more maturely, he was less uncomfortable in her presence than he had been when she was an infant and now paid his daughter more attention. He praised her perspicacity and inquisitiveness as well as the good marks she made in school and devised mock experiments for her to perform. At times, in a playful manner, he role-played with her and pretended that she was a little adult, a future wife and mother. She loved impersonating such a part.

When Plath was five, a tropical hurricane struck the New England coastline. She saw for the first time the destruction and wreckage of which nature is capable. Her grandparent's house withstood the storm, but their property was thrown into great disorder: "Sand buried her [grandmother's] furnace in golden whorls; salt stained the upholster sofa, and a dead shark filled what had been the geranium bed. . . ."[6] At a young age, Plath learned about the fragileness and delicacy of a seemingly so stable world. The point would be driven home a few years later in such a way that it would scar her for the rest of her life. The next few years, her father experienced a prolonged and difficult illness—he feared that he had cancer but in actuality he suffered from diabetes mellitus—the first symptoms of which began to appear the year after the hurricane, but he was too afraid to seek treatment. His illness incapacitated him, making him weak and tired. His temper flared easily and he retired to his study and spent even less time with the children. Sylvia thought that he no longer loved her and felt resentful. As a college student, many years later, she confessed to Nancy Hunter that her father "was an autocrat. I adored and despised him, and I probably wished many times that he were dead. When he obliged me and died, I imagined that I had killed him."[7] In October 1940, Otto Plath's diabetes had progressed to the point where his leg had to be amputated at the thigh. After the surgery was performed, he was not permitted to move but lay immobilized. As a result, he developed an embolus in his lung, from which he died on November 5. Plath connected his death with the hurricane that had struck a few years before. Now her world was truly devastated and thrown into disarray. The image of the dead father would haunt much of her later work. In the poems, he appears in many guises, sometimes positive, more often horrific, but always enigmatic and perplexing, hard to get a firm grip on, slippery as Proteus. He is a shattered colossus his daughter can never piece together properly. He is alternately a murdered god or a suicide, a Nazi as well as a teacher at the blackboard, a vampire and a drowned man, shivering from the wet as well as a bridegroom from whom Plath is separated and to whom she must return. In "Full Fathom Five" the incestuous wedding bed rests on the sea floor and is covered with shells. Plath complains the air she inhales is thick and noxious. She would prefer to join her father in the briny depths. He rises out of the abyss of the ocean and is as much of a natural force, his power as great and just as disruptive, as any tropical storm or hurricane. He bids her inexorably to come to him.

After Otto Plath's death, Sylvia's childhood on the seashore ended. Her mother and grandparents decided to move inland together to the Boston suburb of Wellesley. As Plath wrote in her late essay "Ocean 1212-W," her first nine years of life "sealed themselves off like a ship in a bottle—beautiful, inaccessible, obsolete, a fine, white, flying myth."[8] Paradise had been lost. Her childhood closes shut and she, too big to go backward, is fixed as in a parenthesis. During the years that followed, Aurelia Plath sacrificed for the children and pushed them to achieve. Grandmother Schober took over the household duties while Aurelia earned her livelihood teaching in the medical-secretarial training program at Boston University. To make ends meet, Sylvia's grandfather took a job as a *maitre d'hotel* at the Brookline Country Club. Close to her mother, Sylvia was, for many years, overly dependent on her. In 1943, Aurelia fell ill with a gastric hemorrhage and had to be hospitalized. Sylvia feared that she would die just as her father had when he had been hospitalized. She felt she could influence the outcome of her mother's illness by being a good girl. If she was truly good enough, her mother would return to her. She worked even harder at school, practiced the piano longer, and stood up for her brother when he was picked on by his schoolmates. Aurelia recovered.

During Plath's formative years, her mother saw that she was exposed to numerous cultural activities and took her to concerts and plays. They visited museums and art galleries in Boston on a regular basis. Mrs. Plath also spent hours reading to Sylvia. In addition, she inculcated in her daughter the conviction that she must do well in school, for a good education was the means by which she would rise in the world. Her mother told her that she would have to be a go-getter. She wanted her daughter not to repeat her own mistakes, and told her that she could not count on a husband to take care of her but must be prepared to fend for herself. Later Plath would explore her relationship with her mother in her autobiographical novel, *The Bell Jar*. Esther Greenwood writes that her mother hated having to support her family and hated her husband "for dying and leaving no money because he didn't trust life-insurance salesmen."[9] From her mother's comments, Esther comes to feel that, for a woman, being married was "like being brainwashed, and afterward you went about numb as a slave in some private, totalitarian state."[10] Esther, however, is deeply resentful of her mother. She feels antagonistic to her despite all her self-sacrifice and resents the fact that she always had set goals for her. She feels manipulated and as if she has been jumping through hoops held by Mrs. Greenwood her entire life. She can't stand her mother's presence and feels suffocated by her. Plath undoubtedly shared many of her protagonist's feelings and with time would come to feel great resentment toward her mother; but during childhood and adolescence, she was both demanding and dependent upon her surviving parent, clinging to her tenaciously, fearing to let go. While Plath was in junior high, her mother was offered a position as Dean of Women at Northeastern University in Boston which she had to turn down because of Sylvia. The position would have been one of dignity and stature for Mrs. Plath and would have brought the family more income, but, of course, it would demand that she spend less time with her children. Because of this Sylvia protested and protested vehemently. She angrily told her mother, "For your self-aggrandizement you would make us complete orphans." Aurelia turned the job down. Even at a young age, Sylvia knew what buttons to push to make her mother do what she wanted. The manipulation worked both ways. Sylvia could control and exploit her mother by making her feel guilty.

There were numerous reasons for Plath's breakdown and suicide attempt the summer of 1953. During her tenure in New York City as a guest editor at *Mademoiselle*, her work was harshly criticized by members of the magazine's staff. Suddenly, she felt unprepared for life after college, and her confidence in her writing abilities shrank. Moreover, the world of the fashion magazine, which she initially thought would be so glamorous, seemed increasingly dull and superficial. Her schedule was nonetheless frantic, and she had the feeling that she didn't measure up. Feted by an advertising agency, a number of the guest editors, including Sylvia, contracted ptomaine poisoning from the food served at the luncheon. She was still ill from the effects of the poisoning when Ethel and Julius Rosenberg were electrocuted. She found their deaths horrific. However, the other guest editors thought that the atomic bomb spies only got what they deserved. Finally, shortly before she was to leave New York, Plath went on a date with a Peruvian delegate to the United Nations who proved to be a violent misogynist and who attempted to rape her. She had long had trouble in her relationships with men. Invariably, all the boys she dated "betrayed" her in one way or another. Throughout her college days, she deeply resented the double standard. She felt that she had to remain a virgin but also wanted to give in to various suitors. She had been involved for many years with a Wellesley neighbor, Dick Norton, who had contracted TB while studying to be a doctor, but felt indignant about the fact that he had an affair with a waitress. She saw other men as well but never had sexual relations. Plath returned from New York to the dull world of the suburbs. On her arrival home, she was shaken by the fact that she wasn't accepted into Frank O'Connor's summer fiction writing class at Harvard. Her assurance and self-possession evaporated further when she began preparation for her honor's thesis at Smith. The subject was James Joyce, but she found *Finnegans Wake* impenetrable. She worked for a time as a nurse's aide, feeding ill patients but could not continue with the job. She developed insomnia and she was unable to read or write. A late summer vacation she was to take with Dick Norton also depressed her. Plath started to contemplate suicide, eventually slashing her leg with a razor. Her mother took her to the family doctor, who referred the case to a young psychiatrist who recommended shock treatments on an outpatient basis. Although she feared the therapy, Plath accepted it at her mother's insistence. She found the procedure intensely painful. She writes in "The Hanging Man" that when the current was applied, she felt as if some malign god had seized her by the hair, that she fried and sizzled like cooking meat. Several days after a treatment, she broke into a medicine cabinet and took all the sleeping pills out of a nearly full bottle, but carefully disguised both theft and break-in. She wrote a note to her mother that she was leaving on a short trip and would return the next day, then went down to the basement where she hid in the crawlway behind a pile of a firelogs and swallowed the pills.

After Plath was discovered, she was taken to the hospital and later transferred to a private facility, her expenses paid by Olive Higgins Prouty. She was befriended by a female psychiatrist there but would need both insulin shock treatment and additional electroshock therapy before recovering. By mid-winter, she was well enough to return to Smith. To all appearances, she had made a complete recovery, but much was different about Sylvia. She continued to win contests and to receive A's, but she also began taking lovers. She saw several different men at the same time, including an Amherst English major she had met before her breakdown, a Yale history student who was a relative of the English poet Siegfried Sassoon, and a physics professor from MIT. While having sexual relations with the professor, she suffered a vaginal tear and lost a considerable amount of blood. She lied about taking lovers and with certain men pretended that she was still a virgin.

It was not, however, until she met Ted Hughes in England several years later that Plath found someone whom she could consider her equal. She later confessed that she married him because he was the only man she'd ever met whom she could never boss. He was also an exceptionally gifted poet in his own right, and for a time his career eclipsed hers. They met at Cambridge University and were wed in London on Bloomsday, June 16, 1956. At the time of his marriage, Hughes worked as a reader for J. Arthur Rank at Pinewood Studios. Afterward he took a job in a secondary school in Cambridge while Sylvia finished her studies at the university. In the spring of 1957, they moved to the United States. Prior to their coming to America, Hughes' collection of poems *The Hawk in the Rain* had won the impressive Poetry Center first book prize and would be published by Harper's in the United States and later by Faber and Faber in England. For a time, Plath put Ted's needs over her own. She worked as an instructor in the English department at Smith College but would quit her post after only a short time. She worked at various jobs, mostly part time, while Ted devoted himself totally to his writing. The couple eventually moved to Boston and lived in a small apartment on Beacon Hill. In 1959, Plath attended Robert Lowell's poetry workshop at Boston University where she met a number of up-and-coming poets, including George Starbuck and Anne Sexton. Sexton and Plath spoke frequently about suicide and discussed their experiences of nervous breakdown. Ted Hughes was awarded a Guggenheim fellowship in the spring of 1959. Having decided to return to England the following December, the Hugheses took a cross-country trip through several states during the summer. They hiked during the day and camped at night. Then they spent their autumn at the upstate New York writer's colony of Yaddo. In England in April 1960,

Sylvia gave birth to a daughter, Frieda. Her first poetry collection, *The Colossus*, was accepted for publication by William Heinemann and published in October of the same year. The following winter, she suffered both a miscarriage and an appendectomy. She became pregnant again in the spring of 1961. In the summer of that year, the Hugheses left London and moved to the village of Devon and into an old thatch-roofed country manor. Sylvia had been granted a Eugene F. Saxton Fellowship to complete *The Bell Jar*. She gave birth to her second child, a son, Nicholas, in January 1962. Shortly after his birth, she wrote the play *Three Women*. Like Plath, the play's three characters have just gone through labor. The first woman has had a son, the second has suffered a miscarriage, while the third has had a daughter whom she must shortly put up for adoption.

Life in Devon became particularly hectic for Plath after Nicholas' birth. She found taking proper care of two small children both difficult and time consuming. Ted and Sylvia's relationship began to deteriorate the following spring when Sylvia became aware that her husband had started, or was just about to start, an affair with Assia Wevill, the wife of Canadian poet David Wevill. Upon moving to Devon, the Hugheses had rented the couple their London flat. The poems Plath wrote that spring deal with the problems of marriage which Plath comes to see as a snare or trap. Initially wedded life seemed so full of promise but in the end only bleak and desolate; all hope was extinguished. In these poems, the wife is pictured as victim. She feels lonely and deserted and significantly is already haunted by the specter of death. After Plath listened in on one of Ted's telephone calls early in July, she burned the incomplete manuscript of her new novel which was to have been a fictional celebration of their love. After vacationing briefly in Ireland, the couple decided to separate for a time. Toward the end of August, Sylvia drove the family Morris station wagon off the road and onto an airfield in an apparent suicide attempt. She was not hurt nor was the car damaged. In "Lady Lazarus," she refers to the accident as the second suicide attempt which she has survived. Many of the poems she wrote in October, including her Bee sequence, celebrate survival and the power of womanhood. The old Queen fights against her younger rivals and emerges victorious. As winter approaches, the drones are driven out of the nest by the females to die. The useless, crippled, and crude, they are deserving of death. "Lady Lazarus" also ends with a show of daring and feminine bravado. Plath has passed through her marital crisis. Like the phoenix, she has risen from her funeral pyre. She emerges with flame-colored hair and boasts that she will now consume men like air. On October 12, however, she wrote "Daddy." The poem is complex and has many levels of meaning. It is spoken by a girl whose father died at a time when she believed him to be a god. By dying, he betrayed her. The daughter's fear and love for him are so great that, to live herself and emerge from under his shadow, she has had to banish all memory of him. In effect, she has had to kill him. It is then revealed that the father was a Nazi and the daughter a half-Jew. Throughout her life, Plath found her Germanic background terribly suspect, tainted and called into question by the great events of the century. In *The Bell Jar*, the only subject that Esther Greenwood cannot excel in is German: "the very sight of those dense, barbed-wire letters made my mind shut like a clam."[11] Although Plath loved her father very much, she often wondered if he had remained in Europe whether he might have possibly become a Nazi. It was not unimaginable that her mother, who was Austrian, might have had Jewish blood and thus could have become a victim of the father. Describing the poem, Plath stated that in the daughter "the two strains marry and paralyse each other—she has to act out the awful little allegory before she is free of it."[12] She does so by marrying a man much like her father, a *Doppelgänger* of her own creation, a man in an SS uniform who loves both sex and torture. Plath writes all women love fascists, louts, and brutes who enjoy inflicting pain and abuse. The betrayals of father and husband fuse together and the daughter is "through."

The prospect of spending the winter alone in Devon was too much for Plath, so she decided to move her family back to London. While looking for a flat to rent, she passed Yeats's house with its blue plaque "Yeats lived here" which she had gone by many times before and had longed to live in. To her surprise, she saw a sign in the window advertising flats for rent. She ran to the agent and signed a five-year lease. A few days before Christmas, she and the children moved in. The last months of her life, Plath was at work on a new novel, *Double Exposure*, which dealt with the step-by-step corruption of a young girl by a strong, deceitful man. Sadly, the manuscript would disappear from her posthumous papers. According to Hughes, it was lost around 1970. She was at the height of her creative powers during this time, and, at breakneck speed, she also produced a string of amazing poems. Yet she felt depressed and helpless. It was the coldest winter in a century. Her pipes had frozen solid. She didn't yet have a telephone and felt cut off and isolated. She had renewed trouble with her sinuses, a long-standing and painful affliction with her. She also had difficulty finding adequate help for the children. A few days before her suicide, Plath wrote "Edge," a poem explaining what she hoped killing herself would accomplish. Death perfects a woman. At each of her breasts is a dead child. She has drawn the babes back into herself as if she were a flower closing its petals at nightfall. Yet Plath made sure that whatever happened to her, her children would live. At 6 A.M., she left cups of milk and plates of bread and butter beside their beds. Before turning on the gas, she sealed the kitchen window with tape and shoved towels under the door to prevent the escape of gas. A new *au pair* girl was to arrive the next morning at nine. She came on time but when she rang at the outside there was no response. At eleven o'clock the night before, Plath had borrowed some stamps from the tenant below her, an elderly painter. Standing in his doorway, she heard him say that he would be up well before nine. Had he been and had he let the girl in, Plath would have undoubtedly been saved. She knew that her neighbor was a man of regular habits. Unfortunately for her, his bedroom was directly below her kitchen. Gas seeped down through the floor and rendered him unconscious. Receiving no answer at the door, the *au pair* girl telephoned her agency for instructions. She was told to wait. At eleven, workers arrived to work on the frozen pipes. The girl was admitted. Knocking on Sylvia's apartment door, she noticed the smell of gas and summoned the workers, who then forced the lock. They found Sylvia with her head in the oven, her body still warm. On the kitchen table lay the note with her therapist's phone number asking that he be called—that this was an emergency and that she needed help.

Notes

1. See Nancy Hunter Steiner, *A Closer Look at Ariel: A Memory of Sylvia Plath*, introduction by George Stade (New York: Harper's Magazine Press, 1973), pp. 51–53.

2. Quoted by Eileen Aird, *Sylvia Plath: Her Life and Work* (New York: Harper and Row, 1975), p. 79.

3. Plath, *The Bell Jar* (New York: Harper and Row—BOMC, 1993), p. 36.

4. Quoted by Aird, *Sylvia Plath*, p. 2.

5. Ibid., p. 3.

6. Ibid., p. 4.

7. Steiner, *A Closer Look at Ariel*, p. 45.

8. Quoted by Aird, *Sylvia Plath*, pp. 4–5.

9. *The Bell Jar*, p. 43.

10. Ibid., p. 94.

11. *The Bell Jar*, p. 36.

12. Quoted by Aird, *Sylvia Plath*, p. 79.

Charles Jackson

C HARLES JACKSON SUCCUMBED FROM A SUICIDAL INGESTION OF sleeping pills on September 21, 1968. Several days earlier he had been discovered unconscious in his Chelsea Hotel apartment in New York City. From there he was taken to St. Vincent's Hospital, where he remained comatose and unresponsive until his death. His death was ruled a suicide by the Medical Examiner's office after the performance of an autopsy. Jackson's literary agent disputed the coroner's findings and maintained that the overdose had been accidental, that there had been no suicidal intent on Charles Jackson's part, an understandable but untenable position considering the author's obsession with death as evidenced by his novels and short stories, where the themes of suicide and self-destruction resurface in various guises.

At the time of his death, Jackson was sixty-five years old and three hundred pages into a new novel, *Farther and Wilder,* in which Don Birnam, the hero of his most enduring work of fiction and first published novel, *The Lost Weekend*, reappeared as an older man. The earlier book, brought out by Farrar & Rinehart in January 1944, chronicled several days in the life of this witty and charming alcoholic, depicting in brutal and unflinching detail—from start to finish—one of his periodic drunken binges, a recurrent descent into hell and plumbing of the very depths of self-abasement. It was just one in a succession of many such downward-spiralling sprees, all single in kind, all equally self-destructive. Not only did *The Lost Weekend* receive favorable critical notices—Philip Wylie, writing for "*New York Times* Book Review," called the novel "the most compelling gift to the literature of addiction since De Quincey"[1] and characterized the depiction of Birnam as "a masterpiece of psychological precision"[2]—the book was also a runaway bestseller. The movie rights to the novel were sold to Paramount and the film version, starring Ray Milland, was also a critical and popular success. It won the Academy Award for Best Picture in 1945; Milland also took home the award for best actor. Jackson's three subsequent novels—*The Fall of Valor* (1945), *The Outer Edges* (1948), and *A Second-Hand Life* (1967)—all garnered approving and commendatory reviews, but none of them registered sales anywhere near to *The Lost Weekend*. Like the earlier work, however, the succeeding books are equally hard-boiled and glum, Jackson applying the same naturalistic methods he utilized in his first novel. Each work deals with a seamy or slightly off-color topic, which Jackson nonetheless manages to probe sensitively and sympathetically, and features a protagonist bent on self-destruction. Jackson subjects his characters to an almost microscopic scrutiny and ruthlessly lays bare their flaws and imperfections. His goal is to portray life with complete and objective veracity and to explore "the unhappy and sheltered corners of the mind"[3] that usually go unexamined and unplumbed. Yet, at the same time, Jackson also strives to create empathy and understanding for his aberrant and anomalous heroes and heroines, to make their plights so pitiful and heart-wrenching that the reader is bound to identify and sympathize with these so-called deviants, to accept them as normal and human after all. *The Fall of Valor* tells the story of a marriage on the verge of collapse due to the husband's increasing inattention to his wife resulting from his latent homosexuality, while *The Outer Edges* deals with a mentally deficient man who commits a savage and seemingly senseless murder. A sexually obsessed woman is the focus of *A Second-Hand Life*. Once again Jackson shows the devastating consequences that arise from an oppressive and irresistible addiction.

In addition to the novels, Jackson published two noteworthy collections of short stories, *The Sunnier Side* (1950) and *Earthly Creatures* (1953). The stories in the first volume are all set in the same upstate New York town and take place between the years 1912 and 1918. Many are autobiographical and deal with events of Jackson's youth. Most, as the title of the collection would indicate, are light and comic. Others, however, are dark and disturbing and more in the vein of his novels. In his preface to *The Sunnier Side*, Jackson wrote what amounts to his artistic credo:

> The writer's own mother is no more "safe" from him than a total stranger who might strike his fancy as being likely material for a story. He must essentially draw from life as he sees it, lives it, overhears it, or steals it, and the truer the writer, perhaps the bigger the blackguard. He lives by biting the hand that feeds him.[4]

Elsewhere Jackson wrote that he was never able to write about himself unless it was in the form of fiction. He made special reference to the short stories in *The Sunnier Side*, but this confession is perhaps even more applicable to two of his novels, *The Lost Weekend* and *The Fall of Valor*. An element of self-portraiture went into the characterization of both Don Birnam and Professor John Grandin, the similarly named protagonists of these two works. The "darker side" of Charles Jackson is uncovered and laid bare in both novels. The author shifts his own faults and weaknesses to these two fictional alter egos. Their dilemmas, predicaments, and impasses reflect Jackson's own problems and frustrations. These, no doubt, paved the way for Jackson's eventual suicide—his death wish so clearly arose out of them. After interviewing the author for "The *New York Times* Book Review," Harvey Breit wrote, "The impression one gets on seeing Charles Jackson is single—it's the sense unmistakably felt of the terrible and moving effort in the man to be deeply honest at each and every moment."[5] One receives the same impression from every page of his work. The author is no more "safe" from himself than his own mother—indeed, probably even less safe. His stand-ins Birnam and Grandin share their creator's fascination with death. The reasons why these two men are so beguiled by the notion of extinction, the psychological bases for death's appeal and allure, the powerful force of attraction it exerts upon them, are fully explored in the two books.

Charles Jackson was born in Summit, New Jersey on April 6, 1903, the fourth child of Frederick and Sarah Williams Jackson. His father was English, as were his mother's parents. Jackson grew up in Newark, New York, a little town located in Wayne County. After graduating from the local high school—the extent of his formal education—Jackson lived in Chicago, where he spent two years working in a bookstore. He moved to New York City late in 1926. The following year he contracted tuberculosis. By 1929, Jackson's health was so precarious that he sought treatment in Davos, Switzerland, the same resort area in the Graubunden canton, famous for its high-altitude sanitoria, where Thomas Mann set *The Magic Mountain*. While not remaining seven years in the isolated community of the sick and dying like Hans Castorp, Jackson, who stayed in Davos until July of 1931, made use of his time there, as did Mann's hero, to develop his mind and to discover himself. During his years of illness, breathing in the same rarefied Alpine air that had such sinister yet stimulating effect upon Mann's Castorp, Jackson wiled away the time by reading—primarily "Shakespeare, Proust, the great Russians, and the Bible"[6]—and by trying his hand at writing. At last, however, he was pronounced cured and returned to the States with a sense of vocation. He wanted to be a writer. He encountered great difficulty, however, in establishing himself and suffered through years of rejection. He wrote three novels prior to *The Lost Weekend*, none of which was accepted for publication. He also sent story after story to the magazines, but again met with no success.

The Lost Weekend chronicles a similar difficult stage in Don Birnam's life and is set during the Great Depression, the same time period as Jackson's own troubles. Prior to becoming addicted to alcohol, Birnam had huge artistic aspirations, and, although at the novel's opening he has become greatly debilitated by his habit, overmastered and enslaved to drink, he still envisions tremendous artistic successes for himself, that is, when he is dead drunk. In that besotted condition, he inflates "the image of himself out of all proportion to the miserable truth."[7] Birnam daydreams of writing a novelette about alcoholism comparable in quality to Mann's "Death in

Venice." He sees copies of "In a Glass" stacked in bookshop windows, "piled in tricky pyramids."[8] He imagines rave reviews from the critics—his book would be labeled a *tour de force*, a brilliant performance—and various readers' reactions, including his mother's. She complains that he has written a book which she can't show to the neighbors. As he downs shot after shot, he envisions how the novelette will unfold. The alcohol sets him on fire. His brain becomes "so feverishly alert that it seemed his perceptions. . . could grasp any problem in the world."[9] At dizzying speed, whole sentences come to him, but he has no pencil and paper with which to write them down. The ending of the work also appears to him: "after the long procession of motley scenes from his past life . . . the hero decides to walk out of the bar and somewhere, somehow, that very day . . . commit suicide."[10] He feels superior to those around him, the bartender and the tavern's other patrons, and in his conceit, seeing himself as a spiritual brother of Tonio Kröger, he envies these people their "blessed mediocrity."[11] They do not suffer from the burden of genius and therefore cannot possibly understand what it is to conceive, much less write, a story such as "In a Glass." They are mere drunks. Birnam is something else entirely; he uses alcohol to stimulate his muse. "A multitude of fancies"[12] arise out of his glass. At another point in the novel, sipping scotch while listening to a recording on the gramophone of Schnabel performing the Rondo of *Waldstein*, Birnam casts himself as a virtuoso pianist, "a dream he could re-live forever and had already enjoyed many dozens of times." (Outside of writing and reading, Jackson stated that his chief interest was music.)[13] This fantasy is even more grandiose and improbable than his dream about writing a great novelette. He steps out onto the stage at Carnegie Hall, dressed not in tie or tails but in "grey flannels, comfortable sport-shoes, soft sleeveless sweater, and a white shirt."[14] The house is packed, for tonight Don Birnam has accepted a challenge "unique in music history."[15] He does not know what his program will be but has agreed to perform, without music, any piece requested of him, from Poulenc to Scarlatti, from Buxtehude to Copland. Certainly when sober but even during the course of such fantasies, between his drinks, Birnam becomes disgusted with himself. Euphoria turns to loathing. "Suddenly, sickeningly, the whole thing was so much eyewash. How could he have been seduced, fooled, into dreaming up such a ridiculous piece; in perpetrating, even in his imagination, anything so pat, so contrived, so cheap, so phoney, so adolescent, so (crowning offense) sentimental?"[16] Self-deprecation and manic elevation alternate with one another. One moment Birnam feels scorn and self-reproach, but the next he suddenly has a brilliant idea for a story. He plunges from euphoria to despair and back again as he drinks himself into oblivion and no words get written down.

Prior to the novel's opening, Birnam—like Jackson—spent several years in Davos due to a tubercular condition. Upon his return home, he tried to become a writer (as did his creator) and met with just as little success. He began several novels but could never complete them. He also attempted to write a number of short stories, but they, too, remained unfinished. These defeats and disappointments, among other reasons, led him to drink, for when he is tight (as Birnam himself acknowledges) he can lie back in his chair and enter his favorite fantasies, imagining himself the success that he is not. Birnam realizes that his frustration and disillusionment mirror that of a great number of other people living in the 1930s:

> He supposed he was only one of several million persons of his generation who had grown up and, somewhere around thirty, made the upsetting discovery that life wasn't going to pan out the way you expected it would; and why this realization should have thrown him and not them—or not too many of them—was something he couldn't fathom. Life offered none of those prizes you'd been looking forward to since adolescence (he less than others, but looking forward to them all the same, if only out of curiosity). Adulthood came through with none of the pledges you'd been led somehow to believe in; the future still remained the future—illusion: a non-existent period or a constantly-receding promise, hinting fulfillment yet forever withholding the rewards. All the things that had never happened yet were never going to happen after all. It was a mug's game and there ought to be a law. But there wasn't any law, there was no rhyme or reason; and with the sour-grapes attitude of "Why the hell *should* there be"—which is as near as you ever came to sophistication—you retired within yourself and compensated for the disappointments by drink, by subsisting on daydreams, by living in a private world of your own making (hell or heaven, what did it matter?), by accomplishing or becoming in fancy what you could never bring about in fact.[17]

Throughout the novel Birnam's addiction to literature and writing is equated with his addiction to drink. Indeed, the impetus for his binge is his chance reading of a sentence from James Joyce's *Dubliners*: "The barometer of his emotional nature was set for a spell of riot."[18] Birnam is in the process of "drying out" as the novel opens. Having refrained from drink for several days, he is to attend an afternoon performance of *Tristan* with his brother Wick and his long-suffering girlfriend Helen, and afterward he and his brother plan to spend a long weekend together in the country. At the last moment, encumbered and oppressed, he begs off attending the opera, claiming that his nerves are shot and that he could not possibly sit still for its nearly four-hour duration. His brother reluctantly allows him to remain behind after he promises not to go out, not even to walk the dog. He asks Wick to give his love to Helen and says that he looks forward to their trip together later that evening. Nervous and tense after his brother leaves but determined to keep his promise, he plays a record on the phonograph and skims through an art book before he discovers Joyce's *Dubliners* wedged between the arm and cushion of his chair. He opens the book randomly and, in his keyed-up condition, reads the above-quoted sentence. It has a soothing effect upon him, much as would a first drink: "The burden, the oppression was gone. He felt positively light-headed, joyous. The words had released him from the acute sense of suspense he now realized he had been under since his brother left. This is what he had been waiting for, what he had probably known all along in the back of his mind was bound to happen. It was as though a light-switch had been snapped on or a door sprung open, showing him the way."[19] In a matter of minutes, he is on his way. He rips open an envelope addressed to his brother's cleaning lady on the kitchen table, steals the twenty dollars contained in it, her pay for the month, and heads for the closest bar. His brother will proceed to the country without him, and Birnam will spend the long weekend getting smashed and sinking ever deeper into his degradation. The man with such lofty aspirations will "play the aristocrat before the peasant"[20] and shamelessly borrow money— money he never intends to repay—from an elderly German laundress down the street; steal a purse and be tossed from a ritzy bar in Greenwich village, "Jack's on Charles Street";[21] set a date with a hostess in another bar after telling her an elaborate lie about the suffering he has undergone at the hands of a nonexistent wife—to do the girl a kindness, for a date with a person like him, a real gentleman, was as "near to romance"[22] as someone from her class would ever be given to come—only to forget their appointment and stand her up; lose or misplace most of the money he does have; cross half of New York looking for an open pawnbroker to hock his typewriter, only to find that it is Yom Kippur; wake up in the alcoholic ward of a hospital after falling down the stairs of his apartment; trade his watch for whiskey after leaving the hospital; suffer from hallucinations and contemplate suicide; be dressed and fed by Helen and taken to her place to recover; attempt the next morning to break into her locked hall closet and drink her liquor and, failing that, steal her short leopard coat and pawn it; unexpectedly find twenty-seven dollars he thought he had lost in the breast-pocket of his jacket and with a portion of this windfall purchase six pints of rye at the local liquor store; and finally return to his and his brother's apartment to lie down and wait for Wick to return from the country, after first hiding the pints in various places, including one in the tank of his toilet.

Birnam sees his whole life, not just his frequent alcoholic episodes (only one of which *The Lost Weekend* chronicles), as a great descent into destruction. His attraction to the abyss stems from his artistic nature and personality. Alcoholism is only a symptom of an even greater disease. From his youth onward, Birnam was strangely drawn to self-destructive artists of the past. He felt a mystic kinship to these individuals long before he took his first drink: "The idol of the boy had been Poe and Keats, Byron, Dowson, Chatterton—all the gifted, miserable and reckless men who had burned themselves out in tragic brilliance early and with finality. Not for him the normal happy genius living to a ripe old age (genius indeed! How could a genius be happy, normal, above all, long-lived?), acclaimed by all (or acclaimed in his lifetime?), enjoying honour, love, obedience, troops of friends. . . ."[23] Because of who he is, Birnam searches—is on a quest for—experience, experience of any sort, especially of a dubious nature that involves suffering and humiliation. He constantly pushes the limits and endangers himself in various ways to advance his development as an artist and to learn about himself. He tests boundaries and welcomes pain and disillusionment because these inevitably lead to self-discovery.

When his father deserted the family when he was only a young boy, Don wept his heart out but also self-consciously looked into the mirror to see what a stricken child looked like. All his life, he has cultivated a dual identity as both participant and observer. As a spectator, he enjoys watching himself tumbling down toward the bottom but not sinking under entirely, at least not yet. He never missed an opportunity to engage in some dangerous behavior that could "color and cripple"[24] his life from then on. He remembers with deep shame homosexual experiences from his boyhood. After school he and his friend Melvin would go to the carriage sheds behind the Presbyterian Church, climb into an abandoned buggy and "have fun."[25] On one occasion, he asked Mel what he thought about while they fondled each other, and Mel replied that he pictured himself laying his face on the bare belly of one of their fellow schoolgirls. Don is too ashamed to tell Mel the scene that flashes before his own eyes. He imagines Mel washing his father's back, a ritual Mel dutifully performed whenever his father took a bath and which he casually mentioned to Don, something the latter finds exciting perhaps because he himself no longer has a father at home. He realized that he was different from Mel as soon as the other answered his question and revealed to him his fantasy, and he was no longer able to take joy in their petting and had to stop their regular meetings. Several years later, at age seventeen, he had another crushing homosexual experience. "All the woeful errors of childhood and adolescence came to their crashing climax."[26] During his first month of college, he hero-worshiped and became infatuated with an upperclassman. Because of this behavior, he was drummed out of the fraternity house where he had been pledging and lost his precious annotated copy of *Macbeth*. He dropped out of the university and thereafter was fearful of encountering any of the fraternity brothers. He is still anxious and frightened about the prospect of such a chance meeting at the time of *The Lost Weekend*, years later. Prior to this incident, he had dated a girl (and had taken up the pen to write poetry), and afterward he engaged in a number of love affairs with a number of different women. Nonetheless, Birnam remains insecure about his sexual identity and fears that he will never have the courage or gumption to marry Helen. This aspect of his story is not portrayed or even hinted at in the 1945 Paramount film. Obviously, Jackson did not intend this background material as merely incidental. His protagonist's self-destructive tendencies demonstrably increased after the fraternity episode.

The long years of drinking commenced. Shortly after his leaving school, Birnam overlooked and disregarded his first tubercular hemorrhages and did nothing to arrest the onset of disease, because he felt that to be seriously ill would afford him a rich and rewarding experience. He also began toying with the notion of suicide, sensing that he would find fulfillment in death. While recuperating from tuberculosis in Europe and then during the trip homeward, he contemplated killing himself on numerous occasions and lived in a very reckless fashion. In retrospect, he realizes that the life he has led has had a pattern and this pattern will be complete only when he actually does die. Actually, he has come near death many times.

After his cure in Davos, he traveled for a time in Switzerland and France. He thought about tossing himself from a catwalk over the railroads tracks at Basle. Later, standing at the rail of his ocean liner, he joked with a Norwegian woman about leaping into the Atlantic. Once, in a hotel bar, he exploded a gas-filled balloon with his cigarette. The crepe-paper streamers decorating the place (it was some sort of gala night) caught fire, but then miraculously were extinguished, sparing not only him but the several hundred people sleeping in the rooms above. On numerous occasions, he had burned up his beds, having passed out drunk with a lit cigarette in his hand, to awake to the stench of burning pillow feathers. One year, Birnam reached a point where he almost slit his wrists. He rented a shack on a resort beach for the summer, but before the season ended spent all his money and had no food, and more importantly no drink. Although he went so far as to write three suicide notes, at the last moment he was unable to follow through and gave himself one more chance, another day. He managed to escape that time, but, on another occasion, he could not fight off the urge to do away with himself and overdosed on sodium amytal tablets prescribed to him by a psychiatrist. Two days later he came to, to the great relief of his brother Wick, who had found him while he was comatose. During the course of his drunken weekend, again and again, Birnam feels that his life will end in suicide, that suicide will be his one real accomplishment. His alcoholism is but a symptom of his self-destructive death wish. He realizes that he is slowly drinking himself to an early grave and doesn't care. His heart pounds in his chest and skips beats but he goes on drinking bourbon. As Birnam listens to his heart, he apostrophizes himself, "He died a thousand deaths." He says, "Worse by far than a thousand, it was one death drawn out in endless torture, a death that didn't die. You kept on dying, and dying; you died all day and all night; and still there was dying yet to do, and more dying ahead—it simply did not end and would never end."[27]

If like Don Birnam, Charles Jackson had fears about marriage, he was able to overcome them. In 1938, he married Rhonda Booth, an associate editor of *Fortune* magazine. (The couple would have two daughters, Sarah and Kate.) The following year, he finally had a short story accepted for publication. "Palm Sunday" appeared in the quarterly *Partisan Review*, and the magazine promptly accepted a second story by Jackson, "Rachel's Summer," for its next issue. In addition, two years previously, he had found fulfilling work as a staff writer for CBS. From 1939 to 1944, he freelanced in radio and taught radio-writing at New York University. During these years, Birnam's stories, essays, and book reviews began appearing in a wide number of magazines and newspapers. He also did movie work in Hollywood on three occasions. In 1944, the year *The Lost Weekend* appeared, he and his family took up residence in Orford, New Hampshire. Thereafter Birnam supplemented his income as a visiting professor and guest lecturer at various colleges and universities. He spent a year at Marlboro College in Vermont where he taught a course in the American novel and he frequently led workshops and lectured on writing at Dartmouth College, and at Columbia and New York Universities.

If *The Lost Weekend* treats the dark period in Jackson's life before his marriage and before he gained success as a writer, *The Fall of Valor* reflects his life after success and marriage and deals with the difficulties he encountered as an older man and the tragic flaw he saw in himself—the identity he could not suppress despite marriage and fatherhood and the lie he lived or, at least at some times, concluded and thought that he did. With this work, Charles Jackson indeed attempts to write his own, very personal "Death in Venice."

As the novel opens, Professor John Grandin has just had his book on American literature, *The Tragic Ideal,* accepted for publication and as a result has received promotion to the rank of full professor by his college. He is shortly to leave Manhattan to join his wife, Ethel, for a vacation at the New England seaside resort of Sconset. Ethel left New York City a week earlier with the couple's two boys to visit her parents' home in Maine and will join him while the children remain behind with their grandparents. Grandin realizes that he has been guilty for some time of neglecting his wife. They had fallen in love ten years before, had married and had children together; but, despite his having been a good provider and a faithful husband, habit has taken their marriage over and the couple has slowly drifted apart. They no longer have meaningful and passionate conversations with one another and have fallen into their separate routines. His inattention to his wife's needs, especially her sexual requirements, has grown more pronounced in the last several months. She would go to bed early—he'd hear her go up the steps—and browse through a magazine, while he remained downstairs reading and writing in his study; eventually she would turn out the light—he'd hear this, too, but, absorbed in his labors, he would remain below to toil deep into the night. Grandin blames this neglect on two things: his preoccupation with his work and his apprehension and sadness about World War II, which America had entered two years before. As he makes his preparations to depart, Grandin vows to lay work and cares aside. He is feeling "a holiday mood" and is "anxious to induce as quickly as possible the sense of light-heartedness befitting a vacation."[28] He pledges to make up for his past neglect of his wife during the trip. As Ethel leaves her parents, she, too, is hoping for a reconciliation, but she is also determined to make her husband pay for his sins. During the trip, she plans to confront and have it out with him.

Professor Grandin's new-found holiday disposition masks the grave anxieties and forebodings he has been previously experiencing for the last several weeks and months. These feelings become especially intense after his wife and children leave home:

> Though outwardly his life had been going well indeed, John Grandin had lately found himself living under an emotional suspense. For hours, sometimes, he had a sense that something was about to happen to him, something untoward, per-

verse, impossible to fit into his comfortably ordered life; then the feeling would pass and he would forget it until it came up again. It interrupted his work, interfered with his attentions to his family and to family duties, left his mind far from rest. Working of an afternoon, in broad daylight—he would lift his head, his senses all aware, and catch himself in the act of expressing a baffling thought: When will the blow fall? What would he do when it did fall, what kind of blow would it be? For months his thinking had never been wholly his own, for something or someone seemed to be thinking for him and through him. In the back of his mind lay a vague and fearful uncertainty, a reminder of doom, so that he found himself wondering, even almost casually (it had become so habitual by now): Now what was it I was feeling or supposed to feel bad about?—as if he had lately passed through a harrowing experience which, though he had deliberately put it behind him, still lingered in his mind, sent reverberations of unpleasantness into his everyday thought, and somewhere lay dormant but still menacing, still liable to waken again. When it intruded itself actively, he could almost have declared for his own peace of mind: Very well, I'm guilty, they've found me out, the police will arrive any moment now, Ethel will leave me, the children be taken away, I'll lose everything and have to serve my term—and I'll feel better. . . . But what he would lose, or why, was the mystery.[29]

Grandin's presentiments recall those of both Henry James's John Marcher and Thomas Mann's Gustave von Aschenbach. Like the former he feels something momentous is on verge of happening to him and he is on pins and needles waiting for his beast to spring. He is also experiencing "a spell of riot"[30] similar to that Aschenbach underwent in Munich before departing southward on his impromptu journey to Italy. As was the case with the great German novelist, the oppression that burdens Grandin disrupts his work and causes him to feel the need for a vacation. An unconscious desire for death manifests itself in both characters' craving for a holiday. Death, after all, offers the ultimate respite from life. All earthly burdens and hardships come to an end when we do. Both men travel to the seaside, Grandin to a New England beach, Aschenbach to the Lido and there they fall in love with a member of their own sex, an individual who senses their attention and interest and coquettishly responds to it. Aschenbach's attraction to the Polish boy Tadzio and Grandin's obsession with marine Captain Cliff Hauman represent each man's ultimate degradation, the lowest point of their lives, that nadir to which their death wish has caused them to sink. Homosexuality is equated with death in both works. Despite lifelong homoerotic yearnings, both authors view the love that dare not speak its name as pathetic, sterile, and doomed, as a chaotic force that overthrows order, form, propriety and stateliness and topples its victim into the abyss.

The similarities between the two works do not end there. There are many intimations early on in The Fall of Valor of what is about to befall John Grandin, just as Aschenbach's ultimate fate is adumbrated from the very first pages of Death in Venice. The book that Grandin takes with him on his trip—The Collected Poems of

A. E. Housman—is subconsciously selected because of the theme of the poems: namely, "youth stricken in untimely death."[31] On its way to Grand Central Station, his taxi is blocked on Madison Avenue by a double column of oddly assorted men, inductees to the various branches of the armed services. Grandin exits his cab to walk the short distance to the station, but first takes a long look at the marching barrier of humanity before him. He is disturbed and saddened yet strangely touched at the sight of these men and boys, many of whom are destined for premature death. His unease grows as he watches the parade of inductees until he finally turns and breaks into a run to escape from the scene. Opening the book on his train, he is initially puzzled why he had chosen this particular volume. As he rereads the poems, he is sickened and appalled by them. "Verse after witty verse, so satisfying before, now struck him with repulsion. Beneath the grace of the most lightly turned stanza lay a cynicism bitter beyond even the poet's wonderful words: morbid, macabre, necrophiliac—polluted with an amorousness, a virtual lust for the grave. The verses smelled of rot; no felicity of phrase could mask the underlying sordid horror."[32] In consternation, Grandin slams the book shut and, although he had previously always believed in freedom of expression, he feels that such a volume should have been suppressed. He gets up from his seat and heads to the smoking car which is filled with soldiers. One of these, a large handsome blond boy, springs up and offers him his seat. A startled Grandin declines the offer, the soldier's gesture "so patently that of youth to age, a young man's politeness to an elder,"[33] and finds another seat. After Grandin finishes his cigarette and gets up to leave, the soldier flashes him "a painfully polite and eager smile."[34] This is the professor's first encounter with Cliff Hauman, whom neither he nor the reader yet knows by name. Grandin returns to his seat and opens a copy of *Life* to the Picture-of-the-Week, a full-page photograph of four dead marines laying face down on a beach. Grandin discerns "a melancholy beauty"[35] in the shot and feels ashamed about his earlier reaction against Housman (as the reader will shortly learn, the poet's surname and that of the marine are almost identical; the demoniac appears to be at work here just as it is in Mann): "Who knew better than he [Grandin] that the theme of death-in-youth was more 'suitable' to poetry and had always been more attractive to poets than any other theme in human experience; and while the heart was wrung, the aesthetic sense was exalted and satisfied."[36] He recalls that Whitman "had celebrated death in many a challenging manly chant"[37] and that one of the Bachs had composed the lovely "Come, Sweet Death."[38]

The scene switches back and forth between Grandin traveling on his train and his wife Ethel traveling on hers. In one of the Ethel chapters, we learn that, some months before, Mrs. Grandin had discovered a newspaper clipping tucked under the blotter of Grandin's desk, a photograph of "a battle-exhausted marine lying in a burlap bunk fast asleep, his right arm (as if by habit) around a heavy Garland rifle, a packed kit of some kind resting on his chest, and his left hand relaxed and limp on his stomach—the only part of him which did not seem, in spite of his dead sleep, tensed and ready for instant action."[39] Ethel slipped the photograph of this "rugged, masculine, and mature-looking man"[40] back under the blotter. While she never told her husband that she had found the picture, it revealed to her, like nothing else, Grandin's "tragic even morbid concern" with the war and perhaps "his sense of guilt for being out of it."[41] She felt the war had come between her and her husband, and she remembered feeling puzzled and disturbed about the photograph.

Husband and wife meet at the town of Woods Hole. After exiting their respective trains, they board the ferry to Nantucket. In the boat's small cafeteria, Grandin again encounters the marine who proceeds to introduce him to his wife, who turns out to be one of Grandin's former students. The couple, married only the day before, are on their honeymoon. Grandin also learns that Hauman is not on furlough but on sick list. He entered the marines after graduating from Syracuse University and had fought at Guadalcanal, where he was wounded the previous December. He has been off duty for over half a year. Grandin finds Hauman an attractive but not overly bright individual. He enjoys the younger man's respect and attentiveness and is surprised to learn that, although Cliff could receive an honorable discharge, he intends to return to the fighting as soon as he is able. Grandin feels that he is marked for early death and his attraction toward the marine grows. Aschenbach similarly feels that Tadzio is bound for an early grave. Although the youth is very beautiful, he has a weak constitution and bad teeth. It is the transience of beauty and perfect form, as exemplified by the Polish boy, that affects Aschenbach so profoundly. While the Haumans' marriage has only just begun, that of the Grandins is rapidly deteriorating. On the boat, John and Ethel are nervous and agitated in each other's company. Ethel is prone to tears and full of recriminations. Instead of relaxing and enjoying their vacation, she is spoiling for a fight. In the Haumans' company, however, the Grandins attempt to hide their problems and put the best face on things if only for appearance's sake. The Haumans intend to spend their honeymoon on Nantucket but Grandin invites them, if they can find the time, to call on Ethel and him in Sconset. The two couples disembark from the ferry, and the Grandins take the rickety omnibus to their beachside resort where they register at their hotel, Dune House. They have a bitter argument the first night. Ethel airs all her grievances of the last several months and complains of her husband's neglect night after night. John begs her not to shout and reminds her that only thin walls separate the rooms of the hotel, that their conversation will be overheard. Ethel sobs all the louder and says that she won't sleep with him, now that he wants to do so; she won't let him use this vacation to make up for his past indifference and negligence. At last Grandin asks his wife if she loves him. She replies that she does not know and in anger he leaves their room and slams shut the door. When Grandin returns late that night, Ethel is lying awake in bed, smoking. He tries to get in bed with her, but she still refuses him, gets out of bed, and sits in the wicker chair by the bureau.

The following morning John awakens to find his wife gone. He searches for her in the hotel and then on the beach before at last finding her in the town drugstore.

At her request, he scribbles a note to his sons on a postcard. Just then the bus from Nantucket pulls to the curb and the Haumans get off. The two couples spend the day on the beach. The alert and earnest Cliff remains attentive to the professor and does everything he can to make himself winsome and fetching in the older man's eyes. After swimming, the two men shower together and Grandin inquires about the Haumans' honeymoon. He wonders if the couple is using birth control and feels that they should be if Cliff intends to return to military service. Hauman replies a bit brusquely that everything is taken care of, and Grandin feels that he has been rebuked for his inquisitiveness. He also realizes that he secretly hoped by raising the topic of contraception, to induce Hauman to speak about his sexuality. Despite this incident, a day or two later, the Haumans again return to Dune House, having decided to check into the resort hotel themselves. The two couples are now constantly together: on the beach, in the hotel dining room, in the town. In private, John and Ethel remain cold and antagonistic with one other, but, when in the Haumans' company, they pretend they are having a fine time and enjoying a lovely vacation together. The marine remains very accommodating and considerate to Grandin, always lighting his cigarettes, opening his doors, and quickly performing other courtesies whenever he sees the opportunity to do so. On one occasion, he offers to rub suntan lotion on the older man's back and arms while, together with their wives and another couple, they are sitting on the beach. Grandin pulls violently away, however, surprised at the violence of his reaction. That night, however, the two couples attend a military dance at the Yacht Club in Nantucket. Although Ethel dances with Cliff, Grandin does not dance with Mrs. Hauman. Grandin feels uncomfortable in the military crowd and he and Ethel leave the party early and return to Sconset. At the hotel, Ethel chides her husband not only for not asking Mrs. Hauman onto the dance floor but for the way he acted about the suntan oil on the beach. Exasperated with and angered at his wife, Grandin goes for a walk. It is a foggy night and he loses his way, only to find himself again on the beach (where at night war regulations forbid him to be). He discovers the sun-tan oil bottle and thinks back to the events of the morning. Now he imagines Cliff's "two strong hands moving over his upper arms, shoulders, and back" and to his surprise he discovers that he has an erection. He feels shocked and helpless. Unlike Don Birnam, who had boyhood homosexual experiences, Grandin has had exclusively heterosexual desires until this time.

The following day, Ethel discovers a khaki overseas cap adorned with two bars in her husband's suitcase. Cliff had given it to Grandin as a war souvenir. Recalling the photograph she had earlier found under her husband's desk blotter, she confronts Grandin about the cap, and he attempts to tell her what the marine means to him. He recounts what happened to him the night before, his moment of self-discovery on the beach; however, he assures her that he loves her and that the matter is insignificant: "Maybe it's a definite part of my nature. But till now, my love for you has kept it in the background where it belongs. Our love can do it again."[42] Scandalized, Ethel immediately packs her bags and leaves Sconset to return to her parents in Maine. Grandin remains at the resort. On the beach one morning, Hauman tells Grandin that he reminds him of a former English professor who had been particularly kind to Hauman and his best friend. Both young men were on the football team and had difficulty with English. They would not have been allowed to continue to play ball if they did not pass the man's course; therefore, he helped them out by tutoring them privately. However, one night the professor made sexual advances to Cliff. Hauman rebuffed the man and later learned that he had done the same thing with his friend. Hauman regrets his action, however. The professor was truly a nice person and besides, he was a lot younger then. Grandin can't believe his ears. He decides to take a swim and Cliff follows him. The current is strong and the water choppy. Grandin becomes tired and contemplates drowning himself: "He gave himself up to the rough lull and rocking of it. . . . *Hurry me out of the sight of the land; Cushion me soft, rock me in billowy drowse; Dash me with amorous wet—I can repay you.* . . ."[43] He is determined not to call out, to die quietly; but Cliff, who has already swum back to the beach, discerns his plight, plunges once more into the water, and tows the exhausted Grandin back to shore.

Shortly thereafter, Grandin and the Haumans leave Sconset. Grandin returns to Manhattan while Ethel remains in Maine. One day he receives a telephone call from Cliff asking if he might stop by. At the same time, Ethel Grandin, who is resting on a beach in Maine, has written a letter to her husband that she will be coming home soon; she realizes that what had happened in Sconset meant nothing. Only now does she perceive what had attracted her initially to John Grandin. The weakness that had revealed itself to her husband in Sconset "was one and the same with that sensitiveness of his which, unaware, she had loved him for from the beginning. . . . Had John Grandin been all male, they would not have met on common ground ever."[44] Meanwhile, Hauman arrives alone at the Grandin apartment, a bit flustered, beside himself, and very hot. He asks Grandin if he might take a bath and Grandin nods. He feels that while Cliff is in the tub, he should walk out the door, but he cannot. In ten minutes, Hauman returns to the living room and sits down beside Grandin. He seems nervous and uneasy. Grandin thinks that he may not have passed his physical to return to the marines. Cliff tells him about his and a fellow soldier's sexual escapades in California. They had visited a Hollywood canteen, and he claims to have had sex with a movie star. Feeling that Hauman is exploiting him, Grandin gets up from his seat and walks round the room. Finally he walks back to Cliff. The marine stands up, and Grandin embraces him. Confused by his own feelings, at the moment of crisis, Hauman opts for violence. His response is reflexive and soldier-like; he grabs the brass-handled tongs beside the fireplace and strikes Grandin in the face. The blow that the professor had been waiting for comes at last. The novel ends with Grandin lying on the floor badly beaten up and bleeding. While not actually dead, he has suffered a spiritual decease. His weakness, he feels, will be revealed to the whole world, and he wishes that Cliff would have finished the job.

While *Death in Venice* is a near perfect work, *The Fall of Valor* is not only derivative (owing, as it does, a great debt to the Mann classic) but uneven in quality. The chapters devoted to Ethel (roughly half the book) are melodramatic and unconvincing. The confrontation scenes between husband and wife are also over the top and often unintentionally funny. In comparison to Grandin, the other characters appear flat and two-dimensional, with the possible exception of Captain Hauman, who has something of the sly seducer about him, despite all his Little Abnerisms, the "gee gollys" and "aw shucks" that comprise his speech. Jackson's dialogue is often generic and uninspired. He fills pages with vapid exchanges such as the following:

> "How do you feel, Johnnie?"
> "All right."
> "I suppose you miss Eth."
> "Very much."
> Surprisingly Cliff asked, then: "Rather not talk."
> "No, not especially."
> "I've been thinking of you, Johnnie," he said. "I'm sure going to miss you,
> gosh, when we go away from here."[45]

There are far fewer such passages in *The Lost Weekend*, but there are enough. Other than Don Birnam, the bar patrons speak, for the most part, as if they're in a Sam Spade or Philip Marlowe detective story. As a writer, Jackson is far more interesting when he enters the minds of his protagonists. Indeed, he is really two writers, for there are two very different impulses at work in his fiction. He tries to be maximalist and minimalist—Faulkner and Hemingway both—and shifts back and forth between the two modes throughout his works. When he enters Grandin's or Birnam's head, he allows his prose to become symphonic. The trickle turns into a turbid, churning flood and the writing is often first-rate. In these rapt, spellbound, often deliberately meandering passages (which witless critics will no doubt deride as purple and opaque), Jackson shows himself to be a master of the art of crescendo and decrescendo as the tortured thoughts of his heroes swirl and rise up in intensity as they contemplate the matters closest to their hearts' desire, then descend and taper off as outside, peripheral concerns and circumstances intrude only to swell once more when they again turn back to the objects of their obsession.

Whatever its flaws, *The Fall of Valor* found an admirer in Thomas Mann. Jackson had met the German author and his wife, Katia, at a Hollywood party in 1944 and tried to engage Mann in a conversation about his work. Mann was characteristically reserved and, attempting to turn the conversation away from himself, proceeded to talk shop about publishing concerns—contracts, advances, and like matters. Katia, however, was much more severe with the reverential, fawning American. She told Jackson that one could not truly esteem Mann unless one read him in German and even then only if one had a thorough knowledge of German poetry. Yet despite this inauspicious encounter, Jackson eventually would receive a letter from Mann about *The Fall of Valor*, a candid and intimate note written in faltering English in which Mann credited Jackson "for never denying the knowledge we have retained of the so-called perversions and aberrations of this sphere, namely above all the homosexual component, a phenomenon which, as Goethe says, is in nature, although it seems to be directed against nature."[46] The letter became one of Jackson's most treasured possessions.

In the two novels that followed the *Fall of Valor*, Charles Jackson still wrote about self-destructive characters, but the protagonists of *The Outer Edges* and *A Second-Hand Life* encountered obstacles and dilemmas, albeit sexual in nature, quite different from the author's own. Admittedly, in the short story collection *The Sunnier Side*, Jackson did write about himself, but in this volume of primarily comic tales he fondly recalled his boyhood days in upstate New York. In summoning his early years, he occasionally veered from the sentimental and nostalgic to brave and confront life's darker realities, but for the most part, he kept true to his title and dealt with happier themes. At the time of his suicide, however, he was again writing about Don Birnam and presumably once more faced all his own demons as he stared hard into the mirror a final time.

Jackson was survived by his wife, his two daughters, and a brother, Frederick.

Notes

1. *New York Times* obituary, 22 September 1968.

2. From the Philip Wylie review quoted in the *New York Times* obituary cited.

3. From the dust jacket of *The Fall of Valor* by Charles Jackson (New York: Rhinehart, 1946).

4. Quoted in *New York Times* obituary.

5. Ibid.

6. Quoted in *Twentieth Century Authors, First Supplement*, ed. Stanley J. Kunitz and Vineta Colby (New York: H.W. Wilson, 1955), p. 481.

7. Charles Jackson, *The Lost Weekend* (New York: Carroll and Graf, 1983), p. 16. *The Lost Weekend* was originally published by Rhinehart in 1944.

8. Ibid., p. 18.

9. Ibid., p. 16.

10. Ibid., p. 18.

11. Ibid., p. 19.

12. Ibid., p. 16.

13. Ibid., p. 65.

14. Ibid., pp. 65–66.

15. Ibid., p. 66.

16. Ibid., p. 18.

17. Ibid., pp. 45–46.

18. Ibid., p. 9.

19. Ibid.

20. Ibid., p. 26.

21. Ibid.

22. Ibid., p. 82.

23. Ibid, pp. 15–16.

24. Ibid., p. 51.

25. Ibid., p. 52.

26. Ibid., p. 48.

27. Ibid., p. 175.

28. Jackson, *Fall of Valor*, p. 11.

29. Ibid., pp. 6–7.

30. See footnote 18 above.

31. *Fall of Valor*, p. 32.

32. Ibid.

33. Ibid.

34. Ibid., p. 33.

35. Ibid., p. 40.

36. Ibid., pp. 40–41.

37. Ibid., p. 41.

38. Ibid.

39. Ibid., p. 55.

40. Ibid.

41. Ibid., p. 54.

42. Ibid., p. 255.

43. Ibid., p. 269.

44. Ibid., p. 308.

45. Ibid., p. 266.

46. Quoted by Anthony Heilbut, *Thomas Mann: Eros and Literature* (New York: Knopf, 1996), p. 141.

John Kennedy Toole

AS JOHN KENNEDY TOOLE'S POSTHUMOUSLY PUBLISHED PULITZER prize-winning novel *A Confederacy of Dunces* careens to its comic conclusion, its hero, the obese former graduate student, virgin, and lute player, Ignatius J. Reilly, prepares to flee from his mother's house on Constantinople Street in New Orleans. Circumstances compel him to cut the umbilical cord that has bound him for so long. He must flee, for his mother has reached the end of her tether at last. He's broken her heart so many times that she can't count them up any more. Again and again, she has told him that he's her cross to bear, but she is also his. She has forgiven his outrageous behavior in the past, but now her fat, slothlike son with his blue and yellow eyes, his Mickey Mouse watch, his bushy black moustache, his full fleshy lips with potato chip crumbs protruding from the corners, and his ubiquitous green hunting cap atop his balloon of a head, has gone too far. Ignatius had lived at home with her for years, but as the novel opens events dictate that he at long last find employment. Ignatius and his mother are shopping at the D. H. Holmes department store. Ignatius comes close to being picked up as a suspicious character by undercover policeman Mancusco, who desperately needs to arrest someone in order to get back into the good graces of his superiors at the police station. Mrs. Reilly intervenes and prevents her son from being detained, and she and Ignatius repair to the Night of Joy cocktail lounge, where Mrs. Reilly has one too many beers. On the way home she smashes her car into a house, doing considerable damage to it, damage for which she is liable. Because of this new debt, Mrs. Reilly puts her foot down and makes her Oliver Hardyesque son go to work. Grudgingly, he complies; he can't, however, hold down a job. He fails both as an office worker at a clothing factory and as a hot dog vendor. At the workplace, he is a disaster waiting to happen. His half-

276

hearted attempts to earn a living all end in catastrophe and catastrophe of his own making. One slapstick episode follows another until events culminate in a final madcap debacle. Ignatius's actions precipitate the filing of a half-million-dollar lawsuit against his erstwhile employer at Levy Pants. (Ignatius forged an insulting letter in the name of the company president to an outraged client who promptly instigates a libel suit.) His career selling weenies ends in a wild incident on Bourbon Street. Ignatius passes out in his vendor's costume after being attacked by a cockatoo during a stripper's act inside the Night of Joy club, into which he has been enticed by the black doorman Burma Jones. Fleeing from the club, he is almost run over by a Desire bus. The bar is subsequently raided by patrolman Mancusco, and Ignatius is caught lying in the street "like a drunk bum"[1]—his image (that of a beached whale) snapped by a photographer for a New Orleans newspaper. He is hospitalized for shock, but his name and picture appear on the front page, much to the chagrin of Mrs. Reilly. Enraged by the adverse publicity generated by the Bourbon Street brouhaha, seeing her chances of marrying the elderly pensioner Claude Robichaux spoiled by the incident, and fearful of the impending lawsuit against Levy Pants, she sees no other alternative but to follow the advice of her friend and matchmaker Santa Battaglia and have Ignatius committed to the psychiatric wing of the Charity Hospital. There he would not be liable to prosecution for forgery by Mr. Levy. Aware of his mother's planned course of action and realizing that in a mental ward they "tampered with your soul and mind and worldview,"[2] Ignatius perceives that he must make his escape quickly or else be carted off to the loony bin like Blanche DuBois. Fate unexpectedly aids him. A guitar slung over her shoulder, Myrna Minkoff shows up at his door at his hour of need.

Ignatius's troubles began years before he and his mother walked into the D. H. Holmes store. After receiving his Masters degree in history and traveling to Baton Rouge via Greyhound Scenicruiser for a job interview at Louisiana State University—the only time he had ever been outside of New Orleans in his life—only to become sick on the bus somewhere in the swamps, then be insulted by the chairman of the Medieval Culture Department and have his beloved lumber jacket stolen in the faculty men's room after he ran there in mid-interview, Ignatius swore off work forever. He fled from the bathroom and the building and hailed a taxi to take him back to New Orleans. Ignatius's aversion to work, however, began in graduate school. He lost his teaching assistantship there because his students demanded that he grade and return their accumulated essays and examinations. They gathered outside the window of his office to protest his tardiness in returning their themes, and Ignatius dumped the ungraded papers out the window onto the students' heads. His college "was too small to accept this act of defiance against the abyss of contemporary academia."[3]

After graduating, Ignatius did find work at the New Orleans Public Library pasting checkout slips in the backs of books, but he was fired after only two weeks because some days he could only paste in three or four slips and at the same time feel satisfied with the quality of his work. For three years, Ignatius felt content to remain unemployed and to live at home with his mom, who coddled and spoiled her son between her frequent trips to the kitchen to sneak drinks from a bottle of Gallo muscatel hidden inside her oven. A goof-off and slugabed who is plagued continually by gastro-intestinal problems—his pyloric valve continually snaps shut, filling his stomach with trapped gas—Ignatius would spend his days doing nothing but watching television, eating large quantities of food, and washing it down with Dr. Nut soda pop, desultorily strumming a few measures upon his lute, and occasionally masturbating while thinking about happy hours he spent playing with his now dead collie, Rex, during his high school years. When he climaxes, he can almost hear Rex go, "Woof! Woof! Arf!"[4] He also devotes himself to one other activity, an endeavor well suited for someone with a lot of time on his hands: writing. He spends hours a day in his cloister-like back room scribbling away in his Big Chief tablets, sealed off from society as if he were a latter-day Proust. He fills yellow page after yellow page composing a monumental indictment against modern American society. Like Leo Naphta, the Jewish Jesuit in *The Magic Mountain*, he feels civilization reached its height in the medieval era. Not only does contemporary society need taste and dignity, it lacks theology and geometry as well. Walker Percy correctly states in his introduction that Ignatius wages a "one-man war against everybody—Freud, homosexuals, heterosexuals, Protestants, and the assorted excesses of modern times."[5] Ignatius spends his days drafting his mammoth condemnation of the modern world, constantly deploring the lack of culture in America to anyone who'll lend him an ear, but he secretly enjoys watching television and going to the movies. From his seat in the movie theater, he rails out loud at the scantily clad actresses on the screen as they perform their—to his mind—various indecencies and abominations. In addition to working on his magnum opus—the giant indictment against the modern world—he writes scholarly essays such as "Boethius Observed" and "In Defense of Hroswitha" with an eye toward publication in university journals as well as articles for family magazines, including a tribute to his dead dog, "The Death of Rex," and the tritely titled "Children, the Hope of the World."[6] In order "to crack the Sunday supplement market,"[7] he writes columns such as "The Challenge of Water Safety," "The Danger of Eight-Cylinder Automobiles," and "Abstinence, the Best Method of Birth Control."[8] Although he feels each of his pieces is excellent in its own way, he has never submitted any of them for publication. He did mail a two-page, handwritten monograph, *Blood on Their Hands: The Crime of It All, A study of some selected abuses in sixteenth century Europe*, to the rare books room of Tulane University as a gift. He realizes, however, that it was probably immediately discarded. Although clearly a failure as a writer, Ignatius is content to continue on the course he has chosen, stay at home with his mother, and let posterity be his judge until his mother's accident necessitates his going to work. A good medievalist, he accepts his plight, for although he dreads the prospect of earning a living, he knows misery is the proper condition of man, and he believes in Boethius's conceit of the *rota Fortunae*, or wheel of fortune. Luck comes in cycles. The blind goddess spins the wheel, and what will be will be. He realizes that it is futile to attempt to arrest the beginning of a bad cycle.

Ignatius's erstwhile girlfriend and former fellow graduate student, the crusading Jewish folksinger, fighter of reactionary ideas, and exponent of erotic liberty, Myrna Minkoff of the Bronx, has written him that "great Oedipus bonds"[9] encircle his brain and that these are destroying him. She feels that he not only desperately needs the "therapy of sex,"[10] but that he must emerge from his "womb room"[11] and has been writing to tell him so for years. Ignatius never gave ear to her entreaties or supplications. He would yawn and say "ho hum" or else shout "filth"[12] and tear up her letters. Nonetheless, Myrna's numerous campaigns and quests in the behalf of various liberal causes prompt Ignatius to put into action his own mad schemes for the betterment of society. His worldview is, of course, completely different from hers. Early in the novel, he contemplates founding a Divine Right party in order to establish a monarchy in the United States. At Levy Pants, he leads an abortive strike of the mostly black employees, which he calls "The Crusade for Moorish Dignity."[13] In order to achieve world peace, he attempts to persuade a group of New Orleans homosexuals to enlist in the armed services, hoping to secretly fill the armies of the world with their ranks. Meeting on the battlefield, they would find other things to do with each other than fight. Although Ignatius and Myrna disagree about practically everything, he is nonetheless very glad to see her pull into his mother's driveway at the novel's conclusion. In order to effect his escape, he acts the part of convert and agrees to flee with her back to New York. She has driven all the way to New Orleans from the Bronx because from reading Ignatius's letters she had come to the conclusion that he was sinking fast and about, any moment, to go under. She felt that she had to salvage a mind rotting before her very eyes, so she got in her car and drove all night. She is confident that great thoughts will one day come pouring out of Ignatius's head once they've "cleared away all the cobwebs and taboos and crippling attachments."[14] She says Ignatius's condition is the fault of his mother and that she would like to "outline to that woman what she's done to you."[15] He readily agrees with her conclusion. Before they depart—in the nick of time, for the Charity ambulance passes them on the street—Myrna asks Ignatius if he wants to pack anything, and he replies, "Oh, of course. There are all of my notes and jottings. We must never let them fall into the hands of my mother. She may make a fortune from them. It would be too ironic."[16]

In 1976, while teaching creative writing seminars at Loyola University, Walker Percy began receiving telephone calls from an eccentric, elderly woman whom he did not know—Thelma Ducoing Toole. She kept pestering him to read a manuscript by her deceased son. The novel, *A Confederacy of Dunces*, had been written sometime in the early sixties. On March 26, 1969, its author John Kennedy Toole, then a Ph.D. candidate in English teaching at a New Orleans college, had, at the age of thirty-one, gassed himself to death in his car near the Gulf Coast town of Biloxi, Mississippi. He had lived at home and supported his parents until a short time before his death. His deaf and ailing father had not worked for some time; for much of Toole's life, his mother, Thelma, had been the family breadwinner. She taught elocution lessons at home, first when her husband worked and then after he had become disabled. Such lessons had long been passé, however, and Toole's paychecks, during his army years in Puerto Rico—when he completed *A Confederacy of Dunces*—and then during his career as a college teacher, kept his parents financially afloat. During the fall semester of 1968, Toole began to act strangely on campus. The following January, he vanished from the college. He left home at the same time, and his parents had no further contact with him. They would suffer and worry about his well-being for weeks until a police officer informed them of his suicide the day of his death.

Reluctantly, after much coaxing on Mrs. Toole's part, Percy agreed to take a look at the manuscript. She brought to his office "a badly smeared, scarcely readable carbon,"[17] thrust it theatrically into his hands, and once again stated that the work was a masterpiece. Previously, on the telephone, she had told him that *Confederacy* was a great novel. At first, Percy had declined her invitation to read the book, but she dogged him persistently and at last he relented, hoping the novel would prove bad enough that he could stop reading in good conscience after several pages. At first to bitter frustration then to his growing amazement, he found that he could not put the book down. After finishing the novel, he declared it "a great rumbling farce of Falstaffian dimensions,"[18] and he eventually persuaded Louisiana State University press to publish the work in 1980. It would take the Pulitzer Prize the following year and would be translated into a number of foreign languages. Mrs. Toole would indeed reap a fortune from her son's writing. The harvest, however, had been a long time in coming.

John Kennedy Toole had completed his novel in 1963 and submitted it to Simon and Schuster, where it was given a sympathetic reading by editor Robert Gottlieb. Although he ultimately passed on the book, Gottlieb recognized Toole's talent and wrote to him encouragingly. For two years, Toole revised and redrafted his manuscript; by 1965, however, he had grown disheartened. He determined that he had little or no chance of breaking into print. From a very young age, he had shown himself bright and gifted, demonstrating great ability in art and music. He was born when his mother was thirty-seven. She had been told by her physicians that she would never conceive, but, with a persistence that would parallel her later effort to publish her son's work, she tried to become pregnant until at last she succeeded. Always the apple of his mother's eye, he would twice skip grammar school grades and later would win scholarships to Tulane and Columbia Universities, earning his Master's degree at Columbia. After a two-year stint in the army, Toole would once again pursue his graduate career. Although incredibly precocious as a child, he was shy and secretive as an adolescent and a young man. Only his closest friends knew of his ambitions as a writer. Thelma Toole would later claim that her son's failure to find a publisher for *A Confederacy of Dunces* drove him to suicide. At the time of his death, however, she had not read the book and was perhaps unaware of its existence. She also destroyed, immediately after reading it, his suicide note which was addressed to her and her husband. She never disclosed its contents to anyone, taking whatever secrets it contained with her to the grave. Her relationship to John, her only child, had always been abnormally close. Due to his deafness, Toole's father had difficulty communicating with the boy during his formative years, and, to make up for that lack, Thelma had to devote herself all the more to her son. Not only had she, despite great obstacles, brought John into the world, she had dedicated herself unstintingly to his upbringing for thirty-one years. She felt betrayed by his suicide and by the notion that she had somehow become a burden to him. That "the darling,"[19] as she always called him, would choose to end his life seemed positively spiteful to her. After his death, she saw herself as no longer having any purpose in life—that is, until she discovered the typescript of her son's novel. One wonders how she was initially affected by the depiction of Ignatius's mother. Did the suffocating, mutually destructive relationship between mother and son in the book reflect that between her and her own son, and, if so, would she not have wanted to suppress the manuscript instead of publish it?

Walker Percy notes that despite its being a hugely funny book, *A Confederacy of Dunces* is at the same time also very sad and that "at the heart of Ignatius's great gaseous rages and lunatic adventures"[20] lingers tragedy. John Kennedy Toole made mirth and laughter out of the sad circumstances of his own life. He utilized his anger at being an outcast in modern American society in order to fashion a corrosive satire and side-splitting burlesque. Toole found his novel's title in Jonathan Swift's "Thoughts On Various Subjects, Moral And Diverting." "When a true genius appears in the world," Swift wrote, "you may know him by this sign, that the dunces are all in a confederacy against him."[21] Like his fictional creation Ignatius J. Reilly, John Kennedy Toole felt victimized by "mongoloids" and "subhumans" his entire life. From an early age, he felt that he was destined to do great things, but he learned early on that contemporary American society did not value him. He wanted to spend his life writing great books, but his efforts were ignored. Sports figures, folk singers, and movie stars could blithely go about their business and rake in millions, but he was condemned to earn his livelihood by teaching and correcting papers, underappreciated and underpaid. America's love of kitsch nauseated and outraged Toole. Ignatius shares his rage. On hearing a man in the street whistling "Turkey in the Straw," Ignatius explodes. He tells the man that, with his apparent musical bent, he should be applying himself to something more worthwhile. "I suspect," he says, "that you imagine 'Turkey in the Straw' to be a valuable bit of a Americana. Well, it is not. It is a discordant abomination. . . . Veneration of such things as 'Turkey in the Straw' is at the very root of our current dilemma."[22] Yet Ignatius is not a total élitist. He is sympathetic not just to aspiring artists but to all those subsisting on the fringes of society: an elderly woman who bungles a job she is no longer able to perform because she can't afford to retire, bums on skid row, and the black factory workers at Levy Pants—in short, all people disenfranchised by modern America. Ignatius writes in one of his Big Chief Tablets that to be "a resounding failure in our century" gives a person "a certain spiritual quality."[23] Such a person is easily recognizable; he seems absurdly out of place, out of contact with reality. Even the young street punk George intuits something is very wrong about Ignatius's working as a hot dog vendor. To get on Ignatius's good side, George calls him Professor. He can tell that Ignatius went to school for a long time from the way he talks and concludes that that "was probably what was wrong with him."[24] Ignatius himself feels that he is " a seer and philosopher cast into a hostile century by forces beyond [his] control."[25] All great American artists are similarly out of step with their culture. The "failure to make contact with reality is . . . characteristic of almost all America's 'art.' Any connection between American art and American nature is purely coincidental. . . ."[26] Ignatius feels "a kinship with the colored race because its position is the same as [his: they] both exist outside the inner realm of American society."[27] The only difference is that Ignatius's "exile is voluntary."[28] He feels himself a sort of blood brother to the blacks at Levy Pants. He decides to lead them like a modern-day Kurtz and organizes the crusade for Moorish dignity because they "have better things to do than to loiter about Levy Pants, such as composing jazz or creating new dances."[29] Although funny, Toole's depiction of the factory/sweatshop is both realistic and glum.

Aside from writing, Ignatius sees all work as deviation and exploitation. In one of the novel's darkest moments, he contemplates suicide when first faced with the prospect of finding a job:

> The gyre had widened; The Great Chain of Being had snapped like so many paper clips strung together by some drooling idiot; death, destruction, anarchy, progress, ambition, and self-improvement were to be Pier's new fate. And a vicious fate it was to be: now he was faced with the perversion of having to GO TO WORK.
>
> His vision of history temporarily fading, Ignatius sketched a noose at the bottom of the page. Then he drew a revolver and a little box on which he neatly printed GAS CHAMBER. He scratched the side of the pencil back and forth across the paper and labeled this APOCALYPSE. When he had finished decorating the page, he threw the tablet to the floor among many others that were scattered about.[30]

Because of his mother and his belief in the *rota Fortunae*, Ignatius resigns himself to his fate. Toole also had to shoulder a burden and support his aging parents which he seems to have deeply resented. The last scene of the novel appears to be a form of wish fulfillment on the author's part. Unlike Ignatius, Toole was unable to escape; he had no Myrna to spirit him off to a new life. He remained unborn, trapped in a life that suffocated and stifled him, snared forever inside the maternal womb. One wonders that Thelma did not deeply resent the novel and destroy it, but Toole knew just how deeply sentimental she was. He was after all "the darling." Ignatius is likewise an only child, spoiled and coddled and made to feel guilty as one imagines John also was. Irene Reilly calls her son baby and that perhaps is his strongest identity. At one point, Ignatius imagines how his mother would act if baby were to die:

> Meditating upon the call from the grave which I had almost received, I began to think about my mother, for I have always wondered what her reaction would be were I to die in the cause of paying for her misdeeds. I can see her at the funeral, a shoddy, low-cost affair held in the basement of some dubious funeral parlor. Insane with grief, tears boiling from her reddened eyes, she would probably tear my corpse from the coffin, screaming drunkenly, "Don't take him! Why do the sweetest flowers wither and fall from the stem?" . . . There would be a certain amount of spectacle involved in the proceedings, I imagine. However, with my mother acting as director, the inherent tragedy would soon become melodrama. Snatching the white lily from my lifeless hands, she would break it in half and wail to the throng of mourners, well-wishers, celebrants, and sightseers, "As this lily was, so was Ignatius. Now they are both snatched and broken."[31]

Thelma Toole did grieve and agonize over her son's death. At the time of his suicide, she was sixty-seven. The care of her invalid husband and the management of her and his affairs now devolved completely on her. The couple received $8,000 when John's estate was settled. Thelma also happened on John's manuscript. Whatever her initial reaction to reading the novel might have been, finding a publisher for the work became her new mission in life. Five years of frustration followed. She sent the book to eight houses and each rejected it. "Every time it came back," she later said, "I died a little."[32] During this time, her husband died and her own health deteriorated. In 1976, she cajoled Walker Percy into reading the novel and in 1980 the book at last saw print. As previously noted, it was published to great acclaim, and Thelma Toole basked in her son's new-found celebrity. She touted the novel on television and radio. She even went so far as to stage public performances, singing old chestnuts such as "Sometimes I'm Happy" and "Way Down Yonder in New Orleans" and reading passages from the book. At some point in her performance, she would stop in mid-sentence and declare circumspectly, "I walk in the world for my son."[33] In the years that followed, *Confederacy* would be translated into ten languages and a musical would be based on the book. Mrs. Toole would also reveal the existence of a second novel by "the darling," one he had written at the age of sixteen. The year before, when John had just learned to drive, he chauffeured his mother down Airline Highway. They passed a large concrete structure beside which stood a huge neon sign in the shape of an open book with the words "Holy Bible" illuminated on one page and "Midcity Baptist Church" on the other.[34] Mother and son had laughed at this gaudy piece of Americana. Shortly thereafter, when John visited relatives in rural Mississippi, he transferred church and sign to this country setting in *The Neon Bible*, a nostalgic portrait of small-town life that also warns against the dangers of religious intolerance and bigotry. Thelma hoped to see this earlier work published as well. Unfortunately, the book became the object of a lengthy lawsuit. Due to Louisiana's antiquated Napoleonic code, half the rights to the novel belonged to her husband's brother and his children. They had signed their rights to *Confederacy* over to Mrs. Toole, only to see that novel become a bestseller, and they were not about to do so again. Thelma wrote letters of protest to the governor, various congressmen, and the state supreme court decrying the injustice of the Louisiana state law—all to no avail. Therefore, she decided to hold up publication of the novel. She asked one of Walker Percy's creative writing students, W. Kenneth Holditch, to become "guardian"[35] of the book shortly before her death in August 1984, altering her will to that effect. She asked that he not allow publication until her husband's relatives surrendered their claims or Louisiana law changed. For three years, the matter remained unresolved and Holditch became embroiled in a lengthy court battle. In 1987, a New Orleans judge ordered the manuscript partitioned and put up for public auction. Holditch gave up the fight to see Thelma's wishes respected in order to avoid such an unseemly display and the novel was subsequently published to sterling reviews. No further fictions of Toole were found when Holditch went through Thelma's effects. She had, however, preserved all of John's letters to her over the years as well as numerous essays and examination papers from his college days.

Notes

1. John Kennedy Toole, *A Confederacy of Dunces*, foreword by Walker Percy (New York: Grove Weidenfeld, 1987), p. 349. *A Confederacy of Dunces* was first published in 1980.
2. Ibid., p. 395.
3. Ibid., p. 64.
4. Ibid., p. 43.
5. Walker Percy, "Foreword," *A Confederacy*, p. 8.
6. *A Confederacy*, p. 110.
7. Ibid.
8. Ibid.
9. Ibid., p. 193.
10. Ibid., p. 92.
11. Ibid.
12. Ibid., p. 91.
13. Ibid., p. 149.
14. Ibid., p. 402.
15. Ibid., p. 398.

16. Ibid., pp. 399–400.

17. Percy, p. 7.

18. Ibid., p. 9.

19. Quoted by W. Kenneth Holditch, "Introduction," *The Neon Bible* by John Kennedy Toole (New York: Grove Press, 1989), p. vi.

20. Percy, p. 9.

21. Quoted by John Kennedy Toole, *A Confederacy*, p. 5.

22. *A Confederacy*, p. 166.

23. Ibid., p. 238.

24. Ibid., p. 295.

25. Ibid., p. 300.

26. Ibid., p. 131.

27. Ibid., p. 134.

28. Ibid.

29. Ibid., p. 136.

30. Ibid., p. 41.

31. Ibid., pp. 240–41.

32. Quoted by Holditch, p. vii.

33. Ibid., p. viii.

34. See Holditch, p. ix.

35. Ibid., p. x.

Yukio Mishima

H IS DEATH WAS HIS CROWNING ACHIEVEMENT. HE STAGED HIS RITUAL suicide as if it were the dénouement of his last and greatest play, the final chapter of a majestic novel, or the concluding line of some ultimate poem. Blood would have to flow in copious quantities for Yukio Mishima to realize his youthful desire to make his life a work of art. His name itself was a fabrication. Born Kimitake Hiraoka, he settled on Yukio Mishima for himself at the age of sixteen when his first story, "The Forest in Full Bloom," was accepted for publication. One of his teachers suggested that he use a pen name. Together they decided on the characters used in writing it. Yukio was derived from the Japanese word for snow. Mishima is the name of a town from which the snow-capped peak of Mt. Fuji is clearly visible. He crafted his public persona with the same diligence as he conceived and designed his novels. He would be Japan's Renaissance man, her Leonardo da Vinci. The death Mishima chose for himself would have the greatest possible political impact, but would also serve to underscore the philosophy he developed in his fiction. According to the aesthetic he professed, a metaphysics of love and death entwined, the successful art work would necessarily end in an apotheosis of violence. When asked in an interview, shortly before his suicide, why he glorified ruthlessness and savagery in his fiction, Mishima replied, "This blood and brutality is something we have stylized into a special sense of beauty. It comes from our subconscious. We have always had a special symbolism about blood."[1]

Mishima believed that the beautiful object attained the highest measure of perfection at the moment of its destruction. Again and again in his numerous novels, short stories, and plays, the action inexorably progresses to an act of immolation. Something stunning and gorgeous— be it an art object or a living person—must be annihilated and obliter-

ated. In some instances, the destructive act remains a fantasy in the mind of a character, as in the final scene of the early novel *Confessions of a Mask,* in which the
autobiographical narrator discovers homoerotic yearnings within himself as he
watches a robust and vibrant youth dancing in a café and suddenly visualizes the
young man's chest bleeding and covered with wounds. More often than not the deed
is carried out in fact. Two examples come immediately to mind. In *Thirst For Love,*
the central figure, the young widow Etsuko, strikes down the servant farm boy
Saburo, for whom she has developed an unquenchable passion, with a mattock
snatched from the hands of her aged father-in-law, the repulsive dying man circumstances have forced her to submit to as mistress; in *The Temple Of The Golden
Pavilion,* the failed Buddhist monk Mizoguchi sets fire to the famous temple in
Kyoto whose beauty has haunted and obsessed him ever since he entered it as a
boy-novice.

In contrast to Mizoguchi's act of destruction which is carefully conceived and
planned to the last detail well in advance, the murder of Saburo by Etsuko seems
a sudden insane impulse. Yet in both cases the deed is foreshadowed by smaller
destructive acts on the parts of the two protagonists. Prior to the murder, Etsuko
attempts to inflict both physical and psychological pain on the object of her desire.
First, during the course of a religious festival in which Saburo participates in the
ritual dancing, she slashes his back with her fingernails as he runs to and fro in an
almost trance-like state. Later she forces her father-in-law to dismiss the servant
Miyo, Saburo's pregnant lover, while the latter is away on a pilgrimage. The
destruction of the Golden Temple, on the other hand, is prefigured by an incident
in Mizoguchi's youth. As a schoolboy, he deliberately disfigures the ivory scabbard
of a soldier's sword. Upon entering the temple as an acolyte, Mizoguchi comes
under the spell of the building, one of the great national treasures of Japan. He
feels overpowered by the pavilion's great beauty and almost immediately desires
deliverance from the spell that the edifice casts on him. During the war years, he
fervently hopes that American planes will bomb the shrine, feeling that its destruction will release him from his paralysis. However, the war ends, and the temple
remains intact. No other recourse is left open for Mizoguchi but to embark on a
course of a calculated duplicity and wrong-doing that, step by step, leads to his last
outrageous deed. During his residency at the temple, he performs various acts of
desecration, at one point accepting cigarettes from an American soldier for tram-
pling on the belly of a pregnant prostitute in the temple garden and causing her to
miscarry. These same cigarettes he in turn gives to the superior of the temple. His
master will enjoy the fruits of his crime and thus, he feels, be implicated in it. Later
Mizoguchi spends funds set aside by the temple for his tuition at the Buddhist University at a Kyoto brothel, hoping to bring the wrath of the superior down on his
head. His offense is a personal attack directed at the head of the order as well, for
earlier Mizoguchi had discovered that his master patronized similar establish-
ments. His attempt to effect his dismissal fails although his behavior insures that

he will never be named as the superior's successor, an event which had once seemed likely. Deciding that liberation will come only when the temple is engulfed in flames, he methodically plans the building's destruction. He practices removing nails from the barred back door of the temple to gain entrance after hours, purchases both knife and arsenic as he initially intends to commit suicide after setting his fire, and bides his time until a favorable opportunity presents itself. One day Mizoguchi hears that the temple's fire alarm has been disabled, but that night he cannot carry out his resolve. The following day, a repairman arrives, but it will take several days to fix the alarm. Heaven seems to be smiling on Mizoguchi. He buys some sweets to steady his nerves the night of his arson, calls on a visiting priest and pays his respects as if nothing unusual is taking place, and collects all his belongings—including imperishable objects which will identify him as the perpetrator of the crime—and stores them in a trunk he lugs inside the temple with him. Finally, he steals several bundles of straw from the monastery's workroom to serve as kindling for his fire. He ignites the straw, but as the temple fills with smoke, he finds the door to the Kukyocho, a small golden room at the apex of the temple, locked. It was here that Mizoguchi had planned to take his own life. Thwarted, he retreats down the stairs, passing through the fire itself, and exits the temple through the billowing smoke. He flees into the night and, from a distance, observes the temple as it goes up in flames. A carved phoenix stands on the structure's rooftop, an inspiring if obvious symbol on Mishima's part, a fit emblem for his beauty-in-immolation philosophy.

Both Etsuko and Mizoguchi seem to embody aspects of Mishima's character, and their final destructive deeds surely serve as types for the author's own death. To many Japanese, Mishima's suicide seemed an irrational, insane act—as rash and capricious as Etsuko's murder of Saburo. Such, in fact, was the opinion of Japan's Prime Minister Eisaku Sato, who, on the evening of the author's death, stated to the press that the celebrated novelist had gone over the edge— "was out of his mind."[2] If, however, one examines the author's biography and reads his work, his flirtation with death can be seen, and is reflected, in almost every page he wrote. The fact that he committed suicide—and indeed the manner he chose to end his life—can therefore hardly seem surprising. In retrospect, death at his own hand appears to have been inevitable. Moreover, it quickly becomes evident that Yukio Mishima planned his suicide with all the care and deliberation of a Mizoguchi.

On November 25, 1970, the author paid a visit to the headquarters of Japan's Eastern Ground Self-Defense Forces at the military complex on Ichigaya hill near Tokyo. The military authorities received him graciously. He had made an appointment to visit the facility in advance and was accompanied by four members of the Tatenokai or Shield Society, an organization of young men, mostly university students, which Mishima had founded in 1968 for the express purpose of putting samurai teachings into practice on weekend retreats. The recruits were all personally selected by the author; he even designed the brown uniforms which they all proudly wore. The young men professed an interest in the martial arts but also shared Mishima's right-wing political leanings in that they wished to restore emperor worship in Japan. Due to Mishima's literary reputation, a number of high-ranking Japanese military officers were persuaded to support the organization under the aegis of the Self-Defense Forces. Members of the society routinely took part in military exercises with the regular soldiers. Mishima was at the height of his fame in 1970. Although he was only forty-five years old, he had been nominated for the Nobel Prize on three occasions. In his own country, as well as in Europe and America, he had long been recognized as a literary giant. He had distinguished himself in a wide variety of genres, having written more than a dozen novels, more than fifty short stories, many successful plays both modern and traditional (No and Kabuki), a travel book, and countless essays. His talent, however, was not restricted to his literary endeavors. He acted, directed, and produced for the theater, and appeared in several movies: he committed hari-kari in one film and starred as a gangster in another. Although he had been a weak and sickly child, Mishima had developed into a superb athlete. In 1955, he began a much-promoted regimen of weight lifting and body building. In the spirit of the samurai warriors, he trained himself to be an expert swordsman and became an adept at kendo, the ancient sport of stick fighting. He also mastered several other martial arts forms and earned a reputation as an amateur boxer. Photographs of Mishima participating in various sporting events regularly appeared in Japanese periodicals, but he also worked as a model. As a young boy skimming through an art book, he came across a reproduction of Guido Reni's *Saint Sebastian,* and he became captivated by the painting. Many years later, he posed as the saint for a camera shoot, his body pierced by many arrows, an expression of bliss on his face.

In short, by 1970 Yukio Mishima had long been a prominent figure. Not only was he a writer of world renown, in Japan he had the status and celebrity of an American film star. When asked in an interview who he felt was the greatest writer of the twentieth century, he replied Thomas Mann, but added if he could assume the identity of any person on the planet he would not choose to be Mann or himself, or indeed any other writer, but would instead be Elvis Presley.

Throughout his career, Mishima delighted in shocking the public. The poses he assumed were often conflicting and paradoxical. Mishima's critics claimed that he was a crypto-fascist, although he vigorously denied the charge. Indeed, he championed the traditional samurai spirit, but he claimed that this was not the same as the militarism that had brought Japan into the Second World War. In fact it was the abandonment of the old code that paved the way for his country's defeat. This, according to Mishima, occurred during Japan's period of industrialization and modernization in the late eighteenth and early nineteenth centuries. Thus, Mishima felt, it was a "Westernized, civilized army, which was so close to Fascism and Nazism."[3] Yet despite the fact he revered his country's samurai heritage and the traditional martial spirit of Japan, he himself adopted a western manner of living which astounded and dismayed his associates. He told the press that his ideal was "to live in a house where I sit on a rococo chair wearing an aloha shirt and blue jeans."[4] The house he built in Tokyo was far from traditional; in fact it was western in style and furnished inside and out with Victorian bric-a-brac.

Mishima's sexual proclivities were also far from conventional. Although in 1958, when informed that his mother had terminal cancer, he acceded to his family's wishes and entered into an arranged marriage with Yoko Sugiyama, he had been a practicing homosexual since adolescence. Although he fathered two children by his wife and took an active part in their upbringing, he continued to frequent the gay bars in Tokyo's Ginza district, and at the time of his death was infatuated with Masakatsu Morita, the first student to join the Shield Society and his primary accomplice in his last desperate deed. Although he insisted that the woman selected for him to wed be shorter in stature than himself—Mishima was a diminutive 5'2"—and he boasted to the press that he would rule his wife at home, the author proved to be a courteous and solicitous husband. Flaunting Japanese custom, he permitted Yoko to travel abroad with him and granted her many nontraditional liberties in their daily life. He again behaved in a nontraditional manner by helping his wife rear and care for his two children, a boy and a girl, when they were infants.

Born in Tokyo on January 14, 1925, into an upper-middle-class family, Mishima himself was raised in traditional, if also somewhat peculiar, fashion. Asserting her prerogative, his paternal grandmother demanded that she be entrusted with raising the delicate, sickly infant and, over the protest of the child's mother, Mishima was turned over to her. For the next twelve years, she brought the boy up and indulged him in everything. He was frequently ill, but was also adept at feigning sickness. Mishima later claimed that his grandmother raised and dressed him as if he were a girl. Only when he visited relatives did he have to act like a boy. "The reluctant masquerade had begun,"[5] Mishima wrote. After his grandmother's death, Mishima moved into his parent's home. At about the same time, he was accepted into the prestigious Peers' School. He proved a brilliant scholar and also made his first attempts at writing. He was sixteen when he was first published, and when he graduated in 1944, he received a citation from the emperor for being the school's highest honor student. While attending classes, Mishima also fell in love for the first time. He was attracted to a muscular upperclassman named Omi. "Because of him," he later wrote, "I began to love strength, an impression of overflowing blood, ignorance, rough gestures, careless speech, and savage melancholy inherent in flesh not tainted in any way with intellect."[6]

When the Second World War broke out, Mishima was still a student at the Peers' School. He claimed that he did not enlist in the Japanese army due to his poor constitution and chronic illness. However after his graduation, he was drafted. By that time, the war was already lost, but the army was nonetheless preparing to resist the anticipated American invasion. Mishima would later write in an essay that he "shuddered with a strange delight at the thought of my own death. I felt as if I owned the whole world."[7] Later he professed that he wanted to die in combat. However, he did not pass the final physical and was rejected for service at the last possible moment. After the war, at his father's behest, he attended the Tokyo Imperial University of Jurisprudence from which he graduated in 1947. He then accepted a position at the Ministry of Finance. However, shortly thereafter, he became the protégé of Yasunari Kawabata, who encouraged him to write his first novel. Mishima resigned his post and devoted himself to writing. *Confessions of a Mask* was published the following year.

Mishima continued writing right up to the end. Although he was still producing best-selling novelettes such as *After the Banquet* and *The Sailor Who Fell From Grace with the Sea*, he increasingly devoted himself to the composition of what would prove his masterpiece, a tetralogy of novels known as *The Sea Of Fertility*, in which Mishima would explore the subject of reincarnation. Each volume would feature a different hero or heroine; the protagonists, however, would all be incarnations of the same soul. Three of the volumes, *Spring Snow*, *Runaway Horses*, and *The Temple of Dawn*, had been published by 1970. Mishima finished the last book, *The Decay of the Angel*, prior to visiting the headquarters of the Self-Defense Forces. He placed the completed manuscript on the vestibule table of his home when he left to join the four students on the morning of November 25. He had prepared what would happen next as carefully as his fictional character Mizoguchi had planned the destruction of the Golden Temple. His life and work would come to a conclusion on the same day.

When Mishima and the four students arrived at the Ichigaya complex, they asked for an interview with the commanding officer Lieutenant General Kanetoshi Mashida. He invited them into his office where he and Mishima spoke for approximately a half hour. At the conclusion of their conversation, Mishima drew his sword and the four students jumped the general, taking him hostage and quickly tying him to his chair. The noise of the struggle caught the attention of staff aides outside the office. Sensing that something was wrong, these men attempted to storm the room. However, by that time, the general was already securely bound, and the students had joined Mishima at the door to the office with samurai swords drawn. The besiegers were quickly subdued, six of the aides suffering stab wounds. Mishima demanded that he be given the opportunity to address the Self-Defense Forces at the base. By noon, a crowd of 1,200 soldiers had assembled below the balcony of the three-story white building. His hands on the railing, Mishima harangued the troops for approximately fifteen minutes. He urged the soldiers to foment revolution in order to overturn Japan's post-war constitution which forbade war and to restore the rule of the emperor. He said the Self-Defense Forces had failed to achieve anything during their twenty years of existence and accused its leaders of being spineless. It was up to the servicemen themselves, Mishima said, to restore honor to their country. The reception he received was chilly. The servicemen shouted for him to surrender and to release his hostage. "We can't act in common with fellows like you,"[8] one man shouted. Mishima gave three shouts of "Banzai" and went back inside. Upon returning to the general's office, he told the students, "They didn't seem to hear me too well,"[9] then sat down on the floor and bared his torso. With his knife, he committed hari-kari, suicide by disembowelment or belly cutting, as formerly practiced by the samurai in cases of disgrace or by government order. His disciple Masakatsu Morita then performed the rite known as *Ksithaku*. He stood behind the dying Mishima and beheaded him with his sword. Morita then committed suicide in the same manner, one of the other students in turn severing his head from his shoulders. Horrified by what he saw, still tied to his chair, General Mashida shouted, "Stop it!" and "What are you doing?"[10] After the beheading of Morita, the three remaining students came out of the room, bringing Mashida with them. They surrendered quietly to the police. Undoubtedly, Mishima thought his suicide both beautiful and honorable. He had exited this life in a Saint Sebastian-like fashion, dying a martyr for a cause. He hoped that his death would cause a spiritual awakening among his people, that out of the ashes a phoenix would rise, a Japan more beautiful and golden than before.

Notes

1. Joseph F. Fried, "Japan's Renaissance Man," *New York Times*, 25 November 1970.

2. Quoted by Thomas Cowan, *Gay Men and Women Who Enriched the World* (New Canaan, Conn.: Mulvey Books, 1989), p. 240.

3. Fried, *New York Times*.

4. Quoted by Cowan, *Gay Men and Women*, p. 244.

5. Ibid., p. 241.

6. Ibid., p. 242.

7. Ibid.

8. Quoted by Takashi Oka, "Renowned Author Raids Tokyo Military, Ends Life," *New York Times*, 25 November 1970.

9. Ibid.

10. Ibid.

$\mathcal{Y}$asunari
$\mathcal{K}$awabata

O N APRIL 16, 1972, AT 3 P.M., JAPAN'S FIRST NOBEL-PRIZE laureate in literature left his home in the seaside city of Kamakura, famous throughout the world for its giant statue of Buddha, in order to take a walk. The seventy-two-year-old author, who had been experiencing health problems for some time and who had not produced any major work since the early 1960s, told his wife, Hideko, that he would return shortly. After the sun had set and her husband had still not come home, Mrs. Kawabata dispatched a maid to the adjacent town of Zushi, where Kawabata maintained a room in an apartment house facing the sea which he used as a study and workplace. When the woman arrived, she found the door chained from the inside and smelled gas, so she immediately summoned the police, who proceeded to break into the apartment. They discovered Kawabata's body slumped near the entrance to the bathroom, a gas hose inserted in his mouth. Although he usually wore traditional Japanese kimonos, he had on a business suit and a western polo shirt. An open, nearly drained, bottle of whiskey sat beside him. Autopsy results would later indicate that he had in fact been drinking shortly before his death.

Kawabata's suicide came as a surprise to his family and associates. Although he had suffered periodically from an inflamed gall bladder and had, a decade earlier, undergone hospitalization for toxicosis due to an overreliance upon sleeping pills, the Japanese author seemed zestful and happy during his final days. To be sure, his books had always featured lonely and alienated characters. He would often juxtapose descriptions of nature in all its exquisite beauty against the tormented inner thoughts of a receptive individual who is in some way or another cut off and isolated from the perfection and beauty he perceives, an irreconcilable separation that gives Kawabata's work a melancholy tinge. Yet, despite the sadness of his novels and that of his own early life, Kawabata had always frowned on suicide. Two years prior to his own death, he had been deeply disturbed by his protégé Yukio Mishima committing hari-kari. Despite dissimilar temperaments, the two men felt very close to one another. At the funeral ceremony of the younger writer, Kawabata told the crowd which had gathered at a Tokyo temple to pay their respects and to mourn Mishima's death, to "pray quietly"[1] for his friend's soul. He would not enter into discussion about the rightness or wrongness of the younger man's actions. Prayer and silent meditation, he said, were the only fit response to such a deed.

Two years earlier, however, in 1968, Kawabata had condemned the act of suicide in no uncertain terms in the life-affirming Nobel-prize address he gave in Stockholm. The Swedish Committee had determined in advance to honor a Japanese writer that particular year. A number of authors, including Mishima, were in the running for the award, but ultimately Kawabata received the nod because his works were deemed the most traditionally Japanese of all the writers under consideration. Although in his youth, he had studied English and French literature at Tokyo Imperial University and, influenced by European expressionism and by French symbolist poetry, had participated in the avant-garde Japanese literary movement of the 1920s known as neo-sensationalism, Kawabata forsook literary experimentation by the mid-1930s, returning in his most celebrated work to a more classical Japanese manner. However, he still managed to shock his readership from time to time with his startling, sometimes brutal, scenes. His enthusiasm for symbolist poetry never waned entirely, but he assimilated and refined such western influences to create an end-product distinctly Japanese. Kawabata would later say that he found his primary inspiration in Haiku poetry and Buddhist scripture. He valued the latter texts, he said, "not so much as religious teachings but as literary visions and fantasies."[2] Sparse language and attention to specific detail distinguish his novels. Setting and ritual performance of ceremony are as important as character and plot. There is a vague dreamlike quality to his prose which is full of vivid images despite its ethereal, understated character, its combination of deceptive simplicity and misty open-endedness. Kawabata's novels seem shapeless and non-linear. They swerve and float, they weave and bob, as present and past alternate and memory glides into mirage and hallucination only for reality to reassert itself with the limpidity of a mountain spring. Yet the books do not lack structure, even precise formality. Kawabata claimed to find inspiration in Japanese ceramics and tapestry and, above all, in ritual such as the traditional tea ceremony with its numerous utensils used in specific order according to custom and etiquette. Pattern and framework are provided to certain of his novels through the portrayal and description of the step-by-step unfolding of such prescribed ritual forms. One of his novels, for instance, is built around the moves of an ancient board game.

To this day, Kawabata's literary reputation remains strong. Along with Mishima and Junichiro Tanizaki, he is considered one of Japan's three greatest modern writers. When he received the Nobel prize, which many critics in the West considered more as a signal of good-will to Japanese writers generally than as an acknowledgment of Kawabata's own unique achievement, he was clearly past his prime. The other major contender, the far more prolific Mishima, was then at the height of his powers. Some grumbled that the more important author had been overlooked, while Kawabata himself felt bewildered at his selection. He thought that the tradition that he worked out of posed enormous difficulties for Westerners and believed that his work could only be properly appreciated by the Japanese, that European and American readers would fail to comprehend what he was striving after. Nonetheless, he accepted the honor as a gesture of benevolence and kindly intention on the part of the West. He perceived an interest in his culture and a readiness to learn more, so he used his Nobel lecture which he entitled "Japan the Beautiful and Myself" for pedagogic purposes. The lecture would later be published as a small book. Kawabata declared, "All my life I have been striving for beauty, and this I will continue to do until I die."[3] Broaching the topic of suicide in his talk, he stated, "However alienated one may be from the world, suicide is not a form of enlightenment. However admirable he may be, the man who commits suicide is far from the realm of the saint."[4]

Yasunari Kawabata was born in Osaka on June 11, 1899, the son of a prominent physician. Both his parents died before his third birthday and shortly thereafter he lost both his only sister and his grandmother. He lived with his grandfather, his only surviving family member, until the age of fourteen when the old man followed the others in death. Kawabata chronicled the last weeks of his grandfather's life in his first major literary work, *The Diary of a Young Boy*, which, although written while the beloved old man lay dying, was not published until Kawabata's twenty-sixth year. The book, influenced by Buddhist doctrine, exhibits the same sense of isolation and loss as do the later novels. After his grandfather's death, Kawabata enrolled in an Osaka middle school. He resided there, a child without family or home, until 1917 when he received admittance into the First High School in Tokyo. Before graduating from this prestigious institution, he had already decided upon a literary vocation and had developed a taste for Scandinavian authors. Going on to the Imperial University, he planned to pursue a degree in English literature, but would later change his course of study to Japanese literature. He published several well-received short stories during his college years and graduated from Tokyo Imperial University in 1924. His first novel, the book that cemented his reputation, *The Izu Dancer*, appeared the following year. It concerns the attraction of a painfully shy high school student for a dancing girl from Izu province, a child who embodies for him the virginal ideal.

Upon his graduation from the university, Kawabata would lead a restless, rootless life. Mishima dubbed him the ceaseless traveler, for he never remained in one place for any length of time. He supported himself as a journalist and filed stories from various locations for the twin Osaka and Tokyo newspapers that today bear the

Mainichi banner. A slow and exacting writer, he labored on his next novel, *Snow Country*, from 1934 to 1947. Passive and unresistant when it came to politics, Kawabata nonetheless deplored the jingoism prevalent during the wartime years. However, after the defeat of Japan, he said that he would only be able to write elegies. Although he felt little sympathy for liberalism and democracy, he held himself aloof from politics after the war just as he had done before and during the conflict. His aristocratic disdain delighted Mishima, but Kawabata did not experience any drastic call to action resembling that of his one-time disciple. Unlike Mishima, he did not feel the need to reenergize the nation through a return to Samurai culture. His sympathy lay with the quiet artisans of Japan's past—the master calligraphers, kimono designers, and obi weavers who had mastered their trades and in turn passed down the ancient traditions to the next generation of craftsmen. Kawabata perceived the gradual loss of this legacy and lamented it in his novels. The surrender of tradition—the disappearance of the old ways—meant more in his eyes than military defeat. As Japan westernized, the domestic gave way more and more to the foreign. Kawabata tried to preserve what he could in his books.

Set in a hot springs resort in the cold mountainous region of Western Japan, the snowiest district not only in Japan but all the world, *Snow Country* concerns the love affair of the beautiful young geisha Komako and Shimamura, a cynical, well-to-do dilettante from Tokyo, who abandons the geisha due to ennui and coldness of heart after only three visits to the hot spring. She offers him warmth and the possibility of love, but he rejects the gift she extends him despite his strong attraction to her, thus dooming Komako to waste her youth and beauty as a courtesan. Komako is under no delusions about her lover. From the very beginning, she realizes that he cannot return her love but yields anyway, knowing that she can at least awaken an irresistible sadness in the heart of this wealthy man whose soul is as bleak and desolate as the cold mountains and wintry country of Japan's western coast.

With the completion of *Snow Country*, Kawabata entered his most productive period. His next important work, *A Thousand Cranes*, appeared in 1949. This is the novel that receives its structure from the elaborate tea ceremony. It tells of a young man's romantic fixation with two of his dead father's former mistresses and his inability to forge an identity of his own, caught as he is in the web of his father's past. Nineteen-fifty-four was an especially fruitful year for Kawabata. He completed three major works, the novels *The Master of Go*, *The Sound of the Mountain*, and *The Lake*. He had worked intermittently on all three of them for a great many years. The first two books, like *A Thousand Cranes*, deal with generational problems, the tug of war between old and new modes of thought and action. It is the sound of his own advancing death that old Shingo hears coming from the hills beyond his garden in *The Sound of the Mountain*. The novel depicts the indignities brought on by old age. The endearing protagonist suffers at the hands of his shrewish wife and his discourteous and disrespectful son and daughter. The only person in his family who does not cause him misery is his deferential and attentive daughter-in-law, for whom he feels both strong paternal affection and latent sexual desire. Only from her can he draw strength and life in his last days.

The Master of Go chronicles a six-month championship match of the ancient Japanese board game of Go. The novel has a circular structure, beginning and ending at the same point in time, a pivotal moment in the game. The two contestants, the aged, formerly invincible master Shusai and the impertinent, insolent youth Otake, "the foremost representative"[5] of a younger generation of players who have a more impetuous and impulsive style of play than that of their elders, move pebble counters on a board divided into 361 squares. Despite his skill and superiority, the old man eventually suffers defeat at the hand of the challenger, but placidly accepts the loss, for the old must inevitably give way to the young. The noble Shusai plays supremely well at first, beating back the violent assaults of Otake, "who would avert defeat even if he had to chew the stones to bits."[6] Yet late in the match the initiative slips from the ailing sixty-four-year-old master. The "natural flow" leads "to a close and delicate" finale.[7] At the very end, the never-before-beaten Shusai can't even take advantage of bad moods on his opponent's part and thereby reduce the proportions of Otake's victory. Nor can he unfold any last-minute grand strategy. He will die shortly after the match, yet those who observe the game, shocked as they are by Shusai's defeat, can't deny that he had nonetheless "put everything into [the] game."[8] He had done so expressly because he sensed he was playing "with the next in line, the one who might succeed him."[9] Kawabata characterized this book as a *shosetsu* or, roughly translated, a nonfiction novel. It is based upon an actual 1938 match which Kawabata covered as a journalist. Kawabata reworked his older reportage into the novel but fictionalized certain aspects of the story. The actual Master was indeed named Shusai, but according to those who knew him best, he had little of Kawabata's character's virtue and integrity. Grotesquely short of stature, he seemed sly and devious to adherents of the game. The character of the challenger was more faithfully drawn, but Kawabata assigned him a fictional name in the novel. (His real name was Kitani Minoru. Kawabata does the same thing for himself, adopting the name Uragami.) Kawabata came to see the championship match he witnessed in the late 1930s as a metaphor for a wider cultural conflict taking place in Japan both at that time and then after the Second World War. Although as a young man he himself was attracted to the literature of the West, to foreign and innovative forms, his sympathies in this novel lie with the orthodox master who embodies and embraces the old Japanese way of life. As noted above, Kawabata's early fascination with foreign literatures gave way to an increasing passion for Asian classics. As he grew older, he found himself drawn to the world of Japan's past more and more, but he nonetheless always felt torn and conflicted and *The Master of Go* reflects his own inner struggle.

The Lake explores Kawabata's usual themes of guilt, incurable obsession, the paradoxical nature of love, and the profound isolation and estrangement of the individual. It is perhaps the author's finest novel though also his most amorphous work.

At a pivotal point in the book, the hero, Gimpei Momoi, briefly contemplates suicide but then rejects the notion. The novel opens with the protagonist's visit to a Turkish bath. A homeless man and perpetual traveler, Momoi is perhaps a fugitive from the law as well. He has committed a crime, but does not know if it has been reported to the authorities by the victim. The female attendant washes and massages his body. The girl then pushes him into the steam bath, a square wooden box with a board on the top for the head to fit in. This lid reminds Gimpei of a guillotine and he becomes nervous and wide-eyed inside the box. After the attendant lets him out and he lies down on a couch, he keeps very still as the girl proceeds to soap and towel him, for he fears he will be hit if he accidentally touches her. He is self-conscious about his long toes. The attendant's voice, he says, is that of an angel. Never, he confesses, has he heard a more exquisite sound.

In a flashback, we learn of Gimpei's crime. A woman had recently thrown a blue handbag in his face when he had followed her in the street. He stole a bundle of 1000 yen bills—200,000 yen in all— from the purse. Also inside the bag is the woman's passbook. From it, he learns her name—Miyako Mizuki. We learn from further flashbacks that this woman is not the first one Momoi has stalked and shadowed. He feels compelled to pursue beautiful women whenever he encounters them. He feels that he is an inhabitant of an infernal world. Pleasure, however, is never one-sided. He senses that the women to whom he is attracted are fellow sufferers, that they experience a secret thrill of pleasure at being followed. He is correct in his analysis, for, as it later turns out, Miyako had been stirred by him. She had been followed by other men in the past, and she did not report his crime even though she lost most of her savings that day. Momoi had once been a schoolteacher. The first person he felt compelled to shadow was one of his students, Hisako Tamaki. Once after school, he follows her to the door of her home. She sees him doing it, and he explains that he pursued her because her father knew a good medication for athlete's foot, and he wanted her to ask him the name of it. Although Momoi does not in fact suffer from athlete's foot, Hisako will bring a tube of medicine the next day. Hisako realizes that he is attracted to her, and eventually he will seduce his young pupil after she asks him to follow her again. They will meet several times before another student, a friend of Hisako, reports them, and Gimpei loses his post. Although Hisako changes schools, she and Gimpei continue to meet. Years later, after she is married, Hisako will build her house on the spot of her and Gimpei's former trysts.

Their affair comes to an end after Hisako sneaks Gimpei into the room of her parents' house, and they are caught by her mother and father. After they are discovered, Gimpei fantasizes about murdering Hisako and then killing himself: "And bathed in Hisako's warm blood, even his crooked, gnarled and shriveled toes, which were as long as a monkey's, became as graceful as a mannequin's. The sudden thought that so much blood could never have come from Hisako alone made Gimpei aware of the wound in his own chest. He felt faint, as if wrapped in the five-colored clouds on which Amida Buddha rides to receive the spirits of true believers."[10] The fantasy lasts but a second. He realizes that Hisako does not want him to be violent and that he could not kill her anyway. He climbs out of her bedroom window after tying several sashes together. With this makeshift rope, Hisako lowers him to the ground. Much earlier in his life, Momoi had attempted a murder. He induced his first love, his cousin Yayoi, to step out on the iced-covered lake near his mother's home village in the hopes that the ice would give way and that Yayoi would drown. Earlier his greatest joy had been to walk beside the lake with Yayoi, but she rebuffed and teased him. Gimpei's father had drowned in the same waters. It is not certain whether the death was an accident, a murder, or a suicide, but the villagers maintained that the man's troubled spirit haunted the shore of the lake. Gimpei could never forgive Yayoi for ordering him to throw a mouse which had been killed by her terrier into the lake. He had nonetheless done so. This episode continues to haunt Gimpei throughout his life as does another. During the war, when he was a student, he had impregnated a prostitute or at least had been accused of doing so. A baby girl had been left in a basket at the boarding house where Gimpei stayed, with a note identifying him as the father. He and another student took the child back to the brothel and abandoned it there. Gimpei often ponders what became of the baby. After his relationship with Hisako ended, Momoi continued to follow women. A crime once committed pursues a person until he repeats it. Momoi's feet can't help but chase after women and that is part of the reason he thinks them ugly. He fears that one day he will murder a woman whom he follows, although his fear appears to be unfounded. Old Arita, chairman of the board at Hisako's high school, another character in the novel who on the surface appears a much more respectable man, is far more dangerous in this regard. Arita's wife committed suicide in a fit of jealousy over another woman when Arita was in his thirties. After being fired from his job, Gimpei writes Arita's speeches. He can never use the words "wife" or "marriage" in what he writes.

Miyako Mizuki is the kept mistress of Arita. He enjoys suckling at her breasts, and she feels that she is a mother surrogate for him, but he also envies her youth. Miyako thinks he drains it from her as if he were a vampire. Like Komako in *Snow Country*, she is condemned to waste and lose her beauty. Miyako uses the money that Arita pays her to put her brother Keisuke through a university. Keisuke introduces her to his friend Mizuno and Mizuno's girlfriend Machie. Miyako feels drawn to Machie in a way similar to though less strong than the way the men who follow her are attracted to her. Gimpei Momoi will also fall under Machie's spell. He sees her walking a dog, and she reminds him of Yayoi and Hisako. He stops her in the street and attempts to engage her in conversation, but she quickly moves away. Later he sees her meet Mizuno and notices that her eyes are full of love. They are a lake Momoi wants to swim in. Gimpei confesses to Mizuno that he has been following Machie but tries to explain the innocence of his intentions. He is merely happy to see a young couple in love. Mizuno pushes him down a hill and into a ditch. Momoi recalls an old dream in which he saw fish leaping high in the sky and flying. He wishes that he had the strength to "leap free from the waves of humanity."[11] In his next life, he is sure that he will have beautiful feet. In the days that follow, Momoi continues to spy on Machie. On one occasion, he hides in a ditch in order to watch her walk above him. He sees her again on the night of the firefly festival. That evening he carries a cage full of the insects. When he over-hears her bemoaning the fact that she has caught so few of the released fireflies, he hangs his cage on her belt without her noticing it. After he returns to the city that evening, he notices that an ugly woman is following him in the street. He stops to speak to her and she tells him that she has a daughter to support. He takes her to an eating place for a meal and sake. She wears rubber boots, but Momoi wants to see if her feet are as ugly as his. If they are, he feels the two of them are fated for each other. After leaving the restaurant, they pass a cheap hotel where they might spend the night. Gimpei tells her that she should go home to her child. She col-lapses in the street, then begins tossing stones at his ankles.

Kawabata produced two more important novels, *House of Sleeping Beauties* in 1961 and *Koto* the following year. The first, a brief but potent book, would appear in English translation in 1969, a year after Kawabata won the Nobel prize. The English volume would also contain, in addition to the novel proper, an introduction by Mishima and two of Kawabata's most celebrated short stories, including the Kafkaesque "One Arm." This latter piece would become Kawabata's most widely anthologized work in the West. It begins with a girl offering the narrator the loan of her right arm for the night and, upon his acceptance, her unscrewing it from her body and laying it down upon his knees and ends with him tearing her arm from his shoulder and replacing it with his own, an impulsive action that he likens to an act of murder. After ripping it from his body, he embraces the female arm as if it were "a small child from whom life was going."[12] He brings the fingers to his lips and says, "If the dew of woman would but come from between the long nails and fingertips."[13]

The novel relates the four-night stay of an elderly man named Eguchi in a Japanese brothel, where he sleeps alongside young girls drugged into oblivion. While the book confirms Kawabata's reputation as a maestro of delicate eroticism, it also has a claustrophobic feel and an ominous ending—one of the girls dies in her sleep. The proprietress of the house tells Eguchi that there is always another girl, a remark that strikes the sixty-seven-year-old Eguchi to the core, quelling his lust and causing the facade he has, in Mishima's words, "so carefully and minutely fabricated"[14] to collapse completely. Like Shingo in *The Sound of the Mountain*, Eguchi is aware of the approach of his own death. This awareness is a goad to lust. In his introduction to the volume, Mishima writes, "Lust attaches itself to frag-ments, and, quite without subjectivity, the sleeping beauties themselves are frag-ments of human beings, urging lust to its highest intensity."[15] The remark is applic-able to both the novel and to the short story "One Arm." For Eguchi, the girls are not persons but "living dolls."[16] He forgets their humanity until the dark-skinned girl dies. The part also stands for the whole for the narrator of "One Arm." He wishes to connect physically but not emotionally or intellectually with women, a trait he shares in common with Shimamura in *Snow Country*. Both men reject not only love but, finally, physical intimacy as well. Mishima pushes his analysis further and says: "And, paradoxically, a beautiful corpse, from which the last traces of spirit have gone, gives rise to the strongest feelings of life. From the reflection of these violent feelings of the one who loves, the corpse sends forth the strongest radiance of life."[17] This final comment, however, is probably more indicative of Mishima's own philosophy than Kawabata's.

Koto would not appear in English translation until 1987, when it would be issued under the title *The Old Capital*. The novel was originally serialized in the *Asahi Newspaper* in one hundred installments in 1961 and 1962. Set in the ancient city of Koto or Kyoto, a place of art and high culture for centuries, it is perhaps Kawabata's greatest elegy, his last portrait of a vanishing culture. The Nobel committee cited this novel along with two others when it awarded Kawabata the prize for literature. He called it his "abnormal product"[18] as he strove for an epic, panoramic portrayal of life in the old city instead of his wonted lyricism. Unlike the other novels, this book does not have a narrow focus. Kawabata depicts the various artisans at work at their crafts, a rich and diverse tapestry of a bygone era. He became addicted to sleeping pills while writing the book and checked himself into a hospital for detoxification immediately after he had finished it. In 1988, a year after the American and British publication of *Koto*, a collection of Kawabata's shorter fiction, *Palm-of-the-Hand Stories*, would also appear in English. Kawabata considered these epigrammatic tales, many no longer than a single page, his finest work. They showcase his lyric strengths to an even greater extent than do the novels. As always, intimation, shade, and nuance play a greater role than plot and story line.

After receiving the Nobel prize in 1968, Kawabata lectured widely in the West. In 1969, he was appointed writer-in-residence at the University of Hawaii. His heart, however, always belonged to Japan. The award revitalized interest in Kawabata's work at home as well as prompting notice abroad. It also removed any financial worry the author might have had. It did not, however, spark creative renewal or fresh output on Kawabata's part. He realized that he was a writer in decline, that the last of the novels the Nobel committee had praised him for had been written a decade before and that, since that time, he had produced very little. Privately, he thought Mishima had been more deserving of recognition than himself, which made the latter's suicide even more troubling to the older man. He never approved of his protégé's flamboyance and extroversion; but, like the aging Master of Go, he recognized in the younger man "the one who might succeed him."[19] Mishima's final rash act did succeed, however, in jolting Kawabata into active politics for the first time in his life. Prior to Mishima's suicide, he had been apolitical, a quiet and acquiescent figure, but in 1971 he lent his support to an unsuccessful conservative candidate for the governor of Tokyo. Although he did not wish Japan to revert to her former warlike ways or to see the post-war constitution repealed, Kawabata feared she would lose sight of her traditional culture in the years to come. He did not desire a Westernized future for his nation. Yet, until his suicide, despite his recurrent health problems, and his sadness and shock over Mishima's death, he seemed placid and serene to both his family and friends. It seems equally clear, that at the time of his death, Kawabata was once more experiencing irretrievable loss. The world was moving in a direction not to his liking and he felt more and more out of place in it. He, too, heard the sound of the mountain and realized that it was time for him to move on and join all the others who had gone before him in death. In addition to his wife, Hideko, Kawabata was survived by a daughter and two grandchildren.

Notes

1. Quoted in *New York Times* obituary, 17 April 1972.

2. Ibid.

3. Ibid.

4. Ibid.

5. Yasunari Kawabata, *The Master of Go*, trans. Edward G. Seidensticker (New York: Knopf, 1972), p. 178.

6. Ibid.

7. Ibid.

8. Ibid.

9. Ibid.

10. Kawabata, *The Lake*, trans. Reiko Tsukimura (Tokyo: Kodansha International, 1974), p. 120.

11. Ibid., p. 105.

12. Kawabata. "One Arm," *The House of Sleeping Beauties*, trans. by Edward G. Seidensticker, introduction by Yukio Mishima (Tokyo, Palo Alto: Kodansha International, 1969), p. 124.

13. Ibid.

14. Yukio Mishima, "Introduction," *The House of Sleeping Beauties*, p. 8.

15. Ibid.

16. Ibid., p. 9.

17. Ibid., p. 8.

18. Quoted by J. Martin Holman, "Introduction," *The Old Capital* by Yasunari Kawabata, trans. Holman (San Francisco: North Point Press, 1987), p. i.

19. *The Master of Go*, p. 178.

John Berryman

ANOTHER IN THE LONG LINE OF AMERICAN AUTHORS UNDONE BY
alcohol, John Berryman was, all his life, burdened and obsessed
by the alleged suicide of his father, John Allyn Smith, on June 26, 1926.
Only eleven at the time of his father's death, Berryman never fully overcame his feelings of loss and separation. To survive, the boy had put his
father out of mind, and, on the heels of John Smith's death, when his
mother, Martha, wed John Angus Berryman, the man with whom she was
having an affair at the time of her husband's "suicide," he had acquiesced to the ultimate disloyalty—a change of surname. John Allyn Smith
Jr. became John Allyn Berryman. Although the name change was not his
idea—truth be told, he really did not have a choice in the matter; nor did
the wishes of John Smith's kin factor at all into the equation—and
although he deeply loved his mother and, with time, came to like the
man whom he called "Uncle Jack," John Berryman nonetheless would
suffer from a kind of Hamlet complex. Living with uncertainties and
unresolved conflict his entire life, he would become as hamstrung and
hung up as the Prince of Denmark, and eventually he would develop a
death wish as powerful as Hamlet's own. At fifty-eight, when he jumped
to his death from the Washington Avenue Bridge in Minneapolis, unable
to defeat his alcohol addiction and hoping to spare his wife and children
further grief and hardship on that account, he sought reunion with the
man whom he felt that he had betrayed and forsaken.

His father's death had been such a traumatic experience for the
young Berryman that he repressed not only his memories of the incident
itself but almost all recollection of his father. Daddy had gone away for
good, so he was determined to send him packing, to eliminate and erad-
icate all traces of him. In later life, Berryman retained a clear and distinct image of John Smith's face and physique, but everything else was

hazy and blurred, a half-forgotten, half-remembered dream. Berryman would later claim that, due to his father's death, his childhood had been stolen from him and that he had to begin life all over again. The boy's slate was wiped clean. All that had come before was brusquely and irreversibly erased the morning of June 26th when Martha Smith discovered her husband's body lying outside the Kipling Arms, the apartment building owned by John Angus Berryman where the couple and their two young sons were then residing, a .32 beside his head, a bullet hole in his chest.

In the months following his father's death, the boy's whole world turned topsy-turvy. Uncle Jack, his mother, he, and his younger brother, Robert Jefferson, relocated from Tampa, Florida, to Jackson Heights, Queens. The boys gave up their father's faith, Catholicism, and joined the Episcopalian church, and, in the fall of 1928, Berryman was sent to an Episcopalian boarding school in South Kent, Connecticut. Initially, he had great difficulty adjusting to life in the all-boys school. A geeky and awkward teen who suffered from acne and bad eyesight, Berryman was frequently bullied by his classmates. Underweight and unable to excel at athletics, he did not fit well into the prep school milieu where showing to advantage on the playing field counted above all else. Despite his scrawny build, he strove hard for acceptance, tried out for the "Kids'" football team, struggled to learn to skate, and, in order to avoid being called yellow by his classmates, deliberately provoked fights, fights which he'd not only lose but for which he would, in his own words, "take a razzing for a month."[1]

Shortly after he arrived at South Kent, feeling uprooted and homesick, he dreamed that his mother had died and that he had not been able to return home from the school to see her in time. In real life, his mother had indeed undergone a kind of metamorphosis, if nothing so prodigious as Henry James's "Great Change." At Uncle Jack's request, she dropped the name Martha and now went by "Jill Angel." Nothing in Berryman's world, not even his mother's given name, remained the same. Years later, the poet would christen his eldest daughter Martha, an act of reclamation and defiance. Toward the end of his life, despite his desperate addiction and his continual urge to do away with himself, Berryman experienced an unanticipated religious reawakening and began attending mass; after his death, he was given a Roman Catholic funeral at Saint Frances Cabrini Church in Minneapolis. By returning to his father's faith late in his own life, he succeeded in recovering another small slice of the boyhood of which he had been so suddenly and irrevocably bereft. When he entered South Kent at age thirteen, it seemed as though any trace of that earlier life was gone. It had floated out to sea like a lost ball, disappearing from view as it sank beneath the waves to descend to a watery grave:

> What is the boy now, who has lost his ball,
> What, what is he to do? I saw it go
> Merrily bouncing, down the street, and then
> Merrily over—there it is in the water!
> No use to say 'O there are other balls':

An ultimate shaking grief fixes the boy
As he stands rigid, trembling, staring down
All his young days into the harbour where
His ball went. I would not intrude on him,
A dime, another ball, is worthless. Now
He senses first responsibility
In a world of possessions. People will take balls,
Balls will be lost always, little boy,
And no one buys a ball back. Money is external.
He is learning, well behind his desperate eyes,
The epistemology of loss, how to stand up
And gradually light returns to the street,
A whistle blows, the ball is out of sight,
Soon part of me will explore the deep and dark
Floor of the harbour. I am everywhere,
I suffer and move, my mind and my heart move
With all that move me, under the water
Or whistling, I am not a little boy.[2]

Berryman wrote "The Ball Poem" in 1941. Today, most critics agree that it is the most accomplished of his early lyrics. Berryman himself regarded it as his break-through poem. Years later, he would explain to Howard Nemerov the significance it had for his later development: "[My] discovery here was that a commitment of identity can be 'reserved,' so to speak with an ambiguous pronoun. The poet himself is both left out and put in; the boy does and does not become him. . . . Without this invention . . . I could not have written either of the two long poems that constitute the bulk of my work so far."[3] As Berryman's biographer Paul Mariani writes, the poem presents "a double vision: the child's first realization of loss—a ball floating out into the ocean—and the sudden realization from the adult's perspective—looking forward and simultaneously looking back—that life was inevitably made up of many such losses. . . ."[4] The boy remains on the shore, but the "I" of the poem is carried out to sea with the lost ball and will sink to the floor of the harbor with it. John Allyn Smith had died from a gunshot wound to the chest, but in the weeks preceding his death, he took frequent swims in the Gulf. On the beach, his sons watched him disappear from sight and anxiously awaited his return. Once Smith took his younger son, Robert, swimming with him and he teth-ered the child to his chest with a rope. He swam out so far that Martha grew hys-terical. Convinced that her husband was going to drown both himself and the boy, she sent John Angus Berryman out after the two. When he reached them, he found Smith in a trancelike state. He came to his senses, however, and, at Berryman's bidding, swam back to shore. Martha screamed and shrieked at him when he reached the beach and accused him of trying to murder Robert. Smith's eyes glazed over. He shrugged his shoulders and walked away. His elder son would misremember the episode, thinking that his father had taken him, as well as his younger brother Robert, on the fateful swim.

In later life, John Berryman desperately wanted to recover his past, but his childhood remained elusive and out of reach. He felt the presence of his father's ghost but, maddeningly, it hovered at the very edge, the farthest remove, of sight. Whenever he attempted to close in on it and bring it into sharper focus, it faded and withdrew. He had difficulty separating what he actually remembered about the events leading up to his father's "suicide" from what he had been later told by his mother. He later came to see that many of his recollections were colored and slanted by her point of view, that the memories he did retain were mostly cast and shaped by her. She had told him his father had no *joie de vivre*, that he lacked all passion and ardor, and that the goatee he grew after he had been forced to resign his position as vice president and chief loan officer of the First State Bank in Anadarko, Oklahoma, had given him—in her opinion—the effeminate appearance of a French homosexual. In his appraisal of Berryman accompanying the *New York Times* obituary of the author, Thomas Lask noted the change in Berryman's own looks toward the end of his life. Like his father, he grew a beard, albeit not a trim goatee but a wild flowing one: "In his younger days, Mr. Berryman appeared as a rather solemn, clean shaven professorial type. In his last years, he had grown a full beard and looked like a sailor just home from a long voyage, capable of downing infinite pots of ale or other spirituous liquors and reading off the rollicking rhythms of his own dream songs at a single sitting."[5]

As a boy, Berryman had always taken his mother's version of events as gospel. During his college years, however, he began to question her account of what had happened in Tampa. He continued searching for the truth the rest of his life. While the past would remain as fugitive and inexplicable as always, as early as 1938, Berryman became convinced of one thing: that he had a sacred duty not only to try to remember his father but also to commemorate his life in verse. In October of that year, he wrote the poem "Father and Son" in which he pledges to keep his father's memory alive for future generations. As in many other of Berryman's poems, the father is a victim of drowning:

> The man taken this morning from the water
> Has had his turn, and he is written down
> In all the dusty offices of failure
> But one. Surviving him there is a son
> Who yet may patch the name and memory
> For annalists in the great times to be.[6]

The specter of John Allyn Smith Sr. would continue to haunt much of Berryman's subsequent work. Again and again, with disturbing regularity, the poems return to the topic of Berryman's childhood trauma. Despite all his laborious self-investigation and tortured inner probing (perhaps reflected in the distorted and twisted syntax of his late style)—despite, in the end, a lifelong struggle to exorcise his demons and declare himself dispossessed—Berryman could never really come to terms with the "ultimate shaking grief"[7] that fixed him as a child.

Although a part of him never stopped loving his mother, with the passage of time, Berryman gradually perceived and increasingly resented her calculated and devious manipulation of both himself and others. He felt sure that she had similarly controlled his father. In the end, his resentment would border on hate. An indefatigable monologist, Jill would smother her son with talk. In a good mood, she would chatter on and on, but, if she became angry with her boy for any reason, her volubility would suddenly cease. Endless yapping would give way to icy silence as Jill deliberately attempted to freeze John out. She would ignore him completely for days or even weeks. Berryman felt stymied by both his mother's moods; either way he found communication with her utterly impossible. His frustration at his inability to make his wishes and thoughts known, to speak and be attended to in a conversation with his mother, began to affect his health.

From an early age, he was subject to epileptic attacks. As a man, he came to the conclusion that these seizures were "hysteroid,"[8] a method of handling his mother, a way of making her take notice of him, of asserting himself and fighting free from her domination. Throughout his life, whenever he felt low or blue, Berryman would feign illness or else force himself to actually become sick in order to be nurtured and fussed over by mother surrogates. When life got too hard for him, whenever academic responsibilities or deadline pressures became too burdensome or whenever his alcoholic binges had lasted too long and he needed to undergo detoxication, he checked himself into a hospital. Extremely accident prone, he broke bones—wrists, arms, ribs, ankles, legs—on such a frequent basis that friends thought something was amiss with his appearance if one of his limbs wasn't in a sling or a cast.

Berryman's three wives, Eileen, Ann, and Kate, all had to coddle and baby him. Ann was twenty years younger than he, Kate twenty-five, but in the course of their marriages, both found themselves cast in the role of mother far more often than that of daughter. For all his brilliance as a poet, Berryman could not do—or perhaps disdained to do—even the simplest things for himself. The tasks of everyday living always seemed beyond him. Whenever he was left to his own devices, laundry and dishes would pile up for weeks. Preparing even the most basic meals taxed him terribly. Nor could he master such rudimentary essentials as driving an automobile or balancing his checkbook. His wives waited on him constantly, and he enjoyed having them do so. He demanded from the women he wed the attention and solicitous regard he felt his mother had denied him. He felt entitled to such care and devotion, and his needs and requirements kept increasing as long as the marriage lasted. Eventually they were so time-consuming and of such an onerous nature that they became too much for any of his three wives to handle. Adept at emotional blackmail, Berryman would threaten suicide if he felt that his spouse was shunting him in any way. Toward the end of his life, his forewarnings became so frequent that a perplexed and frightened Kate did not know when to take them seriously.

Berryman made his first attempt at killing himself as a student at South Kent. On a winter day, while he was jogging in order to train for tennis, three upper-formers started taunting him. Soon one was hurling snowballs in his direction. After missing twice, he lifted a chunk of ice and snow off the ground and ran after Berryman. He quickly gained on him, as Berryman had been running for some time and had become winded. Coming up directly behind his unsuspecting quarry, he heaved the hunk of ice hard at Berryman's shoulders and back. A staggered Berryman turned and tried to fight, but a fist struck him full in the face, and he fell to the ground. The upper-former pinned the younger boy's arms with his knees and punched him a half a dozen times. When the older student at last let him up, Berryman heard a train approaching on a nearby track. He ran to the railway and threw himself into the path of the loco-motive. The other boys managed to yank him from harm's way. The train roared past immediately after they had pulled the hysterical Berryman from the track. Later that evening, two of the boys approached him following supper. Contrite and chastened by what had previously happened, they now treated him with exaggerated kindness and promised not to bully him ever again. Berryman learned an important lesson that day. He had found a sure-fire method (or so he thought) of eliciting the sympathy of others. With time, he would grow as expert at manipulation as Jill.

When he grew old enough to comprehend them, the mysterious circumstances of his father's death added to the hostility Berryman felt toward his mother. Did Daddy shoot himself or did Mommy and Uncle Jack murder him as his Aunt Cora had always insisted? John Allyn Smith had the misfortune of dying in the middle of the Florida land bust. A failed banker and restaurateur, Smith fit the profile of ruined businessmen who were killing themselves right and left during the summer of 1926. Jill maintained that during their courtship, Smith had for all intents and purposes raped her. Seven years her senior, he had taken advantage of her naiveté and girlish inexperience. Fearing that she might be pregnant, she consented to marry him. She further contended that both she and her husband had affairs early in their marriage, while they and their two sons still lived in Oklahoma.

When Berryman was old enough, she told him that, in Anadarko, she had fallen "desperately, instantly, totally, forever in love"⁹ with a future governor of Oklahoma. She claimed that her beau wanted her to divorce John Smith and marry him. Although she desired to do what her heart bade her, for the sake of her young boys, she decided not to end the marriage, even when John Allyn, upon learning of her unfaithfulness, embarked on an affair of his own. He had done this solely for retribution's sake. To inflict as much pain on his wife as he could, he had taken one of her closest friends as his lover. The woman accompanied him to Chicago where banking matters frequently took him.

At the time, Berryman was too young to notice the supposed friction developing between his father or mother. (We only have Jill's word that the two had experienced marital troubles so early in their union.) What her son most remembered about this early period in his life were the hours he spent at the Catholic mission church of the Holy Family, where he made his first communion and served as an altar boy. A Belgian priest, Father Boniface Beri, had taken a special interest in him. He recalled taking part in the morning services where he recited the prescribed Latin responses to Beri's formal questions. Berryman would later say that, at the time, he "believed in God and [his] guardian angel to the hilt."[10] The images he recalled of his father were of him working at the First State Bank or dressing up in his National Guard uniform for summer reserve duty. In 1924, Smith resigned from the bank. Jill claimed that he had taken a fishing trip to Colorado at a time when, though on vacation, he had promised to be immediately available for bank business if needed. According to Jill, he was given the option of resigning or being fired. For a time, he found work as an assistant game and fish warden, but eventually he, his wife, and his mother-in-law left Oklahoma for Florida, where they hoped to strike it rich in real estate. Martha's mother already owned some property in Tampa. The Smiths enrolled their two sons in a Catholic boarding school in Oklahoma, promising to return for them in short order. In three months' time, Martha came and fetched them. John Smith opened a restaurant called the Orange Blossom in Tampa, but the business would shortly fail. The couple would vacate more expensive lodgings to move into the Kipling Arms, while Martha drifted into an affair with her landlord. Smith, in turn, took up with a Cuban woman. The couple agreed to divorce, but Smith's mistress dropped him and returned to Cuba. Smith now wanted Martha to come back to him, proposing that they take the children and move somewhere else and start their lives over again. Martha was torn and could not decide between Smith and Berryman. Smith began hitting the bottle hard. He brandished his .32 in a threatening manner and took daily swims far out into the Gulf.

Martha would later tell her son that out of concern for his father, shortly before his death, she removed five bullets from the chamber of his gun. Berryman wondered why she had not taken out all six. On the night of June 25, Smith once again visited his wife and renewed his pleas that she accept him back. John Angus Berryman interceded. Martha would later claim that she fell asleep in the living room as the two men talked and that later in the night she awoke to find her husband passed out in the bedroom. She said she returned to the living room and fell asleep again. When she awoke at six, Smith was gone. She went outside to look for him and found his body spread-eagled on the rear steps of the apartment building. When the authorities arrived, she produced an unsigned note she said she found on her husband's dresser. It read: "Dear Peggy: Again I am not able to sleep—three nights now and the terrible headaches."[11] The police wrote Smith's death off as a suicide, making much of his depression and insomnia at the inquest; but, as Paul Mariani points out, two key facts about the case were glossed over and ignored. First, the pistol Smith supposedly used to kill himself was actually registered in

Martha's name. Smith had bought it for her protection four years before. Contrary to Jill's claims to her son, the gun was her weapon and not Berryman's father's. Second, and most incriminating, no powder burns were found on Smith's blood-stained shirt, an impossibility in the case of a self-inflicted gunshot wound.

John Berryman saw his father's death as a great theft. He would come to view himself as the principal victim of that theft, i.e., as the dispossessed party, but he was never quite sure whom to blame for this act of piracy and sabotage, this early shipwreck of his life. The guilt went all round, and Berryman directed his anger at various targets at different times in his life. For years, his mother was the principal mark of his wrath. Maybe she hadn't pulled the actual trigger. On that score he gave her the benefit of the doubt, but he still held her responsible for John Smith's death. She had demanded a divorce when Smith's world was falling apart, when he was at an emotional ebb and most likely to do himself harm. Furthermore, she had given herself, what properly belonged to his father, not only to Uncle Jack but to a succession of other suitors, both during her marriage to his father's rival and afterward. Berryman hated his mother's promiscuity, but, in an act of transference, he would emulate her behavior in his own marriages and love affairs. Berryman's first sexual experience was a homosexual encounter with a classmate at South Kent, but, apart from this one instance of youthful experimentation, he was heroically heterosexual. From an early age, he cast himself in the role as the tempter and seducer (a persona he would make use of, and have a great time reveling in, in his "Homage to Mistress Bradstreet"). A woman chaser all his life, Berryman was as libertine and abandoned as his mother. Particularly sad and distressing was his compulsion to seduce—or attempt to seduce (he had his share of bitter failures)—the girlfriends and wives of his friends and colleagues, and, later on, those of his best and brightest male students. He could not check his need to betray and double-cross the very people to whom he was closest, for whom he cared most. He cheated on all three of his wives. However, if a woman played him false or if one of his friends put the moves on a girl he was dating or was merely interested in, he would become self-destructive and suicidal.

Although, in 1938, Berryman declared his poetic mission "to patch the name and memory"[12] of his dead father, as he grew older, he began venting his anger at John Smith as well. He could not shake his father's ghost, and eventually the dead man would become just as much a ghoul and vampire for him as Sylvia Plath's father became for her. In February 1956, attempting to find a suitable form for his projected *Dream Songs*, he drafted a poem concerning his father's suicide. In it, he argues that his father's desire for death was selfish. In his haste to do away with himself, Daddy forgot the legacy he was leaving behind for his two sons and the impact his act would inevitably have on them:

> His widow did feel bad.
> However it was only him,
> who *had* swum out with his younger son
> promising not to be a returning two or one,

but he changed his mind & did.
He swam strong, always had,

thing he did best.
Bequeathing the elder, upset son
a seething, troubles less unspeakable than one
vacant in-raging
silence of the younger, lest
a spilt word bomb the world.[13]

Berryman would eventually write 385 Dream Songs. Each poem is divided into three six-line stanzas with lines 1, 2, 4, and 5 in pentameter and lines 3 and 6 in trimeter. Despite the strict stanza form, the tone of the songs is breezy and glib, the diction slangy and contemporary. The songs would be published in two volumes, *77 Dream Songs* (1964) and *His Toy, His Dream, His Rest* (1968). The first collection would bring Berryman the Pulitzer Prize, the second the National Book Award for poetry. In a prefatory note to the second volume, Berryman wrote: "The poem then, whatever its cast of characters, is essentially about an imaginary character (not the poet, not me) named Henry, a white American in early middle age sometimes in blackface, who has suffered an irreversible loss and talks about himself sometimes in the first person, sometimes in the third, sometimes even in the second; he has a friend, never named who addresses him as Mr. Bones and variants thereof."[14] Despite this disclaimer that he and his character are not the same, Berryman is nonetheless instantly recognizable as the source and pattern of Henry Achilles. The songs are essentially confessional; Henry undergoes experiences and ordeals identical to Berryman's own, the cast of characters include many of the poet's actual friends and acquaintances. Berryman considered the *Dream Songs* an epic poem. "Its plot," he wrote, "is the personality of Henry as he moves on in the world" from the age of forty-one to fifty-one. The songs record Henry's personal fears, his addiction to alcohol, his suicidal inclinations, his marital difficulties, and his erotic adventures. The deaths of Henry's friends, a succession of doomed fellow poets, are also recounted. Moving tributes to Randall Jarrell, Theodore Roethke, Sylvia Plath, and Delmore Schwartz, among others, are woven into the tapestry of the second volume, *His Toy, His Dream, His Book*. The "irreversible loss" that Henry experiences as a boy is, of course, the death of his father.

Late in December 1962, Berryman wrote what would become "Dream Song 42." His daughter Martha was born earlier that month. Working on other Dream Songs the previous November, he had been drinking inordinately, using alcohol to fire his muse. Exhausted, he checked himself into a hospital Thanksgiving week but was released prior to his daughter's birth, December 2. After visiting his wife and baby in the maternity ward, he went on a drinking spree. Friends sent him home in a taxi. As he exited the vehicle, the taxi backed over his left foot, snapping his ankle. Once again he found himself in a cast. As New Year's approached, a continually drunken Berryman began work on "Dream Song 42." In it, his alter ego confronts his father's ghost, a monkey on his back, a demon he cannot exorcise. The two are on familiar terms. They "dream of honour, and . . . get along."[15] Nonetheless, a part of Henry hopes that the poem will expel or drive off the evil spirit. Another facet of his personality wants the ghost to hold fast, to never loosen its grip. Henry is a split self, yet, ultimately, even the side of him that wishes his father to stay urges the ghost to disregard this perverse and misguided desire of his and listen to the more rational self's adjuration to be gone:

> Fate winged me, in the person of a cab
> and your stance on the sand.
> Think it across, in freezing wind: withstand
> my blistered wish: flop, there, to his blind song
> who picks up the tab.[16]

Finally in the penultimate poem of *His Toy, His Dream, His Rest*, Berryman relates a visit he paid to his father's grave. His anger and bitterness grow so great that he shrieks: "I spit upon this dreadful banker's grave/ who shot his heart out in a Florida dawn."[17]

In other poems, Berryman expressed his rage at God, the heavenly Father whom for most of his life he dismissed as nonexistent but whom in his verse he indicted for all manner of human suffering, from wars to natural disasters to deadly diseases such as the cancer that claimed his friend and fellow poet Bhain Campbell in 1940. Two years after Campbell's death, as World War II raged in Europe, Berryman drowned his sorrows in alcohol. He proclaimed scotch, ice, and water "the new Trinity."[18] He admitted that they were less comforting "perhaps than the first, and with no such magnificent corollaries as the Virgin."[19] However, he maintained that they were "more available, more real, able to exist in the twentieth-century world, in short the survivor."[20]

While his anger toward John Smith increased with the years, upon admission to the Intensive Alcohol Treatment center at Saint Mary's Hospital in 1970, after having reached rock bottom, Berryman turned to God. While hospitalized, he wrote his "Eleven Addresses to the Lord," a series of poems that dealt with his conversion experience. Berryman knew that he was gradually murdering himself with alcohol, as his friend Dylan Thomas had done before him. Desperate to get well, he reached out for help wherever he could find it. Suddenly he was able to accept the idea of a loving God watching over those who trusted and put their faith in him. He hoped for intercession from above since he himself did not have the power to turn his life around. He would either drink himself to death or else, like his father, commit suicide. For years, he thought persistently, almost on a daily basis, about ending his life. The temptation was so great that he knew he did not have the strength to withstand it alone. Berryman prayed for help and was vouchsafed what he described as an epiphany about the compassionate, caring nature of God. Suddenly he felt a new energy and vitality. This vigor and animation, the result of his conversion experience, can be seen in all eleven poems of the series but especially the middle one, the sixth:

> Under new management, Your Majesty:
> Thine. I have solo'd mine since childhood, since
> my father's suicide when I was twelve
> blew out my most bright candle faith, and look at me.
>
> I served at Mass six dawns a week from five,
> adoring Father Boniface & you,
> memorizing the Latin he explained.
> Mostly we worked alone. One or two women.
>
> Then my poor father frantic. Confusions & afflictions
> followed my days. Wives left me.
> Bankrupt I closed my doors. You pierced the roof
> twice & again. Finally you opened my eyes.
>
> My double nature fused in that point of time
> three weeks ago before yesterday.
> Now, brooding thro' a history of the early Church,
> I identify with everybody, even the heresiarchs.[21]

Berryman's faith did not last. The old compulsions, the urge to drink, the desire to die, reasserted themselves. One of his early favorite poets was Hart Crane, and he often thought of drowning himself in the ocean or leaping to his death from off a bridge. His depression had many triggers: rejection of any sort by friend or lover, world events, nuclear testing, his inability to control his drinking, dissatisfaction with the progress of his writing, domestic and financial difficulties, and anxieties about his performance in the classroom. The list goes on and on. Something as seemingly innocuous as a case of the flu could turn Berryman's thoughts to suicide. His life seemed so disorganized and chaotic to him that death appeared to be the tidiest and most logical solution. In August 1958, Berryman vacationed with his family on Long Island's south shore. Sick and forlorn, he jotted down the following lines:

> Snuffle . . . For Henry has a filthy cold,
> like a sea in the head,
> with slap & lurchings & a sense of congestion
> of weeds just offshore, behind the eyebrows. . . .
> He isn't strong enough just now. He will be.
> Hoho, heehee.
> He cd put everything in order & perish. . . .[22]

As a younger man, Berryman came close to killing himself on several occasions. During the summer of 1946, Berryman and his first wife, Eileen, visited Richard and Helen Blackmur at their summer cottage in Harrington, Maine. Delmore Schwartz had warned Berryman not only that Blackmur and his wife constantly fought, but also that their battles could be quite acrimonious. The couple proved true to form during the Berrymans' stay. Through the thin walls of the cottage, John and Eileen could hear their hosts arguing with one another late at night. The bickering Blackmurs reminded Berryman of his own parents fighting in Tampa. One night, he had difficulty sleeping after the two had quarreled. He read until almost dawn. As the night passed, however, he became terribly depressed. Looking out one of the cottage windows, he stared across the lawn and the bluff beyond it at the Atlantic and was overcome with the desire to walk into the ocean and end it all. He managed to resist the urge to do away with himself that night, but it took every ounce of his willpower. He and Eileen bid their farewells to the Blackmurs the following day. Twenty-six years later, in 1972—not long before he jumped to his death from the Washington Avenue Bridge—in a poem entitled "Henry's Understanding," Berryman would write about his experience that night in Harrington in 1946:

> He was reading late, at Richard's, down in Maine,
> age 32? Richard & Helen long in bed,
> my good wife long in bed.
> All I had to do was strip & get into my bed,
> putting the marker in the book, & sleep,
> & wake to a hot breakfast.
>
> Off the coast was an island, P'tit Manaan,
> the bluff from Richard's lawn was almost sheer.
> A chill at four o'clock.
> It only takes a few minutes to make a man.
> A concentration upon now & here.
> Suddenly, unlike Bach,
>
> & horribly, unlike Bach, it occurred to me
> that *one* night, instead of warm pajamas,
> I'd take off all my clothes
> & cross the damp cold lawn & down the bluff
> into the terrible water & walk forever
> under it out toward the island.[23]

Three years later, in January 1949, Berryman was bringing to a close his biography of Stephen Crane, in the final chapter of which he attempted to explain the novelist's relationship with women. "The woman loved," Berryman wrote, "must involve, first, an 'injured third party'—some other man, that is, who has a right of possession, as husband or betrothed or near friend. She must be, second, 'more or less sexually discredited . . . within the limits of a significant series'. . . . Third, this highly compulsive situation [was] repeated."[24] As he looked over what he had written, Berryman realized that what he said about Crane—that he compulsively seduced married or otherwise attached women as a form of retaliation against his mother—was equally true of himself. He also realized that his interpretation of the late Crane short story "The Veteran" pertained to his own life just as much as it did to the novelist's, if not more so. In this story, Henry Fleming, the hero of *The Red Badge of Courage*, now an old man, rushes into a burning barn to rescue several trapped children, knowing full well that his life will be sacrificed. His suicidal action, he hopes, will make amends for his earlier cowardice on the battlefield. Fleming goes to his death as bravely as Lord Jim. As the roof of the barn collapses and flames and smoke leap skyward, old Henry and young Henry at last become one. Death unites "father and son." Putting his manuscript down, Berryman walked out on to the terrace of the sixth-floor studio where he was working. He wrote in his diary that his brain was "ready to burst."[25] If he could only shut his eyes and let himself drop, the long separation between father and son would at last be over and he would be free from all future worry. Once again, however, as in Maine, Berryman was able to check the suicidal impulse, but the reprieve was short-lived. Seven months later, in July 1949, he and Eileen were vacationing in Cape Cod. One night, while attending a cocktail party, Berryman got into an argument with his friend and Princeton colleague Dwight MacDonald. He ran to the shore and walked into the ocean fully clothed. Friends searched for him for a half hour. At last they found him on the beach drenched and despondent.

Over the years, in numerous poems, Berryman again and again wrote about his urge to kill himself. Of all his lyrics on the subject, his 1970 poem "Of Suicide" is perhaps the most poignant. In it, we see both the perpetual attraction death held for this poet and also the valiant effort he made to resist giving in to his suicidal impulse. The reader learns of his constant vigilance and self-policing and of some of the defenses he used when the desire to die grew strong within him:

> Reflexions on suicide, & on my father, possess me.
> I drink too much. My wife threatens separation.
> She won't 'nurse' me. She feels 'inadequate.'
> We don't mix together.
>
> It's an hour later in the East.
> I could call up Mother in Washington, D.C.
> *But* could she help me?
> And all this postal adulation & reproach?
>
> A basis rock-like of love & friendship
> for all this world-wide madness seems to be needed.
> Epictetus is in some ways my favorite philosopher.
> Happy men have died earlier.
>
> I still plan to go to Mexico this summer.
> The Olmec images! Chichen Itza!
> D.H. Lawrence has a wild dream of it.
> Malcolm Lowry's book when it came out I taught to my
>   precept at Princeton.

I don't entirely resign. I may teach the Third Gospel
this afternoon. I haven't made up my mind.
It seems to me sometimes that others have easier jobs
& do much worse.

Well, we must labour & dream. Gogol was impotent,
somebody in Pittsburgh told me.
I said: At what age? They couldn't answer.
That is a damned serious matter.

Rembrandt was sober. There we differ. Sober.
Terrors came on him. To us too they come.
Of suicide I continually think.
Apparently he didn't. I'll teach Luke.[26]

Berryman did everything he could to hold on to life as long as possible. He
attended AA and tried to remain sober. If that did not work, to fend off his depression, he would drink himself unconscious or else—not being impotent—pursue
women. He planned future trips so he would always have something to look forward
to. He threw himself into his writing and tried to exorcise his demons through his
poetry. He prepared lectures and diligently taught his courses. If he could only
keep busy, he reasoned, he could keep his mind off suicide. He played and romped
with his children, and he tried to find God. He bought books by the cartload and
read his eyes out. Certain works provided him special solace, and he came back to
them again and again. Keats's letters were a yearly consolation. He also frequently
turned to the New Testament and the plays of Shakespeare. Once Berryman
claimed that the fact that he had not read all of Henry James's short stories had prevented him from committing suicide on several occasions. To lengthen his days, he
vowed to read only one new James story a year. He hoped to never come to the end
of the list, to always have a backlog.[27]

John Berryman was born in McAlester, Oklahoma, October 25, 1914. His family,
however, was not southwestern. John Allyn Smith Sr. had been brought up in Minnesota. His father, Leonard Jefferson Smith, a Maine Volunteer, had moved westward after the Civil War. He married an Irish Catholic wife in Minneapolis and supported his family of ten children by working as a lumberman in the town of South
Stillwater. Berryman's father was the couple's last child. Leonard Smith's ancestors
had hailed from the Green Mountains of Vermont. One of his forbears was reputedly the celebrated American Revolutionary infantryman Ethan Allen.

    A famous soldier was also prominent in Martha Little's line. Although born in
Illinois, Berryman's mother's roots were in the South. Her grandfather was Confederate General Robert Glenn Shaver who led the 7th Arkansas Infantry at Shiloh
and later the 38th Arkansas Infantry, the last Southern regiment to surrender to the
North. Shaver helped establish the Ku Klux Klan in Arkansas after the war.

Brought up on Federal charges, he fled to British Honduras for four years. After the warrant for his arrest was rescinded, he returned home to Howard County where he was elected sheriff and practiced law.

Despite his rich military heritage, Berryman was an avowed pacifist, and, although in 1967 he attended a Halloween party dressed as his great-grandfather Shaver, Berryman loathed the South for its treatment of blacks. World War II, Korea, and Vietnam all caused Berryman anxiety and heartache. He felt enormous compassion for the victims of war and for the young soldiers who had made the ultimate sacrifice. On the other hand, he viewed with scorn and contempt the politicians who sought confrontation, thought them power-mad butchers, and feared that the entire human race might be wiped out because of their stupidity. When would "the fire be turned on," he asked in a 1968 poem,

> and by whom?
> heating the memory & soul alike
> until both crisp.
> Not soon, I wonder, but in some lead-shielded room
> mistakes are being made like the Third Reich. . . .[28]

Berryman believed that, due to its military conflicts and wars on a scale without precedent in all of human history, this century was a particularly inimical one for poets. Sensitive souls like himself could not turn a blind eye to all the suffering, to the millions of casualties. They felt compelled to chronicle the horror they beheld, to open all eyes to it, to force those who would avert their gaze to take a hard look at the charnel house, even if such a task would upset their own emotional equilibrium and, in the end, hasten their self-destruction. In 1948, Berryman planned a sequence of poems on the Nazi concentration camps called *The Black Book.* He envisioned the work as a forty-two section "Mass for the Dead." The book obsessed him for the better part of a year, but, in the end, he did not prove up to the task. It was too daunting, too heart-wrenching, too dangerous for his own well-being, to proceed with the series. There was no way he could make "palatable the monstrosity of the thing."[29] The sections he had written were "unrelievedly horrible."[30] He became so depressed and suicidal that he had to put the manuscript away. Seven years later, however, he did publish three poems meant for the book in pamphlet form. Although the Holocaust proved too daunting for his pen, Berryman wrote numerous poems protesting United States police actions in Korea and Vietnam. Both wars saddened and disheartened him as well as aroused his wrath. In 1950, he depicted the murder of Santa Claus as American and UN forces engaged North Korean and Chinese troops along the 38th parallel. America's freedom from sin was over. Guilelessness and guiltlessness had both come to an end:

Santa Claus with blood across his face
Went past out of control; the reindeer cried
Over the deep snow, and the dogs gave chase.

Our youth spent that bitter night outside
Deaf to the hurrying call, awake at one,
Awake at three, clasping their metal bride. . . .

Now in the breath of the dogs the reindeer cry,
Blood dabbles the beautiful snow, and the slack
Reins suggest we have made some one die

No one believed in, who will not come back.[31]

Correct about America's loss of innocence following World War II, Berryman also had the Vietnam conflict pegged as early as 1966:

a war which was no war,
the enemy was not our enemy
but theirs whoever they are
and the treaty-end that might conclude it more
unimaginable than *Alice's* third volume—eee—
and somehow our policy bare

in eighteen costumes kept us unaware
that we were killing Asiatics daily.[32]

Although he came out strongly against the war, Berryman was sympathetically disposed to Vietnam veterans, especially after learning the staggering statistic that "27% of all returned veterans in hospitals are known to have actually tried to kill themselves—a phenomenon unique in history, so far as I know, & blood-curdling."[33] As angry as Berryman was at U.S. policy makers, he was nonetheless honest enough to admit that if the reigns of power had been placed in his hands, he, too, could not have forborne the temptation to crack the whip and wield the power. Thank goodness, he did not have *his* finger on the button. In his own limited way, however, he had added his portion to the world's collective suffering:

Tottered thro' his remorse many Bigger Ones—
the maximum leader, the Secretary, Mao,
Il Duce, El Caudillo
          Soon full backing
helped out his hoores & coccyx. His beard hurled
one deal across the world. . . .[34]

Berryman understood the mindset of America's policy makers for he knew all about denial. He compared his own inability to stop drinking to the United States' unwillingness to pull its forces out of Vietnam, claiming that he and the nation's leaders suffered from a similar arrogance. Neither he nor they were able to face the fact; both preferred delusion to the truth. Although the images of war he saw on his television and the information he read about it in newspapers and magazines upset him and fed his own neuroses, he felt obliged to keep himself informed of the progress of the conflict and of the carnage and the bloodshed. The news augmented his depression. Berryman suspected that it had a similar effect on other people of sensibility. He knew that it was poets who fell like dominoes, not Asiatic countries.

John Berryman had not taken a drink for close to a year when he purchased a bottle of whiskey on January 5, 1972. In that time he had completed a new collection of poems, *Delusions, Etc.*, which would be published shortly after his death, and began a novel, *Recovery*, dealing with his ongoing struggle with alcohol. He had also been awarded a National Endowment for the Humanities grant to finish a critical biography of Shakespeare, a project that he had been working on intermittently for twenty years. In addition, he contemplated writing a *Life of Christ* for children. By December 1971, work had stalled on all of his projects. He was also dissatisfied with the few poems that he was then in the process of drafting. In addition to suffering writer's block, Berryman had been having trouble with his classes at the University of Minnesota. He found his students that semester dull and uncooperative. As for his own teaching, he felt that he was only going through the motions. Again he found himself thinking increasingly about death. On the thirteenth of December, Berryman contemplated checking into a motel and killing himself either with a gun or with his Spanish knife. Instead he went upstairs to his bedroom and fell on his knees and prayed. He felt strengthened and chastened and, once more, vowed to write his life of Jesus.

In the weeks that followed, however, his pen still remained dry. Berryman began to fear that his newly found faith in God was just another of his delusions. The prospect of winter classes nauseated him. On January 5, he bought the whiskey and drank half the bottle that day. Although he had a long and distinguished teaching career that included positions at Wayne State, Harvard, Princeton, and the University of Cincinnati, Berryman could never forget how he had disgraced himself at the University of Iowa in 1954. Drinking had been his undoing there. After a late night binge, a weaving and tottering Berryman had made his way home to his apartment. When his landlord, seeing what a state he was in, refused him entrance, Berryman began shouting obscenities. Finally he unhitched his pants and defecated on the front porch. The landlord's wife telephoned the police and had Berryman arrested and he spent the night in jail. The following day the local newspapers reported the incident, and Berryman was dismissed from his post as a result of the ensuing scandal.

As he drank that January 5, Berryman determined to end his life by jumping from the Washington Avenue bridge. This suicide attempt would have to be successful. He could not endure another Iowa episode. On the afternoon of the fifth, Berryman left a note on the kitchen table that read, "I am a nuisance,"[35] then walked out of his house. He may have gone to the bridge, but he did not jump. Instead he returned home and wrote what would be his final poem:

> Sharp the Spanish blade
> to gash my throat after I'd climbed across
> the high railing of the bridge
> to tilt out, with the knife in my right hand
> to slash me shocked or fainting till I'd fall
> unable to keep my skull down but fearless
>
> unless my wife wouldn't let me out of the house,
> unless the cops noticed me crossing the campus
> up to the bridge
> & clappt me in for observation, costing my job—
> I'd be now in a cell, costing my job—
> well, I missed that;
>
> but here's the terror of tomorrow's lectures
> bad in themselves, the students dropping the course,
> the Administration hearing
> & offering me either a medical leave of absence
> or resignation—Kitticat, they can't fire me—[36]

Berryman put a line through the poem with his pen then tossed it into the waste-basket.

Two days later, early in the morning on January 7, a bitterly cold day, Berryman told his wife that he was going to campus to clean out his office. As he left the house, he said, "You won't have to worry about me any more."[37] At 9:30 A.M., he reached the bridge. He did not bring his knife, however; he saw that it was superfluous. He climbed over the chest-high railing on the north side. Students inside the opposite glass-enclosed walkway watched in disbelief as Berryman waved to them, then leaned back and let go. He fell nearly one hundred feet to the embankment below. His body bounced then rolled. Police identified the poet from a blank check in his billfold. His name was also printed on the bow of his shattered horn-rimmed glasses.

Notes

1. Quoted by Paul Mariani, *Dream Song: The Life of John Berryman* (New York: William Morrow, 1990), p. 23.

2. John Berryman, "The Ball Poem," in *The Norton Anthology of Modern Poetry*, ed. Richard Ellmann and Robert O'Clair (New York: W.W. Norton, 1973), pp. 893–94. "The Ball Poem" was written in 1941. It appeared in the Berryman collection, *The Dispossessed*, published by Farrar, Straus and Giroux in 1948.

3. Berryman, *His Toy, His Dream, His Rest: 308 Dream Songs* (New York: Farrar, Straus and Giroux, 1967), p. ix.

4. Mariani, p. 134.

5. Thomas Lask, "Sought Own True Voice," *New York Times*, 8 January 1972.

6. Quoted by Mariani, *Dream Song*, p. 95. "Father and Son" was written in 1938.

7. "The Ball Poem," p. 894.

8. Quoted by Mariani, *Dream Song*, p. 198.

9. Ibid., p. 8.

10. Ibid., pp. 7–8.

11. Ibid., p. 17.

12. Ibid., p. 95.

13. Ibid., p. 309. This draft for a "Dream Song" was written in 1957.

14. Berryman, "Changes," *Poets on Poetry*, ed. Howard Nemerov (New York: Basic Books, 1966), p. 98.

15. Berryman, "Dream Song 42," *77 Dream Songs* (New York: Farrar, Straus and Giroux, 1964), p. 46.

16. Ibid.

17. Berryman, "Dream Song 384," *His Toy, His Dream, His Rest*, p. 316.

18. Quoted by Mariani, *Dream Song*, p. 142.

19. Ibid.

20. Ibid., pp. 142–43.

21. Berryman, "Eleven Addresses to the Lord," *Love & Fame* (New York: Farrar, Straus and Giroux, 1970), p. 91.

22. Quoted by Mariani, p. 338. Berryman wrote these lines in 1958.

23. Berryman, "Henry's Understanding," *Delusions, Etc.* (New York: Farrar, Straus and Giroux, 1972), p. 53.

24. Quoted by Mariani, *Dream Song*, p. 219.

25. Ibid., p. 220.

26. Berryman, "Of Suicide," *Love & Fame*, pp. 69–70.

27. Related to the author's father by Kathryn N. Weldy, poet and Berryman acquaintance.

28. Berryman, "Uncollected Dream Song," *Henry's Fate and Other Poems, 1967–1972* (New York: Farrar, Straus and Giroux, 1977), p. 28.

29. Quoted by Mariani, *Dream Song*, p. 222.

30. Ibid.

31. Ibid., pp. 232–33. These lines were written by Berryman in 1950.

32. Berryman, "Dream Song 162," *His Toy, His Dream, His Rest*, p. 91.

33. Quoted by Mariani, *Dream Song*, p. 481.

34. Ibid., p. 412. Berryman wrote these lines in 1965.

35. Quoted by Mariani, *Dream Song*, p. 499.

36. Berryman, his final poem, *Henry's Fate and Other Poems*, p. 93.

37. Quoted by Mariani, *Dream Song*, p. 500.

Anne Sexton

T HROUGHOUT HER LIFE, BESET AS SHE WAS OVER THE YEARS BY HER extreme, often incapacitating, mental illness that paradoxically also served as the wellspring of much of her poetry, Anne Sexton repeatedly attempted to kill herself. So, when she at last succeeded on October 4, 1974, her death could have hardly come as a surprise to either her friends or family no matter how much it would, naturally enough, sadden them. For most of her adult life, Sexton simply reveled in self-destruction. Constantly unfaithful to her long-suffering husband, Kayo, she routinely hurt all those closest to her, drove wedges between herself and her two daughters, and even attempted to coerce the older girl into having a sexual relationship with her. Indeed she saw herself as a "possessed witch" haunting the night sky: "dreaming evil, I have done my hitch/ over the plain houses, light by light:/ lonely thing, twelve-fingered, out of mind./ A woman like that is not a woman, quite./ I have been her kind."[1]

Far from resembling an old crone, however, Sexton, with her model's figure, good looks, and flair for fashion, was rather the image of the glamour girl, the long-legged, dark-haired, blue-eyed knockout. She dressed the part and always wore bright red lipstick.[2] She kept her good looks intact right up to the day of her death despite the fact that she was a heavy smoker and substance abuser. Nonetheless, she had done great damage to her body guzzling alcohol and popping pills.[3] She partied with reckless abandon, but also used alcohol and prescription medications as a crutch, as a way to fend off her phobias and allow herself to loosen up. Always shaky before appearing in public whether accepting an award, teaching a class, giving a poetry reading, or appearing with her chamber rock group *Anne Sexton and Her Kind*, she would almost inevitably get loaded beforehand. Only in a beclouded state could she steel herself to step out on stage and face an audience. She also used alcohol and drugs to blot out the anguish and emotional torture that periodically gripped her due to her disease, which could never be diagnosed with complete certainty and, throughout her life, led to numerous hospital stays. Indeed, Sexton overdosed on her prescription medications, antidepressants and tranquilizers for the most part, as well as on over-the-counter sleeping pills, on many occasions. She hoarded all the tablets and capsules she could manage to get her hands on, and her purses, whenever she traveled, always overbrimmed with them. She became so dependent on these medications that she could not sleep without taking a nightly cocktail of various pills mixed together. She also always kept in reserve a bottle of Nembutals that she blithely referred to as her "kill-me" pills should the need for oblivion and death ever grow too pressing and overwhelming. In addition to tranquilizers, her doctors put her on the powerful psychotropic drug Thorazine. In Sexton's case, the drug was prescribed to treat a manic-depressive condition. However, it is more often used to treat schizophrenia and other psychoses. The drug also has a number of disturbing side effects, many of which were as yet unknown when Sexton began taking the medication. No doubt Thorazine also added to the effects of both the alcohol and the other tranquilizers and antidepressants she was taking. Sexton would go on and off the drug according to her own whim—whenever she wanted a suntan (Thorazine makes the user's skin sting and burn whenever it is exposed to sunlight) or, more importantly, whenever she became blocked in her writing and needed a manic high. Such interruptions boded no good for her course of treatment and could precipitate a suicide attempt. As was the case with virtually all the medications she used for legitimate purposes, there came a time when Sexton also used Thorazine (in this instance in combination with other drugs) in order to overdose—she did this in the final year of her life. Discovered comatose a day later, she was rushed to the hospital and saved, though at first it was thought that she had sustained severe brain damage.

In her poem "The Addict," Sexton calls herself a "sleepmonger" and a "deathmonger."[4] She "keeps in practice" with capsules in her "palms each night" for she has "promised to die."[5] She is "merely staying in shape"[6] when she nightly drugs herself into oblivion. She experiences a little death every time she swallows her capsules and crawls under the sheets. For Sexton, pills don't merely resemble colored candy to be greedily swallowed down, they also warm and comfort the user like a loving parent. Taking the drugs, she experiences a prolonged embrace:

> The pills are a mother, but better,
> every color and as good as sour balls.
> I'm on a diet from death.[7]

Indeed, throughout her poetry, Sexton constantly exhibits and investigates her desire for death. Like Robert Lowell whom she studied under along with Sylvia Plath at Boston University in the late 1950s, Sexton primarily wrote poems in an autobiographical or confessional mode. Her topics include not only her parents, her children, her life as a suburban housewife, the twists and turns in her relationship with her husband, her adulterous affairs with both men and women, her physical ailments, her periods, her body parts—she celebrates her uterus in one poem—but also her breakdowns and hospitalizations, her self-abandonment, and her wish for death. She felt that her problems, her madness, her self-hatred, and her death wish mirrored the condition of many others, men and women both, then living in America. These fellow sufferers were "her kind." Whether they affirmed or denied it, Sexton's concerns were also their own: "sometimes in private,/ my kitchen, your kitchen,/ my face, your face."[8] The misery and torment she constantly met kept prompting her to re-ask, both in her own life and in her poetry, Hamlet's famous ontological question. The title of one of her collections *Live or Die* (which would bring her the Pulitzer Prize), paraphrases the Dane's words, though the answer she provides to his question in the book's final poem celebrating the birth of a litter of puppies—to stubbornly endure and persist—effectively begs it. The programmatic concluding lines were written at white heat to meet a publisher's deadline. The finale, "So I won't hang around in my hospital shift,/ repeating the Black Mass and all of it./ I say *Live, Live* because of the sun,/ the dream, the excitable gift"[9] seems uncharacteristically optimistic. Sexton herself would opt for the darker alternative. Death was simply too seductive for her. Could the ultimate choice she would make ever really be in doubt? For years, she contemplated her end, even planned a posthumous volume of what she felt was her best verse. (Ironically she would finally be persuaded to publish *The Death Notebooks* during her lifetime.) Again and again in her poems she expresses her longing for oblivion and extinction. Words such as "dead," "death," "die," and "suicide" frequently appear in their titles, such as "Wanting to Die," "The Truth the Dead Know," "The Suicide Note," "Godfather Death," "The Death of the Fathers," and "For Mr. Death Who Stands with His Door Open," to cite several prominent examples. She communicates her longing most poignantly perhaps in "Wanting to Die." Written in 1966, the poem would appear in her *Live or Die* collection. While the title of the volume suggests that the suicidally inclined person is constantly deliberating between life and death, in the poem itself, Sexton writes that for such individuals the question of living or dying never even arises. The suicide wants death and is determined to do away with himself. Room for debate exists only as to the method of release. Sexton admits to having made two attempts on her own life. Death did not possess her; she possessed death and acquired his magic. She did not concern herself with her body. Considering it dispensable and superfluous, she had no difficulty betraying it. Suicide attempts may fail, but the person who has tried never forgets the beauty and magic: "Still-born they don't always die,/ but dazzled they can't forget a drug so sweet/ that even children would look on and smile."[10]

The first of her many psychiatrists, Martin Orne, however, disagreeing with many of Sexton's family members, holds that the poet's suicide was not inevitable. Had she not been deprived in the last months of her life of the interpersonal braces and supports she had developed over the years in his and his colleagues' therapy sessions, she might have (he feels) very well overcome her difficulties of that time. She could have undergone yet another rebirth similar to the one she experienced at age twenty-nine when she first entered his care following her initial nervous break-down after the birth of her second daughter, and still be alive today. Indeed, through therapy she had not only overcome profound feelings of personal inadequacy, she had also acquired her identity as poet, for it was at Orne's suggestion that she started writing. Sexton never put her demons totally behind her, however. She continued to be quite sick all her adult life, from the time of her daughter Joy's birth in 1955 right up to the day of her death. However, while never completely stable and balanced and always prone to retrogression, sudden mood swings, deep bouts of depression, and even fugue- or trancelike states that could last for hours at a time, she had made impressive strides forward in terms of her health. As a result of her therapy, espe-cially Dr. Orne's exhortation that she take up the pen, Anne Sexton had emerged like a beautiful butterfly from the envelope of silk the ugly worm had spun about itself. An entirely new being or persona sprang from the cocoon. Sexton loved palindromes, her favorite tellingly being "rats live on no evil star."[11] She reveals the relevance this particular instance of verbal magic held for her in an early poem with the unwieldy title "An Obsessive Combination of Ontological Inscape, Trickery and Love":

> Busy, with an idea for a code, I write
> signals hurrying from left to right,
> or right to left, by obscure routes,
> for my own reason; taking a word like "writes"
> down tiers of tries until its secret rites
> make sense; or until, suddenly, RATS
> can amazingly and funnily become STAR[12]

Language had the power not only to save but also to transform. Sexton herself had undergone the miraculous change from rodent to luminary, and the metamorphosis had come about due to the witchery of her wordplay, the magic contained within her pen. It didn't happen instantly. She had to work hard at refining her verse. Although profoundly agoraphobic, she started attending workshops, where she listened to and learned from the criticisms of teachers and peers, and began putting her poems through many drafts. Finally she began submitting her work for publication, which was widely accepted by prestigious periodicals. From there her career really began to streak. In no time at all, Houghton Mifflin agreed to publish her first collection, *To Bedlam and Part Way Back*. The book was accepted in May of 1959, just four years after her initial mental collapse. Six more collections, *All My Pretty Ones*, *Live or Die*, *Love Poems*, *Transformations*, *The Book of Folly*, and *The Death Notebooks*, would follow in her lifetime. Three more—*The Awful Rowing toward God*, *45 Mercy Street*, and *Words for Dr. Y.*—would appear after her death, and still other uncol-lected verse would eventually be published in *Complete Poems* (1981). Sexton also wrote a handful of short stories, authored several children's books in collaboration with Maxine Kumin, and completed several drafts of a play dealing with a suicide who, after her death, reviews her past life and relives an incestuous childhood episode between herself and her father. This is witnessed by a beloved aunt whose own thwarted sexuality had previously found "innocent" release in cuddling sessions with the child. A horrible recognition is forced upon the old lady when she accidentally stumbles upon father and daughter and she is driven mad. One of the play's many incarnations, *Mercy Street*, was produced off-Broadway for a short time in 1969, earning several sterling notices before it closed, but none of the play's various versions have as yet reached print. Sexton also took an unsuccessful stab at writing a comic novel in the manner of John Cheever and John Updike. Tentatively titled *Marriage—USA*, the unfinished fiction deals with a premenopausal suburban housewife whose husband refuses any longer to make love to her. As a result of his rejection, she subsequently seeks solace in the arms of both her priest and her psychiatrist. Chapter drafts and notes for the novel exist but, as of this date, remain unpublished. Like much of Sexton's poetry, the novel would have been at least partially autobiographical. Sexton had a long affair with Dr. Ollie Zweizung, one of her many psychiatrists, making love to him during therapy sessions for which he charged his regular fee, much to the chagrin of various of Sexton's friends and former therapists. She likewise had intimate relations with Dr. Anne Wilder, also a practicing psychiatrist and the second cousin of Thornton Wilder, though Sexton was never one of her patients. Additionally, she wrote flirtatious letters (as was her wont with all her male correspondents, most of whom, however, were fellow poets) to a young monk, Brother Dennis Farrell, while also asking him for spiritual guidance. Farrell, who had written Sexton first due to his admiration for her poetry, thought readers of their correspondence would see the couple as a modern-day Éloïse and Abélard.[13] Sexton's later poems would increasingly dwell on religious themes, including a sequence on Jesus. Although divine, Sexton's Christ is the exemplar of human suffering. He lusts after his mother— "in His dream/ He desired Mary./ His penis sang like a dog"[14]—and thinks only about his own needs and wants and not those of others, and is frightened yet fascinated by his approaching death. He resembles no one so much as Anne Sexton herself (she, too, had a mother named Mary). Indeed, her Christ is decidedly feminine. Tellingly, she presents the Mother as being equally divine. Jesus sheds blood, while Mary transforms her own blood into milk that the Christ child drinks: "When the cow gives blood/ and the Christ is born/ we must all eat sacrifices. We must all eat beautiful women."[15] She enjoyed speaking to Catholic priests during the last few years of her life and felt that, due to her life circumstances, she had attained a special understanding of Jesus all her own. The thirty-nine poems that comprise *The Awful Rowing toward God* also deal with religious themes. Although their correspondence had ended years before, she would dedicate the volume to Farrell as well as to one of her former lovers, the poet James Wright. God was much on Sexton's mind toward the end. She seemed to find a source of solace in religious questioning just as she did in psychotherapy, poetry, pill popping, and promiscuity. While drafts of her incomplete novel and her play remain unpublished, many of Sexton's letters have reached print, collected under the title of *Anne Sexton: A Self-Portrait in Letters in 1977.*

Had it not been for the intervention of others (she had numerous guardians and good Samaritans who watched over her during her lifetime), Sexton's suicide could have come much earlier—when, having written nothing, her suffering would have remained anonymous and her death just another statistic. However, due to her own tenacious effort and because of the suffering forbearance of her family (in becoming a poet, she largely neglected and put aside both her familial duties; her husband and children, however, had to constantly minister to her needs and be ever vigilant in monitoring and watching over her in order to ensure not only her well-being but her very survival), Sexton lived long enough to effect her tremendous makeover. The suicidal, alcoholic suburban housewife with only a finishing school education and average grades, who had been struck down by postpartum depression; who had been unable to manage a household; who would not cook and clean; who preferred to be mothered rather than to mother; who could not cope with the incessant, unrelenting demands of her young children on her time and affection; and who had to be repeatedly institutionalized because of her periodic mental breakdowns, underwent a stunning metamorphosis. Out of the ashes of her old life of pain, mental illness, and bovine domesticity, the new Anne Sexton rose: a nationally recognized poet whose work would bring her success and money beyond all her expectations. Her poems would be widely anthologized; she would enter the canon in her own lifetime. In addition to winning numerous awards and honorary doctorates, Sexton—the mediocre student—would attain a faculty position at Boston University as a professor of poetry. The agoraphobe who could not bear to leave the house to shop at the supermarket and who even during her later years could never bring herself to travel anywhere without a chaperon, would crisscross the country on the lecture and poetry reading circuit, tour with her own musical group, cross the Atlantic and drive all over Europe, and even, in Hemingwayesque fashion, venture out on a safari in Nairobi, Africa. Despite her tragic suicide at age forty-five, Sexton's life still must be regarded as a profound success story. Considering her illness and her many addictions, the strides she made and the obstacles she overcame seem all but miraculous.

On November 9, 1928, Anne Gray Harvey was born in Newton, Massachusetts, the youngest of three daughters. Her parents, Ralph and Mary Gray Staples Harvey, were members of the leisure class, affluent, attractive, affable, and pleasure-seeking. They liked to entertain and mix with other members of their social set. Ralph Harvey was a successful business man, a wool manufacturer, who had established and then ran his own firm, the R. C. Harvey Company. He was on the road a great deal of the time hawking his processed wool to clothing manufacturers and earning fat commissions. He had a lifelong passion for automobiles and liked to race his speedboat. A heavy drinker, philanderer, and general hell raiser, he was, despite his wild, fun-loving nature, nonetheless nothing short of a despot at home. Very painstaking and particular when it came to his dress, he demanded that his children likewise be fastidious about their appearances. Anne, however, could never live up to his (or her own) high and impossible standards and constantly brought down his wrath on herself. He found her noisy and shrill. In his opinion, she also had bad table manners. She wriggled and squirmed and twisted her hair with her fingers. As a result, her father banned her from the dining room until she was eleven. She took her meals with the family nanny, a nurse who oversaw the daily activities of both Anne and her elder sisters when they were children.

Sexton's mother also drank and tended to be cold and distant with her daughters. Anne was always asking for her love, never knowing if her mother would treat her kindly or else, too busy and preoccupied to make time for her, rebuff her advances. Later in life, conflict would persist between mother and daughter. They were very competitive with one another. Mary's father, Arthur Gray Staples, had been a respected newspaper editor and columnist for the *Lewiston Evening Journal*. Although she never worked for her father's paper, Mary was herself something of a writer. She wrote long letters to her husband when he was on the road as well as birthday verses and family skits. Much to Sexton's distress, once she herself began to write poems, her mother followed suit.

Until her death, however, Mary Gray remained sharply critical of Anne. She was skeptical about her daughter's mental illness and suspected her of having affairs when her husband did a stint in the navy early in their marriage and later when he was on the road as a salesman for the R. C. Harvey Company. Anne and Alfred Muller Sexton (nicknamed Kayo after the cartoon character in the *Moon Mullins* strip because, like him, he had been put to bed in a dresser drawer as a baby) had met in 1948 while Anne was attending finishing school in Boston and Kayo was a pre-med major at Colgate University in Hampton, New York. They eloped when Anne mistakenly thought she had become pregnant. Due to the marriage, Kayo had to forgo the rest of his college education, the first of many sacrifices he made for Anne. She deeply loved her husband, but became very susceptible to flirtations whenever he was away for any length of time. Bored and in need of affection, she would continually drift into short-lived casual affairs. Sexton claimed that she had been careful to keep her mother in the dark concerning her various liaisons, but the elder woman nonetheless somehow intuited what was going on. She confronted her daughter and said, "You're just like me—and I know."[16] In 1970, many years after the deaths of both her parents, Sexton received a call from an old family acquaintance, Azel Mack. He dropped a bombshell on her by claiming that he, and not R. C. Harvey, was in actuality her biological father. He brought a lock of hair that he claimed was Anne's, cut for him by Mary Gray when Sexton was a baby, and a print of a studio portrait of Anne at age sixteen. As Mary Gray was dead, there was no way for Sexton to substantiate Mack's claim. Other family members were far from convinced, but the possibility lingered for the poet that her mother had also become lonely and restless when *her* husband was away on business trips, visiting the same clients that Kayo would later regularly see, and that she herself might very well have been an illegitimate child.

Long before Mack's revelation, however, Sexton came to see herself as her mother's double. When Anne first entered treatment and underwent a prolonged hospitalization, Mary Gray took Sexton's eldest daughter, her granddaughter Linda, to live with her for a time while the baby was nursed and cared for by Sexton's mother-in-law Billie. Mary also helped with Anne's expenses, chipping in to pay her psychiatrist and hospital bills. To cheer her daughter up after her release from the mental institution, she commissioned Anne's portrait by a local artist. Sexton's condition nonetheless continued to deteriorate and, shortly after her release, she attempted suicide on two occasions, the first of many attempts to do away with herself. However, when Sexton recovered to the point where she felt she could follow Dr. Orne's advice to enroll in several college courses, she asked her mother to pay the fees and was peremptorily refused. Mary Gray told Anne she would never be able to do the work. Shortly thereafter, Mary developed breast cancer and would have to undergo a radical mastectomy. She claimed that her disease had been caused by stress brought on by her daughter's breakdown and suicide attempts.

While she was recovering from surgery, Mary Gray had her own portrait painted by the same artist in a pose similar to that of her daughter's. Sexton indicates just how much she identified with her mother at this time in her 1958 poem "The Double Image," which refers to the two portraits her mother had commissioned, each of a woman who had undergone a terrible illness and come close to death. The two portraits hung across from each other in the Harvey home: "And this was the cave of the mirror,/ that double woman who stares/ at herself, as if she were petrified."[17] The poem is, however, addressed to Sexton's own daughter Joy. She tells her that she "chose two times / to kill myself"[18] rather than accept the identity of being her mother and explains why she had up to now let her "grow in another place"[19] (i.e., sent her to live with her Grandmother Billie). She ends the poem by declaring her acceptance of the mother's role with Joy's return to her care. She also confesses why she (or a part of herself) initially wanted a child, specifically a baby daughter: "I, who was never quite sure/ about being a girl, needed another / life, another image to remind me./ And this was my worst guilt; you could not cure/ nor soothe it. I made you to find me."[20]

When Mary Gray finally succumbed to cancer in 1959 (Ralph Harvey would die only months later), Sexton felt tremendous guilt but also a great sense of abandonment. She would write many poems memorializing both her parents. Again and again she would address her dead in her verse. One of her consolations, however, was that Mary Gray had lived long enough to read "The Double Image" and say that she liked it. Sexton would continue to identify with her mother throughout her life. Discussing "The Double Image" before reading it on the radio some years later, she would say, "The mother-daughter relationship is more poignant than Romeo and Juliet. Just as Oedipus is more interesting."[21]

Mary Gray Harvey was distant with not just Anne but with her other two daughters as well, forcing each child to seek affection from an alternate source. Anne's eldest sister, Jane, was Ralph Harvey's favorite. She shared his interests in sports, automobiles, and breeding bull terriers. She also had good table manners and did not fidget or speak out of turn. Like Sexton, however, she, too, would commit suicide in middle age. The second sister, Blanche, was the most intellectual of the three during their formative years. She became the darling of her maternal grandfather, the newspaperman Arthur Gray Staples. The most self-controlled and balanced of the three sisters, she was also the only child Ralph and Mary deemed worthy to send to college.

Anne, as a young girl, would turn to her spinster grandaunt Anna Ladd Dingley—or Nana as she called her—who would move into the Harvey home when Anne was eleven. Before then, Anne would see her whenever she visited her grandparents, as Nana then lived with them, her sister Jane being Arthur Gray Staples's wife and Sexton's grandmother. The grandaunt and the young girl would begin to form a strong bond with one another even before Dingley moved into the Harvey household. Nana would frequently cuddle and hug Anne and give her the time and attention that Mary Gray would not. She also liked to rub and massage the girl's back and shoulders and sprinkle them with talcum powder, activities the young Anne delighted in. The old woman quickly became a sort of substitute mother for the girl. As they shared a first name, they called each other "the twins."[22] When Sexton was approximately five years old, she told her grandaunt that she had an invisible brother named Bobby Pressit. Nana played along with Anne and even went so far as to purchase a portrait of a young boy at an antique store—they pretended he was the said Bobby—and hang it in her room at the Staples's house, so that whenever Anne came to visit, Bobby could be there, too.

Significantly, Anna Ladd Dingley had been a writer by profession. She was a reporter for the *Lewiston Evening Journal* and eventually became a part owner of the paper as well as one of its editors. She took an interest early in her career in the plight of the mentally ill and once tried unsuccessfully to have herself committed so she could write an exposé on lunatic asylums. Once she moved into the Harvey home, she and Anne were almost inseparable for the next two years. The love between Nana and Anne, however, continued on an abnormally childlike level. There was no growth or development in their relationship either intellectually or emotionally. They persisted in their cuddling and in their fantasizings about the imaginary Bobby. At age thirteen, Anne began to draw away. She was now interested in socializing with children her own age and chasing after boys. Shortly thereafter Dingley would suffer a mental breakdown after first losing her hearing during the course of a symphony concert. When Anne visited her in her room, the elderly woman struck out at her. Sexton vividly remembered her aunt shouting, "You're not Anne!" and saying that she was "horrible and disgusting."[23] Once she even attacked the teenager with a nail file. The old woman would be sent first to a mental hospital where she would undergo electroshock therapy. Sometime afterward, she would be committed to a nursing home where she would die ten years later. By then, however, her mental condition had vastly improved—indeed, in short order, she would return to normal.

In 1957, during the course of her own therapy with Dr. Orne, Sexton began recalling (or else inventing) memories of having been fondled by her father when she was a child and he was drunk and angry with her. These recollections surfaced after Sexton had entered a trancelike state and an alternate persona named Elizabeth had emerged in her stead. Sexton's father had once called Anne "a little bitch" while paddling her as a child, and, in trance, Sexton associated the name Elizabeth with this phrase. "Elizabeth" claimed to Orne that, as a child, Anne had taken her presence for that of the imaginary brother Bobby and that Aunt Nana was the only adult who could detect the difference between "Elizabeth" and Anne. The memories of the incestuous episode varied greatly from session to session. Sometimes Anne was only five or six but on other occasions she was a young teenager. Alternatively Nana witnessed and did not witness the event. Sexton, however, made a mental connection between the real cuddling sessions she had shared with her grandaunt and her father's alleged gropings. Orne feels that, while the memory seemed real to Anne, the event probably never occurred. Her father had certainly been abusive with her on occasion, but Sexton tended to sexualize everything. Moreover, she had been reading and writing about incest at the time this memory surfaced. Orne also feels that Sexton did not suffer from multiple personality disorder. Once his interest in the Elizabeth persona dropped, so did his patient's. After a time, Elizabeth stopped appearing in their therapy sessions; nor would she ever reemerge before any of Sexton's subsequent doctors.

One characteristic of Sexton's disease, according to Orne, was that she tended to take on or mimic symptoms of other mentally ill patients she came in contact with during her many hospitalizations. She also read a great many books on psychiatry and various mental disorders. Orne suspects that Sexton came across case studies of split personalities, read about hidden childhood memories surfacing during therapy, and consciously or unconsciously parroted and imitated what she had found out in books in her sessions with him.[24] Her family members tend to concur with his analysis and strongly dispute the contention that Ralph Harvey ever sexually molested Anne. Several of Sexton's friends disagree, most notably Lois Ames, a psychiatric social worker. She believes Sexton underwent sexual abuse at the hands of both her grandaunt and her father. Sexton would later dramatize the alleged incident with Ralph Harvey in the various versions of her play. Like Virginia Woolf, who had been molested as a child by her half-brother George Duckworth, Sexton heard voices in her head, or at least claimed that she did. She wrote Orne: "I am looking for Nana—I know she is here—every one who dies follows me. . . . The voices are small in my ear—they are tiny because they are shouting from so far away. Sometimes the voice is a stranger's—but he is dead—I do not know him. The dead people control me—they don't comfort me—they say awful things—I am afraid—they laugh at me—they can see through me."[25] She even went so far as to claim that at times she was possessed by the spirits of the departed, especially by the vengeful ghost of

Nana. In one of her play's numerous drafts, she externalizes these inner voices haunting her. In this version, the Sexton character Daisy finds herself in the after-life surrounded by barkers calling out to her as if she were at a carnival. They try to entice the suicide into their various booths with witty and often obscene come-ons.

Throughout her life, Sexton kept trying to recreate and recapture the love she had for Nana as a child. She told Orne: "I never want to go beyond that moment. I want to lie on the couch and be with Nana where I was loved."[26] For all the years of their marriage, Kayo acted as a Nana surrogate—that is, when he was at home and not on the road, where he could constantly and soothingly reassure his wife that she was a good girl. Had he been able to stay with her constantly, she probably would never had had affairs. Her need for reassurance and personal affirmation, however, pressed forever upon her; it was unremitting and constant. She would have to seek approval (sexual high regard being a particularly potent form of endorsement for her) if love and affection were not permanently showered upon her. When she started gaining notoriety as a poet, she strove to become sexually inti-mate with as many of her male peers as she could. She would try to sexualize her relationships with all her various mentors and fellow practitioners, but her lovers would not be limited to poets. She would take up with all sorts of men—if they could step in and gratify her, for she was needy and insatiable both. Significantly Wilder's first name was also Anne. Once again Sexton found a Nana substitute, a second twin, another Anne. She would characterize her relationship with Wilder in a letter to the psychiatrist as being deeply fulfilling: "It was my need, my overture. Later we'll go into why the need to sexualize the tenderness (the never-had tender-ness for me) of mother. O, Mary, little mother . . ."[27] As her daughters went through puberty and matured into adults, Sexton reversed roles with them. They would start acting the part of mother to her, watching over her constantly and ministering to her many needs. Sexton celebrated her eldest daughter Linda's transformation from girl into woman in the poem, "Little Girl, My String Bean, My Lovely Woman." She tells her daughter men will come to her, "young Romans/ at noon where they belong."[28] They will bring "ladders and hammers" to facilitate their siege:

> But before they enter
> I will have said.
> *Your bones are lovely*,
> and before their strange hands
> there was always this hand that formed.[29]

When Kayo was away, Anne would crawl in bed with Linda. While the girl feigned sleep, the mother would lie beside her and masturbate. Mother and daughter had long been close. Linda's love of Grimm's fairy tales inspired Sexton to rework the stories in a series of dark, humorous poems collected under the title of *Transfor-mations*. They pit children against monsters and witches. Youth and Age grapple for supremacy. The young are tested and must strain under heavy burdens and overcome great afflictions in order to triumph. Linda certainly had to brave great ordeals with her mother. She would later claim that Anne attempted to force the Nana role on her: "It was as if she now needed to cast me in the role of the disapproving parent—Nana at the doorway—because it was inevitable that I would be hurt and disgusted, for my father's sake, by her philandering."[30] She kept making Linda come into her bedroom and sleep with her whenever Kayo was away. Once, when she was fifteen, the girl awoke in the middle of the night unable to breathe. Her mother lay on top of her, rubbing against her and kissing her on the mouth.

For several years, Sexton's husband and daughters provided her life with both structure and security. Because of their watchfulness, she attained a certain level of stability and was able to fulfill her ambitions as poet. At first Kayo did not like her having literary pretensions. He thought her self-absorption selfish and her career as poetess merely an extension of her illness and her willful abandonment of him and the girls. She also was able to thoroughly manipulate him. She would goad him into ugly fights and he would strike her with open hands. Sexton welcomed such marital strife because she knew that after the fires cooled, Kayo would inevitably experience great remorse and try to make up for the fight by becoming particularly affectionate and tender with her. He and Linda would both end up in therapy. Everyone in the family would be seeing psychiatrists. Kayo, however, determined to stick the marriage out. He stood by his wife, even though he knew about her many infidelities. Thus it was particularly difficult for him when Anne sued for divorce in the early seventies. Her chief caretaker would move out. At the same time, her daughters began pursuing their own lives and putting more distance between themselves and their mother. They were less and less willing to serve as her guardians. Sexton's numerous addictions were also gradually taking their toll. Although she continued writing until right before death, her work had begun to seriously atrophy.

However, like Yukio Mishima, Anne Sexton brought an important work to conclusion on the day of her suicide. She and her longtime friend, collaborator, and fellow poet Maxine Kumin met on a lunch date and together went over the galley sheets of *The Awful Rowing toward God,* due out the following March, making last minute revisions and corrections. Earlier in the day—the fourth of October, 1974—Anne had visited her current therapist, Barbara Schwartz. She brought a new poem, "The Green Room," written especially for her. Sexton had been in treatment with Schwartz for nine months. She would leave her cigarettes and lighter in the therapist's office, perhaps a significant signal. After saying goodbye to Kumin after their lunch, Sexton returned home. She wrote no suicide note. After removing her rings from her fingers and depositing them into her purse, she wrapped herself in an old fur coat of her mother's as if to rewomb herself. After drinking several tumblers of vodka, she refilled a glass to take with her to the car, then stepped out to the garage, shutting all the doors before getting into her red Cougar and sitting behind the wheel. She turned the key in the ignition and put on the radio.

Notes

1. Anne Sexton, "Her Kind," *The Complete Poems*, foreword by Maxine Kumin (Boston: Houghton Mifflin, 1981), p. 15.

2. See Diane Middlebrook, *Anne Sexton: A Biography* (Boston: Houghton Mifflin, 1991), pp. 19, 96–97.

3. Ibid., pp. 139–40, 380.

4. Sexton, "The Addict," *Complete Poems*, p. 165.

5. Ibid.

6. Ibid.

7. Ibid.

8. Sexton, "For John Who Begs Me Not to Enquire Further," *Complete Poets*, p. 34.

9. Sexton, "Live," *Complete Poems*, p. 170.

10. Sexton, "Wanting to Die," *Complete Poems*, p. 143.

11. Quoted by Middlebrook, *Anne Sexton: A Biography*, p. 124.

12. Sexton, "An Obsessive Combination of Ontological Inscape, Trickery and Love," *Voices: A Journal of Poetry* 169 (1959): 34.

13. See Middlebnrook, pp. 182–84, 239–40, 259–60.

14. Sexton, "Jesus Asleep," *Complete Poems*, p. 338.

15. Sexton, "The Author of the Jesus Papers Speaks," *Complete Poems*, p. 345.

16. Quoted by Middlebrook, *Anne Sexton*, p. 41.

17. Sexton, "The Double Image," *Complete Poems*, p. 27.

18. Ibid., p. 35.

19. Ibid., p. 36.

20. Ibid., pp. 41–42.

21. Quoted by Middlebrook, *Anne Sexton*, p. 87.

22. Ibid., pp. 14, 38.

23. Ibid., p. 16.

24. Ibid., pp. 55–56.

25. Ibid., p. 219.

26. Ibid., p. 167.

27. Ibid., p. 239.

28. Sexton, "Little Girl, My String Bean, My Lovely Woman," *Complete Poems*, p. 147.

29. Ibid.

30. Quoted by Middlebrook, *Anne Sexton*, p. 325.

Romain Gary

THE NOVELIST, DIPLOMAT, AND WORLD WAR II HERO ROMAIN GARY died from a self-inflicted gunshot wound to the head in his Left Bank apartment in Paris, on December 2, 1980. At the time of his death, he was undergoing treatment for anxiety and nervous tension. He was sixty-six years old. His former wife, the American movie star Jean Seberg, had killed herself fifteen months earlier, on September 8, 1979, at the age of forty. Her final exit had also taken place in Paris, where her body was discovered in the back seat of her car. She succumbed from an overdose of barbiturates and alcohol, leaving Gary despondent.

The novelist alleged that his ex-wife's problems had begun in 1970 when she prematurely went into labor three months after an item concerning her pregnancy appeared in Joyce Haber's gossip column in the *Los Angeles Times*. Seberg was not identified by name in the May 19 column, but referred to only as "Miss A." However, the identity of the actress was immediately recognizable to the cognoscenti, for Haber characterized "Miss A" as a well-known white Hollywood actress who supported the black nationalist cause in America, and Seberg had volubly championed the Black Panther movement and donated large sums of money to the organization. Furthermore, the article specified that Miss A was married to a former official in the French government who also had a second career in the arts. It was abundantly clear to everyone in the know whom Haber was writing about. The item concluded with the following bombshell: "And now, according to all those really 'in' international sources, Topic A is the baby Miss A is expecting and its father. Papa's said to be a rather prominent Black Panther."[1] *Newsweek* picked up the story and named Seberg. The magazine reported that the baby the actress was carrying had been fathered by "a black activist she had met in California."[2] When Seberg saw the *Newsweek* article, she was in the sixth month of her pregnancy. Traumatized by the cruel allegations, she attempted to kill herself in Majorca by overdosing on pills. She was found unconscious on the beach and resuscitated. Gary placed her in a private Swiss clinic. She did not miscarry at the time, but the following month, two months prematurely, she went into labor. Doctors delivered the baby, a daughter named Nina Hart Gary, by Caesarean section. The infant, who was Caucasian, died two days later (August 28, 1970). Presumably Romain Gary had been the father.

The novelist would later claim that his wife became psychotic after the infant's death, and, in a 1974 interview, Seberg herself admitted that she had "cracked up."[3] The couple buried their daughter in Seberg's hometown of Marshalltown, Iowa. In the 1974 interview, the actress described the funeral as follows: "I did the whole deal. We opened the coffin and took 180 photographs and everybody in Marshalltown who was curious what color the baby was got a chance to check it out. A lot of them came to look."[4] Gary and his wife sued *Newsweek* for libel and won $10,000 in damages. The two, however, would drift apart and eventually divorce. Seberg would later marry the Algerian actor Ahmed Hasni. However, she never fully recovered from the death of her child. Shortly after her suicide, Gary revealed that "every year on the anniversary of that still birth she tried to take her life."[5] He also stated for the record that he always believed that the child had been his.

Haber never revealed the identities of her "really 'in' international sources." Shortly after the death of his ex-wife, however, Gary claimed that he had discovered the origin of the information. In an emotional news conference, he revealed to the world that the story had been planted by the Federal Bureau of Investigation as part of its counterintelligence program COINTELPRO. Gary alleged that the FBI had plotted to defame and discredit his wife in retaliation for her financial support of the Black Panther party. He accused the agency of ruining Seberg's life and asserted that its action had caused her suicide. A week later, the FBI conceded that its agents had indeed plotted to leak news of Seberg's pregnancy to the media in 1970, but that the story had been broken independently by Haber shortly after the bureau had given the go-ahead to its Los Angeles division to disseminate the rumor. In addition to admitting that the FBI had planned to sully Seberg's reputation, the bureau's director in 1979, William H. Webster, made public all documents pertinent to the case and gave the following statement:

> The days when the FBI used derogatory information to combat advocates of unpopular causes have long since passed. We are out of that business forever.
>
> The collection and dissemination of information today is carefully regulated by privacy statutes and by Attorney General guidelines which will soon be embodied as a part of a legislative charter for the FBI. Criminal conduct is the key requirement for all domestic investigations of the FBI.[6]

Webster claimed that, early in 1970, a "sensitive source,"[7] whose identity he refused to make public, had disclosed to agents of the Los Angeles office of the FBI that Seberg had engaged in an adulterous affair with a Black Panther leader and had become pregnant with his child. The bureau claimed the putative father was still alive in 1979 and deleted his name from all the documents it released to the press. This, Webster explained, was standard FBI policy whenever the agency issued documents containing the names of living persons. Despite the FBI's protestation that the activist was alive in 1979, reporters speculated that the Black Panther in question was Malcolm X's cousin Allen Donaldson. Donaldson, who took the name Hakim Abdullah Jamal, was brutally murdered in the early 1970s.

In addition to refusing to name Seberg's alleged lover, Webster also declined to reveal the name of the Washington official who authorized the Los Angeles agents to leak the potentially explosive story to the press. He would only divulge that the official was a headquarters supervisor. When queried if other people of note had been similarly targeted by the FBI, Webster replied that he did not know. Today, however, it is a well-known fact that J. Edgar Hoover kept incriminating files on a great many famous people. He prided himself on having the goods on just about every public figure of note in the country, from the president on down. He could use the information he had amassed during his four-decade tenure as director to blackmail or embarrass not only "advocates of unpopular causes" but also any politician who got in his way. It has been further suggested that Hoover's obduracy against investigating organized crime in America in the 1960s—his fanatical insistence that the mob did not exist—was due to the Mafia having the goods on him, that Hoover feared that his own secret—that he was a cross dresser and a homosexual[8]—would be revealed if the FBI targeted the five New York crime families. Hoover repeatedly stonewalled Bobby Kennedy on the issue of organized crime in America and undermined the latter's efforts as attorney general to investigate corrupt organizations and prosecute mobsters.

Whether or not he was subject to blackmail himself, Hoover nonetheless understood the efficacy of extortion and delighted in exposing the foibles of others. His antipathy toward civil rights leader Martin Luther King Jr. was legendary, and the bureau's harassment of King at Hoover's behest has been well chronicled. If the director felt that the moderate Dr. King posed a threat to America, he viewed the Black Panthers as a far greater danger. Hoover ordered the agency to keep strict tabs on the organization, and it also appears that the FBI was instrumental in framing certain of the black radicals for crimes they did not commit. The question that naturally arises is whether the Seberg story was a complete fabrication or whether it had some basis in truth. Did Seberg have an affair or not, and, if she did, did Gary learn of it from reading the *Newsweek* article? In his 1979 press conference, Webster did not say whether the bureau considered the story to be true or not. This much, however, is certain: Despite the fact that Romain Gary had served in the French delegation to the United Nations and, until 1960, as the French consul general in Los Angeles, after his marriage to Seberg later in the decade, the idealistic novelist and war hero increasingly sought the company of left-wing, anti-establishment types in California. The novelist and the actress consorted not only with Hollywood liberals but also with militants and extremists, including Black Panther party members, whose radical views and principles were currently in vogue with the chic Hollywood set. While Seberg lent her support to the black national cause, Gary was suspicious of Hollywood liberalism and in 1970, the year of Seberg's miscarriage, he published the novel *Chien blanc*, or *White Dog*, in which he exposed the hypocrisy and insincerity of Hollywood leftists. While the book attacked white racism (the canines of the title are specifically trained by white bigots to attack blacks), it was also highly critical of black radicalism. In an interview, Gary explained, "In Hollywood, I was mostly dealing with phony liberals. I couldn't just invent the right kind, but I know they exist. In fact American liberals are great. They've got a sense of injustice bigger than anyone else, but not much of a sense of justice—that is, they don't want to face the consequences."[9]

The first document pertaining to Seberg's pregnancy released by the FBI in 1979 was a request from the Los Angeles office to Washington to publicize her condition and then announce that the baby's father was a high-ranking member of the Black Panther party. The Los Angeles office wrote "the possible publication of Seberg's plight could cause her embarrassment and serve to cheapen her image with the general public."[10] The agents proposed to leak the story to a Hollywood gossip columnist by sending out an anonymous letter, and they assured headquarters that "usual precautions would be taken by the Los Angeles Division to preclude identification of the Bureau as the source of the letter if approval is granted."[11] They also submitted a draft of the fraudulent note that they planned to dispatch:

> I was just thinking about you and remembered I still owe you a favor. So I was in Paris last week and ran into Jean Seberg who was heavy with baby. I thought she and Romain had gotten together again but she confided the child belonged to [name deleted] of the Black Panthers. The dear girl is getting around. Anyway, I thought you might get a scoop on the others.[12]

Headquarters authorized the Los Angeles division to proceed. The Washington supervisor, sanctioning the action, wrote back to the West Coast operatives: "Jean Seberg has been a financial supporter of the BPP and should be neutralized. Her current pregnancy by [name deleted] while still married affords an opportunity for such an effort."[13] He instructed the agents, however, to bide their time and not plant the story until Seberg's condition had become more noticeable: ". . . to insure the success of your plan, Bureau feels it would be better to wait approximately two additional months until Seberg's pregnancy would be obvious to everyone."[14] Two weeks after the Los Angeles division received these instructions, Haber's column appeared in the *Los Angeles Times*. A copy of the article was forwarded to Washington with a note indicating that it was connected to an earlier communiqué from the L.A. office. Gary continued to blame the FBI for his ex-wife's death and stated that it was his firm belief that the agency had been responsible for Haber's story. The columnist, who had lost her job with the *Los Angeles Times* in 1975, disputed this. She stated in a telephone interview with the *New York Times*: "If I was used by the FBI, I didn't know it. To my knowledge, I didn't know anyone with the FBI then and I don't now."[15]

Friends said that Gary remained deeply depressed from the time of the FBI press conference on September 14, 1979, until his own death on December 2, 1980. After the novelist's suicide, a manuscript entitled "Life and Death of Émile Ajar" was found among Gary's papers. At the head of the typescript, Gary scribbled the following instructions: "The date on which these revelations are to be made is to be decided by Robert and Claude Gallimard, in agreement with my son."[16] The novelist signed his name and wrote the date: 30 Nov. 1980. Two days later, he would put a bullet in his brain. The novelist had been contemplating his death, however, even before Seberg's suicide, for the typescript itself, which ends with the words, "I've had a lot of fun. Goodbye, and thank you,"[17] was dated 21 March, 1979, and thus was written six months prior to the actress's death.

Gary's disclosures in these papers, which according to his wishes were made public after his death, would prove as riveting in their own way as those made fifteen months earlier by the FBI concerning Jean Seberg's 1970 pregnancy: Gary would reveal to the reading public that he had perpetrated, at least in his own estimation, the greatest literary hoax since Macpherson's *Ossian*. Gary announced that he had successfully created an alter ego for himself. He disclosed that the reclusive and enigmatic French novelist Émile Ajar, whose work had caused such a stir in France in the nineteen seventies, had been no one else but Romain Gary. The identity of "Ajar," who published four successful novels, was widely speculated upon. Gary had not let even his French publishers in on the ruse. Ajar's first manuscript, *Gros câlin*, was sent to Gallimard from Brazil through the offices of Gary's friend Pierre Michaut, who claimed that he had met Ajar in Rio. He said that the young author had gotten himself in trouble with the law and as a result had to flee France to South America where he led a nomadic existence. With the exception of one female editor, the readers at Gallimard were not overly enthusiastic about the novel. She, however, persuaded the publisher to recommend *Gros câlin* to another house—Mercure de France. There, the editor Michel Cournot fell in love with the book and pushed it into print even though, unable to contact Ajar for permission, he had to accede to cuts recommended by his senior colleagues in the author's name. The novel was very well received by the French critics. *Le Nouvel Observateur* suggested that either Raymond Queneau or Aragon was the actual author of the book, for the novel "could only be the work of a great writer."[18] The French newspapers speculated that Ajar was an abortionist, a common-law criminal, a charlatan physician, or Michel Cournot himself. One journal suggested that the novel was the collaborative work of several prominent authors. A scandal sheet claimed that Ajar was in actuality Hamil Raja, a Lebanese terrorist, and Gary eventually would encounter a young woman who claimed to be Ajar's lover. She said the young man was "a terrific fucker."[19] The elderly Gary smiled. None of the professional critics guessed that Gary was responsible for the book, which only at the last moment he decided to publish under a pseudonym. *Gros câlin* was short-listed for the prestigious Theophraste-Renaudot prize. Gary feared that the incumbent publicity would threaten his anonymity, so he withdrew his candidature in a letter purportedly sent from Brazil which was submitted to both the jury and to Mercure de France.

Ajar produced three more novels: *La vie devant soi (Momo)*, *Pseudo*, and *King Solomon*. At the same time, Gary continued to produce novels under his own name. *La vie devant soi*, Ajar's second novel, was a best-seller and would eventually be made into a film starring Simone Signoret. After the novel's publication, the magazine *Le Port* speculated that Ajar might be Gary's nephew Paul Pavlowitch. It seemed to Gary that if Ajar would make a brief appearance in the flesh, only to disappear once again into mystery, the press would stop its search for the true Ajar, so the author asked Pavlowitch to assume the part. He wanted Pavlowitch to observe the strictest incognito and invented a fictitious biography for Ajar, but instead Gary's nephew granted an interview to *Le Monde* in Copenhagen, gave his real biography and, against Gary's wishes, submitted a photograph of himself to the press. Once Pavlowitch's relationship to Gary was known, *Le Port* identified him as Ajar. Some critics opined that Ajar/Pavlowitch was a second-rate writer whose works could not compare to those of his uncle. Others found him far superior to Gary. None guessed the truth. *La vie devant soi* would win one of France's most celebrated literary awards, the *Prix Goncourt*, a prize that Gary had himself earlier won for his war novel *Les racines du ciel*. No French author had ever won the award twice.

Gary's deception would deeply embarrass the French literary establishment. As he had previously exposed the hypocrisy of Hollywood liberals in his novel *White Dog*, Gary, by way of his posthumous revelations, would unmask "the unreliability of current critical opinion in the Parisian journals"[20]—or so John Weightman would write some months later in the *Times Literary Supplement*.

Gary began "Life and Death of Émile Ajar" with the following bleak pronouncement:

> I am writing these lines at a moment when it has become increasingly obvious that, given the way it has been evolving during the last quarter of a century, the world now confronts a writer with a question that is mortal for every kind of artistic expression: that of futility. Not even the lyrical illusion remains of what for so long literature wished, and believed itself to be —a contribution to the development and progress of mankind.[21]

As the writing of serious novels and the reading of books with even a *soupçon* of literary merit had become largely *démodé* during the last decades of the twentieth century both in Europe and North America, Gary realized that his importance to society had been greatly reduced and that he had become something of an anachronism.

In "Life and Death of Émile Ajar," he questions whether anyone in the future will care about his books or the indignities he had suffered over the years at the hands of self-important and time-serving French critics. Nonetheless, if only for form's sake, he assumes that posterity will attach some slight importance to his works and thus will be interested in his travails as a writer. Gary's great grievance against the French literary establishment was that it boxed him in by inventing a persona for him. Just like an actor, he felt typecast. The critics had defined what a Romain Gary novel was and whenever he tried to branch out in a new direction they disregarded or dismissed his efforts. As an author, he "was classified, catalogued, taken for granted, all of which relieved the professionals from the task of really studying [his] work and discovering what it was about."[22] Quoting Witold Gombrowicz, he claimed that he became a prisoner of "the image he [had] been saddled with"[23]—an image, he went on to say, that had nothing to do with either his work or himself. He also found the critics fickle and dishonest in the extreme. In his last essay, Gary speaks of the "literary terror" that persisted in Paris at the height of his career, "of the coteries, of the cliques with their claques, of cronyism, of 'you scratch my back and I'll scratch yours,' of debts repaid or accounts settled,"[24] and relates a depressing anecdote concerning one female reviewer. The lady in question raved about one of his novels but venomously attacked his next book a year later simply because he neglected to write her a thank-you note for the earlier positive review. Having had his fill of such disagreeable incidents, Romain Gary devised, in Weightman's words, "an ingenious act of revenge."[25] In "Life and Death of Émile Ajar" the novelist disclosed the trap he had laid for his various Parisian detractors—a snare he greatly delighted in.

Romain Gary was born Roman Kacew in Vilna, Lithuania, on May 8, 1914. He was the son of Leibja Kacew and Mina Josel. The father, who was of Mongol descent, would desert the family when Gary was but seven years old. In compensation for this loss, the boy would develop an exceptionally strong bond with his mother, the daughter of a Jewish watchmaker who, after her husband's departure, would start a successful hat business in Vilna. She told her son that he could become anything he wanted. Gary wrote in his autobiography *La promesse de l'aube* (*Promise at Dawn*) that Mina convinced him at an early age that he would find within himself "a secret bonanza of genius that would lead [them] both to some supreme triumph, greatness, and material success."[26] She not only approved his decision to pursue the arts, she told her son that some day he would become a great ladies' man and have wealth beyond all his expectations. Infatuated with all things French, she would also instill in her boy at an early age a love of French culture. After the family moved to Nice following the failure of her hat business, she would tell her son, then aged fourteen, that, if he applied himself in school in his adopted country, he might grow up to be a French ambassador. As a youth, Gary tried his hand at acting, singing, dancing, and painting. He also learned how to play the violin, but he did not find the success he was looking for in any of these endeavors. In 1932, while attending school in Nice, Gary distinguished himself in athletics, becoming the pingpong champion of the French seaport that year. He went on to earn a law degree at the University of Paris. Later he obtained a diploma in Slavic languages. At the age of twenty or thereabouts he began work on a novel about youthful alienation and anguish entitled *Vin des morts*, which he abandoned and never published (though he would incorporate passages from it into later books).

In 1937, a year prior to Hitler's invasion of Poland and the outbreak of World War II, Gary enlisted in the French airforce. When France fell to the Nazis, he fled to Great Britain and joined the RAF, serving as a fighter pilot. Finally he fought with the "Lorraine" Free French Air Force Squadron in Africa, Palestine and the Soviet Union. He was wounded on three occasions and was awarded the Croix de la Liberation and the Croix de Guerre, and was also made a Chevalier of the Légion d'Honneur. In 1945, he produced his first important work, the novel *Education européenne* (translated into English as *Forest of Anger*), a series of tales concerning a group of partisans fighting the Nazis in Poland that reflect the resistance experience from a variety of angles. Some of the incidents related in the novel are humorous and bittersweet while others are cruel and harsh. In the pages of the existential review *Les Temps Modernes*, Jean-Paul Sartre predicted that the book would in future years come to be regarded as the best novel about the Resistance. It would win the *Prix des Critiques* for 1945. The same year Gary entered the French diplomatic service. Prior to his appointments to the United Nations and Los Angeles, he would be posted to Sofia, Berne, and London. He would leave the French diplomatic corps in 1960, but would come out of retirement briefly in 1967 to serve in the Ministry of Information under Georges Pompidou.

After writing *Education européenne*, Gary produced seventeen other books. Although the temptation was very strong, for the most part, he did not attempt to duplicate or repeat his earlier successes. Styling himself a literary chameleon, he wrote about widely divergent topics and in a variety of different styles. The French critics tended to prefer his books dealing with the Second World War. He was "saddled with the image"[27] of decorated airman and author of *Forest of Anger*. Later important works would include *Le grande vestiaire* (*The Company of Men*); *Les racines du ciel* (*Roots of Heaven*), *Europa*, *Les enchanteurs*, *Tulipe*, *Clair de femme*, *Pour Sganarelle*, *La danse de Ghengis Cohn* (*The Dance of Ghengis Cohn*), and *Adieu Gary Cooper* (*The Ski Bum*). A collection of Gary's short stories would appear in English under the title of *Hissing Tales*. His two most highly regarded books were probably *The Roots of Heaven* and *The Dance of Ghengis Cohn*, both of which had World War II themes. The former work is set in a German concentration camp. The novel's hero Morel weathers the horrors of his incarceration by focusing his thoughts on wildlife in Africa. Dreams and visions of the beauties of pristine nature bring him solace and succor as he languishes in Nazi hell. *The Dance of Genghis Cohn* concerns a Jewish stand-up comedian who has had a successful career performing in the nightclubs of Berlin. After he is sent to Auschwitz and killed by the Nazis, he returns as a dybbuk and resides in the mind of his executioner.

Gros câlin was not the first book Gary published under a pseudonym. He used the nom de plume Fosco Sinibaldi for *L'homme à la colombe,* which sold only five hundred copies, and Shatan Bogat for *Les têtes de Stéphanie,* which did not initially sell well either. Sales picked up, however, after Gary was identified as its author. Both the critics and the general reading public wanted Gary to continue writing "Romain Garys." He complied for a time but also continued to press forward in new directions with many of his books. These were generally ignored by the critics while the works that conformed to his earlier image earned favorable notices. He decided that he did not want to keep on writing "Garys." The urge to renew himself was too great. So he invented Ajar:

> Perhaps I went along with it, unconsciously. It was easier: the image was ready-made. I only had to adopt it. It meant that I had no need to reveal myself. Above all there was nostalgia for one's youth, for one's début, for one's renewal. To *renew* myself, to relive, to be someone else, was always the great temptation of my existence. I read, at the back of my books: ". . . several very well-filled lives . . . airman, diplomat, writer. . . ." Nothing, zero, straws in the wind, and with the taste of the absolute on my lips. All my as it were official, labelled lives were doubled, tripled, by other, more secret ones, but the old adventure-seeker that I am has never found total satisfaction in any of them. The truth is that I was profoundly affected by the oldest protean temptation of man: that of multiplicity. A craving for life in all its forms and possibilities, which every flavour tasted merely deepened. My impulses, always simultaneous and contradictory, constantly urged me on in every direction, and the only things that enabled me to survive them with my mental stability intact were, I think, sexuality, and the novel—which is a prodigious means of ever-renewed incarnations. I have always been someone else. And whenever I encountered a constant: my son, a love, the dog Sandy, I pushed my attachment to this stability to the point of passion.[28]

In his four hundred-and-fifty-odd page essay *Pour Sganarelle,* Gary attempted to define what to his mind would constitute a "total novel" or "total fiction." He felt that he achieved such a work in the "Ajar" novel *Pseudo.* In this book, he invented an "autobiographical" Paul Pavlowitch and at last succeeded in writing the novel of anguish that he had dreamed of creating when he began *Vin des Morts* as a young man. Many critics believed that the character of Tonton Macoute was a fictional depiction of Romain Gary by his nephew, but in actual fact "instead of Paul Pavlowitch inventing Romain Gary, it was Romain Gary inventing Paul Pavlowitch."[29]

The professionals didn't grasp this, but many of Gary's other readers did. Gary swore them all to silence. In "Life and Death of Émile Ajar," he writes that his charade should have been discernible to all discriminating readers: "To be honest, I don't think a 'dual personality' is possible. The roots of works go too deep, and even when their ramifications seemed varied and very different from one another, they can't stand up to a real examination or what used to be called 'textual analysis.' "[30] In his last essay, he points out that books of Ajar and Gary "often contained the same sentences, the same turns of phrase, the same human beings."[31] He points out how the friends of the young hero in *King Solomon* had all appeared in *Adieu Gary Cooper*. He notes how previously published passages of *Vin des morts* appear verbatim in *Pseudo* and relates how he acquired his information on chemical psychotherapy in the same Ajar novel in a manner reminiscent of how he learned about aphasia for *Clair de femme*. He alludes to the similarity in theme between *Les racines du ciel* and *Gros câlin*, which were both ecological novels. He contrasts two similar passages in *La vie devant soi* and *Le grand vestiaire*. In the former book, Momo gives his dog to a wealthy woman so that it may lead a better life than his own, while, in *Le grand vestiaire*, Luc turns his dog over to a G.I. for similar reasons. Pythons play an important part in both *Gros câlin* and *Chien blanc*. These and other examples of the sameness of Gary and Ajar that Gary puts forward in "Life and Death of Emile Ajar" would cause the faces of many prominent French critics to redden. Gary prided himself in showing up these dilettantes for what they really were.

Gary's suicide remains something of a puzzle. Did he underestimate the seriousness of his marital relationship with Jean Seberg, whose career in Hollywood had not lived up to its initial start-up in the 1950s? Otto Preminger had chosen Seberg after an extended talent search for an unknown to play the title role in his version of Shaw's *Saint Joan*, an ultimately unsuccessful film. The Swedish-American girl from Iowa had learned French somewhere along the way, however, and she made a better impression in her subsequent appearances in the French cinema. Did Gary marry the young, modestly talented American simply as a diversion or did the problematic aspects of Jean Seberg really stimulate his deep love and concern? If so, the Black Panther-FBI scandal must have had a deeply disturbing effect on him. He exposed the scurrilous actions of the FBI to the world but never revealed his personal feelings about Seberg. No doubt, he considered these private and was annoyed by the segment of the public that intrusively snooped and pried. Such feelings surely contributed to Gary's growing disillusionment with the French literary milieu of the late 1970s. Underlying this would have been the prevailing burden of his past very obvious direct involvement in the black events of Europe and the world in mid-century. His suicide alternately suggests ennui, exhaustion, and extremes of pain.

Notes

1. Quoted by Wendall A. Rawls Jr., "FBI Admits Planting a Rumor to Discredit Jean Seberg in 1970," *New York Times*, 15 September 1979.

2. Ibid.

3. Ibid.

4. Ibid.

5. Quoted by Kirk Crivello, "Jean Seberg," *Fallen Angels: The Lives and Untimely Deaths of Fourteen Hollywood Beauties* (Secaucus, N.J.: Citadel Press, 1988), p. 171.

6. Quoted by Rawls, "FBI Admits Planting a Rumor."

7. Ibid.

8. See Athan Theoharis, *J. Edgar Hoover, Sex, and Crime* (Chicago: Ivan R. Dee, 1995), pp. 11–17.

9. Quoted by Josh Barbanel, "Ordered to Be Famous," *New York Times*, 3 December 1980.

10. Quoted by Rawls, "FBI Admits Planting a Rumor."

11. Ibid.

12. Ibid.

13. Ibid.

14. Ibid.

15. Ibid.

16. Romain Gary, "Life and Death of Émile Ajar," *King Solomon*, trans. Barbara Wright, introduction by John Weightman (New York: Harper and Row, 1983), p. 242.

17. Ibid., p. 255.

18. Ibid., p. 248.

19. Ibid.

20. John Weightman, "Introduction," *King Solomon*, p. 7.

21. "Life and Death," p. 243.

22. Ibid., p. 244.

23. Quoted by Gary, "Life and Death," p. 243.

24. "Life and Death," p. 247.

25. Weightman, "Introduction," *King Solomon*, p. 7.

26. Quoted by Barbanel, "Ordered to be Famous."

27. Quoted by Gary, "Life and Death," p. 243.

28. "Life and Death," p. 249.

29. Ibid., p. 245.

30. Ibid., p. 251.

31. Ibid., p. 244.

Arthur Koestler

THE DOUBLE SUICIDE OF THE HUNGARIAN-BORN NOVELIST AND SOCIAL essayist Arthur Koestler and his third wife, Cynthia Jefferies, took place in their home in the Knightsbridge section of London on March 2, 1983. They had ended their lives by overdosing on barbiturate tablets. The Koestlers' maid, Amelia Marino, discovered the bodies when she reported to work the following day. She found the corpses seated in chairs in the living room of the couple's house. The Koestlers had left a note asking the maid to telephone Scotland Yard.

Of all the suicides discussed in this study, Koestler's would have been perhaps the least problematic had he not permitted Cynthia, who was some twenty years his junior and apparently in perfect health, to end her life along with him. Shortly after the couple's joint suicide, a friend of the writer, the editor of *Encounter* magazine, Melvin J. Lasky commented to the press that the Koestlers' marriage "was almost impossibly close; her devotion to him was like no other wife's I have ever known."[1]

At the time of his death, Koestler was seventy-seven years old and suffering from both Parkinson's disease and leukemia. His prognosis was bleak. Had he not taken his life, he would have died within a short time of natural causes, but would have suffered a great deal of needless and unwarranted pain. Both Koestler and Jefferies belonged to the British right-to-die advocacy group Exit, an organization similar to the American Hemlock Society. Both associations endorse the right of terminally ill patients to choose suicide and end their lives with dignity instead of undergoing unnecessary suffering in their final days. Koestler even authored a brochure for the British organization in which he put forth all the standard arguments for euthanasia. He pointed out the discrepancy that exists in the West between the way we treat beloved pets at the close of life and how we deal with dying human beings. The attitude we adopt toward pets, he argues, is far more humane and sensible than the one we adopt for ourselves. While animals are routinely put to sleep in Europe and the United States in order to spare them undue agony, human beings are not allowed to die "peacefully and without fuss in old age"[2] but must often expire in torment and misery.

As we approach the millennium, Koestler's point of view is gaining more and more acceptance. The constitutionality of physician-assisted suicide is currently being debated in federal courts throughout the United States. Several states have either passed or are in the process of passing laws to legalize euthanasia. The religious right vehemently opposes physician-assisted suicide, and various organizations promoting the rights of the elderly, the handicapped, and disabled have expressed fears about the possible abuses of euthanasia, particularly the concern that, if physician-assisted suicide is legalized for the terminally ill, a slippery slope would be created and society, either due to the increased cost of medical care or to changing criteria touching upon quality of life, would judge the lives of the aged and of the mentally and physically debilitated not worth living and would force euthanasia on such individuals in a manner reminiscent of Nazi Germany. Nonetheless, there has been a groundswell of popular support, both in the United States and Europe, for the "right-to-die movement."

In the 1990s, Dr. Jack Kevorkian became the leading advocate of physician-assisted suicide in the United States. From 1990 until 1998, he assisted in 130 suicides in the state of Michigan and was brought to trial five times there on assisted-suicide and murder charges. Before Kevorkian began offering his services to the terminally ill, Michigan had no law in its books against euthanasia. Due to Kevorkian's newfound notoriety, however, a bill against assisted suicide was quickly introduced in the state's legislature, which passed by a large majority. Despite the efforts of zealous prosecutors, the flamboyant doctor was acquitted the first four times he went to trial. Agreeing with Kevorkian's contention that to deny terminally ill patients a painless death and force them to suffer needlessly was both unconscionable and obscene, the four juries uniformly chose to disregard Michigan's new law and practiced jury nullification. In these cases, however, Kevorkian had merely abetted patients who had administered their own suicides. In September 1998, Kevorkian himself injected a dose of lethal drugs into a patient suffering from Lou Gehrig's disease. He videotaped the procedure, and the footage was broadcast on *60 Minutes*. In the subsequent trial, Kevorkian would be convicted of second-degree murder. Nevertheless, Kevorkian's arguments for euthanasia continue to carry much weight with many people in the world.

Kevorkian constantly reiterated his belief that the physician must follow exacting and uncompromising guidelines in determining when it is—and when it is not—appropriate to accede to a suffering patient's request for death. While Koestler undoubtedly would have met Kevorkian's criteria, Cynthia Jefferies would not have. At the time of her death, she suffered from no grave ailment. Despite this fact,

Koestler did not attempt to dissuade her from taking her life. As had previously been the case with Stefan Zweig and Charlotte Altmann, a celebrated novelist and his much younger wife chose to exit this world together. Both women had served as their husbands' secretaries, and Jefferies coauthored the third volume of Koestler's autobiography, *The Stranger in the Square*. It was published a year after the couple's death and details how the two had overcome personal estrangement and alienation to become as close and inseparable as autonomous individuals possibly can.

Over the centuries many lovers have bought into the romantic belief that in death two people can truly become one. Literature, of course, provides countless examples of famous pairs whose love finds consummation in death. That Koestler would subscribe to such a quixotic and sentimental notion at the end of his life and allow his healthy wife to terminate her life prematurely—to perform an act equivalent to the Hindu rite of suttee—is particularly troubling in that the author had bought into other equally romantic and utopian ideals in his younger days, the aims and objectives of world communism. For a time, blinded by those goals and ideals, he had countenanced and rationalized a tremendous amount of human suffering. To his enormous credit, Koestler saw the error of his thinking and became perhaps the greatest whistle blower of his generation. Furthermore, having survived one of history's most turbulent periods, he had witnessed such misery and seen death on such a massive scale that, throughout his life, he spoke out against the unnecessary taking of human life on many occasions. In 1956, he wrote *Reflections on Hanging*, one of the strongest indictments against capital punishment ever put to paper. Koestler described himself as a veteran of Europe's "military and ideological battlefields, concentration camps, hospitals, and prisons."[3] When he was in his forties, he wrote: "At a conservative estimate, three out of every four people whom I knew before I was 30 were subsequently killed in Spain, or hounded to death at Dachau, or gassed at Belsen, or deported to Russia, or liquidated in Russia; some jumped from windows in Vienna or Budapest, others were wrecked by the misery and aimlessness of permanent exile."[4] As a result of all the horror he had beheld, he felt impelled toward political activism and felt it was the moral duty of the individual to do all he could to combat and resist evil. In 1952, he wrote: "Moral indignation did and still does affect me in a direct physical manner. Like most people who suffer from chronic indignation—as others do from chronic indigestion—I can feel, during the attack, the infusion of adrenaline into the bloodstream, the craving of the muscles for violent action."[5] Three years later, Koestler's second wife, Mamaine Paget, whom the novelist had recently divorced, died by her own hand. In his preface to the 1955 collection, *The Trail of the Dinosaur and Other Essays*, the author would write a poignant and touching tribute to his dead wife, but he certainly did not contemplate following her into death. His duty was clearly to remain with the living and continue his crusade against communism. In 1985 a volume of Paget's letters that recount her relationship with the novelist would appear under the title *Living with Koestler: Mamaine Koestler's Letters* (1945–1951).

Koestler's politics evolved and changed during the course of his life. His development began at the age of seventeen when he joined a Zionist fraternity in Vienna where he studied science, engineering, and psychology, first at the Polytechnic High School, then at the University of Vienna. "I started in a relatively narrow movement," Koestler wrote, "as a young duel-fighting Zionist."[6] He would eventually leave the Zionist effort for "a more general cause, the world revolution. . . ."[7] Koestler was hired by the Berlin-based liberal Ullstein newspaper group in 1927 and served as both a correspondent in the Middle East, Paris, and Berlin, and later as science editor for the various Ullstein publications (he was the only journalist invited on the *Graf Zeppelin* arctic expedition). Koestler secretly joined the German Communist party in 1931 after coming to the conclusion that "communism was the only possible solution for Europe—both as a lesser evil compared to fascism and as a road to Utopia."[8] He served as a courier between various party officials. When his activities were discovered, Koestler was fired from the newspaper, after which he joined a communist cell and took part in clandestine party operations. Among other things, he served as the driver for Communist gunmen. He traveled to the Soviet Union and lectured widely; he wrote a play praising the Revolution that he later destroyed. Despite his political convictions, Koestler saw many things in Russia that disturbed him. The poverty of the workers, the backwardness of the people, the brutal repression of all internal enemies by the Stalin régime and the endless propagandizing of the press all disillusioned Koestler for a time, but he did not break faith with the communist cause. After Hitler came to power, he returned to Budapest, then moved on to Paris. He spent the years 1933 to 1935 primarily in the French capital, where he worked for the cause of international communism. In 1935, he married his first wife, Dorothy Ascher, in Zurich, Switzerland. Shortly thereafter, he resumed his career as a journalist. As a correspondent for the *London News Chronicle*, he journeyed to Spain to cover the Civil War on three separate occasions, his reportage heavily biased in favor of the Left. Traveling with Republican troops, he was captured by Franco forces in Malagra. Sentenced to death, Koestler spent time in prisons both in Malagra and Seville. Kept in solitary confinement, during the entire period of his captivity, he believed that he would be shortly shot. The British government, however, protested vigorously in his behalf and eventually gained his release through a prisoners' exchange.

Koestler would later say that incarceration brought out the meditative side of his personality and that from his experiences he learned the value of altruism, the individual, and apolitical ethics. After his release from prison, Koestler would quickly set to work on a memoir about his captivity in Spain. After publishing *Spanish Testament* in 1937, the author would turn to fiction, and his first novel, *The Gladiators*, would appear in 1939. Prior to writing the novel, Koestler resigned from the Communist party. His faith in the world revolution had begun to waver during his incarceration in Spain at the hands of the Nationalists. He had expected a strong protest against his death sentence from Moscow, but the party had not interceded for

Koestler. After his release, he discovered that only a perfunctory effort had been made on his behalf by the Soviet government, and that he owed his life to the British and not the Russians. Koestler had faithfully served the party during the 1930s even though numerous of his friends and acquaintances had been arrested on trumped-up charges in the mass purges of Joseph Stalin. After writing *Spanish Testament*, Koestler learned that his brother-in-law Dr. Ernst Ascher had been among the ruthless dictator's victims. This revelation capped his disenchantment with the Communist system and caused him to sever all ties with the International. Scales, as it were, fell from his eyes. The thousands of victims of Stalin's terror were no longer anonymous and faceless. Koestler suddenly realized that in the name of high-minded ideals while promoting the program of the revolution he had overlooked and rationalized the terrible crimes perpetrated by Stalin and his minions. The horror of these crimes now struck him full force. He was forced to admit that at no time and in no country had "more revolutionaries been killed and reduced to slavery than in Soviet Russia."[9] He saw that he himself had been guilty of a grave crime. To forward the ends of the Communist revolution, as a journalist, he had excused any and all means that the party and its leaders had adopted to achieve those ends.

Koestler was in France when World War II began. He had already begun work on his masterpiece, the novel *Darkness at Noon*, a scathing indictment of the Moscow treason trials of the 1930s and a probing and unsparing psychological study of the Bolshevik mindset, when, in 1940, French police arrested him as a war refugee and confined him in a camp for aliens. (He would write about this internment in the 1941 memoir *Scum of the Earth*.) Once again the British government sought and achieved his release. Before the fall of Paris, Koestler joined the French foreign legion. After the German defeat of France, he fled to Great Britain. In 1941, the year *Darkness at Noon* reached print in English translation, he began two years' service with the British Army's Pioneer Corps, an organization that recruited loyal Allied residents of enemy nationality. After the war, Koestler chose to become a British subject. According to Melvin Lasky, Koestler became an ardent Anglophile but realized that he could never in truth really be an Englishman. Although he became a citizen, he realized that he would always be "a foreigner"[10] in his adopted country and saw himself, finally, as a "rootless cosmopolitan."[11] He stopped writing in Hungarian and German and wrote exclusively in English from 1943.

Darkness at Noon is set in 1938. Although the story obviously takes place in the Soviet Union, the country is never referred to by name in the novel. It is alluded to merely as the country of the revolution. Nor does Stalin's name appear in the text; the dictator is simply dubbed No. 1. The novel concerns the arrest and subsequent interrogations of Nicholas Rubashov, one of the great heroes of the 1917 uprising. The character was a synthesis of a number of men who were victims of the Stalinist purges. Many commentators have linked him in particular with the historical figure of Nikolai Ivanovich Bukharin, one of the most prominent scapegoats of the Moscow trials. Rubashov has faithfully served the cause of world communism for forty years.

The ex-Commissar of the people had been expecting his arrest for a long time. Awakened in the middle of the night by two officials of the People's Commissariat of the Interior (in other words by the secret police), he is informed that a warrant has been issued for his detention. He is taken into custody and driven to one of the state's new model prisons. Electric lights illumine the iron galleries, the austere, whitewashed walls, and the cell doors. Each of these doors bears a namecard and "the black hole of a judas eye,"[12] a round aperture through which a prisoner can be observed from the outside by one of his warders. Rubashov and the guards reach cell 404. He sees his name on the card. Then the guards usher him into the small room, and he hears the door slam shut behind them. He realizes that he has been placed in an isolation cell for political prisoners. From the beginning of his incarceration, Rubashov perceives his eventual fate. He knows that he will be shot.

The following morning Rubashov is awakened by a bugle call but does not stir from his bed. He senses that he is being watched. A short time later, a warder turns a key in the heavy lock of the door and opens it to ask Rubashov why he hasn't gotten up. The former Commissar replies that he has a toothache. After the warder shuffles out of the cell and bangs the door shut, Rubashov rises and begins pacing back and forth across the room, six and a half steps to the window, six and a half steps back. A short time later he hears the sound of several people marching in the corridor. He imagines that a prisoner is about to be beaten and shudders at the prospect of hearing the first screams of the victim. The footsteps grow louder. Rubashov peers through the judas eye into the corridor. Instead of witnessing a prisoner being dragged to torture, he sees guards delivering food to the various isolation cells. He does not receive breakfast himself.

Later in the day, Rubashov becomes conscious of a quiet knocking from the other side of the wall separating him from adjacent cell No. 402. The two prisoners communicate by tapping out the twenty-five letters of the "quadratic alphabet."[13] Being out of practice, Rubashov at first has difficulty visualizing the square of twenty-five compartments, five horizontal rows of five letters each. The first set of taps, from one to five knocks, identifies the number of the horizontal row, while the second set, also between one and five beats, identifies the number of the letter in the row. Rubashov's fellow prisoner, a former soldier and member of the old guard who has opposed the revolution from day one, is surprised to learn the ex-Commissar's identity. He asks Rubashov why the latter has been incarcerated, and Rubashov responds, political divergences, to which the former replies, "Bravo! The wolves devour each other."[14] Despite their ideological differences, the two prisoners continue to communicate with one another. Their mutual, shared situation makes them allies, and each is helpful to the other in the course of the book. The military man has been in prison so long that he longs to hear about women, and, rather pathetically, he begs Rubashov to recount the details of his last sexual encounter. Rubashov responds by tapping out the lyrics of an old cabaret song that greatly pleases and gratifies No. 402. In turn, the soldier will give Rubashov advance warning of events about to take place in the prison, and, at the close of the novel, he keeps Rubashov occupied and entertained as the latter awaits his execution. He tells his comrade that he won't "show the white feather"[15] and that he is a "devil of a fellow."[16] In soldierly fashion, he also urges the ex-Commissar to empty his bladder before the guards come to fetch him.

From his cell window, Rubashov watches the prisoners exercising in the yard. He notices that one of these, a man with a harelip repeatedly glances up at his window. No. 402 informs Rubashov that this prisoner is his neighbor, No. 400, and that he was tortured by steambath the previous day. Like Rubashov, Harelip has been incarcerated for "political divergences."[17] Later in the day, Harelip sends greetings to Rubashov via inmate No. 402, but the man refuses to reveal his name.

Three days later, Rubashov is summoned to the first of his interrogations. The prison official is none other than his old college friend and former battalion commander, Ivanov. During the war, Ivanov had lost his leg in battle and asked Rubashov to procure veronal for him so that he might commit suicide. The two had argued passionately with one another. Ivanov claimed that every man had a right to suicide, but Rubashov disagreed. The individual and his sufferings were nothing, the party was all. Rubashov contended that Ivanov could still be of service to the party. Therefore it was impermissible for him to take his life. The tables are now turned. Rubashov learns from his old comrade that he is accused of belonging to the organized opposition and that he is suspected of hatching an assassination plot against No. 1. Ivanov wants Rubashov to make a public confession that he had in fact joined the opposition, but to deny that he organized or planned an assassination. He is to state that he withdrew from the group when he learned of its terrorist plans. Ivanov tells his friend that his position is precarious and warns him not to be unbending or intransigent. Not confessing, he says, would be tantamount to committing suicide, and Ivanov vows that he will not permit his friend to throw away his life. He reminds Rubashov that the latter had convinced him that "suicide was petty bourgeois romanticism."[18] Ivanov promises a prison sentence instead of the death penalty if Rubashov confesses. He then attempts to persuade Rubashov of his culpability.

While the ex-Commissar never joined any opposition group and is not guilty of any of the specific charges levelled against him, he is forced to admit, during the course of the first interview, that he has not kept faith with the party and has in fact developed an "oppositional"[19] attitude. Ivanov points out to him that, in conversation, he refers to the State and Party as "you," as opposed to "I"[20]—that is, Nicolas Salmanovitch Rubashov. Later, when he has admitted the error of his ways, Rubashov will characterize his shift to the first person singular as "the grammatical fiction."[21] But even as Ivanov speaks, Rubashov is taken aback. He recalls all he fought for and preached during the last forty years and acknowledges that he always believed that "the branch which broke from the tree must wither. . . ."[22]

Ivanov traces Rubashov's disaffection with the party back to the year 1933, when Rubashov was illegally smuggled into Germany shortly after Adolf Hitler's ascension to power. Germany had been a great disappointment to the party. Of all nations, it seemed ripest for a communist takeover in the late 1920s and the early 1930s, but the Nazis seized control instead and effectively squashed their Communist rivals. Rubashov was sent to Germany to carry out "a purging and reorganization of the ranks"[23] of Germany's Communist party. Within a few months, however, he was arrested and he was subsequently imprisoned by the Nazis for two years. Upon his return to Russia, he requested a new mission abroad even though he could have had an important job at home. Ivanov interprets Rubashov's action as follows: "You did not feel at ease here, presumably? During your absence, certain changes had taken place which you evidently did not appreciate."[24] Ivanov attributes Rubashov's desire to leave Russia to the fact that the first of the great purges had already taken place by the time he returned home. Many of his friends and comrades had already been convicted and liquidated. Rubashov admits as much and tells Ivanov that the Revolution had been murdered by the new party leaders, though he still denies he belonged to the opposition. During the interview, Rubashov notices a square patch on the wall and realizes that a famous photograph of the early leaders of the Revolution had once hung there. A number was printed beside each of the bearded heads for identification purposes. Most of these important historical figures had perished in the purges. Rubashov was one of the great men in the photograph. Now he is reduced to being just a number, prisoner No. 404. At this point in the novel, the prison is a microcosm for the Soviet Union itself. Koestler insinuates that, under Communist rule, Russia became one vast gulag and that each of its citizens underwent a diminution similar to Rubashov's. Stripped of all humanity, they became (at least in the eyes of their rulers) abstractions or numbers. Even the dictator of such a nation is reduced. Stalin himself becomes a digit. He is the all powerful numeral one, the least integer of all.

Ivanov reminds Rubashov that he himself has often condoned the sacrifice of an individual if such a sacrifice led to the greater good of the party as a whole or otherwise benefitted the ends of the Revolution. Rubashov recalls a young German Communist, Richard, whom he expelled from the party for not following Moscow directives after the Nazi rise to power. Richard refused to distribute party leaflets that contained boldfaced lies concerning the state of the German Communist party. Richard realized that the communists had been defeated and the party was in shambles in Germany. The leaflets were full of phrases about the communists' "unbroken will to victory."[25] These rang hollow to Richard's ears and reminded him of German government lies during the great war. Richard believed that all the opponents of fascism must unite in the fight against Hitler. Moscow, however, felt that the party had to remain ideologically pure and forbade its members to join forces with the moderates. Richard told Rubashov that the party was mistaken. Rubashov replied that the party could never be mistaken. "You and I can make a mistake. Not the party. The party, comrade, is more than you or I and a thousand others like you and I."[26]

Rubashov also remembers Little Loewy, a hunchbacked, idealistic party member in the docker's section of Belgium's Communist league. Rubashov had to explain to the Belgium dockworkers why Russia was supplying goods to the fascists when the party had earlier called the workers of the world to stand up against fascism. The dockworkers did not accept his arguments and threatened to stop the Russian goods from passing through their ports. Rubashov telegraphed Russia and had the leaders of the dockers' section, including Little Loewy, expelled from the party. Loewy was denounced as an *agent provocateur* in the local Communist paper. He hanged himself in his room three days later.

Finally, Rubashov recalls his private secretary and mistress, Arlova. After Little Loewy's death, Rubashov took over "his new post as leader of the Trade Delegation in B."[27] While the other twelve subordinates at the delegation all got on his nerves, he always felt at ease with the sleepy, indolent Arlova, who reminded him of his sisters at home. It was nearly a month before he spoke to her in a conversational tone. A fortnight later he placed his hands on her shoulders and asked if she would go out with him that evening. Soon the two began an affair. After they slept together, Arlova told him that he would always be able to do whatever he liked with her. In the office, she behaved with her usual circumspection and did not let on to any of her coworkers that she and Rubashov had become intimate. Sometimes Rubashov would make sarcastic asides about No. 1 when he dictated to her. She would stop writing until he finished. Once she even warned him not to say such things since he might be overheard. The second great purge was then taking place in Russia. While the other members of the legation were all on pins and needles calling out to each other "the catch words of the latest Congress manifesto" and protesting against any "false interpretation of what [they] had just said,"[28] Rubashov had "the impression of a queer and ceremonious marionette-play with figures, moving on wires, each saying their set piece."[29] Only Arlova, "with her silent, sleepy manner,"[30] seemed unchanged to him. Upon orders from above, portraits were removed from the legation's walls and books taken from the shelves of its library. Rubashov continued to make sarcastic comments to Arlova. History was being rewritten. Rubashov joked that "a new and revised edition of the back numbers of all newspapers"[31] would have to be published. Orders arrived that a librarian was to be appointed to "take political responsibility"[32] for the contents of the legation library. Arlova was selected for the post. Soon she found herself being attacked from all sides. Opposition works had not been removed while important speeches of No. 1 could not be found. Arlova was given a stern warning by the committee. She stared at Rubashov in the presence of the others. The Legation head became uneasy. He felt something was in store for Arlova and stopped making witty remarks in front of her. Eventually she stopped visiting him at night. One day he was told Arlova's brother and sister-in-law were arrested for treasonable activities in Russia. That day Rubashov walked behind Arlova and glanced down at her neck. He knew that the condemned in Russia were shot through the back of the neck. The next week Arlova was dismissed from her post as librarian and recalled to Russia. Later Rubashov would publicly disavow his secretary. His declaration was decisive in the passing of the death sentence on her.

Rubashov's betrayal of Arlova is particularly revealing of his character. His acquiescence in his mistress's death serves as a potent fictional analogue to Koestler's tacit acceptance and approval of his wife's suicide in London in 1983. In the novel, Rubashov does not lift a finger to prevent the recall and execution of his lover when she is accused of political untrustworthiness by his associates. Indeed, he is in part responsible for her death, for, when she refers to him for exculpation, he denounces her and thus dooms her to her fate. While Koestler cannot be accused of causing Cynthia Jefferies's death, he apparently did nothing to dissuade his young and healthy wife from committing suicide at the time his illness drove him to take his life. Like the character he created, Koestler displayed a blatant, selfish, disregard toward the welfare of the woman he supposedly loved most. While Rubashov condemned Arlova to death, Koestler could have insisted that Cynthia live.

At the end of the first hearing, Ivanov informs Rubashov that he has been granted a fortnight to come to a decision whether or not he will make a public confession. During this interval, his warders treat him much better than they had previously done. He is permitted soap, towels, paper, pencil, and tobacco. He is also allowed to accompany the other prisoners into the courtyard for exercise. He determines that he will admit to the authorities that he has erred and begins keeping a journal in which he affirms his allegiance to the party and attempts to justify the harsh treatment of Soviet dissidents. He hopes to someday write a book on the topic:

> We have learnt history more thoroughly than the others. We differ from all the others in our logical consistency. We know that virtue does not matter to history, and that crimes remain unpunished; but that every error had its consequences and venges itself unto the seventh generation. Therefore we concentrated all our efforts on preventing error and destroying the very seeds of it. Never in history has so much power over the future of humanity been concentrated in so few hands as in our case. Each wrong idea we follow is a crime committed against future generations. Therefore we have to punish wrong ideas as others punish crimes: with death.[33]

The night before Rubashov is to give Ivanov his answer, an execution takes place in the prison. The condemned man, Michael Bogrov, a close friend of Rubashov, and two guards pass by the ex-Commissar's cell. Death had always been an abstraction for Rubashov. A "factor in a logical equation,"[34] it "had lost any intimate bodily feature."[35] For the party, death had neither mystery nor romantic aspect. However, it was rarely spoken of and the word "execution" was hardly ever used. The act of dying was a technical detail. As he observes Bogrov being dragged off, death assumes an entirely different aspect for Rubashov. Bogrov whimpers and cries and calls out Rubashov's name as he is led down the corridor. Rubashov wonders if Arlova sobbed in the same manner at the time of her execution.

Ivanov comes to Rubashov's cell with a bottle of brandy later that night. He explains that Bogrov's execution was arranged by his subordinate Gletkin against his express orders. He admits that it was calculated to have a psychological effect on Rubashov, but he feels that it was a mistake. Bogrov was executed because he advocated the construction of submarines of large tonnage. No. 1 had favored the production of small submarines for coastal defense instead. Ivanov and Rubashov debate late into the night. The former's arguments are familiar to Rubashov; he has used them himself. History cannot be conducted "according to the maxims of the Sunday school."[36] Many will have to die in order that a just, class-free society can be created on the earth. Before the night is over, Rubashov once again accepts the party's doctrine. The following day he writes a letter to the Public Prosecutor in which he repudiates his former oppositional stance.

Rubashov's final hearing, after he has already confessed, is conducted by Gletkin. He is taken to the latter's office and interrogated under blinding lights. Gletkin informs him that Ivanov has been shot for treating him too leniently and that the Public Prosecutor will demand Rubashov's life at his upcoming trial. Gletkin questions whether Rubashov's repentance is real. If it is, he can perform one last service to the party and help heal the rent the opposition has made in it. Gletkin employs the same arguments Rubashov had used on Richard: the party must be united. "It must be as if cast from one mould—filled with blind discipline and absolute trust."[37] Rubashov admits that "Humanitarian weakness and liberal democracy, when the masses are not mature, is suicide for the Revolution."[38] Therefore, he agrees to sacrifice himself for the higher good of the party, yet he still has his pride and makes Gletkin work hard for each concession he wrings out of him. The hearing is a protracted affair, conducted over several days' time. Rubashov is subjected to lengthy interrogation and is only allowed to sleep for the briefest of intervals. The two men engage in a pitched intellectual duel. It is Gletkin's task to make the ex-Commissar confess to all the specific (and false) charges that have been leveled against him. Harelip incriminates Rubashov in a plot to assassinate No. 1, and Rubashov at last recognizes him as the son of his former colleague, the Communist party historian Kieffer, an early victim of the purges. Rubashov is also accused of entering into secret and treasonous negotiations with the Germans. In a manner reminiscent of a chronic or terminal illness, the sessions under the bright lights wear Rubashov down. All he wants to do is sleep and eventually he equates death with sleep. He comes to believe that the only suffering a person should endure is that suffering which is absolutely "inevitable,"[39] in other words, suffering "rooted in biological fatality."[40] All suffering "with a social origin was accidental, hence pointless and senseless."[41] The object of the revolution itself was "the abolition of senseless suffering."[42] Therefore, he enters "an unspoken agreement"[43] with his interrogator: "if Gletkin could prove that the root of [a] charge was right—even when this root was only of a logical, abstract nature—he had a free hand to insert the missing details."[44] At the novel's end, Rubashov makes his public confession, after which he is duly executed. Although, in the end, he finds Gletkin's arguments persuasive and logical, he still has inner doubts and wonders if "reason alone was a defective compass, which led one on such a winding, twisting course that the goal finally disappeared in the mist."[45]

In all, Koestler had been a member of the Communist party for seven years. In his contribution to *The God That Failed*, a 1949 anthology of essays in which a series of influential authors including André Gide, Richard Wright, and Stephen Spender, among others, relate their initial enthusiasm and their later disillusionment with communism, he wrote: "I served the Communist party . . . the same length of time as Jacob tended Laban's sheep to win Rachel, his daughter. When the time was up, the bride was led into his dark tent; only the next morning did he discover that his ardors had been spent not on the lovely Rachel but on the ugly Leah. I wonder whether he ever recovered from the shock of sleeping with an illusion."[46]

Koestler realized that he himself had been blinded by the high-sounding ideals of communism. In *The God That Failed*, he wrote: "How our voices boomed with righteous indignation, denouncing flaws in the procedure of justice in our comfortable democracies; and how silent we were when our comrades, without trial or conviction, were liquidated in the Socialist sixth of the earth."[47] He listed every evil he and other believers in the Communist cause had countenanced: "The necessary lie; the necessary slander; the necessary intimidation of the masses to preserve them from shortsighted error; the necessary liquidation of oppositional groups and hostile classes; the necessary sacrifice of a whole generation in the interest of the next—it may all sound monstrous and yet it was easy to accept while rolling along the single track of faith."[48]

After he split ranks with the communists, Koestler felt that it was his duty to disabuse Western intellectuals who continued to be sympathetically disposed to the Communist cause. He delineated the bleak realities of Soviet life and denounced Communist ideology in countless essays. He predicted the de-Stalinization of Russia in the 1950 book *The Age of Longing* and was the first to use the phrase "balance of terror"[49] in describing postwar American and Soviet relations. He and George Orwell set up the anti-Communist organization, the Congress of Cultural Freedom, which appealed to many conscientious Western scholars and intellectuals. Although he broke with the Communists, Koestler still considered himself a liberal and a leftist. He knew that communism would always hold an attraction for such individuals. He wanted, in particular, to reach out to the "Babbitts of the Left,"[50] seemingly reasonable and fair-minded people who thought: "I am not a Communist. In fact, I dislike Communist politics, but I don't wish to be identified with anti-Communist witch-hunting. Hence I am neither a Communist nor an anti-Communist, but an anti-anti-Communist."[51] He participated in many panel discussions with other writers and academics and debated Jean-Paul Sartre and Simone de Beauvoir on political action. Eventually, however, Koestler felt that he had said his piece and no longer wrote upon political topics or gave political interviews. He explained his decision as follows: "I've written all I have to write on democracy, totalitarianism, communism, and progress, which have obsessed me for the best part of a quarter of a century. Now the errors are atoned for, the bitter passion has burned itself out. Cassandra has gone hoarse and is due for a vocational change."[52] His later books dealt with a wide variety of causes and issues. He never shrank from controversy.

Arthur Koestler was born in Budapest on September 5, 1905, the only child of Henrik and Adela Jeiteles Koestler. While his father was Hungarian, his mother was Viennese. She was also a descendant of a chief rabbi of Prague. Koestler wrote that as a boy he was "lonely, precocious and neurotic, admired for my brains and detested for my character by teachers and schoolfellows alike."[53] In 1914, Koestler's parents moved to Vienna. Although he was chiefly interested in science as a young man, he also displayed a talent for linguistics. At the age of seventeen, Koestler joined the Zionist fraternity movement that had been founded by Theodor Herzl in the 1890s. According to Koestler, Herzl had started the Jewish fencing associations to show the world "that Jews could hold their own in dueling, drinking and singing just like other people."[54] While a student, Koestler became a follower of the militant Zionist leader Vladimir Jabotinsky, who was also an early mentor of the future Israeli prime minister Menachem Begin. For a time, Koestler would serve as Jabotinsky's private secretary. In 1926, at the age of twenty, he withdrew from the University of Vienna "to go to Palestine and till the earth."[55] To demonstrate his dedication to Jabotinsky's Revisionist party, he performed menial jobs and lived in a small collective settlement in the Jezreel Valley. He would later utilize his experiences to write a pro-Zionist novel, *Thieves in the Night*, in 1946. He eventually moved from the settlement and lived variously in Haifa (where he supported himself by selling lemonade), Tel Aviv, and Cairo. In 1927 he became a Middle East correspondent for the Ullstein newspaper chain and eventually returned to Europe.

After the Second World War, Koestler once again espoused the Zionist cause. He monitored the Palestine situation as a correspondent for the *London Times*. In 1949, he wrote *Promise and Fulfillment: Palestine 1917–1949*, a treatise on the Zionist movement and the creation of the state of Israel, as well as numerous articles concerning the emerging Jewish nation for British, American, and French periodicals. While pro-Zionist, Koestler was sharply critical of certain aspects of Jewish character and identity. Some critics alleged that *Thieves in the Night* was, in fact, anti-Jewish. In 1976, Koestler published *The Thirteenth Tribe: The Khazar Empire and Its Heritage*, a provocative yet persuasively argued study that contends "that the bulk of Eastern Jewry—and hence of world Jewry—is of Khazar-Turkish rather than Semitic origin."[56] In the book, Koestler recounts the history of the ancient Khazar Empire, a once great power in Eastern Europe whose importance and significance has been largely overlooked by modern historians and scholars. The empire eventually fell to the forces of Genghis Khan. Koestler contends that the Khazars converted to Judaism in the Middle Ages, in order to resist pressures from the West to become Christian and from the East to adopt Islam. Koestler argues that after the destruction of Khazaria by the Mongols, survivors of the empire migrated to Poland, where they formed the cradle of Western Jewry. In making his case, Koestler writes that "the evidence from anthropology concurs with history in refuting the popular belief in a Jewish race descended from the biblical tribe."[57] While the book won praise from George Steiner, Philip Toynbee, and Sir Fitzroy Maclean, it also had its share of angry detractors. Many Jews argued that Koestler had propounded views and ideas similar to those of Israel's Arab opponents, who contested the legitimacy of Israel's claim to statehood. Koestler countered that his convictions in no way invalidated Israel's right to exist. The novelist Isaac Bashevis Singer was particularly critical of Koestler. In an interview, he said the Hungarian-born novelist had shorn away his identity and become a cipher: "When you take a man like Koestler, who tries so hard to show that the Jews are not even Jews, he fails also as a writer. A Jewish writer who denies his Jewishness is neither a Jew nor does he belong to any other group."[58]

Koestler delighted in writing about controversial subjects and cultivated the image of a subversive thinker and intellectual maverick. He saw himself as a popularizer of scientific and philosophical thought, lectured widely at American universities, and was a Fellow at the Center for Advanced Study in the Behavior Sciences at Stanford in 1964–1965. His later books examine a wide array of subjects. He explores Eastern mysticism and spirituality in the 1961 volume *The Lotos and the Robot*, a chronicle of his travels in Japan and India in which he investigates the Eastern notion of the unity of all creation. He probes the processes of human creativity in the 1964 book *The Act of Creation*, and examines mankind's susceptibility to misconception and error in *The Ghost in the Machine* (1968) in which he argues that as a species we have an absolute penchant for delusion and misleading of the mind. The essays in the 1969 collection *Drinkers of Infinity* treat topics as diverse as extrasensory perception and cruelty to animals while the 1972 volume *The Roots of Coincidence* deals with the topic of parapsychology. *The Case of the Midwife Toad* (1981) examines the case against Darwin's theory of evolution put forward by a heretical Austrian biologist in the 1920s. Koestler returned to the novel with 1973's *The Call Girls* in which he speculates about man's chances of survival in the coming century, and he summarizes and recapitulates what he came to view as the core of his wide-ranging speculations about mankind and human behavior in 1978's *Janus: A Summing Up*. His autobiography consists of three volumes, *Arrow in the Blue*, *The Invisible Writing*, and *The Stranger in the Square*.

Collaborating with her Parkinson's debilitated husband on the concluding volume of his autobiography perhaps compensated Cynthia Jefferies for certain failings and inadequacies in her own life. She may have felt that the time before her marriage to Koestler was unimportant and that her coauthorship of the third volume demonstrated how her and Koestler's lives had essentially become one. If so, the determination to join her husband in suicide could have been all that more easy for her. She died without giving Koestler a child. His two previous marriages were also without offspring.

Notes

1. Quoted by Eric Pace, "Arthur Koestler and Wife Suicides in London," *New York Times*, 4 March 1983.

2. Ibid.

3. Quoted by Walter Goodman, "Arthur Koestler, an Intellectual and Man of Action," *New York Times*, 4 March 1983.

4. Quoted by Pace, "Arthur Koestler and Wife Suicides in London."

5. Ibid.

6. Ibid.

7. Ibid.

8. Ibid.

9. Ibid.

10. Quoted from Melvin J. Lasky, *Encounter*, September–October 1983 in *Literary Exile in the Twentieth Century: An Analysis and Biographical Dictionary*, ed. Martin Tucker (New York: Greenwood Press, 1991), p. 381.

11. Ibid.

12. Arthur Koestler, *Darkness at Noon* (New York: New American Library, 1955), p. 15. *Darkness at Noon* was first published in 1941.

13. Ibid., p. 24.

14. Ibid., p. 26.

15. Ibid., p. 186.

16. Ibid.

17. Ibid., p. 42.

18. Ibid., p. 68.

19. Ibid., p. 64.

20. Ibid., p. 61.

21. Ibid., p. 82.

22. Ibid., p. 62.

23. Ibid., p. 64.

24. Ibid., p. 65.

25. Ibid., p. 35.

26. Ibid., p. 36.

27. Ibid., p. 83.

28. Ibid., p. 86.

29. Ibid.

30. Ibid.

31. Ibid., p. 87.

32. Ibid.

33. Ibid., p. 74.

34. Ibid., p. 99.

35. Ibid.

36. Ibid., p. 111.

37. Ibid., p. 168.

38. Ibid., p. 136.

39. Ibid., p. 181.

40. Ibid.

41. Ibid.

42. Ibid.

43. Ibid., p. 158.

44. Ibid.

45. Ibid., pp. 184–85.

46. Quoted by Pace, "Arthur Koestler and Wife Suicides in London."

47. Quoted by Goodman, "Arthur Koestler."

48. Ibid.

49. Quoted by Pace, "Arthur Koestler and Wife Suicides in London."

50. Quoted by Goodman, "Arthur Koestler."

51. Ibid.

52. Quoted by Pace, "Arthur Koestler and Wife Suicides in London."

53. Ibid.

54. Ibid.

55. Ibid.

56. Arthur Koestler, *The Thirteenth Tribe: The Khazar Empire and Its Heritage* (New York: Random House, 1976), p. 199.

57. Ibid.

58. Quoted by Pace, "Arthur Koestler and Wife Suicides in London."

Jerzy Kosinski

J ERZY KOSINSKI DODGED DEATH DAILY AS A BOY. DURING THE FIRST
weeks of World War II, when Kosinski was six years old, his
affluent Jewish parents (his father was a respected philologist, his
mother a concert pianist) sent him from the city of Lodz to a remote village in the Polish countryside. Numerous other city children, Jew and
Gentile both, made similar exoduses. His parents, who would shortly go
into hiding themselves, thought that sending him away would best guar-
antee his survival during the war. For a sizable sum, a man leaving the
city for the eastern provinces agreed to take the child with him and find
shelter for the boy with a farming family. During the course of the war,
Kosinski's parents lost contact with the individual to whom they had
(perhaps in retrospect foolhardily) entrusted their son, and they had to
face the prospect, even the likelihood, that they would never see the boy
again. Kosinski would later write that his parents "were constantly tortured by the possibility that their decision to send [him] away had been
wrong, that [he] would have been safer with them."[1] His mother told him
that there were "no words . . . to describe their anguish as they saw
young children being herded into the trains bound for the ovens or the
horrendous special camps scattered throughout the country."[2] Although
Kosinski's parents had no way of knowing it, the man kept his word and
found foster parents for Jerzy. The boy, however, did not remain with
these people long.

In *The Painted Bird*, Kosinski's fictionalized account of his nightmarish childhood experiences, the foster mother dies within two months
of the boy's arrival. In the book, the child, called only the Gypsy, roams
alone from village to village. He is abused, starved, and tortured by the
superstitious and cruel peasants who temporarily shelter him, always for
reasons involving their own gain. The boy's features differ markedly from

362

those of the rural Poles and betray his ethnicity. He has olive skin, dark hair, and black eyes. The villagers, for the most part, have fair skin, blond hair, and blue eyes. He also speaks, at least initially, the "language of the educated class,"[3] a speech radically different from the peasants' own dialect and barely intelligible to them.

For a time, the boy lives with the bird catcher Lekh and sets snares for him. Whenever Lekh's lover, Stupid Ludmilla, a mentally disturbed woman who, as a girl, had been raped by a group of drunken peasants after she refused to wed the suitor her parents had selected for her, did not visit Lekh on a regular enough basis, he would grow restive and angry and remove a bird from one of his cages and paint its body in a variety of gaudy colors. He would then release the bird into the air. The bird would be attacked from all sides by members of its own species and pecked to death because of its strange appearance. Stupid Ludmilla is eventually murdered in similar fashion. After her rape, she had retreated to the forest and lived there many years. She still resides in the woods when the abandoned child comes to live with Lekh. She lures any man who pleases her into the bushes and grants him her favors. Often she takes several men in a day. Because he loves her, Lekh accepts this, though he is ridiculed by the other villagers. While the boy is in Lekh's care, a group of peasant women become infuriated with Stupid Ludmilla because their husbands no longer care for their embraces after having been with her. One day they catch Ludmilla, hold her down against the grass and beat her to death with rakes and shovels. Lekh tries to come to her rescue but is knocked down and beaten by the women. The boy flees, terrified after he beholds the attack on Ludmilla and Lekh. He feels an affinity to the madwoman: she and he are both "painted birds." People attack them because they are different from their fellows.

The peasants have ample reason to fear the child. Concealing Jews and Gypsies was a crime. The Germans, who already appropriate the lion's share of the peasants' harvests for the needs of their regular troops and thereby cause great hardship, want, and deprivation for the Poles, would take terrible reprisals against communities that protected Jews and Gypsies, whose place was in the ghettos and extermination camps. For this reason, the child is chased from wherever he goes. If someone in a village takes him in, he must keep a low profile, for if his presence is detected by the others, he will be run off or worse. The majority of the Poles are unwilling to jeopardize their own lives in his behalf. Early in the novel, Polish partisans raid the home of a blacksmith where the boy has found temporary refuge. The blacksmith had supported a rival guerrilla group. There were both white and red partisans. The "whites" opposed both the Germans and the Soviets, whereas the "reds"[4] supported the Russians and fought only the Germans. After beating the blacksmith, his wife, son, and hired hands to death, the partisans enter and plunder the house. They discover the child hiding in the attic and assume that he is a gypsy foundling. After beating him with their fists, they decide that he should he handed over to the Germans. This would make the enemy less suspicious of the village. Upon the instructions of the partisans, several peasants deliver the child to the nearest German outpost. An officer orders a German soldier to take him into the forest and shoot him. He is given a small can of gasoline with which he is to burn the body. Instead of following his orders, the soldier lets the boy go, then simulates the execution by firing two shots into the air.

Many of the Polish peasants the boy subsequently encounters in the other villages and hamlets he passes through fear him not only because of the Germans' harsh penalties for harboring Gypsies and Jews but also for irrational reasons stemming from superstition and ignorance. Thinking that the boy is a gypsy, they fear that he will give them the evil eye or that he will count their teeth and thereby cause their deaths. In one village, a priest compels a farmer named Garbos to take the boy in against his will. Garbos flogs the child constantly, fearing that the boy is casting spells on him in an attempt to contrive his death. He takes the stray into a room and makes him grab hold of two hooks driven into the beams of the ceiling. He then calls his dog Judas into the room. The dog leaps in the air and tries to snap at the boy's feet. The child knows that if he lets go, Judas will attack and kill him. Garbos lets the foundling hang for hours at a time. Everyday he suspends him from the ceiling. He feels that if the boy falls and Judas kills him, he will not be guilty of murder and that his patron, St. Anthony, will therefore grant him absolution for the foundling's "accidental"[5] death. Each day, the child prays as he hangs from the ceiling, believing that Christ will save him. His prayers seem to be answered on Corpus Christi. One of the altar boys falls sick that day and the new priest orders that the child take his place in the service. He is to lift the heavy missal and transfer it from one side of the altar to the other. The muscles in his arms are so sore from all the hours he has spent hanging from Garbos's ceiling that he staggers backward and the missal and its tray fall to the floor. The congregation goes wild and shouts "Gypsy vampire!"[6] The interruption of High Mass will bode evil for the village. The peasants lift the boy up and bear him out of the church and carry him to a large manure pit. In his fear, the child attempts to beg for mercy but he loses the power of speech. The angry peasants toss him into the open sewer, where they believe that he drowns. He manages to climb out of the muck but thereafter remains mute for a period of several years. Only after the war does he regain his voice after he is injured in a skiing accident.

Kosinski may have suffered muteness himself for several years following World War II. As is true with his other semiautobiographical novels or "autofictions," the line between what Kosinski imagines and what happened in actuality is purposely blurred and indeterminate. Kosinski seems to enjoy playing with his readers. One is never sure what is fact and what is fiction, especially in the later books. Kosinski puts a lot of himself into his various heroes; certain events in his life appear only slightly fictionalized. George Levanter, the investor hero of *Blind Date*, shares his creator's working and sleeping habits. A survivor of the holocaust in Eastern Europe, he tricks his way into coming into America. He survives in the hostile environment of New York and marries an industrial heiress who succumbs to a fatal illness shortly thereafter. He has a deteriorating heart condition and his favorite sport is skiing. But there is a great deal of exaggeration and embellishment in the novels as well. Levanter committed a brutal rape as a boy and had an incestuous affair with his mother, a concert pianist, after his father, a "student of ancient languages,"[7] suffered a stroke. In the West, he is an occasional terrorist and assassin and has wilder love affairs than 007.

Kosinski delights in hyperbole and deliberate leg pulling, but there is also an element of wish fulfillment to his fictions, especially when his heroes act as agents of vengeance on the perpetrators of crime and evil in the modern world. Kosinski is honest about his own hate and rage and preaches a Nietzschean gospel. The world of his experience confirms to the Darwinian model: dog eats dog and cat kills cat. In *The Painted Bird*, the Gypsy frequently fantasizes that he is a blond, blue-eyed SS officer in black uniform. In Gregor Samsa-like fashion, he thinks himself an insect in comparison to such a German. What does not kill him indeed makes him stronger. He fights for his life whenever danger comes his way and becomes every bit as brutal and unmerciful as the peasants. He causes a cruel carpenter to fall through a pillbox into an abandoned bunker full of hundreds of rats and watches the sea of animals eat him alive. Outside one village several boys taunt him and he smashes a rock into the largest one's face. When a crowd of men and boys gathers to club him to death with sticks, he detonates a caché of ammunition he has stored in a barn as his pursuers enter the building. After he comes under the protection of Soviet soldiers, he sees himself as a future communist warrior. He and another boy precipitate a train derailment to kill peasants coming into the city to sell their wares following the peace. Although he can't speak, he becomes involved with the black market and associates with prostitutes. Eventually he is arrested and jailed. His puzzled parents secure his release and say nothing.

The hero of Kosinski's next novel, *Steps*, escapes from Eastern Europe to America. Like the boy in *The Painted Bird*, during the war, he was also a horribly mistreated child vagrant hounded and tortured by the peasants. Like the boy in the first book, he commits murder and takes horrible revenge on his tormentors. He feeds the children of a farmer who spit on him bread laced with crushed glass and watches them die in agony. He enjoys placing lighted matches under the rims of jars in which he has placed butterflies he has caught. In the smoke, the insects fly faster and faster, collide with each other, and knock the dust off their wings as they are slowly asphyxiated. Some years after the war, during his student days, he throws beer bottles at an old man standing guard over an abandoned factory. One strikes the man on the head and kills him. In the United States, the *Steps* hero, at least initially, lives from hand to mouth. Once more he must fight for his survival. He speaks little English and sometimes pretends that he is a spastic deaf mute in order to extract himself from messy situations. He works as a menial, scrapes paint from the hulls of ships, parks cars, and drives trucks. He strong-arms another Holocaust survivor, a restaurant owner, into going into business with the mob and races cars illegally in Harlem. He takes drugs and pursues sexual encounter after sexual encounter. George Levanter also seeks deliverance through sexual abandon. When circumstances permit, he, too, takes deadly action against the world's evil doers. Early in *Blind Date*, he blows up a ski gondola in which the Deputy Minister of Indostran and his entourage are riding. The Deputy Minster had been responsible for the mass jailing of university professors, writers, and artists in his country.

Over the years, Kosinski made a number of contradictory statements about *The Painted Bird*. Initially he wanted to keep under wraps the autobiographical nature of the book. To those in the know, he admitted that he had "extended"[8] certain of his experiences for dramatic effect, but he preferred readers who knew nothing of his past and who therefore would approach the novel as entirely fictional. He maintained that the finished work should be able to stand on its own. To this end, he made sure the first editions of the book contained little or no information about himself or his own traumatic boyhood experiences. Fiction and autobiography, he claimed in an afterword to later editions of the book, were very different modes. The reader of an autobiography compares his life to that of the subject, but a reader of fiction does more than compare, he contributes: "he actually enters a fictional role, expanding it in terms of his own experience, his own creative and imaginative powers."[9] In later years, however, Kosinski would insist that every incident in the book was true. Just how much he did or did not embellish his own boyhood experiences in *The Painted Bird* cannot now be readily ascertained. What is certain is that Kosinski did encounter unspeakable horrors as a child.

In the novel, after he is thrown into the manure pit and loses his voice, the boy continues to have a number of close calls with death. The people he encounters in his wanderings remain heartless and barbaric. At one point, he confesses that the German ambition of world conquest puzzles him: "Was such a destitute cruel world worth ruling?"[10] Eventually he is rescued by Communist soldiers and, at last, is reunited with his parents. In real life, Russian soldiers did in fact take mercy on the young Kosinski. Miraculously his parents also had survived the war. The traumatized child did, in fact, find his way home. Father, mother, and son all lived, but they were the only members of a once large and distinguished family of scholars, physicians, lawyers, and financiers who did survive. In 1938, some sixty Kosinski relatives attended a last reunion. With the exception of Kosinski's nuclear family, all would perish in Hitler's Holocaust. His parents wanted to immigrate to Israel following the war but were never granted an exit visa. After recovering from his youthful shocks and blows, Kosinski attended high school, then state-controlled universities in Warsaw and Moscow. He was a brilliant student as an undergraduate but faced expulsion on two occasions for not adequately toeing the Marxist party line. In the mid-1950s, he received two master's degrees from the University of Lodz in history and political science and then became a Ph.D candidate in social psychology. From 1955 until 1957, he served as professor of psychology at the Polish Academy of Sciences in Warsaw and was appointed as an organizer of youth festivals throughout the Soviet bloc. Despite his university honors and the perquisites of his academic position (he spent part of his winters as a ski instructor at a model resort and his summers as a psychological counselor at a spa by the sea), Kosinski came to despise the Marxist system and began to plot his escape to America. Kosinski took up photography, exhibiting widely throughout Poland. This gave Kosinski access to printing plants. He claimed that in 1957 he decided to invent a series of fictional academicians to provide him with recommendations for study abroad. Because he had printing contacts through his photography, he could supply himself with official-looking seals and proper government stationery. Eventually he obtained a passport. Had his various acts of forgery been detected, he could have been imprisoned for a term of fifteen years. While waiting for his travel papers, Kosinski carried a foil-wrapped egg of cyanide with him at all times. He determined to kill himself if his plans were thwarted by state authorities. "One way or another," he said, "they would not keep me against my will."[11] Big Brother was always looking over your shoulder in the East. In *Steps*, Kosinski suggests that the only means one had of securing privacy in Soviet satellite countries was to lock oneself in a lavatory cubicle. There, at last, one could find peace and quiet. Even after migrating to the West, Kosinski remained adept at disappearing from sight. "I have hiding places everywhere," he once commented. "If I were alone in your apartment for a half an hour, I'd find a hiding place there."[12] One of the narrator's acquaintances in *Steps*, a fellow university student, takes refuge in the lavatories for hours at a time. He confesses that he does this because he needs to be alone. He scrubs the antigovernment slogans off the walls so that if he is ever questioned why he spends so much time in the toilets, he can offer a patriotic excuse. One day in class, he rises from his seat to answer a question about a political doctrine recently implemented by the party. He says the doctrine seems "to mirror perfectly the many repressive elements of the total state, and for this reason it lacked all humanity."[13] All the students know that he is through. After being removed from the university for antisocial behavior, he kills himself one day in a toilet.

At the age of twenty-four, Kosinski fled Poland for New York. (He would return to Poland only once again in 1988, at the invitation of the Communist government, having become in the meantime a famous American writer.) When Kosinski arrived in the city in 1957, he could speak (as he later claimed) no English and had but $2.80 to his name. By 1958, "this displaced person in an uncharted landscape"[14] had won a Ford Foundation fellowship to continue his sociological studies at Columbia University. In a half year he had taught himself English, with his philologist father instructing him by mail. He did four further years of postgraduate work. He published two nonfiction works, "a psychological analysis of the totalitarian state," *The Future Is Ours Comrade* (1960), and "a study of totalitarian behavior,"[15] *No Third Path* (1962) under the pen name of Joseph Novak. He wrote both books in English. In 1962, Kosinski married Mary Hayward Weir, the widow of the founder of one of America's largest steel companies. The two would divorce in 1966 after Weir developed an inoperable brain disease. She would die two years later. Kosinski decided to write *The Painted Bird* in 1963 when he and his wife visited Switzerland in order to consult with health specialists. Kosinski would dedicate the book, which appeared in October 1965, to his wife. The work brought Kosinski immediate recognition and won the French Best Foreign Book Award. Eastern Europeans, however, would roundly condemn the novel as a vicious slander of the Polish people. A campaign against the work was launched in Poland, where the work was banned. A famous Eastern European writer who had read the book in French translation and initially praised it in a review was forced to recant. Subsequently he published an "Open Letter to Jerzy Kosinski" in which he accused the novelist of forsaking his native language and of libeling his own people. He predicted that one day a guilt-stricken Kosinski would commit suicide by slitting his "throat in some seedy hotel on the Riviera."[16] A young Polish poetess whom Kosinski had met through the international literary association PEN was forced by Polish authorities to write a short story about her New York encounter with the author of *The Painted Bird*, which portrays Kosinski as a "pervert who had sworn to denigrate all that her motherland had stood for."[17] Reprisals were also made against the author's aging and ill mother, who still lived behind the Iron Curtain in her native Poland. Prior to her death she had to move to another town because angry protesters would descend upon her house on an almost daily basis.

Kosinski's second novel, *Steps*, appeared in 1968. It would win the National Book Award for that year. Kosinski followed *Steps* in 1970 with the satirical novel *Being There*, the tale of Chance, a vapid and platitudinous gardener who is mistaken as a sage by pundits, politicians, business tycoons, and blue-stocking socialites. Chance's entire knowledge of the world, all his supposed wisdom, comes from years and years of television watching. Kosinski continued producing novels in the seventies and eighties. His later works include *The Devil Tree* (1973), *Cockpit* (1975), *Blind Date* (1977), *Passion Play* (1979), *Pinball* (1982), and *The Hermit of 69th Street* (1988), but none of these works would receive anything like the critical approbation accorded to the initial three. In 1967, Kosinski was awarded a Guggenheim Fellowship and in 1968 he was appointed a Fellow of the Center for Advanced Studies at Wesleyan University. He would also teach at both Princeton and Yale. Kosinski was elected president of PEN in 1973. He served two terms and fought for the release of imprisoned writers around the globe. He wrote the screenplay for the 1979 film version of *Being There*, and in 1982, he played the Communist ideologue Grigory Zinoviev in the Warren Beatty film *Reds*. When he was not lecturing or working on Hollywood projects, Kosinski spent much of his later years on the road. He would often disguise himself and from time to time would take temporary employment in corporations and businesses that interested him. He also remained active in the two sports he most loved, downhill skiing and horseback riding. Kosinski's knowledge of the latter sport is reflected in his 1979 novel *Passion Play*, which concerns the modern-day knight-errant Fabian, a professional polo player who drives his Van Home, a combination trailer and stable, across the United States in search of both love and combat with a worthy adversary. Kosinski himself was forced into the lists in 1982 when the *Village Voice* printed a front-page article which alleged that all his novels were ghost written by editors and that the CIA had "played a clandestine role"[18] in the publication of his first two books. Kosinski hotly contested the allegations that would prove unfounded.

In 1986, Kosinski married his second wife, Kiki von Fraunhofer, in the apartment of Marion Javits, the widow of the New York senator. His first novel in six years, *The Hermit of 69th Street,* appeared in 1988. It was something of a comeback book for Kosinski and earned better notices than any of his other later titles, though some critics thought it over-the-top and complained that it read, at least in part, like self-parody. The prose is jazzier and more inventive than that found in his preceding books. In writing *The Hermit of 69th Street,* Kosinski decided to really let go. In none of his other novels does he appear to be having so much fun as he does in this book. For all its droll humor and antic buffoonery, however, the book is a serious meditation on the questions of identity and authorship and seems to be inspired, at least in part, by the *Village Voice* fiasco. It brings to mind the Nabokov of *Pale Fire* but also the tediously self-referential John Barth of *Chimera* and *Letters.* Once again Kosinski mixes fact and fiction. A writer Norbert Kosky leaves his collected papers in the hands of his editor Jay Kay, who exhaustively annotates them. The footnotes contain references to the fiction of Jerzy Kosinski (cited under Kosinski's own name) and to fictional works supposedly written by Norbert Kosky. Some of the latter books, however, are immediately identifiable as Kosinski's own previously published fiction. The trio of Kosky, Jay Kay, and Kosinski parodies the Christian trinity, each representing a different facet of the same personality. The book probes the many different levels of identity. Kosinski contends that everyone wears multiple masks. He, for example, has Jewish, Polish, and American sides to his character and, in his own way, is as multifaceted as Joseph Conrad, to whom a number of pages of the book are devoted. In his last novel, Kosinski argues that reality itself has many planes and layers. He seems to say that its puzzle can never be satisfactorily solved. In his final book, Kosinski satirizes the Hollywood scene with trenchant and biting wit, transferring his own experiences to his alter ego Kosky. The book is crammed with inside jokes and features a hilarious send-up of Warren Beatty. In his final incarnation, Kosky resolves that he must withdraw from the world. Hiding he will see more. In becoming the hermit of the title he begins to resemble another of Kosinski's creations, Chance the gardener. In the end, he effaces himself completely.

Kosinski's near misses with death did not cease once he came to America. He was almost murdered twice. Shortly after the government campaign against *The Painted Bird* began in Poland, the novel began to be attacked in emigré publications in the United States and Kosinski received a slew of threatening letters from naturalized Eastern Europeans. One day, two large burly men forced their way into

Kosinski's Manhattan apartment and threatened to beat the author to death with lengths of steel pipe they had concealed inside the coat sleeves of their raincoats. Kosinski noticed one of the men glancing at a newspaper clipping he had pulled from his pocket. It featured an old blurred photograph of Kosinski—a very bad likeness of him. He immediately insisted that he was not the man in the photograph, but a cousin of the author who was often mistaken for him. The real Kosinski had momentarily left the apartment but would be coming back shortly. The two men sat down on the sofa, gripping their lengths of lead pipe menacingly, to await his return. When Kosinski asked the men what they wanted, one replied that they had come to punish his "cousin" for *The Painted Bird*, a book that defamed their mother country. The second man interjected that, although he and his companion now lived in the United States, they were still patriots. Soon the two were speaking Polish, the same rural dialect Kosinski had come to know so well as a boy. Kosinski offered the men vodka. At first they demurred but soon were drinking heartily. As the men downed a second and third round, Kosinski was able to walk over to one of his bookshelves. He had a revolver hidden there behind his two-volume *Dictionary of Americanisms*. He drew the weapon and demanded the Poles drop theirs. They then pleaded for mercy. Kosinski took a camera out of a desk drawer and snapped five or six photos of the men. He said that he would use the photographs to press charges against the two if they ever troubled him again, then let them go.

Kosinski's second close call with death occurred in 1969. He was traveling from Paris to Los Angeles, where he planned to stay the night at the Beverly Hills home of his boyhood friend and fellow expatriate, Roman Polanski, and his wife, Sharon Tate. During a stopover in New York City, Kosinski's luggage was not transferred to the connecting L.A. flight but sent instead to the inspection ramp. He did not have enough time to go through customs and still make the L.A. connection, and the next plane to L.A. would not leave until the following day. Kosinski cleared customs and reluctantly spent the night in New York. The Charles Manson family invaded the Polanski house that same night. Five people, including the pregnant Sharon Tate, were murdered. Had he not missed his flight, Kosinski would have been there and would have probably perished with the other victims. Kosinski would write about both his experience and the California mass murder itself in *Blind Date*. In the novel, after missing his flight, Levanter attempts to telephone his friends Woytek and Sharon but receives no answer at Sharon's house. The following morning he is awakened by a ringing telephone. It is the Los Angeles police department asking to speak to the next of kin of George Levanter. The police mistakenly think that he was one of the murder victims, having found a telegram he had previously sent to Sharon telling her to expect him the evening of the murders. After realizing his mistake, the officer informs Levanter of his friends' deaths. As he learns what has happened, Levanter, who has suffered a heart ailment for many years, feels his heart lose its rhythm. He gasps and fights for breath. Throughout the novel his heart is affected adversely by bad news and whatever human cruelty he happens to witness. However, when he commits murder himself earlier in the novel (Levanter detonates the plastic explosives hidden in a pair of skis that were placed in the gondola of the Deputy Minister of Indostran and his security guards, blowing the gondola apart, showering bits of metal walls, glass windows, and chunks of bodies into the chasm below), his heart beats regularly and rhythmically. But, as the novel concludes, Levanter's heart rebels a final time, perhaps in part because of his earlier action. Skiing in a snowstorm near the PicSoliel gondola station where he had earlier assassinated the Indostran minister, he loses his way. He skis that day even though he knows how dangerous the weather conditions are, an almost suicidal act. Alone and tired, he stops to rest. He knows that he will freeze to death and calmly awaits his final blind date. Death will find him where once before he had dealt it out.

Earlier in the book, when he learns of the helter-skelter killings, Levanter ponders if the entire human race is intrinsically barbaric:

> Were all people cruel by nature, he wondered, and would they be amused by the games he had seen in some European cities? Would they enjoy the colorful ducks tapping a frenetic dance on a metal platter if they knew the platter was connected to a battery that sent electric shocks through the bird's body each time the webbed feet stepped on it? Would they be entertained by the man who tucks his trousers into his boots, then slips two fierce-looking rats into his baggy pants, buckles up, and waits while blood begins to seep through the fabric? The bystanders move away in horror, sure that his flesh is being eaten away by the rats. He bleeds more and more, and when everyone around appears convinced that he will bleed to death, he smiles and opens his fly: two dead rats fall out, and behind them jumps a little ferret, its jaws still full of hunks of rat meat.[19]

Perhaps what pains Levanter's heart most is the realization that he is as capable of a ruthlessness every bit as merciless and heartless as that shown to him as a child by the Germans and the Russians.

On Thursday, May 2, 1991, Kosinski appeared to be in a particularly good mood. He attended a book signing party for Senator William S. Cohen, Republican of Maine, at the upper-east-side home of author Gay Talese. A crowd had gathered to celebrate the publication of Cohen's book *One-Eyed Kings*. Kosinski conversed with the senator and had him inscribe a copy of the book. Before leaving the affair, he handed Cohen his card. Returning to his West 57th Street apartment, Kosinski spoke briefly with his second wife, Katherina (Kiki) von Fraunhofer, a public relations executive who, prior to her 1986 marriage to Kosinski, had been his editorial assistant for close to twenty years. The couple had separate bedrooms and bathrooms. Kosinski retired at 9 P.M. Von Fraunhofer would later recall that her husband seemed in especially good spirits that night. Fourteen hours later, she would walk into her husband's bathroom. Kosinski lay naked in a bathtub half filled with water, a plastic shopping bag tied around his head. Von Fraunhofer ran from the room to summon help. Paramedics arrived on the scene in short order. Kosinski, however, had been dead for hours from asphyxiation. A suicide note was found among his papers. It read: "I'm going to put myself to sleep now for a bit longer than usual. Call the time Eternity."[20]

In a statement released to the press by a publicity agent later in the day, Fraunhofer said that in recent years her husband had been periodically depressed by a "growing inability to work"[21] and that he suffered from a serious heart condition and was frightened "of becoming a burden to me and his friends."[22] For years, the author suffered from fibrillation. He also occasionally had difficulty breathing. With the exception of *New York Times*' columnist A. M. Rosenthal, who had seen Kosinski earlier in the week and recalled that "he was more down than I've ever seen him,"[23] those who attended the party were shocked by Kosinski's suicide. Even though he knew about Kosinski's health problems, Talese, for one, found it hard to believe that his friend was suffering from severe depression: "I had my arm around him, and we were laughing. The things we were talking about had a future tense to them. I saw him often in April and in recent months. There was nothing in his manner to show he was depressed. . . . Last night he was moving in and out of the crowd as I've seen him on many occasions."[24] Talese found Kosinski's suicide "inexplicable."[25] He said his friend "did something in the last minutes of his life that would have been unbelievable had it been performed by a character in one of his novels."[26]

Anyone who has seen *Reds* knows that Kosinski was a great actor. He had a real talent for imposture, and had a long history of adopting disguises. That he fooled everyone, including Talese and his wife, the night of his suicide should not surprise anyone. Kiki blamed his death on his medical circumstances and on his inability to write, but he had suffered the same health problems for well over a decade. Kosinski's condition in 1991 was much the same as it was in 1977, the year he published *Blind Date*. In that novel, Levanter's ailment is exacerbated by the horrible events he witnesses around the world. Kosinski committed suicide two months after the liberation of Kuwait and the conclusion of Operation Desert Storm. In 1991, civil war had also broken out in Yugoslavia. Croatia and Slovenia wanted the former Communist state to become a loose confederation, while Serbia and Montenegro favored a more centralized form of government. Bosnia and Hercegovina sought a compromise and envisioned a future state that would contain elements of both federalism and confederalism. On March 9, riots occurred in Belgrade, protests against the government of Serbian president Slobodan Milosevic. Army tanks rolled into the streets and put down the unrest, resulting in a number of civilian casualties. The same month, the conflict spread to Croatia where there were numerous skirmishes between the Croat National Guard and police and Serb irregulars backed by the former Yugoslav Peoples' Army. The country continued to disintegrate in April and May, with Croatia calling for a republicwide referendum. There could be little doubt the populace would vote for the creation of an independent Croat state. War and racial division would ensue, and 600,000 people would be displaced in Yugoslavia by year's end. One can imagine the creator of Chance the gardener looking at his television screen with horror, disgust, and heartache.

The events in the Gulf and in Yugoslavia came after the fall of communism in Eastern Europe. No doubt, Kosinski welcomed the downfall of totalitarianism in the former Soviet bloc. A new optimism awoke when the Berlin wall came down, an optimism that would shortly be tempered by events in Kuwait, Iraq, and Yugoslavia. In his afterword to later editions of *The Painted Bird*, Kosinski recalls his 1963 trip to Switzerland with his terminally ill wife Mary Weir. The two took a suite in a palatial hotel. In the corridors of the famous resort, Kosinski stood before portraits of various statesmen who had visited the hotel between the wars and read the gilded plaques commemorating international peace conferences that had been held in the hotel's convention halls after World War I. Kosinski realized that those who fought the war to end all wars and who convened the postwar peace conferences were well-intentioned, humanitarian individuals, but having lived through World War II, he wondered if the authors of the treaties had signed them in good faith. The events that followed the conferences did not support such a conclusion. He and his family "had been forced to experience events far worse than those the treaties so grandiloquently prohibited."[27] History now seemed to be repeating itself. Clearly Kosinski saw that Saddam Hussein had to be put down. Scud missiles exploding over Israel would have certainly outraged him. He would not, however, have been blind to the hypocrisy of the United States. In *Blind Date*, Levanter decries the fact the United States supports right-wing dictators who trample the human rights of their people. The book contains unflattering portraits of a Henry Kissinger-like secretary of state and of an Imelda Marcos type, the wife of an Asian dictator who ruthlessly suppresses his people but who nonetheless receives support from the United States' government. Kosinski also records many instances of American bigotry and small-mindedness in his novels. Our people can be just as cruel as the Germans, Russians, and Poles. Furthermore, Kosinski realized that the "guarantors of peace" often become "the initiators of war"[28] and was surely aware of the fact that Saddam Hussein had been a former U.S. ally and that the American government had secretly helped him build his war machine during the Iran-Iraq war. No doubt Kosinski felt compassion for all the victims of the Gulf conflict, especially the innocent children. The events in Yugoslavia must have recalled his own boyhood. One can envision Kosinski watching his television and, like his fictional avatar Levanter, asking himself again and again, if all people were, by nature, cruel. From the evidence on the TV screen, the answer would appear to be a resounding yes.

Addendum

James Park Sloan's 1996 biography, *Jerzy Kosinski* (which the present author came across and began reading just as *Final Drafts* was going to press), reveals that Kosinski's falsification of the actual facts of his early life was even more extensive than originally supposed. Sloan's research discloses that Kosinski's parents were not separated from their son from the fall of 1939 to the spring of 1945. Indeed, Sloan convincingly documents that the parents accompanied Jerzy both during all stages of his migrations from Lodz to the easternmost parts of Poland in 1939 and during the swerve back to Lodz from 1944 on. Together the family witnessed many horrors. Kosinski experienced profound alienation and isolation during these years and, as a result, became increasingly estranged from his parents. The separation was spiritual and psychological and, evidently, is paralleled by the harrowing fictional experiences the child protagonist in *The Painted Bird* undergoes with the Polish country people and German and eventually Russian soldiers. In later years, Kosinski's mother conspired with her son to maintain the story that, as a young boy, Kosinski was sent into hiding alone. Even in her private correspondence with her son, she preserved this fiction.[29]

Notes

1. Jerzy Kosinski, afterword to *The Painted Bird* (New York: Bantam, 1978), p. 267. *The Painted Bird* was first published in 1965.

2. Ibid.

3. *The Painted Bird*, p. 2.

4. Ibid., p. 69.

5. Ibid., p. 135.

6. Ibid., p. 144.

7. Kosinski, *Blind Date* (New York: Bantam, 1978), p. 9. *Blind Date* was first published in 1977.

8. Afterword to *The Painted Bird*, p. 256.

9. Ibid., p. 258.

10. *The Painted Bird*, p. 94.

11. "On Kosinski," *Blind Date*, p. 272.

12. Quoted by Mervyn Rothstein, "In Novels and Life, a Maverick and an Eccentric," *New York Times*, 4 May 1991.

13. Kosinski, *Steps* (New York: Bantam, 1969), p. 70. *Steps* was first published in 1968.

14. Quoted by Rothstein, "In Novels and Life."

15. "On Kosinski," *Blind Date*, pp. 272–73.

16. Afterword to *The Painted Bird*, p. 260.

17. Ibid., p. 264.

18. Quoted by Rothstein, "In Novels and Life."

19. *Blind Date*, pp. 209–210.

20. Quoted by Matthew Flamm, "Reading Their Last Writes," *Entertainment*, 14 March 1997, p. 72. A book review of *Or Not to Be: A Collection of Suicide Notes*, Riverhead, 1997.

21. Quoted by Alessandra Stanley, "Jerzy Kosinski, The Writer, 57, Is Found Dead," *New York Times*, 4 May 1991.

22. Ibid.

23. Ibid.

24. Ibid.

25. Ibid.

26. Ibid.

27. Afterword to *The Painted Bird*, p. 255.

28. Ibid.

29. James Park Sloan, *Jerzy Kosinski, A Biography* (New York: Dutton, 1996), pp. 17–54, 171, 225.

Other Notables

Jack London (1876–1916)

F OR MANY YEARS, IT WAS ASSUMED THAT THE AMERICAN NOVELIST and short-story writer had died from uremic poisoning, but it has since come to light that on the night preceding his death he took an overdose of a prescribed sleeping medication. He died at his Glen Ellen, California, ranch at 7:45 P.M. on November 22, 1916. A servant found London unconscious early in the morning of the 22nd when he went to his room. Physicians who were summoned from the city of Santa Rosa at first suspected that London suffered from ptomaine poisoning. Later they determined that he was a victim of severe uremia. It is unclear whether they knew about the overdose at the time they were treating him. Later in the day, Dr. J. Wilson Shields, a San Francisco physician who was also a close personal friend of London, arrived at the ranch to attend the comatose author. From the time London was discovered until the hour of his death, he never regained consciousness, although he appeared to rally somewhat toward midday. In the afternoon, however, he suffered a relapse and his condition continued to deteriorate during the hours preceding his demise. London was only forty years old. In his last hours, he was attended by his second wife, Charmian Kittredge London, and his sister Mrs. Eliza Shepherd. He and his wife had only recently returned from a trip of several months to the Hawaiian Islands.

Born in San Francisco on January 12, 1876, London spent his early years on various California ranches. At nine, he and his family moved to Oakland. The following year he entered the Oakland Public Library for the first time. Befriended and guided in his reading by the librarian, the poet Ina Coolbrith, London "discovered the great world beyond the skyline. . . . I read everything, but principally history and adventure, and all the old travels and voyages. I read mornings, afternoons, and nights. . . ."[1] As a boy and youth, London attended public schools but only intermittently. At an early age, he worked as an oysterman and bayman, styling himself as the "Prince of the Oyster Pirates."[2] A double-barreled shotgun clutched in his hands, he managed to steer his sloop with his feet. At nights, when his crew went ashore to sleep, London would go to the Free Library, exchange his books, buy a quarter's worth of candy, sneak back aboard *The Razzle Dazzle*, lock himself in the cabin, lie down on the bed, and spend the night reading and chewing candy. Not all his jobs would be so picturesque. He signed as a common sailor on a sealing schooner along the coast north of the Russian side of the Bering sea. In California, he worked long hours at a jute mill as well. While putting in thirteen-hour-a-day shifts there, London managed to write an essay "Typhoon Off the Coast of China" and enter it in a contest sponsored by the *San Francisco Call*. He took first prize and began to consider a career as a writer. One year, bent on researching social and economic conditions in his home state, he led the life of an itinerant tramp. At the age of nineteen, he enrolled as a student at the University of California, but midway through his freshman year, he was forced to drop out for lack of money. For a time, he worked in a laundry and wrote in his spare hours. In 1897, he sought his fortune in the Klondike during the Alaskan gold rush. One of the few who made it over the Chilcoot pass that winter, London nonetheless did not find gold, and he fell victim to scurvy. Unable to get a homebound steamer, he and two companions embarked on an open boat for the Bering Sea.

London began writing in earnest upon his return to San Francisco. His experiences as a common sailor and prospector in the Klondike provided the background for much of his fiction. London's tough "survival-of-the-fittest" philosophy was informed by his reading of Nietzsche, Marx, and Darwin. He produced a great many novels and short-story collections, including *The Son of the Wolf* (1900), *The God of the Fathers* (1901), *The Call of the Wild* (1903), *White Fang* (1906), and *The Sea Wolf*. His socialist ideals are reflected in *War of the Classes*; *The People of the Abyss* (1903), which examined life in the London slums; and *The Iron Heel*, which depicts a fascist uprising and a Utopian state. *Martin Eden* (1909) reflects London's impoverished youth and boyhood, while *John Barleycorn* (1913) deals with his later drinking problems. His other books include *When God Laughs*, *The Cruise of the Snark*, *The Valley of the Moon*, and *The Abysmal Brute*. London's last six years were plagued by mounting difficulties. His reputation as a writer had waned, and he experienced financial troubles. He tried to supplement his income by planting grapevines and eucalyptus trees on his ranch. His crops, however, failed abysmally. In addition, Wolf House, the large stone home that he had built on his ranch, caught fire and was badly damaged. London was severely depressed when he and his wife returned to California from the Hawaiian islands. Charmian London would erect a second stone home, the House of the Happy Walls, on their Glen Ellen ranch. Today it serves as a Jack London museum.

Sergey Aleksandrovich Yesenin (1895–1925)

Isadora Duncan found a firebrand to marry in Sergey Aleksandrovich Yesenin. The pair wed in Moscow in May 1922 and Duncan brought her blond, curly-haired, handsome Russian husband—tall, muscular, and of pure peasant stock—to America to show him off. Ten years younger than his wife, at twenty-seven, the imagist poet looked as if he were still an adolescent. Naive and puppylike, he stood beside his wife but served merely as a prop to set her off. He belonged to her entourage and knew it, though she called him in public the greatest poet since Pushkin and said that he possessed a genius on the order of Edgar Allan Poe. In the Soviet Union Yesenin was not a mere adjunct but had a reputation of his own. A Bolshevist, he composed Tolstoian hymns to the soil, and wrote poems about horse, plow, and furrowed earth, sowing, reaping, and gathering. He also extolled the Communist revolution in his verse, for which reason the United States held up the couple's entry into America, even though Duncan was a citizen and celebrity. A special board convened, and admission was granted. Much red tape had to be cut through first, however, and Duncan took revenge by dancing conspicuously with a red flag that she waved in every city she visited on her American tour.

Yesenin remained meek and subservient, often appearing childishly naive at Duncan's side as the cameras clicked, but he was transformed completely—and this, too, was eventually reported—as soon as he got a drink. Yesenin had a prodigious capacity for alcohol, drinking great quantities of liquor in a single sitting. He become sentimental and teary-eyed in his cups. A cuddly Russian at first, he could quickly turn into a belligerent, insanely jealous brute. He constantly beat Duncan for real and perceived infidelities. Once he blackened her eye at a party in the Bronx, forcing her to cancel a performance. It took five men to subdue him. He was bound and gagged until he sobered up some hours later. He broke furniture in his rages and smashed everything in sight. His drunken exploits made copy again and again. Duncan seemed to enjoy the publicity and defended her husband in the papers or dismissed his actions with a smile. "Everyone knows he is crazy,"[3] she said. Yesenin accompanied her to Paris, where he continued to fight and cause trouble. Once he attempted to beat two Russian former guardsmen in a Montmartre restaurant. He continued to go into insane rages and rumors that he battered Duncan persisted. At last she grew tired of his abuse and tantrums and shipped him to Moscow from Paris under guard. "Sergey Yesenin," she told the press, "is no more deserving of tears than laughter. He is better off in Russia, where he is loved even if he is foolish. He can smash things in Moscow and nobody cares, because he is a poet."[4] At home, Yesenin caused trouble in cafés. He returned to Paris and took up with Duncan again. They traveled to Berlin together, but he did not change his ways. He had affairs himself but tormented his wife continually about her liaisons. He went back to Moscow, where he was arrested for making anti-Semitic remarks and jailed. He would be released after friends testified he was drunk and out of his mind at the time he made the comments. He moved in with another woman and stated publicly that he was through with Duncan. In November 1923, she decided to sue for divorce. "If it were only women," she said, "I wouldn't mind so much, but Sergey's trouble comes out of the bottle. It is difficult enough for me to carry on my school anyway and with a husband that is always raising Cain it is impossible."[5] The following year, however, Duncan, was still in communication with her husband. She reported to the press that he had gone to the Caucasus to become a bandit.[6] "He writes," she said, "that he is going to be a robber to get thrills. He wants to write poetry about robbery and wants experience as a bandit." When asked about the divorce, Duncan maintained that she no longer considered herself married to Yesenin, as America did not normally recognize Soviet marriages. She joked that it was impossible for her to divorce Yesenin because in Russia it was necessary to fill out a divorce application before noon at the Divorce Commissariat and Sergey never rose until late afternoon because he was up all night drinking. "Now," she concluded, "if the Soviets only had the sense to keep the divorce office open until 12 o'clock midnight we would have been divorced nicely."[7] Because of her marriage, she could not return to France. She was not permitted reentry on Yesenin's Russian passport and thus could not liquidate her property in Paris. At the time of Yesenin's suicide, a degree of divorcement had been entered in the poet's behalf. Yesenin married Sophia Tolstoy, Leo Tolstoy's granddaughter, shortly before his death. His suicide in Leningrad was spectacular. He slashed his wrists and wrote his suicide note (which proved illegible) in his own blood. Bleeding profusely, he proceeded to hang himself. At the time of his death, he was said to be suffering from a nervous breakdown. He was thirty years old.

Charlotte Mew (1870–1928)

She burned a great deal of her work, never satisfied with it. As she is considered one of the finest poets of the Georgian period—Sir Sidney Cockerell compared her verse in its heated fervor and intensity to Emily Brontë's brooding, passionate prose—her act occasioned an irretrievable loss. Mew was born one of four children in Bloomsbury, London, on November 15, 1870, the daughter of Frederick Mew, an architect who died early in life, and Anne Kendall Mew. Frederick's death plunged the family into poverty. Mew's whole adult life would be one of ongoing struggle against destitution and penury. Two of her siblings would eventually be institutionalized in insane asylums. She, her mother, her brother, and two sisters had vowed to care for each other and see to one another's needs throughout their lives. Disease and illness struck frequently. Charlotte would outlive everyone, tending both her mother and her most beloved sister while they were dying. The passing of the latter was too much for her. She spent hours nursing the ailing woman, totally devoted to her. After her sister died, Mew herself collapsed. Her reserve snapped, the facade fell. Committed to a charity home, immured like her siblings in an institution as well as held captive in a failing body, exhausted and terribly ill, she took poison shortly after her admittance to the home, killing herself at fifty-seven, but not before destroying a great many of her poems.

Mew resembles Emily Dickinson in that she was an intensely private woman. Self-educated, she resided for a number of years in Paris. She fell in love once, to whom it is not certain, but never married. She first wrote prose before trying her hand at poetry. Her stories and essays appeared in *Yellow Book* and other periodicals. Her verse, more personal and lapidary in its craftsmanship, won praise from Thomas Hardy, who called her "undoubtedly the greatest woman poet of our day."[8] One of the high points of Mew's life was a pilgrimage she made to see Hardy. He, John Masefield, and Walter de la Mare secured a Civil List pension of seventy-five pounds a year for her in 1923. This made her last years, prior to her final crisis with her sister, tolerable, reducing her want and need somewhat. Her first collection of verse, *The Farmer's Bride*, was published in 1916. She tortured herself over each line of verse and turned out her poems very slowly and secretly. But what she allowed into print was always first rate. Her best work appears in 1929's *The Rambling Sailor*, a posthumous volume of verse that she did not manage to lay her hands on and destroy before her death.

Mew's will had directed this material to be burned as well but fortunately for literature's sake, its provisions weren't followed. Louis Untermeyer wrote: "Her work, like herself, had a deceptive fragility, a cameo cut in steel."[9] Mew's reputation rests on a handful of verse. Her range of subjects is narrow but her unevenly rhymed, halting poems, written in broken meters, are intense, charged as they are with poignant feeling. She displays stylistic finesse in shaping the subjective and giving form to the ineffable. Although her verse seems spontaneous, each line is pieced together with patient precision. Her exactness of detail recalls Hardy at his best. Shy and retiring in life, she appears meek and rather startled and out of place in photographs. Lying ill in the convalescent home, shortly before killing herself, Mew received a poem from Thomas Hardy written in his own eighty-seven-year-old hand. It was her last gift from the world.

Ernst Toller (1893–1939)

A German expressionist playwright and poet, Ernst Toller was born December 1, 1893, in Samotschin, East Prussia (today part of Poland), the son of a Jewish shopkeeper. He attended Jewish grade school, then entered the *Realgymnasium* in Bromberg. In 1910, he began to contribute articles to *Ostdeutsche Rundshau*. After passing the *Abitur* in 1913, he enrolled at the University of Grenoble, attending classes there until the outbreak of the First World War. Toller's earliest surviving poem, "Der Ringende" ("The Striver"), dates from his student days at Grenoble. In

1914, he volunteered for military service in a Bavarian artillery regiment and was posted to the front where he served in both an artillery battalion and in a machine gun unit. Due to heart and stomach disorders, perhaps psychosomatic in nature, he was transferred to a convalescent unit in Munich. He attended university there and met both Rilke and Thomas Mann, who both provided encouragement and constructive criticism to the young poet.

In 1917, Toller was discharged from further military service. He began to participate in antiwar activities and began his antiwar drama *Die Wandlung* (*Transfiguration* 1919). Portions of the play were printed as political tracts. In 1918, he arranged antiwar strikes in Munich and was arrested for treason and placed in a military prison. While incarcerated, he became a socialist and began reading Marx, Lenin, and Rosa Luxemburg. Later in the year, Toller was posted to a reserve battalion in Neu Ulm, then confined in a mental hospital. After his release, he became Deputy Chairman of the *Zentralrat* of the Workers, Peasants, and Soldiers' Council. The following year he was defeated in the January elections to the Regional Parliament. After attending the Second International in Switzerland, he became chairman of the Munich branch of the Independent Social Democrats. He issued a decree for the establishment of a Red Army. He was placed in prison from 1919 until 1924 for his part in the Communist uprising and attempted coup later that year. As Field Commander of the Red Army, Toller had participated in the fighting. After 35,000 soldiers marched on Munich, he helped form a new government but it did not stand long. Munich was shortly retaken by White troops. Banished from Bavaria after serving his sentence, he traveled throughout Europe lecturing and campaigning for the socialist cause. Upon Hitler's rise to power, Toller left Germany and went into exile, living variously in England, Russia, and Switzerland. In 1935, he married the refugee actress Christiane Grautoff. The following year, he traveled to Spain and Portugal before going on to the United States and Canada for a speaking tour. Hired by M.G.M. in 1937, he worked on film scripts in Hollywood for one year.

In 1938, Toller went on a fact-finding tour in Spain and campaigned throughout Europe to raise funds for Spanish refugees before returning to the United States. Toller and his wife would separate later that year. Living in New York City in 1939, Toller was exhausted and careworn. He suffered from insomnia and found himself unable to write. He was worried about the fate of his sister and brother who were still in Europe; moreover, his plays were not being performed in America and he felt isolated in exile. In deepening financial difficulties, he had trouble scraping up enough money for each month's rent. Early in May, he attended and spoke at the International PEN Congress, and, on the 11th, he and the other delegates to the conference visited the White House at the invitation of Eleanor Roosevelt. He and Klaus Mann rode the train back to New York together. Toller, whose spirits had seemed to revive, was planning to return to Europe. That evening, however, he confessed to Mann that he was having great difficulty sleeping. He could not rest at all that night on the train and looked horribly tired the following morning when he disembarked at Pennsylvania Station. Mann recalled that his face was ashen and that his eyes were dark-ringed. Toller could not concentrate when Mann tried to engage him in a conversation about the morning newspaper. Although Toller did not live to see the Nazi-Soviet pact, he had heard rumors that such a deal was in the works and was sickened and disheartened at the prospect. Franco's victory in Spain also greatly depressed him. On Sunday, May 21, he dined at the apartment of his friends the Marcuses. When the conversation at the dinner table turned to suicide, Marcuse took the position that every man had the right to end his own life. Toller dissented strongly. The following day, however, he hanged himself in the bathroom of his apartment at the Mayflower Hotel. He had not slept well the night before and fought that morning on the phone with his agent over royalties. His secretary Ilse Herzfeld left him at the lunch hour. When she returned, she found his body swinging from a hook behind his bathroom door. He had used the cord of his dressing gown to kill himself.

Toller is most remembered today for his crusading, often doctrinaire plays, which called attention to the social injustices of his time, exposed corruption and hypocrisy, championed class struggle, and protested against the unfair treatment of workers. These include *Requiem dem gemordeten Brudern* (1920, *Requiem for Murdered Brothers*); *Masse Mensch* (1920, tr. *Man and the Masses*, 1924); *Die Maschinenstürmer* (1922, tr. *The Machine-Wreckers*, 1923) based on the Luddite riots in England; *Der Entfesselte Wotan* (1923, *Wotan Unchained*); *Hinkeman* (1924, tr. *Broken Bow*, 1926); *Hoppla, wir leben!* (1927, *Hoppla! Such is Life*); *Bourgeois bleibt Bourgeois* (1929, *Once a Bourgeois Always a Bourgeois*); *Feuer aus den Kesseln* (1930 *Draw the Fires*); *Wunder in Amerika* (1931, *Miracle in America*); *Die blinde Göttin* (1932, *The Blind Goddess*); *Nie wieder Freiden* (1937, *No More Peace*) and *Pastor Hall* (1939), whose title character was modeled on the anti-Nazi Protestant theologian Martin Niemoller. Toller's reputation as a lyric poet rests primarily on his 1923 collection *Das Scwalbenbuch* (*The Swallow Book*) which appeared in Germany while he was serving his prison sentence. Two nonfiction books of note are Toller's autobiographical account of his early years, *Eine Jungend in Deutschland* (1933, tr. *I Was a German*, 1934), and *Briefe aus dem Gefängnis* (1935), a collection of letters he wrote while he was jailed in Bavaria. The second volume and *Das Schwalbenbuch* were issued together in English translation under the title *Look through the Bars* in 1937.

Stuart Engstrand (1904–1955)

On September 9, 1955, the American novelist Stuart Engstrand drowned himself in the MacArthur Park Lake at the western edge of downtown Los Angeles. Two boathouse employees, Bill Sherman and Harvey Weaver, observed the man from some distance away as he walked into the water at approximately 12:30 P.M. They pulled Engstrand from the water and then summoned Fire Department paramedics who tried unsuccessfully to resuscitate the victim. Engstrand carried no identification. His body lay in the coroner's office until the following morning when Engstrand's brother-in-law Melvin H. Simon established that the dead man was indeed the novelist. The previous day, two hours after Engstrand drowned himself, his wife, Sophia, had filed a missing person's report with police. She stated that she had last seen her husband at 10 A.M. and that for quite some time he had been severely depressed and that recently he had been exhibiting suicidal inclinations. On the day Engstrand chose to slay himself, his final novel, *More Deaths Than One*, went on sale in bookstores across America—certainly not a coincidence.

Born in Chicago March 13, 1904, Engstrand was the youngest of seven children of Swedish immigrant parents. His parents moved from the city to the country town of Wheaton, Illinois, shortly after Stuart's birth. Engstrand spent his formative years in a bucolic setting. "There were fields to roam and creeks to swim. There were chickens and a cow to tend, which in some small way supplemented my father's earnings as a small merchant."[10] Although he spent his adult years in cities—he spent his last years in Beverly Hills—Engstrand developed "a love for the earth and the things that grew on it"[11] that lasted his entire life. Most of his novels are set in the rural Middle West.

After graduating from high school, Engstrand attended Wheaton College, but finding the school too sectarian for his tastes, he transferred to the Illinois State Teachers College at DeKalb. He funded his education by trimming trees and driving trucks, among other things. By the time he graduated, he already saw himself as a budding writer of some importance and turned down a teaching position offered him, feeling that, if he entered the profession for which he had trained, his "writing ambition and endeavors would be drowned out."[12] Engstrand left the Midwest for the West Coast. Unable to support himself as a writer, he opted for Conradian adventure *à la* Malcolm Lowry and signed as a common sailor on the *Islip*, a freighter bound for China. He stayed at sea for a year and toured various ports of call in the Orient. Impressed by his diligence, Engstrand's superiors tried to persuade him to remain at sea and to study for a captaincy, but once again the young man wanted freedom to pursue his literary aspirations. He rented a room in Los Angeles and again tried his hand at writing. He sent stories off to various magazines, but they were all returned. His savings ran out, and he moved back to Chicago where he once more earned his livelihood as a truck driver.

When he cleared a sufficient sum, Engstrand again quit his job and moved to Ashland County, Wisconsin, where he erected a cedar shack in the woods. For three years, he did nothing but write, turning out novels, short stories, and poems. He sold some of the small pieces but failed to place the larger manuscripts. After his unsuccessful sojourn in the forest, Engstrand sat in on James Weber Linn's writing workshop at the University of Chicago. In Linn, he discovered a sympathetic mentor whose enthusiasm and criticism greatly encouraged him. In 1935, he married Sophia Belzer, an apprentice writer like himself. They moved to Phoenix, Arizona, where Engstrand began *The Invaders*, his first published novel (1937), which concerned the fraught and complex relationships of people living in a deceptively placid northwestern farm community. His second book, *They Sought for Paradise*, appeared in 1939. He dealt with the Nazi occupation of Norway in *Spring 1940* (1941), a work comparable to John Steinbeck's *The Moon Is Down*. His most acclaimed work, *The Sling and the Arrow*, was published six years later in 1947. The novel, very similar in plot and theme to Charles Jackson's *The Fall of Valor*, concerns a marriage destroyed by the husband's latent homosexuality. In his next novel *Beyond the Forest* (1948), Engstrand attempted an American *Madame Bovary*. The book would be made into a movie starring Bette Davis the following year. Although critics in 1949 panned Davis's portrayal of the female lead as overwrought and menopausal, the film featured one of her classic one-liners. Davis says, "What a dump" when she first enters the small but comfortable home her doctor-husband has just purchased for her. Edward Albee found the line memorable and incorporated it strikingly in his 1962 play *Who's Afraid of Virginia Woolf*. Engstrand wrote four more novels: *Son of the Giant* (1950), *A Husband in the House* (1952), *The Scattered Seed* (1953), and *More Deaths Than One* (1955). During his lifetime, his works were compared favorably to those of Theodore Dreiser.

Paul Celan (1920–1970)

Considered by many critics to be the greatest German-language poet since the Second World War, Paul Antschel, who wrote under the pseudonym of Paul Celan, leapt from the Pont Mirabeau into the Seine River late in April 1970. The exact date is uncertain but his death came on or near the Passover holiday. Though a strong swimmer, he drowned without calling attention to himself at the age of forty-nine. A fisherman would discover his body seven miles downstream from Paris on May 1. As mail began to pile up under the door of his flat at 6 Avenue Émile Zola, where he had been living alone, Celan's wife, the graphic artist Gisele Lestrange, telephoned a friend to ask if he knew her husband's whereabouts. She thought that he had perhaps gone to Prague. On his desk, however, a copy of a Hölderlin biography lay open with a single sentence underlined: "Sometimes this genius goes dark and sinks down into the bitter well of the heart."[13] His flat was located across the quay from the Pont Mirabeau, a sad spot Apollinaire had commemorated in a poem of the same name: a melancholic verse of impermanence and loss. Celan had quoted from it in an untitled 1962 poem that continued:

> From the bridge-
> stone, from which he bounded over in-
> to life, fledged by wounds,—from the
> Pont Mirabeau.[14]

In a 1964 poem, he wrote:

> Water needles
> stitch up the split
> shadow—he fights his way
> deeper down,
> free.[15]

Celan was born at Cernowitz, in the Bukovina region of Rumania, in 1920, the son of German-speaking Jews. Bukovina, which Celan later called "a region in which men and books lived,"[16] had been part of the Austrian Empire but had become Rumanian shortly before the poet's birth. After attending the Cernowitz gymnasium, he studied medicine in Tours, France, for half a year beginning in December 1938. He gave up his medical studies and returned to Cernowitz, where he enrolled in the local university and pursued a course in Romance languages and literature. The Soviet Union occupied Bukovina in 1940. Celan remained at the university until the following year, when German and Rumanian troops took the city and began herding Jews into a German-organized ghetto. Both Celan's mother and father would face deportation to a Nazi extermination camp, while Celan himself would be interred for a time in a Rumanian labor camp. By 1944, the Russians had retaken the region. Celan, who had found his way home to Cernowitz by the close of 1943, would resume his studies at the university. In 1945, he left Bukovina to live in Bucharest where he earned his living as both a translator and a reader for a publishing house. In 1947, he departed Bucharest for Vienna, and, the following year, he went on to Paris. There he studied German and linguistics and took a *license en lettres* in 1950. He married Lestrange the same year and he eventually became a French citizen.

Between 1938 and 1970, Celan produced eight hundred poems which began appearing in magazines in 1947. He published his first collection of verse under his own name in 1948. A second book, *Mohn und Gedächtnis* (*Poppy and Memory*), which appeared in 1952, brought him recognition and acclaim in Germany and Austria. His most famous poem, "Todesfugue," which concerns the Nazi concentration camps and Hitler's Final Solution, appeared in both volumes. Begun in Cernowitz in 1944 and revised in Bucharest in 1945, the poem is spoken (or sung) by the inmates as they dig their graves at the order of the Camp Commandant. A Jewish orchestra plays music as the work proceeds: "He shouts jab this earth deeper you others sing up and play/ he grabs for the rod in his belt he swings it his eyes are so blue/ jab your spades deeper you lot there you others play on for the dancing/ Black milk of daybreak we drink you at night/ we drink you at midday and morning we drink you at evening/ we drink and we drink/ a man lives in the house your goldenes Haar Margareta/ your aschenes Haar Shulamith he plays with his vipers/ He shouts plays death more sweetly this Death is a master from Deutschland/ he shouts scrape your strings darker you'll rise then as smoke to the sky/ you'll have a grave then in the clouds there you won't lie too cramped/ Black milk of daybreak we drink you at night/ we drink you at midday Death is a master aus Deutschland."[17]

Much of Celan's work is not easily accessible. He coined new word combinations and employed archaic words. His lines are full of often obscure allusions to music, religion, philosophy, and literature. Hebraic phrases also punctuate his verse. As J. C. Middleton has noted, "his idiom is evasively figurative. . . . Syntax and imagery make few concessions to his readers."[18] The Germans stole everything that meant anything to the young Celan. They ravaged and obliterated his world, took away his home, and made him a displaced person. He would not let them strip from him the one possession he had left: his language, which, ironically, was also theirs. "In the midst of all the losses," Celan wrote, "one thing remained in reach and not lost. . . ."[19] He felt the Germans had marred and defiled their tongue. The Nazis had made weapons out of words. They used propaganda viciously and brilliantly in their campaign against European Jewry. Celan felt that he could repair the damage they had done. He could cleanse and recover his mother tongue, make the German language his own, and create a new home for himself out of words. He was a fractured personality, having both German and Jewish identities. He loved the poetry of Goethe, Hölderlin, and Rilke and felt part of a great German tradition.

The historian Erich Kahler was informed of Celan's death while lying on his own deathbed. Joseph Frank saw and reported his reaction. Kahler "spoke not of himself but, with his hands grasped before him as if in prayer, and with a passion that made his voice tremble and tears come to his eyes, of the terrible psychologic burden—the burden of being a great German poet and a young Central European Jew growing up in the shadow of the concentration camps—which led to the suicide of Paul Celan."[20] Only in death could "the split shadow" be made one.

Henry de Montherlant (1896–1972)

Blindness did not break the Olympians. Sightless as Polyphemus (or so it has at any rate been passed down), Homer sang of Troy's sack by seagoing Akhaians, heroes with sun-bronzed bodies and hair the color of burnished gold. Milton became God's exegete. The scales never fell from his eyes after he lost his sight; nonetheless he performed day labor, justifying the ways of God to man, when light was denied. In glorious and lofty hymns, he celebrated the throne and equipage of the Almighty. The twentieth century gave us "Germ's Choice," aka Shem the Penman, aka James the Joyce. He of the Odin-patch. Of the immense goggling peepers blinking open and shut (shize, I should shee!) behind the goldfishbowl lenses. Slip on those straighteners and the words and letters would begin to weave and bob, to blend, blur, and flip their places for you, too. Nor can we omit from our list the South American Daedalus Jorge Luis Borges, who led us into labyrinths that were in their own way as intricate and devious as those of Joyce himself.

Blindness did not break the Olympians, but to writers of a lower order, mere mortals who so utterly depend upon their eyes to order and arrange words upon a page, what prospect could be more horrifying than that of loss of vision? Approaching blindness, coupled with other indignities brought on by advancing age, made life unbearable, in the end, for that most enigmatic of twentieth-century French writers, Henry de Montherlant. He was a self-indulgent sensualist with a seemingly insatiable appetite for physical pleasure who, despite his libertinage and his inveterate misogyny, also seemed a gallant and honorable throwback to another age, one more amenable to aristocratic pretension. Who but Montherlant would suppress a manuscript for thirty-eight years because publication of the novel in question, *La Rose de sable*, a critique of French colonialism in North Africa, might cause acute embarrassment to elected officials at home, sully France's reputation abroad, and create problems for the soldiers and administrators carrying out their duty in the field? It would be beneath Montherlant's dignity to stoop so low as to put his own interests above those of the nation. Earlier in his life, his code of honor led him to turn down a commission as an officer in the First World War. Class and caste brought preferment in their train. Montherlant would have none it. As a grand gesture, he would serve with the enlisted men—not forgetting for one moment, however, that he was the great-grandson of the Comte Henry de Riancey. Honor determined where the line would be drawn, what one could and what one could not acquiesce to. Montherlant would not submit to the fate of Oedipus and Gloucester. Beethoven went without his ears. Handel composed blind. Such dispensations, however, were not granted to everyone. Moreover, not only his eyes were failing. Old age had reduced Montherlant to a caricature of his former self on many fronts. Deteriorating vision, however, was the final outrage, the insult and humiliation not to be borne. The lesser darkness was as appalling, if not more horrific, than the greater. Indeed the two seemed almost interchangeable in their awfulness, except for the fact that consciousness was not extinguished in the first case. One was awake in the dark and not oblivious of it. That was worse than being dead. What could Montherlant do but meet his fate, embrace his destiny? He had come to the realization early on in life that all men were doomed and underscored the point again and again in his novels and plays. The chaos of life would finally give way to night. Death would claim all: the helmeted soldier on the front, the noble bull chosen for sacrifice in the ring, the aging writer who strove to depict life's acute pleasures as well as its ridiculous futility, its patently absurd aspect. Montherlant did not sing of immortals. If he wrote of Olympians, they were athletes, temporal, transient men, who could attain moments of bliss that, while ecstatic and sublime, were nonetheless short lived. Montherlant's mission as writer, at least initially, seems to have been to capture such moments in his prose, fix them there forever like Cretan friezes. Writing became an act of defiance, a way to defeat time and the abyss. In his early works, Montherlant glorifies youth and adolescence, the period of awakening when life's promise and potentiality loom large, when danger stimulates vitality, and the presence of death adds but another ingredient—one more piquant dash—to an already heady mixture.

It was during his own nonconformist youth that Montherlant felt most alive. His childhood was sheltered and pampered. He attended the best of preparatory schools and received private tutoring by priests. He showed an early penchant for writing. Sienkiewicz's *Quo Vadis* sparked a lifelong interest in Roman history. Montherlant would later claim that he tried to lead his life according to the Roman model. The Romans, he maintained, understood both the art of living and the art of dying. With relish, they pursued all forms of pleasure and sensual gratification, but they also knew how to make an end when their time came, facing death stoically. As A. L. Rowse notes, Montherlant's concupiscent side began to emerge when he was still in school. While attending the Jesuit College Sainte-Croix de Neuilly, Montherlant and several other boys formed a secret society. The clandestine activities the boys engaged in were of such a nature as to severely discomfort the priests who caught them. Singled out as ringleader, Montherlant was expelled from the school at the age of sixteen. The experience devastated him. He felt as if he had been cast out of the garden. His sense of exile did not abate for years. He wrote about his school experience in *La Relève du matin*, a collection of essays published at his own expense in 1920; the play *La Ville dont le Prince est un enfant*; and the novel *Les Garcons*. The essays, written between 1914 and 1918, laud the college and its priests and celebrate with youthful enthusiasm the transformation of the human chrysalis into a butterfly—the period in adolescence when youthful intelligence begins to quicken as a world of new possibilities hitherto unsuspected starts opening up for it. At such a turning point, Montherlant argues, it is not at all amiss for the priests to provoke a crisis of conscience on a pupil's part. Such a crisis will only hasten the process of self-discovery. Montherlant wrote the play and novel in the 1930s, but withheld their publication until 1951 and 1969 respectively. Following his expulsion from Sainte-Croix, Montherlant began law studies in Paris but failed to pass the bar examination. He did not feel comfortable in his parent's milieu. Paris society bored him; therefore he turned to sports for diversion. While he enjoyed track and soccer, his real passion (he had Spanish blood on his father's side) was for the bullfight. His first experience killing bulls came in 1911 during a vacation to Spain.

In 1914, Montherlant's father died. That same year, when he learned that one of his old friends from the secret society at Sainte-Croix had enlisted in the army and would soon be departing for the front, Montherlant asked his terminally ill mother's permission to join up. She would not give it. Montherlant submitted to her wishes and began work on the play *L'Exil*, in which he depicted his dissatisfaction and estrangement from bourgeois society. His mother died shortly after he finished the play. With her death, Montherlant renounced all plans of publication, the first of many noble suppressions in his career (*L'Exil* would finally reach print in 1929; after nineteen years, Montherlant determined that sufficient honor had been paid to his mother's memory), and packed his bags for the front. Though found fit only for limited service, he nonetheless insisted on active duty. After receiving a serious wound in action and convalescing in the hospital, Montherlant was attached to the American army as an interpreter. Later he would claim that the war was "the most tender and moving human experience"[21] of his life. He fictionalized his experiences in the novel *Le Songe*. Montherlant portrays both the savagery and exultation of war, the adrenalin surge of battle as well as the misery and odium it invariably occasions. The novel's hero, Alban de Bricoule, is willing to put his life at risk in order to become part of "a holy virile order,"[22] yet he realizes that he has always had a propensity to sacrifice himself for chimeras. The war is just the latest in a long line of lost causes which he has embraced. Bricoule knows that all human activity, including his participation in the present carnage and bloodshed, is mad and useless. For that reason, a part of him abhors the altars upon which he has performed his service, the myriad chimeras he has wasted his virility on; he continues to serve nonetheless. Realizing the vanity of all endeavor, he still chooses to play the game, to throw himself wholeheartedly into the action at hand.

After the war, Montherlant served as secretary of the fund to erect the Ossuary of Douaumont and wrote his own memorial to the war dead, *Chant funèbre pour les morts de Verdun*. Although he called for the abolition of war in his writings, he missed its "great physical lyricism." He turned to sports for compensation and in the stadium found the same primitive simplicity and clarity which he had loved on the battlefield. In Spain, he fought bulls on stock-breeding ranches and on one occasion was severely gored. After the death of his grandmother in 1925, Montherlant left France for a period of seven years. He traveled widely in Italy and North Africa. During this time, he devoted himself to two activities: writing (his own brand of "useless service"[23]) and the pursuit of pleasure. In the thirties, Montherlant produced a tetralogy of novels detailing his affairs with women. The series *Les jeunes filles*, *Pitié pour les femmes*, *Le démon du bien*, and *Les lepreuses* caused a sensation due to the author's ruthless, at time gleeful, dissection of the feminine character.

That decade also saw the publication of perhaps Montherlant finest novel, *Les célibataires*. The book, which would bring Montherlant the Grand Prix de Littérature from the French Academy, concerns two pathetic bachelors of the noble class, an uncle and a nephew, who cannot fend for themselves after the death of their mutual caretaker, the younger man's mother, the elder's sister. A shift of emphasis can be detected in the novels of the thirties. Montherlant's earlier fiction celebrated life and dealt with vibrant characters determined to prevail in their endeavors, human beings capable of superhuman effort in their attempts to squeeze the utmost out of each and every moment. In his later works, Montherlant's outlook becomes more pessimistic and his focus begins to switch away from the superior individual. The defeated and doomed, the damned and the despairing, the absurd and the ludicrous begin to preoccupy him more and more. The hero of the tetralogy, the writer Pierre Costals, who succeeds in living life on his own terms, is still a hero of the old type if also a cynic and an opportunist. The women he loves and dominates, however, are for the most part weak and silly, flawed and tawdry creatures. The protagonists of *Les célibataires* are male mediocrities, piteous in their ineptness yet all too comfortable in their lassitude. In the forties and fifties Montherlant devoted himself almost exclusively to the theater.

In the judgment of most critics, Montherlant's plays constitute his greatest achievement. He strove for an intellectual classicism in the tradition of Corneille and Racine. His undeniable masterpieces for the stage include *La reine morte* (1942), *Malatesta* (1946), *Le maître de Santiago* (1947), and *La guerre civile* (1965). *Le chaos et la nuit*, Montherlant's first novel in over twenty years, appeared in 1965. It is a dark and bitter tale concerning a Spanish anarchist who has lived past his time and who experiences full force the indifference of his fellow man, an indifference that ultimately kills him. The book portrays the tedium and isolation of old age. Time becomes interminable to Celestino Marcilla. Days pass without visits, mail, or telephone calls. Although his days are now numbered, it seems that he has more time on his hands than ever. Whatever held importance for him in the past now appears meaningless. The hours drag on in unrelieved monotony: he goes to sleep each night to awake to a day identical to the one just past. If his first novels depict the dawn of life, here Montherlant pictures its dusk. Montherlant's subject was man and he always strove to illustrate in the particular what was universal and general. While his personae wear a wide array of masks, they share the same human lot. The abyss yawns for them as it yawns for everyone. After the bright hours comes the void.

In his own life, when the horror of continued existence became worse than the horror of dying, Montherlant opted for release in the Roman manner. As A. L. Rowse comments in *Homosexuals in History*, it is a pity we don't know more about his personal life. His suicide note gives a possible clue: "My dear Claude, I am becoming blind. I am killing myself. I thank you for all that you have done for me. Your mother and you are my sole heirs."[24]

William Inge (1913–1973)

Early in the morning of June 10, 1973, William Inge's sister Helene Connell woke up to the rumbling of an automobile engine. For the last several years, she had been living with her brother, the prize-winning playwright, at his secluded Oriole Drive home in the Hollywood Hills. She leapt out of bed and ran to the garage to find her worst fears realized. Her brother lay slumped in the driver's seat of his Mercedes Benz. For months, he had been deeply depressed. Connell did not know specifically why, and she said Inge did not really know either. On June 2, after attempting to kill himself with an overdose of barbiturates, he had been admitted to the University of California at Los Angeles Medical Center to have his stomach pumped. The following morning, he was transferred to the hospital's psychological ward, but he checked himself out after arguing with his doctor. Connell had been watching him warily since his return home.

At the time of his death, William Inge was sixty years old. Born May 3, 1913 in Independence, Kansas, Inge was the youngest of five children. On his father's side, he was distantly related—or, so his father, a traveling salesman, claimed—to the Booth acting family. From a very early age, William enjoyed performing in public. "I felt the audience reaction," he said. "It meant an awful lot to me. . . . I found a way of getting on with people that I hadn't had."[25] Inge acted in all the plays in high school and upon graduation attended the University of Kansas, where he earned a B.A. in speech and drama in 1935. He acted in summer stock while a college student and wanted ever so badly to go to New York to pursue an acting career. As he had very little money—he subsisted on peanut butter and jelly sandwiches in college—he gave up his dream and determined to become a teacher instead, enrolling at the George Peabody Teachers' College in Nashville. Two weeks before he was due to complete the program, however, Inge "developed a sickness of mood and temper"[26] and dropped out. Returning home without a degree, he drifted aimlessly for a time. In 1938 he joined the drama department at Stephens College for Women in Columbia, Missouri, where he stayed for five years.

In 1943, Inge became a drama critic for the *St. Louis Star-Times*. The following year he would interview Tennessee Williams in St. Louis, while Williams was visiting his parents. The meeting would prove propitious for Inge. Williams liked him and would prove a valuable contact when he launched his own career as a playwright a short time later. Inge claimed the stimulus to write had been awakened in him by Williams. In his capacity as drama critic, he went to Chicago to see *The Glass Menagerie*. The play strongly affected him. "I found it so beautiful and so moving," he later wrote, "that I felt a little ashamed for having led what I felt was an unproductive life."[27] Inge saw how Williams had created great drama out of the sad lives of his mother, sister, and himself, and knew he could do the same for the common everyday folks of his own region. What the former had done with Saint Louisians, Inge felt he could do with the denizens of Kansas small towns. Ordinary people were fit subjects for art. Inge understood the aspirations and disappointments of middle-class American Midwesterners, their unrealized desires, their hypocrisy and dishonesty as well as their steadfastness and nobility of character. He had lived with "his characters" all his life. Suddenly, he realized the dramatic possibilities they offered were endless. Shortly after seeing *The Glass Menagerie*, he set to work on his first play, *Farther Off from Heaven* (1947), a domestic drama he would later rework as *The Dark at the Top of the Stairs*. Williams was instrumental in seeing the work produced. Margo Jones, the codirector of *The Glass Menagerie*, staged it in Dallas at the Little Theater at Williams's recommendation. Inge's career really took off, however, with his next work, the play *Come Back Little Sheba*, which took him two years to write. It proved a big hit in New York, playing 190 performances on Broadway with Shirley Booth and Sidney Blackmer in the roles of Lola and Doc, a middle-aged couple living on spent dreams in a Midwestern city, their lives shattered by past circumstances. Doc had to leave medical school in his third year when he had impregnated Lola, then a happy-go-lucky, dreamy-eyed teenager. Instead of a physician, he became a chiropractor, but his sacrifice was all in vain. The baby died and Lola could bear no future children. He took to drink, and Lola grew fat and sentimental. Each day she looks forward to the return of a long-lost dog, the little Sheba of the title. The couple has taken in a boarder, an attractive art student named Marie. While Lola relishes hearing about Marie's romantic escapades (she is engaged to one young man but steps out on him with another), Doc looks at the girl both as a sort of daughter and as an object of his own deeply repressed sexual desire. One day, as Lola tidies the house and prepares a dinner for Marie and Bruce, her fiancé, Doc catches sight of Turk, the on-the-make jockstrap Marie has taken up with behind Bruce's back, slinking out of her room. In a drunken rage, hating the whole female sex, he attacks Lola and beats her so badly he almost kills her. After one week's hospitalization to be "dried out," he returns home and, pathetic in his degradation, begs Lola to forgive him. She does. Doc becomes the child-in-need whom she has always craved. Sheba has returned to her at long last.

After *Come Back*, Inge produced a sting of hits. He joined Williams and Arthur Miller to become one of the three brightest luminaries of the American theater in the 1950s. In writing his next play, *Picnic*, he recalled a group of women who regularly congregated to talk and gossip on a neighbor's front porch in Kansas. In the play, Inge creates a similar group of ladies who form "a little fortress"[28] that is cracked and battered by a swaggering ne'er-do-well just arrived in the suburbs. The play was not only the hit of the 1953 season, it won the Pulitzer Prize and the New York Drama Critics' Circle Award as well. Inge subsequently took up residence in New York City. He lived at the Dakota and often participated in panel discussions concerning the theater. Self-disciplined, he did not "crack up" like other successful American authors, but remained abstemious and health conscious. At parties, he made it a point to drink ginger ale instead of alcohol. His next two full-length plays, *Bus Stop* and *The Dark at the Top of the Stairs*, were both popular successes. The first, an expanded version of an earlier one-act romantic comedy, deals with a group of passengers who are marooned in a small Kansas town due to a swirling snowstorm. The second, a dark and forbidding but nonetheless comic drama, concerns a family in a conflict over ordinary, mundane matters. However, Inge's next three plays—A *Loss of Roses*, dealing with a brief love affair between a failed actress and a willful and conceited young man; *Natural Affection*, which concerns a woman whose loyalties are divided between her reprobate teenage son and her flawed but vital lover; and *Where's Daddy*, treating the subject of premature parenthood and youth—fared poorly. Panned by the New York critics, they closed after only brief runs. While Inge charged his reviewers of fickleness, his plays had, in truth, slackened into melodrama and routine. "Audience reaction" no longer felt so good. Indeed, it stung. Inge found employment and renewed success in Hollywood. He wrote the 1961 adaptation of *All Fall Down* and the original screenplay for *Splendor in the Grass*, a tale of adolescent love, for which he won an Academy Award. In 1968, the University of California premiered another play, *Don't Go Gentle*, but it received only lukewarm notices and was not produced elsewhere.

In his later years, Inge tried his hand at writing novels. One, *Good Luck, Miss Wyckoff*, enjoyed a moderate success. Published in 1970, the book concerns a woman cut off from society due to a cruel sexual initiation. The same year, Inge mounted a last play in New York, *The Last Pad*, which appeared off off Broadway. Once again the critics lambasted Inge. In addition to his major works, Inge wrote a number of shorter plays in the 1950s and 1960s. These include *To Bobolink, for Her Spirit*; *The Boy in the Basement*; *Bus Riley's Back in Town*; and *Glory in the Flower*.

Richard Brautigan (1935–1984)

A quintessential American novelist of the late 1960s and early 1970s, whose works seemed more and more dated as time went on, Richard Brautigan told friends in 1984 that he was going away on a hunting trip and that he wouldn't be back for some time. In the past, he had disappeared periodically, usually after starting a new novel. He had begun a new book in 1984 when he announced his hunting trip. Even though in recent months, the author had begun to drink heavily and had been depressed because of his declining readership, friends did not worry at his prolonged absence. Two of his associates would eventually drop in at his secluded, Bolinas, California, home to check up on him and discover his badly decomposed body. Brautigan had died from a self-inflicted gunshot wound to the head. The Marin County Coroner's office reported that he had been dead between four and five weeks.

Born in Spokane, Washington, Brautigan became a fixture in the Bay area of California. Like a Hare Krishna devotee passing out flowers and free literature, he stood on street corners in Berkeley and Haight-Ashbury handing out copies of his books to whoever would take them. None of his early poetry collections and novels, printed by the Four Seasons Foundation in San Francisco, initially sold well. Brautigan styled himself as a counter-culture outlaw. He belonged to the literary underground and attacked the establishment. He freely conceded that he was a failure at everything aside from writing (both his marriages ended in divorce), and he took pride in the fact that he never had learned to drive and that he never owned an automobile. He developed a disjointed, hip style, funny and anarchistic, that delighted the California crowd. Brautigan's first important work was 1964's *A Confederate General from Big Sur*. He would go mainstream in 1970. Two years before, he had been taken on by agent Helen Brann, who offered three of his books, two novels and a poetry collection, at an auction. Seymour Lawrence of Delacorte Press made the highest bid. The works—two novels, *Trout Fishing in America* (which had been previously issued by Four Seasons in 1967) and *In Watermelon Sugar*, and a volume of verse, *The Pill versus The Springhill Mining Disaster*—were published together to great acclaim. The novelist Thomas McGuane wrote in the *New York Times Books Review*: "He seems crazy with optimism. Like some widely gifted Rotarian who wants you to come to his town, he seems assured and sincere."[29] Brautigan's quirky novels of life on the Pacific Coast quickly became best sellers. Paperback editions of his books sold briskly on college campuses across America. *Trout Fishing In America* would sell more than two million copies worldwide (his works would be translated into twelve languages). Other volumes such as *Dreaming of Babylon, a private eye novel* and *The Hawline Monster, a gothic Western* would also find wide readership. His admirers claimed that with his easy-to-read yet strange and idiosyncratic prose, Brautigan had created a whole new genre and that people would write "Brautigans" in the future just as novels are written now. By the eighties, however, Brautigan no longer seemed such a novelty. His newer work received only halfhearted reviews and sales fell off in the United States (though he continued to sell well in Japan and France). The poet Barry Yourgrau reviewed the novel *The Tokyo-Montana Express* negatively in the *Times Book Review* in 1980. This review was typical of critical reaction to Brautigan's later work. Yourgrau wrote: "He is now a longhair in his mid-40s, and across his habitually good humor there now creep shadows of ennui and dullness, and too easily aroused sadness."[30] When Brautigan's death was announced, his friend and early supporter Thomas McGuane gave the following statement: "He was a true American genius in the tradition of Twain and Lardner."[31] His opinion, at least, had not changed with the years. Brautigan's volumes of verse include *The Galilee Hitch-hiker, Lay the Marble Tea, The Octopus Frontier, Please Plant This Book, Rommel Drives on Deep into Egypt*, and *Loading Mercury with a Pitchfork*. His short stories from 1962 to 1970 were collected in *Revenge of the Lawn* in 1971. Brautigan's later novels include *The Abortion: An Historical Romance 1966*; *Willard and his Bowling Trophies, a perverse mystery*; *Sombrero Fallout, a Japanese novel*; and *So the Wind Won't Blow It All Away*. On the unconventional and heady opening page of *In Watermelon Sugar*, Brautigan writes about the propinquity of death:

> I live in a shack near iDEATH. I can see iDEATH out the window. It is beautiful. I can also see it with my eyes closed and touch it. Right now it is cold and turns like something in the hand of the child. I do not know what the thing could be.
> There is a delicate balance in iDEATH. It suits us.[32]

The words could serve as his epitaph.

Primo Levi (1919–1987)

At the age of sixty-seven, No. 174517 threw himself down a stairwell of his home, the house where he had been born in the Crocetta neighborhood of Turin. Ostensibly he killed himself due to his failing health. Apart from his physical ailments, Primo Levi suffered from acute depression. Everything seemed more bleak than normal the last several months of his life. His ninety-two-year-old mother had suffered a stroke the previous year and had been partially paralyzed ever since. Her condition deeply upset her son who had recently undergone minor surgery himself and was not well. According to his son Renzo, he felt helpless and impotent, unable to ameliorate his mother's condition or his own. The specter of Auschwitz and the other Nazi extermination camps continued to haunt and obsess him. He had survived his incarceration, but his scars had never really healed. He had been staring death in the face ever since. Levi had seen the worst that man can do to his fellow man and as a result, although he had been liberated, he had never really left hell.

Born July 31, 1919, Primo Levi had descended from Jewish settlers of the Piedmont who had been previously expelled from Spain. His ancestors had belonged to the middle class, and, long before Primo's birth, they had assimilated into mainstream Italian culture. In his early years, Levi did not concern himself much with his Hebrew roots and heritage. For him, a Jew was "someone who at Christmas does not have a tree, who shouldn't eat salami but does, who has learned a little bit of Hebrew at 13 and then forgotten it."[33] Levi studied chemistry at the University of Turin, taking his degree in 1941 despite the fact that Benito Mussolini had barred all Jews from attending Italian universities in 1938. For two years, Levi worked at a Milan pharmaceutical factory but left his job in 1943 to fight with the Italian partisans against both the German army and Italian Fascist forces. Levi later said that he had been an ineffectual guerilla. An informer betrayed his unit, and he was turned over to the Germans after first being interrogated by the Italians. Herded onto a train along with hundreds of other Jews, he was transported to Auschwitz. Assigned to the Monowitz factory section of the camp, he eked out his existence as a slave laborer until the camp was at last liberated. A trained chemist, Levi could contribute to the German war effort and thus was permitted to live. The Nazis tattooed his prison number several inches above the wrist of his left arm, then put him to work in a synthetic rubber factory. A fellow inmate, an Italian bricklayer who was not Jewish, took mercy on Levi and saved him from starvation by smuggling him bread and soup.

Returning to Italy after the war, Levi worked once more as a chemist. Employed by SIVA, a Turin paint manufacturer, he stayed with the company thirty years, becoming the plant's general manager in 1961. Upon his return home, however, he immediately began writing about his experiences in the Nazi death camp. Although "a chemist by conviction," after Auschwitz, Levi felt "an absolute need to write. Not only as a moral duty but as a psychological need."[34] His first book, *Survival in Auschwitz*, later retitled *If This Is a Man*, appeared in 1947. Levi spiced his Italian with the disappearing picturesque pidgin of the Piedmontese Jews, which synthesized Hebrew roots with local endings and inflections. In *The Reawakening*, the first of two sequels to *Survival in Auschwitz*, published in 1962,

Levi recounted his protracted, surreal journey home to Italy after the war. The third volume of his memoirs and perhaps his best book, *The Periodic Table*, came out in 1984. He interweaves reflections on the orderly nature of matter and the regularly recurrent variation in properties of the chemical elements into a final, highly subjective reminiscence about his experiences in Nazi hell. Levi also wrote two volumes of individual portraits of various prisoners he encountered in the camps: *Moments of Reprieve* and *The Drowned and the Saved*. Levi also wrote fiction, some of which he published under the pen name Damiano Malabello. During his last decade, he devoted himself increasingly to the production of novels and short stories. He revisited his Partisan days in the 1982 novel *If Not Now, When?* which dealt with a group of East European Jews fighting the Germans at the close of the war and dreaming about a future life in Palestine. In addition to writing fiction and nonfiction, Levi regularly contributed poems to the Turin newspaper *La Stampa*. He won the Strega Prize in 1979 and shared the Kenneth B. Smilen fiction award with Saul Bellow in 1985.

Bruno Bettelheim (1903–1990)

Nursing homes haven't improved much since Charlotte Mew's day. However modern, however sanitized, they remain death houses, and to a patient such as child therapist Bruno Bettelheim, who, like Paul Celan and Primo Levi, survived incarceration in Nazi concentration camps, such a facility would bring back bad memories. Rudolph Ekstein, a Los Angeles psychoanalyst and personal friend of the pioneering theorist and controversial author, reported that Bettelheim had said to him "that once you were in a camp, you could never escape the cruelty."[35] Born in Vienna on August 28, 1903, Bettelheim had an unhappy childhood. Nearsighted and slight of build, he was very self-conscious about his physical appearance. He was also subject to frequent depression. Bettelheim attended university in Vienna and earned advanced degrees. His doctorate, however, was in philosophy, not psychology or medicine. He became intrigued with the ideas of Hans Vaihinger, taking to heart his view of the *als ob*. According to this "as if" philosophy, it is permissible for individuals to cultivate fictive lives if they act meaningfully on the basis of their falsehoods. The fabrications are justified if they make life more tolerable or enable a person to succeed in the world.

Since Bettelheim's death, it has come to light that he misrepresented much of his past, though not his internment in Buchenwald and Dachau. Bettelheim claimed that, as a youth, he worshiped Siegmund Freud, and that, by the age of fourteen, he had read most of the psychoanalytic literature of the day. His interest in the topic, he said, had been sparked by a female classmate for whom he had a crush and who had ignored him in favor of an older boy who had already studied the subject. According to the story, Bettelheim retained a deep interest in psychoanalysis long after the girl had ceased to be important to him. Bettelheim further boasted that, as a teenager, he would go a great distance out of his way just to walk by Freud's house and that later Freud had supported Bettelheim's decision to become an analyst and had recommended him personally for training in the field. No proof exists that he and Freud ever met or that Bettelheim formally studied the discipline he would later practice. As noted earlier, his doctorate was in philosophy. Nonetheless, Bruno Bettelheim adopted this fiction upon arriving in America and maintained it for the rest of his life. He further claimed that, early in his career in Austria, he had become intrigued with the childhood disorder of autism. He professed that he had grown dissatisfied with the prevailing approach to the disease and had challenged the then widely held notion that it was incurable. He postulated that a specially structured environment could be created in which the autistic child, seemingly so withdrawn from the world, could learn to communicate and interact with others. According to this myth, he brought such a child (he called her Patsy) into his home in 1932 to test his theories; he was making slow but sure progress with her when the Nazis invaded Austria in 1938, and his research came to an abrupt end. Bettelheim had, in fact, been running his family's lumber business during the 1930s. It was his first wife, Gina Alstadt, who treated the girl. Following the Nazi takeover, Bettelheim spent nearly two years in Dachau and Buchenwald. Governor Herbert Lehman of New York and First Lady Eleanor Roosevelt campaigned for the release of prisoners holding advanced academic degrees. Bowing to international pressure, the Germans complied and Bettelheim and his second wife, the former Gertrud Weinfeld, immigrated to the United States.

In 1944, Bettelheim was appointed the director of the Sonia Shankman Orthogenic School in Chicago, which developed under his direction into one of America's premier treatment centers for autistic and emotionally troubled children. As Robert Coles, a child psychiatrist at Harvard University rightly maintains, "His [Bettelheim's] impact on the culture went far beyond psychoanalysis." Coles goes on: "He was an enormously gifted writer and social essayist, with a great literary and moral sensibility. And he had personal heroism, in dedicating himself to find a way to treat the hardest-to-reach children—demanding exhausting work."[36] Upon arriving in America, Bettelheim dealt with his experiences in the two Nazi camps in an article entitled "Individual and Mass Behaviour in Extreme Situations," which described how the prisoners were methodically stripped of their dignity to such a degree that their personalities all but disintegrated. While the article shot Bettelheim to prominence in American intellectual circles, it aroused wrath among Bettelheim's fellow Jews, for he argued, as did Stefan Zweig, that Jews bore some measure of responsibility for provoking the actions of the Nazis. Bettelheim claimed that the only reason he was able to preserve his sanity and maintain his sense of self in the camps was his study of psychoanalysis.

Bettelheim returned to his camp experiences again and again in his career, most significantly in his book *The Informed Heart* and in "Surviving," a 1976 *New*

Yorker article in which he argued that those who had made it through the camps had done so not for life's sake but for cultural and religious reasons beyond the fact of mere continued existence. The ordeals he faced daily in Dachau and Buchenwald influenced everything he put his hands to subsequently, especially the therapeutic methods he devised for disturbed children at the Orthogenic school. He admitted that he had learned from his Nazi captors, but while they strove to dehumanize their victims, he reversed their process. As Ekstein observed, "he turned [Nazi methods] upside down" and created "a protected, caring environment, the mirror opposite of the camps. The door was locked to the outside, but always open to the inside."[37] He called for a "total therapeutic milieu."[38] The children would be treated with utmost respect from dusk to dawn. Therapy continued all day long. The meals were wonderful and served on fine china. The institution resembled a "home" rather than a hospital. Bettelheim claimed his methods had an eighty-five percent success rate. Although he had his critics who disputed the efficacy of his methods, the idea that children profit from a "total milieu" is today generally accepted. Bettelheim's views continued to modify and shift with the years. These changes are recorded in the pages of his numerous books on child rearing, autism, and other childhood disorders. These include *Love Is Not Enough*, *Truants from Life*, *The Empty Fortress*, *A Home for the Heart*, and *A Good Enough Parent: A Book on Child-Rearing*, which was published in 1987 and which Bettelheim called "a summation of my life work."[39] Bettelheim once held that autism was brought on by the behavior of schizophrenic mothers. He repudiated such views as ridiculous in his last book, arguing that children are naturally good and most parents are "good enough."[40] Early in his career, some maintained that he was too indulgent in his treatment of children and derided him as "Dr. Yes."[41] In the late sixties, however, he attacked the youthful Vietnam war protesters, calling them neo-Nazis, and chastising their parents for failure to instill proper fear and respect in them. He later admitted he had gone too far in his statements. Bettelheim's wife died in 1984.

Illness later forced him to become a resident in a Silver Spring, Maryland, nursing home. Althought it was a first-class facility and plush by most standards, he did not adapt to life in the institution. Once again, as in the Nazi camps, he felt dehumanized and stripped of his identity. His life had come full circle. On the fifty-second anniversary of the *Anschluss*, Bettelheim killed himself in the nursing facility. He tied a plastic bag around his head and died from asphyxiation at the age of eighty-six. In the years following his death, his detractors have become increasingly vocal. Some scholars have charged that, despite the felicity of his writing, Bettelheim was not an original thinker; that many of "his" ideas, were borrowed, without credit, from other psychoanalysts. Having a far greater literary gift than most of his colleagues, he could communicate such ideas in a breezy and provocative way that would attract readers. The insights might not have always been his own but the manner of their presentation was. His prose was neither dry nor didactic, and his books proved inspiring to innumerable readers. Some former students of the Sonia

Shankman Orthogenic school, however, have made allegations in the years following Bettelheim's death that are far more shocking than the charge of plagiarism. They allege that they were psychically and physically abused by Bettelheim and that the abuse was a secret part of the doctor's treatment program. Perhaps, if the charges are true, Bettelheim had learned all to well from the Nazis. Therefore, guilt and anxiety about being eventually unmasked for the fraud he, at least to some extent, was, may have also played a part in his decision to kill himself.

Michael Dorris (1945–1997)

On April 11, 1997, the fifty-two-year-old National Book Award-winning author Michael Dorris was found dead in a Concord, New Hampshire, motel room, where he had registered under an assumed name. He had tied a plastic bag over his head after swallowing a lethal coctail of sleeping pills and vodka. This suicide technique is nearly identical to that employed by the thirty-eight Heaven's Gate cult members, intent upon leaving their "containers"[42] to rendezvous with a UFO supposedly hiding in the tail of the Hale-Bopp comet, several weeks before. The type of pills differed but the booze was the same. Dorris took over-the-counter medication instead of the prescription phenobarbital, but, just as the androgynous cult members had done, he drank vodka and then slipped a plastic bag over his head to quicken asphyxiation. Unlike the followers of Marshall Herff Applewhite, Dorris did not believe that the approaching millennium was going to have deleterious effects on the Earth—that the planet was about to be, in Applewhite's words, "recycled."[43] Nor was he trying to advance to a level beyond human, but, like the cultists, he was bent on escape from approaching catastrophe—in his case not cosmic but personal.

Allegations had been made against Dorris that he felt would destroy his life. At the time of his death, he believed his own world to be in imminent peril. One of Dorris's three biological daughters—Persia Andromeda, thirteen, Pallas Antigone, twelve, and Aza Marion, eight—had told their mother, Dorris's estranged wife, novelist and poet Louise Erdrich, that she had been molested by her father. The allegations surfaced a year after the couple had separated. At the time, Dorris and Erdrich were in the middle of divorce proceedings. In recent years, such charges have become almost routine during custody battles in the United States. After Dorris's death, however, Erdrich denied that the couple had been engaged in a custody fight. In an interview with the *New York Times*, she said that she had sued for divorce because of Dorris's chronic depression. She claimed that he had talked of suicide from the second year of their fifteen-year marriage and that she could no longer lend him the emotional support he desperately and constantly required. "He had descended inch by inch," she said, "fighting all the way."[44] She also indicated that Dorris had agreed to give her custody of their three daughters months before the abuse allegation was made. She had reported her daughter's charge to a health-care professional, who contacted the police as required by state law. Nine days before Dorris's death, police conducted a search of his Minneapolis home. Authorities from Hennepin County, Minnesota, also visited Denver to interview Dorris's two surviving adopted children, Jeffrey Sava, twenty-five, and Madeline Hannah, twenty-one, to see whether they had ever been abused. When he learned of the allegations against him, Dorris telephoned his friend Douglas Foster, director of school affairs for the Graduate School of Journalism at the University of California, Berkeley, and the former editor of *Mother Jones* magazine, and told him that his life was over. In an interview with the Associated Press, Foster said, "He didn't know how to fight without making things worse, and he had a realistic idea that no matter how baseless the allegations were, they were going to have a strong negative effect on his family and his work."[45] Foster also disputed Erdrich's claim that Dorris had a long history of depression and had shown suicidal tendencies for years. He said that Dorris was a "relatively cheerful, even-keeled, generous, outgoing person,"[46] whose depression arose from the end of his marriage and the charge of sexual molestation. Erdrich's story, however, would receive corroboration from Anthony Rolo, the editor of a Native American newspaper in Minneapolis. Rolo alleged that Dorris would take his depression out on his wife and that he devoted himself to work instead of seeking treatment for his worsening condition. Rolo said that he was surprised that Louise "managed to keep her sense of self-identity."[47] He further contends that Erdrich believed that by separating from her husband she would incite him to seek help: "When she ended it, she believed she was doing it for his benefit as well as hers."[48]

Dorris made an earlier suicide attempt on March 28 (Good Friday)—surely not a coincidental date. Because of the sex-abuse charge, he felt like Christ crucified. He ingested pills and alcohol at a cottage on the farm he and his wife had formerly shared in Cornish, New Hampshire. Serendipitously, Foster telephoned him shortly after he had swallowed the medication. During their conversation, Dorris admitted that he had "activated the kit"[49] then lost consciousness. Foster contacted the state police, who broke into the cottage and saved Dorris's life. After the unsuccessful attempt, the author checked himself into a psychiatric facility, where his outlook seemed to improve during the week he spent there. Dorris's friend Ruth Coughlin telephoned him several times a day. She learned that Dorris had begun a new children's book and had seemed pleased with the way the work was progressing. On Thursday, April 12, the author left the facility on a pass. He rented a car and drove to Concord, where he ended his life in the motel room. Police found his body after the institution filed a missing person's report. Another of his friends, Jeanne Friedman, a fund raiser at Berkeley, commented: "Michael saw no way out. He felt the charges would destroy his family, would destroy the body of work he had built up over his lifetime. He kept saying, 'All across the country, my books are in schools with young people. What do you think they're going to do when they hear about these charges?' "[50] After Dorris's suicide, Erdrich filed a motion in court to seal the police records concerning the sex-abuse allegation.

Michael Dorris was part Modoc Indian. He was born January 30, 1945, in Louisville, Kentucky, the son of Jim and Mary Besy (Burkhardt) Dorris. He attended Georgetown and Yale Universities and in 1972, founded Dartmouth College's Native American studies program which he headed until 1985. He met Erdrich, who is also part Native American, at Dartmouth, where she was a student and later a writer-in-residence. Prior to their marriage, Dorris, at age twenty-six, became one of the first single men in America to legally adopt a child, a three-year-old Sioux Indian named Reynold Abel who suffered mental and physical disabilities due to fetal alcohol syndrome. Dorris would record his son's trials in his 1989 memoir *The Broken Cord*. A best seller, the book would reveal the dangers of women drinking during pregnancy to a wide audience. It would bring Dorris the National Book Award and become a 1992 made-for-TV movie. The book also helped spark interest in the syndrome in Congress, where hearings on the subject were later held. Before marrying Erdrich in 1981, Dorris adopted Jeffrey and Madeline, two more American Indian children who suffered from fetal-alcohol problems. For years Dorris and Erdrich seemed to have an ideal marriage. They had complete trust in one another and were close literary collaborators. In an interview, Dorris once stated that a manuscript never left their home without "consensus on every word."[51] The dedications of their various books, always to each other, seem to confirm this. The inscription at the beginning of Erdrich's *The Beet Queen*, reads: "To Michael, Complice in every word, essential as air."[52] Dorris's 1987 novel *A Yellow Raft in Blue Water* begins: "For Louise, Companion through every page, through every day. Compeer."[53] In 1991, they coauthored the nonfiction *Route Two and Back* and the best-selling novel *Crown of Columbus*. Author Martin Cruz Smith commented: "They were like a twin star system, I can't think of another pair of writers who worked like that."[54] Ruth Coughlin reminisced about seeing the pair dance. They moved in perfect sync, flawlessly attuned to one another: "Scott and Zelda without the alcohol."[55]

Dorris's adopted children, however, caused them continual trouble and heartache. Abel died in a car crash in 1991. Four years later, the couple pressed extortion charges against Jeffrey. Then living in Denver, Jeffrey had been arrested and incarcerated on misdemeanor charges for battering his girlfriend. Awaiting trial, he wrote a long, rambling letter to his parents. Addressing his father, he charged: "Think about what we put up with as helpless children. You beat us senseless, you terrorized us, you made us walk on eggshells, we feared you, and then Louise comes onto the picture. Instead of stopping his abuse, she kicks in."[56] Jeffrey claimed that his own problems had their origins in childhood abuse and demanded $15,000 from Erdrich and help publishing a manuscript. "Very simple, people," he wrote, "you owe me! You owe me a childhood, you owe me a life."[57] Dorris's and Erdrich's case against Jeffery went to trial twice. The couple were so frightened of their son, that, on leave from Dartmouth, they went into hiding, first in Montana, and then in Minneapolis. Jeffrey's public defender, Lisa Wayne, claimed that the extortion charges against her client were an attempt on Dorris's and Erdrich's part "to shut [him] up,"[58] that he had been mentally and physically abused by the couple since childhood. She claimed that, in the course of ten years, Jeffrey had written about the abuse in many letters. The first trial ended in a hung jury. At the second proceeding, Jeffrey was acquitted of the charge involving Dorris, but the jury could not reach a verdict in the charge involving Erdrich. The couple's lawyer, Craig Truman, would later claim that Dorris had been a bad witness: "He was too sensitive to go through the hurly-burly world of the criminal-justice system. He was reaching out to Jeffrey. He was always worried that he was too thin and not eating right."[59] A month before his suicide, during a reading in Washington, when asked about his adopted children, Dorris said, "I don't think I was by any means the best parent my children could have found."[60]

Dorris's other adult titles include the nonfiction works *Native Americans: Five Hundred Years After* (1977), *A Guide to Research on North American Indians* (1983), and *Rooms in the House of Stone* (1993); the short story collection *Working Men* (1993); and *Paper Trail: Collected Essays, 1967–1992*. In 1992, he published his first book for children, *Morning Girl*, a tale of two young Bahamians living in 1492. The title character prefers the day while her counterpart, Star Boy, favors the night. Both witness Christopher Columbus's arrival to the Americas. The novel ends with the crew of the *Nina* landing on their island. Reviewing the book in the *Los Angeles Times*, Suzanne Curley wrote: "This sad, lovely and timely tale gives us an alternate view of America's 'discovery.' "[61] In the *New York Times Book Review*, Alice McDermott described *Morning Girl* as "a warm story full of real characters and situations, told in marvelous language that makes it a pleasure to read out loud."[62] Other works for young adults include *Guests* (1994) and *Amory Goes Wild* (1995).

Notes

1. Quoted in "About Jack London," *White Fang* (New York: Scholastic Book Service, 1973), p. i.

2. Ibid.

3. Quoted in *New York Times* obituary, 29 December 1925.

4. Ibid.

5. Ibid.

6. Ibid.

7. Ibid.

8. Quoted in *The Avenel Companion to English and American Literature, Britain and the Commonwealth* (New York: Avenel Books, 1981), p. 359.

9. Quoted in *Twentieth Century Authors: A Biographical Dictionary of Modern Literature*, ed. Stanley J. Kunitz and Howard Haycraft (New York: H.W. Wilson, 1942), p. 952.

10. Quoted in *Twentieth Century Authors, First Supplement*, ed. Stanley J. Kunitz and Vineta Colby (New York: H. W. Wilson, 1955), p. 308.

11. Ibid.

12. Ibid.

13. Quoted by John Felstiner, *Paul Celan: Poet, Survivor, Jew* (New Haven and London: Yale University Press, 1995), p. 287.

14. Paul Celan, untitled poem, trans. John Felstiner, *Paul Celan*, p. 286.

15. Celan, untitled poem, trans. Felstiner, *Paul Celan*, pp. 286–87.

16. Quoted in *World Authors, 1950–1970*, ed. John Wakeman (New York: H.W. Wilson, 1975), p. 290.

17. Celan, "Death Fugue," trans. Felstiner, *Paul Celan*, p. 31.

18. Quoted in *World Authors*, p. 290.

19. Ibid.

20. Quoted by Felstiner, *Paul Celan*, p. 287.

21. Quoted by A. L. Rowse, *Homosexuals in History* (New York: Dorset Press, 1983), p. 332.

22. Quoted by Lucille Becker, *Henry de Montherlant: A Critical Biography* (Carbondale: Southern Illinois University Press, 1970), p. 5.

23. Ibid, p. 6.

24. Quoted by Rowse, *Homosexuals in History*, p. 334.

25. Quoted by Paul L. Montgomery, "Sheba an Instant Success," *New York Times*, 11 June 1973.

26. Ibid.

27. Ibid.

28. Ibid.

29. Quoted by Edwin McDowell, "Richard Brautigan, Novelist, A Literary Idol of the 1960s," *New York Times*, 26 October 1984.

30. Ibid.

31. Ibid.

32. Richard Brautigan, *In Watermelon* Sugar (New York: Dell, 1974), p. 1.

33. Quoted by John Tagliabue, "Primo Levi, Holocaust Writer, Is Dead at 67," *New York Times*, 12 April 1987.

34. Ibid.

35. Quoted by Daniel Goleman, "Bruno Bettelheim Dies at 86; Psychoanalyst of Vast Impact," *New York Times*, 14 March 1990.

36. Ibid.

37. Ibid.

38. Ibid.

39. Ibid.

40. Ibid.

41. Ibid.

42. Quoted by Elizabeth Gleick, "The Marker We've Been . . . Waiting For," *Time* (7 April 1997), p. 31.

43. Ibid.

44. Quoted by Elizabeth Gleick, "An Imperfect Union," *Time* (28 April 1997), p. 68.

45. Quoted in "Family Seeks to Seal Record of Abuse Allegation Against Late Author," AP Wire Story, week of 11 April 1997.

46. Quoted by Gleick, "An Imperfect Union," p. 68.

47. Ibid., p. 69.

48. Ibid.

49. Ibid.

50. Ibid., pp. 68–69.

51. Ibid., p. 68.

52. Ibid.

53. Ibid.

54. Ibid.

55. Ibid.

56. Ibid., p. 69.

57. Ibid.

58. Ibid.

59. Ibid.

60. Ibid.

61. Quoted in *Something About the Author*, vol. 75, ed. Diane Telgen (Detroit, Washington, D.C., and London: Gale Research Inc., 1994), p. 43.

62. Ibid.

More Suicides Still

George Sterling (1869–1926)

GEORGE STERLING, WHOSE CARMEL, CALIFORNIA, HOME, BECAME the informal meeting place of the Piedmont writers' group, whose members all believed in the right of suicide, killed himself by ingesting cyanide. For years, this American poet kept a vial of the poison on his person should the need to do away with himself ever arise. Of all the Piedmont writers, Sterling was perhaps the strongest advocate of suicide. One member of the group, the poet Nora May French, used Sterling's Carmel home to kill herself. Earlier, French had attempted to murder her lover James Hopper by offering him a poisoned sandwich. She accidentally dropped the sandwich to the floor, however, before serving it to Hopper; a dog snatched it up and ate it and died instantly, whereupon Hopper immediately fled the scene. Sterling's own death followed a bout of heavy drinking that aggravated his ulcer condition and gave him a severe headache of three days' duration. H. L. Mencken had announced his intention of attending the November 17, 1926, banquet of the Bohemian Club, which Sterling was to have directed and to have presided over as the evening's toastmaster. Sterling and one of his associates drank a large quantity of wine set aside for the occasion, and Sterling became quite ill and was subsequently unable to attend the banquet. That evening, in his room at the Bohemian Club, he drank his vial of cyanide instead.

George Sterling was born in Sag Harbor, Long Island, New York, on December 1, 1869, the eldest son of Dr. George Ansel and Mary Parker (Havens) Sterling. When Sterling was in high school, his father converted from Episcopalianism to Roman Catholicism and the whole family followed suit, though George did not take this change in religion very seriously. However, he did attend St. Charles College, Ellicott City, Maryland. Sterling's father wanted him trained for the priesthood, but he dropped out of college and never went on to the seminary. Instead, he fled west to California where his maternal uncle had become something of a real estate mogul. Sterling clerked in the office from 1890 to 1905, reluctantly to be sure. At last his aunt set him up for life, and he purchased land in Carmel on which he built his future home. Sterling resided variously in San Francisco, Oakland, Piedmont, and Carmel. Ambrose Bierce championed his verse. Jack London succeeded for a time in converting him to socialism, at least intellectually if not in practice. The East Coast ignored him completely. He was a San Francisco property only, published as he was almost exclusively in that city, but the press there praised him to the skies, claiming that his orotund, deliberately old-fashioned verse equalled that of Shelley and Poe. In 1896, Sterling married Caroline Rand, but they separated in 1912 when Sterling became enmeshed in one of numerous love affairs. While he skirted across the continent back to New York, Rand committed suicide in Berkeley. Sterling would never remarry, though he continued to engage in romantic dalliances the rest of his life. His first volume of verse, *Testimony of the Suns*, is probably his best. In addition to his poetry, Sterling wrote several of the infamous Grove plays performed at the Bohemian Club's "summer high jinks"[1] at Bohemian Grove on the Russian River.

Harry Crosby (1898–1929)

In his introduction to Crosby's posthumously published collection of poems, *Transit of Venus*, T. S. Eliot writes: "I doubt whether we can understand the poetry of a contemporary, especially if we are engaged in writing ourselves. When I first read some of his poems I concluded merely that he was a young man in a hurry . . . in a hurry, I think because he was aware of direction, and ignorant of the destination, only conscious that time was short and the terminus a long way off."[2] The Boston-born Crosby knew where he wanted to go. "I want a long straight road into the Sun," he wrote, "and a car with the cut out wide open speeding a mile a minute into the Sun with a princess by my side."[3] While serving in the American Ambulance Corps during the First World War, Crosby earned a reputation for heroics and risk-taking. Like Hemingway, he displayed an eagerness to brave danger and chance extinction. He lived with reckless abandon and liked to call attention to himself, to offend and appall. Delighting in decadence, he smoked hashish and opium on a regular basis. A mad prophet in the Nietzschean tradition, his work is a call to arms, his poems wild tirades, vehicles to display his megalomaniacal vision of world destruction:

> I am the harbinger of a New Sun World
> I bring the Seed of a
> New Copulation
> I proclaim the Mad Queen

I stamp out vast empires
I crush palaces in my rigid
    hands
I harden my heart against
    churches

I blot out cemeteries
I feed the people with
stinging nettles
I resurrect madness
I thrust my naked sword between the world
I murder the world![4]

During the last decade of his life, Crosby frequently wrote about the attraction death held for him. In "Assassin," he predicts, "I the Murderer of the World shall in my fury murder myself. I shall cut out my heart take it into my joined hands and walk towards the Sun without stopping until I fall down dead."[5] In "Sun-Death," he celebrates suicides past—Diogenes, Socrates, Sappho, Samson, Cleopatra—and exhorts his reader to "Die at the right time when your entire life, when your soul and your body, your spirit and your sense, are reduced to a pin-point, the ultimate gold point, the point of finality, irrevocable as the sun, sun-point, then is the time, and not until then, and not after then (o horror of anticlimax from which there is no recovering) for us to penetrate into the cavern of the Sombre Slave-girl of death, to enjoy explosion with the sombre Slave-girl of death, in order to be reborn, in order to become what you wish to become, tree or flower or star or sun, or even dust and nothingness. . . ."[6] In 1929 he entered into a murder-suicide pact with his mistress Mrs. Josephine Rotch Bigelow, reminiscent to that, a century before, of the Prussian dramatist Heinrich von Kleist and Henrietta Vogel. Twenty-four hours prior to their deaths, Bigelow gave Crosby a poem she had written that concluded with the words "Death is our marriage."[7] The following day the pair went to their friend Stanley Mortimer's suite at the New York Hotel des Artistes. They took off their shoes and reclined together on the bed. Crosby then placed the barrel of a .25 caliber pistol against the left temple of Bigelow's head and fired the weapon. For two hours, he cuddled and hugged her body before pointing the gun at his own fore-head and pulling the trigger.

Robert E. Howard (1906–1936)

The creator of "Conan the Barbarian" deeply loved his mother. A sickly child growing up in West Texas, Howard was frequently beaten up by bullies in his early youth. His father, a family doctor, was away on calls much of the time, so it fell to Mrs. Howard to comfort the boy. She did so by reading the child poetry as well as myths and legends of various nations. During his teens, Howard began lifting weights. He spent hours at body-building, shaping his physique over the years into that of a muscular athlete. As an adult, he stood six feet tall and weighed two hundred pounds. In the mid–1930s, Howard's mother fell into a coma and on June 11, 1936, doctors pronounced her terminal. The same day, after being informed of the physicians' diagnosis, Howard drove home and parked his car in the driveway. He did not exit the vehicle but sat there some time. Finally, he pulled a gun and shot himself in the head. His mother died the following day. The epitaph on his marker in the Howard family plot in Greenleaf Cemetery in Brownwood, Texas, reads:

> They were lovely and pleasant in their lives
> And in their death they were not divided.[8]

Carole Landis (1919–1948)

Better known to the world for her movie career, Carole Landis qualifies for inclusion because she did write a book: *Four Jills in a Jeep*. In 1942, as part of a USO tour, along with fellow actresses Martha Raye, Kay Francis, and Mitzi Mayfair, Landis entertained American troops in Bermuda, Northern Ireland, and England. In London, she impulsively married her third husband, Captain Thomas Wallace, whom she had previously met in California. Prior to Pearl Harbor, Wallace had joined the Eagle Squadron of the RAF and had fought in the Battle of Britain. He subsequently transferred to the United States Air Force. Three days after the wedding, the "Jills" proceeded to the front lines in North Africa. Quite close to the fighting, often within earshot of artillery fire, Landis experienced terror and panic on an almost daily basis. She trembled at the prospect of being accidentally killed—catching a stray bullet, being blown up by a randomly flung shell or when her jeep drove over a land mine. The chance of falling into enemy hands frightened her perhaps even more. On stage in Algiers, Landis experienced aerial bombings by the Germans. Nonetheless, despite the stress and fear, she felt it was her duty to carry on with the tour, to put on a brave and nonchalant front before the boys. The "Jills" returned to the United States in March 1943 and Landis began her book. *Four Jills in a Jeep* was published serially in the *Saturday Evening Post* and later by Random House. Landis continued performing before servicemen at the Hollywood Canteen. A movie version of her book was filmed in 1944, with the Jills playing themselves. The film, however, was attacked in the press, with the Jills being accused of shameless self-promotion. The film's "recurrent theme of 'Look what we girls did for our country' is almost sickening,"[9] sniped the movie critic of the *New York Herald Tribune*. Nonetheless, later that year, Landis went on tour again. She came down with amoebic dysentery in North Africa and contracted malaria in the South Pacific. Pneumonia almost killed her in New Guinea. Landis survived her sojourns in North Africa and the Pacific only to commit suicide in 1948. She overdosed on Seconal because her lover at that time, Rex Harrison, refused to divorce his wife, Lili Palmer, and marry her. Landis had divorced Thomas Wallace in 1945. That same year, she had a short-lived lesbian affair with Jacqueline Susann. She then wed millionaire producer Horace Schmidlapp, to whom she was still married at the time of her death.

Landis is of particular interest in the annals of twentieth-century suicides because her death marked the beginning of a wave of suicides among Hollywood actresses and actors—she was the first "domino" to fall—that continued unabated into the 1960s, a phenomenon comparable in terms of victims to the surge of suicides among authors during the past one hundred years. Her book started another trend. *Four Jills in a Jeep* was the first of numerous reminiscence and confessional books by Hollywood notables. Many other stars would pen or dictate memoirs in the succeeding four decades.

T. O. Heggen (1919–1949)

On May 19, 1949, a maid discovered the body of Thomas Heggen, the author of the hit novel *Mister Roberts*, in the bathtub of the East Sixty-second Street, New York City, duplex apartment that he shared with fellow tenant Alan Campbell, a screenwriter and former husband of Dorothy Parker, who at the time of Heggen's death was working in Hollywood. The author's body was immersed in fourteen inches of water, his head submerged beneath the surface; he had been dead approximately eleven hours. Police found a razor blade at the bottom of the tub, but no cuts or slashes appeared on the body. On a washstand, however, sat a bottle of sleeping pills with six tablets left in it. Police said it had originally contained fifty. The police made a preliminary finding of asphyxiation by drowning; autopsy results would later show that Heggen had ingested a large quantity of sleeping pills. Heggen wrote no suicide note. When, prior to the autopsy, the press informed Alan Campbell of Heggen's death, Campbell told them that Heggen was hard at work on a new play and was under doctor's orders to take a sleeping pill at night. He theorized that Heggen had taken an extra pill to sleep better, had lost consciousness while bathing, and had accidentally drowned. "I talked to him yesterday," Campbell said, "and he was in wonderful spirits, feeling fine, and he said his work was going well. A young guy with that much money, such a great success, busy and thanking his stars to be out of the Navy could never have killed himself."[10] When apprised of the razor blade found in the tub, Campbell had no recourse but to crack a joke: "I'm surprised that they didn't find a pair of shoes."[11] Still, Heggen's suicide seems baffling for the very reasons Campbell stated. Heggen did appear to have everything to live for at the very time he killed himself. He had divorced his wife, the former Carol Lynn Gilmer, to whom he had dedicated his novel, but he had survived that crisis and appeared to have gotten on with his life. He had no financial worries. The hardback edition of *Mr. Roberts*, published by the Houghton Mifflin Company in 1946, had sold extremely well. At the time of Heggen's death, more than 100,000 copies had been purchased in the United States. In 1949, Pocket Books brought out the paperback. In the months prior to Heggen's suicide, 750,000 books had already been purchased—at the rate of 30,000 a month. With Joshua Logan, the director and producer of the musical *South Pacific*, Heggen had coauthored a play based on his novel that was subsequently published by Random House. Six thousand copies of the play had sold, and it was running on Broadway with Logan directing and Henry Fonda in the lead at the time of Heggen's death. A second company performed the work nightly on the Chicago stage as well. Heggen received weekly royalty checks of between $4,000 and $4,500; his total earnings from the play had reached $200,000. Had he lived, he would have received additional windfalls. The play had already been sold to Hollywood (Fonda would reprise the title role in the movie version). Heggen would have earned further royalties from the continuing Broadway production, from the film, and from the foreign rights to the book and play. The author's death shocked Fonda and the rest of the Broadway cast. The actor would have to deal with yet another suicide during the course of the play's run. His wife Frances Seymour Brokaw Fonda killed herself by slashing her throat with a razor blade a year after Heggen's death. She had suffered a nervous breakdown and had been committed to the Craig House Sanatorium after suing Fonda for divorce. Informed of his wife's death, Fonda asked Joshua Logan if he should go on that night. The director answered in the affirmative, and Fonda played the part of Mister Roberts for the 883d consecutive time.

Born December 23, 1919 in Fort Dodge, Iowa, T. O. Heggen attended the University of Minnesota, earning a Bachelor of Arts degree in 1941. Following the Japanese attack on Pearl Harbor, he enlisted in the United States Navy, serving five years at sea—one in the Atlantic, four in the Pacific—aboard a variety of vessels including a tanker, a cargo ship, an assault transport, and a battleship. He took part in the Guam, Peleliu, Iwo Jima, and Okinawa campaigns and, before his discharge, attained the rank of lieutenant. After the war, Heggen joined the staff of *Reader's Digest* and began writing about his navy experiences: *Mister Roberts* slowly began to take shape. Heggen set his novel aboard a navy supply ship in the Pacific. Behind the battle lines, the *Reluctant* cruises tediously back and forth between the ports of "Tedium" and "Apathy," with occasional stopovers at "Monotony" and "Ennui." The crew—a motley assortment of genial blackguards—is tyrannized by the *Reluctant's* puffed-up, self-important captain who constantly comes into conflict with the title character, the conscience of the ship and the novel's one estimable character. Prior to the book's publication, selections from the novel appeared in the *Atlantic Monthly*. Although Campbell and others claimed that Heggen was at work on a new play at the time of his death, no manuscript was ever found. Perhaps, like Ross Lockridge, Heggen had difficulty mounting a new project after achieving his first success.

F. O. Matthiessen (1902–1950)

On March 31, 1950, the noted American critic and Harvard professor F. O. Matthiessen leaped to his death from the twelfth-story window of the Manger Hotel in Boston. For the previous five years, he had been severely depressed—ever since the 1945 death of his lover, Russell Cheney, whom he had met in the mid-1920s while crossing the Atlantic by ocean liner; their relationship, however, was often tempestuous and troubled for the next twenty years. As early as 1938, Matthiessen thought of suicide. That year, he had recurrent dreams of falling to his death after jumping out of a high window. In the years following Cheney's death, Matthiessen became increasingly withdrawn and lonely. A homosexual who espoused left-wing politics, Matthiessen was deeply troubled by the Cold War conflict between Russia and the United States. His disenchantment at the world situation closely resembled that of Klaus Mann. (The two men would commit suicide within a year of each other.) Matthiessen championed the work of Klaus's father, Thomas Mann, when it increasingly came under attack in the late 1940s due to the elder Mann's leftward-leaning politics and his refusal to repudiate the newly installed Communist regime in East Germany. The right-wing press in America attacked Mann's political stances and his critical reputation—at least in certain circles—began to plummet. While his Harvard colleague Harry Levin changed his famous seminar "Proust, Joyce, and Mann" to "Proust, Joyce, and Kafka" and lambasted *Dr. Faustus* in the pages of the *New York Times Book Review*, Matthiessen continued to staunchly defend Mann. He particularly liked the Joseph novels, finding strongly American themes in the tetralogy, especially the final volume, *Joseph the Provider*, in which Mann portrays Joseph as a biblical FDR. Matthiessen compared Mann favorably to the American authors whom he most loved: Melville, Whitman, and Henry James.

Knowing that he was severely depressed, Matthiessen's friends watched him closely in his last years, but he gave his retainers the slip on March 31 when he checked into the Manger Hotel. Prior to jumping to his death, he placed his Yale Skull and Bones pin, several sealed letters written a few days before to certain of his friends, his apartment keys, and his suicide note written on two three-by-five file cards, on the desk in his hotel room. The note read as follows:

> I have taken this room in order to do what I have to do. My will is to be found on my desk in my apartment at 87 Pincknev St., Boston. Here are the keys. Please notify Harvard University—where I have been a professor.
>
> I am exhausted. I have been subject to so many severe depressions during the past few years that I can no longer believe that I can continue to be of use to my profession and my friends. I hope that my friends will be able to believe that I still love them in spite of this desperate act.
>
> F. O. Matthiessen[12]

On the flip side of one of the two file cards he used to write his suicide note, Matthiessen added these further instructions and reflections:

> I should like to be buried beside my mother in the cemetery at Springfield, Mass. My sister . . . will know about this
>> *but not until morning*
>> Please notify, Kenneth B. Murdock . . . and Jonathan Ogden Bulkley . . . who will notify my other
>> *but not until morning*
>> Yale friends . . . I would like them to go to my apartment and to see that the letters on the desk are mailed. How much the state of the world has to do with my state of mind I do not know. But as a Christian and a socialist believing in international peace, I find myself terribly oppressed by the present tensions[.][13]

Louis Verneuil (1893–1952)

The French dramatist Louis Verneuil (pseudonym of Louis Collin-Barbié du Bocage), by himself and in collaboration with Georges Berr, wrote more than sixty plays, most of them boulevard comedies. Among the most successful of French playwrights, he also acted and directed. His earlier comedies dealt primarily with complications in love while his later works tended to satirize current world political situations. Many of his plays appeared on Broadway, including *Mlle. ma mère* (1920) as *Oh, Mama* (1925); *Boom Boom* (1929); *Pile ou face* (English title *First Love* [1926]); *Le mariage de maman* (1925), adapted as *Matrimony Pfd.* by Grace George and James Forbes; and *Jealousy*, a two-character piece that had a successful run not only in New York but across America as well. In 1950, Verneuil wrote, in English, *Affairs of State*, which lampooned life in the diplomatic service. Performed on Broadway with Celeste Holm in the lead role, it ran for 610 performances. Verneuil's French successes include 1919's *La jeune fille au bain* (*The Young Girl Bathing*) and *Le traité d'Auteuil*; 1921's *L'amant de coeur*; 1922's *Régine Armand* which featured Sarah Bernhardt, whose granddaughter Verneuil married and later divorced, in one of her last roles; 1923's *Le fauteuil 47*, his greatest French success; 1923's *Ma cousine de Varsovie* (*My Cousin from Warsaw*); and 1931's *La Banque Nemo* (*Nemo's Bank*); which depicts the meteoric rise of a newsboy into a financial magnate. Verneuil's twenty-odd collaborations with Berr include 1916's *La charrette anglaise* (*The Dogcart*); 1917's *Monsieur Beverly*; 1933's *Parlez-moi d'amour* (*Speak to me of Love*); and 1935's *Le train pour Venise* (*The train to Venice*). Despite his popular success, Verneuil was prone to depression. He felt that he had never written a serious or substantial work, only entertaining fluff. On November 3, 1952, his body was discovered in the bathroom of his apartment. He slit his throat in his tub. Verneuil was fifty-nine years old.

Winfield Townley Scott (1910–1968)

No, he was not related to his namesake, the famous American general. Some of his ancestors arrived in America as early as 1620. Others, Scotch-English farmers and millworkers, came to New England in the 1840s. None of his forebears had artistic or literary pretensions, though two had been cabinetmakers of some skill. One of his grandfathers had earned his livelihood as a shoemaker, the other ran a hardware store. Scott's father worked for both men and practiced both professions. Born a few days after Mark Twain died and thus under Halley's Comet, Scott grew up in Haverhill, Massachusetts, and Newport, Rhode Island. As a young boy, he enjoyed being in the company of elderly women, sitting transfixed as he listened to their stories of the past. He graduated at a young age from listening to stories to reading books, and sometime before his tenth birthday, he decided he wanted to be a writer and began to industriously scribble stories of his own. While a sophomore at Haverhill High School, Scott discovered poetry. One day his English teacher, Miss R. Elaine Croston, read "The Rime of the Ancient Mariner" to the class. The young Scott experienced something akin to religious awe, and at that moment, he determined to write poetry himself.

Scott's early efforts appeared in the high school newspaper and in *Scholastic* magazine. Scott went on to attend Brown University. Graduating in 1931 at the height of the Great Depression, he found work at the Providence *Journal*. He would stay with the newspaper for twenty years, eventually rising to the position of literary editor. In the course of his career, he would teach briefly at Brown and New York Universities. Chosen Phi Beta Kappa poet of Harvard and Tufts universities in 1944, he would go on to win many other awards and honors for his poetry, though he would never take home any of the more prestigious prizes. Scott would publish nine books of verse in his lifetime, and his poems would be widely anthologized. He felt, however, that he had never received indubitable proof of his success. He waited his entire life for the recognition he thought that he deserved. A New England poet in the tradition of Dickinson, Robinson, and Frost, his folksy yet meticulously crafted verse celebrates the powers of individual perception and the beauties of the New England landscape. His descriptive power is evident in poems such as "Tidal River":

> . . . Grass voluptuous in the
>   river water
> Exhales a pre-dawn rain. But
>   no rain now. A fuss of
>   finches
> Flusters the low light rising
>   through alder tangle. A
>   tin can
> Winks in the mud, is angled
>   to shoot the sun.[14]

Scott was not a flamboyant and cliquish poet. He knew his verse appeared unassuming and unpretentious if nonetheless impeccably crafted. His more colorful and faddish colleagues might eclipse him for a time. He saw himself as a tortoise in a race with a field of far too many hares, but he would eventually receive his due. His flashy and exhibitionistic competitors would peter out and fall to the wayside in the long run—proper recognition would come his way, he just knew, if he could only hold on and wait.

Scott married Savila B. Harvey in 1932. After the couple divorced in 1946, Scott married Eleanor Metcalf, whose personal wealth enabled Scott to resign from the *Journal* in 1951. Although Scott devoted himself to his literary career for the remainder of his life, he nonetheless felt like a kept person and held it against Eleanor. He took increasingly to drink and often became combative and vindictive in his cups, directing his wrath at Eleanor and his three children. The Scotts eventually moved from New England to Santa Fe, New Mexico, where they purchased a handsome adobe home. Eleanor fell ill with the flu shortly before the couple's twenty-second wedding anniversary on April 26, 1968. She forgot the occasion, only realizing what day it was when flowers and a card sent by the Scotts' youngest son, nine-year-old Douglas, arrived in the afternoon. Eleanor apologized to her husband for her forgetfulness. He kept up a dignified reserve throughout the day. Their eldest son, Lindsay, and some of his college friends joined the poet for cocktails in the evening and all seemed well when Eleanor retired for the night. She feared that her omission might have further depressed her husband, who had been morose since the appearance of his last book, *New and Selected Poems*, published the previous year. He had high hopes for the volume, but it had not attracted the notice that he thought it would, though one reviewer had called him "the most under-estimated talent among contemporary poets."[15] Scott seemed in good spirits, however, when his wife went to bed. But the following day, as the two lunched at a restaurant several blocks from their home, Scott confronted his wife. "Is the idea of being married to me all these years so dreadful that you had to forget our anniversary?"[16] he asked. She attempted to evade the question and speak about his upcoming birthday a few days later on April 30. When she asked what he wanted in the way of gifts, he told her she needn't go out of her way. He wanted a pair of slippers and a few new books. His mood improved as he downed several luncheon martinis. They returned home, and he took his afternoon nap. They had plans that evening to attend a party given by a friend, Tom Jameson. Scott did not feel like putting in an appearance, but Eleanor nonetheless made him dress and go. Scott seemed to enjoy himself more and more as the night wore on. He refused to eat, however, and drank instead. Knowing that her husband was subject to irrational fits of jealous rage, Eleanor did not engage in extended conversations with any of the men attending the party.

When it came time to leave, Scott asked Bob Saam to come home with Eleanor and him for a nightcap. When they arrived, Scott was spoiling for a fight. First he complained that Douglas had left the living room a mess. Then after failing to light a fire in the bedroom, he began castigating himself. He said that he was a failure, that he couldn't write any more and that he was no good in bed. He concluded that his family would be better off with him dead. The Scott's teenage daughter Jeannette arrived home with a date but, seeing what the situation was, left again. Scott then proceeded to accuse Eleanor of being unfaithful with Saam, a ridiculous charge. Again and again he repeated that she and the children would be better off without him. Such scenes were commonplace in the last few years. Scott eventually left the room to retire to the guest house for the evening, taking his bottle with him. Eleanor believed the show to be over for the night and felt relieved when Scott departed. Forty-five minutes later, she went to the guest house, to see that her husband was tucked in for the night. She found Scott unconscious. He had swallowed a dozen or more 500-milligram capsules of Placidyl. She telephoned for an ambulance, but, by the time it arrived, Scott was dead. The sleeping pills and the alcohol he had drunk earlier in the evening combined to cause a massive circulatory collapse. Scott would be buried two days later on his fifty-eighth birthday.

Scott's books of poetry include *The Dark Sister*, a long narrative poem concerning Lief Ericson's hideous half-sibling Freydis, who is responsible for mass murder in Vinland; *Scrimshaw*; *Mr. Whittier and other poems*; *Change of Weather*; *To Marry Strangers*; *The Sword on the Table*; and *Wind the Clock*. He also published *Exiles and Fabrications*, a volume of critical essays.

Tom McHale (1942–1982)

Carbon monoxide poisoning killed Pennsylvania novelist Tom McHale. On March 30, 1982, at age forty, the author took his life in Pembroke Pines, Florida. A cover story blaming his death on a heart attack was put in circulation; early obituary notices indicated death by natural causes. A month after the author's passing, however, *Time* in a "death-revealed milestone" reported that McHale's death had been self-inflicted. Born in 1942 and raised in Scranton, Pennsylvania, McHale grew up in a blue-collar, right-wing, urban milieu where, in his words, everyone seemed "Catholic, pro-McCarthy, and very patriotic."[17] The familiars of his youth would become the future butts of his satire. He found more bull's eyes—new unsuspecting marks for his wit—in Philadelphia, which lent a lot of the local color to his early work, providing the setting for his first two novels. The city became McHale's back yard and stomping ground during the years he attended Temple University, where he earned a B.A. in biology in 1963. His studies would take him abroad for a year at the Sorbonne. Back home, he would complete additional course work at the University of Pennsylvania and later would go on to earn a Master of Fine Arts degree at Iowa.

In 1972 McHale became writer-in-residence at Monmouth College, in West Long Branch, New Jersey. During the lean apprentice years before his rise to prominence as an author, McHale supported himself by waiting tables. He also lived (or perhaps more correctly took refuge) on a kibbutz. His early fictions, black comedies concerning the societal and moral dilemmas of Irish and Italian Catholic Americans of differing income brackets and social stature, brought recognition and kudos. His first novel, *Principato*, which appeared in 1970, won acclaim for both its trenchant satire and for its expert technical execution. According to a *Time* book reviewer, with his first book McHale had already attained "formal mastery."[18] In *Principato*, McHale displays an inspired talent for grotesquerie. One important thread in the book's tapestry is the title character's hero worship of his dying father, a magisterial figure dwarfing all who surround him. As the novel opens, Angelo Principato recalls sitting, as a boy, small and naked beside his great and imposing father in a steam room at the San Giorgio Baths. The son's respect and reverence for his father bring him into conflict with the dark and sinister person of Monsignor Allergucci. The two older men have been locked in a private duel for decades. For thirty-five years, the elder Principato has refused to walk into a church. This defiance, as Allergucci terms it, is something the son has grown up with. It was always there and Angelo accepted it just as he accepted the Catholic faith he himself was reared in, for, while the father resolutely refused to go to mass, he never interfered with the Catholic upbringing of the son insisted upon by the boy's mother. Nor did he ever explain the cause of his own falling away from the faith. It falls to Allergucci to do that. Shortly before the old man's death, he summons Angelo to call on him by Western Union messenger. At the meeting, the Monsignor claims that he himself is responsible for the old man's fall from grace. As a young priest during the Depression, Allergucci was assigned to the Principatos's parish. Once two little girls walked into the church for mass without shoes. When Allergucci ordered them to leave, they ran away crying. The elder Principato challenged the young priest. Did he really care what his charges wore? Perhaps the girls did not even own shoes. Allergucci responded that the Italians did not come to America yesterday. He could not condone their going barefoot in the house of God. Principato asked if Allergucci was speaking as a priest of the Church, and when he replied that he was, Principato swore to never set foot in a church again. Allergucci realizes that he will bear the guilt of the man's eternal damnation if Principato fails now to reembrace the church. He vows to the son that he will be in the death room; indeed, the elder Principato will demand that he be there. The Monsignor fears that the old man is still not done punishing him, that he will refuse salvation to the very end and make "the final inevitable turn of the screw."[19] He begs now for Angelo's assistance. The dying man must make his confession and receive absolution. Allergucci warns Angelo that his veneration is misplaced, that there is a Satanic quality to the elder Principato's obstinacy and opposition:

> In revering your father, you revere a false god. You think you revere his Defiance because it takes strength and integrity to maintain an old view. But it's not that at all. The Defiance, the name applied years ago to his righteous anger, is only a veneer. Deep down, he's mocking us by having us believe in falsehood. . . .[20]

Within a year, McHale followed *Principato* with *Farragan's Retreat*. The second book concerns the demise of a middle-class Irish Catholic family whose members the author knocks off one by one in an elaborately engineered plan of gleeful extermination. The novel opens with Farragan rehearsing an array of murder schemes. The intended victim of each scenario is none other than his own son, a being whom he "loved in essence but was compelled to despise in principle":[21]

> Farragan had absolutely no intention of murdering his son, Simon: fathers did not usually quash their own seed, after all, given the time and trouble it took to make it grow. Even if a number of people thought Simon definitely needed quashing.
>
> But it occasionally disturbed him that he so positively enjoyed fantasizing the killer poses. This August Sunday morning, between the Offertory and Communion of the Mass, he was into them again for perhaps the thirtieth time. Pose one was doggedly simple. Farragan, with revolver already in hand, had only to pull the trigger after aiming point-blank at the victim's heart the instant the latter opened his apartment door in response to Farragan's knock.[22]

The reasons Simon deserves death are manifold: his inability to stick to one course of a study as a university student, his renunciation of the Catholic faith, his disinclination to work as a team player, the fact that he dodged the draft while his cousins paid the ultimate price in Vietnam.

Like *Principato*, *Farragan's Retreat* earned numerous favorable reviews. McHale continued building upon his comic vision, working the narrow but nonetheless rich vein he had staked for his own, in four subsequent novels: *Dooley's Delusion* (1971), *Alinsky's Diamond: A Love Story* (1974), *School Spirit* (1976), and *The Lady from Boston* (1978). *School Spirit* received the Thomas More medal and won a National Book Award nomination. While much of the time caustically critical of the church he grew up in, the former Jesuit high school graduate leavened his gall with humor. While mercilessly acerbic toward his subjects, he still held them in something like affectionate regard. His jabs were often of a sentimental, nostalgic sort. In a review of *School Spirit*, Richard Lingeman likened McHale to "one of those impish, irreverent carved figures, often with their tongues sticking out, that medieval craftsmen hid under seats and in other visually inaccessible places in cathedrals."[23]

James Tiptree Jr. (1915–1987)

James Tiptree Jr. was a nom de plume—the surname came from a brand of marmalade—though Alice Sheldon so successfully pulled off her masquerade that few people guessed the true sex of this brilliant science fiction writer. Sheldon created a persona for herself as complex as any of her characters. Tiptree resided in Washington and worked for the Pentagon. His letters to his fans were persuasively masculine: dynamic, funny, and to the point. The male characters in his fiction were likewise three-dimensional and believable, though they often had difficulties fathoming the vagaries of Tiptree's women. She wrote one clearly feminist story, "The Women Men Don't See." The two principal female characters opt at the story's end to leave the earth aboard a UFO. The tale concludes with the unsettling line: "Two of our opossums are missing."[24] They have spent their entire lives in the background, forced into obscurity and oblivion by the loud and flashy men who surround them. Although unable to make heads or tails of the women, the chief male character is nonetheless drawn sympathetically. He comes forth as a compassionate and friendly individual, someone very much like the author James Tiptree himself.

As a child, Sheldon traveled a great deal in the company of her parents. Her mother, a productive author in her own right, often wrote about her daughter (in various fictional guises) in her books. Little is known about Sheldon's first marriage. She supported herself as an art critic and married a second time in 1945. The following year she published a traditional story in the *New Yorker* under her own name. In 1967, she earned a Ph.D. in psychology. In 1968, at the age of fifty-two, she began to publish science fiction under the pseudonym of Tiptree—"his" first piece, "Birth of a Salesman," appeared in *Astounding* that year—and continued to work in this genre for the rest of her life. Tiptree's first short-story collection, *Ten Thousand Light Years from Home*, fifteen voyages through space and time, appeared in 1973.

Sheldon's stories, while energetic and celebratory of life, are also often quite dark. Almost all her tales conclude with a death. All life, all joy, eventually ceases. Death comes in the end for everyone and everything. In "The Last Flight of Doctor Ain," perhaps Sheldon's most grim work, she sees humanity as nothing more than a deadly, rapidly multiplying virus. A scientist ruthlessly wipes out the human population of a planet in order to save the world from total destruction. Her other short-story collections include *Warm Worlds and Otherwise* (1975), *Star Songs of an Old Primate* (1978), *Byte Beautiful* (1985), *The Starry Rift* (1986), and *Tales of the Quintana Roo* (1986). She also wrote five novels: *Up the Walls of the World* (1978), *Brightness Falls from the Air* (1985), *The Girl Who Was Plugged In* (1989), *Houston, Houston, Do You Read?* (1989), and *The Color of Neanderthal Eyes* (1990). In 1987, Sheldon's second husband was suffering from Alzheimer's disease, and she, too, was in poor health. She shot him and then herself.

Lewis B. Puller Jr. (1936–1994)

Lewis Puller Jr. found it a terrible burden to be the son of General Lewis "Chesty" Puller, the most highly decorated marine in history, yet he joined the corps and served in Vietnam as a second lieutenant and combat platoon leader, where he earned the Silver Star, two Purple Hearts, the Navy Commendation Medal, and the Vietnam Cross of Gallantry. In 1968, when he tripped an enemy land mine, he lost both his legs as well as fingers from each of his hands. He described the blast in his 1992 Pulitzer-prize winning autobiography *Fortunate Son*:

> I thought initially that the loss of my glasses in the explosion accounted for my blurred vision, and I had no idea that the pink mist that engulfed me had been caused by the vaporization of most of my right and left legs. As shock began to numb my body, I could see through a haze of pain that my right thumb and little finger were missing, as was most of my left hand, and I could smell the charred flesh which extended from my right wrist upward to the elbow. I knew that I had finished serving my time in the hell of Vietnam.[25]

In *Fortunate Son*, Puller records the cold reception that he and other vets received upon returning stateside and details his lengthy, painful convalescence, his growing disenchantment with his country, and his subsequent addiction to alcohol and pain killers. The book purports to recount how he overcame his pain and despair and conquered his alcoholism. His victory was short-lived, however. Two years after *Fortunate Son*'s publication, Puller committed suicide by shooting himself. At the time of his death, Puller had taken a leave of absence from the Pentagon, where he worked as a lawyer, to teach at the George Mason University. He had previously served as a director of the Vietnam Memorial Association, a nonprofit organization that fosters reconciliation between the United States and Vietnam. Puller was experiencing marital difficulties at the time of his suicide. In a statement to the press, his wife Linda T. "Toddy" Puller stated that he had suffered terrible wounds that had never really healed. Buried in Arlington National Cemetery with full military honors, Puller is survived by a son, Lewis B. Puller III, and a daughter, Maggie.

Jay Anthony Lukas (1933–1997)

The two-time Pulitzer prize-winning author J. Anthony Lukas died of "suicide by strangulation"[26] on June 5, 1997, in New York City, where he was born on April 25, 1933, the son of Edwin Jay, a prominent attorney, and Elizabeth Schamberg Lukas. The younger Lukas attended Harvard University where he earned a B.A. and graduated magna cum laude in 1955. He did further graduate study at the Free University of Berlin in 1956. From 1958 until 1962, he served as city hall correspondent for the *Baltimore Sun*. Lukas switched newspapers in 1962 and became a reporter for the *New York Times*. He had a long association with the paper and wore many different hats over the years. First he worked in the *Time*'s Washington and United Nations bureaus. In the mid-sixties, he served as an overseas correspondent, first in the Congo and then in India. In 1967, he became a member of the paper's metropolitan staff. Two years later, his title was "roving national correspondent."[27] In his final two years with the *New York Times* (1970–1971), Lukas served as a staff writer for the paper's Sunday magazine. After 1971, Lukas earned his living as a freelance writer, a visiting lecturer at Yale, Boston, and Harvard Universities, and as a radio host for station WOR in New York City. During his years as a correspondent, Lukas reported on controversial issues, social injustice, and America's counterculture. His first books, *The Barnyard Epithet and Other Obscenities: Notes on the Chicago Conspiracy Trial* (1970) and *Don't Shoot—We Are Your Children!* (1971) had their geneses in newspaper articles. The second grew out of a 1968 piece "The Two Worlds of Linda Fitzpatrick" concerning the 1967 murder of an upper-class Connecticut teenager and her hippie boyfriend. The article brought Lukas his first Pulitzer. *Don't Shoot—We Are Your Children!* not only profiles Fitzpatrick and her lover, it features biographical sketches of eight other young people of the period as well. The subjects came from a variety of ethnic and economic backgrounds. In the *New York Times Book Review*, Ross Macdonald wrote that "an eleventh young American, a few years older than the others, comes to be known in these pages. Their author, Mr. Lukas. His eloquence as a writer, his tenacity in research, his respect for other human beings, have combined to give us a beautiful and important book which I think may become a classic."[28] Lukas's next book, *Nightmare: The Underside of the Nixon Years*, came out in 1975. He contributed a chapter to the anthology *My Harvard, My Yale* in 1982.

From 1974 until 1985, Lukas was preoccupied with the most ambitious project he had yet undertaken, the work which would ultimately bring him his second Pulitzer, the mammoth *Common Ground: A Turbulent Decade in the Lives of Three American Families*. The 1400-page book ostensibly deals with the issue of school busing in the city of Boston. The three families of the title—the Divers, the Twymons, and the McGoffs—represent "the socioeconomic spectrum of the city."[29] Two are white, one affluent, the other working class. The third is black. The book was a huge critical success. Writing in the *Chicago Tribune Book World*, Robert B. Parker hailed the work as a journalistic masterpiece. Like many other critics, he thought that the volume transcended its basic subject, busing: "This is a book of such force and clarity that its just praise would require language rendered empty by jacket blurbs. To say that *Common Ground* is about busing in Boston is like saying that *Moby Dick* is about whaling in New Bedford, but it is a start."[30] In a *New York Times* article, Lukas suggests the work's deeper import: "I believe what happened in Boston was not a series of random events but the acting out of the burden of American history."[31] Not only does Lukas give us a vivid portrait of a modern city and three contemporary families, he goes to great pains to document the ancestry and historical background of his subjects. He visited Ireland to learn about the McGoff forebears; located the Twymons's ancestors, slaves in Georgia; and traced the Divers line to the period before the Revolutionary War. *Common Ground* presents a powerful generational view of history. According to Mark Zanger, how people "respond when they are cheated, how their families are strained and how they go on living and find new understanding"[32] are Lukas's real themes. Prior to his suicide, Lukas completed another work, *Big Trouble*.

Notes

1. Quoted in *Twentieth Century Authors: A Biographical Dictionary of Modern Literature*, ed. Stanley J. Kunitz and Howard Haycraft (New York: H.W. Wilson, 1942), p. 1341.

2. Quoted by Geoffrey Wolff, *Black Sun: The Brief Transit and Violent Eclipse of Harry Crosby* (New York: Random House, 1976), p. 237.

3. Ibid., p. 273.

4. Harry Crosby, "Assassin," quoted in Wolff, *Black Sun*, p. 241. "Assassin" appeared in *Mad Queen* (Paris: Black Sun Press, 1929).

5. Ibid.

6. Harry Crosby, "Sun Death," quoted in Wolff, *Black Sun*, p. 242. "Sun Death" appeared in *Mad Queen*.

7. Quoted in *American Literary Almanac*, ed. Karen L. Rood (New York, Oxford: Bruccoli, Clark, Layman, Inc. Facts on File, 1988), p. 353.

8. Ibid., p. 356.

9. Quoted by Kirk Crivello, *Fallen Angels: The Lives and Untimely Deaths of Fourteen Hollywood Beauties* (Secaucus, N.J.: Citadel Press, 1988), p. 96.

10. Quoted in *New York Times* obituary, 20 May 1949.

11. Ibid.

12. Quoted in *American Literary Almanac*, p. 358.

13. Ibid.

14. Winfield Townley Scott, "Tidal River," *Change of Weather* (New York: Doubleday, 1964), p. 21.

15. Quoted by Scott Donaldson, *Poet in America: Winfield Townley Scott* (Austin: University of Texas Press, 1972), p. 8.

16. Ibid., p. 7.

17. Quoted in *Contemporary Authors*, volumes 77–80, ed. Frances C. Locker (Detroit: Gale Research, Co, 1979), p. 369.

18. Ibid.

19. Tom McHale, *Principato* (New York: Viking, 1970), p. 204.

20. Ibid.

21. McHale, *Farragan's Retreat* (New York: Viking, 1971), p. 3.

22. Ibid.

23. Quoted in *Contemporary Authors*, p. 369.

24. James Tiptree Jr., "The Women Men Don't See," *Warm Worlds and Otherwise*, introduction by Robert Silverberg (New York: Ballantine Books, 1975), p. 164.

25. Lewis B. Puller Jr., *Fortunate Son* (New York: Grove Weidenfeld, 1991), p. 157.

26. Anna Holmes, "Monitor," *Entertainment*, 20 June 1997, p. 14.

27. Linda Metzger, ed., *Contemporary Authors, New Revision Series*, vol. 19 (Detroit, Michigan: Gale Research Co., 1987), p. 307.

28. Ibid., p. 308.

29. Ibid., p. 308.

30. Ibid., p. 308.

31. Ibid., p. 309.

32. Ibid., p. 308.

Seven Possibles

Ambrose Bierce (1841–1913?)

MBROSE BIERCE'S DISAPPEARANCE IN 1913 HAS BEEN THE SUBJECT of much speculation over the years. While Carlos Fuentes's 1985 novel *The Old Gringo* offers one imaginative answer to the question, the mystery persists to this day. The last authenticated sighting of the Ohio-born newspaperman and short-story writer occurred in Chihuahua, Mexico, December 26, 1913. From there he rode into the Mexican desert and was never seen again. In a Christmas letter, he wrote that he planned to travel further south. Rumors of his death proliferated during the next several months. Some held that Bierce had joined the army of Pancho Villa in the border war then taking place between the United States and Mexico and that he was slain in one of that conflict's numerous skirmishes. Others maintained that he was waylaid by Mexican bandits. Certain of his associates were convinced that he had committed suicide in the desert. Prior to his trip to Mexico, Bierce had been experiencing acute financial difficulties. His monetary hardships, they argued, had driven him to this extreme measure. This last view is bolstered by the fact that, while residing in California, Bierce associated with the Piedmont writers who promoted, in George Sterling's words, "leaving the world in a good temper when one selected the hour of one's going."[1] In addition to Sterling, these proponents of suicide included Nora May French and Joaquin Miller. Jack London also fraternized with a number of these same writers. Bierce's *Tales of Soldiers and Civilians*, published in 1891, revised and retitled *In the Midst of Life* in 1898, remains one of the finest collections of Civil War-inspired stories ever written. Other works include *The Devil's Dictionary*, a witty and misanthropic digest of definitions (happiness, for example, is "the contemplation of the misery of another"[2]); *Write It Right*, a manual of style; and *Can Such Things Be?*, a collection of macabre and fantastical tales, many focusing on death, which Bierce brought out in 1893. His single most famous story is the haunting "An Occurrence at Owl Creek Bridge," which concerns the execution by hanging of Confederate spy Peyton Farquhar. Most of the story "takes place" the split second between Farquhar's plunging downward from the makeshift gallows and his neck breaking when the rope goes taut. The Alabama planter stands on one end of a plank spanning three cross-ties of a railroad bridge while a Union soldier stands at the other. At a signal from his commanding officer, the latter steps aside, the plank tilts, and Farquhar goes down between the ties. Time slows down. Not only does Farquhar recall all his past life, he fantasizes that the rope snaps and that he falls into the river and swims away from his captors, one of whom manages to draw a pistol and fire several shots at him but to no avail. Farquhar crosses to the far river bank and runs into the forest. He travels hard all day and at nightfall reaches the gate of his own house, where his wife and children come running to greet him. As he stretches to embrace his wife, he "feels a stunning blow upon the back of his neck."[3]

In his fiction, Bierce often speculated what the moment of death might be like. Like Virginia Woolf, he conceives a mystical revelation—a cross-over vision of arresting beauty—at the end of life. Farquhar experiences the following:

> Objects were represented by their colors only; circular horizontal streaks of color—that was all he saw. He had been caught in a vortex and was being whirled on with a velocity of advance and gyration that made him giddy and sick. . . . The sudden arrest of his motion, the abrasion of one of his hands on the gravel, restored him, and he wept with delight. He dug his fingers in the sand, threw it over himself in handfuls and audibly blessed it. It looked like diamonds, rubies, emeralds; he could think of nothing beautiful which it did not resemble. The trees upon the bank were giant garden plants; he noted a definite order in their arrangement, inhaled the fragrance of their blooms. A strange, roseate light shone through the spaces among their trunks and the wind made in their branches the music of aeolian harps. He had no wish to perfect his escape. . . .[4]

T. E. Lawrence (1888–1935)

Lawrence of Arabia undertook two great projects in his lifetime. During the First World War, he waged a guerrilla campaign against the Turks in the hopes of establishing a single Arab state, his exploits and heroics inspiring the British army and nation as well as winning him love and renown in the Arab world. In the years following the war, he wrote *Seven Pillars*, an epic narrative, a half-million words long, of his adventures in the Arab campaign. According to his biographer Vyvyan Richards, Lawrence had very high ambitions for his memoir. Not only did he wish to produce a historical account of the military operations he participated in and led, he also desired to create a work of art that would disclose his inner complexities, divulge the workings of his mind—in short, reveal him heart and soul. Lawrence completed the first draft of his manuscript only to lose it in Paris. Not at all disheartened, he immediately set to work rewriting the text from his notes, producing up to 30,000 words in a twenty-four hour period. Known for his mood swings, he remained driven and enthusiastic during the course of his book's composition. He revised, polished, and rewrote until he was satisfied that he fulfilled all his ambitions for the book, that he had indeed produced a great work of art. Lawrence then arranged to have *Seven Pillars* published in a deluxe edition of a hundred copies with specially commissioned illustrations and hand-crafted bindings. A condensed version of the work, *Revolt in the Desert*, sold briskly. Lawrence used the profits he earned from it to pay the high printing costs of *Seven Pillars*. To his great disappointment, the book did not receive the literary acclaim that he thought it deserved.

Born August 15, 1888, in Tremadoc, North Wales, Lawrence developed a love for archeology in his youth. He took a first-class degree in history at Oxford, then traveled to Syria in 1909 to study its French medieval fortresses. He returned to the Middle East a short time later to work at the Carchemish archaeological excavation. At this time, he developed a profound knowledge of both local Arab customs and of the geological region. These insights led to his being assigned to British military intelligence in Cairo within a few months of war breaking out in 1914. Since Turkey had allied with Germany, Lawrence took on the role of agitator. He proved to be a hypnotic, charismatic figure and began inciting rebellion in Turkish-controlled Arab areas. He joined Feisal al Hussein in the latter's uprising against the Turks, leading guerrilla attacks for which he earned the nickname "Amir Dynamite."[5] He exhorted the independent sheiks to unite in the cause of a single Arab state and roused them by his own courageous acts and the promise of the plunder and spoils of war. Captured and tortured by the Turks, Lawrence escaped in time to take part in a victory parade in Jerusalem after the war. He left the army as a lieutenant colonel, declining the Order of the Bath and the DSO from George V, saying that he did not wish fame or recognition for his military service. He tried to withdraw from public life by enlisting in the RAF as an ordinary aircraftman under an assumed name. His ruse, however, was almost immediately discovered, and he was released from duty. He proceeded to enlist in the army, once again under a false name. Caught once more, he was permitted to transfer back to the RAF, but was discharged for the final time in 1935. At the age of forty-six, Lawrence retired to his estate at Clouds Hill, Dorset, and died in a motorcycle accident May 13, 1935. At the inquest investigating the mishap, Lawrence's death was ruled accidental. Two young boys testified that he had swerved to avoid hitting them as they rounded a corner on their bicycles. Rumors circulated, however, that Lawrence had deliberately killed himself due to his profound despondency. The only adult witness at the inquest, Lawrence's neighbor Corporal Ernest Catchpole, testified that moments before the crash he had seen Lawrence driving wildly on his motorbike at a high rate of speed, probably in excess of sixty miles per hour. In the years following his death, most of Lawrence's biographers dismissed the idea that it was anything other than accidental. In 1996, however, six letters Lawrence wrote shortly before the accident were unearthed by the writer Paul Marriott. Their contents lend new credence to the view that Lawrence took his life, that he had suicide on his mind May 13 when he left home on his motorbike. One letter, to Lawrence's close friend Eric Kennington, is particularly convincing. Lawrence appears at a loss what to do now that he has been discharged from the RAF. He feels with his career over, only death remains. The letter reads in part:

> You wonder what I am doing? Well, so do I in truth. Days seem to dawn, suns to shine, evenings to follow, and then I sleep. What I have done, what I am doing, what I am going to do, puzzle and bewilder me. Have you ever been a leaf and fallen from your tree in autumn and been really puzzled about it? That's the feeling. . . . I am sitting in my cottage rather puzzled to find out what has happened to me, is happening and will happen. At present the feeling is mere bewilderment. I imagine leaves must feel like this after they have fallen from their tree and until they die.[6]

James Weldon Johnson (1871–1938)

In "The Doomed in Their Sinking," his joint 1972 review of A. Alvarez's *The Savage God* and Jacques Choron's *Suicide*, William H. Gass writes: "Nowadays the significance of a suicide for the suicide and the significance of that suicide for society are seldom the same. If, according to the social workers' comforting cliché, they are often a cry for help, they're just as frequently a solemn vow of silence. Nevertheless, it is easy to imagine circumstances under which some of our conventional kinds of suicide would be impossible because we would refuse to recognize them. The liver fails. The veins collapse. Sleep seizes the wheel. No suicides there."[7]

In our introduction, we have already discussed the phenomenon of psychological suicides, writers who lived in a reckless, self-destructive manner that considerably shortened their lives, but who resisted the temptation to "cash in" and do away with themselves in quick fashion. The list of writers who harmed and hurt themselves from overindulgence in alcohol, as we have seen, is quite long. Dylan Thomas's heavy drinking led to his tragically premature death at thirty-nine in a New York hospital. On a lecture tour of America, Thomas, who showed little regard for his health his entire adult life, collapsed in his room at the Chelsea Hotel after a long night of drinking. He succumbed from a cerebral ailment. His drinking, however, was considered a contributory cause. Tennessee Williams abused both drugs and alcohol. He did not die, however, from cirrhosis of the liver, but choked to death on a plastic nasal spray cap. Williams had often spoken about the possibility of his doing himself in. His brother Dakin, however, scoffed at the notion that his death was a possible suicide. If alcohol did not contribute to the deaths of Faulkner and Fitzgerald, it certainly took a toll on their writing. Every page of *A Fable* was written when Faulkner was dead drunk. Several prominent authors this century have died in automobile crashes. In most cases, when such accidents are revisited, they seem to be exactly that. The circumstances of the wreck rule out suicidal intent. At the age of forty-six, Albert Camus, for example, died when the car in which he was riding struck a tree some seventy miles southeast of Paris in 1960. Camus was not driving. Michel Gallimard, a member of the French publishing family, was at the wheel of the Facel Vega sports sedan. The left rear wheel of the car blew out as the vehicle sped at eighty miles an hour. Gallimard, his wife, and eighteen-year-old daughter were thrown clear of the wreckage, though all three sustained severe injuries. Camus, who sat in the front passenger seat, was thrown into the back. The car bounced off one tree then careened into another, and Camus died instantly. In 1940, Nathanael West ran a stop sign and crashed into another car in Imperial County, California. He and his wife, Eileen McKenney, were returning from a hunting trip in Mexico. Driving conditions were poor at the time; it had been raining and the highway was slick. Both West and McKenney died of skull fractures.

No accident was more spectacular, however, than that which claimed the life of James Weldon Johnson, the African American author, poet, composer, educator, and early crusader for civil rights, who died in a Maine Central Railroad grade crossing accident near his summer home in Dark Harbor, Maine. Johnson drove the car in which he and his wife, Grace Nail, were riding into the path of an oncoming train. Both Johnson's legs and his skull were fractured. He died within minutes. His wife sustained severe head and leg injuries but survived. Freak accidents happen all the time, and Johnson's death may have simply been the result of one. The circumstances of his death, however, are such that the possibility of suicide can't be totally ruled out. Johnson's talents were many and he died in the prime of life. Born in Jacksonville, Florida, six years after the close of the Civil War, he earned B.A. and M.A. degrees at Atlanta University in 1894 and 1904. He served as a teacher and principal of a negro school in Jacksonville. In 1897, he became the first negro admitted to the Florida bar since the Civil War. In 1901, he moved to New York, and, in collaboration with his brother J. Raymond Johnson, a graduate of the Boston Conservatory of Music, and vaudevillian Bob Cole, he became a song writer. In addition to penning many of the popular tunes of the day, Johnson and his brother composed several light operas. The trio earned $13,000 on one song alone. After establishing himself in the world of music and vaudeville, Johnson served his country for a time as a diplomat. He functioned as a United States Consul, first in Venezuela and then in Nicaragua. In 1912, two years after his marriage to Nail, he began his literary career, writing both verse and prose. His works include the novel *Autobiography of an Ex-Colored Man*, published anonymously that year and reissued under the author's rightful name in 1927; *Fifty Years* and Other Poems (1917); Self-Determining Haiti (1920); God's Trombones (poems, 1927); Black Manhattan (1930); Saint Peter Relates an Incident of the Resurrection Day (verse, 1930); Negro Americans, What Now? (1934); an autobiography, Along This Way (1934); and Selected Poems (1936). He edited The Book of American Negro Poetry in 1921 and two books of negro spirituals published respectively in 1925 and 1926. He also wrote an English version of the grand opera Goyescas that was produced by the Metropolitan Opera Company in 1915.

John Horne Burns (1916–1953)

Shortly after he and his male lover, an Italian doctor, severed relations, the American novelist John Horne Burns, who was then living in Leghorn, Italy, went sailing. The official line, supported by his biographer John Mitzel, goes as follows: Burns fell into a coma while sunbathing and died six hours later from a cerebral hemorrhage at the age of thirty-six. Supposition that he took his own life, however, continues to this day. His parents, both devout Catholics, never approved or understood their son. Although Burns was first interred in Florence, they had his body exhumed and reburied with full Catholic rites in Holyhood Cemetery, Brookline, Massachusetts. Born in Massachusetts and educated at Harvard, Burns served with the American armed forces in Africa and Italy during the Second World War. He wrote three books: The Gallery (1947), a collection of fictionalized sketches concerning GIs in Naples which show how democratic ideals become corrupted in war; Lucifer with a Book (1949), a novel satirizing progressive private schools in America; and A Cry of Children (1952), which examines the difficult and complicated love shared between two ex-Catholics. Although Burns' reputation as a writer has grown considerably in the years following his death, a final novel, The Stranger's Guise, remains unpublished.

Randall Jarrell (1914–1965)

On October 15, 1965, the American poet Randall Jarrell went out for an evening walk in Greensboro, North Carolina, where he taught at the university. Facing oncoming traffic, Jarrell made his way down U.S. Highway 15–501, which was congested but poorly illuminated. At 7:30 P.M. Jarrell stepped into the path of a car. The driver said that the man he hit, whom he had seen walking along the highway's berm, had suddenly turned and thrown himself into the side of his automobile. The driver reported that his speed had not been in excess of forty-five miles per hour. Jarrell, nonetheless, fractured his skull and died within five minutes of impact. The death was ruled accidental. Nine months earlier, however, in January 1965, Jarrell had attempted to commit suicide by slitting his left wrist and for a time had to be committed to the psychological ward at North Carolina Hospital. In May, he was again hospitalized at the same facility for treatment of manic-depressive disorder. He recommenced teaching at the University of North Carolina at Greensboro in the fall of 1965, but continued to receive treatment at North Carolina Memorial. That month he also underwent hand therapy due to his wrist wounds at the Hand Rehabilitation Center at Chapel Hill. Most Jarrell scholars today believe that he took his own life.

Born in Nashville, Tennessee, Jarrell served in the air force in World War II. Later he became a consultant in poetry at the Library of Congress and wrote criticism for the *Nation*. His first volume of verse, *Blood for a Stranger*, appeared in 1942. He followed it with *Little Friend, Little Friend* (1945), *The Seven-League Crutches* (1951), *Selected Poems* (1955), *The Woman at the Washington Zoo* (1960), and *The Lost World* (1965). His *Complete Poems* appeared in 1969 as did *The Death of a Ball Turret Gunner*. Jarrell's fraught and compassionate verse examines the plight of the victims of war and historical mischance. Except for childhood, existence is ugly and sordid, and man is responsible for much of his own suffering, Jarrell seems to argue. The horrors of the war had colored his thought and continued to haunt him in later life. He used his verse to exorcise these demons. In his later poems, conscious of his own shortcomings and quirks, Jarrell ironically questions his right to evaluate and condemn his fellow human beings, but proceeds to censure and rebuke the greed and stupidity of those who start wars and otherwise profiteer from human suffering. In addition to his poems, he published volumes of criticism, including 1953's *Poetry and the Age* and 1962's *A Sad Heart in the Supermarket*, a novel, *Pictures from an Institution*—an academic satire that comments wryly on the hopeless state of education in certain American liberal arts colleges—and a memorable translation of Goethe's *Faust*.

Seth Morgan (1949–1990)

In hindsight it seems that he was destined to perish in a traffic fatality. He smashed up automobiles and motorbikes with reckless abandon and had been arrested at least nine times for driving under the influence. The night before his last ride, Morgan had been busted on the same red-and-white Harley he would be thrown to his death from twenty-four hours later. He had steered the bike into the wrong lane and was swerving around oncoming vehicles when the cops nabbed him and hauled him off to jail. He called a long-suffering, much put-upon ex-girlfriend, Suzy Levine, to bail him out. He showed up drunk at the pub where she worked in New Orleans's French Quarter, toward the end of her shift the next night, insisting that she close up so the two could go out for a ride. The four remaining patrons recalled Levine's terrified reaction. Over and over again, she said: "No way I'm getting on that fuckin' motorcycle with you."[8] Morgan followed her behind the bar and tried to grab hold of her, losing his balance and almost falling. She helped him into a seat and began telephoning friends, looking for someone to take him off her hands. No such luck. He wanted alcohol, so she began pouring him shots. She had been hitting the bottle herself on and off during the night and now tossed back a few more as the other customers, sensing trouble, hurriedly finished their drinks and headed for the door. She locked up as soon as the last had left. A few latecomers found the place closed when they tried the door at 11:30 P.M. Peering through the window, they saw that Suzy and Seth had left in a hurry. The television was still on. The empties had not been cleared from the bar. Dishes lay unwashed in the sink. Shortly before midnight on October 17, 1990, witnesses near the Saint Claude Bridge saw a couple fly past on a motorcycle, the female passenger clutching the man with one hand while she beat his back with the other. What did the pummeling signify? Did she want him to slow down? Did she want off? The witnesses could only guess. Neither driver nor passenger were wearing helmets. The seventy-one-year-old St. Claude Avenue Bridge narrows to just two lanes for one segment of its span. An abutment of eight telephone poles painted bright yellow and covered with reflectors sits one hundred feet away from the roadway just where the two-lane stretch begins, its purpose to secure and safeguard the bridge's warning gates. Crossing the bridge, Morgan aimed for the right lane but did not steer hard enough. The motorcycle hit the medium strip dividing the roadway and both driver and passenger were catapulted into the air. Morgan slammed into the piling face first, Levine was thrown beyond it. She landed forty-five feet further down the roadway. Both died instantly. Blood tests revealed that Morgan had both cocaine and Percodan in his system. His blood alcohol content was .3, three times the legal limit. Levine's BAC was almost as high: .28.

Running amok on booze and drugs was nothing new for Seth Morgan. He had been battling his demons for decades. Born in 1949, he was the son of the distinguished poet Frederick Morgan, founder and editor of the *Hudson Review* quarterly. The family was one of means, having amassed a fortune selling soap. As a young man, Seth received between $26,000 and $30,000 annually from a trust fund. Early on, he exhibited a precocious talent for self-expression, but his childhood had been lonely and unhappy. His mother was an alcoholic. Cold and unaffectionate, she drank herself to death before Morgan reached sixteen. The son bore incredible resentment toward his mother. The bitterness she provoked in Morgan caused him, he would later concede, to spend years "planning the strategic degradation of women."[9] Not only did he believe that he inherited his addictive personality from her, he also claimed that she had been responsible for his brother's suicide. Fate decreed that two of Frederick Morgan's children would die on bridges. Years before Seth's crash, his brother leaped to his death from the Oakland Bay overpass in California.

Seth went to a number of private schools as a boy, including the American School in Switzerland, and earned a youthful reputation for being a troublemaker. He attended the University of California at Berkeley but dropped out in 1970. That same year he met the singer Janis Joplin while delivering cocaine to her Marin

County home. The two became lovers and might have married had not Joplin overdosed on heroin. A born ladies' man, Morgan took numerous lovers after Joplin's death. He married a Sausalito waitress he had injured in a motorcycle accident when the pair crashed into a former residence of Jack London. The wreck left the muscles in the woman's face paralyzed. Morgan married her to stem a possible lawsuit. In San Francisco he worked as a barker for a striptease club and became progressively addicted to heroin. Morgan married a second time. His new bride worked as a prostitute, and he pimped for her. He sank so low that, to support his habit, he began pulling off armed robberies. On one occasion, he struck a knife through a victim's hand into a floor. In 1977, after being apprehended by police during the commission of a crime, Morgan did a thirty-month stint in prison. After serving his sentence, he went back to work as a strip joint barker. In 1986, he moved to New Orleans, where he was arrested for DWI twice in six months. He had gone south, he later admitted, to drink himself to death. But something awoke in him and he authored a book instead. He claimed that he wrote *Homeboy*, a novel based on his drug and prison experiences, during a six-month sober period in 1987. One of his numerous girlfriends, Vicki Vanderford, would later dispute this. According to her, Morgan had been working on the novel for at least ten years. She said that it was all he ever did. Whichever version of the novel's composition comes closer to the truth, the book was published to huge critical acclaim by Random House early in 1990. Both Norman Mailer and William Styron praised the book. The novel also received a front-page rave from the *New York Times Book Review*. Morgan earned a $50,000 advance for the paperback rights; a $425,000 movie deal was also in the works. Seth and his father reconciled, and the younger Morgan began work on a second novel provisionally entitled *Mambo Mephiste*. Once he achieved success, however, Morgan began hitting the booze and drugs again. Shortly after the publication of *Homeboy*, he was involved in a hit-and-run accident. A week after that, he was again arrested for DWI. According to Vanderford, one reason for Morgan's renewed bingeing was writer's block. He could not get on with *Mambo Mephiste*; the success of *Homeboy* intimidated him. He felt that he could never produce work of the same caliber again. During his last months, Morgan lived with a succession of accommodating females. Whenever his alcohol and drug abuse became too much for his girlfriend of the moment to handle, he moved on. One or two of the women tried to get him into therapy. When the subject was broached, he would appear receptive at first, but when it came time to act, he would invariably change his mind.

During the last year of his life, Morgan blew money left and right. He shot cocaine all the time and, in no shape to have sex himself, paid prostitutes and junkies to perform sex acts in front of him. He bought vehicle after vehicle and totaled them all. After one wreck in which he broke his nose and received twenty-five stitches to his face, he told Levine's teenage son Joey that he wished that faces were disposable. "This one is about shot," he said, "I wish I could hang it up and put on a new one."[10] In an interview with the New Orleans' *Times-Picayune* shortly after the publication of *Homeboy*, Morgan called himself a con man and an addict-alcoholic. He said that if he couldn't create, he would destroy—first his loved ones then himself. When Morgan purchased the Harley, Joey warned, "You know you just bought your own death."[11] Morgan did not rebut or deny it.

Eugene Izzi (1953–1996)

He wrote detective thrillers, but Izzi's own end would prove more cryptic and puzzling than any of his fictions. The police originally approached the novelist's death as a possible homicide, but a Chicago medical examiner would eventually find that the author had committed suicide. In the coroner's view, the evidence could support only one conclusion. A second explanation of Izzi's odd death has, however, been proposed, and it, too, seems feasible. While murder can legitimately be ruled out, accident and plain stupidity cannot. Whether Izzi's end resulted from suicide or from overzealous research may never be known for certain. On the morning of December 7, 1996, a corpse was seen dangling outside the fourteenth floor window of an office highrise along Chicago's Loop; it had been spotted by pedestrians passing below. Someone notified the police. The office in question proved to be that of Eugene Izzi. It was locked from the inside, but upon entering it, the police found signs of a struggle. A loaded revolver lay on the floor and a hole had been punched into one of the room's plasterboard walls. The rope tied around the novelist's neck was secured to the leg of a desk inside the building. The dead man was wearing a bullet proof vest. Searching through Izzi's pockets, the police found a canister of Mace aerosol, a set of brass knuckles, several hundred dollars, and three computer disks. The disks did not contain a suicide note but a dramatic scenario: White militia members storm the office of a detective writer who has satirized their organization in one of his novels. They jump the author, who, resisting their assault, flails his fists and bashes a hole in the wall. The extremists toss a noose over their intended victim's neck, then struggle to eject him from his office window. At last, they heave him through. The writer, however, manages to catch hold of the rope with his hands and breaks his fall. Having averted death, he pulls himself up through the window, and puts paid to his would-be assailants with his pistol.

Eugene Izzi strove for authenticity in his novels and had a reputation for being an obsessive researcher, combing the newspapers for stories and plots. He used real people and incidents in his books, fictionalizing them only slightly. His friends claim that he wanted every page of his fiction to ring true; they have suggested that on December 7, he was attempting to act out the scene on the computer disks: that in order to portray the event accurately, he had to find out how it felt to fall out of an office window with a rope slipknotted around his neck. Others argue that the novelist wanted to kill himself and that he was intent on self-promotion. His death was his last creative act, a gruesome publicity stunt. He created a final mystery that would provoke media attention, arouse curiosity, and kindle speculation. The buzz would insure sales for his seventeenth and last novel, *A Matter of Honor*, which had been accepted for publication some months before his death but had not yet appeared. Izzi had been a moderately successful writer but none of his books had achieved best sellerdom, which galled and vexed him. Born in Chicago, Izzi grew up in the Hegewisch neighborhood of the city. Before writing crime novels, he worked as a steel worker and did a stint in the U.S. Army. After his tour in Germany, he wrote six novels, none of which he was ever able to sell. His first published book was 1987's *The Take*, a story about a cop turned criminal. His other works include *Bad Guys* (1988); *The Booster* (1989), which charts a mob boss's bid to take over a rival's territory; *Invasions* (1990); *The Prime Roll* (1990); *Prowlers* (1991), another novel with a mob theme; *Tribal Secrets* (1992); and Izzi's most successful book, the paperback original *King of the Hustlers* (1993), which recounts an aborted bank robbery. Izzi received a large advance for the last book. Because of its success, he was able to sell the movie rights to several of his other novels.

Notes

1. Quoted in *American Literary Almanac*, ed. Karen L. Rood (New York, Oxford: Bruccoli, Clark, Layman, Inc. Facts on File, 1988), p. 360.

2. Quoted in *The Avenal Companion to English and American Literature, United States of America*, ed. David Daiches, Malcolm Bradbury, and Eric Mottram (New York: Avenel Books, 1981), p. 33. *The Devil's Dictionary* appeared in 1906.

3. Ambrose Bierce, "An Occurrence at Owl Creek Bridge," *A Treasury of Civil War Stories*, ed. Martin H. Greenberg and Bill Pronzini (New York: Bonanza Books, 1991), p. 351. "An Occurrence" appeared in *Tales of Soldiers and Civilians*, published in 1891.

4. Ibid., p. 350.

5. Quoted by Rajeev Syal, "Letters Hint at Lawrence's Death," *London Times*, 1 September 1996.

6. Ibid.

7. William H. Gass, "The Doomed in Their Sinking," *The World Within the Word* (Boston: Godine, 1979), p. 8.

8. Quoted by Mike Capuzzo, "Seth Morgan's Last Ride," *Esquire* (February 1991), p. 94.

9. Ibid.

10. Ibid, p. 97.

11. Ibid, p. 96.

Envoi

Manic-Depression: A Genetic Predisposition for Creativity and Suicide?

THE TWENTIETH CENTURY HAS WITNESSED A SLEW OF AUTHOR SUI-cides. In no other era have so many writers fallen by their own hand. The other arts have also seen a marked increase in such deaths. Toward the conclusion of *The Savage God*, during a discussion of modernism, A. Alvarez makes the succinct observation that "one of the most remarkable features of the arts in this century has been the sudden, sharp rise in the casualty-rates among the artists."[1] He further states that "before the twentieth century . . . the artists who killed themselves or were even seriously suicidal were rare exceptions."[2]

As we have seen, the numbers bear him out in terms of actual *felos-de-se*. However, Alvarez's claim that artists with suicidal bents were few and far between before 1900, that such a self-destructive disposition among writers is only a relatively recent development, seems highly suspect, a surprising statement for the author of a book which presents a great deal of compelling albeit inferential evidence to the contrary.

One of Alvarez's stated purposes in writing his groundbreaking study was to track society's evolving attitude toward suicide from the Middle Ages to modern times through the specialized lens of literature. Indeed, he succeeds admirably in showing how suicide meant different things to writers of various ages and epochs. One fact, however, emerges quite clearly to the reader of *The Savage God* and seems all but indisputable; namely, that suicide has been a topic of undying fascination to authors, a subject that has exerted a profound and perennial pull on the creative imagination in all eras. Why, we must ask, were authors in all time periods so consistently and in such large numbers drawn to the question of suicide? Could it be that the suicidal impulse was not a foreign one to the great majority of the writerly guild or brotherhood but an impetus all too keenly felt, if also in most cases successfully resisted? The answer seems to be not simply yes, but a resounding yes.

Since the publication of *The Savage God* in 1971, the link between artistic inventiveness and manic depression has been explored in depth in works such as Kay Jamison's *Touched by Fire: Manic Depression and the Artistic Temperament* and Julian Lieb and D. Jablow Hershman's *Manic Depression and Creativity*. It is the provocative thesis of Lieb's and Hershman's book that "manic-depression is almost, but not absolutely, essential in genius. . . ."[3]

A long-recognized inherited mental disorder, bipolar syndrome, also known as manic depression, affects approximately one percent of the population. It consists of two contrasting states, each marked by a subtle change in brain chemistry. The person who suffers from this kind of mental illness—a mood disorder—enters into both states, and is thus subject to alternating episodes of mania and depression. The order of episodes is often unpredictable. Mania doesn't necessarily trigger depression, nor does depression invariably give way to mania. Periods of normalcy may intervene. In most cases, however, some sort of cyclical or seasonal pattern does eventually emerge. The duration and degree of each kind of episode vary widely among patients: some are predominately manic, others predominately depressive. Some patients experience only mild mania or depression while others are subject to far severer attacks. The mood and behavior of the sufferer, however, can be transformed dramatically in either instance.

During a manic phase or period, the mind of a bipolar patient shifts into a higher gear, with the afflicted individual perceiving a heightening of his or her abilities and powers. It seems as if the heavenly fire of the gods has been lent or imparted to the person, as if he or she, singled out for blessing and elevation to the highest, has been struck by the lighting bolt of Zeus himself and, rather than falling dead, has been catapulted into a state of transport and inspiration, an exhilarating condition akin to drunken intoxication.

Instead, however, of experiencing a diminishment of faculties, a blurring or blunting of sensation, "the God-touched and Muse-kissed" is favored with an enhanced acuity, a sharpening or refinement of impression. The moment he is lifted to empyreal heights, the thunderheads disperse and scatter. Whereas below all appeared dark, unjust and sorrowful, on high, everything seems clear and luminous. The sun shines down from the blue sky, and the one-set-apart surges with energy as if he has an overactive thyroid or has taken a highly effective or potent amphetamine.

Some manics are able to harness their excess energy and to channel it into creative endeavor. They prove capable of sustained concentration and exhibit a rare singleness of purpose. The lucky few are so empowered. They find within themselves the wherewithal for staggering, seemingly superhuman labor and, tapping their magical reserves of energy, seem up to any task or challenge. More often, a manic person can't keep focused or has trouble doing so. His interest fluctuates, and he capriciously leapfrogs from activity to activity, spreading himself far too thin. Pleasures wave and beckon all the more beguilingly for the manic due to his already electrified state and in many cases, to the detriment of his work, he gives in to his temptations.

The manic's sleep requirements may decrease markedly. He may also not feel the need to take nourishment. Inhibitions vanish. Often he finds himself in a state of sexual arousal, and so the search for physical fulfillment may increasingly and obsessively take up his time. Alcohol and drugs provide illusory gateways, points of entry into unknown regions of dazzling beauty. Already in a state of exaltation, the manic feels as indestructible as a pumped-up high school teenager on the day of the big game. He can chance a wild joy ride, for he is at an emotional pinnacle and believes that he is immune from peril.

Up there, where the view is radiant and shining, he feels he has vitality and stamina to spare. Blindly optimistic, he will spend all his money on a drinking binge or else will gamble it away, sure of its eventual return, for he is a winner who will inevitably reap what he has sown. After attaining such heights, his stature and importance seem crystal clear to him. The world is his oyster. He feels that special dispensation has been, and will continue to be, granted him.

The manic person will often become suddenly convivial, especially after a depressive period in which he has shunned the company of others. Outgoing and sociable, he will seek the companionship of sycophants and acolytes. Friends not seen for months will be awakened in the middle of the night. Long put-off visits will be paid or new associates and hangers-on will be found. Friends, however, cease to be friends the moment their usefulness ends and will be unceremoniously, even brutally, dropped.

In conversation, the manic person is voluble and expansive. Despite her occasional acute need to be around people, she is still self-involved, in her own little world, and she scarcely pays attention or heed to any of her associates. In conversation, she is a perpetual monologist, and ignores or disregards the interpolations of those about her. If someone continues to interrupt or contradict her, she may fly into a fit of virulent rage. Often she suffers from a persecution complex or else feels that she is surrounded by incompetents.

If the manic doesn't give in to her temptations and she applies herself to her work, she often finds the floodgates open. Ideas succeed one another at breakneck pace. The god, the muse, whispers continuously into the manic's ear. Illusive, long-sought solutions suddenly materialize and a breakthrough is made where there had been formerly an impasse. If the manic person is writing or composing, she may experience such ease and facility that it seems as if she is not working at all but merely taking dictation and it appears to her that whatever she sets down comes out copperplate and flawless. The manic-depressive's ability to assess her work, however, is skewed by her disease. When she is in high spirits, she is uncritical and subject to feelings of grandeur. She suffers from an inflated sense of self-importance and is puffed to the gills with pride. The quality of the work she produces when viewed objectively may or may not conform with her high estimation of it.

When his mood shifts to deep depression, the bipolar person is plummeted to the darkest pit or bottom. Mired in the slough of despond, banished to the bench of desolation, he is visited by another deity. The grim god of the lower depths spreads his dark cape about him and the manic-depressive feels as if he has been snatched or kidnapped. Suddenly he finds himself, as the poet Hölderlin put it, in "Orchus's realm," where the life-giving rays of the sun god no longer reach him. In this shadowy world of silence and black cloud, deserted by his muse, he can only grub blindly in the dark.

Once again symptoms differ among patients. The depressive individual suffers from low self-esteem. He often is unable to concentrate; with the passage of time, his mental processes will slow to a creep or perhaps even come to a deadlock or full stop. His sexual drive may dwindle or fade or the sexual act may suddenly appear so bestial and revolting that all desire is scotched in an instant. Other bodily functions such as eating likewise may become repulsive and odious. All that was formerly relished will turn to dust. The depressive will often become languid, listless and withdrawn. If the depressive period persists for any length of time, he may become profoundly agoraphobic. He will often disregard his appearance, and he may go long periods without bathing. Sleep may elude him or he may retire to his bed for longer and longer intervals, increased sleeping serving as yet another means of escape from his world of troubles. To dispel his depression, the depressive may self-medicate, try to improve his disposition by turning to drugs and alcohol. He may succeed for a time, but his black mood will often return, and his agony will be redoubled. As the days pass, he will grow increasingly apathetic about all aspects of his life. What formerly excited him will now leave him unmoved and indifferent.

Once the emotional pendulum has swung downward, the creative manic-depressive is seldom able to get much work done. When depressed, a bipolar writer often becomes hypercritical when it comes to evaluating his productions. While writing, he may become stymied and mired, unable to develop a forward momentum to his narrative or poem. Like Joseph Grand, the thwarted would-be novelist of Camus's *The Plague*, he may not be able to move beyond the opening paragraph of his opus but will find himself interminably revising it. He may amass draft after draft in which only a single adjective or verb has changed from one version to the next. In addition, passages that pleased the writer while manic may now fill him with nausea and disgust. A phrase that formerly seemed choice will suddenly appear meretricious. His mood at the time has a profound effect on the manic-depressive's power of assessment. His judgment can be faulty and wide of the mark in both directions. Henry James realized this and remarked: "Our judgments are all dictated by feeling—a feeling of undue elation or undue depression and the verdict we come to is apt to be preposterous in either case alike."[4] Not all bipolar people come to creative standstills while depressed. As Hershman and Lieb point out, some enterprising manic-depressives who get to know their rhythms and develop an understanding of the pattern and repetition in their cycles can learn to adapt "work phase to mood."[5] During depressive periods, they polish and improve the material they drafted at lightning speed while manic.

Depression can be so deep and so long lasting that the sufferer may become delusional or psychotic. He may feel that he has committed a heinous crime or unpardonable sin or that he is personally responsible for all the wrongs of the world. This guilt can weigh so heavily on his conscience that he yearns for castigation and punishment. Some depressives develop extreme self-loathing, even suicidal self-hatred. Others develop what Hershman and Lieb call "negative grandeur"[6] and feel as if God has graven the mark of Cain upon their brows and set them aside for special persecution. Such individuals take perverse pride in the deluded belief that they have been damned by the Almighty. Concluding that they suffer afflictions comparable to those of Job, they attempt heroic resistance, seeing themselves as Lears venturing forth into the storm in order to shake their fists at the deity. Caught in the grip of delusional depression, bipolar individuals often suffer from extreme paranoia. They often feel that they are being targeted by family members, governmental agencies, the police, or malign neighbors. They may become haunted by financial worries and feel that destitution or bankruptcy is imminent. Such fears are often irrational; nonetheless they are intensely frightening to the depressive. We have already mentioned how depressive people can be subject to hypochondriacal hallucinations. Such illusions intensify when depression becomes severe. Some delusional depressives enter into catatonic stupors. Others become increasingly suicidal. As noted above, some sufferers grow to despise themselves and, in towering self-directed rages, desire to brutally and ruthlessly rub themselves out. Others don't experience such self-loathing but develop an increasing fatalism. They may fear death greatly but they know that it is certain and inescapable. This awareness can become so powerful and overwhelming that certain individuals may decide that there is no point in putting off any longer what must eventually come anyway and so elect to die at their own hands without further delay. When depression becomes severe, hope and optimism vanish altogether.

Yet if the manic depressive is cognizant of the cyclical nature of his affliction, he knows that he will inevitably emerge from the tomb, and once more be elevated to the upper circles, the brisk and invigorating summits. In the depths of his depression, it may seem as if "his muse is hoarse" and "dreary death does haste." However, reprieve may be just around the corner. Winter's siege can be prolonged, but spring will inevitably come.

The motif of resurrection has fascinated writers and poets from time immemorial. It informs the poetry of both Hart Crane and Sylvia Plath, but predates them by millennia. The theme resurfaces with astonishing regularity in many signal works of the literary canon. In 1579, for example, Edmund Spenser made use of it in his first important work, his sequence of twelve eclogues titled *The Shepherd's Calendar*. These poems examine the ruthless authority of the seasons which govern the agricultural round. The *Calendar's* central figure, Colin Clout, is a type of the pastoral poet and an idealized projection of Spenser himself. During spring and summer, he is complacent and at ease in nature, but by December he becomes an image of winter and old age. In January, the first month of the *Calendar*, he breaks his pipe. He repeats the action in December, the concluding month. As the poem ends, Colin bids his final adieus and lies down to die. December, however, does not mark Colin's last appearance in Spenser's work. He would revive the character in his subsequent pastoral "Colin Clout's Come Home Again" and in *The Faerie Queene*.

In "Colin Clout Come Home Again," the shepherd returns to his bucolic homeland after a long absence. He relates to a group of fellow shepherds how he crossed the ocean to a far country, Queen Cynthia's land—a place very different from his native hearth, a kingdom where "learned arts" flower and "wits are held in peerless price," but also a domain where corruption and debauchery flourish. Its denizens uniformly fail to see "their own misfaring/ For either they be puffed up with pride,/ Or fraught with envy that their galls do Swell,/ Or they their days to idleness divide,/ Or drowned lie in Pleasure's wasteful well,/ In which like moldwarps nuzzling still they lurk,/ Unmindful of chief parts of manliness. . . ." (11.731–737).

Colin tells his fellow swains that, after viewing firsthand both the positive and negative aspects of Cynthia's land, he "chose back to his sheep to tourne" and recrossed the ocean. The Colin who returns is not the old man of December. He has also circled back from a place far more remote, and, like the other man who harrowed Hell, he has the power to raise the dead,

> Whilst thou wast hence all dead in dole did lie:
> The woods were heard to wail full many a sithe,
> And all the birds with silence to complain:
> The fields with faded flowers did seem to mourn,
> And all their flocks from feeding to refrain:
> The running waters wept for thy return,
> And all their fish with languor did lament:
> But now both woods and fields and floods revive,
> Sith thou art come, their cause and merriment,
> That us late dead, has made again alive. (11.22–31)

Not only does Colin's death and resurrection reflect the annual decay and revival of vegetation, they also recall the cyclical recurrent births and deaths of such pagan deities as Osiris, Adonis, Dionysus, and Persephone, all of whom make an appearance in *The Faerie Queene*.

Such figures are common in man's earliest literature. The ancients believed rebirth to be a fact of life in the universe. During the course of his life, a man would "die" to issue from the grave of his body many times. Indeed, he would live in a succession of bodies—those of a child, a youth, a mature adult, and finally an aged person. Only death could put a stop to these human metamorphoses, which mirrored, as did the larger cycles of birth, procreation, and death, the seasonal changes of nature. Could they also have reflected internal emotional rhythms as well? Were the ancient storytellers more attuned to these inner mood cycles than their fellows? Were they themselves subject to extreme and outlandish temperamental swings and shifts that differentiated them pronouncedly from their peers?

As Hershman and Lieb point out in *Manic Depression and Creativity*, from the ancient Greeks onward, genius has been consistently associated with insanity. Socrates claimed that the poet has "no invention in him until he has been inspired and is out of senses."[7] Greek physicians such as Hippocrates and Areteus were among the first to recognize "mania and depression as medical problems,"[8] and Areteus understood that "mania and depression could alternate in the same person."[9] During the Renaissance, genius became increasingly linked with melancholy. The rationalists of the Enlightenment who subscribed to the theory that reason was the supreme criterion for knowledge did their best to debunk such a view, but, as Alvarez notes, the association "survived . . . in a less extreme form and with a different name. [Melancholy] became 'spleen,' a more rationally anatomical term, as befits the Augustans, for a more circumscribed and controlled gloom which found its outlet not in despair but in the rancour and mean-mindedness of the great age of satire."[10]

For the Romantics, reason and logic took a back seat to ardor and emotion. They felt that genius was inextricably intertwined with suffering and premature death. According to the Romantic ideal, the poet spent his short, turbulent life in pensive meditation. Frequent depression of spirit was the price paid for a life of passion, fervor, and intensity. Willing to expend himself for his art, the poet welcomed the afflictions that periodically visited him. He had no desire to live to old age, but yearned to blaze brightly for a moment and then load his "sparkless ashes" into an "unlamented urn." Hershman and Lieb believe "the Romantic concept of genius" to be "a catalogue of manic-depressive symptoms. . . ."[11] Celebrating as it did being "half in love with easeful Death," Romanticism colored a generation and profoundly influenced both the nineteenth- and twentieth-century image of the artist. The Romantic belief that artists must suffer in order to create persists, albeit in weakened and diluted form, to this day.

Hershman and Lieb effectively make the case that manic depression is a chronic artistic disease. They uncover many symptoms of bipolar disorder, including suicidal thoughts and tendencies, in the lives of many outstanding creative personalities of the past. The careers of Newton, Beethoven, Dickens, and Van Gogh are examined in detail but the lives of many other luminaries—Coleridge, Rousseau, Byron, Goethe, Swift, Charlotte Brontë, Chopin, Wagner, de Musset, and Dostoyevsky, to name but a few—are touched on as well. Hershman and Lieb reveal the enormous impact of manic depression on the lives of these geniuses.

During the course of their lives, many of the writers discussed in *Final Drafts* also exhibited clear signs of manic depression. What differentiates them from their predecessors in previous centuries was their far greater readiness to give in to their suicidal inclinations. Most of the geniuses examined by Hershman and Lieb died natural deaths. Even among the Romantics, suicide was rare. Keats, Shelley, and Byron all embodied the ideal of the poet dying young, but were at best, as we termed in the introduction, psychological suicides. Many other notables of the Romantic period, such as Wordsworth and Goethe, lived well into middle or old age.

Like Colin Clout, we have come full circle and once more find ourselves posing the same question: why was the twentieth century such a lethal one? Manic depression was certainly a factor in the deaths of a number of the authors examined in this study. The disease, the underlying disposition, however, serves only as a partial explanation for "the sudden, sharp rise" in author casualties. In our introduction and elsewhere, we have already explored in some detail additional reasons for the marked increase in author suicides this century, several of which merit brief repeating.

The last one hundred years have been the bloodiest and most angst-ridden in all of recorded history. As the century progressed, it became increasingly difficult for writers to remain myopic. World events—the Great Depression, World Wars I and II, the nuclear arms race—demanded their attention. Heightened awareness of human suffering evoked various reactions—anger, pity, or hopelessness. For some—Woolf and Zweig—the world seemed so brutal and barbarous that death appeared preferable to living. In their zeal to effect social change, others—Mayakovski and Koestler—embraced Utopian socialist ideologies only to become disillusioned and horror-struck when the revolution went wrong. A number of writers—Celan, Kosinski, and Levi—were victims of war and totalitarianism. The wounds inflicted on them in their formative years festered for a lifetime and no doubt influenced their decisions to die. Several writers recognized an affinity between themselves and either the dictator who seized power in their nation or the enemy or foreign invader who despoiled their native country. Thomas Mann called Hitler "a brother." The best and worst in the German character, to his mind, were inextricably bound. In his revenge fantasies, if not in fact, Jerzy Kosinski was as vicious and remorseless as the German and Russian soldiers he encountered in his youth. In the course of their lives, a number of authors saw actual combat. Trakl's suicide was triggered by the horrors he witnessed on the front. The lives of Bierce, Lawrence, Hemingway, Crosby, Toller, Pavese, Gary, Heggen, Jarrell, and Lewis Puller were all colored by their battle experience. The cultural changes that resulted in Japan after its defeat in 1945 led to the suicide of Mishima and factored into that of Kawabata. By 1942, Stefan Zweig had come to the conclusion that the world of his youth, the European civilization that he had known and loved, had passed away altogether. Post-World War II tensions between the United States and Russia troubled Klaus Mann. In 1968, John Berryman wondered when "the fire would be turned on." The prospect of atomic annihilation also worried Malcolm Lowry and Sylvia Plath.

As the twentieth century wore on, serious writers became increasingly less important to their societies. Perhaps Romain Gary put it best in his "Life and Death of Émile Ajar":

> I am writing these lines at a moment when it has become increasingly obvious that, given the way it has been evolving during the last quarter of a century, the world now confronts a writer with a question that is mortal for every kind of artistic expression: that of futility. Not even the lyrical illusion remains of what for so long literature wished, and believed itself to be—a contribution to the development and progress of mankind.[12]

Indeed "celeb non-books" and scandal sheets have become the order of the day. Actors, sports stars, and rock-and-roll musicians are afforded far more acclaim and attention from the general public than serious fiction writers and poets. Will authors continue to slay themselves in such large numbers in the future? As the millennium rapidly approaches, the case appears undecided.

Notes

1. A. Alvarez, *The Savage God* (New York: W. W. Norton, 1990), p. 258.

2. Ibid., p. 259.

3. D. Jablow Hershman and Julian Lieb, *Manic Depression and Creativity* (Amherst, New York: Prometheus Books, 1998), p. 12.

4. Ibid., p. 202.

5. Ibid., p. 200.

6. Ibid., p. 35.

7. Ibid., p. 8.

8. Ibid., p. 19.

9. Ibid.

10. Alvarez, *The Savage God*, p. 193.

11. Hershman and Lieb, *Manic Depression and Creativity*, p. 9.

12. Romain Gary, "Life and Death of Émile Ajar," *King Solomon*, trans. Barbara Wright, introduction by John Weightman (New York: Harper and Row, 1983), p. 243.

Bibliography

Books and Articles

Aird, Eileen. *Sylvia Plath: Her Life and Work.* New York: Harper and Row, 1975.

Allday, Elizabeth. *Stephen Zweig: A Critical Biography.* Chicago: J. Philip O'Hara, 1972.

Alvarez, A. *The Savage God: A Study of Suicide.* New York: W. W. Norton, 1990. *The Savage God* was originally published by Penguin Books in 1971.

Aronowitz, Alfred G., and Peter Hamill. *Ernest Hemingway: The Life and Death of A Man.* New York: Lancer Books, 1961.

Anissimov, Myriam. *Primo Levi, Tragedy of an Optimist.* Translated by Steve Cox. New York: The Overlook Press, 1999.

Baker, Carlos. *Ernest Hemingway: A Life Story.* New York: Charles Scribner's Sons, 1969.

Bareham, Tony. *Malcolm Lowry.* Houndmills, Basingstoke, Hampshire, and London: Macmillan Education Ltd., 1989.

Becker, Lucille. *Henry de Montherlant: A Critical Biography.* Carbondale: Southern Illinois University Press, 1970.

Bell, Quentin. *Virginia Woolf: A Biography.* New York: Harcourt, Brace and Jovanovitch, 1972.

Berryman, John. *Delusions, Etc.* New York: Farrar, Straus and Giroux, 1972.

———. *77 Dream Songs.* New York: Farrar, Straus and Giroux, 1964.

———. *Henry's Fate and Other Poems, 1967–1972.* New York: Farrar, Straus and Giroux, 1977.

———. *His Toy, His Dream, His Rest: 308 Dream Songs.* New York: Farrar, Straus and Giroux, 1967.

———. *Love & Fame.* New York: Farrar, Straus and Giroux, 1970.

Bielschowsky, Albert. *The Life of Goethe.* Vol. 1. New York: Haskell House Publishers, 1969.

Blake, Patricia. "The Two Deaths of Vladimir Mayakovsky." Introduction to *The Bedbug and Selected Poetry* by Vladimir Mayakovski, 9–50. Translated by

Max Hayward and George Reavey. Edited by Patricia Blake. Bloomington: Indiana University Press, 1975. Reprint of the 1960 New York Meridian Books edition.

Bogard, Travis. "Notes and Chronology." In Eugene O'Neill, *Complete Plays*. Vol. 1. New York: Library of America, 1988.

Brautigan, Richard. *In Watermelon Sugar*. New York: Dell, 1974. This novel was first published in 1968.

Bürgin, Hans, and Hans-Otto Mayer. *Thomas Mann: A Chronicle of His Life*. Translated by Eugene Dobson. Alabama: University of Alabama Press, 1969.

Capuzzo, Mike. "Seth Morgan's Last Ride." *Esquire*, February 1991, 92–97.

Carlsson, Anni, and Volker Michels, eds. *The Hesse/Mann Letters*. Translated by Ralph Manheim. Foreword by Theodore Ziolkowski. New York: Harper and Row, 1975.

Clute, John, ed. *Science Fiction: The Illustrated Encylopedia*. London, New York, Stuttgart: Dorling-Kindersley, 1995.

Colby, Vineta, ed. *World Authors, 1975–1980*. New York: H. W. Wilson, 1985.

Conquest, Robert. *The Great Terror: A Reassessment*. New York and Oxford: Oxford University Press, 1990.

Costa, Richard Hauer. *Malcolm Lowry*. New York: Twayne Publishers, 1972.

Cowan, Thomas. *Gay Men and Women Who Enriched the World*. New Canaan, Conn: Mulvey Books, 1989.

Crane, Hart. *The Complete Poems and Selected Letters and Prose of Hart Crane*. Edited with Introduction and Notes by Brom Weber. New York: Liveright Publishing Corporation, 1966.

Crivello, Kirk. *Fallen Angels: The Lives and Untimely Deaths of Fourteen Hollywood Beauties*. Secaucus, New Jersey: Citadel Press, 1988.

Daiches, David, Malcolm Bradbury, and Eric Mottram, eds. *The Avenel Companion to English and American Literature*. New York: Avenel Books, 1981.

Davidson, John. *Ballads and Songs*. London: John Lane, 1895. Boston: Copeland and Day, 1895.

———. *Fleetstreet Eclogues*. London: E. Mathews and J. Lane, 1893.

———. *Fleetstreet Eclogues*. London: John Lane, 1896. New York: Dodd, Mead, 1896.

———. *God and Mammon: Mammon and His Message*. London: G. Richards, 1908.

———. *The Man Forbid and Other Essays*. Edited by E. J. O'Brien. Boston: Ball Publishing, 1910.

———. *Triumph of Mammon*. London: E. G. Richards, 1907.

Day, Douglas. *Malcolm Lowry: A Biography*. New York: Oxford University Press, 1973.

Dembo, L. S. *Hart Crane's Sanskrit Charge: A Study of The Bridge*. Ithaca, New York: Cornell University Press, 1960.

De Salvo, Louise. " 'Tinder-and-Flint' Virginia Woolf and Vita Sackville-West." *Significant Others: Creativity and Intimate Partnership*. Edited by Whitney Chadwick and Isabelle De Courtivron. New York: Thames and Hudson, 1993.

Donaldson, Scott. *Poet in America: Winfield Townley Scott*. Austin: University of Texas Press, 1972.

Dove, Richard. *He was a German: A Biography of Ernst Toller*. Preface by Frank Trommler. London: Liberis, 1990.

Dozois, Gardner R. *The Fiction of James Tiptree Jr*. New York: Agol Press, 1977.

Drake, William. *Sara Teasdale: Woman and Poet*. San Francisco: Harper and Row, 1979.

Edel, Leon. *Henry James: A Life*. New York: Harper and Row, 1985.

————. *Henry James: The Complete Biography*. 5 vols. New York: Avon Books, 1978. The five volumes of *The Complete Biography* were originally published by the J. B. Lippincott company. Volume one appeared in 1953, volumes two and three in 1962, volume four in 1969, and volume five in 1972.

Ellmann, Richard. *James Joyce: New and Revised Edition*. Oxford and New York: Oxford University Press, 1982.

Ellmann, Richard, and Robert O'Clair, eds. *The Norton Anthology of Modern Poetry*. New York: W. W. Norton, 1973.

"An Epistle of Davidson." *Academy* 75 (14 November 1908): 462–63.

Epstein, Edward Z. *Portrait of Jennifer*. New York: Simon and Schuster, 1995.

Faulkner, William. *Flags in the Dust*. Edited with an Introduction by Douglas Day. New York: Vintage Books, 1974.

Felstiner, John. *Paul Celan: Poet, Survivor, Jew*. New Haven and London: Yale University Press, 1995.

Fiedler, Leslie. "Introducing Cesare Pavese." *Kenyon Review* 16 (Autumn 1954): 536–53.

Flamm, Matthew. "Reading Their Last Writes." *Entertainment*, 14 March 1997, 72. A book review of *Or Not to Be: A Collection of Suicide Notes* by Marc Etkind, Riverhead, 1997.

Flores, Angel, ed. *An Anthology of German Poetry from Hölderlin to Rilke in English Translation*. Gloucester, Mass: Peter Smith, 1965.

Gary, Romain. "Life and Death of Émile Ajar." *King Solomon*. Translated by Barbara Wright. Introduction by John Weightman. New York: Harper and Row, 1983.

Gass, William H. *The World Within the Word*. Boston: Godine, 1979. Reprint of the 1978 Alfred A. Knopf edition.

Gerard, James W. " 'A Hymn of Hate,' *My Battle*, by Adolf Hitler." *New York Times Book Review*, 15 October 1933. Reprinted in the *New York Times Book Review 100*, 6 October 1996, 42.

Gessel, Van C. *Three Modern Novelists: Soseki, Tanizaki, Kawabata*. Tokyo: Kodansha International, 1993.

Gilman, Sander L. *Jewish Self-Hatred*. Baltimore and London: John Hopkins University Press, 1990.

Gleick, Elizabeth. "An Imperfect Union." *Time*, 28 April 1997, 68–69.

————. "The Marker We've Been . . . Waiting For." *Time*, 7 April 1997, 31–36.

Goethe, Johann Wolfgang von. *The Collected Works*. Vol. 10. Introduction by Jane K. Brown. Translations by Jan van Heurck and Krishna Winston. Princeton, New Jersey: Princeton University Press, 1995.

Graziano, Frank, ed. *Georg Trakl: A Profile*. Introduction by Graziano. Manchester: Carcanet, 1984.

————. *Georg Trakl: A Profile*. Introduction by Michael Hamburger. Durango, Colorado: Logbridge-Rhodes, 1983.

Greenberg, Martin H., and Bill Pronzini, eds. *A Treasury of Civil War Stories*. New York: Bonanza Books, 1991.

Hamilton, Edith. *The Greek Way*. New York: W. W. Norton, 1964.

————. *The Roman Way*. New York: W. W. Norton,, 1967.

Hamilton, Nigel. *The Brothers Mann*. New Haven: Yale University Press, 1979.

Hayman, Ronald. *Thomas Mann: A Biography*. New York: Scribner, 1995.

Hazo, Samuel. *Hart Crane: An Introduction and Interpretation*. New York: Barnes and Noble, 1963.

Heilbut, Anthony. *Thomas Mann: Eros and Literature*. New York: Knopf, 1996.

Hemingway, Ernest. *Across the River and into the Trees*. New York: Charles Scribner's Sons, 1950.

———. *A Moveable Feast*. New York: Charles Scribner's Sons, 1964.

———. *The Old Man and the Sea*. New York: Charles Scribner's Sons, 1952.

———. *For Whom the Bell Tolls*. New York: Charles Scribner's Sons, 1940.

Hemingway, Mary Welsh. *How It Was*. New York: Knopf, 1976.

Hershman, D. Jablow, and Julian Lieb. *Manic Depression and Creativity*. Amherst, New York: Prometheus Books, 1998.

Hitler, Adolf. *Mein Kampf*. Translated by Ralph Manheim. Boston: Houghton Mifflin, 1971.

Hochman, Stanley, ed. *Encyclopedia of World Drama*. 2d ed. New York. McGraw-Hill, 1984.

Holmes, Anna. "Monitor." *Entertainment*, 20 June 1997, 14. J. Anthony Lukas suicide death notice.

Hornstein, Lillian Herlands, G. D. Percy, and Sterling A. Brown, eds. *The Reader's Companion to World Literature*, 2d ed. New York: New American Library, 1973.

Horton, Philip. *Hart Crane: The Life of an American Poet*. 2d ed. New York: Viking Press, 1957.

Jackson, Charles. *The Fall of Valor*. New York: Rinehart, 1946.

———. *The Lost Weekend*. New York: Carrol and Graf, 1983. *The Lost Weekend* was originally published in 1944.

James, Henry. *Literary Criticism*. Vol 2. New York: Library of America, 1984.

Jamison, K. R. *Touched by Fire*. New York: The Free Press, 1993.

Johnson, Paul. *A History of the Jews*. New York: Harper and Row, 1987.

Johnson, Robert B. *Henry de Montherlant*. New York: Twayne Publishers, 1968.

Jones, Howard Mumford. "A Minor Prometheus." *Freeman*, 25 October 1922, 153.

Joyce, James. *Ulysses: The Corrected Text*. Edited by Hans Walter Gabler with Wolfhard Steppe and Claus Melchior. New York: Vintage Books, 1986.

Kaplan, Fred. *Henry James: The Imagination of Genius*. New York: William Morrow, 1992.

Kawabata, Yasunari. *The House of the Sleeping Beauties*. Translated by Edward G. Seidensticker. Introduction by Yukio Mishima. Tokyo, Palo Alto: Kodansha International, 1969.

———. *The Lake*. Translated by Reiko Tsukimura. Tokyo: Kodansha International, 1974.

———. *The Master of Go*. Translated by Edward G. Seidensticker. New York: Knopf, 1972.

———. *The Old Capital*. Translated by J. Martin Holman. San Francisco: North Point Press, 1987.

———. *Snow Country*. Translated by Edward G. Seidensticker. New York: Knopf, 1956.

Kindermann, Heinz, Margarete Dietrich, and Ernst Johann, eds. *Lexikon Der Deutschen Literatur*. München: Verlag Lebendiges Wissen, 1958.

Koestler, Arthur. *Darkness at Noon*. New York: New American Library, 1955. *Darkness at Noon* was first published in 1941.

———. *The Thirteenth Tribe: The Khazar Empire and Its Heritage*. New York: Random House, 1976.

Kosinski, Jerzy. *Blind Date*. New York: Bantam, 1978. *Blind Date* was first published in 1977.

———. *The Painted Bird*. New York: Bantam, 1978. *The Painted Bird* was first published in 1965.

———. *Steps*. New York: Bantam, 1969. *Steps* was first published in 1968.

Kunitz, Stanley J., and Vineta Colby, eds. *Twentieth Century Authors, First Supplement*. New York: H. W. Wilson, 1955.

Kunitz, Stanley J., and Howard Haycraft, eds. *Twentieth Century Authors: A Biographical Dictionary of Modern Literature*. New York: H. W. Wilson, 1942.

Leibowitz, Herbert A. *Hart Crane: An Introduction to the Poetry*. Foreword by John Unterecker. New York: Columbia University Press, 1968.

Lewis, R. W. B. *The Jameses: A Family Narrative*. New York: Farrar, Straus and Giroux, 1991.

Lindsay, Vachel. *Collected Poems*. New York: Macmillan, 1941.

———. *Selected Poems*. Edited with Introduction by Mark Harris. New York: Collier Books, 1963.

Locker, Frances C., ed. *Contemporary Authors*. Volumes 77–80. Detroit, Michigan: Gale Research Co., 1979.

Lockridge, Larry. *Shade of the Raintree: The Life and Death of Ross Lockridge Jr.* New York: Viking, 1994.

Lockridge, Ross, Jr. *Raintree County*. Boston: Houghton Mifflin, 1948.

London, Jack. *White Fang*. New York: Scholastic Book Services, 1973. *White Fang* was first published in 1906.

Lowry, Malcolm. "Autopsy." *Canadian Literature* 8 (Spring 1961): 23.

———. *October Ferry to Gabriola*. Edited by Margerie Lowry. New York, London, and Scarborough, Ontario: New American Library, 1971. Reprint of the 1970 first edition of the World Publishing Co.

———. *Under the Volcano*. Introduction by Stephen Spender. New York and Scarborough, Ontario: New American Library, 1971. Reprint of the 1965 J. B. Lippincott edition. *Under the Volcano* was first published in 1947.

Maass, Joachim. *Kleist: A Biography*. Translated by Ralph Manheim. New York: Farrar, Straus and Giroux, 1983.

McHale, Tom. *Farragan's Retreat*. New York: Viking, 1971.

———. *Principato*. New York: Viking, 1970.

Mann, Klaus. *Mephisto*. Translated by Robin Smyth. New York: Penquin Books, 1985. Robin Smyth's translation of *Mephisto* was first published in 1977.

———. *The Pious Dance*. Translated by Laurence Senelick. New York: PAJ Publications, 1987.

Mann, Thomas. *Death in Venice and Seven Other Stories*. Translated by H. T. Lowe-Porter. New York: Triangle Classics—BOMC, 1993.

———. *Order of the Day*. Translated by H. T. Lowe-Porter, Agnes E. Meyer, and Eric Sutton. New York: Knopf, 1942.

———. *Pro and Contra Wagner*. Translated by Allan Blunden. Introduction by Erich Heller. Chicago: The University of Chicago Press, 1985.

———. *Stories of Three Decades*. Translated by H. T. Lowe-Porter. New York: Knopf, 1936.

Mariani, Paul. *Dream Song: The Life of John Berryman*. New York: William Morrow, 1990.

Massa, Ann. *Vachel Lindsay: Fieldworker For the American Dream*. Bloomington: Indiana University Press, 1970.

Masters, Edgar Lee. *Vachel Lindsay: A Poet in America*. New York: Biblo and Tannen, 1969. Masters' biography first appeared in 1935.

Matthiessen, F. O. *The James Family: A Group Biography*. New York: Vintage Books, 1980. *The James Family* was first published by Knopf in 1947.

Mayakovsky, Vladimir. *The Bedbug and Selected Poetry*. Translated by Max Hayward and George Reavey. Edited with an Introduction, "The Two Deaths of Vladimir Mayakovsky" by Patricia Blake, 9–50. Bloomington: Indiana University Press, 1975. Reprint of the 1960 New York Meridian Books edition.

———. *The Complete Plays of Vladimir Mayakovsky*. Translated by Guy Daniels. Introduction by Robert Payne. New York: Washington Square Press, 1968.

———. *Selected Works in Three Volumes*. Translated from the Russian. Foreword, "Mayakovsky, Poet of a New World" by Alexander Ushakov, translated by Dorian Rottenberg, 7–28. Vol. 1. Moscow: Raduga, 1985, 1987.

———. *Vladimir Ilyich Lenin*. Translated by Dorian Rottenberg. Moscow: Progress Publishers, 1967.

Metzger, Linda, ed. *Contemporary Authors*. New Revision Series. Vol. 19. Detroit, Michigan: Gale Research Co., 1987.

Middlebrook, Diane Wood. *Anne Sexton: A Biography*. Boston: Houghton Mifflin, 1991.

Milano, Paolo. "Pavese's Experiments in the Novel." *New Republic*, 4 May 1953, 18, 23.

Mishima, Yukio. *The Sea of Fertility—A Cycle of Novels: Spring Snow, Runaway Horses, The Temple of Dawn, The Decay of the Angel*. New York: Pocket Books, 1975. Translations by Michael Gallagher, E. Dale Saunders, Cecilia Segawa Seigle, and Edward G. Seidensticker. The translations of the books comprising Mishima's tetralogy were originally published by Knopf. *Spring Snow* appeared in 1972, *Runaway Horses* and *The Temple of Dawn* in 1973, and *The Decay of the Angel* in 1974.

———. *The Temple of the Golden Pavilion*. Translated by Ivan Morris. Introduction by Donald Keene. New York: Knopf, 1994. Ivan Morris' translation of *The Temple of the Golden Pavilion* was first published in 1959.

———. *The Temple of the Golden Pavilion*. Translated by Ivan Morris. Introduction by Nancy Wilson Ross. New York: Berkley Publishing Corporation, 1971.

———. *Thirst for Love*. Translated by Alfred H. Marks. Introduction by Donald Keene. New York: Berkley Publishing Corporation, 1971. Alfred H. Marks' translation of *Thirst for Love* was first published in 1969.

Nathan, John. *Mishima: A Biography*. Boston: Little Brown, 1974.

Nemerov, Howard, ed. *Poets on Poetry*. New York: Basic Books, 1966.

Nicolson, Nigel. *Portrait of a Marriage*. New York: Atheneum, 1973.

O'Brien, Edna. *Virgina: A Play*. New York and London: Harcourt, Brace and Jovanovich, 1981.

O'Connor, Mary. *John Davidson*. Edinburgh: Scottish Academic Press, 1987.

Pavese, Cesare. *The Moon and the Bonfires*, New York: Farrar, Straus and Young, 1953.

———. *The Selected Works of Cesare Pavese*. Introduction and translation by R. W. Flint. New York: Farrar, Straus and Giroux, 1968.

Payne, Robert. *The Life and Death of Adolf Hitler*. New York: Dorset Press, 1989. *The Life and Death of Adolf Hitler* was originally published in 1973.

Petersen, Gwenn Boardman. *The Moon in the Water: Understanding Tanizaki, Kawabata, and Mishima*. Honolulu: University Press of Hawaii, 1979.

Peterson, Carroll V. *John Davidson*. New York: Twayne Publishers, 1972.

Plath, Sylvia. *Ariel*. Foreword by Robert Lowell. New York: Harper and Row, 1966.

———. *Crossing the Water, Transitional Poems*. New York: Harper and Row in 1971.

————. *The Bell Jar*. New York: Harper and Row—BOMC, 1993. First published in Great Britain under the pseudonymn Victoria Lucas in 1963 by William Heinemann, Ltd., later published in the United States by Harper and Row in 1971.

————. *The Collected Poems*. Edited by Ted Hughes. New York: Harper and Row, 1981.

Prater, Donald. *European of Yesterday: A Biography of Stefan Zweig*. Oxford: Clarendon Press, 1972.

————. *Thomas Mann: A Life*. Oxford, New York: Oxford University Press, 1995.

Puller, Lewis B., Jr. *Fortunate Son*. New York: Grove Weidenfeld, 1991.

Quinn, Vincent. *Hart Crane*. New York: Twayne Publishers, 1963.

Reich-Ranicki, Marcel. *Thomas Mann and His Family*. Translated by Ralph Manheim. London: Collins, 1989.

Richards, Vyvyan. *T. E. Lawrence*. London: Duckworth, 1939.

Rood, Karen L., ed. *American Literary Almanac*. New York, Oxford: Bruccoli, Clark, Layman, Inc. Facts on File, 1988.

Rowse, A. L. *Homosexuals in History*. New York: Dorset Press, 1983. Reprint of the 1977 Macmillan edition.

Ruggles, Eleanor. *The West-going Heart: A Life of Vachel Lindsay*. New York. W. W. Norton, 1959.

Sabor, Rudolph. *The Real Wagner*. London: Cardinal, 1989.

Sanders, Gerald De Witt, John Herbert Nelson, and M. L. Rosenthal. *Poets of America*. Vol. 2 of *Chief Modern Poets of Britain and America*. 5th ed. New York: Macmillan, 1970.

Schoen, Carol B. *Sara Teasdale*. Boston: Twayne Publishers, 1986.

Schoenbaum, S. *William Shakespeare: A Compact Documentary Life*. New York: Oxford University Press, 1977.

Scott, Winfield Townley. *Change of Weather*. New York: Doubleday, 1964.

Scott-Stokes, Henry. *The Life and Death of Yukio Mishima*. New York: Farrar, Straus and Giroux, 1974.

Seinfelt, Frederick W. *George Moore: Ireland's Unconventional Realist*. Philadelphia: Dorrance, 1975.

Sexton, Anne. "An Obsessive Combination of Ontological Inscape, Trickery and Love," *Voices: A Journal of Poetry* 169 (1959): 34.

————. *The Complete Poems*. Foreword by Maxine Kumin. Boston: Houghton Mifflin, 1981.

Sloan, James Park. *Jerzy Kosinski: A Biography*. New York: Dutton, 1996.

Sloan, John. *John Davidson: First of the Moderns*. Oxford, New York: Clarendon Press, 1995.

Sloan, John, ed. *Selected Poems and Prose of John Davidson*. New York: Clarendon Press, 1995.

Spears, Monroe K. *Hart Crane*. Minneapolis: University of Minnesota Press, 1965.

Steiner, Nancy Hunter. *A Closer Look at Ariel: A Memory of Sylvia Plath*. Introduction by George Stade. New York: Harper's Magazine Press, 1973.

Stoddart, Jane. "An Interview with John Davidson." *Bookman*, February 1895, 85.

Strouse, Jean. *Alice James*. Boston: Houghton Mifflin, 1980.

Teasdale, Sara. *The Collected Poems of Sara Teasdale*. New York: Macmillan, 1966.

————. *Mirror of the Heart: Poems of Sara Teasdale*. Edited with Introduction by William Drake. New York: Macmillan, 1984.

Telgen, Diane, ed. *Something About the Author*. Vol. 75. Detroit, Washington, D.C., and London: Gale Research Inc, 1994.

Tennant, Roger. *Joseph Conrad*. New York: Atheneum, 1981.

Theoharis, Athan. *J. Edgar Hoover, Sex, and Crime: An Historical Antidote*. Chicago: Ivan R. Dee, 1995.

Thomas, Bob. *Selznick*. New York: Pocket Books, 1972. This book was originally published by Doubleday in 1970.

Tiptree, James, Jr. *Warm Worlds and Otherwise*. Introduction by Robert Silverberg. New York: Ballantine Books, 1975.

Toland, John. *Adolf Hitler*. New York: Ballantine Books, 1981. This book was first published by Ballantine in 1977.

———. *The Last 100 Days*. New York: Bantam Books, 1967. This book was originally published by Random House in 1966.

Toole, John Kennedy. *A Confederacy of Dunces*. Foreword by Walker Percy. New York: Grove Weidenfeld, 1987. *A Confederacy of Dunces* was first published in 1980.

———. *The Neon Bible*. Introduction by W. Kenneth Holditch. New York: Grove Press, 1989.

Troyat, Henri. *Tolstoy*. Translated by Nancy Amphoux. New York: Doubleday, 1967.

Tucker, Martin, ed. *Literary Exile in the Twentieth Century: An Analysis and Biographical Dictionary*. New York and London: Greenwood Press, 1991.

Ueda, Makoto. *Modern Japanese Writers*. Stanford: Stanford University Press, 1976.

Unterecker, John. *Voyager: A Life of Hart Crane*. New York: Farrar, Straus and Giroux, 1969.

Untermeyer, Louis, ed. *Modern American Poetry*. New York: Harcourt Brace, 1950.

———. *Modern British Poetry*. New York: Harcourt Brace, 1950.

Ushakov, Alexander. "Mayakovsky, Poet of a New World." Translated by Dorian Rottenberg, 7–28. Vol. 1. Foreword to *Selected Works in Three Volumes* by Vladimir Mayakovsky. Moscow: Raduga, 1985, 1987.

Wagner-Martin, Linda W. *Sylvia Plath: A Biography*. New York: Simon and Schuster, 1987.

Wakeman, John, ed. *World Authors, 1950–1970*. New York: H.W. Wilson, 1975.

———. *World Authors, 1970–1975*. New York: H. W. Wilson, 1980.

Watson, Derek. *Richard Wagner: A Biography*. London: J. M. Dent and Sons, 1979.

Weber, Brom. *Hart Crane: A Biographical and Critical Study*. New York: Bodley Press, 1948.

West, Paul. *Sheer Fiction*. Vol. 1. New Paltz, New York: McPherson, 1987.

———. *Sheer Fiction*. Vol. 3. Kingston, New York: Macpherson, 1994.

Winston, Richard. *Thomas Mann: The Making of an Artist, 1975–1911*. New York: Knopf, 1982. Afterword by Clara Winston.

Wolff, Geoffrey. *Black Sun: The Brief Transit and Violent Eclipse of Harry Crosby*. New York: Random House, 1976.

Woolf, Virginia. *Mrs. Dalloway*. Introduction by Nadia Fusini. New York: Knopf, 1993. *Mrs. Dalloway* was originally published in 1925.

———. *Orlando: A Biography*. New York and London: Harcourt, Brace and Jovanovich, 1956. *Orlando* was originally published in 1928.

———. *Orlando: A Biography*. New York: Triangle Classics—BOMC, 1993.

———. *The Captain's Death Bed and Other Essays*. New York: Harcourt Brace and Jovanovich, 1978. *The Captain's Death Bed and Other Essays* was originally published in 1950.

———. *The Waves*. New York: Harcourt, Brace and Jovanovich, 1978. *The Waves* was originally published in 1931.

Zweig, Stefan. *Beware of Pity*. Translated by Phyllis and Trevor Blewitt. Evanston, Illinois: Northwestern University Press, 1996.

———. *The Royal Game and Other Stories*. Translated by Jill Sutcliffe. Introduction by John Fowles. New York: Harmony Books, 1981.

———. *Marie Antoinette*. Translated by Eden and Cedar Paul. New York: Harmony Books, 1984. The Eden and Cedar Paul translation of *Marie Antoinette* was originally published by Viking Press in 1933.

———. *The World of Yesterday: An Autobiography*. New York: Viking Press, 1942.

Newspapers

New York Times

Rawls, Wendall, Jr., "FBI Admits Planting a Rumor to Discredit Jean Seberg in 1970." 15 September 1979.

Obituaries and accompanying articles with author creditation cited in this book:

Barbanel, Josh. "Ordered to be Famous." 3 December 1980.

Fried, Joseph F. "Japan's Renaissance Man." 25 November 1970.

Goleman, Daniel. "Bruno Bettelheim Dies at 86; Psychoanylyst of Vast Impact." 14 March 1990.

Goodman, Walter. "Arthur Koestler, an Intellectual and Man of Action." 4 March 1983.

Lask, Thomas. "Sought Own True Voice." 8 January 1972.

McDowell, Edwin. "Richard Brautigan, Novelist, a Literary Idol of the 1960s." 26 October 1984.

Montgomery, Paul L. "Sheba an Instant Success." 11 June 1973.

Oka, Takashi. "Renowned Author Raids Tokyo Military, Ends Life." 25 November 1970.

Pace, Eric. "Arthur Koestler and Wife Suicides in London." 4 March 1983.

Rothstein, Mervyn. "In Novels and Life, a Maverick and an Eccentric." 4 May 1991.

Stanley, Alessandra. "Jerzy Kosinski, the Writer, 57, Is Found Dead." 4 May 1991.

Tagliabue, John. "Primo Levi, Holocaust Writer, Is Dead t 67." 12 April 1987.

New York Times obituaries without author creditation cited in this book:

Thomas Heggen	20 May 1949
Charles Jackson	22 September 1968
Yasunari Kawabata	17 April 1972
Vachel Lindsay	6 December 1931
Ross Lockridge Jr.	8 March 1948
Klaus Mann	23 May 1949
Teasdale, Sara	30 January 1933
Sergey Yesenin	29 December, 1925

New York Times obituaries consulted for this book:

John Berryman	8 January 1972
Albert Camus	5 January 1960
Hart Crane	28 April 1932
John Davidson	3 October 1909
Stuart Engstrand	10 September 1955
Mrs. Henry Fonda	15 April 1950
Romain Gary	3 December 1980
Ernest Hemingway	3 July 1961
William Inge	11 June 1973
James Weldon Johnson	27 June 1938
Carole Landis	6 July 1948
Jack London	23 November 1916
Dylan Thomas	10 November 1953
Louis Verneuil	4 November 1952
Tennessee Williams	27 February 1983
Virginia Woolf	3 April 1941
Stefan Zweig	24 February 1942

London Times

Syal, Rajeev. "Letters Hint at Lawrence's Death." 1 September 1996.

AP Wire Story

"Family Seeks to Seal Record of Abuse Allegation Against Late Author," week of 11 April 1997.

Index